Probability, Stochastic Processes and Optimization

Probability, Stochastic Processes and Optimization

Editors

Alexandru Agapie
Denis Enachescu
Vlad Stefan Barbu
Bogdan Iftimie

 Basel • Beijing • Wuhan • Barcelona • Belgrade • Novi Sad • Cluj • Manchester

Editors

Alexandru Agapie
Department of Applied
Mathematics
The Bucharest University of
Economic Studies
Bucharest, Romania

Denis Enachescu
Doctoral School of Computer
Science
University of Bucharest
Bucharest, Romania

Vlad Stefan Barbu
Laboratory of Mathematics
Raphaël Salem
University of
Rouen-Normandy
Saint Étienne du Rouvray,
France

Bogdan Iftimie
Department of Applied
Mathematics
Bucharest University of
Economic Studies
Bucharest, Romania

Editorial Office
MDPI
St. Alban-Anlage 66
4052 Basel, Switzerland

This is a reprint of articles from the Special Issue published online in the open access journal *Mathematics* (ISSN 2227-7390) (available at: https://www.mdpi.com/si/mathematics/Probab_Stoch_Process_Optim).

For citation purposes, cite each article independently as indicated on the article page online and as indicated below:

Lastname, A.A.; Lastname, B.B. Article Title. *Journal Name* **Year**, *Volume Number*, Page Range.

ISBN 978-3-0365-9436-1 (Hbk)
ISBN 978-3-0365-9437-8 (PDF)
doi.org/10.3390/books978-3-0365-9437-8

© 2023 by the authors. Articles in this book are Open Access and distributed under the Creative Commons Attribution (CC BY) license. The book as a whole is distributed by MDPI under the terms and conditions of the Creative Commons Attribution-NonCommercial-NoDerivs (CC BY-NC-ND) license.

Contents

About the Editors vii

Alexandru Agapie
Spherical Distributions Used in Evolutionary Algorithms
Reprinted from: *Mathematics* **2021**, *9*, 3098, doi:10.3390/d14020121 1

Alexandru Agapie
Evolution Strategies under the 1/5 Success Rule
Reprinted from: *Mathematics* **2023**, *11*, 201, doi:10.3390/math11010201 17

Cong Wang, Jun He, Yu Chen and Xiufen Zou
Influence of Binomial Crossover on Approximation Error of Evolutionary Algorithms
Reprinted from: *Mathematics* **2022**, *10*, 2850, doi:10.3390/math10162850 37

Marius Giuclea and Costin-Ciprian Popescu
On Geometric Mean and Cumulative Residual Entropy for Two Random Variables with Lindley Type Distribution
Reprinted from: *Mathematics* **2022**, *10*, 1499, doi:10.3390/math10091499 61

Jimmy Reyes, Mario A. Rojas, Pedro L. Cortés and Jaime Arrué
A More Flexible Asymmetric Exponential Modification of the Laplace Distribution with Applications for Chemical Concentration and Environment Data
Reprinted from: *Mathematics* **2022**, *10*, 3515, doi:10.3390/math10193515 71

Cristina-Liliana Pripoae, Iulia-Elena Hirica, Gabriel-Teodor Pripoae and Vasile Preda
Fisher-like Metrics Associated with ϕ-Deformed (Naudts) Entropies
Reprinted from: *Mathematics* **2022**, *10*, 4311, doi:10.3390/math10224311 91

Alexander Zhdanok and Anna Khuruma
Decomposition of Finitely Additive Markov Chains in Discrete Space
Reprinted from: *Mathematics* **2022**, *10*, 2083, doi:10.3390/math10122083 117

Yoon Tae Kim and Hyun Suk Park
Fourth Cumulant Bound of Multivariate Normal Approximation on General Functionals of Gaussian Fields
Reprinted from: *Mathematics* **2022**, *10*, 1352, doi:10.3390/math10081352 139

Gerrit Lodewicus Grobler, Elzanie Bothma and James Samuel Allison
Testing for the Rayleigh Distribution: A New Test with Comparisons to Tests for Exponentiality Based on Transformed Data
Reprinted from: *Mathematics* **2022**, *10*, 1316, doi:10.3390/math10081316 157

Refah Alotaibi, Ehab M. Almetwally, Qiuchen Hai and Hoda Rezk
Optimal Test Plan of Step Stress Partially Accelerated Life Testing for Alpha Power Inverse Weibull Distribution under Adaptive Progressive Hybrid Censored Data and Different Loss Functions
Reprinted from: *Mathematics* **2022**, *10*, 4652, doi:10.3390/math10244652 175

Taras Lukashiv, Yuliia Litvinchuk, Igor V. Malyk, Anna Golebiewska and Petr V. Nazarov
Stabilization of Stochastic Dynamical Systems of a Random Structure with Markov Switches and Poisson Perturbations
Reprinted from: *Mathematics* **2023**, *11*, 582, doi:10.3390/math11030582 199

Tudor Sireteanu, Ana-Maria Mitu, Ovidiu Solomon and Marius Giuclea
Approximation of the Statistical Characteristics of Piecewise Linear Systems with Asymmetric Damping and Stiffness under Stationary Random Excitation
Reprinted from: *Mathematics* **2022**, *10*, 4275, doi:10.3390/math10224275 . . . . **221**

Gurami Tsitsiashvili, Marina Osipova and Yury Kharchenko
Estimating the Coefficients of a System of Ordinary Differential Equations Based on Inaccurate Observations
Reprinted from: *Mathematics* **2022**, *10*, 502, doi:10.3390/math10030502 . . . . **237**

Daniel Homocianu
Exploring the Predictors of Co-Nationals' Preference over Immigrants in Accessing Jobs—Evidence from World Values Survey
Reprinted from: *Mathematics* **2023**, *11*, 786, doi:10.3390/math11030786 . . . . **247**

Gil Cohen
Algorithmic Strategies for Precious Metals Price Forecasting
Reprinted from: *Mathematics* **2022**, *10*, 1134, doi:10.3390/math10071134 . . . . **277**

About the Editors

Alexandru Agapie

Alexandru Agapie is a Full Professor in the Department of Applied Mathematics at The Bucharest University of Economic Studies, Bucharest, Romania, and a Senior Researcher with the "Gheorghe Mihoc—Caius Iacob" Institute of Mathematical Statistics and Applied Mathematics of the Romanian Academy, Bucharest. He received his Lic. and Ph.D. degrees in Mathematics from the University of Bucharest, Romania, in 1993 and 2001, respectively. He has worked with the National Institute for Microtechnology, Bucharest, and the Fraunhofer Institute for Autonomous Intelligent Systems, Sankt Augustin, Germany. His fields of interest are stochastic processes applied to evolutionary algorithms and to socio-economic models. Dr. Agapie was a DAAD Research Fellow at TU Dortmund, Germany, in 2011, a NATO-COBASE Research Fellow at Montana University, Missoula, USA, in 2000 and received a Student Fellowship Award at the IEEE International Conference on Evolutionary Computation, Nagoya, Japan, in 1996. He has also been serving as the Scientific Secretary of the Romanian Society for Probability and Statistics since 2012, has been a Member of the European Cooperation in Science and Technology (COST) since 2009, and has been an Expert for the National Research Council, Romania, since 2011.

Denis Enachescu

Denis Enăchescu is currently a Ph.D. supervisor at the Computer Science Doctoral School and an emeritus professor at the University of Bucharest, Bucharest, Romania. He received his Lic. and Ph.D. degrees in Mathematics from the University of Bucharest, Romania, in 1975 and 1980, respectively. He was the Deputy Dean of the Faculty of Mathematics and Computer Science from 2008 to 2015. His research fields include simulation methods, particularly the Monte Carlo method, data mining methods, especially factorial methods, cluster and discriminant analysis, artificial intelligence, neuronal networks and support vector machines for supervised and unsupervised statistical learning and biostatistics, especially statistical methods for bioavailability and bioequivalence. He was awarded the "Ghe. Lazăr" Prize of the Romanian Academy in 1985. He has been a member of the International Association for Statistical Computing—IASC, a member of the Gesellschaft fur Angewandte Mathematik und Mechanik—GAMM, and an elected ordinary member of the International Statistical Institute—ISI. He is also a founding member of the Romanian Society of Probability and Mathematical Statistics, a member of the Association of Balkan Statisticians—ABS, a member of the International Biometric Society—IBS, and a member of the International Society for Clinical Biostatistics—ISCB.

Vlad Stefan Barbu

Vlad Stefan Barbu has been an Associate Professor at the Laboratory of Mathematics Raphaël Salem (LMRS) at the University of Rouen, Normandy, France, since 2006. He received his Ph.D. in Statistics from the University of Technology of Compiègne, France, in 2005. In 2017, he received his HDR (Habilitation to Conduct Research) in Statistics. His main research fields lie in Markov and Hidden Markov processes, statistical inference for stochastic processes, parametric and nonparametric estimation, hypotheses testing, stochastic methods in reliability and survival analysis. He is also a serving member of the French Statistical Society—SFdS (elected member of the Council of the group Reliability and Uncertainty), a member of the Romanian Society of Probability and Statistics—SPSR (elected scientific secretary), a member of the French Society of Applied and Industrial Mathematics—SMAI, a member of the Romanian Society of Applied and Industrial

Mathematics—ROMAI (elected vice-president), a member of the Society for International Stochastic Modeling Techniques and Data Analysis—SMTDA, and member of the Institute of Complex Systems in Normandy—ISCN.

Bogdan Iftimie

Bogdan Iftimie is a Full Professor in the Department of Applied Mathematics and the Vice Dean of the Faculty of Economic Cybernetics, Statistics and Informatics at the Bucharest University of Economic Studies, Bucharest, Romania. He received his Ph.D. in mathematics from the Institute of Mathematics of the Romanian Academy in 2001. His research interests include stochastic processes in finance, stochastic partial differential equations, and financial models with advanced or delayed information.

Article

Spherical Distributions Used in Evolutionary Algorithms

Alexandru Agapie [1,2]

[1] Department of Applied Mathematics, Faculty of Economic Cybernetics, Statistics and Informatics, Bucharest University of Economic Studies, Calea Dorobantilor 15-17, 010552 Bucharest, Romania; alexandru.agapie@csie.ase.ro
[2] "Gheorghe Mihoc—Caius Iacob" Institute of Mathematical Statistics and Applied Mathematics of the Romanian Academy, 050711 Bucharest, Romania

Abstract: Performance of evolutionary algorithms in real space is evaluated by local measures such as success probability and expected progress. In high-dimensional landscapes, most algorithms rely on the normal multi-variate, easy to assemble from independent, identically distributed components. This paper analyzes a different distribution, also spherical, yet with dependent components and compact support: uniform in the sphere. Under a simple setting of the parameters, two algorithms are compared on a quadratic fitness function. The success probability and the expected progress of the algorithm with uniform distribution are proved to dominate their normal mutation counterparts by order $n!!$.

Keywords: probabilistic optimization; spherical distribution; multi-variate calculus; hypergeometric functions; transition kernel

1. Introduction

Probabilistic algorithms are among the most popular optimization techniques due to their easy implementation and high efficiency. Their roots can be traced back to the first random walk problem proposed by Pearson in 1905: "*A man starts from a point O, and walks ℓ yards in a straight line; he then turns through any angle whatever, and walks another ℓ yards in a second straight line. He repeats this process n times. I require the probability that after these n stretches he is at a distance between r and r + dr from his starting point O.*" [1–4].

Using the ability of computers to generate and store large samples from multi-variate distributions, physicists and engineers have transformed the original random walk into a powerful optimization tool. Probabilistic algorithms do not require additional information on the fitness function, they simply *generate* potential candidate solutions, *select* the best, and move on.

Sharing the same random generator, yet differing with respect to the selection phase, two classes of probabilistic algorithms became more popular over the last decades: *simulated annealing* (also known as Metropolis or Hastings algorithm) [5] and *evolutionary algorithms* (EAs) [6,7]. Only the latter will be discussed in this paper.

EAs are assessed based on local quantities, such as success probability and progress rate, respectively, on global measures, like expected convergence time. Performance depends on both the fitness landscape, and on the particular probabilistic scheme (leading to a probability distribution) involved in the generating-selection mechanism. A popular test problem consists in minimizing the quadratic *SPHERE* function (To avoid confusion, we use uppercase for the fitness function, and lowercase for the uniform distribution in/on the sphere.), with optimum in the origin.

$$\mathcal{F}: \Re^n \to \Re \qquad \mathcal{F}(x_1, \ldots, x_n) = \sum_{i=1}^{n} x_i^2. \tag{1}$$

An elitist (that is, keeping always the best solution found so far), one-individual, mutation+selection EA is depicted below (Algorithm 1).

Algorithm 1 An elitist, one-individual, mutation+selection EA.

Set $t = 0$ and the initial point of the algorithm, x^0
Repeat
$\quad t := t + 1$
$\quad$ *Mutation*: generate a new point $x \in \Re^n$ according to a multi-variate distribution
$\quad$ *Selection*:if $\mathcal{F}(\mathbf{x}) < \mathcal{F}(\mathbf{x}^{t-1})$ then $\mathbf{x}^t := \mathbf{x}$
$\quad\quad$ else $x^t := x^{t-1}$
Until $t = t_{\max}$, for some fixed $t_{\max}$

The region of success of Algorithm 1 is

$$R_x^S = \{y \in \Re^n | \mathcal{F}(y) < \mathcal{F}(x)\}. \tag{2}$$

A rigorous description of the long-term behavior of EAs involves renewal processes, drift analysis, order statistics, martingales, or other stochastic processes [7–13]. However, the basic structure is that of a Markov chain, as the algorithm's state at the next iteration depends only on its current state. Difficulties occur when, even for simple fitness functions, SPHERE included, the actual position of the algorithm affects significantly the local behavior, such that the process lacks homogeneity; so begins the search for powerful mathematical tools, able to describe the transition kernel, which encapsulates the local probabilistic structure of the algorithm [6,7].

For any fitness function $\mathcal{F}$ and fixed point $x \in \Re^n$, assumed as current state, the transition kernel provides the probability of the algorithm to be in set $A \subset \Re^n$ at the next step. Even if the mutation distribution has a probability density function (pdf), discontinuity occurs due to the disruptive effect of elitist selection. To make that clear, let us denote the mutation random variable by $\mathbf{Y}$, its pdf by f, and cumulative distribution function (cdf) by F. The singular (Dirac) distribution, that loads only one point, is denoted δ. Index x designates conditioning by the current state. The finite time behavior of the algorithm is inscribed in the random variable $\mathbf{Z}_x$ and the next state of the algorithm, provided the current state, is x.

$$\mathbf{Z}_x(\omega) = \begin{cases} \mathbf{Y}_x(\omega), & \mathbf{Y}_x(\omega) \in R_x^S \\ x, & \mathbf{Y}_x(\omega) \in \Re^n \setminus R_x^S \end{cases}. \tag{3}$$

while the (Markov) *transition kernel* carries the local transition probabilities

$$P_x(A) = \int_{A \cap R_x^S} f(y) dy + \left[1 - \int_{A \cap R_x^S} f(y) dy\right] \cdot \delta_x(A). \tag{4}$$

As the mutation distribution is entirely responsible for the evolution of the algorithm, let us take a look at the possible candidates, the multi-variate distributions.

Let $\mathbf{x} = (\mathbf{x}_1, \ldots, \mathbf{x}_n)$ denote some n-dimensional random variable, and the euclidean norm in $\Re^n$ be $||x|| = (x'x)^{1/2} = \left(\sum_{i=1}^n x_i^2\right)^{1/2}$. The n-dimensional sphere of radius 1, its surface and volume are given by [14]

$$S_n = \{x \in \Re^n \mid ||x|| \leq 1\}, \quad \delta S_n = \{x \in \Re^n \mid ||x|| = 1\}, \quad V_n = \frac{2\pi^{\frac{n}{2}}}{n\Gamma_{\frac{n}{2}}}. \tag{5}$$

We use 'bold-face' for (single, or multi-variate) random variables, and 'normal-face' for real numbers (or vectors). When partitioning the n dimensions into two sets $\{1, \ldots, m\}$

and $\{m+1,\ldots,n\}$ with $1 \leq m < 1$, we use the compact notation $x = (x_{(1)}, x_{(2)}) = ((x_1,\ldots,x_m),(x_{m+1},\ldots,x_n))$, for either vectors or random variables. Unless otherwise stated, **Beta**$_{a,b}$ denotes the beta random variable with support $(0,1)$ and parameters a, b, while β and Γ stand for the corresponding coefficients. The (one-dimensional) uniform random variable with support (a,b) is denoted $\mathbf{U}_{(a,b)}$. The sign $\stackrel{d}{=}$ denotes two random variables with identical cdf.

The class of spherical distributions can be defined in a number of equivalent ways, two of which are depicted below ([15], pp. 30, 35) (See the excellent monograph of Fang et al. [15] for an exhaustive introduction to spherical distributions.):

Definition 1.
- *An n-dimensional random variable* $\mathbf{x}$ *is said to have spherically symmetric distribution* (or simply spherical distribution) *if*

$$\mathbf{x} \stackrel{d}{=} \mathbf{r} \cdot \mathbf{u}^n \qquad (6)$$

for some one-dimensional random variable (radius) $\mathbf{r}$, *and the uniform distribution on the unit sphere* $\mathbf{u}^n$. *Moreover,* $\mathbf{r}$ *and* $\mathbf{u}^n$ *are independent, and also*

$$\mathbf{r} = ||\mathbf{x}|| \geq 0, \qquad \mathbf{u}^n \stackrel{d}{=} \frac{\mathbf{x}}{||\mathbf{x}||}. \qquad (7)$$

- *If the spherical distribution has pdf* g, *then* g *satisfies* $g(x) = g(||x||)$, *and there is a special connection between* g *and* f, *the pdf of* $\mathbf{r}$, *namely,*

$$f(r) = \frac{2\pi^{n/2}}{\Gamma_{\frac{n}{2}}} r^{n-1} g(r^2). \qquad (8)$$

Three spherical distributions are of particular interest in our analysis:
- the uniform distribution *on* the unit sphere, with support δS_n, denoted $\mathbf{u}^n$;
- the uniform distribution *in (inside)* the unit sphere, with support S_n, denoted simply UNIFORM in this paper; and
- the standard normal distribution, denoted $\mathbf{N}(\mathbf{0}, \mathbf{I_n})$ or simply NORMAL.

A comparison of the previous distributions can be performed from many angles. NORMAL was the first discovered, applied, and thoroughly analyzed in statistics, as being one of the only spherical distributions with independent and identically distributed marginals. By contrast, the components of uniform distributions on/in the sphere are not independent, neither uniform (However, the conditional marginals are uniform, see Theorem 5). Recently, the scientific interest shifted to uniform multi-variate distributions, following the increasing application of directional statistics to earth sciences and quantum mechanics [16,17], and also the application of Dirichlet distribution (which lies at the basis of spherical analysis) to Bayesian inference, involved in medicine, genetics, and text-mining [18].

From the computer science point of view, uniform and normal distributions share an entangled history, in at least two areas: random number generators and probabilistic optimization algorithms. With respect to the first area, early approaches to sampling from the uniform distribution on sphere were actually using multi-normal random generators to produce a sample x, which was further divided by $||x||$, following Equation (7). Nowadays, the situation changed, with the appearance of a new class of algorithms which circumvent the usage of the normal generator by using properties of marginal uniform distributions on/in spheres [17,19]. The comparison of mean computation times demonstrates that the uniform sampling method outperforms the normal generator for dimensions up to $n = 7$ [20].

Concerning global optimization, the probabilistic algorithms based on the two distribution types evolved at the same time, although with few overlaps. In the theory and practice of real space (continuous) EA-*evolution strategy* being their most popular, the representative-normal distribution has played, from the beginning, the central role. Therefore, there is a great amount of literature stressing out the advantages of this distribution [6,21,22].

Occasionally, the supremacy of the normal operator has been challenged by theoretical studies that proposed different mutation distributions, such as uniform in the cube (which is non-spherical) [10], uniform *on* the sphere [7,23], uniform *in* the sphere [9], or even the Cauchy distribution [24]. An attempt to solve the problem globally, by considering the whole class of *spherical* (*isotropic*) distributions, was made in [25,26]. These approaches yielded only limited results (valid either for small space dimension n, or for $n \to \infty$), or not so tight lower/upper bounds for the expected progress of the algorithm.

The study of EAs with uniform distribution in the sphere recently culminated with two systematic studies, one for RIDGE [27], the other for SPHERE [28], comparable to classical theory of evolution strategies [6,29]. Under a carefully constructed normalization of mutation parameters (equalizing the expectations of normal and uniform multi-variates as $n \to \infty$), those studies demonstrate the same behavior for the respective EA variants. Intuitively, the explanation is that for large dimensions, both normal and uniform distributions concentrate *on* the surface of the sphere. The present paper differs from the previous analyses in the way that it does not apply any normalization of parameters. As a consequence, the results are different from those in [28] and an actual comparison between the two algorithms can be achieved.

Section 2 discusses the general framework of spherical multi-variate distributions, with special focus on uniform and normal. Then, two algorithms, one with uniform mutation and the other with normal mutation, are compared on the SPHERE fitness function with respect to their local performance in Section 3.

2. Materials and Methods. Spherical Distributions

In light of Definition 1, the spherical distributions are very much alike. They all exhibit stochastic representation (6), that is, each can be generated as a product of two independent distributions, the n-dimensional uniform on the sphere $\mathbf{u^n}$ and some scalar, positive random variable $\mathbf{r}$. As the distribution of $\mathbf{r}$ makes the whole difference, we point out the form of this random variable in the three cases of interest.

- $\mathbf{u^n}$-$\mathbf{r}$ is obviously the Dirac distribution in 1:

$$\delta_1(x) = 1, \quad x = 1. \tag{9}$$

- NORMAL-$\mathbf{r}$ is the χ distribution with n degrees of freedom, with pdf ([7], p. 20):

$$f(x) = \frac{1}{2^{\frac{n}{2}-1}\Gamma\frac{n}{2}} e^{-\frac{x^2}{2}} x^{n-1}, \quad x \in (0,\infty). \tag{10}$$

- UNIFORM-$\mathbf{r}$ is distributed $\mathbf{Beta}_{n,1}$, with pdf ([15], p. 75):

$$f(x) = nx^{n-1}, \quad x \in (0,1). \tag{11}$$

Using as primary source the monograph [15], we next discuss in more detail the stochastic properties of the UNIFORM and NORMAL multi-variates, the two candidates for the mutation operator of the algorithm.

2.1. Uniform in the Sphere

The local analysis of the EA is based on two particular marginal distributions: the first component $\mathbf{x_1}$, and the joint marginal of the remaining $n-1$ components, $\mathbf{x_{(2)}}$. As already pointed out, the marginals of UNIFORM are not independent random variables, and we shall see that neither are they uniform. A general formula for the marginal density is provided in [15] (p. 75):

Theorem 1. *If $x = (x_{(1)}, x_{(2)})$ is uniformly distributed in the unit sphere, with $x_{(1)}$ of dimension k, $1 \leq k < n$, then the marginal density of $x_{(1)}$ is*

$$f(x_{(1)}) = \frac{\pi^{-\frac{k}{2}} \Gamma_{\frac{n+2}{2}}}{\Gamma_{\frac{n-k+2}{2}}} \left(1 - ||x_{(1)}||\right)^{\frac{n-k}{2}}, \quad ||x_{(1)}||^2 < 1. \tag{12}$$

Corollary 1. *The pdf of the first component of UNIFORM is*

$$f(x) = \frac{1}{\beta_{\frac{n+1}{2}, \frac{1}{2}}} (1 - x^2)^{\frac{n-1}{2}}, \quad x \in (-1, 1). \tag{13}$$

Using the symmetry with respect to the origin and substituting $x^2 = t$ in function (13), we obtain an interesting result, previously unreported in spherical distributions literature.

Corollary 2. *The square of the first component of UNIFORM is $\mathbf{Beta}_{\frac{n+1}{2}, \frac{1}{2}}$, with pdf*

$$f(x) = \frac{1}{\beta_{\frac{n+1}{2}, \frac{1}{2}}} (1 - x)^{\frac{n-1}{2}} x^{-\frac{1}{2}}, \quad x \in (0, 1). \tag{14}$$

The density of the last $n - 1$ components can be derived also from Theorem 1.

Corollary 3. *The joint pdf of the last $n - 1$ components of UNIFORM is*

$$f(x_{(2)}) = n\pi^{-\frac{n}{2}} \Gamma_{\frac{n}{2}} \left(1 - ||x_{(2)}||^2\right)^{\frac{1}{2}}, \quad ||x_{(2)}||^2 < 1. \tag{15}$$

As function of several variables, formula (15) might not look very appealing; however, a basic result from spherical distribution theory transforms the corresponding multiple integral into a scalar one ([15], p. 23).

Theorem 2 (Dimension reduction).

$$\int f\left(\sum_{i=1}^m x_i^2\right) dx_1, \ldots, dx_m = \frac{\pi^{\frac{m}{2}}}{\Gamma_{\frac{m}{2}}} \int_0^\infty y^{\frac{m}{2}-1} f(y) dy. \tag{16}$$

One can see now that, if x is uniformly distributed in the unit sphere, the sum of squares of the last $n - 1$ components is **Beta** distributed.

Corollary 4. *Let $x = (x_1, x_{(2)})$ be UNIFORM. Then, the one-dimensional random variable $||x_{(2)}||^2$ is $\mathbf{Beta}_{\frac{n-1}{2}, \frac{3}{2}}$, with pdf*

$$f(x) = \frac{1}{\beta_{\frac{n-1}{2}, \frac{3}{2}}} (1 - x)^{\frac{n-3}{2}} x^{\frac{1}{2}}, \quad x \in (0, 1). \tag{17}$$

Proof. Apply transformation (16) to (15), $m = n - 1$ and $f(y) = (1 - y)^{(n-1)/2}$. □

As the components of the uniform distribution on/in the sphere are not independent, a better understanding of the nature of such distributions is provided by conditioning one component with respect to the others. In case of uniform distribution *on* the sphere, the work in [15] (p. 74) states that all the conditional marginals are also uniform *on* the sphere.

We shall see that a similar characterization holds true for the uniform *in* the sphere. This result is not presented in [15] and, to the best of our knowledge, in no other reference on spherical distributions. Therefore, an additional theorem is needed ([30], p. 375).

Theorem 3. *Let* $\mathbf{x} \stackrel{d}{=} \mathbf{r} \cdot \mathbf{u}^n$ *be a spherical distribution and* $\mathbf{x} = (\mathbf{x}_{(1)}, \mathbf{x}_{(2)})$, *where* $\mathbf{x}_{(1)}$ *is m-dimensional,* $1 \leq m < n$. *Then the conditional distribution of* $\mathbf{x}_{(1)}$ *given* $\mathbf{x}_{(2)} = h$ *with* $||h|| = a$ *is given by*

$$\left(\mathbf{x}_{(1)} \mid \mathbf{x}_{(2)} = h\right) \stackrel{d}{=} \mathbf{r}_{a^2} \cdot \mathbf{u}^m. \tag{18}$$

For each $a \geq 0$, $\mathbf{r}_{a^2}$ *and* $\mathbf{u}^m$ *are independent, and the cdf of* $\mathbf{r}_{a^2}$ *is given by*

$$\text{prob}(\mathbf{r}_{a^2} \leq t) = \frac{\int_a^{\sqrt{t^2+a^2}} (r^2 - a^2)^{m/2 - 1} r^{-(n-2)} dF(r)}{\int_a^{\infty} (r^2 - a^2)^{m/2 - 1} r^{-(n-2)} dF(r)}, \tag{19}$$

for $t \geq 0$, $a > 0$ *and* $F(a) < 1$, F *being the cdf of* $\mathbf{r}$.

We prove now the result on conditional marginals of the uniform distribution *in* the unit sphere. As conditioning the first component with respect to all others is the most relevant for EA analysis, this particular case is stressed out.

First, an old result from probability theory is needed, similar to the convolution operation, but for the *product* of two independent random variables [31].

Theorem 4 (Mellin's formula). *Let* $\mathbf{y}$ *and* $\mathbf{z}$ *be two independent, non-negative random variables, with densities g and h. Then,* $\mathbf{x} = \mathbf{y} \cdot \mathbf{z}$ *has pdf*

$$f(x) = \int_0^{\infty} \frac{1}{z} g\left(\frac{x}{z}\right) h(z) dz, \quad x \in (0, \infty). \tag{20}$$

Note that Mellin's formula still holds, if only one of the random variables is continuous, the other being discrete, see, e.g., in [15] (p. 41).

Theorem 5.

- *Let* $\mathbf{x} = (\mathbf{x}_{(1)}, \mathbf{x}_{(2)})$ *be UNIFORM, where* $\mathbf{x}_{(1)}$ *is m-dimensional,* $1 \leq m < n$. *The conditional distribution of* $\mathbf{x}_{(1)}$ *given* $\mathbf{x}_{(2)} = a$ *is UNIFORM in the m dimensional sphere with radius* $(1 - ||a||^2)^{1/2}$.
- *If* $m = 1$ *and* $\mathbf{x}_{(2)} = h$ *is a point in* S_{n-1} *with* $||h|| = a$, *the conditional distribution of* x_1 *given* $\mathbf{x}_{(2)} = h$ *is*

$$\left(x_1 \mid \mathbf{x}_{(2)} = h\right) \stackrel{d}{=} \mathbf{U}_{(-\sqrt{1-a^2}, \sqrt{1-a^2})}. \tag{21}$$

Proof. We begin with the last part, case $m = 1$.

Equation (18) gives the conditional first component as a product of two independent random variables, the second being the one-dimensional UNIFORM-the discrete random variable that loads -1 and 1 with equal probability, $1/2$.

The cdf of the first random variable is given by (19), as a fraction of two integrals, both with respect to F, the cdf of $\mathbf{r}$. In case of UNIFORM, $\mathbf{r}$ is $\text{Beta}_{n,1}$ given by (11), thus $dF(r) = f(r)dr = nr^{n-1}dr$.

If $t \geq \sqrt{1 - a^2}$, the upper and lower integrals in (19) are equal, so the probability is 1. If $0 \leq t < \sqrt{1 - a^2}$, the upper integral is

$$n \int_a^{\sqrt{t^2+a^2}} r(r^2 - a^2)^{-1/2} dr = nt,$$

while the lower one is

$$n \int_a^1 r(r^2 - a^2)^{-1/2} dr = n\sqrt{1 - a^2}.$$

Thus, for any fixed $a < 1$, the cdf of the conditional radius is

$$prob(\mathbf{r}_{a^2} \leq t) = \frac{t}{\sqrt{1-a^2}}, \quad t \in (0, \sqrt{1-a^2}),$$

while the corresponding pdf is

$$\mathbf{r}_{a^2} \stackrel{d}{=} \mathbf{U}_{(0,\sqrt{1-a^2})}.$$

Back to the application of Theorem 3, Equation (18). The conditional first component of UNIFORM is a product of two independent random variables: one continuous, the other discrete. This is the easy version of Mellin's formula, and the result is the continuous uniform random variable with support $(-\sqrt{1-a^2}, \sqrt{1-a^2})$ from Equation (21).

As for a larger dimension, $m > 1$, the cdf in (19) becomes

$$prob(\mathbf{r}_{a^2} \leq t) = \frac{t^m}{(1-a^2)^{\frac{m}{2}}}, \quad t \in \left(0, (1-a^2)^{\frac{m}{2}}\right),$$

with corresponding pdf

$$f(t) = \frac{mt^{m-1}}{(1-a^2)^{\frac{m}{2}}}, \quad t \in \left(0, (1-a^2)^{\frac{m}{2}}\right),$$

which is **Beta**$_{m,1}$, yet with reduced support.

Summing up, Equation (18) provides the conditional marginal as a product of the uniform in the unit sphere and a reduced **Beta**$_{m,1}$. According to representation (11), the result is UNIFORM, in m dimensions, with the center being the origin and reduced radius $r = (1-a^2)^{m/2}$. □

2.2. Normal

As we did with UNIFORM, we denote the first component of the standard normal multi-variate distribution by $\mathbf{x}$, and the remaining $n-1$ components by $\mathbf{x}_{(2)}$. Due to independence of the marginals, one can write a compact equivalent of Propositions 1 and 3, see, e.g., in [6] (p. 54).

Proposition 1. *Let $\mathbf{x} = (\mathbf{x}_1, \mathbf{x}_{(2)})$ be NORMAL.*

- *The pdf of the first component, $\mathbf{x}_1$, is*

$$f(x) = \frac{1}{\sqrt{2\pi}} e^{-\frac{x^2}{2}}, \quad x \in \Re. \tag{22}$$

- *The joint pdf of the last $n-1$ components, $\mathbf{x}_{(2)}$, is*

$$f(x_{(2)}) = \frac{1}{\left(\sqrt{2\pi}\right)^{n-1}} e^{-\frac{\|x_{(2)}\|^2}{2}}, \quad x_{(2)} \in \Re^{n-1}. \tag{23}$$

Due to sphericity of the joint $n-1$ components, one obtains again a compact form for the sum of squares.

Corollary 5. *The one-dimensional random variable $\|x_{(2)}\|^2$ is χ^2 with $n-1$ degrees of freedom, with pdf*

$$f(x) = \frac{2^{-\frac{n-1}{2}}}{\Gamma_{\frac{n-1}{2}}} x^{\frac{n-3}{2}} e^{-\frac{x}{2}}, \quad x \in (0, \infty). \tag{24}$$

3. Results

We restrict the study to the case P (current algorithm position) nearby O (optimum of SPHERE) and analyze the local performance of two EAs, one with uniform, the other with normal mutation, in terms of success probability and expected progress. Namely, we assume $R = |OP| \leq 1/2$, such that success region R_P^S is the sphere with center O and radius R, Figure 1.

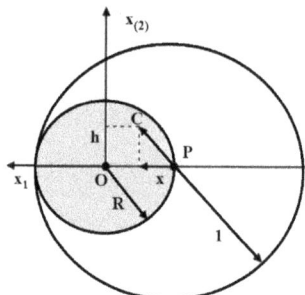

Figure 1. Success region of Algorithm 1 with uniform mutation on SPHERE.

Re-set P as the origin of the coordinate system, and measure the algorithm's progress in the positive direction of the first axis-write x for x_1, h for $x_{(2)}$ and u for $||h||^2$. The success probability and the expected progress are provided by the first term of transition kernel (4), respectively, by the upper part of random variable (3). They obey to the uniform continuous mutation distribution with pdf $f(x) = 1/V_n$ and compact support, the sphere with center P and radius 1.

The calculus of success probability and expected progress resides in integrating the random variable (3) over R_P^S. For UNIFORM mutation this calculus is analytically tractable. For NORMAL mutation, the analytic integration is impossible, see in [6] (p. 56) and Theorem 8, but the theory of incomplete Gamma functions makes the comparison tractable.

Note that, if the success probability bears only one possible definition (the volume of success region), the situation is different with respect to the expected progress. As the random variable $\mathbf{Z}_x$ from (3) characterizes the local behavior of the algorithm, one would normally associate the expected progress to the expected value of this random variable. However, $\mathbf{Z}_x$ is n-dimensional, and such is $E(\mathbf{Z}_x)$, so there is a need to mediate somehow among the n components.

One could consider only the first component of the expected value, the one pointing towards the optimum, which has been applied on a different fitness landscape, the inclined plane [21]. (Yet in another landscape, the RIDGE, it is customary to consider the progress along the perpendicular component h, see in [6,27] for an inventory of fitness functions used in EA testing, the reader is referred to the work in [32].) For UNIFORM mutation, a simplified version of the expected progress may be defined as the centroid of the corresponding success region [9,10]. However, a more traditional view is followed here ([6], p. 54):

$$\mathbf{progress} = R - \sqrt{(R - x)^2 + u}. \tag{25}$$

This corresponds to the difference in distance $|OP| - |OC|$, provided $\mathbf{C}$ is a random point generated by mutation, Figure 1.

3.1. Uniform Mutation

If the UNIFORM mutation in the unit sphere with center P is applied, one cannot use for integration the ensemble of Propositions 1 and 3, as the marginals of UNIFORM are not independent. Instead, one should use the conditional first component from Theorem 5, together with the joint $n-1$ dimensional distribution from Proposition 3. The integration region is

$$\begin{cases} u = ||h||^2 \in (0, R^2) \\ x \in \left(R - \sqrt{R^2 - u}, R + \sqrt{R^2 - u}\right) \end{cases}.$$

Theorem 6. *Let an EA with UNIFORM mutation minimizing the SPHERE be situated at current distance R from the origin, $R \in (0, 1/2)$. The success probability is*

$$prob^U = R^n. \tag{26}$$

Proof. The use of Equations (4), (15), (16) and (21) yields

$$prob^U = \int_{S_n^O} 1_{S_n^p} dx$$

$$= n\pi^{-\frac{n}{2}} \Gamma_{\frac{n}{2}} \int_{h \in S_{n-1}^O} \left(1 - ||h||^2\right)^{\frac{1}{2}} \times \frac{1}{2\sqrt{1 - ||h||^2}} \int_{R - \sqrt{R^2 - ||h||^2}}^{R + \sqrt{R^2 - ||h||^2}} 1 \, dx \, dh$$

$$= \frac{n\pi^{\frac{n-1}{2} - \frac{n}{2}} \Gamma_{\frac{n}{2}}}{\Gamma_{\frac{n-1}{2}}} \int_0^{R^2} y^{\frac{n-1}{2} - 1} \sqrt{R^2 - y} \, dy = \frac{n \Gamma_{\frac{n}{2}}}{\sqrt{\pi} \Gamma_{\frac{n-1}{2}}} \int_0^{R^2} y^{\frac{n-3}{2}} \sqrt{R^2 - y} \, dy = R^n. \tag{27}$$

□

Theorem 7. *Let an EA with UNIFORM mutation minimizing the SPHERE be situated at current distance R from the origin, $R \in (0, 1/2)$. The expected progress is*

$$\phi^U = \frac{R^{n+1}}{n+1} \tag{28}$$

Proof. Following the proof of Theorem 6 and inserting factor (25), one gets

$$\phi^U = \frac{1}{2} \frac{n \Gamma_{\frac{n}{2}}}{\sqrt{\pi} \Gamma_{\frac{n-1}{2}}} \times \int_{u=0}^{R^2} u^{\frac{n-3}{2}} \int_{R - \sqrt{R^2 - u}}^{R + \sqrt{R^2 - u}} \left(R - \sqrt{(R-x)^2 + u}\right) dx \, du$$

$$= C \int_{u=0}^{R^2} u^{\frac{n-3}{2}} \int_{R - \sqrt{R^2 - u}}^{R + \sqrt{R^2 - u}} R \, dx \, du - C \int_{u=0}^{R^2} u^{\frac{n-3}{2}} \int_{R - \sqrt{R^2 - u}}^{R + \sqrt{R^2 - u}} \sqrt{(R-x)^2 + u} \, dx \, du$$

$$= C I_1 - C I_2.$$

We treat separately I_1 and I_2. I_1 is simply (27), multiplied by the constant R, thus

$$C I_1 = R^{n+1}. \tag{29}$$

For I_2 one can apply formula ([33], p. 13)

$$\int (x^2 + a)^{\frac{1}{2}} dx = \frac{x}{2}(x^2 + a)^{\frac{1}{2}} + \frac{a}{2} \ln\left(x + (x^2 + a)^{\frac{1}{2}}\right).$$

in order to get

$$I_2 = \int_{u=0}^{R^2} u^{\frac{n-3}{2}} R \sqrt{R^2 - u} \, du + \int_{u=0}^{R^2} u^{\frac{n-3}{2}} \frac{u}{2} \ln \frac{R + \sqrt{R^2 - u}}{R - \sqrt{R^2 - u}} \, du = I_3 + I_4. \tag{30}$$

Again, I_3 is the integral (27), multiplied by $R/2$, thus

$$C I_3 = \frac{R^{n+1}}{2}. \tag{31}$$

The substitution $y = u/R^2$ on I_4 provides

$$I_4 = \frac{R^{n+1}}{2} \int_0^1 y^{\frac{n-1}{2}} \ln \frac{1 + \sqrt{1-y}}{1 - \sqrt{1-y}} dy$$

while partial integration gives

$$I_4 = \frac{R^{n+1}}{n+1} \int_0^1 y^{\frac{n+1}{2}} \cdot \frac{1}{y\sqrt{1-y}} dy = \frac{R^{n+1}}{n+1} \beta_{\frac{n+1}{2}, \frac{1}{2}}.$$

Bringing in the constant C, one gets

$$C I_4 = \frac{1}{2} \frac{n\Gamma_{\frac{n}{2}}}{\sqrt{\pi}\Gamma_{\frac{n-1}{2}}} \cdot \frac{R^{n+1}}{n+1} \beta_{\frac{n+1}{2}, \frac{1}{2}} = \frac{1}{2} \frac{n-1}{n+1} R^{n+1}. \qquad (32)$$

Summing up (29)–(32) one gets the desired result. □

The results from Theorems 6 and 7 are also presented in [28], yet with different proofs. Equations (26) and (28) point out a remarkable property of the EA with UNIFORM mutation on the SPHERE.

Corollary 6. *In the conditions of Theorems 6 and 7, the success probability is the derivative of the expected progress.*

3.2. Normal Mutation

Setting $\sigma = 1$ and avoiding the transformation $\sigma^* = \sigma n/R$, one obtains the success probability and the expected progress for the EA with standard normal mutation following closely the proof in ([6], pp. 54–56). The incomplete Gamma function is ([33], p. 260):

$$P(a, x) = \frac{1}{\Gamma_a} \int_0^x e^{-t} t^{a-1} dt. \qquad (33)$$

The following expressions are not restricted to the case of algorithm nearby optimum, due to the unbounded support of the normal distribution. Unfortunately, integration is impossible.

Theorem 8. *Let an EA with NORMAL mutation minimizing the SPHERE be situated at current distance R from the origin.*

- *The success probability is*

$$\text{prob}^N = \frac{1}{\sqrt{2\pi}} \int_{x=0}^{2R} e^{-\frac{x^2}{2}} P\left(\frac{n-1}{2}, Rx - \frac{x^2}{2}\right) dx. \qquad (34)$$

- *The expected progress is*

$$\phi^N = \frac{2^{-\frac{n-1}{2}}}{\sqrt{2\pi}\Gamma_{\frac{n-1}{2}}} \int_{x=0}^{2R} \int_{u=0}^{2Rx-x^2} e^{-\frac{x^2}{2}} u^{\frac{n-1}{2}-1} e^{-\frac{u}{2}} \text{ progress } dudx. \qquad (35)$$

Proof.

$$prob^N = \frac{2^{-\frac{n-1}{2}}}{\sqrt{2\pi}\Gamma_{\frac{n-1}{2}}} \int_{x=0}^{2R} \int_{u=0}^{2Rx-x^2} e^{-\frac{x^2}{2}} u^{\frac{n-1}{2}-1} e^{-\frac{u}{2}} du\, dx$$

$$= \frac{2^{-\frac{n-1}{2}}}{\sqrt{2\pi}\Gamma_{\frac{n-1}{2}}} \int_{x=0}^{2R} e^{-\frac{x^2}{2}} \left(\int_{u=0}^{2Rx-x^2} u^{\frac{n-1}{2}-1} e^{-\frac{u}{2}} du \right) dx$$

$$= \frac{1}{\sqrt{2\pi}} \int_{x=0}^{2R} e^{-\frac{x^2}{2}} \left(\frac{1}{\Gamma_{\frac{n-1}{2}}} \int_{t=0}^{Rx-\frac{x^2}{2}} t^{\frac{n-1}{2}-1} e^{-t} dt \right) dx$$

$$= \frac{1}{\sqrt{2\pi}} \int_{x=0}^{2R} e^{-\frac{x^2}{2}} P\left(\frac{n-1}{2}, Rx - \frac{x^2}{2}\right) dx. \tag{36}$$

The same calculus applies for the expected progress, with the addition of the factor corresponding to the one dimensional progress along the x axis, Equation (25). □

3.3. Comparison

Due to the analytic intractability of integral representations (34) and (35), a theoretical comparison between two variants of Algorithm 1-one with UNIFORM, the other with NORMAL mutation-must resort to inequalities. Therefore, a deeper insight into the prolific theory of Euler and hypergeometric functions is required. We start with an upper bound for the incomplete Gamma function (33) ([34], p. 1213).

Proposition 2. *The following inequality holds*

$$P(a, x) \leq \frac{x^a}{a(a+1)\Gamma_a}(1 + ae^{-x}). \tag{37}$$

More results are gathered from in [35], [36] (p. 240), [37] (pp. 890, 894), [38] (pp. 53, 57).

Proposition 3 (Hypergeometric functions).

- For any real set of parameters a, b, a_i, b_i and any real number x, define

$${}_1F_1(a, b \mid x) = \sum_{k=0}^{\infty} \frac{(a)_k}{(b)_k} \frac{x^k}{k!} \tag{38}$$

$${}_2F_2(a_1, a_2; b_1, b_2 \mid x) = \sum_{k=0}^{\infty} \frac{(a_1)_k (a_2)_k}{(b_1)_k (b_2)_k} \frac{x^k}{k!} \tag{39}$$

where $(a)_k = a(a+1)\ldots(a+k-1) = \Gamma_{a+k}/\Gamma_a$ is the Pochhammer symbol, with

$$(a)_{2k} = \left(\frac{a}{2}\right)_k \left(\frac{a+1}{2}\right)_k 2^{2k}. \tag{40}$$

- If $A = (a_1, \ldots, a_q)$ and $B = (b_1, \ldots, b_q)$, we write $B \prec^W A$, if

$$0 < a_1 \leq \ldots \leq a_q, \quad 0 < b_1 \leq \ldots \leq b_q$$

$$\sum_{i=1}^{k} a_i \leq \sum_{i=1}^{k} b_i, \quad k = 1, \ldots, q.$$

- If $B \prec^W A$, the following inequality holds:

$$_pF_p(A, B \mid x) \leq 1 - \theta + \theta e^x, \quad (41)$$

$$\theta = \begin{cases} \frac{a}{b}, & p = 1, \ (A, B) = (a, b) \\ \frac{a_1 a_2}{b_1 b_2}, & p = 2, \ (A, B) = (a_1, a_2; b_1, b_2) \end{cases}.$$

We can prove now the main result stating that, for an EA acting on the SPHERE with current position at maximal range $1/2$ from the origin, the UNIFORM mutation provides a larger success probability than the NORMAL mutation, for the arbitrary dimension n. We denote by $n!!$ the double factorial (semi-factorial), that is, the product of all integers from 1 to n of same parity with n.

Theorem 9. *Let an EA minimizing the SPHERE be situated at current distance R from the origin, such that $R \leq 1/2$. For any $n \geq 3$, the following holds:*

$$\frac{prob^N}{prob^U} < \frac{1}{n!!}. \quad (42)$$

Proof. Apply inequality (37) to Equation (34)

$$prob^N \leq \frac{1}{\sqrt{2\pi}\Gamma_{\frac{n-1}{2}}} \int_{x=0}^{2R} e^{-\frac{x^2}{2}} \frac{4\left(Rx - \frac{x^2}{2}\right)^{\frac{n-1}{2}}}{n^2 - 1} \left(1 + \frac{n-1}{2} e^{\frac{x^2}{2} - Rx}\right) dx$$

$$= \frac{4}{\sqrt{2\pi}(n^2-1)\Gamma_{\frac{n-1}{2}}} \int_{x=0}^{2R} e^{-\frac{x^2}{2}} \left(Rx - \frac{x^2}{2}\right)^{\frac{n-1}{2}} dx$$

$$+ \frac{2}{\sqrt{2\pi}(n+1)} \int_{x=0}^{2R} e^{-Rx} \left(Rx - \frac{x^2}{2}\right)^{\frac{n-1}{2}} dx$$

$$= \frac{R^n 2^{\frac{n+5}{2}}}{\sqrt{2\pi}(n^2-1)\Gamma_{\frac{n-1}{2}}} \int_{x=0}^{1} e^{-2R^2 t^2} t^{\frac{n-1}{2}} (1-t)^{\frac{n-1}{2}} dt \quad (43)$$

$$+ \frac{R^n 2^{\frac{n+3}{2}}}{\sqrt{2\pi}(n+1)\Gamma_{\frac{n-1}{2}}} \int_{x=0}^{1} e^{-2R^2 t} t^{\frac{n-1}{2}} (1-t)^{\frac{n-1}{2}} dt.$$

Using the series expansion of the exponential, the second integral in (43) becomes a hypergeometric function of type (38). The interchange of the integral and the sum is justified by the absolute convergence of the series.

$$\int_{x=0}^{1} e^{-2R^2 t} t^{\frac{n-1}{2}} (1-t)^{\frac{n-1}{2}} dt = \int_{x=0}^{1} t^{\frac{n-1}{2}} (1-t)^{\frac{n-1}{2}} \sum_{k=0}^{\infty} \frac{(-2R^2 t)^k}{k!} dt$$

$$= \sum_{k=0}^{\infty} \frac{(-2R^2)^k}{k!} \int_{x=0}^{1} t^{\frac{n-1}{2} + k} (1-t)^{\frac{n-1}{2}} dt = \sum_{k=0}^{\infty} \frac{(-2R^2)^k}{k!} \frac{\Gamma_{\frac{n+1}{2}+k} \Gamma_{\frac{n+1}{2}}}{\Gamma_{n+1+k}}$$

$$= \beta_{\frac{n+1}{2},\frac{n+1}{2}} \sum_{k=0}^{\infty} \frac{(-2R^2)^k}{k!} \frac{\left(\frac{n+1}{2}\right)_k}{(n+1)_k} = 2^{-n} \beta_{\frac{n+1}{2},\frac{1}{2}} {}_1F_1\left(\frac{n+1}{2}, n+1 \mid -2R^2\right). \quad (44)$$

Identity (40) reduces the first integral in (43) to a hypergeometric function (39).

$$\int_{x=0}^{1} e^{-2R^2 t^2} t^{\frac{n-1}{2}} (1-t)^{\frac{n-1}{2}} dt = \int_{x=0}^{1} t^{\frac{n-1}{2}} (1-t)^{\frac{n-1}{2}} \sum_{k=0}^{\infty} \frac{(-2R^2 t^2)^k}{k!} dt$$

$$= \sum_{k=0}^{\infty} \frac{(-2R^2)^k}{k!} \int_{x=0}^{1} t^{\frac{n-1}{2}+2k} (1-t)^{\frac{n-1}{2}} dt = \sum_{k=0}^{\infty} \frac{(-2R^2)^k}{k!} \frac{\Gamma_{\frac{n+1}{2}+k} \Gamma_{\frac{n+1}{2}}}{\Gamma_{n+1+k}}$$

$$= \beta_{\frac{n+1}{2}, \frac{n+1}{2}} \sum_{k=0}^{\infty} \frac{(-2R^2)^k}{k!} \frac{\left(\frac{n+1}{2}\right)_{2k}}{(n+1)_{2k}} = \beta_{\frac{n+1}{2}, \frac{n+1}{2}} \sum_{k=0}^{\infty} \frac{(-2R^2)^k}{k!} \frac{\left(\frac{n+1}{4}\right)_k \left(\frac{n+3}{4}\right)_k 2^{2k}}{\left(\frac{n+1}{2}\right)_k \left(\frac{n+2}{2}\right)_k 2^{2k}}$$

$$= 2^{-n} \beta_{\frac{n+1}{2}, \frac{1}{2}} \,_2F_2 \left(\frac{n+1}{4}, \frac{n+3}{4}; \frac{n+1}{2}, \frac{n+2}{2} \Big| -2R^2 \right). \qquad (45)$$

Summing up Equations (43)–(45), and using inequality (41) for $p = 1, 2$, one gets

$$prob^N \leq \frac{R^n}{2^{\frac{n+2}{2}} (n+1) \Gamma_{\frac{n+2}{2}}} \left[(n-1)\left(1 + e^{-2R^2}\right) + 4 - \frac{n+3}{n+2}\left(1 - e^{-2R^2}\right) \right]$$

$$< \frac{R^n}{2^{\frac{n+2}{2}} (n+1) \Gamma_{\frac{n+2}{2}}} [2(n-1) + 4] = R^n \frac{1}{2^{\frac{n}{2}} \Gamma_{\frac{n+2}{2}}} = R^n \frac{1}{2^{\frac{n}{2}} \frac{n}{2} \frac{n-2}{2} \cdots} = prob^U \frac{1}{n!!}.$$

In the last equality we have used Equation (26) and the definition of the double factorial, for n even. Obviously, for n odd the constant $\sqrt{2}/\sqrt{\pi}$ will appear at the tail of the product, yet this is a minor difference that may be neglected. □

The result for the expected progress follows now easily.

Theorem 10. *Let an EA minimizing the SPHERE be situated at current distance R from the origin, such that $R \in (0, 1/2)$. For any $n > 3$, the following holds:*

$$\frac{\phi^N}{\phi^U} < \frac{n+1}{n!!} \approx \frac{1}{(n-2)!!}. \qquad (46)$$

Proof. The expected progress of NORMAL mutation (35) differs from success probability (34) only by the integration factor (25). As **progress** $< R$, inequality (46) is a simple consequence of Theorems 7 and 9. □

4. Discussion

Within evolutionary algorithms acting on real space, the use of normal distribution makes the implementation easier: in order to generate an n dimensional point, one simply generates n times from the normal uni-variate. Unfortunately, simplicity of the practical algorithm does not transfer to the theoretical analysis, making EA experts go long distances in order to estimate performance quantities like the success probability and the expected progress. In the end, the normal mutation only provides asymptotic formulas, valid for large n.

This paper analyzes a different mutation operator, based on the uniform multi-variate in the sphere, with dependent components. Using deeper insights into the spherical distributions theory, the local performance of the algorithm with uniform mutation was measured on the SPHERE fitness function. Close expressions for the success probability and the expected progress of the EA with uniform mutation have been derived, valid for arbitrary n. Compared to the performance of the normal operator-which, due to the intractability of integral formulas in Theorem 8, required inequalities with hypergeometric functions-, the success probability and the expected progress of the algorithm with uniform mutation are both larger, by a factor of order $n!!$.

5. Conclusions

From a broader perspective, this paper can be seen, together with the works in [27,28], as an attempt of revisiting the classical theory of continuous evolutionary algorithms. Even if practitioners in the field will continue to use the normal multi-variate as mutation distribution, we claim that the theory can benefit from the uniform distribution inside the sphere. First, as demonstrated in this paper, a particular setting of parameters (the natural choice $\rho = \sigma = 1$) provides better performance for the uniform mutation operator on the SPHERE landscape, if current position of the algorithm is nearby the optimum. However, in light of the "no free-lunch theorem for optimization" paradigm [39], one cannot expect general dominance of an algorithm over all others, irrespective of the fitness function. Rather, specific algorithms with particular operators should be analyzed separately, on different optimization landscapes. This is where the second advantage of the new uniform distribution occurs, in terms of more tractable mathematical analysis, yielding close formulas, previously not attained by normal mutation theory—see the studies of the RIDGE landscape in [28] and of the elitist evolutionary algorithm with mutation and crossover on SPHERE in [27].

A theory of continuous evolutionary algorithms could not be complete without the analysis of global behavior and adaptive mutation parameter. These cases have already been treated in [27,28]—under a normalization of mutation sphere radius which makes algorithm behave similarly to the one with normal mutation, in terms of difference and differential equations, following the works in [6,29]. This opens the way for the challenging task, previously unattempted in probabilistic optimization literature, of linking the theory of continuous evolutionary algorithms to that of differential optimization techniques such as particle swarm optimization [40] and differential evolution [41].

Funding: The work was supported by the Bucharest University of Economic Studies, Romania, through Project "Mathematical modeling of factors leading to subscription or un-subscription from email and SMS lists, forums and social media groups".

Acknowledgments: The author is grateful to his colleague Ovidiu Solomon for guidance through the jungle of Hypergeometric functions.

Conflicts of Interest: The authors declare no conflict of interest.

References

1. Pearson, K. The problem of the random walk. *Nature* **1905**, *72*, 294. [CrossRef]
2. Kluyver, J.C. A local probability problem. *Nederl. Acad. Wetensch. Proc.* **1905**, *8*, 341–350.
3. Watson, G.N. *A Treatise on the Theory of Bessel Functions*; University Press: Cambridge, UK, 1995.
4. Zhou, Y. On Borwein's conjectures for planar uniform random walks. *J. Aust. Math. Soc.* **2019**, *107*, 392–411. [CrossRef]
5. Dunson, D.B.; Johndrow, J.E. The Hastings algorithm at fifty. *Biometrika* **2020**, *107*, 1–23. [CrossRef]
6. Beyer, H.-G. *The Theory of Evolution Strategies*; Springer: Heidelberg, Germany, 2001.
7. Rudolph, G. *Convergence Properties of Evolutionary Algorithms*; Kovać: Hamburg, Germany, 1997.
8. Agapie, A.; Wright, A.H. Theoretical analysis of steady state genetic algorithms. *Appl. Math.* **2014**, *59*, 509–525. [CrossRef]
9. Agapie, A.; Agapie, M.; Rudolph, G.; Zbaganu, G. Convergence of evolutionary algorithms on the n-dimensional continuous space. *IEEE Trans. Cybern.* **2013**, *43*, 1462–1472. [CrossRef] [PubMed]
10. Agapie, A.; Agapie, M.; Zbaganu, G. Evolutionary Algorithms for Continuous Space Optimization. *Int. J. Syst. Sci.* **2013**, *44*, 502–512. [CrossRef]
11. Agapie, A. Estimation of Distribution Algorithms on Non-Separable Problems. *Int. J. Comp. Math.* **2010**, *87*, 491–508. [CrossRef]
12. Agapie, A. Theoretical analysis of mutation-adaptive evolutionary algorithms. *Evol. Comp.* **2001**, *9*, 127–146. [CrossRef]
13. Auger, A. Convergence results for the $(1,\lambda)$-SA-ES using the theory of ϕ-irreducible Markov chains. *Theor. Comput. Sci.* **2005**, *334*, 35–69. [CrossRef]
14. Li, S. Concise Formulas for the Area and Volume of a Hyperspherical Cap. *Asian J. Math. Stat.* **2011**, *4*, 66–70. [CrossRef]
15. Fang, K.-T.; Kotz, S.; Ng, K.-W. *Symmetric Multivariate and Related Distributions*; Chapman and Hall: London, UK, 1990.
16. Mardia, K.V.; Jupp, P.E. *Directional Statistics*; Wiley: New York, NY, USA, 2000.
17. Watson, G.S. *Statistics on Spheres*; University of Arkansas Lecture Notes in the Mathematical Sciences; Wiley: New York, NY, USA, 1983.
18. Blei, D.M.; Ng, A.Y.; Jordan, M.I. Latent Dirichlet allocation. *J. Mach. Learn. Res.* **2003**, *3*, 993–1022.

19. Fang, K.-T.; Yang, Z.; Kotz, S.; Ng, K.-W. Generation of multivariate distributions by vertical density representation. *Statistics* **2001**, *35*, 281–293. [CrossRef]
20. Harman, R.; Lacko, V. On decompositional algorithms for uniform sampling from n-spheres and n-balls. *J. Multivar. Anal.* **2010**, *101*, 2297—2304. [CrossRef]
21. Rechenberg, I. *Evolutionsstrategie: Optimierung Technischer Systeme Nach Prinzipiender Biologischen Evolution*; Frommann-Holzboog Verlag: Stuttgart, Germany, 1973.
22. Schwefel, H.-P. *Evolution and Optimum Seeking*; Wiley: New York, NY, USA, 1995.
23. Schumer, M.A.; Steiglitz, K. Adaptive Step Size Random Search. *IEEE Trans. Aut. Control* **1968**, *13*, 270–276. [CrossRef]
24. Rudolph, G. Local convergence rates of simple evolutionary algorithms with Cauchy mutations. *IEEE Trans. Evol. Comp.* **1997**, *1*, 249–258. [CrossRef]
25. Jägersküpper, J. Analysis of a simple evolutionary algorithm for minimisation in Euclidean spaces. In *International Colloquium on Automata, Languages, and Programming*; Lecture Notes in Computer Science; Springer: New York, NY, USA, 2003; Volume 2719, pp. 1068–1079.
26. Jägersküpper, J.; Witt, C. Rigorous runtime analysis of a $(\mu + 1)$ ES for the sphere function. In Proceedings of the 7th Annual Conference on Genetic and Evolutionary Computation, Washington, DC, USA, 25–29 June 2005; pp. 849–856.
27. Agapie, A.; Solomon, O.; Giuclea, M. Theory of (1+1) ES on the RIDGE. *IEEE Trans. Evol. Comp.* **2021**, *2021*, 3111232. [CrossRef]
28. Agapie, A.; Solomon, O.; Bădin, L. Theory of (1+1) ES on SPHERE revisited. **2021**, under review.
29. Beyer, H.-G. On the performance of $(1, \lambda)$-evolution strategies for the ridge function class. *IEEE Trans. Evol. Comput.* **2001**, *5*, 218–235. [CrossRef]
30. Cambanis, S.; Huang, S.; Simons, G. On the Theory of Elliptically Contoured Distributions. *J. Mult. Anal.* **1981**, *11*, 368–385. [CrossRef]
31. Huntington, E.V. Frequency Distribution of Product and Quotient. *Ann. Math. Statist.* **1939**, *10*, 195–198. [CrossRef]
32. Huang, H.; Su, J.; Zhang, Y.; Hao, Z. An Experimental Method to Estimate Running Time of Evolutionary Algorithms for Continuous Optimization. *IEEE Trans. Evol. Comput.* **2020**, *24*, 275–289. [CrossRef]
33. Abramowitz, M.; Stegun, I.A. (Eds.) *Handbook of Mathematical Functions*, 9th ed.; Dover: New York, NY, USA, 1972.
34. Neuman, E. Inequalities and Bounds for the Incomplete Gamma Function. *Results Math.* **2013**, *63*, 1209–1214. [CrossRef]
35. Volkmer, H.; Wood, J.J. A note on the asymptotic expansion of generalized hypergeometric functions. *Anal. Appl.* **2014**, *12*, 107–115. [CrossRef]
36. Slater, L.J. *Generalized Hypergeometric Functions*; University Press: Cambridge, UK, 1966.
37. Karp, D.B. Representations and Inequalities for Generalized Hypergeometric Functions. *J. Math. Sci.* **2015**, *207*, 885—897. [CrossRef]
38. Luke, Y.L. Inequalities for generalized hypergeometric functions. *J. Approx. Theory* **1972**, *5*, 41–65. [CrossRef]
39. Wolpert, D.H.; Macready, W.G. No free lunch theorems for optimization. *IEEE Trans. Evol. Comp.* **1997**, *1*, 67–82. [CrossRef]
40. Kadirkamanathan, V.; Selvarajah, K.; Fleming, P.J. Stability analysis of the particle dynamics in particle swarm optimizer. *IEEE Trans. Evol. Comp.* **2006**, *10*, 245–255. [CrossRef]
41. Dasgupta, S.; Das, S.; Biswas, A.; Abraham, A. On stability and convergence of the population-dynamics in differential evolution. *AI Commun.* **2009**, *22*, 1–20. [CrossRef]

Review

Evolution Strategies under the 1/5 Success Rule

Alexandru Agapie [1,2]

[1] Department of Applied Mathematics, Faculty of Economic Cybernetics, Statistics and Informatics, Bucharest University of Economic Studies, Calea Dorobantilor 15-17, 010552 Bucharest, Romania; alexandru.agapie@csie.ase.ro

[2] "Gheorghe Mihoc—Caius Iacob" Institute of Mathematical Statistics and Applied Mathematics of the Romanian Academy, 050711 Bucharest, Romania

Abstract: For large space dimensions, the log-linear convergence of the elitist evolution strategy with a 1/5 success rule on the sphere fitness function has been observed, experimentally, from the very beginning. Finding a mathematical proof took considerably more time. This paper presents a review and comparison of the most consistent theories developed so far, in the critical interpretation of the author, concerning both global convergence and the estimation of convergence rates. I discuss the local theory of the one-step expected progress and success probability for the (1+1) ES with a normal/uniform distribution inside the sphere mutation, thereby minimizing the SPHERE function, but also the adjacent global convergence and convergence rate theory, essentially based on the 1/5 rule. Small digressions into complementary theories (martingale, irreducible Markov chain, drift analysis) and different types of algorithms (population based, recombination, covariance matrix adaptation and self-adaptive ES) complete the review.

Keywords: continuous evolutionary algorithm; Markov chain; martingale; drift analysis; Wald's equation; computational complexity

MSC: 68W50

Citation: Agapie, A. Evolution Strategies under the 1/5 Success Rule. *Mathematics* **2023**, *11*, 201. https://doi.org/10.3390/math11010201

Academic Editor: Davide Valenti

Received: 29 October 2022
Revised: 22 December 2022
Accepted: 23 December 2022
Published: 30 December 2022

Copyright: © 2022 by the author. Licensee MDPI, Basel, Switzerland. This article is an open access article distributed under the terms and conditions of the Creative Commons Attribution (CC BY) license (https:// creativecommons.org/licenses/by/ 4.0/).

1. Introduction

It is within the human nature to favor short, simple and intuitive constructs in abstract sciences. This is the case with the 1/5 success rule, proposed in 1965 by Rechenberg for the adaptation of the normal mutation parameter in evolution strategies (ES) [1]. According to Auger and Hansen [2], the idea of step-size adaptation for probabilistic algorithms was also independently proposed by other authors around that time, e.g., [3]. Without any theoretical explanation, the adaptation rule performed surprisingly well in experiments, providing global convergence for various algorithmic designs and fitness landscapes. The magical aura around the rule began to unravel in 2000, with the apparition of convergence proofs for the ES on SPHERE [4–6]. We use uppercase when referring to the fitness function and lowercase for the uniform distribution inside the sphere. Obviously, the optimum (minimum) of SPHERE is located at the origin of $\Re^n$.

$$\mathcal{F}: \Re^n \to \Re \quad \mathcal{F}(x_1,\ldots,x_n) = \sum_{i=1}^{n} x_i^2. \quad (1)$$

Apart from the adaptation mechanism provided by the 1/5 rule, the ES design is very simple: a random walk for generating new individuals (mutation), plus elitist selection, the natural principle of discarding worse offspring. Together, the three procedures build up an efficient algorithm, simple in form but complicated in theory. The local behavior is difficult to estimate because of the discontinuous and inhomogeneous Markov transition kernel induced by mutation and selection, though global convergence is hard to prove due to the empirical application of the 1/5 rule. The Markov character of the ES is lost upon the application of the 1/5 rule, which observes not one, but several previous iterations of the algorithm.

In order to gain a better grip on these difficulties, we introduce first the spherical distributions, a class of multi-variate random variables (r.v.s) which includes the normal distribution and also the uniform on/inside the sphere [7].

Definition 1.

- An n-dimensional r.v. **x** is said to have a spherical distribution if

$$\mathbf{x} \stackrel{d}{=} \mathbf{r} \cdot \mathbf{u}^n \tag{2}$$

for some one-dimensional r.v. (radius) **r**, and a uniform distribution on the unit sphere $\mathbf{u}^n$. Moreover, **r** and $\mathbf{u}^n$ are independent, and also

$$\mathbf{r} = ||\mathbf{x}|| \geq 0, \qquad \mathbf{u}^n \stackrel{d}{=} \frac{\mathbf{x}}{||\mathbf{x}||}. \tag{3}$$

- If the spherical distribution has pdf g, then $g(\mathbf{x}) = g(||\mathbf{x}||)$, and there is a special connection between g and f, the pdf of **r**:

$$f(||\mathbf{x}||) = \frac{2\pi^{n/2}}{\Gamma_{\frac{n}{2}}} x^{n-1} g(\mathbf{x}). \tag{4}$$

The basic algorithm discussed in this paper is the following.

The mutation operator yields new, potentially better solutions from the fitness landscape. Classical ES theory, developed mainly by Rechenberg, Schwefel and Beyer, uses the normal mutation distribution with normalized standard deviation $\sigma = \rho/\sqrt{n}$ [1,4,8]. Rudolph applied the uniform *on* sphere [9], and a recent study proved that, under proper scaling of the mutation parameter, the uniform distribution inside the sphere of radius ρ and the averaged sum of uniforms perform, both locally and globally, similarly to the normal operator [10].

Under a constant mutation rate, a real ES stagnates in the vicinity of the optimum. This is where the 1/5 rule applies, by modifying (decreasing) the mutation parameter ρ. Algorithm 1 depicts Rechenberg's original (symmetric) version of the 1/5 rule, commonly applied in both practical and theoretical studies [1,4,6,11,12]. A simplified, asymmetric rule that only decreases but never increases ρ works as well [10].

There are different ways to describe the sequence of r.v.s $\{Z_t\}_{t \in \mathbb{N}}$ generated by the ES evolution over successive iterations. Contrary to random walk, the Markov kernel induced by mutation and selection is inhomogeneous, since the current state changes the one-step transition (success) probabilities. For arbitrary space dimension n, an exact calculus involving the local transition kernel is intractable, opening the way for various approximations and making the ES convergence one of the most studied problems in literature. The stochastic models proposed so far include renewal processes, drift analysis and martingales [6,9,13–15]. Markov chain models have also been tested, first for constant mutation ES, without (or prior to) the step-size adaptation procedure provided by the 1/5 rule [16,17]. Decomposing the algorithm into a sequence of constant mutation cycles (mathematically, a sequence of Markov chains) has also been considered [2,10,18,19], which is similar to theoretical studies of closely related probabilistic algorithms such as simulated annealing and random heuristic search [20,21]. It is also worth mentioning the large number of theoretical studies that do not presume any stochastic structure at all [4,12,22–24].

Algorithm 1 Elitist ES with 1/5 success rule.

1. Set $t = 0$, t_{max}, initial point $\mathbf{x}^0$ and initial mutation parameter ρ
2. repeat
   - $t := t + 1$
   - *Mutation*: generate a new point $\mathbf{x}$ in $\Re^n$ using some spherical mutation distribution with radius mean ρ
   - *Selection*: if $\mathcal{F}(\mathbf{x}) < \mathcal{F}(\mathbf{x}^{t-1})$ then $\mathbf{x}^t := \mathbf{x}$
     else $\mathbf{x}^t := \mathbf{x}^{t-1}$
   - *1/5 success rule*: if $t \equiv 0$ modulo n, compute the success frequency over the last n iterations
   $$SF = \#S/n$$

   Change ρ according to
   $$\begin{aligned}(i) & \quad \rho = \rho/2, & \text{if } SF < 1/5 \\ (ii) & \quad \rho = 2\rho, & \text{if } SF > 1/5\end{aligned}$$

3. until $t = t_{max}$

Let us take a closer look at the success region, a key concept in the algorithm's local behavior. This is the integration region for both success probability and expected progress. Let $x \in \Re^n$ be the current ES position, $A \subset \Re^n$ an open set and the mutation be defined by a probability density function (pdf) f. The cumulative effect of elitist selection yields the success region R_x^S and transition kernel $P_x(A)$. The transition kernel is discontinuous due to $\delta_x(A)$, the Dirac measure in x—defined as 1 if $x \in A$ and 0 otherwise.

$$R_x^S = \{y \in \Re^n | \mathcal{F}(y) < \mathcal{F}(x)\} \tag{5}$$

$$P_x(A) = \int_{A \cap R_x^S} f(y) dy + \left[1 - \int_{A \cap R_x^S} f(y) dy\right] \delta_x(A). \tag{6}$$

If $A = R_x^S$, Equation (6) reduces to the first term, understood as success probability and denoted P^S.

Under uniform mutation inside the sphere, the modification of the success region—and also the inhomogeneous Markov kernel—can be observed as the ES approaches the optimum in Figure 1, from right to left. In case (a), R_x^S is the intersection of two spheres (corresponding to mutation and fitness). As the algorithm approaches the optimum, assuming ρ has not changed, R_x^S becomes a full (fitness) sphere, case (b). The ES stagnates at this point, the 1/5 rule is activated and ρ is halved, such that R_x^S becomes again the intersection of two spheres, case (c).

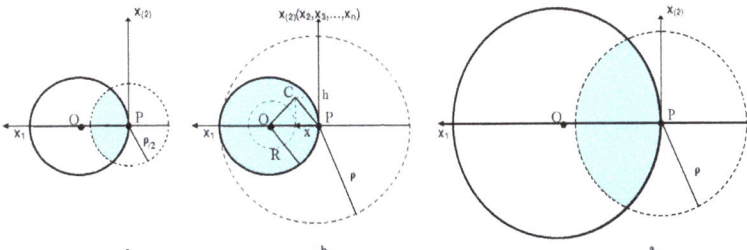

Figure 1. Elitist ES on SPHERE: success region (blue) of uniform mutation. The solid line circle (centered in optimum O) represents the fitness sphere; the dotted circle (centered in current position P) stands for the mutation sphere. As the ES approaches O from sub-figure (**a**–**c**), mutation radius ρ is halved under the 1/5 success rule.

Among the many studies devoted to the convergence of elitist ES with the 1/5 success rule on SPHERE and similar quadratic fitness functions, we review in this paper only what we consider to be complete theories, which follow the general pattern presented in Algorithm 1 and also achieve proofs of global convergence. Consequently, we distinguish between classic ES theory, in Section 2, and general theories, in Section 3. In classic ES theory, the accent falls on local behavior, with global convergence being a consequence of the best-case local scenario. General theories, on the other hand, provide a unitary solution to the convergence paradigm. To classic ES theory we assimilate the works of Rechenberg, Schwefel, Beyer, Rudolph and Jägerskupper; and to general theories the analyses of Auger and Hansen of Akimoto, Auger and Glasmachers. Note that the papers of Jägerskupper fall somehow in between, since they build on local behavior, but also provide a global convergence proof outside the best-case local scenario. The adaptation mechanisms used in population-based ES—with multiple offspring, multiple parents and recombination, self-adaptation or covariance matrix adaptation—are briefly discussed as generalizations of the 1/5 success rule in Section 4.

We underline the fact that this review paper is not an exhaustive survey of the ES state-of-the-art—we defer to [25] for that purpose—but a personal reading of the convergence theories built in this field at the intersection of probability theory, computational complexity and statistics.

2. Classic ES Theory

As in Figure 1b, assume the algorithm and the center of the coordinate system are both in P; the distance to global optimum O is $R = |OP|$; denote x_1 by x and the remaining $n-1$ components $x_{(2)}$ by h. The classic ES theory focuses on the local, one-step behavior of the algorithm, where the mutation rate ρ can be assumed constant.

If C is a random point generated by mutation, the progress becomes a one-dimensional r.v. corresponding to the difference in distance to optimum between the current ES position and the next. Due to the elitist selection, progress is non-negative. For a successful mutation, C is inside region R_x^S, the blue area in Figure 1. Apply Pythagoras to OC and $u = ||h||^2$; then, progress becomes [10] and ([4], p. 54).

$$progress = |OP| - |OC| = R - \sqrt{(R-x_1)^2 + \sum_{i=2}^{n} x_i^2} = R - \sqrt{(R-x)^2 + u}. \quad (7)$$

Insert progress into the integral and set $A = R_x^S$; then Equations (6) and (7) build the so-called ES' expected progress:

$$\phi = \int_{R^S} \left(R - \sqrt{(R-x)^2 + u} \right) f(x, u) dx du. \quad (8)$$

In order to approximate the above integral, two distinct cases occur: (i) ES close to optimum, or large step size (Figure 1b); (ii) ES far from the optimum, or small step size (Figure 1a,c).

With the same uniform mutation distribution, ref. [24] refined the results of both [13,26], and came closer to the analysis reviewed below by considering, in the estimation of local expected progress, the same two cases. However, without a deeper insight into spherical distributions, the study yielded only upper bounds for the expected progress and thus lower bounds for the global convergence time. Additionally, [23] analyzed an EA with $\lambda > 1$ individuals in the population, acting on the SPHERE, with uniform mutation inside the sphere. However, the analysis is confined to the case where optimum is within the mutation sphere—that means, large step size, for which only asymptotic ($\lambda \to \infty$) results are derived; again, a comparison to (32) is intractable. Noteworthy, yet again incomparable to the results reviewed below, are theoretical analyses of mutation distributions that are uniform but non-spherical [22,27].

2.1. Large Step Size

This case is defined by the inequality $\rho \geq 2R$, such that success region R_x^S is completely included in the mutation sphere, Figure 1b. We assume uniform mutation inside the sphere, but an ES with normal mutation performs similarly, for large n and a proper parameter scaling [10,28].

Mathematically, this is the unique situation when Formula (8) is tractable, allowing for a closed-form derivation of the expected progress. However, the case did not receive much attention in the literature, since it corresponds to the worst case scenario (stagnation), calling for an emergency application of the mutation adaptation rule.

A first rigorous result concerning this case was provided by Rudolph, with the analysis of pure random search, an algorithm that generates offspring independently, using the uniform distribution inside the sphere with a fixed center and constant radius ρ ([9], pp. 168–169). The minimal distance to optimum out of the first t trials, R_t, is computed, for large t, by order statistics [29]. The second approximation is with respect to large space dimension n.

$$R_t \approx \rho\, t^{-1/n} \Gamma_{1+\frac{1}{n}} \approx \rho\, t^{-1/n}. \tag{9}$$

The following definitions are used in computational complexity analysis [5,10].

Definition 2.

- A statement $Z(n)$ holds for large enough n if there is $N \in \mathbb{N}$ such that for all $n \geq N$, $Z(n)$ holds.
- For $g(n) > 0$, we say $g(n) = \mathcal{O}(n)$ if there exists $c > 0$ such that $g(n) \leq cn$, for a large enough n. Similarly, $g(n) = \Omega(n)$ if $g(n) \geq cn$, for a large enough n. If $g(n)$ is both $\mathcal{O}(n)$ and $\Omega(n)$, we say that $g(n) = \Theta(n)$.
- We say $g(n) = o(n)$ if $g(n)/n \to 0$ as $n \to \infty$.
- A sequence $p_n \geq 0$ is exponentially small in n if $p_n \leq e^{-\mathcal{O}(n)}$.
- An event A_n happens with overwhelming probability (w.o.p.) in n if $1 - P(A_n)$ is exponentially small in n.

Rudolph argues that the convergence rate of elitist, constant mutation ES decreases to the asymptotics (9), estimated, after re-noting $R_t = \epsilon$, as

$$t = \Theta\left[\left(\frac{1}{\epsilon}\right)^n\right] \tag{10}$$

and classified as poor, compared to the performance of adaptive mutation ES.

One can note in Figure 1b that progress is minimal (zero) if the randomly generated point C is P and maximal (R) if the generated point is O. The success probability in the large step size case is simply the ratio of two n-sphere volumes, $(R/\rho)^n$. A complete description of the progress r.v. (7) is provided in the following.

Proposition 1. *Assume the elitist ES with one individual and uniform mutation inside the sphere of radius ρ, minimizing the SPHERE, is at distance R from the origin, $\rho \geq 2R$. Then, the progress is*

- *cdf*

$$F(x) = P(R - |OC| \leq x) = \begin{cases} 0, & x < 0 \\ 1 - \left(\frac{R}{\rho}\right)^n, & x = 0 \\ 1 - \left(\frac{R-x}{\rho}\right)^n, & x \in (0, R) \\ 1, & x \geq R \end{cases} \tag{11}$$

- *and partial pdf*

$$f(x) = \begin{cases} \frac{n}{\rho^n}(R-x)^{n-1}, & x \in (0, R) \\ 0, & \text{other} \end{cases} \tag{12}$$

Proof. It is easy to see that progress is non-negative, discontinuous and $P(progress = 0) = 1 - (R/\rho)^n$. For $x \in (0, R)$, the point C can be seen as generated by the uniform distribution inside the sphere of radius ρ, but with center O. Then, $|OC|$ corresponds to $\mathbf{r}$, the radius of the uniform distribution inside the ρ-sphere, truncated to $S^O(R)$, the n-sphere with center O and radius R. Note the difference between the radius r.v. $\mathbf{r}$ from Definition 1, and the positive real number ρ, the radius of the mutation sphere.

However, $\mathbf{r}$ is $Beta(n, 1)$ in the case of the uniform inside the sphere of radius ρ, with pdf [10]:

$$g(r) = \frac{1}{\rho^n} n r^{n-1}, \quad r \in (0, \rho). \tag{13}$$

Restricted to $(0, R)$, the pdf (13) provides the (partial) cdf:

$$G(r) = \left(\frac{r}{\rho}\right)^n, \quad r \in (0, R), \tag{14}$$

such that

$$F(x) = P(R - \mathbf{r} \leq x) = 1 - P(\mathbf{r} \leq R - x) = 1 - G(R - x) = \tag{15}$$

$$= 1 - \left(\frac{R - x}{\rho}\right)^n, \quad x \in (0, R). \tag{16}$$

A simple derivation with respect to x provides the pdf (12). □

The progress r.v. is depicted in Figure 2, for $\rho = 1$, $R = 1/2$ and different space dimensions n. To each n corresponds a bar at zero—the Dirac measure δ_0, that is, the discrete part of the progress—and a thin line with the same color representing the partial pdf of the continuous part of the progress.

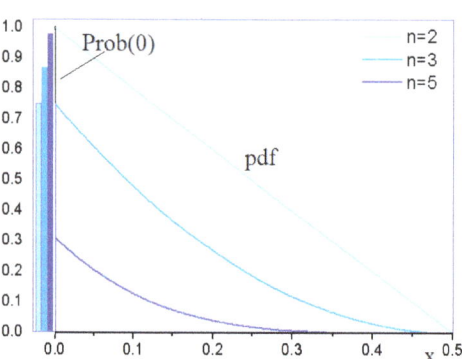

Figure 2. Progress of elitist ES on SPHERE: Dirac (bar) and pdf of continuous part (line)—large step size.

The following result is a slight generalization of a similar result (on the particular case $\rho = 1$) from [30]. However, the proof presented below is easier than the one in [30], building on the exact formulas provided by Proposition 1.

Theorem 1. *In the conditions of Proposition 1,*
- *the success probability is*

$$P^S = \left(\frac{R}{\rho}\right)^n, \tag{17}$$

- the expected progress is

$$\phi = \frac{R^{n+1}}{\rho^n(n+1)}. \tag{18}$$

Proof. The success probability has already been derived geometrically. However, in a unitary setting, both success probability and expected progress are obtained by integration of partial pdf (12) over the success region $(0, R)$.

$$P^S = \int_0^R \frac{n}{\rho^n}(R-x)^{n-1}dx = \left(\frac{R}{\rho}\right)^n.$$

$$\phi = E(progress) = \int_0^R \frac{nx}{\rho^n}(R-x)^{n-1}dx = \frac{R^{n+1}}{\rho^n(n+1)},$$

where the second calculus yields from partial integration. □

Theorem 1 points out an outstanding analytical property of the uniform mutation operator, in case of the algorithm with a large step size: *The success probability is the derivative, with respect to distance to optimum, of the expected progress.*

This result relies on the non-centrality property of the uniform distribution inside the sphere. Namely, we can regard the random point C as being generated from a uniform centered in O, not in P, then apply the radius r.v. for the random distance $|OC|$. This procedure can be applied only for Figure 1b, not for Figure 1a or 1c, and neither for other spherical mutation like the normal distribution. The uniform distribution *on* the sphere provides zero progress if $\rho \geq 2R$, so that case is also tractable but not interesting, corresponding to pure stagnation.

Finally, we confirm and generalize Rudolph's result (10) on the convergence time of the elitist ES on the SPHERE, under constant, large-step-size mutation.

Theorem 2. *In the conditions of Proposition 1, the time required by the algorithm to reach distance ϵ from optimum is*

$$t = \Theta\left[\left(\frac{\rho}{\epsilon}\right)^n\right]. \tag{19}$$

Proof. Start from Equation (18) and the definition of progress (7).

$$\phi = |OP| - |OC| = R_t - R_{t+1} = \frac{R_t^{n+1}}{\rho^n(n+1)} \tag{20}$$

$$\Rightarrow R_{t+1} - R_t = -\frac{R_t^{n+1}}{\rho^n(n+1)}. \tag{21}$$

We transform the above difference equation into a differential equation, with separable variables, which we solve.

$$y' = -\frac{y^{n+1}}{\rho^n(n+1)} \tag{22}$$

$$\Rightarrow \int \frac{y'}{y^n}dy = -\int \frac{\rho^n}{n}dx \tag{23}$$

$$\Rightarrow y^{n-1} = \frac{n}{n-1}x^{-1} \tag{24}$$

$$\Rightarrow y = \left(\frac{n}{n-1}\right)^{n-1}\left(\frac{x}{\rho^n}\right)^{-\frac{1}{n-1}} \approx x^{-\frac{1}{n}}\rho. \tag{25}$$

At the last step, we remove the factors/exponents that converge to one as $n \to \infty$.

If we denote $y = R_t = \epsilon$ and $x = t$, we get

$$\epsilon \approx t^{-\frac{1}{n}}\rho \quad \Rightarrow \quad t \approx \left(\frac{\rho}{\epsilon}\right)^n. \qquad (26)$$

□

One should note that the relevance of the above analysis is purely theoretical. Inspection of Equations (17) and (18) shows that both success probability and expected progress attain their maximum for $\rho = 2R$, where the two quantities are of order $1/2^n$, a rather low value, leading to stagnation. The situation is avoided in Algorithm 1 by halving ρ, such that the ES enters (again) the small step size situation of Figure 1c.

2.2. Small Step Size

This case is defined by the inequality $\rho < 2R$, such that success region R_x^S is the intersection of the mutation and fitness spheres; see Figure 1a,c.

If the ES uses uniform mutation inside the ρ-sphere, the following equation transforms the original radius into a new parameter, equivalent (asymptotically) to the standard deviation (σ) of the normal mutation [10,28].

$$a = \frac{\rho}{\sqrt{n}}. \qquad (27)$$

Under the assumption $a \approx \sigma$, the local behavior of Algorithm 1 does not depend on the mutation distribution used: normal with standard deviation σ or uniform inside the sphere of radius ρ—one can treat these two ES versions as one. Apply next a second normalization of both new mutation parameter a and expected progress ϕ ([4], p. 32):

$$a^* = a\frac{n}{R}, \qquad \phi^* = \phi\frac{n}{R}. \qquad (28)$$

The random local behavior of the algorithm can be expressed by the following compact formulas ([4], pp. 67–68), [10]. The cumulative distribution function (cdf) of the standard normal (Gaussian) distribution $N(0,1)$ is $\Phi(x) = \frac{1}{\sqrt{2\pi}}\int_{-\infty}^{x} e^{-\frac{t^2}{2}} dt$.

Theorem 3. *Let a elitist ES minimize the SPHERE, with either uniform mutation inside the sphere of radius ρ or normal mutation with standard deviation $a = \rho/\sqrt{n}$. Then, for large n, the following approximations hold:*

- *Success probability:*

$$Prob \approx 1 - \Phi\left(\frac{a^*}{2}\right). \qquad (29)$$

- *Normalized expected progress:*

$$\phi^* \approx \frac{a^*}{\sqrt{2\pi}}e^{-\frac{a^{*2}}{8}} - \frac{a^{*2}}{2}\left[1 - \Phi\left(\frac{a^*}{2}\right)\right]. \qquad (30)$$

The asymptotics of success probability and expected progress are depicted in Figure 3. The particular form of ϕ^* as function of a^* is essential for proving the global convergence of the adaptive ES. Note that the function (30) is uni-modal, with a maximum at $a^* = 1.224$, $\phi^*_{max} = \phi^*(1.22) = 0.202$.

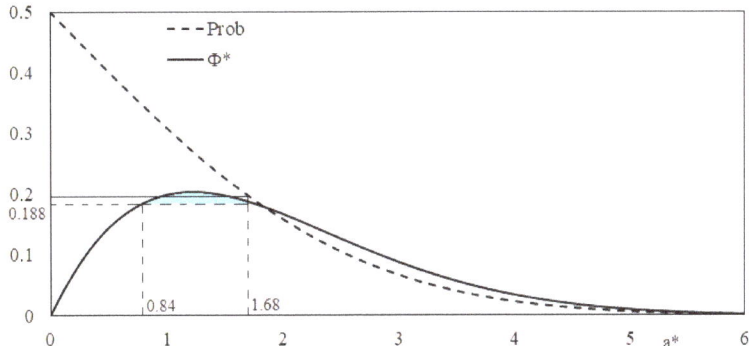

Figure 3. Success probability (29), expected progress (30) and evolution window (blue) of elitist ES on SPHERE.

The blue area corresponding to the a^*-interval $[0.84, 1.68]$ is the 'evolution window' of Algorithm 1. In classic ES theory, the term is used in the broader sense of the region with expected progress being significantly greater than zero, e.g., $a^* \in [0.1, 5]$ in Figure 3 [1], ([4], p. 69), [31]. However, we use here the more restrictive definition from [10], which ensures also global convergence of the ES under the $1/5$ rule. Using the success probability formula, Formula (29), we identify first the critical value $a^* = 1.68$, corresponding to $Prob(1.68) = 1/5 = 0.2$. Then, we apply the expected progress formula, Formula (30), get $\phi^*(1.68) = 0.188$ and use again (30) to get $\phi^*(0.84) = 0.188$. One could say that the evolution window in this case is defined by the condition $\phi^* \geq 0.188$.

Observing the possible benefits of different mutation distributions, the authors of [3,9] developed an analysis based on uniform mutation *on* the sphere. Using the random angle $\theta = \angle CPO$ between the mutated point and the optimum direction, and the same parameter normalization, Rudolph solved the low-dimensional case, $n = 3$. The general case proved intractable, so he resorted to the same approximation of a random variable through its expected value, yielding an asymptotic progress which is the double of Formula (30) ([9], pp. 170–172). Note that a different progress definition applies, usually referred to as *quality gain*:

$$progress' = R^2 - |OC|^2 \tag{31}$$
$$\phi' = 2\phi^*. \tag{32}$$

By applying another spherical mutation operator to the same problem, the Cauchy distribution, Rudolph obtained a different expression of progress, valid for the case $n = 3$ [32]. Like the normal multivariate, the Cauchy distribution is with un-bounded support, can be constructed from independent identical components and exhibits the rare property of being closed to addition. Under quadratic definition (31), the expected progress ϕ_C depends on the mutation parameter δ:

$$\phi_C = 1 - \frac{1}{\delta\pi}\left[\frac{3}{\delta}\arctan(2\delta) + \frac{2\delta^2 - 1}{2\delta^2}\log(4\delta^2 + 1) - 4\right]. \tag{33}$$

Unfortunately, the generalization to larger dimensions failed, due to the intractability of radius **r** from Equation (2), in the case of the Cauchy distribution.

Considering yet another spherical distribution, the (averaged) sum of two independent uniforms inside the sphere, $\mathbf{x} = (\mathbf{x}_1 + \mathbf{x}_2)/2$ [10], also showed that ϕ_S, the expected progress of this new mutation operator, is

$$\phi_S(a^*) = \phi^*\left(\frac{a^*}{\sqrt{2}}\right). \tag{34}$$

Note that if $\mathbf{x}_{1,2}$ are uniformly distributed inside the sphere with radius ρ, the expected value of the radius r.v. $\mathbf{r}$ from Equation (1) is also ρ—asymptotically for large space dimension n. On the other hand, the expected value of the radius of $\mathbf{x}$ is $\rho/\sqrt{2}$, so the scaling factor of the argument in Equation (34) is actually the ratio between the different expected radiuses [10].

2.3. Global Convergence

For decades, the algorithm's global convergence was only a marginal subject in classic ES theory, regarded as a consequence of the ability—un-explained theoretically, though supported by empirical evidence—of the 1/5 success rule to keep the expected progress around its maximal value during the whole evolution. We illustrate this with Beyer's reasoning and apply Formula (30) to express the ES's expected progress between time t and $t+1$ ([4], pp. 48–50).

$$R_t - R_{t+1} = \phi(a_t) \quad \Rightarrow \quad R_{t+1} - R_t = -R_t \frac{\phi^*(a_t^*)}{n}. \tag{35}$$

One obtains a separable differential equation from the difference equation.

$$R'_t = -R_t \frac{\phi^*(a_t^*)}{n}. \tag{36}$$

If the 1/5 rule manages to keep a_t^* approximately constant at its maximum, $\phi^*(a_t^*) \approx \phi^*_{max} = 0.202$; the differential equation solves to the following (note that R_0 is the initial distance to optimum):

$$R_t = R_0 \, e^{-\frac{0.202\, t}{n}}. \tag{37}$$

Apply next the logarithm to get

$$\ln\left(\frac{R_t}{R_0}\right) = \frac{-0.202\, t}{n}, \tag{38}$$

and then reverse Equation (38); denote $R_t = \epsilon > 0$ and $1/0.202 = C$, such that

$$t = C\, n \, \log \frac{R_0}{\epsilon}. \tag{39}$$

According to Definition 2, Equation (39) reads as linear convergence time, with respect to both space dimension n and the logarithm of initial distance to optimum R_0. The only problem is that the above analysis is based on the optimistic assumption that the 1/5 rule keeps expected progress around the value of 0.202. Rigorously, this is only a best-case scenario, so one should actually read the above equalities as inequalities and (39) as a lower bound on convergence time [10]. The ES convergence time is $\Omega[n \cdot \log(R_0/\epsilon)]$.

$$t \geq C\, n \, \log \frac{R_0}{\epsilon}. \tag{40}$$

However, the practical efficiency of Equation (37), expressed by its ability in predicting the behavior of the real algorithm, is undeniable. Following [10], we present here another derivation of Formula (37) with a slightly different exponential parameter (0.178 instead of 0.202) but obtained as an average, not extreme case value.

Rudolph considered first the stochastic nature of the ES, using a martingale model to derive sufficient conditions for global convergence. The following definitions and results are from ([9], pp. 25–26, 52, 166) and ([33], pp. 94, 109, 127–128, 131).

Definition 3.

- The conditional expectation $E(R_{t+1}|R_t)$ is a r.v., with values $E(R_{t+1}|R_t = R)$ and probabilities of R_t, such that $E[E(R_{t+1}|R_t)] = E(R_{t+1})$.
- A sequence of r.v.s $\{R_t\}_{t\in\mathbb{N}}$ is called

- Non-negative supermartingale if, for all t,

$$E(|R_t|) < \infty \text{ and } E(R_{t+1} \mid R_t) \leq R_t \tag{41}$$

- Uniformly integrable (UI) if, for any $\epsilon > 0$, there is $K \geq 0$ such that, for all t

$$E\left(|R_t| \cdot 1_{\{|R_t|>K\}}\right) < \epsilon. \tag{42}$$

Proposition 2. *Let $\{R_t\}_{t\in\mathbb{N}}$ be a sequence of r.v.s.*
- *A sufficient condition for UI is: there is $K > 0$ such that $|R_t| < K$ for all t.*
- *If $\{R_t\}_{t\in\mathbb{N}}$ is a non-negative supermartingale, it converges a.s. to a finite r.v. If $\{R_t\}_{t\in\mathbb{N}}$ is also UI, convergence is also in the mean.*

Let X_t be the r.v. elitist ES at iteration t, f a function with minimum zero and $R_t = f(X_t)$. Then, $\{R_t\}_{t\in\mathbb{N}}$ is a non-negative supermartingale due to the elitist selection, and UI since $R_t \leq R_0$. Due to Proposition 2, R_t converges a.s. and in mean to a finite r.v. What remains to be proved is:
- Global convergence—the limit is exactly zero;
- Convergence rates.

Sufficient convergence conditions are provided in ([9], pp. 165–167). Note that part (a) of Theorem 4 is also presented in [34], and part (b), in terms of dynamical systems and *Lyapunov functions*, is also in ([15], p. 154).

Theorem 4. *Let $\{X\}_{t\in\mathbb{N}}$ be generated by some ES optimizing a fitness function f with global minimum at zero, and $R_t = f(X_t) > 0$.*

(a) *If the ES employs an elitist selection rule and there exist sequences $\epsilon_t, \delta_t \in (0,1)$ such that for all t*

$$\delta_t \leq \text{Prob}\{R_{t+1} \leq (1-\epsilon_t)R_t | R_t\} \tag{43}$$

and

$$\sum_{t=0}^{\infty} \epsilon_t \cdot \delta_t = \infty \tag{44}$$

then the ES converges to zero a.s and in mean, and the approach is exponentially fast with rate $c = 1 - \delta \cdot \epsilon \in (0,1)$.

$$E_{R_{t+1}} \leq E_{R_t} c \implies E_{R_t} \leq E_{R_0} c^t. \tag{45}$$

(b) *Regardless of the selection rule, if there is a constant $c \in (0,1)$ such that for all t*

$$E(R_{t+1} \mid R_t) \leq c \cdot R_t \quad a.s. \tag{46}$$

then the ES converges to zero a.s. and in mean, and the approach is exponentially fast with rate c.

The key r.v.s and parameters used in this study are summarized in Table 1.

Rudolph used Theorem 4 (b) to justify global convergence on SPHERE, for the elitist ES with uniform mutation *on* sphere ([9], pp. 170–172). However, the reasoning is unrealistic: it assumes a mutation radius proportional, at each moment, to distance to the optimum of $\rho_t = \gamma R_t$, with the parameter set to optimal value $\gamma^* = 1.224$.

The problem is that a real ES, modeled as a sequence of (decreasing) constant-mutation phases, delimited by the application of the 1/5 rule, does not fulfill Equations (43)–(46) per se. Assuming a 'good' starting point (see Theorem 7), there is a constant $c > 0$ such that (46) holds as long as the ES is within some narrow evolution window, such as the one depicted in Figure 3. However, as the algorithm reaches the upper limit of the evolution window, at some random time T, there is an exponentially small probability for the ES to continue the descent such that (46) is precluded. Since mutation adaptation is necessary for global convergence, we are interested in the (large probability) event 'the 1/5 rule applies at iteration T'. The situation resembles Theorem 4 (a), with the difference being that $E(R_{T+1}|R_T) = R_T$ for the 1/5 rule applies only in unsuccessful iterations, such that $\epsilon_T = 0$ and (43) is precluded as well.

Table 1. Mathematical concepts used in ES analysis.

X_t	n-dim r.v. 'ES position at time t'
R_t	1-dim r.v. 'ES distance to optimum at time t'
R	positive real number
$(R_{t+1}|R_t = R)$	1-dim r.v. 'ES distance to optimum at $t+1$, conditioned by dist. R at t'
$E(R_{t+1}|R_t = R)$	positive real number, mean of the above
$E(R_{t+1}|R_t)$	1-dim r.v. 'ES distance to optimum at $t+1$, conditioned by distance at t'
$\phi_t(R,n,\rho) = R - E(R_{t+1}|R_t = R)$	non-negative real number, mean progress between time t and $t+1$
$\phi_t^*(a^*) = \phi_t n / R$	non-negative real number, normalized mean progress
T_d	1-dim r.v. 'first hitting time of distance d'

Summing up, Theorem 4 is not strong enough to derive upper bounds on the global convergence time of the elitist ES with the 1/5 success rule. As one can see in the following, the mathematical difficulty resides not in the multi-variate calculus, but in the computational complexity analysis of the 1/5 rule. The linear upper bounds were proved for the first time by Jägerskupper, who regarded the elitist ES as a sequence of n-length *phases* with a constant mutation rate in each phase, during which the success frequency of mutation was observed before the application of the 1/5 rule [5,26,35,36].

Removing line (ii) from the 1/5 rule in Algorithm 1—that is, parameter ρ decreases if success frequency is less than 1/5, but never increases—and using A uniform mutation inside the sphere instead of normal mutation, [10] proved that all of Jägerskupper's results still hold. Moreover, under the simplified 1/5 rule, the constant-mutation phase extends to a number of phases, called a cycle. The r.v. 'length of a cycle' will play a key role in connecting the two (otherwise distinct) parts of the convergence analysis, local and global, leading to an exponential formula able to predict the behavior of the real ES, similar to Equation (37).

We resume next the results from [5,10,26,35,36] in a unitary setting, covering both types of 1/5 rule and both mutation distributions, normal and uniform inside the sphere. The results hold also for the sum of two uniforms; see [10] for details. For the local behavior, Jägerskupper avoided the calculus from Section 2.2 and used instead the decomposition (2) of the normal mutation distribution with standard deviation σ, $N(0, \sigma I_n)$, into r.v.s uniform on sphere $\mathbf{u^n}$ and radius ℓ. Recall that ρ is the radius parameter of the uniform mutation inside the sphere, R the current distance to optimum, *Prob* the success probability and $\mathbf{r}$ the radius r.v. from Equation (1). We also apply the normalization $a = \rho/\sqrt{n}$ in order to equalize the asymptotic mean radiuses of the two distributions, normal and uniform, such that a can be identified to σ and $\mathbf{r}$ to ℓ.

Lemma 1. *Let Algorithm 1 with any spherical mutation minimizing the SPHERE be in current point P; $|OP| = R$. The mutant C is accepted with Prob $\in [\epsilon, 1/2 - \epsilon]$, $\epsilon > 0$, if and only if $|PC| = \Theta(R/\sqrt{n})$.*

Lemma 2. *If X is uniform inside the sphere of radius ρ or normal with standard deviation $\sigma = \rho/\sqrt{n}$, and $\mathbf{r}$ is the corresponding r.v. radius, then*

$$P(|\mathbf{r} - \rho| \leq \delta\rho) \geq 1 - \mathcal{O}\left(\frac{1}{n\delta^2}\right). \tag{47}$$

If $X_1, \ldots, X_n$ are independent copies of X, then for any $\lambda \in (0,1)$, there exist $a_\lambda, b_\lambda > 0$ such that the r.v. cardinal number of $\{i \mid a_\lambda \rho \leq r_i \leq b_\lambda \rho\}$ is $\geq \lambda n$ w.o.p.

The first part of Lemma 2 is actually Chebyshev inequality. Note that the inequality $|\mathbf{r} - \rho| \leq \delta\rho$ is equivalent to $|\mathbf{r} - \rho|/\rho \leq \delta$, so the result holds for the original (that is, before normalization $\rho = a\sqrt{n}$) uniform distribution inside the sphere, for the normalized uniform and also for the normal distribution.

Lemma 3. *Let Algorithm 1 with mutation X, as in Lemma 2, minimize the SPHERE. The following are equivalent:*

(i) $\sigma = \Theta(R/n)$
(ii) $\rho = \Theta(R/\sqrt{n})$
(iii) *There exists $\epsilon > 0$ such that Prob $\in \left[\epsilon, \frac{1}{2} - \epsilon\right]$ for a large enough n—that is, Prob is $\Omega(1)$ and $1/2 - \Omega(1)$.*

Lemma 4. *If $\mathbf{r} = \Theta(R/\sqrt{n})$, then progress is $\Theta(R/n)$, with probability $\Omega(1)$, and within expectation.*

The radius $\mathbf{r}$ in Lemma 4 corresponds to the normalized ($\rho = a\sqrt{n}$) uniform inside the sphere, and hence also to the normal distribution.

Let $i, i+1$ denote the states of the algorithm at the beginning/end of this phase, respectively.

Lemma 5. *Let Algorithm 1 with mutation X as in Lemma 2 minimize the SPHERE. Consider two variants of the 1/5 rule: (i and ii).*

(i)   *If $\rho_i = \Theta(R_i/\sqrt{n})$, then $R_i - R_{i+1} = \Theta(R_i)$ w.o.p.; that is, w.o.p. the approximation error is reduced by a constant fraction in the i-th phase.*
(ii) *If ρ_i is doubled (or respectively not modified) after the i-th phase, then $\rho_i = \mathcal{O}(R_i/\sqrt{n})$.*
(iii) *If ρ_i is halved after the i-th phase, then $\rho_{i+1} = \Omega(R_{i+1}/\sqrt{n})$.*

Lemma 6. *Let Algorithm 1 be as in Lemma 5. If the 1/5 rule causes a $(k+1)$-sequence of phases, $1 \leq k = n^{\mathcal{O}(n)}$, such that in the first phase ρ is halved and in all the following it is doubled (respectively left unchanged), or the other way around, then w.o.p. the distance from optimum is k times reduced by a constant fraction in these phases.*

We can state now the main global convergence result, valid for the ES with either uniform or normal mutation, with either complete (i–ii) or simplified (i) 1/5 success rule [5,10,35].

Theorem 5. *Let Algorithm 1, defined as in Lemma 5, start at distance R_0 from optimum, with mutation parameter $\rho_0 = \Theta(R_0/\sqrt{n})$. If t satisfies $1 \leq t = n^{\mathcal{O}(1)}$, then the number of iterations to reach distance R_t with $R_t \leq R_0/2^t$ is $\Theta(t \cdot n)$, w.o.p. and within expectation.*

For $t = 1$, Theorem 5 states the existence of two constants $a, b > 0$, such that for a large enough n, the random time T required to halve the initial distance to optimum R_0 satisfies

$$a n \leq E(T) \leq b n. \tag{48}$$

Even if the result does not state convergence to zero of r.v. R_t, as $t \to \infty$, neither in expectation, nor a.s. nor w.o.p., it accounts for a form of linear convergence, with respect to both t and n.

Remark 1. *For an arbitrary initial point, outside the prescribed range $\rho_0 = \Theta(R_0/\sqrt{n})$, Jägersküpper conjectured in [35] that: 'For other starting conditions, the number of steps until the theorem's assumption is met must be estimated before the theorem can be applied—by estimating the number of steps until the scaling factor is halved at least once. This is a rather simple task when utilizing the strong results presented in Lemma 5'. Empirical evidence for this fact can be found in [10].*

This is the point where Jägersküpper's convergence time analysis stops, without providing a formula similar to (37), to be tested against the behavior of the real ES. To fill in the gap, reference [10] applied the uniform mutation inside the sphere and the simplified 1/5 rule—obtained by removing line (ii) from Algorithm 1—and made use of the r.v. T = 'length of a constant-mutation ES cycle', defined as a stopping time ([33], pp. 97–98).

Definition 4. *A r.v. T with state space $\{0, 1, \ldots, \infty\}$ is said to be a stopping time for the sequence of r.v.s $\{X_t\}_{t \in \mathbb{N}}$ if one can decide whether the event $\{T = t\}$ has occurred only by observing $X_1, \ldots, X_t$. Note that, since the ES is a Markov chain, we do not assume independence of $X_1, X_2, \ldots$, as in Wald's equation and renewal theory [37].*

Stopping time will be considered the first hitting time of distance $d > 0$ from the initial point X_0.
$$T_d = \min\{t \mid X_1 + \ldots + X_t \geq d\}. \tag{49}$$
A key role in the analysis is played by the following generalization of Wald's equation ([37], p. 38), as introduced in [10]. Note that we define, for some r.v. X and $P(A) > 0$, the conditional expectation $E(X|A) = E(X \cdot \mathbf{1}_A)/P(A)$.

Proposition 3 (Wald's inequality [10]). *Let $c, d, \delta_\ell, \delta_u > 0$ and $\{X_t\}_{t \in \mathbb{N}}$ be non-negative r.v.s such that $X_0 = c$ and $\delta_\ell \leq E(X_t|T_d \geq t) \leq \delta_u$ for $t \geq 1$. Then*
$$\frac{d}{\delta_u} \leq E(T_d) \leq \frac{d + \delta_u}{\delta_\ell}. \tag{50}$$

We set in our ES analysis $X_0 = c = R_0 > d$ and $X_{t+1} = R_t - R_{t+1}$; hence, $X_1 + \ldots + X_t = R_0 - R_t$ for all $t \geq 0$.

Another form of Wald's inequality can be obtained from the additive drift theorem, derived by Lehre and Witt in [38]—which, as the authors mention, adapts for the continuous case the discrete space drift theorem of He and Yao [14]. We apply a formalization similar to Proposition 3.

Theorem 6 (Additive Drift). *Let $\{X_t\}_{t \in \mathbb{N}}$ be a stochastic process, adapted to a filtration $\{\mathcal{F}_t\}_{t \in \mathbb{N}}$, over some state space $S \subseteq \Re$; let $d, \delta_\ell, \delta_u > 0$ and $T_0 = \min\{t \mid X_t > 0\}$. Then, if $0 \leq X_t \leq d = X_0$ and $\delta_\ell \leq E(X_t - X_{t+1}; X_t > 0 \mid \mathcal{F}_t) \leq \delta_u$ for all t*
$$\frac{d}{\delta_u} \leq E(T_0|\mathcal{F}_0) \leq \frac{d}{\delta_\ell}. \tag{51}$$

To be comparable with Wald's inequality, one should set $X_{t+1} = d - (R_0 - R_{t+1})$ in the Adaptive Drift theorem. However, we consider the assumption $X_t \geq 0$ for all t, implying $X_{T_d} = 0$, to be unrealistic for $d < R_0$. On the other hand, if one sets $d = R_0$ as above, the lower bound $\delta_\ell > 0$ does not exist (independent of t) in the continuous case, e.g., the SPHERE. The existence of a strictly positive lower bound on either success probability or expected progress can be seen as a sufficient convergence condition for continuous space algorithms—see also Theorem 4—yet it is only satisfied in discrete space.

Back to the application of Wald's inequality in deriving convergence rates for the ES model. Let n be arbitrarily fixed; $d < R_0$; and consider the two a^*-values corresponding to the lower and upper limits of the evolution window depicted in Figure 3, $a_1^* = 0.84$ and $a_2^* = 1.68$. The normalized distance d^* between these points corresponds to the un-normalized distance

$$d = R_{0.84} - R_{1.68} = \rho\sqrt{n}\left(\frac{1}{0.84} - \frac{1}{1.68}\right), \qquad (52)$$

which further leads, using Wald's inequality (see [10] for details), to

Theorem 7. *Let Algorithm 1 be as in Theorem 5, starting in point* $a^* = 0.84$, *and let* $d^* = 1.68 - 0.84$. *Then, for large* n

$$2.5n \leq E(T_d) \lesssim 5.3n. \qquad (53)$$

The resemblance between Equations (48) and (53) is obvious. According to Theorem 7, if the elitist ES is currently (initially) in point $a_0^* = 0.84 = \rho\sqrt{n}/R_0$, the expected time to reach $2a_0^* = 1.68 = \rho\sqrt{n}/(R_0/2)$ is within $[2.5n, 5.3n]$. One could use these limits as lower and upper bounds on $E(T)$, or search for some value in between, to be used as an estimate for $E(T)$. In [10] the simple arithmetical mean 3.9 has been used, yet we choose here the estimate 3.5, as suggested by the new empirical evidence presented in Figure 4. The experiments were conducted with Algorithm 1 and uniform mutation inside the sphere, on the SPHERE fitness function, with different space dimensions and initial points, all corresponding to $a^* = 0.84$. The results were averaged over 100 independent runs. In each run, the maximal number of iterations was set to $t_{max} = 50,000$, and the last, incomplete cycle was discarded.

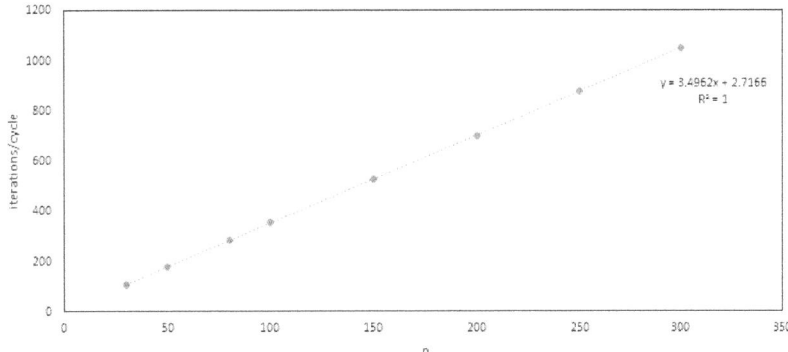

Figure 4. Expected number of iterations per cycle, as a function of space dimension n. Trend-line equation with R^2 value, displayed by Excel.

Using the value 3.5 for the expected value estimate of the r.v. T = 'No. of iterations per constant-mutation ES cycle', we obtained

$$R_{3.5n} \approx \frac{R_0}{2}. \qquad (54)$$

By iterating Equation (54) s times and substituting in $3.9ns = t$, we get

$$R_{3.5ns} = \frac{R_0}{2^s} \implies R_t = R_0 \, 2^{-\frac{t}{3.5n}}, \qquad (55)$$

which further implies, with $\log 2/3.5 = 0.192$,

$$R_t = R_0 \, e^{-\frac{0.192\, t}{n}}. \tag{56}$$

Using $R_t = \epsilon$ and a derivation similar to the one inferred from Equation (37), the linear convergence of the elitist ES on SPHERE is finally obtained.

$$\text{elitist ES convergence time} = \Theta\left(n \cdot \log \frac{R_0}{\epsilon}\right).$$

As demonstrated in [10], Formula (56) can be used, with very good experimental results, as a theoretical predictor of the algorithm's global behavior. Note that the slightly different exponential coefficient, 0.192 instead of 0.178 in [10], is not disruptive.

On the other hand, the above model, indicating identical behavior of the elitist ES within each constant mutation cycle, offers an intuitive insight into the algorithm's dynamics, seen as a sequence of cycles, that are independent and with identical expected length.

3. General 1/5-Rule Theories

Different convergence theories for the elitist ES with 1/5 success rule exist, building up mathematical rigor and complexity, yet, by imposing supplementary conditions, they usually lack compact results such as Theorem 3 and Formula (56). Some relevant examples are reviewed in the following.

Rudolph's stochastic analysis based on martingales, presented already in Section 2.3, provides only sufficient global convergence conditions for the algorithm. A different stochastic process—a random system with complete connections—was used with a similar outcome in [16]. With a deeper insight into the theory of the irreducible Markov chain, which identifies the discrete states to the so-called small sets and extrapolates the basic features of a discrete homogeneous Markov chain onto the continuous space [39,40], Dorea proved, under elitist selection, the global convergence of ES and of a continuous version of simulated annealing to an ϵ-vicinity of the optimum [17]. However, since the mutation distribution is decoupled from the current position, the result is of little practical use. Bienvenüe and Francois applied a different Markov model to an adaptive ES, but under a different, problem-related adaptation rule that multiplies at each iteration the mutation parameter ρ with the current distance to optimum R_t, then searches for 'optimal universal step lengths on the basis of the convergence of the dynamics' [41]. The same adaptation rule was used by Rudolph in his convergence analysis of the elitist ES on SPHERE ([9], p. 70). Connecting the mutation rate to the current position works for the SPHERE centered on the origin, but failed for a slightly modified problem, e.g., for a SPHERE with a different center—where Algorithm 1, adapting the mutation rate according to the 1/5 rule, works very well.

Unaware of Dorea's work, Auger and Hansen re-iterated the irreducible Markov chain modeling, but on the more practical premises used by Jägersküpper [2,18]. Similarly to Bienvenüe and Francois, but without their over-simplifying assumption, Auger and Hansen achieved, at the mathematical peak of ES literature, linear convergence of the elitist ES with the 1/5 rule on scaling-invariant functions (SPHERE included) by studying the stability of the normalized Markov chain $Z_t = R_t/\sigma$ [19]. A compact formula similar to (56) was proved.

$$R_t = R_0 \, e^{-CR\, t}, \tag{57}$$

where $CR > 0$ depends on the asymptotic success probability PS and on the 1/5 rule parameters γ, q.

$$\begin{cases} CR = -\ln \gamma \left(\frac{q+1}{q} PS - \frac{1}{q}\right) \\ \text{increasing 1/5 rule factor} \quad \gamma \\ \text{decreasing 1/5 rule factor} \quad \gamma^{-1/q}. \end{cases} \tag{58}$$

A supplementary condition is imposed on the parameters, which reads for the SPHERE

$$\frac{1}{2}\left(\frac{1}{\gamma}+\gamma^{\frac{1}{q}}\right)<1. \tag{59}$$

Bringing some clarity and a new stochastic formalization to the previous approach, Akimoto, Auger and co-workers employed drift analysis to prove the linear convergence time [6,11,42]. However, since their theory is still avoiding the expected progress calculus, a verification against the behavior of real algorithms can be performed only in terms of upper and lower bounds—see also the critique of adaptive drift theorem from Section 2.3.

4. Extensions of the 1/5-Rule—Population-Based ES

As noticed from the very beginning, the ES performance depends strongly on the value of the mutation parameter σ (or ρ). The 1/5 success rule discussed so far is the simplest, yet not the only way of adapting the parameter during the algorithm's evolution. Two of the most efficient techniques are the σ-self-adaptation [1,4,8] and the covariance matrix adaptation (CMA), which allows for different σ-values on the independent components (of normal mutation), aiming at accelerating the evolution in certain directions of the n-dimensional space [12,25,43,44].

As Beyer pointed out, each of these popular adaptation techniques borrows something from the original 1/5 success rule. The CMA techniques 'have an operating mechanism similar to the 1/5 rule: they analyze the statistical features of the selected mutations in order to change the strategy parameters towards the optimal value' ([4], p. 258). Namely, the pdf of multivariate normal mutation in CMA-ES is

$$f(\mathbf{x}) = \frac{1}{(\sqrt{2\pi})^n \sqrt{\det(C)}} e^{-\frac{\mathbf{x}^T C^{-1} \mathbf{x}}{2}} \tag{60}$$

with symmetric covariance matrix C depending on $n(n+1)/2$ mutation parameters. If one considers all these parameters as independent r.v.s and switches from a single to a multiple offspring algorithm—one parent, λ offspring and no elitist selection being the simplest case, known as $(1, \lambda)$ ES—Rudolph argues that a very large number of individuals is required in order to obtain a good approximation of the optimal matrix C. Pointing out that, in case of quadratic-convex fitness functions, the optimal C is the inverse of the function's Hessian matrix, he suggests that the CMA update rules should follow the deterministic iterative methods of approximating the Hessian matrix, based on the information gathered from previous samples ([9], p. 198); see also [43]. According to the recent survey of the state-of-art in ES for continuous optimization [25], 'we still lack a rigorous analysis of the one-step approximation of the covariance matrix'.

As a general remark in case of population-based algorithms—with multiple offspring, as for the $(1, \lambda)$ ES discussed above or the $(\mu/\mu, \lambda)$ ES with multiple parents, offspring and recombination/crossover [45,46], the explicit reduction of the mutation parameter induced by the 1/5 success rule is not necessary anymore, its exploitation effect being accomplished by the (minimum) order statistics of the λ offspring sample and/or by the μ/μ recombination of the parent population. Intuitively, the explanation is provided by the following fact: The average of two multivariate uniform distributions inside the sphere of radius ρ is also spherical, but with a smaller (expected value) radius, $\rho/\sqrt{2}$ instead of ρ; see [28] for details.

On the other hand, in self-adaptation, the dynamics of the mutation parameter is not based on some success-related statistics, but included in the evolution itself, subject to the basic algorithmic operators. Since mutation parameter σ becomes in this case part of the individual, 'the question reduces to the manner in which σ should be mutated. The answer is: *multiplicatively*, in contrast to the additive mutations of object parameters' ([4], p. 259). Obviously, the multiplicative character of the adaptation is inspired by the 1/5 rule.

5. Conclusions

Using the elitist, single-individual algorithm with mutation and the 1/5 success rule as the adaptation procedure and the SPHERE fitness function, the paper provides a bird eye's view over the theory of evolution strategies, an important class of probabilistic optimization algorithms for multi-dimensional real space.

Despite their easy implementation and huge success in applications, the mathematical models are complicated, and global convergence results are rather scarce. Taking into account some recent studies applying the uniform distribution inside the sphere as a mutation operator, the review centered on the classic evolution strategy theory, built on the one-step behavior of the algorithm and on local quantities such as success probability and expected progress. For the first time in the literature, the three main building blocks of classic theory were presented together in a coherent formalization:

- the asymptotic (w.r.t. large space dimension) local expected progress formula,
- the computational complexity analysis proving lower and upper linear bounds for global convergence,
- a probabilistic analysis—using an adaptation of Wald's equation—of the cyclic behavior of the algorithm with constant mutation rate, connecting the local and global behavior into a prediction formula for the (expected) convergence time of the real algorithm.

Different theories, based on martingales, irreducible Markov chain and drift analysis, were also reviewed, and their results were compared with those of classic theory.

As for population based algorithms—$(1, \lambda)$, $(\mu/\mu, \lambda)$, CMA and self-adaptive ES—the role of the 1/5 rule is transferred to the selection and crossover operators, yielding a reduction in the mutation parameter for local improvement.

Since the 1/5 rule is devoted to exploitation, not to the exploration phase of the algorithm, the case of multi-modal fitness functions was not tackled in this paper.

Funding: This research received no external funding.

Data Availability Statement: No new data were created.

Acknowledgments: The author acknowledges support over the years by the old Chair Informatics 11, Dortmund University, especially from Günter Rudolph, Hans-Paul Schwefel, Hans-Georg Beyer and Thomas Bäck.

Conflicts of Interest: The author declares no conflict of interest.

References

1. Rechenberg, I. *Evolutionsstrategie: Optimierung Technischer Systeme nach Prinzipien der Biologischen Evolution*; Frommann-Holzboog Verlag: Stuttgart, Germany, 1973.
2. Auger, A. Convergence results for the $(1, \lambda)$-SA-ES using the theory of ϕ-irreducible Markov chains. *Theor. Comput. Sci.* **2005**, *334*, 35–69. [CrossRef]
3. Schumer, M.A.; Steiglitz, K. Adaptive Step Size Random Search. *IEEE Trans. Aut. Control* **1968**, *13*, 270–276. [CrossRef]
4. Beyer, H.-G. *The Theory of Evolution Strategies*; Springer: Berlin/Heidelberg, Germany, 2001.
5. Jägerskupper, J. How the elitist ES using isotropic mutations minimizes positive definite quadratic forms. *Theor. Comp. Sci.* **2006**, *361*, 38–56. [CrossRef]
6. Akimoto, Y.; Auger, A.; Glasmachers, T. Drift theory in continuous search spaces: Expected hitting time of the (1 + 1)-ES with 1/5 success rule. In Proceedings of the GECCO '18: Genetic and Evolutionary Computation Conference, Kyoto Japan, 15–19 July 2018; pp. 801–808,.
7. Fang, K.-T.; Kotz, S.; Ng, K.-W. *Symmetric Multivariate and Related Distributions*; Chapman and Hall: London, UK, 1990.
8. Schwefel, H.-P. *Evolution and Optimum Seeking*; Wiley: New York, NY, USA, 1995.
9. Rudolph, G. *Convergence Properties of Evolutionary Algorithms*; Kovač: Hamburg, Germany, 1997.
10. Agapie, A.; Solomon, O.; Bădin, L. Theory of (1+1) ES on SPHERE revisited. *IEEE Trans. Evol. Comp.* **2022**, 3217524. [CrossRef]
11. Akimoto, Y.; Auger, A.; Glasmachers, T.; Morinaga, D. Global Linear Convergence of Evolution Strategies on more than Smooth Strongly Convex Functions. *SIAM J. Optim.* **2020**, *32*, 1402–1429. . [CrossRef]
12. He, X.; Zheng, Z.; Zhou, Y. MMES: Mixture Model-Based Evolution Strategy for Large-Scale Optimization. *IEEE Trans. Evol. Comp.* **2021**, *25*, 320–333. [CrossRef]

13. Agapie, A.; Agapie, M.; Rudolph, G.; Zbaganu, G. Convergence of evolutionary algorithms on the n-dimensional continuous space. *IEEE Trans. Cybern.* **2013**, *43*, 1462–1472. [CrossRef]
14. He, J.; Yao, X. A study of drift analysis for estimating computation time of evolutionary algorithms. *Nat. Comput.* **2004**, *3*, 21–35. [CrossRef]
15. Rudolph, G. Stochastic Convergence. In *Handbook of Natural Computing*; Rozenberg, G., Bäck, T., Kok, J., Eds.; Springer: Berlin/Heidelberg, Germany, 2013; pp. 847–869.
16. Agapie, A. Theoretical analysis of mutation-adaptive evolutionary algorithms. *Evol. Comput.* **2001**, *9*, 127–146. [CrossRef]
17. Dorea, C.C. Stationary Distribution of Markov Chains in R^d with Application to Global Random Optimization. *Bernoulli* **1997**, *3*, 415–427. [CrossRef]
18. Auger, A.; Hansen, N. Linear Convergence of Comparison-based Step-size Adaptive Randomized Search via Stability of Markov Chains. *SIAM J. Optim.* **2016**, *26*, 1589–1624. [CrossRef]
19. Auger, A.; Hansen, N. Linear Convergence on Positively Homogeneous Functions of a Comparison-based Step-size Adaptive Randomized Search: The Elitist ES with Generalized One-fifth Success Rule. *arXiv* **2013**, arXiv:1310.8397.
20. Haario, H.; Saksman, E. Simulated Annealing Process in General State Space. *Adv. Appl. Prob.* **1991**, *23*, 866–893. [CrossRef]
21. Vose, M.D. *The Simple Genetic Algorithm: Foundations and Theory*; MIT Press: Cambridge, MA, USA, 1999.
22. Chen, Y.; He, J. Average convergence rate of evolutionary algorithms in continuous optimization. *Inf. Sci.* **2021**, *562*, 200–219. [CrossRef]
23. Meunier, L.; Chevaleyre, Y.; Rapin, J.; Royer, C.W.; Teytaud, O. On Averaging the Best Samples in Evolutionary Computation. In *Parallel Problem Solving from Nature—PPSN XVI: 16th International Conference, PPSN 2020, Leiden, The Netherlands, 5–9 September 2020*; Bäck, T., Preuss, M., Deutz, A., Wang, H., Doerr, C., Emmerich, M., Trautmann, H., Eds.; Springer: Berlin/Heidelberg, Germany, 2020.
24. Jiang, W.; Qian, C.; Tang, K. Improved Running Time Analysis of the (1+1)-ES on the Sphere Function. In Proceedings of the 14th International Conference, Wuhan, China, 15–18 August 2018; Springer: Berlin/Heidelberg, Germany, 2018; pp. 729–739.
25. Li, Z.; Lin, X.; Zhang, Q.; Liu, H. Evolution strategies for continuous optimization: A survey of the state-of-the-art. *Swarm Evol. Comput.* **2020**, *56*, 100694. [CrossRef]
26. Jägersküpper, J. Analysis of a simple evolutionary algorithm for minimisation in Euclidean spaces. In Proceedings of the 30th International Conference on Automata, Languages and Programming, Eindhoven, The Netherlands, 30 June–4 July 2003; Volume 2719, pp. 1068–1079.
27. Agapie, A.; Agapie, M.; Zbaganu, G. Evolutionary Algorithms for Continuous Space Optimization. *Int. J. Syst. Sci.* **2013**, *44*, 502–512. [CrossRef]
28. Agapie, A.; Solomon, O.; Giuclea, M. Theory of (1+1) ES on the RIDGE. *IEEE Trans. Evol. Comp.* **2022**, *26*, 501–511. [CrossRef]
29. David, H.A. *Order Statistics*; Wiley: New York, NY, USA, 1981.
30. Agapie, A. Spherical Distributions Used in Evolutionary Algorithms. *Mathematics* **2021**, *9*, 3098. [CrossRef]
31. Beyer, H.-G.; Schwefel, H.-P. Evolution strategies. A comprehensive introduction. *Nat. Comput.* **2002**, *1*, 3–52. [CrossRef]
32. Rudolph, G. Local convergence rates of simple evolutionary algorithms with Cauchy mutations. *IEEE Trans. Evol. Comp.* **1997**, *1*, 249–258. [CrossRef]
33. Williams, D. *Probability with Martingales*; Cambridge University Press: Cambridge, UK, 1991.
34. Rapple, G. On linear convergence of a class of random search algorithms. *Z. Für Angew. Math. Und Mech. (ZAMM)* **1989**, *69*, 37–45. [CrossRef]
35. Jägersküpper, J. Algorithmic analysis of a basic evolutionary algorithm for continuous optimization. *Theor. Comp. Sci.* **2007**, *379*, 329–347. [CrossRef]
36. Jägersküpper, J.; Witt, C. Rigorous runtime analysis of a (μ+1) ES for the sphere function. In Proceedings of the 7th Annual Conference on Genetic and Evolutionary Computation, Washington, DC, USA, 25–29 June 2005; ACM: Washington, DC, USA, 2005; pp. 849–856.
37. Ross, S. *Applied Probability Models with Optimization Applications*; Dover: New York, NY, USA, 1992.
38. Lehre, P.C.; Witt, C. Concentrated hitting times of randomized search heuristics with variable drift. In Proceedings of the 25th International Symposium, ISAAC 2014, Jeonju, Republic of Korea, 15–17 December 2014; Springer: Berlin/Heidelberg, Germany, 2014; pp. 686–697.
39. Meyn, S.; Tweedie, R. *Markov Chains and Stochastic Stability*; Springer: New York, NY, USA, 1993.
40. Nummelin, E. *General Irreducible Markov Chains and Non-Negative Operators*; Cambridge University Press: Cambridge, UK, 1984.
41. Bienvenüe, A.; Francois, O. Global convergence for evolution strategies in spherical problems: Some simple proofs and difficulties. *Theor. Comput. Sci.* **2003**, *306*, 269–289. [CrossRef]
42. Akimoto, Y.; Auger, A.; Hansen, N. Quality gain analysis of the weighted recombination evolution strategy on general convex quadratic functions. *Theoret. Comput. Sci.* **2020**, *832*, 42–67. [CrossRef]
43. Hansen, N. The CMA Evolution Strategy: A Tutorial. INRIA, 2005. Available online: https://hal.inria.fr/hal-01297037 (accessed on 10 June 2022).
44. Kumar, A.; Das, S.; Mallipeddi, R. A Reference Vector-Based Simplified Covariance Matrix Adaptation Evolution Strategy for Constrained Global Optimization. *IEEE Trans. Cybern.* **2020**, *52*, 3696–3709. [CrossRef]

45. Arnold, D.V.; Salomon, R. Evolutionary Gradient Search Revisited. *IEEE Trans. Evol. Comp.* **2007**, *11*, 480–495. [CrossRef]
46. Beyer, H.-G.; Melkozerov, A. The Dynamics of Self-Adaptive Multirecombinant Evolution Strategies on the General Ellipsoid Model. *IEEE Trans. Evol. Comp.* **2014**, *18*, 764–778. [CrossRef]

Disclaimer/Publisher's Note: The statements, opinions and data contained in all publications are solely those of the individual author(s) and contributor(s) and not of MDPI and/or the editor(s). MDPI and/or the editor(s) disclaim responsibility for any injury to people or property resulting from any ideas, methods, instructions or products referred to in the content.

Article

Influence of Binomial Crossover on Approximation Error of Evolutionary Algorithms

Cong Wang [1], Jun He [2], Yu Chen [1,*] and Xiufen Zou [3,4]

1 School of Science, Wuhan University of Technology, Wuhan 430070, China
2 Department of Computer Science, Nottingham Trent University, Clifton Campus, Nottingham NG11 8NS, UK
3 School of Mathematics and Statistics, Wuhan University, Wuhan 430072, China
4 Computational Science Hubei Key Laboratory, Wuhan University, Wuhan 430072, China
* Correspondence: ychen@whut.edu.cn

Abstract: Although differential evolution (DE) algorithms perform well on a large variety of complicated optimization problems, only a few theoretical studies are focused on the working principle of DE algorithms. To make the first attempt to reveal the function of binomial crossover, this paper aims to answer whether it can reduce the approximation error of evolutionary algorithms. By investigating the expected approximation error and the probability of not finding the optimum, we conduct a case study comparing two evolutionary algorithms with and without binomial crossover on two classical benchmark problems: OneMax and Deceptive. It is proven that using binomial crossover leads to the dominance of transition matrices. As a result, the algorithm with binomial crossover asymptotically outperforms that without crossover on both OneMax and Deceptive, and outperforms on OneMax, however, not on Deceptive. Furthermore, an adaptive parameter strategy is proposed which can strengthen the superiority of binomial crossover on Deceptive.

Keywords: binomial crossover; differential evolution; fixed-budget analysis; evolutionary computation; approximation error

MSC: 90C15

1. Introduction

Evolutionary algorithms (EAs) are a family of randomized search heuristics inspired from biological evolution, and many empirical studies demonstrate that crossovers that combine genes of two parents to generate new offspring could be helpful to the convergence of EAs [1–3]. Meanwhile, theoretical results on runtime analysis validate the promising function of crossover in EAs [4–15], whereas there are also some cases that crossover cannot be helpful [16,17].

By exchanging components of target vectors with donor vectors, differential evolution (DE) algorithms implement crossover operations in a different way. Numerical results show that continuous DE algorithms can achieve competitive performance on a large variety of complicated problems [18–21], and its competitiveness is to great extent attributed to the employed crossover operations [22]. However, the binary differential evolution (BDE) algorithm [23], which simulates the working mechanism of continuous DE, is not as competitive as its continuous counterpart. Analysis of the working principle indicates that the mutation and update strategies result in poor convergence of BDE [24], but there were no theoretical results reported on how crossover influences the performance of discrete-coded DE algorithms.

This paper is dedicated to investigating the influence of binomial crossover by introducing it to the (1 + 1)EA, excluding the impacts of population and mutation strategies of DE. Although the expected hitting time/runtime is popularly investigated in the theoretical study of randomized search heuristics (RSHs), there is a gap between runtime analysis

and practice because their optimization time to reach an optimum is uncertain and could be even infinite in continuous optimization [25]. Due to this reason, optimization time is seldom used in computer simulation for evaluating the performance of EAs, and their performance is evaluated after running finite generations by solution quality such as the mean and median of the fitness value or approximation error [26]. In theory, solution quality can be measured for a given iteration budget by the expected fitness value [27] or approximation error [28,29], which contributes to the analysis framework named fixed-budget analysis (FBA). An FBA on immune-inspired hypermutations led to theoretical results that are very different from those of runtime analysis but consistent with the empirical results, which demonstrates that the perspective of fixed-budget computations provides valuable information and additional insights for the performance of randomized search heuristics [30].

Accordingly, we evaluate the solution quality of an EA after running finite generations by the expected approximation error and the error tail probability. The former measures the fitness gap between a solution and optimum, and the latter is the probability distribution of the error over error levels, which measures the probability of finding the optimum. An EA is said to outperform another if, for the former EA, its error and tail probability are smaller. Furthermore, an EA is said to asymptotically outperform another if, for the former EA, its error and tail probability are smaller after a sufficiently large number of generations.

The research question of this paper is whether the binomial crossover operator can help reduce the approximation error of EA. As a pioneering work on this topic, we investigate a $(1+1)EA_C$ that performs the binomial crossover on an individual and an offspring generated by mutation, and compare a $(1+1)EA$ without crossover and its variant $(1+1)EA_C$ on two classical problems, OneMax and Deceptive. By splitting the objective space into error levels, the analysis is performed based on the Markov chain models [31,32]. Given the two EAs, the comparison of their performance is drawn from the comparison of their transition probabilities, which are estimated by investigating the bits preferred by evolutionary operations. Under some conditions, $(1+1)EA_C$ with binomial crossover outperforms $(1+1)EA$ on OneMax, but not on Deceptive; however, by adding an adaptive parameter mechanism arising from theoretical results, $(1+1)EA_C$ with binomial crossover outperforms $(1+1)EA$ on Deceptive too.

This work presents the first study on how binomial crossover influences the expected runtime and tail probability of randomized search heuristics. Meanwhile, we also propose a feasible routine to get adaptive parameter settings of EAs from theoretical results. The rest of this paper is organized as follows. Section 2 reviews related theoretical work. Preliminary contents for our theoretical analysis are presented in Section 3. Then, the influence of the binomial crossover on transition probabilities is investigated in Section 4. Section 5 conducts an analysis of the asymptotic performance of EAs. To reveal how binomial crossover works on the performance of EAs for consecutive iterations, the OneMax problem and the Deceptive problem are investigated in Sections 6 and 7, respectively. Finally, Section 8 presents the conclusions and discussions.

2. Related Work

2.1. Theoretical Analysis of Crossover in Evolutionary Algorithms

To understand how crossover influences the performance of EAs, Jansen et al. [4] proved that an EA using crossover can reduce the expected optimization time from superpolynomial to a polynomial of small degree on the function Jump. Kötzing et al. [5] investigated crossover-based EAs on the functions OneMax and Jump and showed the potential speedup by crossover when combined with a fitness-invariant bit shuffling operator in terms of optimization time. For a simple GA without shuffling, they found that the crossover probability has a drastic impact on the performance on Jump. Corus and Oliveto [6] obtained an upper bound on the runtime of standard steady-state GAs to hillclimb the OneMax function and proved that the steady-state EAs are 25% faster than their mutation-only counterparts. Their analysis also suggests that larger populations may be faster than populations of size 2. Dang et al. [7] revealed that the interplay between crossover and mutation may result in a sudden burst of diversity on the Jump test function and reduce the expected optimization time compared to mutation-only algorithms such as (1 + 1) EA. For royal road functions and OneMax, Sudholt [8] analyzed uniform crossover and k-point crossover and proved that crossover makes every $(\mu + \lambda)$ EA at least twice as fast as the fastest EA using only standard bit mutation. Pinto and Doerr [9] provided a simple proof of a crossover-based genetic algorithm (GA) outperforming any mutation-based black-box heuristic on the classic benchmark OneMax. Oliveto et al. [10] obtained a tight lower bound on the expected runtime of the (2 + 1) GA on OneMax. Lengler and Meier [11] studied the positive effect of using larger population sizes and crossover on Dynamic BinVal.

For non-artificial problems, Lehre and Yao [12] proved that the use of crossover in the $(\mu + 1)$ steady-state genetic algorithm may reduce the runtime from exponential to polynomial for some instance classes of the problem of computing unique input–output (UIO) sequences. Doerr et al. [13,14] analyzed EAs on the all-pairs shortest path problem. Their results confirmed that the EA with a crossover operator is significantly faster in terms of the expected optimization time. Sutton [15] investigated the closest string problem and proved that a multi-start $(\mu + 1)$ GA required less randomized fixed-parameter tractable (FPT) time than that with disabled crossover.

However, there is some evidence that crossover is not always helpful. Richter et al. [16] constructed Ignoble Trail functions and proved that mutation-based EAs optimize them more efficiently than GAs with crossover. The later need exponential optimization time. Antipov and Naumov [17] compared crossover-based algorithms on RealJump functions with a slightly shifted optimum, which increases the runtime of all considered algorithms on RealJump. The hybrid GA fails to find the shifted optimum with high probability.

2.2. Theoretical Analysis of Differential Evolution Algorithms

Most existing theoretical studies on DE are focused on continuous variants [33]. By estimating the probability density function of generated individuals, Zhou et al. [34] demonstrated that the selection mechanism of DE, which chooses mutually different parents for the generation of donor vectors, sometimes does not work positively on the performance of DE. Zaharie and Micota [35–37] investigated the influence of the crossover rate on both the distribution of the number of mutated components and the probability for a component to be taken from the mutant vector, as well as the influence of mutation and crossover on the diversity of the intermediate population. Wang and Huang [38] attributed the DE to a one-dimensional stochastic model, and investigated how the probability distribution of population is connected to the mutation, selection, and crossover operations of DE. Opara and Arabas [39] compared several variants of the differential mutation using characteristics of their expected mutants' distribution, which demonstrated that the classic mutation operators yield similar search directions and differ primarily by the mutation range. Furthermore, they formalized the contour fitting notion and derived an analytical model that links the differential mutation operator with the adaptation of the range and direction of search [40].

By investigating the expected runtime of BDE, Doerr and Zhang [24] performed a first fundamental analysis on the working principles of discrete-coded DE. It was shown that BDE optimizes the important decision variables, but is hard to find the optima for decision variables with a small influence on the objective function. Since BDE generates trial vectors by implementing a binary variant of binomial crossover accompanied by the mutation operation, it has characteristics significantly different from classic EAs or estimation-of-distribution algorithms.

2.3. Fixed-Budget Analysis and Approximation Error

To bridge the wide gap between theory and application, Jasen and Zarges [27] proposed an FBA framework of RSHs, by which the fitness of random local search and (1 + 1)

EA were investigated for given iteration budgets. Under the framework of FBA, Jasen and Zarges [41] analyzed the any-time performance of EAs and artificial immune systems on a proposed dynamic benchmark problem. Nallaperuma et al. [42] considered the well-known traveling salesperson problem (TSP) and derived the lower bounds of the expected fitness gain for a specified number of generations. Based on the Markov chain model of RSHs, Wang et al. [29] constructed a general framework of FBA, by which they found the analytic expression of approximation error instead of asymptotic results of expected fitness values. Doerr et al. [43] built a bridge between runtime analysis and FBA, by which a huge body of work and a large collection of tools for the analysis of the expected optimization time could meet the new challenges introduced by the new fixed-budget perspective.

Noting that hypermutations tend to be inferior to typical example functions in terms of runtime, Jansen and Zarges [30] conducted an FBA to explain why artificial immune systems are popular in spite of these proven drawbacks. It was shown that the inversely fitness-proportional mutation (IFPM) and the somatic contiguous hypermutation (CHM) could perform better than the single point mutation on OneMax while FBA is performed by considering different starting points and varied iteration budgets. It indicates that the traditional perspective of expected optimization time may be unable to explain the observed good performance, which is due to the limited length of runs. Therefore, the perspective of fixed-budget computations provides valuable information and additional insights.

3. Preliminaries

3.1. Problems

Considering a maximization problem

$$\max f(\mathbf{x}), \quad \mathbf{x} = (x_1, \ldots, x_n) \in \{0,1\}^n,$$

denote its optimal solution by $\mathbf{x}^*$ and optimal objective value by f^*. The quality of a solution $\mathbf{x}$ is evaluated by its approximation error $e(\mathbf{x}) := |f(\mathbf{x}) - f^*|$. The error $e(\mathbf{x})$ takes finite values, called error levels:

$$e(\mathbf{x}) \in \{e_0, e_1, \ldots, e_L\}, \quad 0 = e_0 \leq e_1 \leq \cdots \leq e_L,$$

where L is a non-negative integer. $\mathbf{x}$ is called *at the level i* if $e(\mathbf{x}) = e_i, i \in \{0, 1, \ldots, L\}$. The collection of solutions at level i is denoted by $\mathcal{X}_i$.

We investigate the optimization problem in the form

$$\max f(|\mathbf{x}|), \tag{1}$$

where $|\mathbf{x}| := \sum_{i=1}^n x_i$. Error levels of (1) take only $n+1$ values. Two instances, the unimodal OneMax problem and the multi-modal Deceptive problem, are considered in this paper.

Problem 1 (OneMax).

$$\max f(\mathbf{x}) = \sum_{i=1}^n x_i, \quad \mathbf{x} = (x_1, \ldots, x_n) \in \{0,1\}^n.$$

Problem 2 (Deceptive).

$$\max f(\mathbf{x}) = \begin{cases} \sum_{i=1}^n x_i, & \text{if } \sum_{i=1}^n x_i > n-1, \\ n-1-\sum_{i=1}^n x_i, & \text{otherwise,} \end{cases} \quad \mathbf{x} = (x_1, \ldots, x_n) \in \{0,1\}^n.$$

For the OneMax problem, both exploration and exploitation are helpful to the convergence of EAs to the optimum, because exploration accelerates the convergence process and exploitation refines the precision of approximation solutions. However, for the Deceptive problem, local exploitation leads to convergence to the local optimum, but it in turn increases the difficulty to jump to the global optimum. That is, exploitation hinders convergence to the global optimum of the Deceptive problem, thus, the performance of EAs is dominantly influenced by their exploration ability.

3.2. Evolutionary Algorithms

For the sake of analysis on binomial crossover excluding the influence of population and mutation, the $(1+1)EA$ presented in Algorithm 1 is taken as the baseline algorithm in our study. Its candidate solutions are generated by the bitwise mutation with probability p_m. The binomial crossover is appended to $(1+1)EA$, getting $(1+1)EA_C$ which is illustrated in Algorithm 2. The $(1+1)EA_C$ first performs bitwise mutation with probability q_m, and then applies binomial crossover with rate C_R to generate a candidate solution for selection.

The EAs investigated in this paper can be modeled as homogeneous Markov chains [31,32]. Given the error vector

$$\tilde{\mathbf{e}} = (e_0, e_1, \ldots, e_L)', \tag{2}$$

and the initial distribution

$$\tilde{\mathbf{q}}^{[0]} = (q_0^{[0]}, q_1^{[0]}, \ldots, q_L^{[0]})' \tag{3}$$

the transition matrix of $(1+1)EA$ and $(1+1)EA_C$ for the optimization problem (1) can be written in the form

$$\tilde{\mathbf{R}} = (r_{i,j})_{(L+1)\times(L+1)}, \tag{4}$$

where

$$r_{i,j} = \Pr\{\mathbf{x}_{t+1} \in \mathcal{X}_i \mid \mathbf{x}_t \in \mathcal{X}_j\}, \quad i,j = 0, \ldots, L.$$

Algorithm 1 $(1+1)EA$

1: counter $t = 0$;
2: randomly generate a solution $\mathbf{x}_0 = (x_1, \ldots, x_n)$;
3: **while** the stopping criterion is not satisfied **do**
4:    generate the mutant $\mathbf{y}_t = (y_1, \ldots, y_n)$ by bitwise mutation:

$$\text{for } i = 1, \ldots, n, \quad y_i = \begin{cases} 1 - x_i, & \text{if } rnd_i < p_m, \\ x_i, & \text{otherwise,} \end{cases} \quad rnd_i \sim U[0,1]; \tag{5}$$

5:    **if** $f(\mathbf{y}) \geq f(\mathbf{x}_t)$ **then**
6:       $\mathbf{x}_{t+1} = \mathbf{y}_t$;
7:    **else**
8:       $\mathbf{x}_{t+1} = \mathbf{x}_t$;
9:    **end if**
10:   $t = t + 1$;
11: **end while**

Algorithm 2 $(1+1)EA_C$

1: counter $t = 0$;
2: randomly generate a solution $\mathbf{x}_0 = (x_1, \ldots, x_n)$;
3: **while** the stopping criterion is not satisfied **do**
4:     Generate the mutant $\mathbf{v} = (v_1, \ldots, v_n)$ by bitwise mutation:

$$\text{for } i = 1, \ldots, n, \quad v_i = \begin{cases} 1 - x_i, & \text{if } rnd1_i < q_m, \\ x_i, & \text{otherwise,} \end{cases} \quad rnd1_i \sim U[0,1]; \quad (6)$$

5:     set $rndi \sim U\{1, 2, \ldots, n\}$;
6:     generate the offspring $\mathbf{y} = (y_1, \ldots, y_n)$ by performing binomial crossover on $\mathbf{v}$:

$$\text{for } i = 1, \ldots, n, \quad y_i = \begin{cases} v_i, & \text{if } i = rndi \text{ or } rnd2_i < C_R, \\ x_i, & \text{otherwise,} \end{cases} \quad rnd2_i \sim U[0,1]; \quad (7)$$

7:     **if** $f(\mathbf{y}) \geq f(\mathbf{x}_t)$ **then**
8:         $\mathbf{x}_{t+1} = \mathbf{y}_t$;
9:     **else**
10:         $\mathbf{x}_{t+1} = \mathbf{x}_t$;
11:     **end if**
12:     $t = t + 1$;
13: **end while**

Recalling that the solutions are updated by the elitist selection, we know $\tilde{\mathbf{R}}$ is an upper triangular matrix that can be partitioned as

$$\tilde{\mathbf{R}} = \begin{pmatrix} 1 & \mathbf{r}_0 \\ 0 & \mathbf{R} \end{pmatrix},$$

where $\mathbf{r}_0$ represents the probabilities to transfer from non-optimal statuses to the optimal status, and $\mathbf{R}$ is the transition submatrix depicting the transitions between non-optimal statuses.

3.3. Transition Probabilities

Transition probabilities can be confirmed by considering generation of a candidate $\mathbf{y}$ with $f(\mathbf{y}) \geq f(\mathbf{x})$, which is achieved if "$l$ preferred bits" of $\mathbf{x}$ are changed. If there are multiple solutions that are better than $\mathbf{x}$, there could be multiple choices for both the number l and the location of "l preferred bits".

Example 1. *For the OneMax problem, $e(\mathbf{x})$ equals to the amount of '0'-bits in $\mathbf{x}$. Denoting $e(\mathbf{x}) = j$ and $e(\mathbf{y}) = i$, we know $\mathbf{y}$ replaces $\mathbf{x}$ if and only if $j \geq i$. Then, to generate a candidate $\mathbf{y}$ replacing $\mathbf{x}$, "l preferred bits" can be confirmed as follows.*

- *If $i = j$, "l preferred bits" consist of $l/2$ '1'-bits and $l/2$ '0'-bits, where l is an even number that is not greater than $\min\{2j, 2(n-j)\}$.*
- *While $i < j$, "l preferred bits" could be combinations of $j - i + k$ '0'-bits and k '1'-bits ($l = j - i + 2k$), where $0 \leq k \leq \min\{i, n-j\}$. Here, k is not greater than i, because $j - i + k$ could not be greater than j, the number of '0'-bits in $\mathbf{x}$. Meanwhile, k does not exceed $n - j$, the number of '1'-bits in $\mathbf{x}$.*

If an EA flips each bit with an identical probability, the probability of flipping l bits are related to l and independent of their locations. Denoting the probability of flipping l bits by $P(l)$, we can confirm the connection between the transition probability $r_{i,j}$ and $P(l)$.

As presented in Example 1, transition from level j to level i ($i < j$) results from flips of $j - i + k$ '0'-bits and k '1'-bits. Then, transition probabilities for OneMax are confirmed as

$$r_{i,j} = \sum_{k=0}^{M} C_{n-j}^{k} C_{j}^{k+(j-i)} P(2k + j - i), \tag{8}$$

where $M = \min\{n - j, i\}$, $0 \leq i < j \leq n$.

According to definition of the Deceptive problem, we get the following map from $|\mathbf{x}|$ to $e(\mathbf{x})$.

$$\begin{array}{c|ccccc} |\mathbf{x}|: & 0 & 1 & \cdots & n-1 & n \\ e(\mathbf{x}): & 1 & 2 & \cdots & n & 0 \end{array} \tag{9}$$

Transition from level j to level i ($0 \leq i < j \leq n$) is attributed to one of the following cases.

- If $i \geq 1$, the amount of '1'-bits decreases from $j - 1$ to $i - 1$. This transition results from a change of $j - i + k$ '1'-bits and k '0'-bits, where $0 \leq k \leq \min\{n - j + 1, i - 1\}$;
- if $i = 0$, all of $n - j + 1$ '0'-bits are flipped, and all of its '1'-bits keep unchanged.

Accordingly, transition probabilities for Deceptive are confirmed as

$$r_{i,j} = \begin{cases} \sum_{k=0}^{M} C_{n-j+1}^{k} C_{j-1}^{k+(j-i)} P(2k + j - i), & i \geq 1, \\ P(n - j + 1), & i = 0, \end{cases} \tag{10}$$

where $M = \min\{n - j + 1, i - 1\}$.

3.4. Performance Metrics

To evaluate the performance of EAs, we propose two metrics for a given iteration budget, the expected approximation error (EAE) and the tail probability (TP) of EAs for t consecutive iterations.

Definition 1. *Let $\{\mathbf{x}_t, t = 1, 2 \ldots\}$ be the individual sequence of an individual-based EA.*

(1) *The expected approximation error (EAE) after t consecutive iterations is*

$$e^{[t]} = \mathbb{E}[e(\mathbf{x}_t)] = \sum_{i=0}^{L} e_i \Pr\{e(\mathbf{x}_t) = e_i\}. \tag{11}$$

(2) *Given $i > 0$, the tail probability (TP) of the approximation error that $e(\mathbf{x}_t)$ is greater than or equal to e_i is defined as*

$$p^{[t]}(e_i) = \Pr\{e(\mathbf{x}_t) \geq e_i\}. \tag{12}$$

EAE is the fitness gap between a solution and the optimum. It measures solution quality after running t generations. TP is the probability distribution of a found solution over non-optimal levels where $i > 0$. The sum of TP is the probability of not finding the optimum.

Given two EAs $\mathcal{A}$ and $\mathcal{B}$, if both EAE and TP of Algorithm $\mathcal{A}$ are smaller than those of Algorithm $\mathcal{B}$ for any iteration budget, we say Algorithm $\mathcal{A}$ outperforms Algorithm $\mathcal{B}$ on problem (1).

Definition 2. *Let $\mathcal{A}$ and $\mathcal{B}$ be two EAs applied to problem (1).*

1. *Algorithm $\mathcal{A}$ outperforms $\mathcal{B}$, denoted by $\mathcal{A} \succeq \mathcal{B}$, if it holds that*
   - $e_{\mathcal{A}}^{[t]} - e_{\mathcal{B}}^{[t]} \leq 0, \forall t > 0$;
   - $p_{\mathcal{A}}^{[t]}(e_i) - p_{\mathcal{B}}^{[t]}(e_i) \leq 0, \forall t > 0, 0 < i < L$.

2. Algorithm $\mathcal{A}$ asymptotically outperforms $\mathcal{B}$ on problem (1), denoted by $\mathcal{A} \succsim^a \mathcal{B}$, if it holds that
   - $\lim_{t \to \infty} e_{\mathcal{A}}^{[t]} - e_{\mathcal{B}}^{[t]} \leq 0$;
   - $\lim_{t \to +\infty} p_{\mathcal{A}}^{[t]}(e_i) - p_{\mathcal{B}}^{[t]}(e_i) \leq 0$.

The asymptotic outperformance is weaker than the outperformance.

4. Comparison of Transition Probabilities of Two EAs

In this section, we compare transition probabilities of $(1+1)EA$ and $(1+1)EA_C$. According to the connection between $r_{i,j}$ and $P(l)$, a comparison of transition probabilities can be conducted by considering the probabilities of flipping "l preferred bits".

4.1. Probabilities of Flipping Preferred Bits

Denote probabilities of $(1+1)EA$ and $(1+1)EA_C$ to flip "l preferred bits" by $P_1(l, p_m)$ and $P_2(l, C_R, q_m)$, respectively. By (5), we know

$$P_1(l, p_m) = (p_m)^l (1 - p_m)^{n-l}. \tag{13}$$

Since the mutation and the binomial crossover in Algorithm 2 are mutually independent, we can get the probability by considering the crossover first. When flipping "l preferred bits" by $(1+1)EA_C$, there are $l + k$ ($0 \leq k \leq n - l$) bits of $\mathbf{y}$ set as v_i by (7), the probability of which is

$$P_C(l+k, C_R) = \frac{l+k}{n}(C_R)^{l+k-1}(1 - C_R)^{n-l-k}.$$

If only "l preferred bits" are flipped, we know,

$$P_2(l, C_R, q_m) = \sum_{k=0}^{n-l} C_{n-l}^k P_C(l+k, C_R)(q_m)^l (1 - q_m)^k$$

$$= \frac{1}{n}[l + (n-l)C_R - nq_m C_R](C_R)^{l-1}(q_m)^l(1 - q_m C_R)^{n-l-1}. \tag{14}$$

Note that $(1+1)EA_C$ degrades to $(1+1)EA$ when $C_R = 1$, and $(1+1)EA$ becomes the random search while $p_m = 1$. Thus, we assume that p_m, C_R, and q_m are located in $(0,1)$. A fair comparison of transition probabilities is investigated by considering the identical parameter setting

$$p_m = C_R q_m = p, \quad 0 < p < 1. \tag{15}$$

Then, we know $q_m = p/C_R$, and Equation (14) implies

$$P_2(l, C_R, p/C_R) = \frac{1}{n}\left[(n-l) + \frac{l-np}{C_R}\right]p^l(1-p)^{n-l-1}. \tag{16}$$

Subtracting (13) from (16), we have

$$P_2(l, C_R, p/C_R) - P_1(l, p) = \left\{\frac{1}{n}\left[(n-l) + \frac{l-np}{C_R}\right] - (1-p)\right\}p^l(1-p)^{n-l-1}$$

$$= \left(\frac{1}{C_R} - 1\right)\left(\frac{l}{n} - p\right)p^l(1-p)^{n-l-1}. \tag{17}$$

From the fact that $0 < C_R < 1$, we conclude that $P_2(l, C_R, p/C_R)$ is greater than $P_1(l, p)$ if and only if $l > np$. That is, the introduction of the binomial crossover in $(1+1)EA$ leads to the enhancement of the exploration ability of $(1+1)EA_C$. We get the following theorem for the case that $p \leq \frac{1}{n}$.

Theorem 1. *While $0 < p \leq \frac{1}{n}$, it holds for all $1 \leq l \leq n$ that $P_1(l, p) \leq P_2(l, C_R, p/C_R)$.*

Proof. The result can be obtained directly from Equation (17) by setting $p \leq \frac{1}{n}$. □

For the popular setting where the mutation probability of (1+1)EA is set as $1/n$, the introduction of binomial crossover does increase the ability to generate new candidate solutions. Then, we investigate how this improvement contributes to change of transition probabilities.

4.2. Comparison of Transition Probabilities

To validate that algorithm $\mathcal{A}$ is more efficient than algorithm $\mathcal{B}$, it is assumed that the probability of $\mathcal{A}$ to transfer to promising statuses could be not smaller than that of $\mathcal{B}$.

Definition 3. Let $\mathcal{A}$ and $\mathcal{B}$ be two EAs with an identical initialization mechanism. $\tilde{\mathbf{A}} = (a_{i,j})$ and $\tilde{\mathbf{B}} = (b_{i,j})$ are the transition matrices of $\mathcal{A}$ and $\mathcal{B}$, respectively. It is said that $\tilde{\mathbf{A}}$ **dominates** $\tilde{\mathbf{B}}$, denoted by $\tilde{\mathbf{A}} \succeq \tilde{\mathbf{B}}$, if it holds that

1. $a_{i,j} \geq b_{i,j}, \quad \forall 0 \leq i < j \leq L$;
2. $a_{i,j} > b_{i,j}, \quad \exists 0 \leq i < j \leq L$.

Denote the transition probabilities of $(1+1)EA$ and $(1+1)EA_C$ by $p_{i,j}$ and $s_{i,j}$, respectively. For the OneMax problem and Deceptive problem, we get the relation of transition dominance on the premise that $p_m = C_R q_m = p \leq \frac{1}{n}$.

Theorem 2. For $(1+1)EA$ and $(1+1)EA_C$, denote their transition matrices by $\tilde{\mathbf{P}}$ and $\tilde{\mathbf{S}}$, respectively. On the condition that $p_m = C_R q_m = p \leq \frac{1}{n}$, it holds for problem (1) that $\tilde{\mathbf{S}} \succeq \tilde{\mathbf{P}}$.

Proof. Denote the collection of all solutions at level k by $\mathcal{S}(k), k = 0, 1, \ldots, n$. We prove the result by considering the transition probability

$$r_{i,j} = \Pr\{\mathbf{y} \in \mathcal{S}(i) \mid \mathbf{x} \in \mathcal{S}(j)\}, \quad (i < j).$$

Since the function values of solutions are merely related to the number of '1'-bits, the probability to generate a solution $\mathbf{y} \in \mathcal{S}(i)$ by performing mutation on $\mathbf{x} \in \mathcal{S}(j)$ depends on the Hamming distance $l = H(\mathbf{x}, \mathbf{y})$. Given $\mathbf{x} \in \mathcal{S}_j$, $\mathcal{S}(i)$ is partitioned as $\mathcal{S}(i) = \bigcup_{l=1}^{L} \mathcal{S}_l(i)$, where $\mathcal{S}_l(i) = \{\mathbf{y} \in \mathcal{S}(i) \mid H(\mathbf{x}, \mathbf{y}) = l\}$, and L is a positive integer that is smaller than or equal to n.

Accordingly, the probability to transfer from level j to i is confirmed as

$$r_{i,j} = \sum_{l=1}^{L} \Pr\{\mathbf{y} \in \mathcal{S}_l(i) \mid \mathbf{x} \in \mathcal{S}(j)\} = \sum_{l=1}^{L} |\mathcal{S}_l(i)| P(l),$$

where $|\mathcal{S}_l(i)|$ is the size of $\mathcal{S}_l(i)$, $P(l)$ the probability to flip "l preferred bits". Then,

$$p_{i,j} = \sum_{l=1}^{L} \Pr\{\mathbf{y} \in \mathcal{S}_l(j) \mid \mathbf{x}\} = \sum_{l=1}^{L} |\mathcal{S}_l(j)| P_1(l, p), \tag{18}$$

$$s_{i,j} = \sum_{l=1}^{L} \Pr\{\mathbf{y} \in \mathcal{S}_l(j) \mid \mathbf{x}\} = \sum_{l=1}^{L} |\mathcal{S}_l(j)| P_2(l, C_R, p/C_R). \tag{19}$$

Since $p \leq 1/n$, Theorem 1 implies that

$$P_1(l, p) \leq P_2(l, C_R, p/C_R), \quad \forall 1 \leq l \leq n.$$

Combining it with (18) and (19) we know

$$p_{i,j} \leq s_{i,j}, \quad \forall 0 \leq i < j \leq n. \tag{20}$$

Then, we get the result by Definition 2. □

Example 2 (Comparison of transition probabilities for the OneMax problem). *Let $p_m = C_R q_m = p \leq \frac{1}{n}$. By (8), we have*

$$p_{i,j} = \sum_{k=0}^{M} C_{n-j}^{k} C_{j}^{k+(j-i)} P_1(2k+j-i, p), \tag{21}$$

$$s_{i,j} = \sum_{k=0}^{M} C_{n-j}^{k} C_{j}^{k+(j-i)} P_2(2k+j-i, C_R, p/C_R). \tag{22}$$

where $M = \min\{n-j, i\}$. Since $p \leq 1/n$, Theorem 1 implies that

$$P_1(2k+j-i, p) \leq P_2(2k+j-i, C_R, p/C_R),$$

and by (21) and (22) we have $p_{i,j} \leq s_{i,j}, \forall\, 0 \leq i < j \leq n$.

Example 3 (Comparison of transition probabilities for the Deceptive problem). *Let $p_m = C_R q_m = p \leq \frac{1}{n}$. Equation (10) implies that*

$$p_{i,j} = \begin{cases} \sum_{k=0}^{M} C_{n-j+1}^{k} C_{j-1}^{k+(j-i)} P_1(2k+j-i, p), & i > 0, \\ P_1(n-j+1, p), & i = 0, \end{cases} \tag{23}$$

$$s_{i,j} = \begin{cases} \sum_{k=0}^{M} C_{n-j+1}^{k} C_{j-1}^{k+(j-i)} P_2(2k+j-i, C_R, \frac{p}{C_R}), & i > 0, \\ P_2(n-j+1, C_R, p/C_R), & i = 0, \end{cases} \tag{24}$$

where $M = \min\{n-j+1, i-1\}$. Similar to the analysis of Example 2, we get the conclusion that $p_{i,j} \leq s_{i,j}, \forall\, 0 \leq i < j \leq n$.

The results demonstrate that when $p \leq 1/n$, the introduction of binomial crossover leads to transition dominance of $(1+1)EA_C$ over $(1+1)EA$. In the following section, we would like to answer if transition dominance leads to outperformance of $(1+1)EA_C$ over $(1+1)EA$.

5. Analysis of Asymptotic Performance

In this section, we will prove that $(1+1)EA_C$ asymptotically outperforms $(1+1)EA$ using the average convergence rate [25,32].

Definition 4. *The average convergence rate (ACR) of an EA for t generation is*

$$R_{EA}(t) = 1 - \left(e^{[t]}/e^{[0]}\right)^{1/t}. \tag{25}$$

Lemma 1 ([32], Theorem 1). *Let $\mathbf{R}$ be the transition submatrix associated with a convergent EA. Under random initialization (i.e., the EA may start at any initial state with a positive probability), it holds*

$$\lim_{t \to +\infty} R_{EA}(t) = 1 - \rho(\mathbf{R}), \tag{26}$$

where $\rho(\mathbf{R})$ is the spectral radius of $\mathbf{R}$.

Lemma 1 presents the asymptotic characteristics of the ACR, by which we get the result on the asymptotic performance of EAs.

Proposition 1. *If $\tilde{\mathbf{A}} \succeq \tilde{\mathbf{B}}$, there exists $T > 0$ such that*

1. $e_{\mathcal{A}}^{[t]} \leq e_{\mathcal{B}}^{[t]}, \forall\, t > T;$

2. $p_{\mathcal{A}}^{[t]}(e_i) \leq p_{\mathcal{B}}^{[t]}(e_i)$, $\forall t > T$, $1 \leq i \leq L$.

Proof. By Lemma 1, we know $\forall \epsilon > 0$, there exists $T > 0$ such that

$$e^{[0]}(\rho(\mathbf{R}) - \epsilon)^t < e^{[t]} < e^{[0]}(\rho(\mathbf{R}) + \epsilon)^t, \quad t > T. \tag{27}$$

From the fact that the transition submatrix $\mathbf{R}$ of an RSH is upper triangular, we conclude

$$\rho(\mathbf{R}) = \max\{r_{1,1}, \ldots, r_{L,L}\}. \tag{28}$$

Denote

$$\tilde{\mathbf{A}} = (a_{i,j}) = \begin{pmatrix} 1 & \mathbf{a}_0 \\ 0 & \mathbf{A} \end{pmatrix}, \quad \tilde{\mathbf{B}} = (b_{i,j}) = \begin{pmatrix} 1 & \mathbf{b}_0 \\ 0 & \mathbf{B} \end{pmatrix}.$$

While $\tilde{\mathbf{A}} \succeq \tilde{\mathbf{B}}$, it holds

$$a_{j,j} = 1 - \sum_{i=0}^{j-1} a_{i,j} < 1 - \sum_{i=0}^{j-1} b_{i,j} = b_{j,j}, \quad 1 \leq j \leq L.$$

Then, Equation (28) implies that

$$\rho(\mathbf{A}) < \rho(\mathbf{B}).$$

Applying it to (27) for $\epsilon < \frac{1}{2}(\rho(\mathbf{B}) - \rho(\mathbf{A}))$, we have

$$e_{\mathcal{A}}^{[t]} < e^{[0]}(\rho(\mathbf{A}) + \epsilon)^t < e^{[0]}(\rho(\mathbf{B}) - \epsilon)^t < e_{\mathcal{B}}^{[t]}, \tag{29}$$

which proves the first conclusion.

Noting that the tail probability $p^{[t]}(e_i)$ can be taken as the expected approximation error of an optimization problem with an error vector

$$\mathbf{e} = (\underbrace{0, \ldots, 0}_{i}, 1, \ldots, 1)',$$

by (29) we have

$$p_{\mathcal{A}}^{[t]}(e_i) \leq p_{\mathcal{B}}^{[t]}(e_i), \quad \forall t > T, 1 \leq i \leq L.$$

The second conclusion is proven. □

By Definition 2 and Proposition 1, we get the following theorem for comparing the asymptotic performance of $(1+1)EA$ and $(1+1)EA_C$.

Theorem 3. *If $C_R = C_R q_m = p \leq \frac{1}{n}$, the $(1+1)EA_C$ asymptotically outperforms $(1+1)EA$ on problem (1).*

Proof. The proof can be completed by applying Theorem 2 and Proposition 1. □

On condition that $C_R = C_R q_m = p \leq \frac{1}{n}$, Theorem 3 indicates that after sufficiently many number of iterations, $(1+1)EA_C$ can performs better on problem (1) than $(1+1)EA$. A further question is whether $(1+1)EA_C$ outperforms $(1+1)EA$ for $t < +\infty$. We answer the question in next sections.

6. Comparison of the Two EAs on OneMax

In this section, we show that the outperformance introduced by binomial crossover can be obtained for the uni-modal OneMax problem based on the following lemma [29].

Lemma 2 ([29], Theorem 3). *Let*

$$\tilde{\mathbf{e}} = (e_0, e_1, \ldots, e_L)', \quad \tilde{\mathbf{v}} = (v_0, v_1, \ldots, v_L)',$$

where $0 \leq e_{i-1} \leq e_i, i = 1, \ldots, L$, $v_i > 0, i = 0, 1, \ldots, L$. *If transition matrices $\tilde{\mathbf{R}}$ and $\tilde{\mathbf{S}}$ satisfy*

$$s_{j,j} \geq r_{j,j}, \qquad \forall \, 1 \leq j \leq L, \tag{30}$$

$$\sum_{l=0}^{i-1}(r_{l,j} - s_{l,j}) \geq 0, \qquad \forall \, 0 \leq i < j \leq L, \tag{31}$$

$$\sum_{l=0}^{i}(s_{l,j-1} - s_{l,j}) \geq 0, \qquad \forall \, 0 \leq i < j-1 < L, \tag{32}$$

it holds

$$\tilde{\mathbf{e}}' \tilde{\mathbf{R}}^t \tilde{\mathbf{v}} \leq \tilde{\mathbf{e}}' \tilde{\mathbf{S}}^t \tilde{\mathbf{v}}.$$

For the EAs investigated in this study, conditions (30)–(32) are satisfied thanks to the monotonicity of transition probabilities.

Lemma 3. *When $p \leq 1/n$ ($n \geq 3$), $P_1(l, p)$ and $P_2(l, C_R, p/C_R)$ are monotonously decreasing in l.*

Proof. When $p \leq 1/n$, Equations (13) and (14) imply that

$$\frac{P_1(l+1, p)}{P_1(l, p)} = \frac{p}{1-p} \leq \frac{1}{n-1}, \tag{33}$$

$$\frac{P_2(l+1, C_R, p/C_R)}{P_2(l, C_R, p/C_R)} = \frac{(l+1)(1-C_R) + nC_R(1-p/C_R)}{l(1-C_R) + nC_R(1-p/C_R)} \frac{p}{1-p} \leq \frac{l+1}{l}\frac{p}{1-p} \leq \frac{l+1}{l}\frac{1}{n-1}, \tag{34}$$

all of which are not greater than 1 when $n \geq 3$. Thus, $P_1(l, p)$ and $P_2(l, C_R, p/C_R)$ are monotonously decreasing in l. □

Lemma 4. *For the OneMax problem, $p_{i,j}$ and $s_{i,j}$ are decreasing in j.*

Proof. We validate the monotonicity of $p_{i,j}$ for $(1+1)EA$, and that of $s_{i,j}$ can be confirmed in a similar way.

Let $0 \leq i < j < n$. By (21) we know

$$p_{i,j+1} = \sum_{k=0}^{M} C_{n-j-1}^{k} C_{j+1}^{i-k} P_1(2k+j+1-i, p), \tag{35}$$

$$p_{i,j} = \sum_{k=0}^{M} C_{n-j}^{k} C_{j}^{i-k} P_1(2k+j-i, p), \tag{36}$$

where $M = \min\{n-j-1, i\}$. Moreover, (33) implies that

$$\frac{C_{j+1}^{i-k} P_1(2k+j+1-i, p)}{C_{j}^{i-k} P_1(2k+j-i, p)} = \frac{j+1}{(j+1)-(i-k)} \frac{p}{1-p} \leq \frac{j+1}{2} \frac{1}{n-1} < 1,$$

and we know

$$C_{j+1}^{i-k} P_1(2k+j+1-i, p) < C_{j}^{i-k} P_1(2k+j-i, p). \tag{37}$$

Note that

$$\min\{n-j-1, i\} \geq \min\{n-j, i\}, \quad C_{n-j-1}^{k} < C_{n-j}^{k}. \tag{38}$$

From (35)–(38) we conclude that
$$p_{i,j+1} < p_{i,j}, \quad 0 \le i < j < n.$$

Similarly, we can validate that
$$s_{i,j+1} < s_{i,j}, \quad 0 \le i < j < n.$$

In conclusion, $p_{i,j}$ and $s_{i,j}$ are monotonously decreasing in j. □

Theorem 4. *On condition that $p_m = C_R q_m = p \le \frac{1}{n}$, it holds for the OneMax problem that*
$$(1+1)EA_C \succsim (1+1)EA.$$

Proof. Given the initial distribution $\tilde{\mathbf{q}}^{[0]}$ and transition matrix $\tilde{\mathbf{R}}$, the level distribution at iteration t is confirmed by
$$\tilde{\mathbf{q}}^{[t]} = \tilde{\mathbf{R}}^t \tilde{\mathbf{q}}^{[0]}. \tag{39}$$

Denote
$$\tilde{\mathbf{e}} = (e_0, e_1, \ldots, e_L)', \quad \tilde{\mathbf{o}}_i = (\underbrace{0, \ldots, 0}_{i}, 1, \ldots, 1)'.$$

By premultiplying (39) with $\tilde{\mathbf{e}}$ and $\tilde{\mathbf{o}}_i$, respectively, we get
$$e^{[t]} = \tilde{\mathbf{e}}' \tilde{\mathbf{R}}^t \tilde{\mathbf{q}}^{[0]}, \tag{40}$$
$$p^{[t]}(e_i) = \Pr\{e(\mathbf{x}_t)\} \ge e_i\} = \tilde{\mathbf{o}}_i' \tilde{\mathbf{R}}^t \tilde{\mathbf{q}}^{[0]}. \tag{41}$$

Meanwhile, by Theorem 2 we have
$$q_{j,j} \le s_{j,j} \le p_{j,j}, \tag{42}$$
$$\sum_{l=0}^{i-1}(q_{l,j} - s_{l,j}) \ge 0, \quad \sum_{l=0}^{i-1}(s_{l,j} - p_{l,j}) \ge 0, \quad \forall\, i < j, \tag{43}$$

and Lemma 4 implies
$$\sum_{l=0}^{i}(s_{l,j-1} - s_{l,j}) \ge 0, \quad \sum_{l=0}^{i}(p_{l,j-1} - p_{l,j}) \ge 0 \quad \forall\, i < j-1. \tag{44}$$

Then, (42)–(44) validate satisfaction of conditions (30)–(32), and by Lemma 2 we know
$$\tilde{\mathbf{e}}' \tilde{\mathbf{S}}^t \tilde{\mathbf{q}}^{[0]} \le \tilde{\mathbf{e}}' \tilde{\mathbf{P}}^t \tilde{\mathbf{q}}^{[0]}, \quad \forall\, t > 0;$$
$$\tilde{\mathbf{o}}_i' \tilde{\mathbf{S}}^t \tilde{\mathbf{q}}^{[0]} \le \tilde{\mathbf{o}}_i' \tilde{\mathbf{P}}^t \tilde{\mathbf{q}}^{[0]}, \quad \forall\, t > 0,\ 1 \le i < n.$$

Then, we get the conclusion by Definition 2. □

The above theorem demonstrates that the dominance of transition matrices introduced by the binomial crossover operator leads to the outperformance of $(1+1)EA_C$ on the uni-modal problem OneMax.

7. Comparison of the Two EAs on Deceptive

In this section, we show that the outperformance of $(1+1)EA_C$ over $(1+1)EA$ may not always hold on Deceptive. Then, we propose an adaptive strategy of parameter setting arising from the theoretical analysis, with which $(1+1)EA_C$ performs better in terms of tail probability.

7.1. Numerical Demonstration for Inconsistency between the Transition Dominance and the Algorithm Outperformance

For the Deceptive problem, we first present a counterexample to show even if the transition matrix of an EA dominates another EA, we cannot conclude that the former EA outperforms the latter.

Example 4. *We construct two artificial Markov chains as the models of two EAs. Let $EA_\mathcal{R}$ and $EA_\mathcal{S}$ be two EAs starting with an identical initial distribution*

$$\mathbf{p}^{[0]} = \left(\frac{1}{n}, \frac{1}{n}, \ldots, \frac{1}{n}\right)^t,$$

and the respective transition matrices are

$$\tilde{\mathbf{R}} = \begin{pmatrix} 1 & \frac{1}{n^3} & \frac{2}{n^3} & \cdots & \frac{n}{n^3} \\ & 1-\frac{1}{n^3} & \frac{1}{n^2} & & \\ & & 1-\frac{1}{n^2}-\frac{2}{n^3} & \ddots & \\ & & & \ddots & \frac{n-1}{n^2} \\ & & & & 1-\frac{1}{n} \end{pmatrix}$$

and

$$\tilde{\mathbf{S}} = \begin{pmatrix} 1 & \frac{2}{n^3} & \frac{4}{n^3} & \cdots & \frac{2n}{n^3} \\ & 1-\frac{2}{n^3} & \frac{1}{n^2}+\frac{1}{2n} & & \\ & & 1-\frac{n^2+2n+8}{2n^3} & \ddots & \\ & & & \ddots & \frac{n-1}{n^2}+\frac{n-1}{2n} \\ & & & & 1-\frac{n^2+n+2}{2n^2} \end{pmatrix}.$$

Obviously, it holds $\tilde{\mathbf{S}} \succeq \tilde{\mathbf{R}}$. Through computer simulation, we get the curve of EAE difference of the two EAs in Figure 1a and the curve of TPs difference between the two EAs in Figure 1b. From Figure 1b, it is clear that $EA_\mathcal{R}$ does not always outperform $EA_\mathcal{S}$ because the difference of TPs is negative at the early stage of the iteration process but later positive.

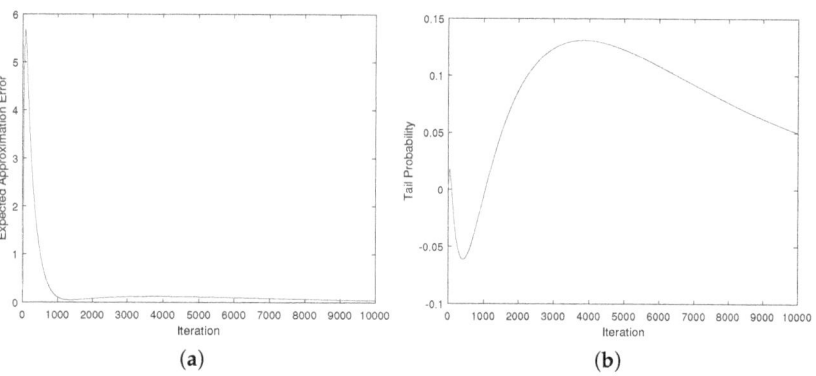

Figure 1. Simulation results on the difference of EAEs and TPs for the counterexample. (**a**) Difference of expected approximation errors (EAEs). (**b**) Difference of tail probabilities (TPs).

Now we turn to discuss $(1+1)EA$ and $(1+1)EA_C$ on Deceptive. We demonstrate $(1+1)EA_C$ may not outperform $(1+1)EA$ over all generations although the transition matrix of $(1+1)EA_C$ dominates that of $(1+1)EA$.

Example 5. In $(1+1)EA$ and $(1+1)EA_C$, set $p_m = C_R q_m = 1/n$. For $(1+1)EA_C$, let $q_m = \frac{1}{2}$, $C_R = \frac{2}{n}$. The numerical simulation results of EAEs and TPs for 5000 independent runs are depicted in Figure 2. It is shown that when $n \geq 9$, both EAEs and TPs of $(1+1)EA$ could be smaller than those of $(1+1)EA_C$. This indicates that the dominance of the transition matrix does not always guarantee the outperformance of the corresponding algorithm.

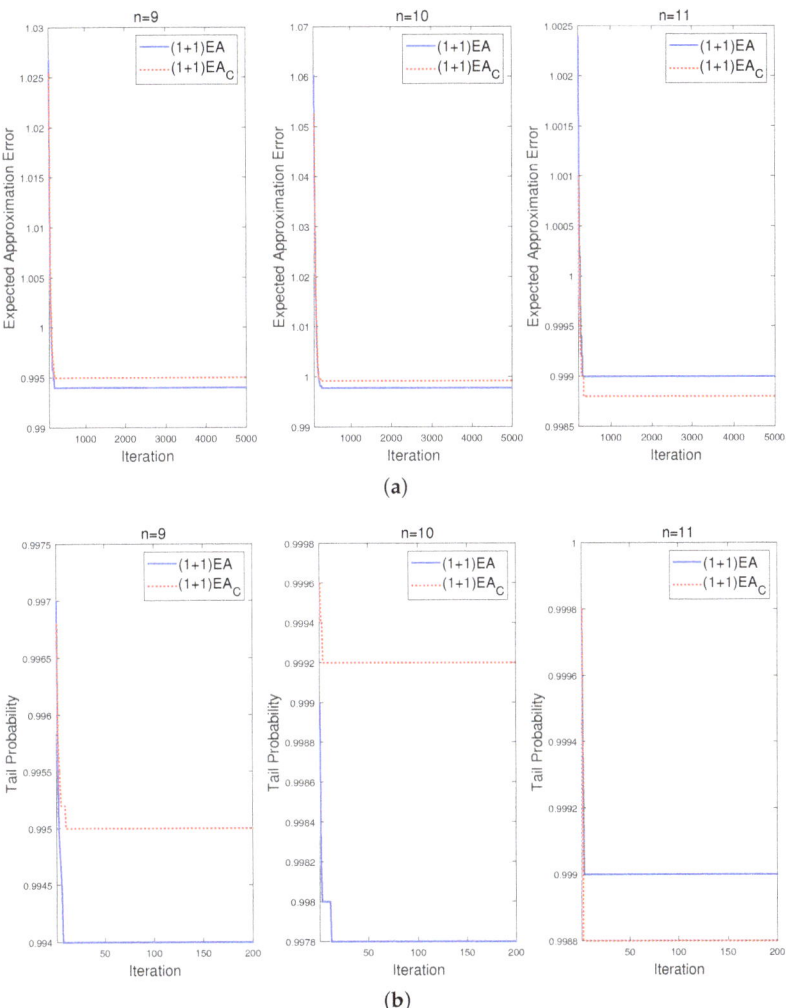

Figure 2. Numerical comparison for $(1+1)EA$ and $(1+1)EA_C$ applied to the Deceptive problem, where n refers to the problem dimension. (**a**) Numerical comparison of expected approximation errors (EAEs). (**b**) Numerical comparison of tail probabilities (TPs).

With $p_m = C_R q_m = p \leq 1/n$, although the binomial crossover leads to transition dominance of $(1+1)EA_C$ over $(1+1)EA$, the enhancement of exploitation plays a governing role in the iteration process. Thus, the imbalance of exploration and exploitation leads to poor performance of $(1+1)EA_C$ at some stage of the iteration process. As shown in the previous two examples, the outperformance of $(1+1)EA_C$ cannot be drawn from the dominance of transition matrices.

The fitness landscape of Deceptive confirms that global convergence of EAs on Deceptive is principally attributed to the direct transition from level j to level 0, quantified by the transition probability $r_{0,j}$. By investigating the impact of binomial crossover on the transition probability $r_{0,j}$, we arrive at an adaptive strategy for the regulation of the mutation rate and the crossover rate, by which performance of both $(1+1)EA$ and $(1+1)EA_C$ are enhanced.

7.2. Comparisons on the Probabilities to Transfer from Non-Optimal Statuses to the Optimal Status

A comparison between $p_{0,j}$ and $s_{0,j}$ is performed by investigating their monotonicity. Substituting (13) and (14) into (23) and (24), respectively, we have

$$p_{0,j} = P_1(n-j+1, p_m) = (p_m)^{n-j+1}(1-p_m)^{j-1}, \tag{45}$$

$$s_{0,j} = P_3(n-j+1, C_R, q_m)$$
$$= \frac{1}{n}[(j-1)(1-C_R) + nC_R(1-q_m)]C_R^{n-j}(q_m)^{n-j+1}(1-q_mC_R)^{j-2}. \tag{46}$$

We first investigate the maximum values of $p_{0,j}$ to get the ideal performance of $(1+1)EA$ on the Deceptive problem.

Theorem 5. *While*

$$p_m^\star = \frac{n-j+1}{n}, \tag{47}$$

$p_{0,j}$ *gets its maximum values* $p_{0,j}^{max} = \left(\frac{n-j+1}{n}\right)^{n-j+1}\left(\frac{j-1}{n}\right)^{j-1}$.

Proof. By (45), we know

$$\frac{\partial}{\partial p_m}p_{0,j} = (n-j+1-np_m)p_m^{n-j}(1-p_m)^{j-2}.$$

While $p_m = \frac{n-j+1}{n}$, $p_{0,j}$ gets its maximum value

$$p_{0,j}^{max} = P_1(n-j+1, \frac{n-j+1}{n}) = \left(\frac{n-j+1}{n}\right)^{n-j+1}\left(\frac{j-1}{n}\right)^{j-1}.$$

□

Influence of the binomial crossover on $s_{0,j}$ is investigated on condition that $p_m = q_m$. By regulating C_R, we compare $p_{0,j}$ with the maximum value $s_{0,j}^{max}$ of $s_{0,j}$.

Theorem 6. *On condition that $p_m = q_m$, the following results hold.*
1. $p_{0,1} = s_{0,1}^{max}$.
2. *If $q_m > \frac{n-1}{n}$, $p_{0,2} < s_{0,2}^{max}$; otherwise, $p_{0,2} = s_{0,2}^{max}$.*
3. $\forall j \in \{3,\ldots,n-1\}$, $p_{0,j} \leq s_{0,j}^{max}$ *if $q_m > \frac{n-j}{n-1}$; otherwise, $s_{0,j}^{max} = p_{0,j}$.*
4. *if $q_m > \frac{1}{n}$, $p_{0,n} < s_{0,n}^{max}$; otherwise, $s_{0,n}^{max} = p_{0,n}$.*

Proof. Note that $(1+1)EA_C$ degrades to $(1+1)EA$ when $C_R = 1$. Then, if the maximum value $s_{0,j}^{max}$ of $s_{0,j}$ is obtained by setting $C_R = 1$, we have $s_{0,j}^{max} = p_{0,j}$; otherwise, it holds $s_{0,j}^{max} > p_{0,j}$.

1. For the case that $j = 1$, Equation (46) implies

$$s_{0,1} = q_m^n(C_R)^{n-1}.$$

Obviously, $s_{0,1}$ is monotonously increasing in C_R. It gets the maximum value while $C_R^\star = 1$. Then, by (45) we get $s_{0,1}^{max} = p_{0,1}$.

2. While $j = 2$, by (46) we have

$$\frac{\partial s_{0,2}}{\partial C_R} = \frac{n-1}{n} q_m^{n-1}(C_R)^{n-3}(n-2+(1-nq_m)C_R).$$

- If $0 < q_m \leq \frac{n-1}{n}$, $s_{0,2}$ is monotonously increasing in C_R, and gets its maximum value while $C_R^\star = 1$. For this case, we know $s_{0,2}^{max} = p_{0,2}$.
- While $\frac{n-1}{n} < q_m < 1$, $s_{0,2}$ gets its maximum value $s_{0,2}^{max}$ by setting

$$C_R^\star = \frac{n-2}{nq_m - 1}. \quad (48)$$

Then, we have $s_{0,2}^{max} > p_{0,2}$.

3. For the case that $3 \leq j \leq n-1$, we denote

$$s_{0,j} = \frac{n-j+1}{n} q_m^{n-j+1} I_1 + \frac{(j-1)(1-q_m)}{n} q_m^{n-j+1} I_2,$$

where

$$I_1 = (C_R)^{n-j}(1 - q_m C_R)^{j-1},$$
$$I_2 = (C_R)^{n-j+1}(1 - q_m C_R)^{j-2}.$$

Then,

$$\frac{\partial I_1}{\partial C_R} = (C_R)^{n-j-1}(1 - q_m C_R)^{j-2}(n-j-(n-1)q_m C_R),$$

$$\frac{\partial I_2}{\partial C_R} = (C_R)^{n-j}\left(1 - \frac{C_R}{n}\right)^{j-3}(n-j+1-(n-1)q_m C_R).$$

- While $0 < q_m \leq \frac{n-j}{n-1}$, both I_1 and I_2 are increasing in C_R. For this case, $s_{0,j}$ gets its maximum value when $C_R^\star = 1$, and we have $s_{0,j}^{max} = p_{0,j}$.
- If $\frac{n-j+1}{n-1} \leq q_m \leq 1$, I_1 gets its maximum value when $C_R = \frac{n-j}{(n-1)q_m}$, and I_2 gets its maximum value when $C_R = \frac{n-j+1}{(n-1)q_m}$. Then, $s_{0,j}$ get its maximum value $s_{0,j}^{max}$ at some

$$C_R^\star \in \left(\frac{n-j}{(n-1)q_m}, \frac{n-j+1}{(n-1)q_m}\right). \quad (49)$$

Accordingly, we know $s_{0,j}^{max} > p_{0,j}$.

- If $\frac{n-j}{n-1} < q_m < \frac{n-j+1}{n-1}$, I_1 gets its maximum value when $C_R = \frac{n-j}{(n-1)q_m}$, and I_2 is monotonously increasing in C_R. Then, $s_{0,j}$ get its maximum value $s_{0,j}^{max}$ at some

$$C_R^\star \in \left(\frac{n-j}{(n-1)q_m}, 1\right], \quad (50)$$

and we know $s_{0,j}^{max} > p_{0,j}$.

4. While $j = n$, Equation (46) implies that

$$\frac{\partial s_{0,n}}{\partial C_R} = (n-1)(1 - q_m C_R)^{n-3}(1 - 2q_m - (n-1-nq_m)q_m C_R).$$

Denoting

$$g(q_m, C_R) = 1 - 2q_m - (n-1-nq_m)q_m C_R,$$

we can confirm the sign of $\partial s_{0,n}/\partial C_R$ by considering

$$\frac{\partial}{\partial C_R} g(q_m, C_R) = -(n - 1 - nq_m)q_m.$$

- While $0 < q_m \leq \frac{n-1}{n}$, $g(q_m, C_R)$ is monotonously decreasing in C_R, and its minimum value is

$$g(q_m, 1) = (nq_m - 1)(q_m - 1).$$

The maximum value of $g(q_m, C_R)$ is

$$g(q_m, 0) = 1 - 2q_m.$$

(a) If $0 < q_m \leq \frac{1}{n}$, we have

$$g(q_m, C_R) \geq g(q_m, 1) > 0.$$

Thus, $\frac{\partial s_{0,n}}{\partial C_R} \geq 0$, and $s_{0,n}$ is increasing in C_R. For this case, $s_{0,n}$ get its maximum value when $C_R^\star = 1$, and we have $s_{0,n}^{max} = p_{0,n}$.

(b) If $\frac{1}{n} < q_m \leq \frac{1}{2}$, $s_{0,n}$ gets the maximum value $s_{0,n}^{max}$ when

$$C_R^\star = \frac{1 - 2q_m}{q_m(n - 1 - nq_m)}.$$

Thus, $s_{0,n}^{max} > p_{0,n}$.

(c) If $\frac{1}{2} < q_m \leq \frac{n-1}{n}$, $g(q_m, 0) < 0$, and then, $s_{0,n}$ is decreasing in C_R. Then, its maximum value is obtained by setting $C_R^\star = 0$, and we know $s_{0,n}^{max} > p_{0,n}$.

- While $\frac{n-1}{n} < q_m \leq 1$, $g(q_m, C_R)$ is increasing in C_R, and its maximum value is

$$g(q_m, 1) = (nq_m - 1)(q_m - 1) < 0.$$

Then, $s_{0,n}$ is monotonously decreasing in C_R, and its maximum value is obtained by setting $C_R^\star = 0$. Accordingly, we know $s_{0,n}^{max} > p_{0,n}$.

In summary, $s_{0,n}^{max} > p_{0,n}$ while $q_m > \frac{1}{n}$; otherwise, $s_{0,n}^{max} = p_{0,n}$.

□

Theorems 5 and 6 present the "best" settings to maximize the transition probabilities from non-optimal statuses to the optimal level, by which we get a parameter adaptive strategy that greatly enhances the exploration of compared EAs.

7.3. Parameter Adaptive Strategy to Enhance Exploration of EAs

Since the level index j is equal to the Hamming distance between **x** and **x***, improvement of level index j is bounded by reduction of the Hamming distance obtained by replacing **x** with **y**. Then, while the local exploitation leads to a transition from level j to a non-optimal level i, the practically adaptive strategy of parameters can be obtained according to the Hamming distance between **x** and **y**.

When $(1+1)EA$ is located at the solution **x** at status j, Equation (47) implies that the "best" setting of mutation rate is $p_m^\star(j) = \frac{n-j+1}{n}$. Once it transfers to solution **y** at status $i (i < j)$, the "best" setting changes to $p_m^\star(i) = \frac{n-i+1}{n}$. Then, the difference of "best" settings is $\frac{j-i}{n}$, bounded from above by $\frac{H(\mathbf{x},\mathbf{y})}{n}$. Accordingly, the mutation rate of $(1+1)EA$ can be updated to

$$p_m' = p_m + \frac{H(\mathbf{x}, \mathbf{y})}{n}. \tag{51}$$

For $(1+1)EA_C$, the parameter q_m is adapted using the strategy consistent to that of p_m to focus on influence of C_R. That is,

$$q'_m = q_m + \frac{H(\mathbf{x}, \mathbf{y})}{n}. \tag{52}$$

Since $s_{0,j}$ demonstrates different monotonicity for varied levels, one cannot get an identical strategy for the adaptive setting of C_R. As a compromise, we would like to consider the case that $3 \leq j \leq n-1$, which is obtained by random initialization with overwhelming probability.

According to the proof of Theorem 6, we know C_R should be set as great as possible for the case $q_m \in (0, \frac{n-j}{n-1}]$; while $q_m \in (\frac{n-j}{n-1}, 1]$, $C_R^\star$ is located in intervals whose boundary values are $\frac{n-j}{(n-1)q_m}$ and $\frac{n-j+1}{(n-1)q_m}$, given by (49) and (50), respectively. Then, while q_m is updated by (52), the update strategy of C_R can be confirmed to satisfy that

$$C'_R q'_m = C_R q_m + \frac{H(\mathbf{x}, \mathbf{y})}{n-1}.$$

Accordingly, the adaptive setting of C_R could be

$$C'_R = \left(C_R q_m + \frac{H(\mathbf{x}, \mathbf{y})}{n-1} \right) / q'_m, \tag{53}$$

where q'_m is updated by (52).

By incorporating the adaptive strategy (51) to $(1+1)EA$, we compare the performance of its adaptive variant with the adaptive $(1+1)EA_C$ that regulates its mutation rate and crossover rate by (52) and (53), respectively. For 13–20 dimensional Deceptive problems, numerical simulation of the tail probability is implemented by 10,000 independent runs. The initial value of p_m is set as $\frac{1}{n}$. To investigate the sensitivity of the adaptive strategy on initial values of q_m, the mutation rate q_m in $(1+1)EA_C$ is initialized with values $\frac{1}{\sqrt{n}}$, $\frac{3}{2\sqrt{n}}$ and $\frac{2}{\sqrt{n}}$, and the corresponding variants are denoted by $(1+1)EA_C^1$, $(1+1)EA_C^2$ and $(1+1)EA_C^3$, respectively.

The converging curves of averaged TPs are illustrated in Figure 3. Compared to the EAs with fixed parameters during the evolution process, the performance of the adaptive EAs on Deceptive has been significantly improved. Furthermore, we also note that the converging curves of adaptive $(1+1)EA_C$ are not sensitive to the initial mutation rate. Although transition dominance does not necessarily lead to outperformance of $(1+1)EA_C$ over $(1+1)EA$, the proposed adaptive strategy can greatly enhance global exploration of $(1+1)EA_C$ to a large extent, and consequently, we get the improved adaptive $(1+1)EA_C$ that is not sensitive to initial mutation rates.

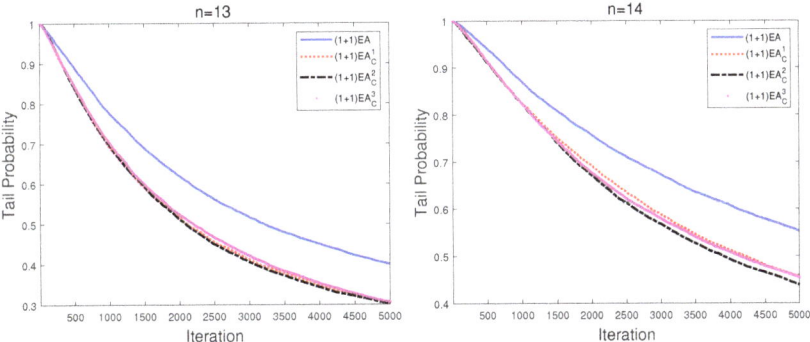

Figure 3. *Cont.*

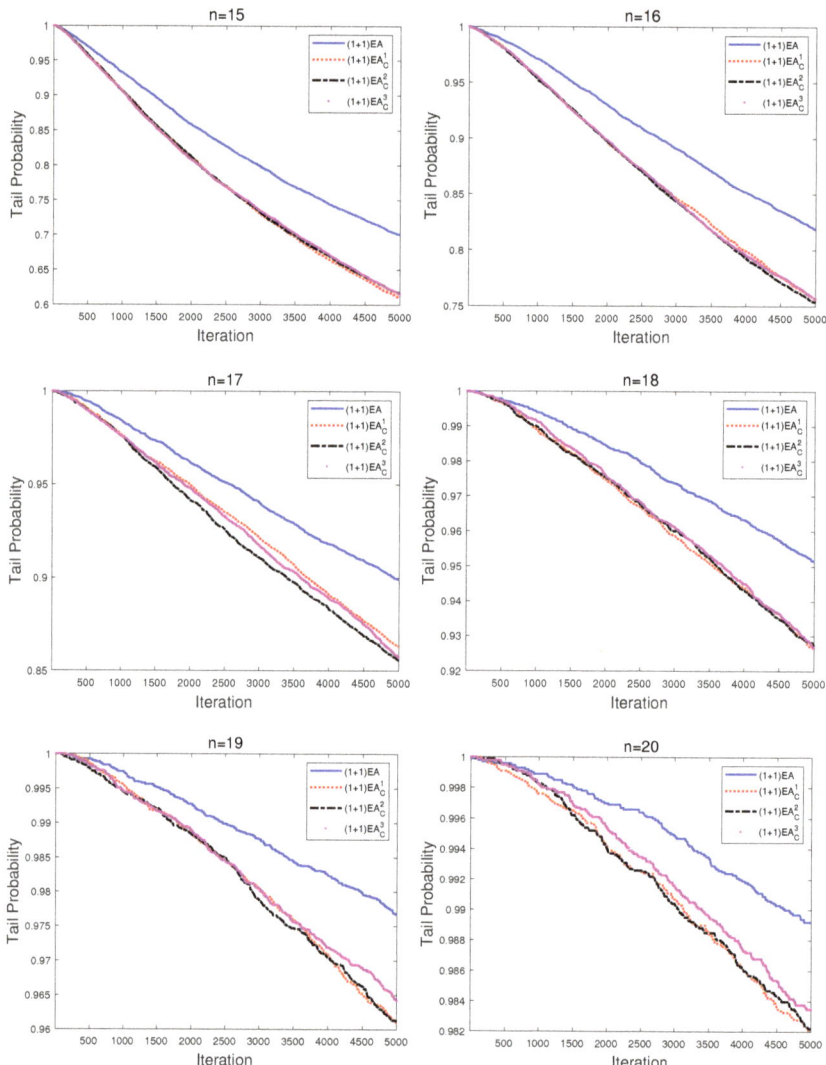

Figure 3. Numerical comparison on tail probabilities (TPs) of adaptive $(1+1)EA$ and $(1+1)EA_C$ applied to the Deceptive problem, where n is the problem dimension. $(1+1)EA_C^1$, $(1+1)EA_C^2$, and $(1+1)EA_C^3$ are three variants of $(1+1)EA_C$ with q_m initialized as $\frac{1}{\sqrt{n}}$, $\frac{3}{2\sqrt{n}}$, and $\frac{2}{\sqrt{n}}$, respectively.

8. Conclusions and Discussions

Under the framework of fixed-budget analysis, we conduct a pioneering analysis of the influence of binomial crossover on the approximation error of EAs. The performance of EAs after running finite generations is measured by two metrics: the expected value of the approximation error and the error tail probability, by which we make a case study by comparing the performance of $(1+1)EA$ and $(1+1)EA_C$ with binomial crossover.

Starting from the comparison of the probability of flipping "*l preferred bits*", it is proven that under proper conditions, incorporation of binomial crossover leads to the dominance of transition probabilities, that is, the probability of transferring to any promising status is improved. Accordingly, the asymptotic performance of $(1+1)EA_C$ is superior to that of $(1+1)EA$.

It is found that the dominance of transition probability guarantees that $(1+1)EA_C$ outperforms $(1+1)EA$ on OneMax in terms of both expected approximation error and tail probability. However, this dominance does lead to the outperformance on Deceptive. This means that using binomial crossover may improve the performance on some problems but not on other problems.

For Deceptive, an adaptive strategy of parameter setting is proposed based on the monotonicity analysis of transition probabilities. Numerical simulations demonstrate that it can significantly improve the exploration ability of both $(1+1)EA_C$ and $(1+1)EA$, and superiority of binomial crossover is further strengthened by the adaptive strategy. Thus, a problem-specific adaptive strategy is helpful for improving the performance of EAs.

Our future work will focus on a further study for the adaptive setting of crossover rate in population-based EAs on more complex problems, as well as the development of adaptive EAs improved by the introduction of binomial crossover.

Author Contributions: Conceptualization, J.H. and X.Z.; formal analysis, C.W.; writing—original draft preparation, C.W.; writing—review and editing, Y.C. and J.H.; funding acquisition, Y.C. All authors have read and agreed to the published version of the manuscript.

Funding: This research was funded by the Fundamental Research Funds for the Central Universities grant number WUT:2020IB006.

Institutional Review Board Statement: Not applicable.

Informed Consent Statement: Not applicable.

Data Availability Statement: Not applicable.

Conflicts of Interest: The authors declare no conflict of interest.

References

1. Tam, H.H.; Leung, M.F.; Wang, Z.; Ng, S.C.; Cheung, C.C.; Lui, A.K. Improved adaptive global replacement scheme for MOEA/D-AGR. In Proceedings of the 2016 IEEE Congress on Evolutionary Computation (CEC), Vancouver, BC, Canada, 24–29 July 2016; pp. 2153–2160.
2. Tam, H.H.; Ng, S.C.; Lui, A.K.; Leung, M.F. Improved activation schema on automatic clustering using differential evolution algorithm. In Proceedings of the 2017 IEEE Congress on Evolutionary Computation (CEC), San Sebastian, Spain, 5–8 June 2017; pp. 1749–1756.
3. Gao, W.; Li, G.; Zhang, Q.; Luo, Y.; Wang, Z. Solving nonlinear equation systems by a two-phase evolutionary algorithm. *IEEE Trans. Syst. Man Cybern. Syst.* **2021**, *51*, 5652–5663. [CrossRef]
4. Jansen, T.; Wegener, I. The analysis of evolutionary algorithms—A proof that crossover really can help. *Algorithmica* **2002**, *34*, 47–66. [CrossRef]
5. Kötzing, T.; Sudholt, D.; Theile, M. How crossover helps in pseudo-boolean optimization. In Proceedings of the 13th Annual Conference on Genetic and Evolutionary Computation, Dublin, Ireland, 12–16 July 2011; pp. 989–996.
6. Corus, D.; Oliveto, P.S. Standard steady state genetic algorithms can hillclimb faster than mutation-only evolutionary algorithms. *IEEE Trans. Evol. Comput.* **2017**, *22*, 720–732. [CrossRef]
7. Dang, D.C.; Friedrich, T.; Kötzing, T.; Krejca, M.S.; Lehre, P.K.; Oliveto, P.S.; Sudholt, D.; Sutton, A.M. Escaping local optima using crossover with emergent diversity. *IEEE Trans. Evol. Comput.* **2017**, *22*, 484–497. [CrossRef]
8. Sudholt, D. How crossover speeds up building block assembly in genetic algorithms. *Evol. Comput.* **2017**, *25*, 237–274. [CrossRef]
9. Pinto, E.C.; Doerr, C. A simple proof for the usefulness of crossover in black-box optimization. In Proceedings of the International Conference on Parallel Problem Solving from Nature, Coimbra, Portugal, 8–12 September 2018; Springer: Berlin/Heidelberg, Germany, 2018; pp. 29–41.
10. Oliveto, P.S.; Sudholt, D.; Witt, C. A tight lower bound on the expected runtime of standard steady state genetic algorithms. In Proceedings of the the 2020 Genetic and Evolutionary Computation Conference, Cancun, Mexico, 8–12 July 2020; pp. 1323–1331.
11. Lengler, J.; Meier, J. Large population sizes and crossover help in dynamic environments. In Proceedings of the International Conference on Parallel Problem Solving from Nature, Leiden, The Netherlands, 5–9 September 2020; Springer: Berlin/Heidelberg, Germany, 2020; pp. 610–622.
12. Lehre, P.K.; Yao, X. Crossover can be constructive when computing unique input output sequences. In Proceedings of the Asia-Pacific Conference on Simulated Evolution and Learning, Melbourne, Australia, 7–10 December 2008; Springer: Berlin/Heidelberg, Germany, 2008; pp. 595–604.

13. Doerr, B.; Happ, E.; Klein, C. Crossover can provably be useful in evolutionary computation. *Theor. Comput. Sci.* **2012**, *425*, 17–33. [CrossRef]
14. Doerr, B.; Johannsen, D.; Kötzing, T.; Neumann, F.; Theile, M. More effective crossover operators for the all-pairs shortest path problem. *Theor. Comput. Sci.* **2013**, *471*, 12–26. [CrossRef]
15. Sutton, A.M. Fixed-parameter tractability of crossover: Steady-state GAs on the closest string problem. *Algorithmica* **2021**, *83*, 1138–1163. [CrossRef]
16. Richter, J.N.; Wright, A.; Paxton, J. Ignoble trails-where crossover is provably harmful. In Proceedings of the International Conference on Parallel Problem Solving from Nature, Dortmund, Germany, 13–17 September 2008; Springer: Berlin/Heidelberg, Germany, 2008; pp. 92–101.
17. Antipov, D.; Naumov, S. The effect of non-symmetric fitness: The analysis of crossover-based algorithms on RealJump functions. In Proceedings of the the 16th ACM/SIGEVO Conference on Foundations of Genetic Algorithms, Virtual, 6–8 September 2021; pp. 1–15.
18. Das, S.; Suganthan, P.N. Differential evolution: A survey of the state-of-the-art. *IEEE Trans. Evol. Comput.* **2011**, *15*, 4–31. [CrossRef]
19. Das, S.; Mullick, S.S.; Suganthan, P. Recent advances in differential evolution—An updated survey. *Swarm Evol. Comput.* **2016**, *27*, 1–30. [CrossRef]
20. Sepesy Maučec, M.; Brest, J. A review of the recent use of differential dvolution for large-scale global optimization: An analysis of selected algorithms on the CEC 2013 LSGO benchmark suite. *Swarm Evol. Comput.* **2019**, *50*, 100428. [CrossRef]
21. Pant, M.; Zaheer, H.; Garcia-Hernandez, L.; Abraham, A. Differential evolution: A review of more than two decades of research. *Eng. Appl. Artif. Intell.* **2020**, *90*, 103479. [CrossRef]
22. Lin, C.; Qing, A.; Feng, Q. A comparative study of crossover in differential evolution. *J. Heuristics* **2011**, *17*, 675–703. [CrossRef]
23. Gong, T.; Tuson, A.L. Differential evolution for binary encoding. In *Soft Computing in Industrial Applications*; Saad, A., Dahal, K., Sarfraz, M., Roy, R., Eds.; Springer: Berlin/Heidelberg, Germany, 2007; pp. 251–262.
24. Doerr, B.; Zheng, W. Working principles of binary differential evolution. *Theor. Comput. Sci.* **2020**, *801*, 110–142. [CrossRef]
25. Chen, Y.; He, J. Average convergence rate of evolutionary algorithms in continuous optimization. *Inf. Sci.* **2021**, *562*, 200–219. [CrossRef]
26. Xu, T.; He, J.; Shang, C. Helper and equivalent objectives: Efficient approach for constrained optimization. *IEEE Trans. Cybern.* **2022**, *52*, 240–251. [CrossRef] [PubMed]
27. Jansen, T.; Zarges, C. Performance analysis of randomised search heuristics operating with a fixed budget. *Theor. Comput. Sci.* **2014**, *545*, 39–58. [CrossRef]
28. He, J. An analytic expression of relative approximation error for a class of evolutionary algorithms. In Proceedings of the 2016 IEEE Congress on Evolutionary Computation (CEC), Vancouver, BC, Canada, 24–29 July 2016; pp. 4366–4373.
29. Wang, C.; Chen, Y.; He, J.; Xie, C. Error analysis of elitist randomized search heuristics. *Swarm Evol. Comput.* **2021**, *63*, 100875. [CrossRef]
30. Jansen, T.; Zarges, C. Reevaluating Immune-Inspired Hypermutations Using the Fixed Budget Perspective. *IEEE Trans. Evol. Comput.* **2014**, *18*, 674–688. [CrossRef]
31. He, J.; Yao, X. Towards an analytic framework for analysing the computation time of evolutionary algorithms. *Artif. Intell.* **2003**, *145*, 59–97. [CrossRef]
32. He, J.; Lin, G. Average convergence rate of evolutionary algorithms. *IEEE Trans. Evol. Comput.* **2016**, *20*, 316–321. [CrossRef]
33. Opara, K.R.; Arabas, J. Differential evolution: A survey of theoretical analyses. *Swarm Evol. Comput.* **2019**, *44*, 546–558. [CrossRef]
34. Zhou, Y.; Yi, W.; Gao, L.; Li, X. Analysis of mutation vectors selection mechanism in differential evolution. *Appl. Intell.* **2016**, *44*, 904–912. [CrossRef]
35. Zaharie, D. Influence of crossover on the behavior of differential evolution algorithms. *Appl. Soft Comput.* **2009**, *9*, 1126–1138. [CrossRef]
36. Zaharie, D. Statistical properties of differential evolution and related random search algorithms. In *COMPSTAT 2008: Proceedings in Computational Statistics*; Brito, P., Ed.; Physica: Heidelberg, Germany, 2008; pp. 473–485.
37. Zaharie, D.; Micota, F. Revisiting the analysis of population variance in differential evolution algorithms. In Proceedings of the 2017 IEEE Congress on Evolutionary Computation (CEC), San Sebastian, Spain, 5–8 June 2017; pp. 1811–1818.
38. Wang, L.; Huang, F.Z. Parameter analysis based on stochastic model for differential evolution algorithm. *Appl. Math. Comput.* **2010**, *217*, 3263–3273. [CrossRef]
39. Opara, K.R.; Arabas, J. Comparison of mutation strategies in differential evolution—A probabilistic perspective. *Swarm Evol. Comput.* **2018**, *39*, 53–69. [CrossRef]
40. Opara, K.R.; Arabas, J. The contour fitting property of differential mutation. *Swarm Evol. Comput.* **2019**, *50*, 100441. [CrossRef]
41. Jansen, T.; Zarges, C. Evolutionary algorithms and artificial immune systems on a bi-stable dynamic optimisation problem. In Proceedings of the 16th Annual Conference on Genetic and Evolutionary Computation, Vancouver, BC, Canada, 12–16 July 2014; pp. 975–982.

42. Nallaperuma, S.; Neumann, F.; Sudholt, D. Expected fitness gains of randomized search heuristics for the traveling salesperson problem. *Evol. Comput.* **2017**, *25*, 673–705. [CrossRef]
43. Doerr, B.; Jansen, T.; Witt, C.; Zarges, C. A method to derive fixed budget results from expected optimisation times. In Proceedings of the the 15th Annual Conference on Genetic and Evolutionary Computation, Amsterdam, The Netherlands, 6–10 July 2013; pp. 1581–1588.

Article

On Geometric Mean and Cumulative Residual Entropy for Two Random Variables with Lindley Type Distribution

Marius Giuclea [1,2,*] and Costin-Ciprian Popescu [1]

[1] Department of Applied Mathematics, Bucharest University of Economic Studies, Calea Dorobanți, 15-17, 010552 Bucharest, Romania; ciprian.popescu@csie.ase.ro
[2] Institute of Solid Mechanics, Romanian Academy, 15 Constatin Mille, 010141 Bucharest, Romania
* Correspondence: marius.giuclea@csie.ase.ro

Abstract: In this paper, we focus on two generalizations of the Lindley distribution and investigate, for each one separately, some special properties related to the geometric mean (GM) and the cumulative residual entropy (CRE), both of them being of great importance from the theoretical as well as from the practical point of view.

Keywords: random variable; mean; geometric mean; entropy; cumulative residual entropy; Lindley distribution

MSC: 60E05

1. Introduction

One of the most widely used numerical characteristics of a random variable is its mean. If X is a continuous random variable whose values are strictly positive and the probability density function of X is $f(x)$, then the geometric mean [1,2] is

$$GM(X) = e^{\int_0^\infty (\ln x) f(x) dx}, \tag{1}$$

where $x > 0$.

The concept of geometric mean has various uses [1,3–7] in many fields of science. A detailed approach can be found in [1]. The formulas for the geometric mean of some probability distributions are also provided in [1]. In the present work, one of the topics of discussion is the geometric mean of two continuous random variables that will be specified in the next section.

Another look at a random variable is given by information theory. In this framework, a central role is played by the concept of entropy, which is a measure of uncertainty. If X is a discrete random variable with possible values $x_i, i = 1, ..., n, n \in \mathbb{N}^*$ and

$$p_i = P(X = x_i), i \in \{1, ..., n\},$$

Shannon entropy of X [8] is

$$H(X) = -\sum_{i=1}^n p_i \log_a p_i. \tag{2}$$

The basis of the logarithm can be 2 but, more generally, it can be chosen depending on the application. If this base is equal to the number e, then it is obtained

$$H(X) = -\sum_{i=1}^n p_i \ln p_i. \tag{3}$$

If X is a continuous random variable with the probability density function $f(x)$ and D is the set where $f(x)$ is strictly positive, then the differential entropy of X [9] is

$$h(x) = -\int_D f(x) \ln f(x) dx. \tag{4}$$

The differential entropy of a continuous random variable has some interesting properties [9] but compared to Shannon entropy for the discrete case it has certain limitations [10] that must be taken into account. For example, the Shannon entropy is positive but the differential entropy does not always have this property. To overcome such inconveniences, another measure of uncertainty is proposed [10], namely the cumulative residual entropy. If X is a non-negative random variable with cumulative distribution function $F(x)$, then the cumulative residual entropy of X is

$$\mathcal{E}(X) = -\int_0^\infty \overline{F}(x) \ln \overline{F}(x) dx, \tag{5}$$

where

$$\overline{F}(x) = 1 - F(x). \tag{6}$$

In [10] some properties of the cumulative residual entropy are given and the relationship between it and the differential entropy is established. Also in [10], the usefulness of CRE in reliability engineering and computer vision is shown. In various works, the concept of CRE is a good starting point for obtaining new and interesting results. For instance, in [11], the Bayesian estimator of the dynamic cumulative residual Rényi entropy is discussed. In [12], there are studied some properties of dynamic cumulative residual entropy and in [13] is investigated the CRE for coherent and mixed systems where the component lifetimes are identically distributed. In [14] is generated the CRE for the case of fractional order and its properties are given, and in [15] is proposed a consistent estimator for CRE, which has the property that its asymptotic distribution is normal.

The Lindley distribution [16,17] is one of the random variables that is important not only for its direct applications but also for the many theoretical developments that have followed it. For instance, in [17], some of its characteristics such as moments, entropies and so on, are extensively studied. In addition, the Lindley distribution is proposed for modeling the waiting time in a bank [17]. The probability density function of the Lindley distribution is

$$f(x;\theta): (0,\infty) \to \mathbb{R}, f(x;\theta) = \frac{\theta^2}{\theta+1}(1+x)e^{-\theta x}, \tag{7}$$

with $\theta > 0$.

The cumulative distribution function of the Lindley distribution [17] is

$$F(x;\theta) = 1 - \frac{1+\theta+\theta x}{1+\theta} e^{-\theta x}, x > 0.$$

Regarding the developments based on the Lindley distribution, it is worth noting the introduction of new random variables [18–27]. In [18], two new families of distributions with applications in repairable data are considered. A new model, namely the generalized Lindley of integer order is given in [19] and its application in studying some medical data is also emphasized. In [20], a new distribution that can be used in insurance is proposed. The model of distribution discussed in [21] is suitable in reliability and fatigue life probems. In [22], a three-parameter Lindley distribution is introduced. A five-parameter generalized Lindley distribution is given in [23]. It was used in the study of four data sets, among them a set of medical data and a set of data regarding the strength of glass in a certain environment [23]. A discrete Lindley distribution is given in [24]. It is compared with geometric and Poisson distributions and its usefulness in analyzing some data sets, including medical data, is studied. A Lindley distribution of discrete type is given in [25] and it is employed in the study of automobile claim data, a situation in which it is compared with the Poisson model. In [26], a distribution called exponential-modified discrete Lindley distribution is proposed and used in modelling exceedances of flood peaks for a river or the period between earthquakes having a certain magnitude. The three-parameter Lindley distribution given in [22] is considered in [27] where some medical data are modeled. In the present paper, two continuous distributions [22,23] that generalize the Lindley distribution are discussed. Following the results already obtained [22,23], some new relationships regarding these two distributions are given.

2. Preliminaries Materials and Methods

This work focuses on two random variables that are related to the Lindley distribution. It is about a continuous random variable with three parameters [22] and one with five parameters [23]. For each one, the geometric mean and the cumulative residual entropy will be determined. There is a relationship between cumulative residual entropy and differential entropy [10] but in this paper the formulas for the cumulative residual entropy will be deduced using only its definition. For both random variables that will be analyzed we will consider that all parameters are strictly positive, except for β that is nonnegative. The three-parameter Lindley distribution X [22] has the probability density function

$$f_X(x;\theta,\alpha,\mu):(0,\infty)\to\mathbb{R},\ f_X(x;\theta,\alpha,\mu)=\frac{\theta^2}{\theta\alpha+\mu}(\alpha+\mu x)e^{-\theta x}. \tag{8}$$

The corresponding cumulative distribution function is [22]

$$F_X(x;\theta,\alpha,\mu):\mathbb{R}\to\mathbb{R},\ F_X(x;\theta,\alpha,\mu)=\begin{cases} 1-\left(1+\frac{\theta\mu x}{\theta\alpha+\mu}\right)e^{-\theta x}, & x>0 \\ 0, & x\leq 0 \end{cases}.$$

The five-parameter Lindley distribution Y [23] has the probability density function

$$f_Y(y;\delta,\alpha,\eta,\theta,\beta):(\beta,\infty)\to\mathbb{R},\ f_Y(y;\delta,\alpha,\eta,\theta,\beta)=\frac{\theta}{\delta\alpha+\eta}[\delta\alpha+\eta\theta(y-\beta)]e^{-\theta(y-\beta)}. \tag{9}$$

In this case, the cumulative distribution function is [23]

$$F_Y(y;\delta,\alpha,\eta,\theta,\beta):\mathbb{R}\to\mathbb{R},\ F_Y(y;\delta,\alpha,\eta,\theta,\beta)=\begin{cases} 1-\left[1+\frac{\theta\eta(y-\beta)}{\delta\alpha+\eta}\right]e^{-\theta(y-\beta)}, & y>\beta \\ 0, & y\leq\beta \end{cases}.$$

The three-parameter distribution [22] can be viewed as a sub-model of the five-parameter distribution [23] because the five-parameter distribution reduces to the three-parameter distribution for $\beta=0$, $\delta=\theta$ and $\eta=\mu$ [23]. Some details about the relations between the parameters of these two random variables are given in [23].

In the next section of the paper, some notions and results related to mathematical analysis will be used. These are briefly presented below.

The Euler–Mascheroni constant is

$$\gamma=\lim_{n\to\infty}\left(\sum_{k=1}^{n}\frac{1}{k}-\ln n\right)\approx 0.57721$$

and one of the ways this constant can be written [28] is

$$\gamma=-\int_0^\infty e^{-x}\ln x\,dx. \tag{10}$$

If $p>0$, gamma function [29] is defined as

$$\Gamma(p) = \int_0^\infty x^{p-1} e^{-x} dx. \tag{11}$$

Among the many properties of the gamma function [29], there are the following relationships:

$$\Gamma(1) = \int_0^\infty e^{-x} dx = 1 \tag{12}$$

and

$$\Gamma(n) = (n-1)!, \text{ for } n \in \mathbb{N}, n \geq 2. \tag{13}$$

The integral

$$E_1(x) = \int_x^\infty \frac{e^{-t}}{t} dt \tag{14}$$

is related to the exponential integral [30].

3. Results

Theorem 1. *If X is a random variable having the probability density function*

$$f_X(x;\theta,\alpha,\mu) : (0,\infty) \to \mathbb{R}, \; f_X(x;\theta,\alpha,\mu) = \frac{\theta^2}{\theta\alpha + \mu}(\alpha + \mu x)e^{-\theta x},$$

with $\theta > 0$, $\alpha > 0$, $\mu > 0$, then

$$GM(X) = \frac{1}{\theta} e^{\frac{\mu}{\theta\alpha + \mu} - \gamma}, \tag{15}$$

where γ is the Euler–Mascheroni constant.

Proof. We have

$$GM(X) = e^{I_1},$$

where

$$I_1 = \int_0^\infty (\ln x) f_X(x;\theta,\alpha,\mu) dx.$$

Consider the integrals

$$J_1 = \int_0^\infty (\ln x) e^{-\theta x} dx, \; J_2 = \int_0^\infty x (\ln x) e^{-\theta x} dx.$$

We have

$$J_1 = \int_0^\infty (\ln x) e^{-\theta x} dx = \int_0^\infty \left(\ln \frac{t}{\theta}\right) e^{-t} \frac{1}{\theta} dt =$$

$$= \frac{1}{\theta} \left[\int_0^\infty (\ln t) e^{-t} dt - \ln\theta \int_0^\infty e^{-t} dt \right] = \frac{-\gamma - \ln\theta}{\theta}.$$

Consider

$$J_{21} = \int_0^w x(\ln x) e^{-\theta x} dx, \; J_{22} = \int_w^\infty x(\ln x) e^{-\theta x} dx,$$

where $w \in (0,\infty)$.

We have

$$J_{21} = \lim_{\substack{u \to 0 \\ u > 0}} \int_u^w x(\ln x) e^{-\theta x} dx = \lim_{\substack{u \to 0 \\ u > 0}} \int_u^w x(\ln x) \left(\frac{e^{-\theta x}}{-\theta}\right)' dx =$$

$$= \lim_{\substack{u \to 0 \\ u > 0}} \left\{ -\frac{1}{\theta}\left[w(\ln w)e^{-\theta w} - u(\ln u)e^{-\theta u}\right] + \frac{1}{\theta}\int_u^w (1 + \ln x) e^{-\theta x} dx \right\} =$$

$$= -\frac{1}{\theta}w(\ln w)e^{-\theta w} + \frac{1}{\theta}\lim_{\substack{u\to 0\\ u>0}}\int_{\theta u}^{\theta w}\left(1+\ln\frac{t}{\theta}\right)e^{-t}\frac{1}{\theta}dt =$$

$$= -\frac{1}{\theta}w(\ln w)e^{-\theta w} + \frac{1}{\theta^2}\lim_{\substack{u\to 0\\ u>0}}\left[\int_{\theta u}^{\theta w}(\ln t)e^{-t}dt + (1-\ln\theta)\int_{\theta u}^{\theta w}e^{-t}dt\right]$$

and

$$J_{22} = \lim_{v\to\infty}\int_w^v x(\ln x)e^{-\theta x}dx = \lim_{v\to\infty}\int_w^v x(\ln x)\left(\frac{e^{-\theta x}}{-\theta}\right)'dx =$$

$$= \lim_{v\to\infty}\left\{-\frac{1}{\theta}\left[v(\ln v)e^{-\theta v} - w(\ln w)e^{-\theta w}\right] + \frac{1}{\theta}\int_w^v(1+\ln x)e^{-\theta x}dx\right\} =$$

$$= \frac{1}{\theta}w(\ln w)e^{-\theta w} + \frac{1}{\theta}\lim_{v\to\infty}\int_{\theta w}^{\theta v}\left(1+\ln\frac{t}{\theta}\right)e^{-t}\frac{1}{\theta}dt =$$

$$= \frac{1}{\theta}w(\ln w)e^{-\theta w} + \frac{1}{\theta^2}\lim_{v\to\infty}\left[\int_{\theta w}^{\theta v}(\ln t)e^{-t}dt + (1-\ln\theta)\int_{\theta w}^{\theta v}e^{-t}dt\right].$$

We obtain

$$J_2 = J_{21} + J_{22} = \frac{1}{\theta^2}\left[\int_0^\infty(\ln t)e^{-t}dt + (1-\ln\theta)\int_0^\infty e^{-t}dt\right] = \frac{1}{\theta^2}(-\gamma + 1 - \ln\theta).$$

Finally,

$$I_1 = \int_0^\infty(\ln x)f(x;\theta,\alpha,\mu)dx = \frac{\theta^2}{\theta\alpha+\mu}\int_0^\infty(\ln x)(\alpha+\mu x)e^{-\theta x}dx =$$

$$= \frac{\theta^2}{\theta\alpha+\mu}(\alpha J_1 + \mu J_2) = \frac{\theta^2}{\theta\alpha+\mu}\left(\alpha\frac{-\gamma-\ln\theta}{\theta} + \mu\frac{-\gamma+1-\ln\theta}{\theta^2}\right) =$$

$$= -\ln\theta + \frac{\mu}{\theta\alpha+\mu} - \gamma$$

and

$$GM(X) = e^{I_1} = \frac{1}{\theta}e^{\frac{\mu}{\theta\alpha+\mu}-\gamma}.$$

□

Theorem 2. *If Y is a random variable having the probability density function*

$$f_Y(y;\delta,\alpha,\eta,\theta,\beta):(\beta,\infty)\to\mathbb{R},\ f_Y(y;\delta,\alpha,\eta,\theta,\beta) = \frac{\theta}{\delta\alpha+\eta}[\delta\alpha+\eta\theta(y-\beta)]e^{-\theta(y-\beta)},$$

with $\delta,\alpha,\eta,\theta\in(0,\infty)$, $\beta\in[0,\infty)$, *then*

$$GM(Y) = \begin{cases} e^{I_2}, \beta > 0 \\ \frac{1}{\theta}e^{\frac{\eta}{\delta\alpha+\eta}-\gamma}, \beta = 0 \end{cases}, \tag{16}$$

where

$$I_2 = \ln\beta + \frac{\eta}{\delta\alpha+\eta} + \left(1 - \frac{\eta\theta\beta}{\delta\alpha+\eta}\right)e^{\theta\beta}E_1(\theta\beta). \tag{17}$$

Proof. If $\beta > 0$, we have

$$I_2 = \int_\beta^\infty(\ln y)f_Y(y;\delta,\alpha,\eta,\theta,\beta)dy = \frac{1}{\delta\alpha+\eta}\lim_{v\to\infty}\int_\beta^v(\ln y)[\delta\alpha+\eta\theta(y-\beta)]\theta e^{-\theta(y-\beta)}dy =$$

$$= \frac{1}{\delta\alpha + \eta} \lim_{v\to\infty} \int_0^{\theta(v-\beta)} \left(\ln \frac{\theta\beta + z}{\theta}\right)(\delta\alpha + \eta z)e^{-z}dz =$$

$$= \frac{1}{\delta\alpha + \eta} \lim_{v\to\infty} \int_0^{\theta(v-\beta)} \left(\ln \frac{\theta\beta + z}{\theta}\right)(\delta\alpha + \eta z)(-e^{-z})'dz =$$

$$= \frac{1}{\delta\alpha + \eta} \lim_{v\to\infty} \left\{ \left[\left(\ln \frac{\theta\beta + z}{\theta}\right)(\delta\alpha + \eta z)(-e^{-z})\right]\Big|_0^{\theta(v-\beta)} + \right.$$

$$\left. + \int_0^{\theta(v-\beta)} \left(\frac{\delta\alpha + \eta z}{\theta\beta + z} + \eta \ln \frac{\theta\beta + z}{\theta}\right)e^{-z}dz \right\} =$$

$$= \frac{\delta\alpha \ln\beta}{\delta\alpha + \eta} + \frac{1}{\delta\alpha + \eta} \lim_{v\to\infty} \int_0^{\theta(v-\beta)} \left(\eta + \frac{\delta\alpha - \eta\theta\beta}{\theta\beta + z} + \eta \ln \frac{\theta\beta + z}{\theta}\right)e^{-z}dz =$$

$$= \frac{\delta\alpha \ln\beta}{\delta\alpha + \eta} + \frac{1}{\delta\alpha + \eta} \lim_{v\to\infty} \left[\eta \int_0^{\theta(v-\beta)} e^{-z}dz + \int_0^{\theta(v-\beta)} \frac{\delta\alpha - \eta\theta\beta}{\theta\beta + z} e^{-z}dz + \right.$$

$$\left. + \eta \int_0^{\theta(v-\beta)} \left(\ln \frac{\theta\beta + z}{\theta}\right)e^{-z}dz\right] =$$

$$= \frac{\eta\Gamma(1) + \delta\alpha \ln\beta}{\delta\alpha + \eta} + \frac{1}{\delta\alpha + \eta} \lim_{v\to\infty} \left[\int_0^{\theta(v-\beta)} \frac{\delta\alpha - \eta\theta\beta}{\theta\beta + z} e^{-z}dz + \right.$$

$$\left. + \eta \int_0^{\theta(v-\beta)} \left(\ln \frac{\theta\beta + z}{\theta}\right)(-e^{-z})'dz\right] =$$

$$= \frac{\eta + \delta\alpha \ln\beta}{\delta\alpha + \eta} + \frac{1}{\delta\alpha + \eta} \lim_{v\to\infty} \left\{\int_0^{\theta(v-\beta)} \frac{\delta\alpha - \eta\theta\beta}{\theta\beta + z} e^{-z}dz - \right.$$

$$\left. -\eta \left[\left(\ln \frac{\theta\beta + z}{\theta}\right)e^{-z}\right]\Big|_0^{\theta(v-\beta)} + \eta \int_0^{\theta(v-\beta)} \frac{e^{-z}}{\theta\beta + z}dz\right\} =$$

$$= \frac{\eta + (\delta\alpha + \eta)\ln\beta}{\delta\alpha + \eta} + \frac{1}{\delta\alpha + \eta} \lim_{v\to\infty} \left[(\delta\alpha - \eta\theta\beta)\int_0^{\theta(v-\beta)} \frac{e^{-z}}{\theta\beta + z}dz + \eta \int_0^{\theta(v-\beta)} \frac{e^{-z}}{\theta\beta + z}dz\right] =$$

$$= \ln\beta + \frac{\eta}{\delta\alpha + \eta} + \frac{\delta\alpha - \eta\theta\beta + \eta}{\delta\alpha + \eta} \lim_{v\to\infty} \int_0^{\theta(v-\beta)} \frac{e^{-z}}{\theta\beta + z}dz =$$

$$= \ln\beta + \frac{\eta}{\delta\alpha + \eta} + \left(1 - \frac{\eta\theta\beta}{\delta\alpha + \eta}\right)e^{\theta\beta} \lim_{v\to\infty} \int_0^{\theta(v-\beta)} \frac{e^{-\theta\beta - z}}{\theta\beta + z}dz =$$

$$= \ln\beta + \frac{\eta}{\delta\alpha + \eta} + \left(1 - \frac{\eta\theta\beta}{\delta\alpha + \eta}\right)e^{\theta\beta} \lim_{v\to\infty} \int_{\theta\beta}^{\theta v} \frac{e^{-t}}{t}dt =$$

$$= \ln\beta + \frac{\eta}{\delta\alpha + \eta} + \left(1 - \frac{\eta\theta\beta}{\delta\alpha + \eta}\right)e^{\theta\beta} \int_{\theta\beta}^{\infty} \frac{e^{-t}}{t}dt =$$

$$= \ln\beta + \frac{\eta}{\delta\alpha + \eta} + \left(1 - \frac{\eta\theta\beta}{\delta\alpha + \eta}\right)e^{\theta\beta} E_1(\theta\beta).$$

If $\beta = 0$, we have
$$GM(Y) = e^{I_3},$$
where
$$I_3 = \int_0^\infty (\ln y) \frac{\theta}{\delta\alpha + \eta}(\delta\alpha + \eta\theta y)e^{-\theta y}dy = \frac{\theta}{\delta\alpha + \eta}(\delta\alpha J_1 + \eta\theta J_2) =$$
$$= \frac{\theta}{\delta\alpha + \eta}\left(\delta\alpha \frac{-\gamma - \ln\theta}{\theta} + \eta\theta \frac{-\gamma + 1 - \ln\theta}{\theta^2}\right) = -\ln\theta + \frac{\eta}{\delta\alpha + \eta} - \gamma.$$

□

Theorem 3. *If Y is a random variable having the cumulative distribution function*

$$F_Y(y;\delta,\alpha,\eta,\theta,\beta): \mathbb{R} \to \mathbb{R}, \; F_Y(y;\delta,\alpha,\eta,\theta,\beta) = \begin{cases} 1 - \left[1 + \dfrac{\theta\eta(y-\beta)}{\delta\alpha+\eta}\right]e^{-\theta(y-\beta)}, & y > \beta \\ 0, & y \leq \beta \end{cases},$$

with $\delta,\alpha,\eta,\theta \in (0,\infty)$, $\beta \in [0,\infty)$, then

$$\mathcal{E}(Y) = \frac{1}{\theta(\delta\alpha+\eta)}\left[\delta\alpha + 2\eta - \eta e^{\frac{\delta\alpha+\eta}{\eta}} E_1\left(\frac{\delta\alpha+\eta}{\eta}\right)\right]. \tag{18}$$

Proof. We have

$$\overline{F}_Y(y;\delta,\alpha,\eta,\theta,\beta) = \left[1 + \frac{\theta\eta(y-\beta)}{\delta\alpha+\eta}\right]e^{-\theta(y-\beta)}, \text{ for } y > \beta,$$

and

$$\mathcal{E}(Y) = -\int_\beta^\infty \overline{F}_Y(y;\delta,\alpha,\eta,\theta,\beta)\ln \overline{F}_Y(y;\delta,\alpha,\eta,\theta,\beta)dy =$$

$$= -\lim_{v\to\infty}\int_\beta^v \left[1 + \frac{\theta\eta(y-\beta)}{\delta\alpha+\eta}\right]e^{-\theta(y-\beta)}\ln\left\{\left[1 + \frac{\theta\eta(y-\beta)}{\delta\alpha+\eta}\right]e^{-\theta(y-\beta)}\right\}dy =$$

$$= -\frac{1}{\theta}\lim_{v\to\infty}\int_0^{\theta(v-\beta)} \left(1 + \frac{\eta z}{\delta\alpha+\eta}\right)e^{-z}\ln\left[\left(1 + \frac{\eta z}{\delta\alpha+\eta}\right)e^{-z}\right]dz =$$

$$= -\frac{1}{\theta}\lim_{v\to\infty}\int_0^{\theta(v-\beta)} \left(1 + \frac{\eta z}{\delta\alpha+\eta}\right)e^{-z}\left[-z + \ln\left(1 + \frac{\eta z}{\delta\alpha+\eta}\right)\right]dz =$$

$$= \frac{1}{\theta}\lim_{v\to\infty}\int_0^{\theta(v-\beta)}\left\{ze^{-z} + \frac{\eta}{\delta\alpha+\eta}z^2 e^{-z} - \left(1 + \frac{\eta z}{\delta\alpha+\eta}\right)\left[\ln\left(1 + \frac{\eta z}{\delta\alpha+\eta}\right)\right]e^{-z}\right\}dz =$$

$$= \frac{1}{\theta}\left\{\Gamma(2) + \frac{\eta}{\delta\alpha+\eta}\Gamma(3) - \lim_{v\to\infty}\int_0^{\theta(v-\beta)}\left(1 + \frac{\eta z}{\delta\alpha+\eta}\right)\left[\ln\left(1 + \frac{\eta z}{\delta\alpha+\eta}\right)\right]e^{-z}dz\right\} =$$

$$= \frac{1}{\theta}\left[\Gamma(2) + \frac{\eta}{\delta\alpha+\eta}\Gamma(3) - \lim_{v\to\infty}\int_0^{\theta(v-\beta)}\frac{\delta\alpha+\eta+\eta z}{\delta\alpha+\eta}\left(\ln\frac{\delta\alpha+\eta+\eta z}{\delta\alpha+\eta}\right)e^{-z}dz\right] =$$

$$= \frac{1}{\theta}\left(1 + \frac{2\eta}{\delta\alpha+\eta}\right) - \frac{1}{\theta}\lim_{v\to\infty}\int_0^{\theta(v-\beta)}\frac{\delta\alpha+\eta+\eta z}{\delta\alpha+\eta}\left(\ln\frac{\delta\alpha+\eta+\eta z}{\delta\alpha+\eta}\right)(-e^{-z})'dz =$$

$$= \frac{\delta\alpha+3\eta}{\theta(\delta\alpha+\eta)} - \frac{1}{\theta}\lim_{v\to\infty}\left\{\left[\frac{\delta\alpha+\eta+\eta z}{\delta\alpha+\eta}\left(\ln\frac{\delta\alpha+\eta+\eta z}{\delta\alpha+\eta}\right)(-e^{-z})\right]\Big|_0^{\theta(v-\beta)} + \right.$$

$$\left. + \frac{\eta}{\delta\alpha+\eta}\int_0^{\theta(v-\beta)}\left(1 + \ln\frac{\delta\alpha+\eta+\eta z}{\delta\alpha+\eta}\right)e^{-z}dz\right\} =$$

$$= \frac{\delta\alpha+3\eta}{\theta(\delta\alpha+\eta)} - \frac{\eta}{\theta(\delta\alpha+\eta)}\lim_{v\to\infty}\int_0^{\theta(v-\beta)}\left[e^{-z} + \left(\ln\frac{\delta\alpha+\eta+\eta z}{\delta\alpha+\eta}\right)e^{-z}\right]dz =$$

$$= \frac{\delta\alpha+3\eta}{\theta(\delta\alpha+\eta)} - \frac{\eta}{\theta(\delta\alpha+\eta)}\left[\Gamma(1) + \lim_{v\to\infty}\int_0^{\theta(v-\beta)}\left(\ln\frac{\delta\alpha+\eta+\eta z}{\delta\alpha+\eta}\right)(-e^{-z})'dz\right] =$$

$$= \frac{\delta\alpha+3\eta}{\theta(\delta\alpha+\eta)} - \frac{\eta}{\theta(\delta\alpha+\eta)} - \frac{\eta}{\theta(\delta\alpha+\eta)}\lim_{v\to\infty}\left[\left(-e^{-z}\ln\frac{\delta\alpha+\eta+\eta z}{\delta\alpha+\eta}\right)\Big|_0^{\theta(v-\beta)} + \right.$$

$$\left. + \int_0^{\theta(v-\beta)}\frac{\eta}{\delta\alpha+\eta+\eta z}e^{-z}dz\right] =$$

$$= \frac{\delta\alpha+2\eta}{\theta(\delta\alpha+\eta)} - \frac{\eta}{\theta(\delta\alpha+\eta)}\lim_{v\to\infty}\int_0^{\theta(v-\beta)}\frac{\eta}{\delta\alpha+\eta+\eta z}e^{-z}dz =$$

$$= \frac{\delta\alpha+2\eta}{\theta(\delta\alpha+\eta)} - \frac{\eta}{\theta(\delta\alpha+\eta)}e^{\frac{\delta\alpha+\eta}{\eta}}\lim_{v\to\infty}\int_0^{\theta(v-\beta)}\frac{\eta}{\delta\alpha+\eta+\eta z}e^{-z-\frac{\delta\alpha+\eta}{\eta}}dz =$$

$$= \frac{\delta\alpha+2\eta}{\theta(\delta\alpha+\eta)} - \frac{\eta}{\theta(\delta\alpha+\eta)}e^{\frac{\delta\alpha+\eta}{\eta}}\lim_{v\to\infty}\int_{\frac{\delta\alpha+\eta}{\eta}}^{\theta(v-\beta)+\frac{\delta\alpha+\eta}{\eta}}\frac{1}{t}e^{-t}dt =$$

$$= \frac{\delta\alpha + 2\eta}{\theta(\delta\alpha + \eta)} - \frac{\eta}{\theta(\delta\alpha + \eta)} e^{\frac{\delta\alpha+\eta}{\eta}} \int_{\frac{\delta\alpha+\eta}{\eta}}^{\infty} \frac{1}{t} e^{-t} dt =$$

$$= \frac{1}{\theta(\delta\alpha + \eta)} \left[\delta\alpha + 2\eta - \eta e^{\frac{\delta\alpha+\eta}{\eta}} E_1\left(\frac{\delta\alpha + \eta}{\eta}\right) \right].$$

□

Theorem 4. *If X is a random variable having the cumulative distribution function*

$$F_X(x;\theta,\alpha,\mu): \mathbb{R} \to \mathbb{R}, \quad F_X(x;\theta,\alpha,\mu) = \begin{cases} 1 - \left(1 + \frac{\theta\mu x}{\theta\alpha + \mu}\right) e^{-\theta x}, & x > 0 \\ 0, & x \leq 0 \end{cases},$$

with $\theta > 0$, $\alpha > 0$, $\mu > 0$, then

$$\mathcal{E}(X) = \frac{1}{\theta(\theta\alpha + \mu)} \left[\theta\alpha + 2\mu - \mu e^{\frac{\theta\alpha+\mu}{\mu}} E_1\left(\frac{\theta\alpha + \mu}{\mu}\right) \right]. \tag{19}$$

Proof. The proof comes directly from Theorem 3, by choosing $\beta = 0$, $\delta = \theta$ and $\eta = \mu$. □

4. Discussion

Regarding the characteristics of the random variables, one can notice that in some papers the geometric mean is considered [1–7]. In the field of the study of uncertainty related to a random variable, the cumulative residual entropy [10] overcomes some drawbacks of differential entropy.

In this paper, two generalizations of the Lindley distribution [22,23] were discussed. The three-parameter distribution [22] is a submodel of the five-parameter [23] one. The work focused on the geometric mean and cumulative residual entropy of these two distributions. The cumulative residual entropy of the one with three parameters can be deduced directly from the one with five parameters, as shown in Theorems 3 and 4.

In connection with the geometric mean, remark that the integral I_2 from Theorem 2 can be transformed as follows:

$$I_2 = \ln\beta + \frac{\eta}{\delta\alpha + \eta} + \left(1 - \frac{\eta\theta\beta}{\delta\alpha + \eta}\right) e^{\theta\beta} E_1(\theta\beta) =$$

$$= \ln\beta + \frac{\eta}{\delta\alpha + \eta} + \left(1 - \frac{\eta\theta\beta}{\delta\alpha + \eta}\right) e^{\theta\beta} \int_{\theta\beta}^{\infty} \frac{e^{-t}}{t} dt =$$

$$= \ln\beta + \frac{\eta}{\delta\alpha + \eta} + \left(1 - \frac{\eta\theta\beta}{\delta\alpha + \eta}\right) e^{\theta\beta} \lim_{v\to\infty} \int_{\theta\beta}^{v} \frac{e^{-t}}{t} dt =$$

$$= \ln\beta + \frac{\eta}{\delta\alpha + \eta} + \left(1 - \frac{\eta\theta\beta}{\delta\alpha + \eta}\right) e^{\theta\beta} \lim_{v\to\infty} \int_{\theta\beta}^{v} e^{-t} (\ln t)' dt =$$

$$= \ln\beta + \frac{\eta}{\delta\alpha + \eta} + \left(1 - \frac{\eta\theta\beta}{\delta\alpha + \eta}\right) e^{\theta\beta} \lim_{v\to\infty} \left[(e^{-t}\ln t)\big|_{\theta\beta}^{v} + \int_{\theta\beta}^{v} e^{-t} \ln t\, dt \right] =$$

$$= \ln\beta + \frac{\eta}{\delta\alpha + \eta} + \left(1 - \frac{\eta\theta\beta}{\delta\alpha + \eta}\right) \left(-\ln\theta - \ln\beta + e^{\theta\beta} \int_{\theta\beta}^{\infty} e^{-t} \ln t\, dt \right) =$$

$$= \frac{\eta}{\delta\alpha + \eta} + \frac{\eta\theta\beta \ln\beta}{\delta\alpha + \eta} + \left(1 - \frac{\eta\theta\beta}{\delta\alpha + \eta}\right) \left(-\ln\theta + e^{\theta\beta} \int_{\theta\beta}^{\infty} e^{-t} \ln t\, dt \right).$$

We have

$$\lim_{\substack{\beta \to 0 \\ \beta > 0}} \left[\frac{\eta}{\delta\alpha + \eta} + \frac{\eta\theta\beta \ln\beta}{\delta\alpha + \eta} + \left(1 - \frac{\eta\theta\beta}{\delta\alpha + \eta}\right) \left(-\ln\theta + e^{\theta\beta} \int_{\theta\beta}^{\infty} e^{-t} \ln t\, dt \right) \right] =$$

$$= \frac{\eta}{\delta\alpha + \eta} - \ln\theta + \int_0^{\infty} e^{-t} \ln t\, dt = -\ln\theta + \frac{\eta}{\delta\alpha + \eta} - \gamma.$$

Therefore the geometric mean of the five-parameter distribution is right continuous at zero with respect to the parameter β. By taking, in Theorem 2, $\beta = 0$ and then making the substitutions $\delta = \theta$, $\eta = \mu$, the geometric mean of the three-parameter distribution with three parameters can be deduced from the geometric mean of the five-parameter distribution. Due to the special position of the parameter β in the calculation of integrals, the geometric mean was independently calculated for each distribution, as seen in Theorems 1 and 2.

5. Conclusions

From the rather large set of Lindley-type distributions, two related distributions were selected for study. For each of them, the formulas for geometric mean and cumulative residual entropy were obtained. These results are in addition to those already known from previous works, thus increasing the area of knowledge concerning the theme of Lindley-type distributions.

Author Contributions: Conceptualization, M.G. and C.-C.P.; methodology, M.G. and C.-C.P.; writing—original draft preparation, M.G. and C.-C.P. All authors have read and agreed to the published version of the manuscript.

Funding: This research received no external funding.

Institutional Review Board Statement: Not applicable

Informed Consent Statement: Not applicable

Data Availability Statement: Not applicable

Conflicts of Interest: The authors declare no conflict of interest.

References

1. Vogel, R.M. The geometric mean? *Commun. Stat.—Theory Methods* **2022**, *51*, 82–94. [CrossRef]
2. Feng, C.; Wang, H.; Tu, X.M. Geometric mean of nonnegative random variable. *Commun. Stat.—Theory Methods* **2013**, *42*, 2714–2717. [CrossRef]
3. Abyani, M.; Asgarian, B.; Zarrin, M. Sample geometric mean versus sample median in closed form framework of seismic reliability evaluation: a case study comparison. *Earthq. Eng. Eng. Vib.* **2019**, *18*, 187–201. [CrossRef]
4. Mahajan, S. Don't demean the geometric mean. *Am. J. Phys.* **2019**, *87*, 75–77. [CrossRef]
5. Martinez, M.N.; Bartholomew, M.J. What does it "mean"? A review of interpreting and calculating different types of means and standard deviations. *Pharmaceutics* **2017**, *9*, 14. [CrossRef]
6. Selvadurai, P.A.; Selvadurai, A.P.S. On the effective permeability of a heterogenous porous medium: The role of the geometric mean. *Philos. Mag.* **2014**, *94*, 2318–2338. [CrossRef]
7. Thelwall, M. The precision of the arithmetic mean, geometric mean and percentiles for citation data: An experimental simulation modelling approach. *J. Inf.* **2016**, *10*, 110–123. [CrossRef]
8. Shannon, C.E. A mathematical theory of communication. *Bell Syst. Tech. J.* **1948**, *27*, 379–423. [CrossRef]
9. Cover, T.M.; Thomas, J.A. *Elements of Information Theory*, 2nd ed.; John Wiley & Sons, Inc.: Hoboken, NJ, USA, 2006; pp. 243–259.
10. Rao, M.; Chen, Y.; Vemuri, B.C.; Wang, F. Cumulative residual entropy: a new measure of information. *IEEE Trans. Inf. Theory* **2004**, *50*, 1220–1228. [CrossRef]
11. Almarashi, A.M.; Algarni, A.; Hassan, A.S.; Zaky, A.N.; Elgarhy, M. Bayesian analysis of dynamic cumulative residual entropy for Lindley distribution. *Entropy* **2021**, *23*, 1256. [CrossRef]
12. Asadi, M.; Zohrevand, Y. On the dynamic cumulative residual entropy. *J. Stat. Plan. Inference* **2007**, *137*, 1931–1941. [CrossRef]
13. Toomaj, A.; Sunoj, S.M.; Navarro, J. Some properties of the cumulative residual entropy of coherent and mixed systems. *J. Appl. Probab.* **2017**, *54*, 379–393. [CrossRef]
14. Xiong, H.; Shang, P.; Zhang, Y. Fractional cumulative residual entropy. *Commun. Nonlinear Sci. Numer. Simul.* **2019**, *78*. [CrossRef]
15. Zardasht, V.; Parsi, S.; Mousazadeh, M. On empirical cumulative residual entropy and a goodness-of-fit test for exponentiality. *Stat. Pap.* **2015**, *56*, 677–688. [CrossRef]
16. Lindley, D.V. Fiducial distributions and Bayes' theorem. *J. R. Stat. Soc. Ser. B* **1958**, *20*, 102–107. [CrossRef]
17. Ghitany, M.E.; Atieh, B.; Nadarajah, S. Lindley distribution and its application. *Math. Comput. Simul.* **2008**, *78*, 493–506. [CrossRef]
18. Abd El-Bar, A.M.T.; da Silva, W.B.F.; Nascimento, A.D.C. An extended log-Lindley-G family: Properties and experiments in repairable data. *Mathematics* **2021**, *9*, 3108. [CrossRef]
19. Abouammoh, A.; Kayid, M. A new flexible generalized Lindley model: Properties, estimation and applications. *Symmetry* **2020**, *12*, 1678. [CrossRef]

20. Gómez-Déniz, E.; Sordo, M.A.; Calderín-Ojeda, E. The Log-Lindley distribution as an alternative to the beta regression model with applications in insurance. *Insur. Math. Econ.* **2014**, *54*, 49–57. [CrossRef]
21. Korkmaz, M.Ç.; Yousof, H.M. The one-parameter odd Lindley exponential model: Mathematical properties and applications. *Stochastics Qual. Control* **2017**, *32*, 25–35. [CrossRef]
22. Shanker, R.; Shukla, K.K.; Shanker, R.; Leonida, T.A. A three-parameter Lindley distribution. *Am. J. Math. Stat.* **2017**, *7*, 15–26. [CrossRef]
23. Tharshan, R.; Wijekoon, P. A comparison study on a new five-parameter generalized Lindley distribution with its sub-models. *Stat. Transit. New Ser.* **2020**, *21*, 89–117. [CrossRef]
24. Bakouch, H.S.; Jazi, M.A.; Nadarajah, S. A new discrete distribution. *Statistics* **2014**, *48*, 200–240. 02331888.2012.716677. [CrossRef]
25. Gómez-Déniz, E.; Calderín-Ojeda, E. The discrete Lindley distribution: Properties and applications. *J. Stat. Comput. Simul.* **2011**, *81*, 1405–1416. [CrossRef]
26. Yilmaz, M.; Hameldarbandi, M.; Kemaloglu, S.A. Exponential-modified discrete Lindley distribution. *SpringerPlus* **2016**, *5*, 1660. [CrossRef] [PubMed]
27. Thamer, M.K.; Zine, R. Comparison of five methods to estimate the parameters for the three-parameter Lindley distribution with application to life data. *Comput. Math. Methods Med.* **2021**, *2021*, 2689000. [CrossRef]
28. Lagarias, J.C. Euler's constant: Euler's work and modern developments. *Bull. Amer. Math. Soc.* **2013**, *50*, 527–628. [CrossRef]
29. Whittaker, E.T.; Watson, G.N. *A Course of Modern Analysis*, 4th ed.; Cambridge University Press: Cambridge, UK, 1996; pp. 235–264.
30. Gautschi, W.; Cahill, W.F. Exponential integral and related functions. In *Handbook of Mathematical Functions with Formulas, Graphs and Mathematical Tables*; Abramowitz, M., Stegun, I.A., Eds.; Dover Publications: New York, NY, USA, 1965; pp. 227–252.

Article

A More Flexible Asymmetric Exponential Modification of the Laplace Distribution with Applications for Chemical Concentration and Environment Data

Jimmy Reyes, Mario A. Rojas, Pedro L. Cortés and Jaime Arrué *

Departamento de Matemáticas, Facultad de Ciencias Básicas, Universidad de Antofagasta, Antofagasta 1270300, Chile
* Correspondence: jaime.arrue@uantof.cl

Abstract: In this work, a new family of distributions based on the Laplace distribution is introduced. We define this new family by its stochastic representation as the sum of two independent random variables, one with a Laplace distribution and the other with an exponential distribution. Using a Monte Carlo simulation study, the statistical performance of the estimators obtained by the moments and maximum likelihood methods were empirically evaluated. We studied the coverage probabilities and mean length of the confidence intervals of the corresponding parameters based on the asymptotic normality of these estimators. This simulation study reported a good statistical performance of these estimators. Fits were made to three real data sets with the new distribution, two related to chemical concentrations and one to the environment, comparing it with three similar distributions given in the literature. We have used information criteria for the selection of models. These results showed that the exponentially modified Laplace model can be an alternative distribution to model skewed data with high kurtosis. The new approach is a contribution to the tools of statisticians and various professionals interested in modeling data with high kurtosis.

Keywords: exponentially modified Laplace distribution; moments; skewness and kurtosis coefficients

MSC: 62P12

1. Introduction

There are several investigations that use the Laplace distribution to model data from certain fields based on an empirical fit using goodness-of-fit techniques. For example, in environmental problems, the Laplace distribution is used to analyze (or model) random variables that determine maximum pollution values and describe times of high pollution. In mining, the Laplace distribution is used to analyze the mineral content in soil samples [1,2].

However, not all data related to these types of problems have a symmetric behavior. For this reason, other distributions have been proposed that are capable of better modeling this type of data. In this sense, Agu and Onwukwe [3] presented the modified Laplace distribution (ML), Grushka [4] presented the exponentially modified Gaussian distribution (EMG) and Reyes et al. [5] presented the exponentially modified logistic distribution ($EMLOG$). One of the advantages of these new probability distributions obtained through mixtures is that the obtained distributions generally have longer tails than the base distribution, thus giving rise to better fits for empirical frequency distributions, [4,5].

Our research is based on the theory of probability distributions and based on the process of mixtures of probability distributions, it proposes a new parametric probability distribution using the Laplace distribution. The new distribution depends on three parameters and is obtained by adding two independent random variables: one with a Laplace distribution and the other with an exponential distribution. This distribution can be used as an alternative to some existing distributions. The density function of the new distribution is obtained using the stochastic representation $Y = \sigma(X + V) + \mu$ where X and V are independent random variables, such that X is standard Laplace distribution and V is exponentially distributed with parameter λ, where μ is the location parameter, σ is the scale parameter, and λ is the skewness parameter. This document is organized as follows Section 2, in order to make this work self-contained, presents the probability distributions of the Laplace, exponential, modified Laplace, exponentially modified Gaussian, and exponentially modified logistic distributions with some characteristics of these that will be useful later. In Section 3, the exponentially modified Laplace probability distribution is constructed, obtaining the density and the main characteristics of the distribution. In Section 4, the methods of moments and maximum likelihood are presented to estimate the parameters of the distribution. A simulation study for the theoretical validation of the model is also presented. Section 5 shows a comparative analysis and a discussion of the results obtained by fitting the different data sets with the modified Laplace (ML), exponentially modified Gaussian (EMG), and exponentially modified logistic distributions (EMLOG) and the proposed exponentially modified Laplace distribution (EML). Finally, in Section 6, conclusions are drawn from the work.

2. Preliminaries

The classical Laplace distribution (also known as Laplace's first law) is a probability distribution, given by the density function

$$f(x; \theta, s) = \frac{1}{2s} e^{-\frac{|x-\theta|}{s}}, \ x \in \mathbb{R}$$

where $-\infty < \theta < \infty$ and $s > 0$ are the location and scale parameters, respectively (Johnson et al. [6]), and we will denote it as $X \sim L(\theta, s)$. When the location parameter is equal to zero and the scale parameter is equal to one, then the standard Laplace distribution function is obtained, denoted by $L(0,1)$. The nth moment for a random variable $X \sim L(0,1)$, is given by:

$$E(X^n) = \frac{1}{2} n! \{1 + (-1)^n\} \ n = 1, 2, \ldots \quad (1)$$

The continuous random variable, say X, is said to have an exponential distribution if it has the following probability density function:

$$f(x; \lambda) = \begin{cases} \lambda e^{-\lambda x} & si \quad x > 0 \\ 0 & si \quad x \leq 0 \end{cases}$$

where λ is called the rate of the distribution and will be represented as $X \sim exp(\lambda)$. The nth moment for a random variable $X \sim exp(\lambda)$ is given by the following expression:

$$E(X^n) = \frac{n!}{\lambda^n}, \ n = 1, 2, \ldots \quad (2)$$

Agu and Onwukwe [3] presented the modified Laplace distribution whose density function is given by

$$f_X(x) = \begin{cases} \frac{\lambda}{2\sigma} \left(\frac{1}{2} e^{\frac{x-\mu}{\sigma}}\right)^{\lambda-1} e^{\frac{x-\mu}{\sigma}} &, \ x \leq \mu \\ \frac{\lambda}{2\sigma} \left(1 - \frac{1}{2} e^{-\frac{x-\mu}{\sigma}}\right)^{\lambda-1} e^{-\frac{x-\mu}{\sigma}} &, \ x > \mu \end{cases}$$

$x \in \mathbb{R}$, which is denoted by $X \sim ML(\mu, \sigma, \lambda)$.

The pdf of a random variable with an exponentially modified Gaussian distribution EMG (Grushka [4]) is given by:

$$f_Y(y; \mu, \sigma, \lambda) = \frac{\lambda}{2} e^{-\frac{\lambda}{2}(2y - 2\mu - \lambda\sigma^2)} erfc\left(\frac{2\mu + \lambda\sigma^2 - y}{\sqrt{2\sigma^2}}\right), \ x \in \mathbb{R}$$

and is denoted as $Y \sim EMG(\mu, \sigma, \lambda)$, where $erfc(z) = \frac{2}{\sqrt{\pi}} \int_z^\infty e^{-t^2}\, dt$.

A random variable X has a logistic distribution with location parameter $\alpha \in \mathbb{R}$ and scale parameter $\beta > 0$ if its density function is:

$$f_X(x; \alpha, \beta) = \frac{e^{-(x-\alpha)/\beta}}{\beta(1 + e^{-(x-\alpha)/\beta})^2},\ x \in \mathbb{R}$$

which is denoted as $X \sim LOG(\alpha, \beta)$. When the location parameter is 0 and the scale parameter is 1, then the standard logistic distribution function is obtained.

Reyes et al. [5], using the methodology given by [4], introduces the exponentially modified logistic distribution by the following stochastic representation:

$$Y = Z + T,$$

where $Z \sim LOG(\alpha, \beta)$ and $T \sim exp(1/\beta)$ are random independent variables and are denoted by $Y \sim EMLOG(\alpha, \beta)$, transforming this into a more flexible distribution in terms of working with data that have high kurtosis. Its function is given by:

$$f_Y(y|\alpha, \beta) = \frac{1}{\beta^2} e^{\frac{y-\alpha}{\beta}} \int_0^\infty e^{-\frac{2w}{\beta}} \left[1 + e^{\frac{y-w-\alpha}{\beta}}\right]^{-2} dw,\ -\infty < y < \infty$$

and we denote as $Y \sim EMLOG(\alpha, \beta)$.

3. Exponentially Modified Laplace Distribution

In this section, the exponentially modified Laplace distribution (EML) is presented using the Grushka methodology [4], considering the location and scale parameters. This distribution is obtained by substituting the normal distribution for the standard Laplace distribution in the stochastic representation. The flexibility of this new distribution allows better capture of outliers. We will start by deriving its density function.

3.1. Density Function

The exponentially modified Laplace distribution admits the following stochastic representation as

$$Y = \sigma(X + V) + \mu, \tag{3}$$

where X and V are independent random variables such that $X \sim L(0,1)$ and $V \sim exp(\lambda)$, where μ is the location parameter, σ is the scale parameter, and λ is the skewness parameter, so we say that Y follows an exponentially modified Laplace distribution and is denoted by $Y \sim EML(\mu, \sigma, \lambda)$.

Proposition 1. *Let Y be a random variable such that $Y \sim EML(\mu, \sigma, \lambda)$. Then, its probability density function (pdf) is given by*

$$f_Y(y; \mu, \sigma, \lambda) = \begin{cases} \frac{\lambda}{2\sigma(\lambda-1)}\left[e^{-\frac{y-\mu}{\sigma}} - \left(\frac{2}{\lambda+1}\right)e^{-\lambda\left(\frac{y-\mu}{\sigma}\right)}\right], & y > \mu,\ \lambda \neq 1 \\[6pt] \left[\frac{2\left(\frac{y-\mu}{\sigma}\right)+1}{4\sigma}\right]e^{-\frac{y-\mu}{\sigma}}, & y > \mu,\ \lambda = 1 \\[6pt] \frac{\lambda}{2\sigma(\lambda+1)}e^{\frac{y-\mu}{\sigma}}, & y < \mu \end{cases} \tag{4}$$

Proof. Using the stochastic representation in (3), we have

$$X \sim L(0,1) \Rightarrow f_X(x) = \frac{1}{2}e^{-|x|}, \quad -\infty < x < \infty,$$
$$V \sim exp(\lambda) \Rightarrow f_V(v) = \lambda e^{-\lambda v}, \quad v > 0$$

and the Jacobian transformation approach, it follows that:

$$\left. \begin{array}{l} Y = \sigma(X+V) + \mu \\ W = V \end{array} \right\} \Rightarrow \begin{array}{l} X = \frac{Y-\mu}{\sigma} - W \\ V = W \end{array} \Rightarrow J = \begin{vmatrix} \frac{\partial x}{\partial y} & \frac{\partial x}{\partial w} \\ \frac{\partial v}{\partial y} & \frac{\partial v}{\partial w} \end{vmatrix} = \begin{vmatrix} \frac{1}{\sigma} & -1 \\ 0 & 1 \end{vmatrix} = \frac{1}{\sigma}.$$

Then,

$$f_{Y,W}(y,w) = |J| f_{X,V}\left(\frac{y-\mu}{\sigma} - w, w\right)$$
$$f_{Y,W}(y,w) = \frac{1}{\sigma} f_X\left(\frac{y-\mu}{\sigma} - w\right) f_V(w)$$
$$f_Y(y) = \int_0^\infty \frac{1}{\sigma} f_X\left(\frac{y-\mu}{\sigma} - w\right) f_V(w)\, dw$$
$$f_Y(y) = \frac{\lambda}{2\sigma} \int_0^\infty e^{-\lambda w} e^{-\left|\frac{y-\mu}{\sigma} - w\right|} dw, \quad -\infty < y < \infty,$$

solving the integral, for $\lambda \neq 1$ and $\lambda = 1$, the result (4) is obtained. □

Proposition 2. *If $Y \sim EML(\mu, \sigma, \lambda)$ and $\lambda \to \infty$, then $Y \sim L(\mu, \sigma)$.*

Proof. If $\lambda \to \infty$ in the density function given in (4), the result is obtained. □

Figure 1 graphically illustrates the behavior of the density function of the exponentially modified Laplace distribution and the standard Laplace for different values of λ (upper), it is observed that as the parameter λ decreases, the tails become heavier. On the other hand, on the lower portion of the figure, the densities of the standard Laplace, modified Laplace, and exponentially modified Laplace distributions are plotted, in which greater flexibility is observed in the *EML* model.

Proposition 3. *Let Y be a random variable such that $Y \sim EML(\mu, \sigma, \lambda)$, then its cdf is given by*

$$F_Y(t; \mu, \sigma, \lambda) = \begin{cases} \frac{\lambda}{2(\lambda+1)} + \frac{\lambda}{2(\lambda-1)}\left[1 - e^{-\frac{t-\mu}{\sigma}} - \frac{2}{\lambda(\lambda+1)}\left(1 - e^{-\lambda\left(\frac{t-\mu}{\sigma}\right)}\right)\right] &, \quad t > \mu, \lambda \neq 1 \\ \frac{1}{4}\left[4 - 3e^{-\frac{t-\mu}{\sigma}} - \frac{2(t-\mu)}{\sigma}e^{-\frac{t-\mu}{\sigma}}\right] &, \quad t > \mu, \lambda = 1 \\ \frac{\lambda}{2(\lambda+1)} e^{\frac{t-\mu}{\sigma}} &, \quad t < \mu. \end{cases} \quad (5)$$

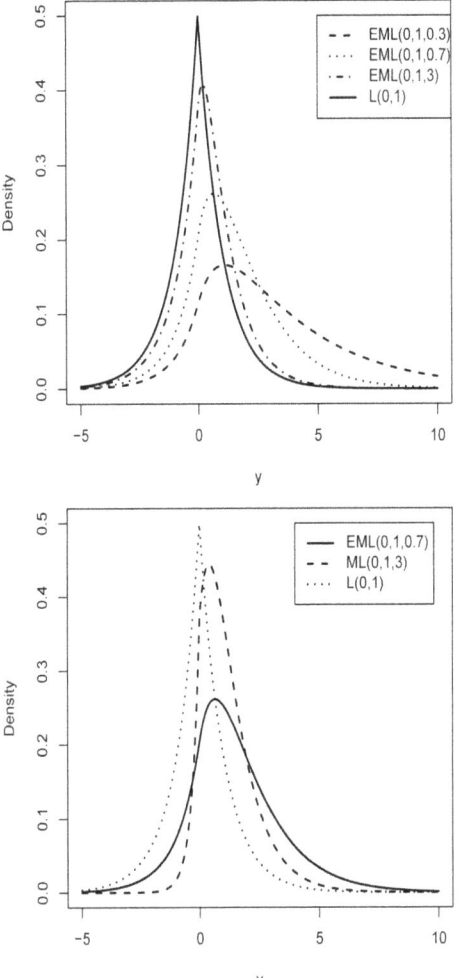

Figure 1. Graphical comparison of EML distributions with L for different values of λ (**upper**) and with ML and L (**lower**).

Proof. Using the definition of cdf, we have

$$F_Y(t;\mu,\sigma,\lambda) = \int_{-\infty}^{t} \frac{\lambda}{2\sigma} \int_{0}^{\infty} e^{-\lambda w} e^{-\left|\frac{y-\mu}{\sigma}-w\right|} \, dw \, dy, \quad -\infty < t < \infty,$$

solving the integral for, $\lambda \neq 1$ and $\lambda = 1$, the result (5) is obtained. □

Corollary 1. *Let Y be a random variable such that* $Y \sim EML(\mu,\sigma,\lambda)$. *Then, the reliability function defined as* $R(y) = P(Y > y) = 1 - F_Y(y)$, $y > 0$ *is given by*

$$R(y) = \begin{cases} 1 - \frac{\lambda}{2(\lambda+1)} - \frac{\lambda}{2(\lambda-1)}\left[1 - e^{-\frac{t-\mu}{\sigma}} - \frac{2}{\lambda(\lambda+1)}\left(1 - e^{-\lambda\left(\frac{t-\mu}{\sigma}\right)}\right)\right] &, t > \mu, \lambda \neq 1 \\ 1 - \frac{1}{4}\left[4 - 3e^{-\frac{t-\mu}{\sigma}} - \frac{2(t-\mu)}{\sigma}e^{-\frac{t-\mu}{\sigma}}\right] &, t > \mu, \lambda = 1 \quad (6) \\ 1 - \frac{\lambda}{2(\lambda+1)}e^{\frac{t-\mu}{\sigma}} &, t < \mu. \end{cases}$$

Proof. Using the reliability function definition $R(y)$ and (5), the result is directly obtained. □

Through Figure 2, we graphically illustrate the behavior of the cumulative distribution function (cdf) for the exponentially modified Laplace distribution. Compared to the standard Laplace distribution, it reflects a slower growth, implying a greater capture of outlier data.

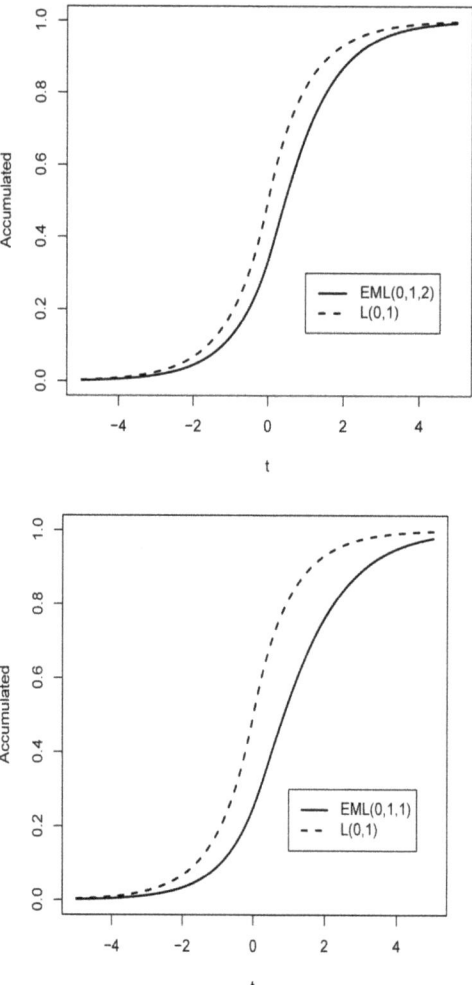

Figure 2. Comparison of the cdf of the EML distribution (solid line) for $\lambda = 2$ (**upper**) and $\lambda = 1$ (**lower**) with the cdf of the distribution L (dashed line).

3.2. Reliability Function Comparison of ML, EMLOG, EMG, and EML Distributions

The reliability function of a random variable Y indicates the probability that a variable exceeds the value of y. In this section, using Table 1, for a fixed value of $\lambda = 0.7$, we make a brief comparison where it is observed that the tails of the EML distribution are heavier than those of the ML, $EMLOG$, and EMG distributions.

Table 1. Reliability function comparison for distributions ML, $EMLOG$, EMG, and EML.

Distribution	$P(Y > 2)$	$P(Y > 2.5)$	$P(Y > 3)$	$P(Y > 3.5)$	$P(Y > 4)$	$P(Y > 4.5)$	$P(Y > 5)$
ML	0.2444	0.1543	0.0958	0.0530	0.0361	0.0220	0.0134
$EMLOG$	0.2878	0.2116	0.1517	0.1065	0.0735	0.0501	0.0377
EMG	0.3073	0.2202	0.1561	0.1102	0.0775	0.0547	0.0385
EML	0.3256	0.2449	0.1820	0.1339	0.0978	0.0711	0.0515

Likewise, observing the graphical illustration represented in Figure 3, it can be seen that the tails of the EML distribution are heavier than those of the ML, $EMLOG$, and EMG distributions.

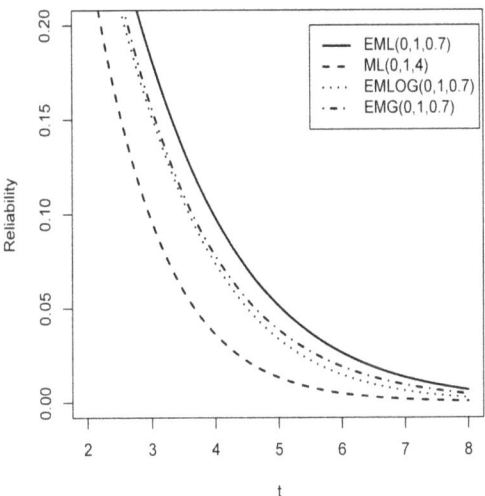

Figure 3. Comparison of the reliability function of the EML distribution (solid line) for $\lambda = 0.7$ with the reliability function of the ML, $EMLOG$, and EMG distributions (dashed line, dotted line, dash-dotted line).

3.3. Moments

The following proposition presents us with a formula that, with the use of numerical techniques, allows us to calculate the rth moment of an exponentially modified Laplace distribution.

Proposition 4. *If $Y \sim EML(\mu, \sigma, \lambda)$, the rth moment of Y is given by:*

$$\mu_r = E[Y^r] = \sum_{j=0}^{r} \binom{r}{j} \sigma^j \mu^{r-j} \left[\sum_{k=0}^{j} \binom{j}{k} \frac{k!\{1 + (-1)^k\}(j-k)!}{2\lambda^{j-k}} \right]$$

Proof. Using the stochastic representation given in (3), applying the binomial theorem and the moments of the standard Laplace and exponential distributions given in (1) and (2), respectively, the result is obtained. □

Corollary 2. Let $Y \sim EML(\mu, \sigma, \lambda)$, then

$$\mu_1 = \frac{\sigma}{\lambda} + \mu$$
$$\mu_2 = 2\sigma^2\left(1 + \frac{1}{\lambda^2}\right) + \frac{2\sigma\mu}{\lambda} + \mu^2$$
$$\mu_3 = \frac{6\sigma^3}{\lambda}\left(1 + \frac{1}{\lambda^2}\right) + 6\sigma^2\mu\left(1 + \frac{1}{\lambda^2}\right) + \frac{3\sigma\mu^2}{\lambda} + \mu^3$$
$$\mu_4 = 24\sigma^4\left(1 + \frac{1}{\lambda^2} + \frac{1}{\lambda^4}\right) + \frac{24\sigma^3\mu}{\lambda}\left(1 + \frac{1}{\lambda^2}\right) + 12\sigma^2\mu^2\left(1 + \frac{1}{\lambda^2}\right) + \frac{4\sigma\mu^3}{\lambda} + \mu^4$$

Proof. Using Proposition 4 with $r = 1, 2, 3, 4$ we obtain the results. □

Corollary 3. Let $Y \sim EML(\mu, \sigma, \lambda)$. Then, the mean and variance are given, respectively, by

$$E(Y) = \mu + \frac{\sigma}{\lambda}$$
$$Var(Y) = \sigma^2\left(2 + \frac{1}{\lambda^2}\right)$$

Proof. Using μ_1 and μ_2 obtained in Corollary 2, and substituting in $V(Y) = \mu_2 - (\mu_1)^2$, we obtain the results. □

Corollary 4. Let $Y \sim EML(\mu, \sigma, \lambda)$, then the asymmetry and kurtosis coefficient of Y is given by

$$\sqrt{\beta_1} = \frac{2}{(2\lambda^2 + 1)^{\frac{3}{2}}}$$
$$\beta_2 = \frac{24\lambda^4 + 12\lambda^2 + 9}{(2\lambda^2 + 1)^2}$$

Proof. Using the standardized skewness and kurtosis coefficients of Y, the result is reached. □

Figure 4 shows that the kurtosis coefficient for the distribution (EML) takes values in the interval $[5, 9]$, decreasing for values of λ between $[0, 1]$ and increasing for values greater than one.

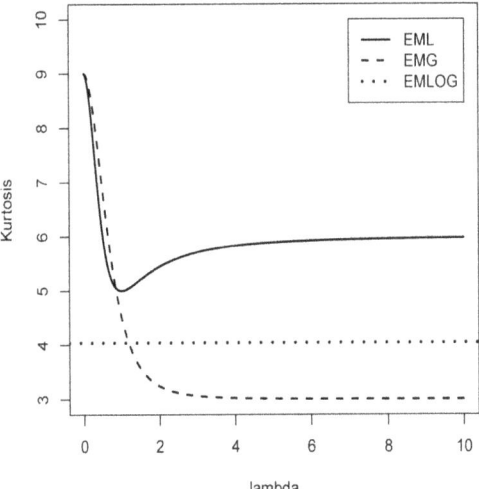

Figure 4. Graphical comparison of the kurtosis coefficient between the exponentially modified Laplace distribution (solid line), the exponentially modified Gaussian distribution (dashed line), and the exponentially modified logistic distribution (dotted line).

4. Estimation
4.1. Moment Estimators

The following proposition shows analytic expressions for the moment estimators of μ, σ, and λ for the exponentially modified Laplace distribution (EML).

Proposition 5. Let $y_1, y_2, \ldots, y_n$ be a random sample from the distribution of random variable $Y \sim EML(\mu, \sigma, \lambda)$, so that the moment estimators for $\theta = (\mu, \sigma, \lambda)$ are obtained by solving the following numerical equation for μ:

$$\mu^3 - 8\bar{y}\mu^2 + 15\overline{y^2}\mu - 6\overline{y^3} - 3\bar{y}s^2 + \overline{y^3} = 0,$$

later, the moment estimator for σ is obtained by substituting the moment estimator for μ ($\widehat{\mu}_M$), in the following equation:

$$\widehat{\sigma}_M = \sqrt{\frac{\overline{y^2} - 2\bar{y}(\bar{y} - \widehat{\mu}_M) - \widehat{\mu}_M^2}{2}}$$

and finally, the estimator of moments for λ is obtained:

$$\widehat{\lambda}_M = \frac{\widehat{\sigma}_M}{\bar{y} - \widehat{\mu}_M}$$

where $\bar{y}, \overline{y^2}, \overline{y^3}$, and s^2 are the sample moments, and sample variance, respectively.

Proof. Equating the first three population moments to the sample moments, we obtain:

$$\bar{y} = \frac{\sigma}{\lambda} + \mu$$
$$\overline{y^2} = 2s^2 - 2\sigma^2 + \left(\frac{\sigma}{\lambda} + \bar{y}\right)\mu$$
$$\overline{y^3} = 6s^2\left(\frac{\sigma}{\lambda} + \mu\right) + \left(\frac{\sigma}{\lambda} + \bar{y}\right)\mu^2,$$

solving the system, we arrive at the result. □

4.2. Likelihood Function

Consider a random sample of size n, $y_1, \ldots, y_n$, from the distribution $EML(\mu, \sigma, \lambda)$ So, the log-likelihood function for $\theta = (\mu, \sigma, \lambda)^T$ can be expressed as

$$\ell(\theta) = n \log \lambda - n \log 2 - n \log \sigma + \sum_{i=1}^{n} \log G(y_i, \theta), \tag{7}$$

where $G(y_i, \theta) = \int_0^\infty e^{-\lambda w} e^{-\left|\frac{y_i - \mu}{\sigma} - w\right|} dw$.

Maximum likelihood estimators (MLEs) were acquired maximizing the likelihood function given in (7). Since there is no analytical solution, we used the iterative numerical method "BFGS", created by Byrd et al. [7]. The "BFGS" method is a limited-memory quasi-Newton method for approximating the Hessian matrix of the target distribution. This method allows us to numerically obtain the maximum likelihood estimates of the parameters of a distribution and their respective standard errors derived from the Hessian matrix.

4.3. Simulation Study

We used the Monte Carlo method to generate random numbers from the distribution $EML(\mu, \sigma, \lambda)$. The results obtained are a sequence of n random numbers that are stored inside an array that we call n-vector. For this, we used 1000 samples of size 50, 100, 200 and 500, obtaining the estimates of the parameters by means of the moment and maximum likelihood methods. In addition, we analyze the standard deviation, average length of the confidence intervals, and the empirical coverage, for the parameters of the distribution, based on a 95% confidence level.

To develop the algorithm (Algorithm 1) we will use the following notation:

1. n: The length of the n-vector.
2. Y: A random variable with the distribution EML.
3. $f_Y(y)$: The PDF of EML.
4. $L1$: Number of samples of size n.
5. μ, σ, λ: Parameters.

Algorithm 1: Monte Carlo algorithm to generate random numbers from the $EML(\mu, \sigma, \lambda)$ distribution

1. Start
   Input: $f_Y(y), L1, n, \mu, \sigma, \lambda$.
   Output: n-vector.
2. Generate a random variable $X \sim L(0, 1)$.
3. Generate a random variable $V \sim exp(\lambda)$.
4. Compute $Y = X + V$.
5. Since $Y \sim EML(\mu, \sigma, \lambda)$, append y to n-vector.
6. Repeat steps 2–5 for each sample of size n obtained.
7. For each estimate, the 95% confidence interval is obtained and the length calculated. Additionally, the number of intervals containing the value of each parameter is counted. By obtaining the average of these 1000 values, the value ali and the empirical coverage c are obtained.
8. end.

Table 2 contains the values of the estimates of the parameters, standard deviation, average interval length, and empirical coverage, based on a 95% confidence interval from simulations obtained by the method of moments for 1000 generated samples of size $n = 50$, 100, 200, and 500 from the population with distribution $EML(\mu, \sigma, \lambda)$. These estimates were obtained by solving the system of equations given in Proposition 5. Similarly, Table 3 shows the results of the simulation studies, illustrating the behavior of the MLEs. For each sample generated, MLEs are calculated numerically using the Newton–Raphson [8] procedure. In both tables, it can be seen that the simulations carried out by these methods show that the average estimates of the parameters are close to the proposed values. Additionally, the standard deviation and the average length of the interval decrease as the sample size increases. This is an expected result, since the ME and MLE are asymptotically consistent. On the other hand, the empirical coverage is adequate since it is close to 95%.

Table 2. ME simulation of 1000 iterations of the model $EML(\mu, \sigma, \lambda)$.

n	μ	σ	λ	$\tilde{\mu}$	$sd(\tilde{\mu})$	$ali(\tilde{\mu})$	$c(\tilde{\mu})$	$\tilde{\sigma}$	$sd(\tilde{\sigma})$	$ali(\tilde{\sigma})$	$c(\tilde{\sigma})$	$\tilde{\lambda}$	$sd(\tilde{\lambda})$	$ali(\tilde{\lambda})$	$c(\tilde{\lambda})$
50	0	1	0.3	0.0341	0.1189	0.4661	93.9	1.0341	0.1189	0.4661	93.9	0.3341	0.1189	0.4661	93.9
100	0	1	0.3	0.0123	0.0650	0.2548	95.2	1.0123	0.0650	0.2548	95.2	0.3123	0.0650	0.2548	95.2
200	0	1	0.3	0.0066	0.0411	0.1612	94.7	1.0066	0.0411	0.1612	94.7	0.3066	0.0411	0.1612	94.7
500	0	1	0.3	0.0036	0.0245	0.0959	94.6	1.0036	0.0245	0.0959	94.6	0.3036	0.0245	0.0959	94.6
50	0	1	0.7	−0.1249	0.2589	1.0150	97.4	0.8751	0.2589	1.0150	97.4	0.5751	0.2589	1.0150	97.4
100	0	1	0.7	−0.1162	0.2293	0.8989	96.1	0.8838	0.2293	0.8989	96.1	0.5838	0.2293	0.8989	96.1
200	0	1	0.7	−0.0785	0.1901	0.7451	91.0	0.9215	0.1901	0.7451	91.0	0.6215	0.1901	0.7451	91.0
500	0	1	0.7	−0.0434	0.1540	0.6038	93.8	0.9566	0.1540	0.6038	93.8	0.6566	0.1540	0.6038	93.8
50	0	1	1	−0.1006	0.3208	1.2576	92.7	0.8994	0.3208	1.2576	92.7	0.8994	0.3208	1.2576	92.7
100	0	1	1	−0.0399	0.2174	0.8522	96.7	0.9601	0.2174	0.8522	96.7	0.9601	0.2174	0.8522	96.7
200	0	1	1	−0.0149	0.1373	0.5381	97.3	0.9851	0.1373	0.5381	97.3	0.9851	0.1373	0.5381	97.3
500	0	1	1	−0.0038	0.0760	0.2978	93.7	0.9962	0.0760	0.2978	93.7	0.9962	0.0760	0.2978	93.7
50	0	1	1.2	−0.0525	0.2984	1.1698	96.6	0.9475	0.2984	1.1698	96.6	1.1475	0.2984	1.1698	96.6
100	0	1	1.2	−0.0114	0.1827	0.7161	98.1	0.9886	0.1827	0.7161	98.1	1.1886	0.1827	0.7161	98.1
200	0	1	1.2	0.0004	0.1118	0.4383	96.0	1.0004	0.1118	0.4383	96.0	1.2004	0.1118	0.4383	96.0
500	0	1	1.2	−0.0024	0.0637	0.2499	94.3	0.9976	0.0637	0.2499	94.3	1.1976	0.0637	0.2499	94.3
50	−1	2	0.3	−0.9902	0.0641	0.2512	94.7	2.0098	0.0641	0.2512	94.7	0.3098	0.0641	0.2512	94.7
100	−1	2	0.3	−0.9923	0.0462	0.1810	94.9	2.0077	0.0462	0.1810	94.9	0.3077	0.0462	0.1810	94.9
200	−1	2	0.3	−0.9958	0.0301	0.1181	94.7	2.0042	0.0301	0.1181	94.7	0.3042	0.0301	0.1181	94.7
500	−1	2	0.3	−0.9987	0.0185	0.0723	94.8	2.0013	0.0185	0.0723	94.8	0.3013	0.0185	0.0723	94.8

sd corresponds to the standard deviation, ali (average length of interval) is the average length of the confidence interval, and c the empirical coverage of the respective ME of the parameters, based on a 95% confidence interval.

Table 3. MLE simulation of 1000 iterations of the model $EML(\mu, \sigma, \lambda)$.

n	μ	σ	λ	$\hat{\mu}$	$sd(\hat{\mu})$	$ali(\hat{\mu})$	$c(\hat{\mu})$	$\hat{\sigma}$	$sd(\hat{\sigma})$	$ali(\hat{\sigma})$	$c(\hat{\sigma})$	$\hat{\lambda}$	$sd(\hat{\lambda})$	$ali(\hat{\lambda})$	$c(\hat{\lambda})$
50	0	1	0.3	0.0470	0.5226	2.0486	93.6	0.9327	0.3885	1.5229	94.2	0.3175	0.2096	0.8216	96.2
100	0	1	0.3	0.0326	0.3439	1.3480	94.2	0.9822	0.2534	0.9933	94.8	0.3081	0.1139	0.4463	94.9
200	0	1	0.3	0.0093	0.2300	0.9015	94.5	0.9937	0.1746	0.6843	95.4	0.3035	0.0706	0.2769	95.1
500	0	1	0.3	−0.0061	0.1408	0.5521	95.0	0.9956	0.1087	0.4260	95.3	0.2999	0.0444	0.1740	94.6
50	0	1	0.7	−0.0023	0.3834	1.5031	94.5	0.9491	0.2611	1.0237	95.6	0.7974	0.5617	2.2017	94.8
100	0	1	0.7	0.0255	0.2872	1.1257	94.1	0.9692	0.1913	0.7498	94.6	0.7607	0.3987	1.5630	95.7
200	0	1	0.7	0.0261	0.2011	0.7882	94.9	1.0004	0.1396	0.5471	95.9	0.7527	0.2750	1.0779	96.1
500	0	1	0.7	0.0084	0.1211	0.4747	95.2	0.9968	0.0829	0.3249	94.9	0.7130	0.1229	0.4816	94.8
50	0	1	1.0	−0.0149	0.3755	1.4718	95.4	0.9182	0.2369	0.9286	93.7	1.2052	1.0383	4.0701	93.8
100	0	1	1.0	0.0176	0.2805	1.0997	94.7	0.9654	0.1697	0.6653	95.0	1.1874	0.8215	3.2204	93.7
200	0	1	1.0	0.0248	0.2150	0.8428	94.6	0.9898	0.1266	0.4962	94.3	1.1528	0.6274	2.4595	94.8
500	0	1	1.0	0.0106	0.1361	0.5337	94.7	0.9924	0.0842	0.3300	94.7	1.0473	0.3208	1.2574	96.5
50	0	1	1.2	−0.0644	0.3430	1.3444	94.8	0.8979	0.2139	0.8385	92.1	1.2577	0.9488	3.7195	95.5
100	0	1	1.2	−0.0013	0.2758	1.0812	94.6	0.9568	0.1629	0.6384	93.5	1.3821	0.9002	3.5287	93.1
200	0	1	1.2	0.0090	0.2123	0.8322	94.9	0.9849	0.1200	0.4704	95.1	1.3675	0.7209	2.8259	94.2
500	0	1	1.2	0.0123	0.1373	0.5383	94.5	0.9969	0.0792	0.3104	94.6	1.2831	0.4290	1.6819	95.5
50	−1	2	0.3	−0.8821	0.9899	3.8805	95.0	1.8777	0.7352	2.8819	93.8	0.3135	0.2027	0.7946	97.3
100	−1	2	0.3	−0.9601	0.6781	2.6582	96.1	1.9483	0.5054	1.9813	94.6	0.3071	0.1150	0.4507	95.5
200	−1	2	0.3	−0.9681	0.4653	1.8239	95.0	1.9917	0.3324	1.3030	94.9	0.3061	0.0702	0.2754	94.5
500	−1	2	0.3	−0.9883	0.2807	1.1004	94.6	1.9960	0.2197	0.8612	94.7	0.3021	0.0448	0.1755	94.9

sd corresponds to the standard deviation, ali (average length of interval) is the average length of the confidence interval, and c the empirical coverage of the respective EMV of the parameters, based on a 95% confidence interval.

5. Three Illustrative Examples with a Real Data Set

In this section, three applications are presented in which the parameter estimators are obtained based on the maximum likelihood method (MLE) for (μ, σ and λ) through of the fitted models ML, $EMLOG$, EMG, and EML to a set of real data. The numerical illustrations below are intended to show that the EML model is an alternative to unimodal data modeling in different areas.

5.1. Illustrative Example 1

In our first illustration, the data set corresponds to the nickel content in soil samples analyzed at the Department of Mining (Department of Mines) of the University of Atacama, Chile, (see Appendix A, Table A1). Table 4 presents summary statistics for the data set of nickel content in soil samples, where γ_1 and γ_2 are the skewness and kurtosis coefficients of the sample, respectively. The moment estimators for these data are given by: $\widehat{\theta}_M = (\widehat{\mu}_M, \widehat{\sigma}_M, \widehat{\lambda}_M) = (6.7497, 5.0626, 0.3412)$.

Table 4. Summary Statistics for the Nickel Concentration Data Set.

n	$\bar{y}$	s_y	γ_1	γ_2
85	21.3372	16.6391	2.3559	11.1917

Table 5 shows the maximum likelihood estimates and the standard deviations for the ML, $EMLOG$, EMG, and EML models. In addition, we report the values of the Akaike [9] (AIC), Bayesian information criteria [10] (BIC), Akaike information criterion consistent [11] (CAIC), and Hannan—Quinn information criterion [12] (HQIC). On the other hand, Figure 5 shows the histogram with estimated pdf. This indicates that the EML model fits the data better than the ML, $EMLOG$, and EMG models. This result is supported by Figure 6 based on theoretical versus empirical (QQ) quantile plots.

Table 5. Maximum likelihood estimators for ML, $EMLOG$, EMG, and EML models for the soil nickel concentration data set, with their corresponding standard deviations in parentheses and comparison criteria AIC, BIC, CAIC, and HQIC.

Parameter Estimates	ML	EMLOG	EMG	EML
$\widehat{\mu}$	11.0020 (0.0657)	18.9149 (1.4048)	10.0433 (0.0771)	7.020 (0.0462)
$\widehat{\sigma}$	11.6843 (1.21645)	7.6833 (0.7231)	9.0165 (0.0766)	5.1452 (0.0258)
$\widehat{\lambda}$	2.2279 (0.2418)		0.7810 (0.0610)	0.3733 (0.0443)
AIC	687.022	699.207	685.0531	682.053
BIC	694.385	704.092	692.381	689.381
CAIC	695.548	705.092	693.381	690.381
HQIC	690.168	701.172	688.001	685.001

Figure 5 presents the histogram of the data with adjustment of the modified Laplace, exponentially modified Laplace, exponentially modified Gaussian, and exponentially modified logistic (upper) distributions, fitted with the values of the maximum likelihood estimators of their parameters. Notice that the fitted exponentially modified Laplace distribution has heavier tails and a magnification of the upper tails of the soil nickel concentration data (lower).

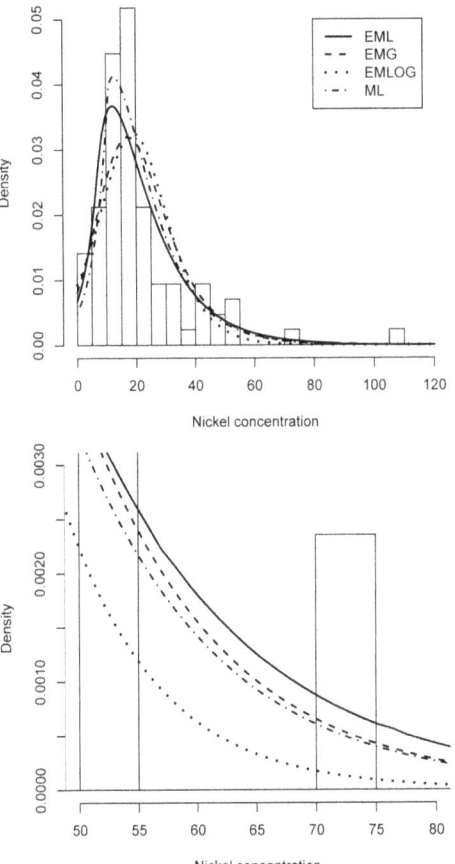

Figure 5. Histogram (**upper**) and tail (**lower**) for nickel concentration data set. Overlaid on top is the density EML with parameters estimated via MLE (solid line), exponentially modified Gaussian density with parameters estimated via MLE (dotted line), exponentially modified logistic (dashed line), and modified Laplace (dash-dotted line).

On the other hand, Figure 6 shows the QQ plot of the fitted models. From these results, it can be seen that the exponentially modified Laplace distribution provided a better fit than the other distributions in consideration.

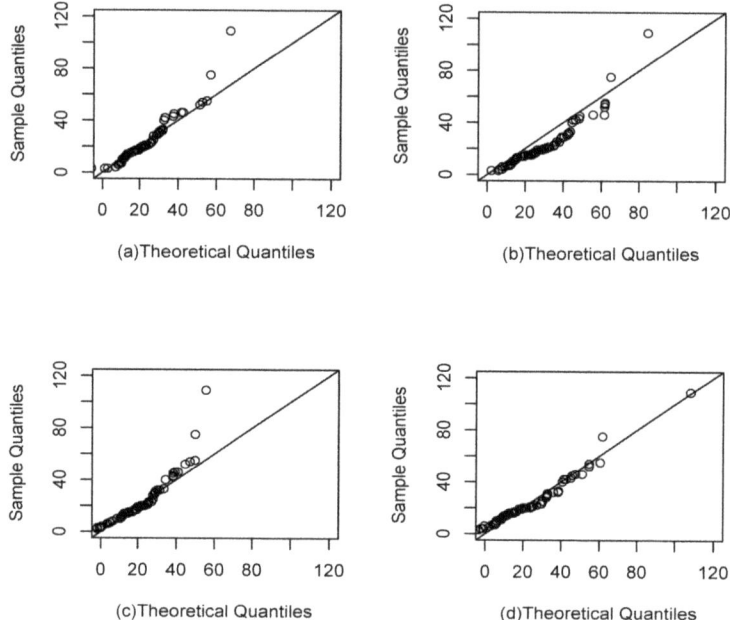

Figure 6. QQ plot for nickel concentration data set. The modified Laplace density (**a**), exponentially modified logistic density (**b**), exponentially modified Gaussian density (**c**), and exponentially modified Laplace density (**d**).

5.2. Illustrative Example 2

The second illustration is related to the neodymium content in soil samples analyzed at the Department of Mining (Department of Mines) of the University of Atacama, Chile (see Appendix A, Table A2). Table 6 presents summary statistics for the data set of the neodymium content in soil samples, where γ_1 and γ_2 are the skewness and kurtosis coefficients of the sample, respectively. The moment estimators for these data are given by: $\widehat{\theta}_M = (\widehat{\mu}_M, \widehat{\sigma}_M, \widehat{\lambda}_M) = (4.2094, 10.3030, 0.5868)$.

Table 6. Summary statistics for neodymium concentration data.

n	$\bar{y}$	s_y	γ_1	γ_2
86	35.1032	34.3307	3.8847	17.3951

The modified Laplace, exponentially modified logistic, exponentially modified Gaussian, and exponentially modified Laplace distributions were fitted to the data set. Table 7 shows the maximum likelihood estimates of the parameters, with the corresponding standard deviations (*sd*) in parentheses, for the three mentioned distributions. The adjustment criteria (AIC, BIC, CAIC, and HQIC) indicate that the data fit better to the exponentially modified Laplace model, because they present a smaller or lower value.

Figure 7 shows the histogram plots and a magnification of the upper tails of the soil neodymium concentration data with the modified Laplace, exponentially modified logistic, exponentially modified Gaussian, exponentially modified Laplace, and distributions fitted with the maximum likelihood estimators of its parameters where the fit of outliers is best observed. In addition, Figure 8 shows the QQ plot of the fitted models, observing that the proposed model achieves a better capture of extreme values.

Table 7. Maximum likelihood estimators for models ML, $EMLOG$, EMG, and EML for the neodymium concentration data set in the soil, with their corresponding standard deviations in parentheses and comparison criteria AIC, BIC, CAIC, and HQIC.

Parameter Estimates	ML	$EMLOG$	EMG	EML
$\hat{\mu}$	13.0001 (0.2804)	29.0578 (2.1736)	15.3836 (2.8609)	10.44577 (0.0388)
$\hat{\sigma}$	18.9313 (1.8033)	12.4762 (1.1937)	17.9653 (1.0407)	6.8136 (0.0091)
$\hat{\lambda}$	2.9883 (0.3412)		0.9147 (0.1363)	0.2831 (0.0339)
AIC	768.088	802.523	792.496	763.294
BIC	775.451	807.432	799.859	770.567
CAIC	776.451	808.432	800.859	771.657
HQIC	771.051	804.499	795.459	766.257

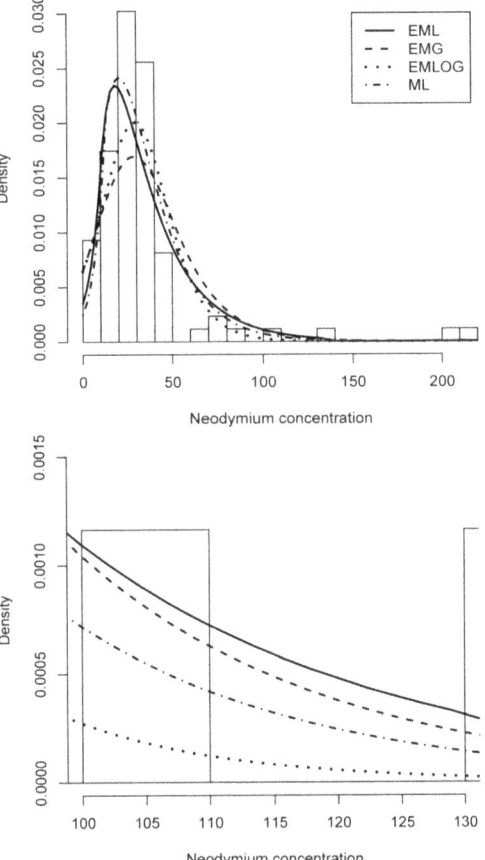

Figure 7. Histogram (**upper**) and tail (**lower**) for the neodymium concentration data set. The first graph shows the densities of the exponentially modified Laplace (solid line), Gaussian modified exponentially (dashed line), exponentially modified logistic (dotted line), and modified Laplace (dash-dotted line) distributions, with their parameters estimated by MLE.

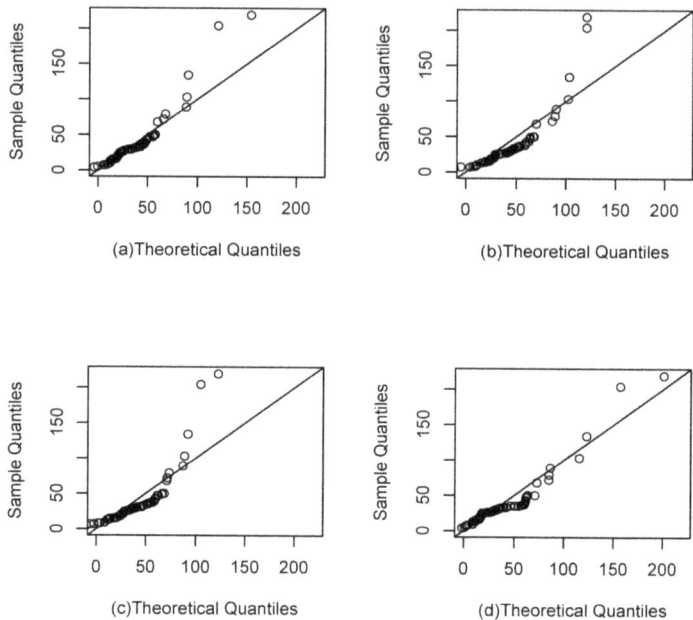

Figure 8. QQ plot for the neodymium concentration data set. The modified Laplace density (**a**), exponentially modified logistic density (**b**), exponentially modified Gaussian density (**c**), and exponentially modified Laplace density (**d**).

5.3. Illustrative Example 3

In this application, we used daily nitrogen concentration data obtained by chromatography [13]. Data are given in the Appendix A (Tabla A3). Table 8 presents summary statistics for the nitrogen concentration data set, where γ_1 and γ_2 are the sample skewness and kurtosis coefficients, respectively. Moment estimators for these data are given by: $\hat{\theta}_M = (\hat{\mu}_M, \hat{\sigma}_M, \hat{\lambda}_M) = (0.0965, 1.0965, 2.0965)$. Table 9 shows the maximum likelihood estimates for the parameters with their corresponding standard deviations (sd) in parentheses for the modified Laplace, exponentially modified logistic, exponentially modified Gaussian and exponentially modified Laplace distributions. The fit criteria used, AIC, BIC, CAIC and HQIC, indicate that the exponentially modified Laplace model fits the data better.

Table 8. Summary statistics for nitrogen concentration data.

n	$\bar{y}$	s_y	γ_1	γ_2
367	0.6189	0.0078	−1.3205	12.4692

Figure 9 shows the histogram plots and a magnification of the lower tails of the nitrogen concentration data with the modified Laplace, exponentially modified logistic, exponentially modified Gaussian, and exponentially modified Laplace distributions fitted with the maximum likelihood estimators of its parameters where the fit of outliers is best observed. In addition, Figure 10 shows the QQ plot of the fitted models, observing that the proposed model achieves a better capture of extreme values.

Table 9. Comparison of the maximum likelihood estimators for nitrogen concentration data between the ML, $EMLOG$, EMG, and EML distributions with their corresponding standard deviations in parentheses and comparison criteria AIC, BIC, CAIC and HQIC.

Parameter Estimates	ML	$EMLOG$	EMG	EML
$\hat{\mu}$	0.6165 (0.0007)	0.6192 (0.0003)	0.6132 (0.0005)	0.6147 (0.0005)
$\hat{\sigma}$	0.0065 (0.0003)	0.0041 (0.0001)	0.0064 (0.0002)	0.0045 (0.0002)
$\hat{\lambda}$	1.5045 (0.1761)		1.0049 (0.0969)	0.9616 (0.1368)
AIC	−2549.257	−2062.155	−2465.067	−2560.045
BIC	−2530.541	−2054.345	−2453.351	−2548.329
CAIC	−2536.541	−2053.344	−2452.351	−2547.329
HQIC	−2544.602	−2059.052	−2460.412	−2555.390

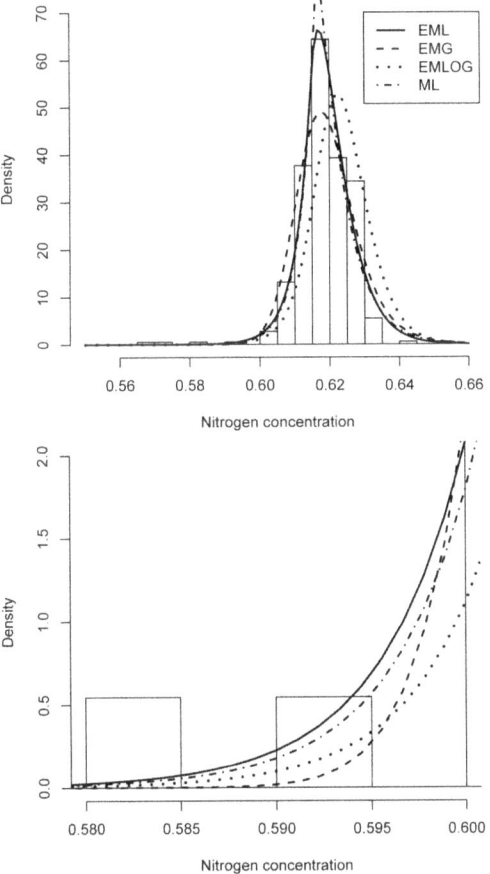

Figure 9. Histogram (**upper**) and tail (**lower**) for nitrogen concentration data set. The first graph shows the densities of exponentially modified Laplace (solid line), Gaussian modified exponentially (dashed line), exponentially modified logistic (dotted line) and modified Laplace (dash-dotted line) distributions, with their parameters estimated by MLE.

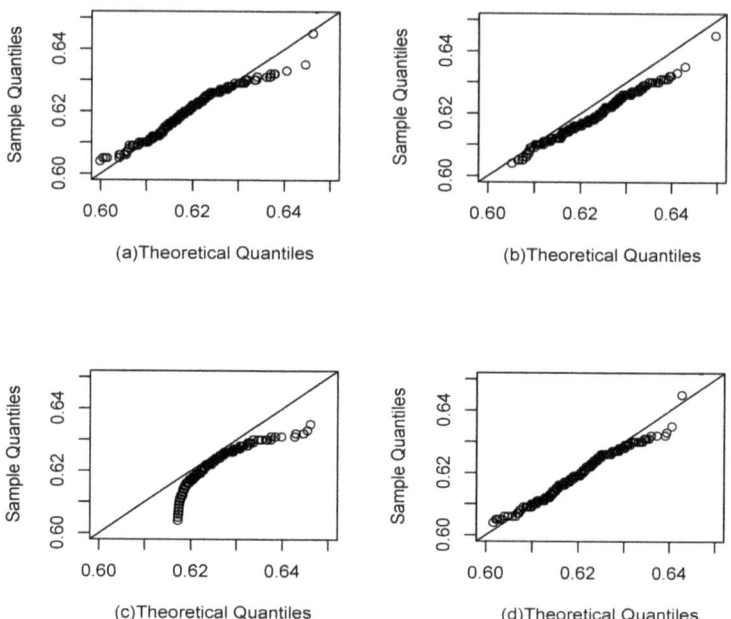

Figure 10. QQ plot for Nitrogen concentration data set. The density *ML* (**a**), *EMLOG* (**b**), *EMG* density (**c**), and *EML* (**d**).

6. Conclusions

In this paper, a new and more flexible distribution, called the exponentially modified Laplace distribution, has been proposed. We estimate the parameters of the model by the moment and maximum likelihood methods. Likewise, we apply information criteria to select the models and evaluate the goodness of fit of the new distribution compared to other similar distributions in the current literature. We performed a Monte Carlo simulation study to empirically assess the statistical performance of the estimates obtained. In addition, we study the standard deviations, the mean length of the confidence intervals, and the empirical coverage based on 95% confidence intervals. This simulation study reported a good statistical performance of these estimates. Three illustrations were made using data related to the chemical and environmental concentrations, comparing them with three similar distributions presented in the literature. The analyses reported a good performance of the new distribution compared to similar distributions, providing evidence that the proposed model is a good alternative for modeling skewed and high-kurtosis data. These results reported that the exponentially modified Laplace model can be an alternative to analyze this type of data. The new approach is a contribution to the tools of statisticians and various professionals interested in data modeling. From these applications, we have obtained useful information that can be used by professionals and users of statistics. A limitation of the proposed distribution is the loss of goodness of fit for data sets whose sample kurtosis is less than five. Some topics for future research based on this new distribution are related to the study of multivariate procedures, quantile regression, spatial methods, temporal methods, partial least squares, principal components, etc.

Author Contributions: Data curation, J.R.; formal analysis, J.R., M.A.R., P.L.C. and J.A.; investigation, J.R., M.A.R., P.L.C.; methodology, J.R., M.A.R., P.L.C. and J.A.; writing—original draft, J.R., M.A.R., P.L.C. and J.A.; writing—review and editing, M.A.R., P.L.C. and J.A.; funding acquisition, J.R., M.A.R. and J.A. All authors have read and agreed to the published version of the manuscript.

Funding: Research of J.R., M.A.R. and J.A. was supported by the Universidad de Antofagasta through project SEMILLERO UA 2022.

Data Availability Statement: The analyzed data are available in the Appendix A of the article.

Conflicts of Interest: The authors declare no conflict of interest.

Appendix A

Table A1. Nickel Data.

2	3	3	3	4	4	6	6	7	7	7	8	8	10	10	11	11	11
12	12	13	13	14	14	14	14	14	14	14	15	15	15	15	15	16	16
16	16	16	16	17	17	17	17	17	19	19	19	19	19	20	20	20	20
20	20	21	21	21	21	22	23	23	25	25	28	29	29	30	31	32	32
33	40	42	42	43	45	46	46	52	54	55	75	109					

Table A2. Neodymium Data.

47	26	29	22	33	16	7	13	4	31	27	13	36	8	42	15	5	29
25	29	36	18	16	50	18	28	16	29	10	31	7	15	32	33	35	31
72	89	37	43	29	35	14	25	21	8	26	49	47	19	14	33	35	21
25	30	15	27	27	9	26	33	13	204	33	38	25	22	35	31	39	24
50	103	28	219	134	68	25	37	21	26	36	32	79	19				

Table A3. Nitrogen Data.

0.607	0.605	0.606	0.606	0.609	0.631	0.617	0.626
0.610	0.611	0.610	0.606	0.610	0.612	0.614	0.613
0.614	0.614	0.615	0.616	0.616	0.616	0.616	0.615
0.616	0.616	0.616	0.618	0.617	0.617	0.617	0.617
0.617	0.617	0.617	0.619	0.619	0.618	0.618	0.622
0.619	0.620	0.620	0.619	0.617	0.616	0.614	0.617
0.611	0.611	0.612	0.611	0.612	0.612	0.612	0.613
0.610	0.612	0.613	0.614	0.613	0.612	0.610	0.609
0.613	0.612	0.616	0.612	0.611	0.611	0.613	0.609
0.612	0.612	0.612	0.605	0.604	0.615	0.620	0.622
0.617	0.619	0.621	0.622	0.630	0.626	0.616	0.617
0.621	0.623	0.625	0.626	0.624	0.618	0.618	0.618
0.621	0.623	0.625	0.626	0.624	0.618	0.618	0.618
0.622	0.623	0.623	0.608	0.624	0.620	0.619	0.615
0.611	0.615	0.612	0.620	0.623	0.627	0.628	0.625
0.627	0.628	0.626	0.627	0.626	0.625	0.625	0.625
0.624	0.626	0.627	0.626	0.628	0.626	0.619	0.618
0.627	0.626	0.626	0.627	0.626	0.626	0.628	0.629
0.627	0.627	0.627	0.627	0.625	0.625	0.629	0.623
0.619	0.573	0.565	0.585	0.595	0.608	0.614	0.614
0.612	0.615	0.616	0.617	0.615	0.615	0.615	0.614
0.610	0.610	0.611	0.611	0.611	0.612	0.610	0.609
0.611	0.614	0.617	0.617	0.620	0.622	0.619	0.618
0.619	0.622	0.618	0.619	0.620	0.619	0.620	0.621
0.617	0.620	0.621	0.623	0.626	0.627	0.626	0.626
0.627	0.626	0.628	0.626	0.624	0.624	0.621	0.620
0.621	0.619	0.621	0.626	0.627	0.624	0.622	0.622
0.622	0.622	0.622	0.625	0.622	0.621	0.618	0.616
0.621	0.619	0.623	0.626	0.625	0.624	0.619	0.620
0.630	0.629	0.630	0.631	0.632	0.624	0.625	0.628
0.623	0.628	0.626	0.629	0.628	0.630	0.618	0.607
0.631	0.630	0.629	0.630	0.629	0.631	0.632	0.633
0.625	0.619	0.619	0.653	0.624	0.622	0.645	0.619

Table A3. Cont.

0.619	0.622	0.622	0.618	0.620	0.620	0.619	0.619
0.620	0.619	0.618	0.620	0.620	0.621	0.618	0.614
0.617	0.616	0.616	0.616	0.615	0.616	0.617	0.616
0.615	0.617	0.616	0.614	0.616	0.617	0.616	0.617
0.618	0.618	0.619	0.622	0.622	0.623	0.622	

References

1. Oosterbaan, R.J. Chapter 6, Frequency and Regression Analysis. In *Drainage Principles and Applications, Publication 16*; En Ritzema, H.P., Ed.; International Institute for Land Reclamation and Improvement (ILRI): Wageningen, The Netherlands, 1994; pp. 175–224. ISBN 90-70754-33-9.
2. Burke, E.J.; Perry, R.H.; Brown, S.J. An extreme value analysis of UK drought and projections of change in the future. *J. Hydrol.* **2010**, *388*, 131. [CrossRef]
3. Agu, F.I.; Onwukwe, E. Modified Laplace Distribution, Its Statistical Properties and Applications Asian. *J. Probab. Stat.* **2019**, *4*, 49277. [CrossRef]
4. Grushka, E. Characterization of Exponentially Modified Gaussian Peaks in Chromatography. *Anal. Chem.* **1972**, *44*, 1733–1738.
5. Reyes, J.; Venega, O.; Gómez, H.W. Exponentially Modified Logistic Distribution with Application to Mining and Nutrition. *Appl. Math. Inf. Sci.* **2018**, *12*, 1–8. [CrossRef] [PubMed]
6. Johnson, N.L.; Kotz, S.; Balakrishnan, N. *Continuous Univariate Distributions*, 2nd ed.; Wiley: New York, NY, USA, 1995. [CrossRef]
7. Byrd, R.H.; Lu, P.; Nocedal, J.; Zhu, C. A Limited Memory Algorithm for Bound Constrained Optimization. *SIAM J. Sci. Comput.* **1995**, *16*, 1190–1208.
8. Tjalling, J.Y. Historical development of the Newton-Raphson method. *SIAM Rev.* **1995**, *37*, 531–551. [CrossRef]
9. Akaike, H. A new look at the statistical model identification. *IEEE Trans. Autom. Control* **1974**, *19*, 716–723.
10. Schwarz, G. Estimating the dimension of a model. *Ann. Stat.* **1978**, *6*, 461–464. [CrossRef]
11. Bozdogan, H. Model selection and Akaike's information criterion (AIC): The general theory and its analytical extensions. *Psychometrika* **1987**, *52*, 345–370. [CrossRef]
12. Hannan, E.J.; Quinn, B.G. The Determination of the order of an autoregression. *J. R. Stat. Soc. Ser. B* **1979**, *41*, 190–195. [CrossRef]
13. Torres de Young, S. *Introduccion a la Cromatografía*; Universidad Nacional de Colombia: Palmira, Colombia, 1994; 134p. ISBNS 9581701192/9789581701193. [CrossRef]

Article

Fisher-like Metrics Associated with ϕ-Deformed (Naudts) Entropies

Cristina-Liliana Pripoae [1], Iulia-Elena Hirica [2], Gabriel-Teodor Pripoae [2,*] and Vasile Preda [2,3,4]

[1] Department of Applied Mathematics, The Bucharest University of Economic Studies, Piata Romana 6, RO-010374 Bucharest, Romania
[2] Faculty of Mathematics and Computer Science, University of Bucharest, Academiei 14, RO-010014 Bucharest, Romania
[3] "Gheorghe Mihoc-Caius Iacob" Institute of Mathematical Statistics and Applied Mathematics of Romanian Academy, 2. Calea 13 Septembrie, nr.13, Sect. 5, RO-050711 Bucharest, Romania
[4] "Costin C. Kiritescu" National Institute of Economic Research of Romanian Academy, 3. Calea 13 Septembrie, nr.13, Sect. 5, RO-050711 Bucharest, Romania
* Correspondence: gpripoae@yahoo.com or gpripoae@fmi.unibuc.ro

Abstract: The paper defines and studies new semi-Riemannian generalized Fisher metrics and Fisher-like metrics, associated with entropies and divergences. Examples of seven such families are provided, based on exponential PDFs. The particular case when the basic entropy is a ϕ-deformed one, in the sense of Naudts, is investigated in detail, with emphasis on the variation of the emergent scalar curvatures. Moreover, the paper highlights the impact on these geometries determined by the addition of some group logarithms.

Keywords: ϕ-deformed (Naudts) entropy; divergence; relative group entropy; generalized Fisher metric; Fisher-like metric; MaxEnt problem

MSC: 53B12; 22E70; 94A17; 53B20

1. Introduction

1.1. History

Entropy is a a very versatile measure of order (or of chaos). In the last few several decades, the growing needs of modeling for stochastic phenomena contributed to the apparition of many new different families of entropy functionals, with increasing levels of generality, reliability and applicability [1–19]. One of the recent interesting new directions of study uses the relative group entropies, based on group logarithms (see [20,21] and references therein).

The geometrization method, a powerful tool in modelization, was applied in the investigation of some statistical relevant parameters sets, beginning with the work of the pioneers: Fisher, Rao, Efron and Amari [12,22,23]. This bridge allows the use of the differential geometric machinery to understand the local and the global behavior of statistical objects.

In particular, the Fisher (semi-Riemannian) metrics correspond to the Fisher Information matrices. Their invariants, especially those tensor fields expressing different kinds of curvature properties, are used in the parameters estimation theory as control tools. For example, the scalar curvature function measures the average statistical uncertainty of a density matrix [12,20,24].

Consider a statistical model, governed by a given entropy, and two or more fixed parameterized probability density functions (PDFs) within it. Various divergences ("distance-like functionals") can be defined in this framework, able to detect how these PDFs relate to each other. A kind of infinitesimal variation of such divergences, w.r.t. the parameters, may provide interpretations for some Fisher-like metrics. Several types of divergences are used, including the Kullback–Leibler and the Bregman ones. For recent viewpoints upon divergences, see [14,25,26].

In 2002, Naudts introduced ([27]) the "ϕ-deformed entropy", via a positive strictly increasing function ϕ, which plays the role of a "generalized logarithm". (We shall call it "ϕ-deformed (Naudts) entropy" and not simply "ϕ-deformed entropy", in order to avoid confusion and to distinguish it from other "deformed" entropies, all originating—sooner or later—from the Boltzman–Gibbs–Shannon (BGS) germ). This new entropy extends (with some technical precautions) the Tsallis and the Kaniadakis entropies, among other ones. Using it, new Fisher metrics were defined [27–29], ranging from simple ones to some more "baroque" constructions. Their applicability covers a wide area, from Physics (the starting point) to Information geometry [29–32].

Using a ϕ-deformed (Naudts) exponential family of PDFs, Matsuzoe et al. [33] investigated the geometry of statistical manifolds derived from a sequence of escort expectations.

Korbel et al. [30] studied properties of the Fisher metrics associated with the ϕ-deformed (Naudts) entropies, in the case of exponential-type PDFs. Particular choices of the function ϕ provided examples based on (c,d)-entropies. Dealing with the MaxEnt problem, they use the Fisher information of the ϕ-deformed (Naudts) exponential entropies, in order to reveal a duality between the cases with linear constraints and those based on escort constraints.

Inspired by these previous works, we believe that a systematic study of semi-Riemannian metrics, canonically associated with the ϕ-deformed (Naudts) entropy, is necessary and might provide useful statistical tools in the future. Our paper suggests a method of research, which combines the beaten path with some new speculative ideas.

1.2. The Content of the Paper

In Section 2, we recall (in a creative manner) the notations and fix the conventions concerning (the different variants of) entropy and divergence; we closely follow [34]. We make some comments about the place of the Naudts' ϕ-deformed entropy in the "Universe" of generalized entropies. We recall here some other examples of remarkable entropies (Tsallis, Kaniadakis, Sharma–Taneja–Mittal). Our main new idea is the distinction we made between the "quotient" divergence and the "difference" divergence, in the context of generalized logarithms; in the particular case of the Neperian logarithm, these two notions coincide, but in other cases (such that of the ϕ-deformed (Naudts) entropy) they are distinct.

In Section 3, we fix the needed notions concerning the generalized Fisher-like metrics associated with the entropies and to the relative (group) entropies, following (especially) [20]. Following the previous distinction we made in Section 2, between the two kinds of divergences, we introduce two generalized Fisher-like metrics (GFM1 and GFM2), which coincide in the classical setting with the Fisher metric. Three other Fisher-like metrics are defined, in a formal way, as auxiliary (but eventually useful) by-products of the former ones.

In Section 4, we determine the semi-Riemannian geometries of the generalized Fisher-like metrics, associated with group relative entropies based on ϕ-deformed (Naudts) entropies and divergences. Their coefficients are expressed in terms of both PDFs and of the ϕ-deformed logarithm and may depend on a group logarithm too.

In the next section, we give seven families of examples of such metrics, for the case when the involved PDFs are exponential. The scalar curvatures functions are computed, and their variation is studied.

In Section 6, we define and solve the MaxEnt problem based on the ϕ-deformed (Naudts) entropy, for univariate PDFs, and we generalize some thermodynamic relations.

1.3. Conventions

Implicitly, the integrals are supposed to be correctly defined and to commute with their derivatives. "Differentiable" means "smooth", even if, sometimes, a weaker assumption would be enough. When a symmetric matrix is called "a (semi-Riemannian) metric", we assume, implicitly that it is non-degenerate; the positive definiteness is not assumed, in general, unless otherwise stated.

2. Entropies and Divergences—A Breviary

We consider a real valued random variable x on a domain $X \subset \mathbb{R}^m$. We denote by $\rho = \rho(x)$ a fixed probability density function (PDF); then, $\rho(x) \geq 0$ and $\int_X \rho(x)dx = 1$. We fix a real valued differentiable function φ, as a "controlling tool". In this setting, the generalized (normalized) entropy is

$$H[\rho] = -\int_X \rho(x)\varphi(\rho(x))dx. \tag{1}$$

We shall use a similar notation for other entropy-like functionals too. In the literature, the avatars of the "generalized logarithm" φ are subject to additional restrictions, imposed through applications inspired axioms.

Let $F : [0, \infty) \times [0, \infty) \to \mathbb{R}$ a smooth function and σ an additional fixed PDF. We define

$$D(\rho, \sigma) := \int_X F(\rho(x), \sigma(x))dx. \tag{2}$$

We suppose that $D(\rho, \sigma) \geq 0$ and $D(\rho, \sigma) = 0$ if and only if $\rho = \sigma$. The number $D(\rho, \sigma)$ is called the (generalized) divergence between ρ and σ and measures to what extent σ influences ρ. Sometimes, additional properties of the divergence function are added, axiomatically.

Example 1. *With the previous notations, we recall some well-known examples of entropies ([35–37]).*

(i) In the particular case when $\varphi(y) := \log(y)$, from Formula (1), we obtain the Boltzmann–Gibbs–Shannon (BGS) entropy.

(ii) Consider a fixed parameter $q \in \mathbb{R} \setminus \{1\}$. The Tsallis q-logarithm

$$\varphi^T_{\{q\}}(y) := \frac{y^{1-q} - 1}{1-q} \tag{3}$$

provides a Tsallis entropy. Usually, for $\varphi^T_{\{q\}}$, we use the notation $\log^T_{\{q\}}$. When $q \to 1$, the BGS entropy is recovered.

(iii) Let us fix $k \in [-1, 1] \setminus \{0\}$. The Kaniadakis k-logarithm

$$\varphi^K_{\{k\}}(y) := \frac{y^k - y^{-k}}{2k} \tag{4}$$

defines a Kaniadakis entropy (named also k-deformed entropy). Usually, $\varphi^K_{\{k\}}$ is denoted $\log^K_{\{k\}}$. When $k \to 0$, we recover again the BGS entropy.

(iv) Fix two real parameters k and r. The Sharma–Taneja–Mittal (k, r)-logarithm

$$\varphi^{STM}_{\{(k,r)\}}(y) := y^r \cdot \frac{y^k - y^{-k}}{2k}$$

provides a Sharma–Taneja–Mittal (STM) entropy (also named (k, r)-deformed entropy). Instead of $\varphi^{STM}_{\{(k,r)\}}$, we shall denote $\log^{STM}_{\{(k,r)\}}$. The Kaniadakis k- logarithm and the Tsallis q-logarithm are recovered as particular cases, for $r = 0$ and for $r = \pm |k|$, respectively. When $(k, r) \to (0, 0)$, we recover the BGS entropy. Sometimes, additional restrictions are imposed on the domain of the parameters, required by convergence conditions imposed on some integrals (see [38–40] for details).

(v) ([27]) Let $\phi : (0, \infty) \to \mathbb{R}$ a positive, differentiable, strictly-increasing function. (Sometimes, in the literature, "non-decreasing" is required, instead of the "strictly-increasing" condition). Define the ϕ-deformed (Naudts) logarithm

$$\log_\phi^N(y) := \int_1^y \frac{1}{\phi(z)} dz. \quad (5)$$

The function $\varphi_\phi^N := \log_\phi^N$ defines the ϕ-deformed (Naudts) entropy. The previous formula may also be read "backwards":

$$\phi(y) = (\frac{\partial}{\partial_x} \varphi_\phi^N(y))^{-1}. \quad (6)$$

Moreover, given an arbitrary "generalized logarithm" φ as in (1), Formula (6) always provides a differentiable function ϕ; if it is positive and strictly-increasing, we expressed φ like a ϕ-deformed (Naudts) logarithm. Sometimes, this procedure works for some restrictions of the involved parameters only. For example, the preceding four entropies are recovered as particular cases of ϕ-deformed (Naudts) entropies, as follows: BGS for $\phi := id$; Tsallis for $\phi(y) := y^q$ with the restrictions $q > 0$ and $y \in (0, \infty)$; Kaniadakis $\phi(y) := 2(y^{k-1} + y^{-k-1})^{-1}$ with the additional restriction

$$y^{2k} < \frac{k+1}{k-1},$$

for $y \in (0, \infty)$; STM for

$$\phi(y) := 2k[(k+r)y^{k+r-1} + (k-r)y^{r-k-1}]^{-1},$$

with the additional restriction

$$y^{2k} < \frac{(r-k)(r-k-1)}{(r+k)(r+k-1)},$$

for $y \in (0, \infty)$. These additional restrictions are imposed in order ϕ to be strictly-increasing.

(vi) Let $G = G(t)$ be a formal group logarithm, which is a differentiable real valued function with some special algebraic properties, inspired from the formal series linking Lie groups to Lie algebras. More precisely,

$$G(t) := \sum_{i=0}^{\infty} c_i \frac{t^{i+1}}{i+1},$$

where $c_0 = 1$ and $c_i \in \mathbb{Q}$. Its inverse is

$$F(s) := \sum_{i=0}^{\infty} \gamma_i \frac{s^{i+1}}{i+1},$$

where $\gamma_i \in \mathbb{Q}$, $\gamma_0 = 1$, $\gamma_1 = -c_1$, $\gamma_2 = \frac{3}{2}c_1^2 - c_2$ and so on. (We refer to [20,21,41] for details about these functions). The simplest example is $G(t) = t$.

We define the generalized group entropy functional (GGEF) associated with (1) by

$$S_G(\rho) := \int_X \rho(x) G(\varphi \circ \rho(x)) dx. \quad (7)$$

In particular, for $\varphi := -\log$, we recover the well-known group entropy functional ([20,41]) associated with (1)

$$S_G(\rho) := \int_X \rho(x) G(\log \rho(x)^{-1}) dx. \quad (8)$$

Similar GGEFs can be provided by replacing the Neperian logarithm by other "generalized" logarithms (e.g., Tsallis, Kaniadakis, STM, etc). In Section 3, we shall introduce the geometries associated with the GGEF, based on ϕ-deformed (Naudts) entropies. Accordingly, we shall use the generalized logarithm $\log_\phi^N$ from (5).

Example 2. *With the previous notations, we recall some well-known examples of divergences.*

(i) An important particular case is the generalized (quotient) relative entropy (a.k.a. generalized divergence) between ρ and σ (see [34,42])

$$\tilde{D}(\rho \parallel \sigma) := \int_X \rho(x) \varphi\left(\frac{\rho(x)}{\sigma(x)}\right) dx. \tag{9}$$

The function $F(z,y) := z\varphi(\frac{z}{y})$. We accept (formally) that $0 \cdot \varphi(\frac{0}{0}) = 0$, $\rho \cdot \varphi(\frac{\rho}{0}) = 0$ and $\varphi(1) = 0$. In particular, when $\varphi := \log$, we recover the Kullback–Leibler divergence ([20]).

Another particular case considers $f : [0, \infty) \to (-\infty, \infty]$ to be a convex function, with $f(1) = 0$ and $f(0) = \lim_{t \to 0^+} f(t)$. For $\varphi(y) := \frac{1}{y} f(y)$, we recover the f-divergence ([43] and references therein). The slightly more general notion of (f, Γ)-divergence (see [44]) may be recovered in a similar way.

(ii) In a similar way, we define the generalized (difference) relative entropy between ρ and σ, as

$$D(\rho \parallel \sigma) := \int_X \rho(x) [\varphi(\rho(x)) - \varphi(\sigma(x))] dx. \tag{10}$$

The function $F(z,y) := z[\varphi(z) - \varphi(y)]$. In particular, when $\varphi := \log$, $\tilde{D}$ coincides with D and we recover the Kullback–Leibler divergence, as in (i). When $\varphi := \log_\phi^N$, the divergence D was considered in [27]; we mention that, in this case, $\tilde{D}$ does not coincide with D.

In general, a necessary and sufficient condition on φ, ρ and σ, in order that $D = \tilde{D}$, is the vanishing of the mean function $\varphi(\frac{\rho}{\sigma}) - \varphi(\rho) + \varphi(\sigma)$. A sufficient (but quite strong) condition is provided by the functional equation $\varphi(\frac{\rho}{\sigma}) = \varphi(\rho) - \varphi(\sigma)$.

(iii) In the hypothesis of Example 1 (vi), we can define generalized divergences as relative group entropies, which combine the formal group logarithm G, the φ-likelihood function and the previous quotient or difference operation upon two PDFs. For example, the analogue of (10) is

$$D_G(\rho \parallel \sigma) := \int_X \rho(x) \cdot G\Big(\varphi(\rho(x)) - \varphi(\sigma(x))\Big) dx.$$

(iv) Consider two fixed PDFs ρ_1 and ρ_2. Denote $\psi : \mathbb{R} \to \mathbb{R}$ as a fixed convex differentiable function. In this setting, the Bregman divergence is

$$D_\psi(\rho_1 \parallel \rho_2) := \int_X \{\psi(\rho_1(x)) - \psi(\rho_2(x)) - (\rho_1(x) - \rho_2(x))\psi'(\rho_2(x))\} dx. \tag{11}$$

We mention that the function $F(z,y) := \psi(z) - \psi(y) - (z - y) \cdot \psi'(y)$ is convex too.

Let $\rho = \rho(x,t)$ be a *time-dependent* PDF, where $x, t \in \mathbb{R}$. Then, the entropy in (1) will also depend on the parameter t, so $H[\rho] = H[\rho](t)$. We consider a *potential energy function* $V = V(x)$ and its associated *energy average function*

$$U[\rho](t) := \int_\mathbb{R} V(x) \rho(x,t) dx. \tag{12}$$

(If needed, restriction of these functions to open subsets is possible). This particular framework will be used in Section 6 only.

3. Fisher-like Metrics Associated with Generalized Entropies and Generalized Divergences

In this section, we recall the notion of Fisher metric associated with a family of (generalized) entropies or divergences, defined on the space of parameters of an arbitrary PDF, using mainly [20,34]. For a more general setting, see [34].

Consider the case when the PDF ρ in Section 2 depends, moreover, on n real parameters $\theta^1, \ldots, \theta^n$, with $\theta := (\theta^1, \ldots, \theta^n) \in \Theta$, where Θ is an open set of $\mathbb{R}^n$. Thus, $\rho : X \times \Theta \to \mathbb{R}$, $\rho = \rho(x, \theta)$. Let $\varphi : \mathbb{R} \to \mathbb{R}$ be a differentiable controlling function, $\varphi = \varphi(y)$. The dependence on θ leads to a generalized entropy function $H : \Theta \to \mathbb{R}$, canonically derived from Formula (1):

$$H(\theta) = -\int_X \rho(x,\theta) \cdot \varphi(\rho(x,\theta))dx. \tag{13}$$

In a similar natural way, we can define generalized divergence functions, by θ-parameterizing (2) and its avatars.

Define

$$g_{ij}(\theta) := -\int_X \rho(x,\theta) \frac{\partial^2 \varphi(\rho(x,\theta))}{\partial \theta^i \partial \theta^j} dx \quad, \quad i,j = \overline{1,n} \tag{14}$$

and

$$\tilde{g}_{ij}(\theta) := \int_X \rho(x,\theta) \frac{\partial \varphi(\rho(x,\theta))}{\partial \theta^i} \cdot \frac{\partial \varphi(\rho(x,\theta))}{\partial \theta^j} dx \quad, \quad i,j = \overline{1,n}. \tag{15}$$

We suppose that the matrices $(g_{ij})_{i,j=\overline{1,n}}$ and $(\tilde{g}_{ij})_{i,j=\overline{1,n}}$ are non-degenerated, and g has constant index on Θ. We call g and $\tilde{g}$ *generalized Fisher metrics of type 1 and type 2*, respectively, and denote GFM1 and GFM2. Both metrics are "means", w.r.t. ρ, of some φ-mediated "information matrices": the Hessian of $\varphi \circ \rho$ and the matrix of the gradient of $\varphi \circ \rho$ with its transpose, respectively. The diagonal coefficients $\tilde{g}_{ii}(\theta)$, $i = \overline{1,n}$, generalize the Fisher Information Numbers from [45], which can be recovered when φ is the Tsallis logarithm.

In general, the semi-Riemannian metric g and the Riemannian metric $\tilde{g}$ differ from each other and differ from the Hessian (semi-Riemannian metric if non-degenerated)

$$h_{ij}(\theta) := \frac{\partial^2 H(\theta)}{\partial \theta^i \partial \theta^j}. \tag{16}$$

We define, in a formal way, two auxiliary symmetric tensors of (0,2)-type α and β, given by

$$\alpha_{ij}(\theta) := \int_X \frac{\partial^2 \rho(x,\theta)}{\partial \theta^i \partial \theta^j} \cdot \varphi(\rho(x,\theta)) dx \tag{17}$$

and

$$\beta_{ij}(\theta) := \int_X \left\{ \frac{\partial \rho(x,\theta)}{\partial \theta^i} \cdot \frac{\partial \varphi(\rho(x,\theta))}{\partial \theta^j} + \frac{\partial \rho(x,\theta)}{\partial \theta^j} \cdot \frac{\partial \varphi(\rho(x,\theta))}{\partial \theta^i} \right\} dx. \tag{18}$$

We remark that, if non-degenerated, α and β provide semi-Riemannian metrics. In this case, these metrics are also of Fisher type, as they express "means" w.r.t. the PDF ρ of two "derived information matrices", of coefficients $\rho^{-1} \cdot \rho_{ij} \cdot \varphi(\rho)$ and $\rho^{-1} \cdot (\rho_i \cdot \varphi_j(\rho) + \rho_j \cdot \varphi_i(\rho))$, respectively.

Example 3. *Consider the particular case of the BGS-entropy, with $\varphi := \log$.*

(i) In this case, both previous GFM1 and GFM2 coincide with the classical (Riemannian) Fisher metric g^0 associated with H (or φ) [20].

In the general case, it would be interesting to find all the controlling functions φ, for which g coincides with $\tilde{g}$. Does this property necessarily imply that φ is proportional with $\log$, modulo a non-null constant? A further step would be to look for appropriate functions φ, in order that g and $\tilde{g}$: be homothetic or conformal; have the same geodesics; have the same curvature, etc. To this differential geometric viewpoint, a statistical counterpart may eventually correspond.

(ii) Let $X \subset \mathbb{R}^m$ be an open set and let $C = C(x)$, $F_1 = F_1(x), \ldots, F_n = F_n(x)$, $\nu = \nu(\theta)$ be smooth functions on X. Consider $\rho : X \times \mathbb{R}^n \to \mathbb{R}$ the PDF of exponential type, given by

$$\rho(x,\theta) := exp\{C(x) - \nu(\theta) + \sum_{i=1}^n F_i(x)\theta^i\}.$$

The associated Fischer metric is $g = Hess_\nu$, which is a Hessian metric.

(iii) For this choice of the function φ, we obtain $\alpha_{ij} = \rho^{-1} \cdot \rho_{ij} \cdot \log(\rho)$ and $\beta_{ij} = 2\rho^{-2} \cdot \rho_i \cdot \rho_j$, for $i,j = \overline{1,n}$. The "perturbed" Hessian matrix associated with α is similar to the one studied in some recent statistical applications (see, for example, [46]).

Remark 1. *(i) We give an interpretation and a motivation for the definition of the GFM1, in a slightly more general case than [20]. Consider φ a fixed controlling function. Let $\rho = \rho(x, \theta)$ and $\sigma := \rho(x, \theta_0)$ be two families of parameterized PDFs over $X \subset \mathbb{R}^m$, with $\theta, \theta_0 \in \mathbb{R}^n$, and let*

$$D(\rho \parallel \sigma)(\theta, \theta_0) := \int_X \rho(x, \theta) \cdot [\varphi(\rho(x, \theta)) - \varphi(\sigma(x, \theta_0))] dx$$

be the generalized (difference) relative entropy between them, as in (10). Denote $\Delta \theta := \theta - \theta_0$ and suppose its norm to be infinitesimally small. We know that $D(\rho \parallel \sigma)$ has a unique minimum for $\rho = \sigma$, i.e., for $\theta_0 = \theta$. The Taylor decomposition around $\theta = \theta_0$ gives

$$D(\rho \parallel \sigma)(\theta_0, \theta_0) = -\frac{1}{2} \int_X \rho(x, \theta_0) \cdot \Delta \theta^i \cdot \Delta \theta^j \cdot \left(Hess_{\varphi \circ \rho}\right)_{ij} (\theta_0) \, dx + \mathcal{O}((\Delta \theta)^3) =$$

$$= \frac{1}{2} \cdot \Delta \theta^i \cdot \Delta \theta^j \cdot g_{ij}(\theta_0) + \mathcal{O}((\Delta \theta)^3).$$

The second order approximation of this expression is precisely half of the GFM1 g, calculated in θ_0.

When $\varphi := \log$, we recover the interpretation given in [20].

(ii) We do not know a similar interpretation for the GFM2 $\tilde{g}$.

(iii) The generalized group relative divergences from Example 2 (iii) provide analogous formulas. We shall study them in the next section, in the particular case of the ϕ-deformed (Naudts) entropy.

(iv) The definition of Fisher metrics described previously is closely related to the need for understanding a variation of a PDF w.r.t. another (reference) one; the output of this "variational calculus factory" are functions. We signal here the forthcoming book [47], containing new revolutionary ideas in Variational calculus, including invariants of tensorial type, motivated by differential geometric problems; this source provides new insights for the definition and the study of divergence-like tensor fields, as a path toward a new bundle spaces approach in Statistics.

(v) All the previous tensor fields g, $\tilde{g}$, h, α, and β have constant index, one each connected component of their definition domains.

An open problem is to find the more general hypothesis such that these tensor fields be non-degenerated (in order to define semi-Riemannian metrics). Locally, the answer is simple: let θ_0 be a point in the parameters space, such that the determinant of the corresponding matrix, calculated in θ_0, is not null. Then, the tensor field is non-degenerated in an open neighborhood of θ_0. For many families of examples (and in Section 5 we add several more ones), this property holds true. A common practice in the literature is to stop here, without investigating global conditions which are fulfilled in general cases. To our knowledge, global existence results for Fisher metrics, in the general setting, are not proven yet. Moreover, the eventual singular points have an interest in their own, as they may signal—in a suitable statistical model—a phase transition ([48]).

We consider it useful to point out here the paper [49], where a different but correlated problem is studied: namely, to what extent the Fisher metric is (globally) unique, modulo the action of a diffeomorphism group.

4. The Fisher Geometries Associated with GGEFs Based on ϕ-Deformed (Naudts) Entropies and Divergences

We particularize now the results from Section 3, for the case of the Naudts entropies. Let us fix the context more precisely.

Consider ϕ a positive, differentiable and strictly-increasing function as in Example 1 (v) and the ϕ-deformed (Naudts) logarithm log_ϕ^N defined in Formula (5). Let $\rho : X \times \Theta \to \mathbb{R}$, $\rho = \rho(x, \theta)$ be a family of parameterized PDFs, as in Section 3. The associated GFM1 g and the GFM2 $\tilde{g}$ are obtained as particular cases from (14) and (15):

$$g_{ij}(\theta) := - \int_X \rho(x, \theta) \frac{\partial^2 log_\phi^N(\rho(x, \theta))}{\partial \theta^i \partial \theta^j} dx \quad , \quad i,j = \overline{1,n} \qquad (19)$$

and
$$\tilde{g}_{ij}(\theta) := \int_X \rho(x,\theta) \frac{\partial \log_\phi^N(\rho(x,\theta))}{\partial \theta^i} \cdot \frac{\partial \log_\phi^N(\rho(x,\theta))}{\partial \theta^j} dx \quad, \quad i,j = \overline{1,n}. \tag{20}$$

We suppose, as usual, that g and $\tilde{g}$ are non-degenerated and that $\tilde{g}$ has a constant index on X.

We also consider, via (16), the associated Hessian metric $h = h(\theta)$

$$h_{ij}(\theta) = -\frac{\partial^2}{\partial \theta^i \partial \theta^j}\left\{ \int_X \rho(x,\theta) \cdot \log_\phi^N(\rho(x,\theta)) dx \right\} \quad, \quad i,j = \overline{1,n}. \tag{21}$$

Proposition 1. *With the previous notations, for every $i,j = \overline{1,n}$, we have*

$$g_{ij}(\theta) = \int_X \rho(x,\theta) \left\{ \frac{\partial \rho(x,\theta)}{\partial \theta^i} \cdot \frac{\partial \rho(x,\theta)}{\partial \theta^j} \cdot \phi^{-2}(\rho(x,\theta)) \cdot \phi'(\rho(x,\theta)) - \right. \tag{22}$$

$$\left. - \frac{\partial^2 \rho(x,\theta)}{\partial \theta^i \partial \theta^j} \cdot \phi^{-1}(\rho(x,\theta)) \right\} dx,$$

$$\tilde{g}_{ij}(\theta) := \int_X \rho(x,\theta) \cdot \frac{\partial \rho(x,\theta)}{\partial \theta^i} \cdot \frac{\partial \rho(x,\theta)}{\partial \theta^j} \cdot \phi^{-2}(\rho(x,\theta)) dx, \tag{23}$$

and

$$h_{ij}(\theta) = \int_X \left\{ \rho(x,\theta) \frac{\partial \rho(x,\theta)}{\partial \theta^i} \cdot \frac{\partial \rho(x,\theta)}{\partial \theta^j} \cdot \phi^{-2}(\rho(x,\theta)) \cdot \phi'(\rho(x,\theta)) - \right. \tag{24}$$

$$\left. - \frac{\partial^2 \rho(x,\theta)}{\partial \theta^i \partial \theta^j} \cdot \log_\phi^N(\rho(x,\theta)) - 2\frac{\partial \rho(x,\theta)}{\partial \theta^i} \cdot \frac{\partial \rho(x,\theta)}{\partial \theta^j} \cdot \phi^{-1}(\rho(x,\theta)) - \right.$$

$$\left. -\rho(x,\theta) \cdot \frac{\partial^2 \rho(x,\theta)}{\partial \theta^i \partial \theta^j} \cdot \phi^{-1}(\rho(x,\theta)) \right\} dx.$$

In this case, α and β are given by

$$\alpha_{ij}(\theta) := \int_X \frac{\partial^2 \rho(x,\theta)}{\partial \theta^i \partial \theta^j} \cdot \log_\phi^N(\rho(x,\theta)) dx$$

and

$$\beta_{ij}(\theta) := \int_X \left\{ \frac{\partial \rho(x,\theta)}{\partial \theta^i} \cdot \frac{\partial \log_\phi^N(\rho(x,\theta))}{\partial \theta^j} + \frac{\partial \rho(x,\theta)}{\partial \theta^j} \cdot \frac{\partial \log_\phi^N(\rho(x,\theta))}{\partial \theta^i} \right\} dx.$$

Corollary 1. *In a condensed form, we have the following relation*

$$h = g - \alpha - \beta.$$

We consider now, in addition, a fixed formal group logarithm G, as in Example 1 (vi). Let $\sigma := \rho(x,\theta_0)$ be the associated parameterized PDFs and $D_{G,\phi} = D_{G,\phi}(\rho \parallel \sigma)(\theta,\theta_0)$ be the generalized (difference) group relative entropy (a.k.a. the generalized (difference) group divergence), as particularization from (10) and Remark 1 (i), (iii), written as

$$D_{G,\phi}(\rho \parallel \sigma)(\theta,\theta_0) = \int_X \rho(x,\theta) \cdot G\Big(\log_\phi^N(\rho(x,\theta)) - \log_\phi^N(\rho(x,\theta_0))\Big) dx.$$

Denote the generalized group Fisher metric associated with $D_{G,\phi}$ by

$$\hat{g}_{jk}(\theta_0) := \frac{\partial^2 D_{G,\phi}(\rho \parallel \sigma)(\theta,\theta_0)}{\partial \theta^j \partial \theta^k}\Big|_{\theta=\theta_0}. \tag{25}$$

This Hessian-type metric will be calculated in the next result.

Proposition 2. *With the previous notations, we have the relation*

$$\hat{g}_{jk}(\theta_0) = G'(0) \cdot \left\{ \int_X \frac{\partial^2 \rho(x,\theta_0)}{\partial \theta^j \partial \theta^k} \cdot \frac{\rho(x,\theta_0)}{\phi(\rho(x,\theta_0))} dx + \right. \tag{26}$$

$$+ 2 \int_X \phi(\rho(x,\theta_0)) \cdot \frac{\partial}{\partial \theta^j} log_\phi^N(\rho(x,\theta_0)) \cdot \frac{\partial}{\partial \theta^k} log_\phi^N(\rho(x,\theta_0)) dx -$$

$$- \left. \int_X \rho(x,\theta_0) \cdot \phi'(\rho(x,\theta_0)) \cdot \frac{\partial}{\partial \theta^j} log_\phi^N(\rho(x,\theta_0)) \cdot \frac{\partial}{\partial \theta^k} log_\phi^N(\rho(x,\theta_0)) dx \right\} +$$

$$+ G''(0) \cdot \int_X \rho(x,\theta_0) \cdot \frac{\partial}{\partial \theta^j} log_\phi^N(\rho(x,\theta_0)) \cdot \frac{\partial}{\partial \theta^k} log_\phi^N(\rho(x,\theta_0)) dx,$$

which may be re-written as depending only on ϕ and ρ, in

$$\hat{g}_{jk}(\theta_0) = G'(0) \cdot \left\{ \int_X \frac{\partial^2 \rho(x,\theta_0)}{\partial \theta^j \partial \theta^k} \cdot \frac{\rho(x,\theta_0)}{\phi(\rho(x,\theta_0))} dx + \right. \tag{27}$$

$$+ 2 \int_X \phi^{-1}(\rho(x,\theta_0)) \cdot \frac{\partial}{\partial \theta^j} \rho(x,\theta_0) \cdot \frac{\partial}{\partial \theta^k} \rho(x,\theta_0) dx -$$

$$- \left. \int_X \rho(x,\theta_0) \cdot \phi'(\rho(x,\theta_0)) \cdot \phi^{-2}(\rho(x,\theta_0)) \cdot \frac{\partial}{\partial \theta^j} \rho(x,\theta_0) \cdot \frac{\partial}{\partial \theta^k} \rho(x,\theta_0) dx \right\} +$$

$$+ G''(0) \cdot \int_X \rho(x,\theta_0) \cdot \phi^{-2}(\rho(x,\theta_0)) \cdot \frac{\partial}{\partial \theta^j} \rho(x,\theta_0) \cdot \frac{\partial}{\partial \theta^k} \rho(x,\theta_0) dx.$$

Proof. We follow the line of reasoning from [20]. As

$$log_\phi^N(\rho(x,\theta)) = \int_1^{\rho(x,\theta)} \frac{1}{\phi(y)} dy,$$

we calculate

$$\frac{\partial}{\partial \theta^k} log_\phi^N(\rho(x,\theta)) = \frac{\partial \rho(x,\theta)}{\partial \theta^k} \cdot \frac{1}{\phi(\rho(x,\theta))}.$$

Suppose, for the moment, that θ_0 is constant. Denote

$$A(\theta) := D_{G,\phi}(\rho(x,\theta) \| \rho(x,\theta_0)).$$

We calculate successively

$$\frac{\partial A}{\partial \theta^k}(\theta) = \int_X \left\{ \frac{\partial \rho(x,\theta)}{\partial \theta^k} \cdot G\left(log_\phi^N(\rho(x,\theta)) - log_\phi^N(\rho(x,\theta_0))\right) + \right.$$

$$+ \left. \rho(x,\theta) \cdot G'\left(log_\phi^N(\rho(x,\theta)) - log_\phi^N(\rho(x,\theta_0))\right) \cdot \frac{\partial}{\partial \theta^k} log_\phi^N(\rho(x,\theta)) \right\} dx =$$

$$= \int_X \left\{ \frac{\partial \rho(x,\theta)}{\partial \theta^k} \cdot G\left(log_\phi^N(\rho(x,\theta)) - log_\phi^N(\rho(x,\theta_0))\right) + \right.$$

$$+ \left. \rho(x,\theta) \cdot G'\left(log_\phi^N(\rho(x,\theta)) - log_\phi^N(\rho(x,\theta_0))\right) \cdot \frac{1}{\phi(\rho(x,\theta))} \frac{\partial \rho(x,\theta)}{\partial \theta^k} \right\} dx =$$

$$= \int_X \frac{\partial \rho(x,\theta)}{\partial \theta^k} \cdot \left\{ G\left(log_\phi^N(\rho(x,\theta)) - log_\phi^N(\rho(x,\theta_0))\right) + \right.$$

$$+ \left. \frac{\rho(x,\theta)}{\phi(\rho(x,\theta))} \cdot G'\left(log_\phi^N(\rho(x,\theta)) - log_\phi^N(\rho(x,\theta_0))\right) \right\} dx$$

and

$$\frac{\partial^2 A}{\partial \theta^j \partial \theta^k}(\theta) = \int_X \frac{\partial^2 \rho(x,\theta)}{\partial \theta^j \partial \theta^k} \cdot \left\{ G\left(log_\phi^N(\rho(x,\theta)) - log_\phi^N(\rho(x,\theta_0))\right) + \right.$$

$$+\frac{\rho(x,\theta)}{\phi(\rho(x,\theta))}\cdot G'\Big(\log_\phi^N(\rho(x,\theta))-\log_\phi^N(\rho(x,\theta_0))\Big)\Big\}+$$

$$+\frac{\partial\rho(x,\theta)}{\partial\theta^k}\cdot\Big\{\frac{\partial}{\partial\theta^j}\log_\phi^N(\rho(x,\theta))\cdot G'\Big(\log_\phi^N(\rho(x,\theta))-\log_\phi^N(\rho(x,\theta_0))\Big)+$$

$$+G'\Big(\log_\phi^N(\rho(x,\theta))-\log_\phi^N(\rho(x,\theta_0))\Big)\cdot\frac{\frac{\partial\rho(x,\theta)}{\partial\theta^j}\cdot[\phi(\rho(x,\theta))-\rho(x,\theta)\cdot\phi'(\rho(x,\theta)]}{\phi^2(\rho(x,\theta))}+$$

$$+\frac{\rho(x,\theta)}{\phi(\rho(x,\theta))}\cdot G''\Big(\log_\phi^N(\rho(x,\theta))-\log_\phi^N(\rho(x,\theta_0))\Big)\cdot\frac{\partial}{\partial\theta^j}\log_\phi^N(\rho(x,\theta))\Big\}dx=$$

$$=\int_X \frac{\partial^2\rho(x,\theta)}{\partial\theta^j\partial\theta^k}\cdot\Big\{G\Big(\log_\phi^N(\rho(x,\theta))-\log_\phi^N(\rho(x,\theta_0))\Big)+$$

$$+\frac{\rho(x,\theta)}{\phi(\rho(x,\theta))}\cdot G'\Big(\log_\phi^N(\rho(x,\theta))-\log_\phi^N(\rho(x,\theta_0))\Big)\Big\}+$$

$$+\frac{\partial\rho(x,\theta)}{\partial\theta^j}\cdot\frac{\partial\rho(x,\theta)}{\partial\theta^k}\cdot\frac{1}{\phi(\rho(x,\theta))}\cdot\Big\{G'\Big(\log_\phi^N(\rho(x,\theta))-\log_\phi^N(\rho(x,\theta_0))\Big)+$$

$$+G'\Big(\log_\phi^N(\rho(x,\theta))-\log_\phi^N(\rho(x,\theta_0))\Big)\cdot\frac{\phi(\rho(x,\theta))-\rho(x,\theta)\cdot\phi'(\rho(x,\theta))}{\phi(\rho(x,\theta))}+$$

$$+\frac{\rho(x,\theta)}{\phi(\rho(x,\theta))}\cdot G''\Big(\log_\phi^N(\rho(x,\theta))-\log_\phi^N(\rho(x,\theta_0))\Big)\Big\}dx.$$

We replace $\theta:=\theta_0$, and we use the property $G(0)=0$. It follows that

$$\hat{g}_{jk}(\theta_0):=\frac{\partial^2 A}{\partial\theta^j\partial\theta^k}\Big|_{\theta=\theta_0}=\int_X \frac{\partial^2\rho(x,\theta_0)}{\partial\theta^j\partial\theta^k}\cdot\Big\{G(0)+\frac{\rho(x,\theta_0)}{\phi(\rho(x,\theta_0))}\cdot G'(0)\Big\}+$$

$$+\frac{\partial\rho(x,\theta_0)}{\partial\theta^j}\cdot\frac{\partial\rho(x,\theta_0)}{\partial\theta^k}\cdot\frac{1}{\phi(\rho(x,\theta_0))}\cdot\Big\{G'(0)+\frac{\rho(x,\theta_0)}{\phi(\rho(x,\theta_0))}\cdot G''(0)+$$

$$+G'(0)\cdot\frac{\phi(\rho(x,\theta_0))-\rho(x,\theta_0)\cdot\phi'(\rho(x,\theta_0))}{\phi(\rho(x,\theta_0))}\Big\}dx=$$

$$=G'(0)\cdot\int_X \frac{\partial^2\rho(x,\theta_0)}{\partial\theta^j\partial\theta^k}\cdot\frac{\rho(x,\theta_0)}{\phi(\rho(x,\theta_0))}dx+$$

$$+\int_X \phi(\rho(x,\theta_0))\cdot\frac{\partial}{\partial\theta^j}\log_\phi^N(\rho(x,\theta_0))\cdot\frac{\partial}{\partial\theta^k}\log_\phi^N(\rho(x,\theta_0))\cdot$$

$$\cdot G'(0)\cdot\Big\{2-\frac{\rho(x,\theta_0)\cdot\phi'(\rho(x,\theta_0))}{\phi(\rho(x,\theta_0))}\Big\}dx+$$

$$+G''(0)\cdot\int_X \rho(x,\theta_0)\cdot\frac{\partial}{\partial\theta^j}\log_\phi^N(\rho(x,\theta_0))\cdot\frac{\partial}{\partial\theta^k}\log_\phi^N(\rho(x,\theta_0))dx.$$

From the last suite of formulas, we obtain both (26) and (27). □

Suppose, moreover, that $G(t)=t$. Then, we have

$$\hat{g}_{jk}(\theta_0)=\int_X\Big\{\frac{\partial^2\rho(x,\theta_0)}{\partial\theta^j\partial\theta^k}\cdot\frac{\rho(x,\theta_0)}{\phi(\rho(x,\theta_0))}+2\frac{\partial\rho(x,\theta_0)}{\partial\theta^j}\cdot\frac{\partial\rho(x,\theta_0)}{\partial\theta^k}\cdot\frac{1}{\phi(\rho(x,\theta_0))}-\quad(28)$$

$$-\frac{\partial\rho(x,\theta_0)}{\partial\theta^j}\cdot\frac{\partial\rho(x,\theta_0)}{\partial\theta^k}\cdot\frac{\rho(x,\theta_0)\cdot\phi'(\rho(x,\theta_0))}{\phi^2(\rho(x,\theta_0))}\Big\}dx.$$

We re-write this formula in a condensed form, and we obtain the following result, which completes Corollary 1.

Corollary 2. *With the previous notations, for $G(t) = t$, we obtain*

$$\hat{g} = -h - \alpha.$$

By analogy, starting with a generalized (quotient) group relative entropy (a.k.a. the generalized (quotient) group divergence) $\tilde{D}_{G,\phi} = \tilde{D}_{G,\phi}(\rho \parallel \sigma)(\theta, \theta_0)$, as particularization from (9), we shall obtain, in the sequel, other Fisher-like metrics, similar to the ones in Proposition 2 and Corollary 2.

Denote the generalized group Fisher metric associated with $\tilde{D}_{G,\phi}$ by

$$\tilde{g}_{jk}(\theta_0) := \frac{\partial^2 \tilde{D}_{G,\phi}(\rho \parallel \sigma)(\theta, \theta_0)}{\partial \theta^j \partial \theta^k} \bigg|_{\theta=\theta_0}. \tag{29}$$

Proposition 3. *With the previous notations, we have the relation*

$$\tilde{g} = \left\{ G'(0) \cdot \left[\frac{2}{\phi(1)} - \frac{\phi'(1)}{\phi^2(1)} \right] + G''(0) \cdot \frac{1}{\phi^2(1)} \right\} \cdot g^0, \tag{30}$$

where g^0 denotes the classical Fisher metric.

Proof. We adapt the proof of Proposition 2, from the divergence $D_{G,\phi}$ to the divergence $\tilde{D}_{G,\phi}$. Suppose that θ_0 is constant. Denote

$$\tilde{A}(\theta) := \tilde{D}_{G,\phi}(\rho(x,\theta) \parallel \rho(x,\theta_0)).$$

It follows that

$$\frac{\partial \tilde{A}}{\partial \theta^k}(\theta) = \int_X \left\{ \frac{\partial \rho(x,\theta)}{\partial \theta^k} \cdot G\left(\log_\phi^N \left[\frac{\rho(x,\theta)}{\rho(x,\theta_0)} \right] \right) + \right.$$

$$\left. + \rho(x,\theta) \cdot G'\left(\log_\phi^N \left[\frac{\rho(x,\theta)}{\rho(x,\theta_0)} \right] \right) \cdot \frac{\partial}{\partial \theta^k} \log_\phi^N \left[\frac{\rho(x,\theta)}{\rho(x,\theta_0)} \right] \right\} dx =$$

$$= \int_X \left\{ \frac{\partial \rho(x,\theta)}{\partial \theta^k} \cdot G\left(\log_\phi^N \left[\frac{\rho(x,\theta)}{\rho(x,\theta_0)} \right] \right) + \right.$$

$$\left. + \rho(x,\theta) \cdot G'\left(\log_\phi^N \left[\frac{\rho(x,\theta)}{\rho(x,\theta_0)} \right] \right) \cdot \phi^{-1}\left(\frac{\rho(x,\theta)}{\rho(x,\theta_0)} \right) \cdot \rho^{-1}(x,\theta_0) \cdot \frac{\partial \rho(x,\theta)}{\partial \theta^k} \right\} dx =$$

$$= \int_X \frac{\partial \rho(x,\theta)}{\partial \theta^k} \cdot \left\{ G\left(\log_\phi^N \left[\frac{\rho(x,\theta)}{\rho(x,\theta_0)} \right] \right) + \right.$$

$$\left. + \rho(x,\theta) \cdot G'\left(\log_\phi^N \left[\frac{\rho(x,\theta)}{\rho(x,\theta_0)} \right] \right) \cdot \phi^{-1}\left(\frac{\rho(x,\theta)}{\rho(x,\theta_0)} \right) \cdot \rho^{-1}(x,\theta_0) \right\} dx$$

and

$$\frac{\partial^2 A}{\partial \theta^j \partial \theta^k}(\theta) = \int_X \frac{\partial^2 \rho(x,\theta)}{\partial \theta^j \partial \theta^k} \cdot \left\{ G\left(\log_\phi^N \left[\frac{\rho(x,\theta)}{\rho(x,\theta_0)} \right] \right) + \right.$$

$$\left. + \rho(x,\theta) \cdot \phi^{-1}\left(\frac{\rho(x,\theta)}{\rho(x,\theta_0)} \right) \cdot \rho^{-1}(x,\theta_0) \cdot G'\left(\log_\phi^N \left[\frac{\rho(x,\theta)}{\rho(x,\theta_0)} \right] \right) \right\} +$$

$$+ \frac{\partial \rho(x,\theta)}{\partial \theta^k} \cdot \left\{ \phi^{-1}\left(\frac{\rho(x,\theta)}{\rho(x,\theta_0)} \right) \cdot \rho^{-1}(x,\theta_0) \cdot \frac{\partial \rho(x,\theta)}{\partial \theta^j} \cdot G'\left(\log_\phi^N \left[\frac{\rho(x,\theta)}{\rho(x,\theta_0)} \right] \right) + \right.$$

$$\left. + G'\left(\log_\phi^N \left[\frac{\rho(x,\theta)}{\rho(x,\theta_0)} \right] \right) \cdot \phi^{-2}\left(\frac{\rho(x,\theta)}{\rho(x,\theta_0)} \right) \cdot \frac{\partial \rho(x,\theta)}{\partial \theta^j} \right..$$

$$\cdot \left[\rho^{-1}(x,\theta_0) \cdot \phi\big(\frac{\rho(x,\theta)}{\rho(x,\theta_0)}\big) - \rho(x,\theta) \cdot \rho^{-2}(x,\theta_0) \cdot \phi'\big(\frac{\rho(x,\theta)}{\rho(x,\theta_0)}\big)\right] +$$

$$+\rho(x,\theta) \cdot \phi^{-2}\big(\frac{\rho(x,\theta)}{\rho(x,\theta_0)}\big) \cdot \rho^{-2}(x,\theta_0) \cdot G''\Big(\log_\phi^N\Big[\frac{\rho(x,\theta)}{\rho(x,\theta_0)}\Big]\Big) \cdot \frac{\partial \rho(x,\theta)}{\partial \theta^j}\Big\}dx .$$

We assign $\theta := \theta_0$, and we use the property $G(0) = 0$. We obtain

$$\bar{g}_{jk}(\theta_0) := \frac{\partial^2 A}{\partial \theta^j \partial \theta^k}\Big|_{\theta=\theta_0} = \int_X \frac{\partial^2 \rho(x,\theta_0)}{\partial \theta^j \partial \theta^k} \cdot \Big\{G(0) + \frac{1}{\phi(1)} \cdot G'(0)\Big\} +$$

$$+ \frac{\partial \rho(x,\theta_0)}{\partial \theta^j} \cdot \frac{\partial \rho(x,\theta_0)}{\partial \theta^k} \cdot \frac{1}{\rho(x,\theta_0)} \cdot \Big\{\frac{1}{\phi(1)} \cdot G'(0) + \frac{1}{\phi^2(1)} \cdot G''(0) +$$

$$+ G'(0) \cdot \frac{\phi(1)) - \phi'(1)}{\phi^2(1)}\Big\}dx = \Big[G'(0 \cdot \Big(\frac{2}{\phi(1)} - \frac{\phi'(1)}{\phi^2(1)}\Big) + G''(0) \cdot \frac{1}{\phi^2(1)}\Big] \cdot$$

$$\cdot \int_X \rho^{-1}(x,\theta_0)) \cdot \frac{\partial \rho(x,\theta_0)}{\partial \theta^j} \cdot \frac{\partial \rho(x,\theta_0)}{\partial \theta^k} + G'(0) \cdot \frac{1}{\phi(1)} \cdot \int_X \frac{\partial^2 \rho(x,\theta_0)}{\partial \theta^j \partial \theta^k}dx.$$

The first integral equals $g^0_{jk}(\theta_0)$. The second integral is null because $\int_X \rho(x,\theta)dx = 1$. We obtained Formula (30). □

Remark 2. *(i) In Proposition 1, we establish the basic formulas for the future development of associated Riemannian geometries determined by g, g̃, h, α, β, in terms of the function φ-deformed (Naudts) entropy (curvature, geodesics, Riemannian distance in the positive definite case). Examples of scalar curvature functions derived from these formulas will be shown in the next section. The coefficients of GFM1 g extend known ones from [29], derived for PDFs of exponential type and for particular functions φ. The other Fisher metrics are new.*

An interesting consequence of Proposition 1 is the fact that g and g̃ do not coincide, as in the case of the Neperian logarithm. This can be seen directly, by comparing their φ-dependent coefficients.

(ii) In Proposition 2, we derive the Fisher-like metric ĝ associated with the divergence $D_{G,\phi}$, as a generalization of a construction in [30] for the case of a Kullback–Leibler divergence, of a trivial group logarithm $G = id$ and for PDFs of exponential type.

(iii) In Proposition 3, the Fisher-like metric ĝ associated with the divergence $\tilde{D}_{G,\phi}$ is—to our knowledge—completely new.

The metrics in Formula (30) are homothetic, via a constant $k_{G,\phi}$ supposed—implicitly—to be not null. It is interesting that $k_{G,\phi}$ depends only on the behavior of the deformation function φ, for or around 1 and on G, around 0. Its independence on the PDFs gives $k_{G,\phi}$ an "universality" feature, which corresponds—probably—to some special uncovered property of the statistical model.

Suppose, moreover, that $G(t) = t$. We replace in (30) the values $G'(0) = 1$ and $G''(0) = 0$, and we obtain

$$\bar{g} = \Big[\frac{2}{\phi(1)} - \frac{\phi'(1)}{\phi^2(1)}\Big] \cdot g^0. \tag{31}$$

5. Examples

We particularize now the results from Section 4, for the case when ρ is an exponential PDF and $m = 1$, $n = 2$. The deforming function φ will be chosen conveniently, in order to be able to compute the integrals.

Let $X := \mathbb{R}$ and $\rho : \mathbb{R} \times \mathbb{R} \times (0,\infty) \to \mathbb{R}$ be the exponential (normal) PDF given by

$$\rho(x;\theta^1,\theta^2) = \frac{1}{\sqrt{2\pi\theta^2}} \cdot e^{-\frac{(x-\theta^1)^2}{2(\theta^2)^2}}. \tag{32}$$

We denote the partial derivatives of ρ, with respect to the variables θ^1 and θ^2, by ρ_1, ρ_2, ρ_{11}, ρ_{12}, ρ_{22}. A short calculation ([34]) leads to the formulas

$$\rho_1 = \frac{x - \theta^1}{(\theta^2)^2} \cdot \rho \quad , \quad \rho_2 = \{\frac{(x - \theta^1)^2}{(\theta^2)^3} - \frac{1}{\theta^2}\} \cdot \rho,$$

$$\rho_{11} = \{\frac{(x - \theta^1)^2}{(\theta^2)^4} - \frac{1}{(\theta^2)^2}\} \cdot \rho \quad , \quad \rho_{12} = \{\frac{(x - \theta^1)^3}{(\theta^2)^5} - \frac{3(x - \theta^1)}{(\theta^2)^3}\} \cdot \rho,$$

$$\rho_{22} = \{\frac{(x - \theta^1)^4}{(\theta^2)^6} - \frac{5(x - \theta^1)^2}{(\theta^2)^4} + \frac{2}{(\theta^2)^2}\} \cdot \rho.$$

The classical Fisher metric g^0 has the coefficients $g^0_{11} = (\theta^2)^{-2}$, $g^0_{12} = g^0_{21} = 0$ and $g^0_{22} = 2(\theta^2)^{-2}$ (see, for example, [2,34]).

For future calculations, we shall use the following simple result.

Lemma 1. *Let c, k_1, k_2 be fixed real constants, with $k_1 \neq 0$, $k_2 \neq 0$. Then, the semi-Riemannian metric*

$$y^{-c} \cdot \begin{bmatrix} k_1 & 0 \\ 0 & k_2 \end{bmatrix}$$

on the set $y \neq 0$ in $\mathbb{R}^2$ has the scalar curvature

$$-\frac{c}{2k_2} \cdot y^{c-2}.$$

In the sequel, we give examples of the semi-Riemannian metrics from Propositions 1–3, under various particular assumptions.

I—The case of g. Suppose $\phi(t) := t^c$, with $c \in (0,2)$ an arbitrary fixed parameter. From Formula (22), we calculate the coefficients

$$g_{11} = K_1(c) \cdot (\theta^2)^{c-3} \quad , \quad g_{12} = g_{21} = 0 \quad , \quad g_{22} = K_2(c) \cdot (\theta^2)^{c-3},$$

where

$$K_1(c) = (2-c)^{-\frac{3}{2}} \cdot (\sqrt{2\pi})^{c-1} \quad , \quad K_2(c) = (c^3 - 4c^2 + 6c - 1) \cdot (2-c)^{-\frac{5}{2}} \cdot (\sqrt{2\pi})^{c-1}.$$

There exists a unique $c_0 \in (0.18, 0.19)$ such that $K_2(c_0) = 0$. For this value, g is degenerated. The metric g is Lorentzian, when $c \in (0, c_0)$ and is Riemannian, when $c \in (c_0, 2)$.

The scalar curvature $S^{\{c\}} = S^{\{c\}}(\theta)$ of g is

$$S^{\{c\}}(\theta) = \frac{1}{2K_2(c)} \cdot (c - 3) \cdot (\theta^2)^{1-c}.$$

The scalar curvature $S^{\{c\}}$ does not vanish anywhere, and its sign is the opposite sign of $K_2(c)$. Moreover, $S^{\{c\}}$ is constant if and only if $c = 1$, i.e., only in the case when g is the classical Fisher metric g_0. If we decide to use the scalar curvature as a control, this may lead to a quick criterion to distinguish the BGS entropy case from the ϕ-deformed (Naudts) entropy case. (The statistical interpretation of the scalar curvature of the Fisher metrics may be found in [20]).

We depicted in Figure 1 (and magnified in Figure 2 around $c = 1$ and in Figure 3 around $c = 0.19$) how $S^{\{c\}}$ varies w.r.t. c and θ^2 (denoted t).

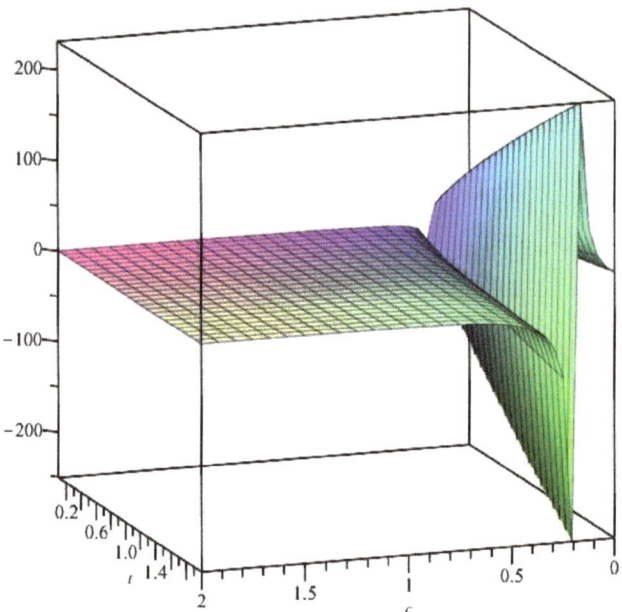

Figure 1. The variation of $S^{\{c\}}$ w.r.t. $c \in (0, c_0) \cup (c_0, 2)$ and $\theta^2 := t$.

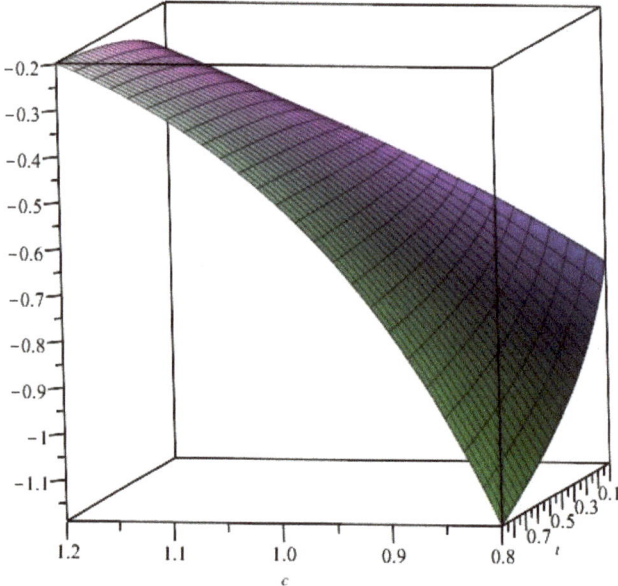

Figure 2. The variation of $S^{\{c\}}$ w.r.t. $c \in (0.8, 1.2)$ and $\theta^2 := t$.

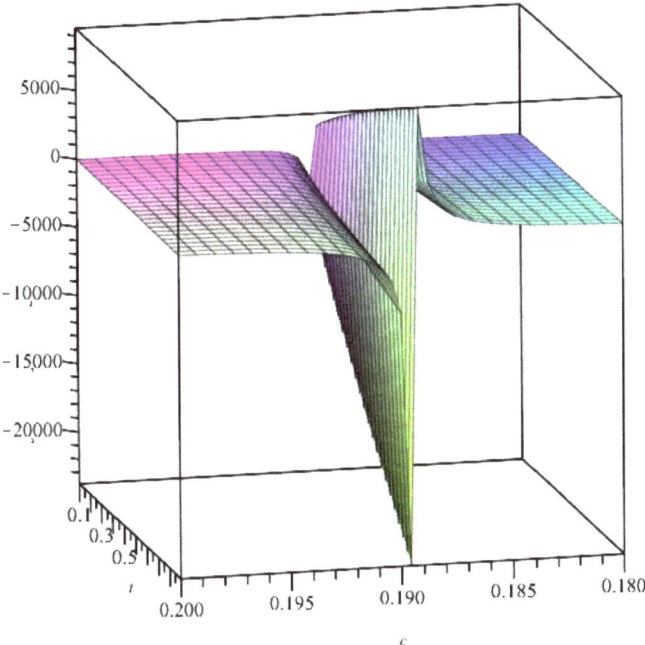

Figure 3. The variation of $S^{\{c\}}$ w.r.t. $c \in (0.18, 0.20)$ and $\theta^2 := t$.

II—The case of $\tilde{g}$. Suppose $\phi(t) := t^c$, with $c \in (0, \frac{3}{2})$ an arbitrary fixed parameter. From Formula (23), we calculate the coefficients

$$\tilde{g}_{11} = \tilde{K}_1(c) \cdot (\theta^2)^{2c-4} \quad , \quad \tilde{g}_{12} = \tilde{g}_{21} = 0 \quad , \quad \tilde{g}_{22} = \tilde{K}_2(c) \cdot (\theta^2)^{2c-4},$$

where

$$\tilde{K}_1(c) = (3 - 2c)^{-\frac{3}{2}} \cdot (\sqrt{2\pi})^{2c-2} \quad , \quad \tilde{K}_2(c) = (4c^2 - 8c + 6) \cdot (3 - 2c)^{-\frac{5}{2}} \cdot (\sqrt{2\pi})^{2c-2}.$$

The scalar curvature $\tilde{S}^{\{c\}} = \tilde{S}^{\{c\}}(\theta)$ of the Riemannian metric $\tilde{g}$ is

$$\tilde{S}^{\{c\}}(\theta) = \frac{1}{\tilde{K}_2(c)} \cdot (c - 2) \cdot (\theta^2)^{2-2c}.$$

We mention that: the scalar curvature is negative; it decreases indefinitely as the variable θ^2 grows and the parameter c goes to 0; it tends to 0 as c goes to $\frac{3}{2}$. We depicted in Figure 4 how $\tilde{S}^{\{c\}}$ varies w.r.t. c and θ^2 (denoted t).

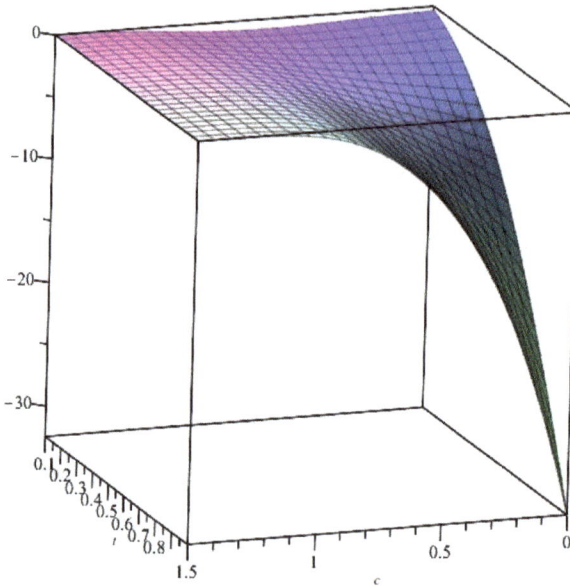

Figure 4. The variation of $\tilde{S}^{\{c\}}$ w.r.t. c and $\theta^2 := t$.

III—The case of h. Suppose $\phi(t) := t^c$, with $c \in (0,2)$ an arbitrary fixed parameter. From Formula (24), we calculate the coefficients

$$h_{11} = h_{12} = h_{21} = 0 \quad , \quad h_{22} = K_4(c) \cdot (\theta^2)^{c-3},$$

where

$$K_4(c) = -(2-c)^{\frac{1}{2}} \cdot (\sqrt{2\pi})^{c-1}.$$

As the (0,2)-type tensor field h is degenerated, it does not define a semi-Riemannian metric. In this case, there is no scalar curvature to compute.

IV—The case of α. Suppose $\phi(t) := t^c$, with $c \in (0,2)$ an arbitrary fixed parameter. From Formula (17) or from Proposition 1, we calculate the coefficients

$$\alpha_{11} = K_5(c) \cdot (\theta^2)^{c-3} \quad , \quad \alpha_{12} = \alpha_{21} = 0 \quad , \quad \alpha_{22} = K_6(c) \cdot (\theta^2)^{c-3},$$

where

$$K_5(c) = -(\sqrt{2\pi})^{c-1} \cdot (2-c)^{-\frac{3}{2}} \quad , \quad K_6(c) = (1-2c) \cdot (2-c)^{-\frac{5}{2}} \cdot (\sqrt{2\pi})^{c-1}.$$

The (0,2)-type tensor field α is degenerated for $c = \frac{1}{2}$. If $c \in (0, \frac{1}{2})$, then α is a Lorentzian metric. If $c \in (\frac{1}{2}, 2)$, then $(-\alpha)$ is a Riemannian metric.

The scalar curvature $U^{\{c\}} = U^{\{c\}}(\theta)$ of $(-\alpha)$ is

$$U^{\{c\}}(\theta) = \frac{1}{2K_6(c)} \cdot (3-c) \cdot (\theta^2)^{1-c}.$$

and has the sign of K_6. We depicted in Figure 5 how $U^{\{c\}}$ varies w.r.t. c and θ^2 (denoted t).

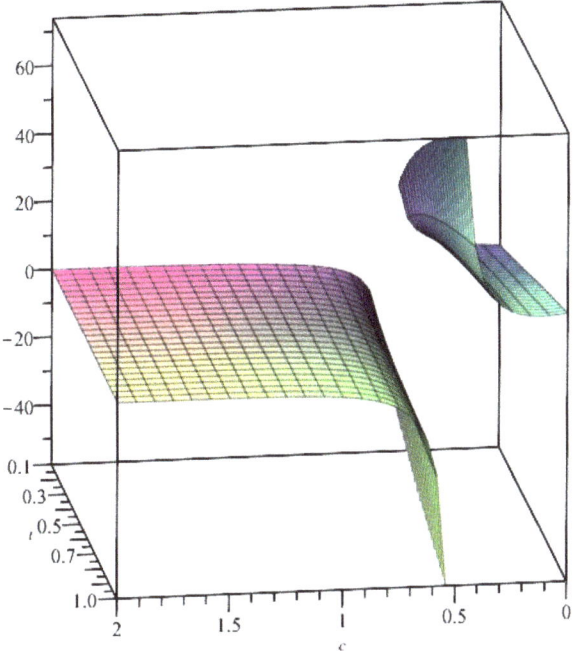

Figure 5. The variation of $U^{\{c\}}$ w.r.t. c and $\theta^2 := t$.

V—The case of β. Suppose $\phi(t) := t^c$, with $c \in (0,2)$ an arbitrary fixed parameter. From Formula (18) or from Proposition 1, we calculate the coefficients

$$\beta_{11} = K_7(c) \cdot (\theta^2)^{c-3}, \quad \beta_{12} = \beta_{21} = 0, \quad \beta_{22} = K_8(c) \cdot (\theta^2)^{c-3},$$

where

$$K_7(c) = 2(\sqrt{2\pi})^{c-1}(2-c)^{-\frac{3}{2}}, \quad K_8(c) = 2(c^2 - 2c + 3) \cdot (2-c)^{-\frac{5}{2}} \cdot (\sqrt{2\pi})^{c-1}.$$

The scalar curvature $V^{\{c\}} = V^{\{c\}}(\theta)$ of β is

$$V^{\{c\}}(\theta) = \frac{1}{2K_8(c)} \cdot (c-3) \cdot (\theta^2)^{1-c}.$$

and takes negative values. We depicted in Figure 6 how $V^{\{c\}}$ varies w.r.t. c and θ^2 (denoted t).

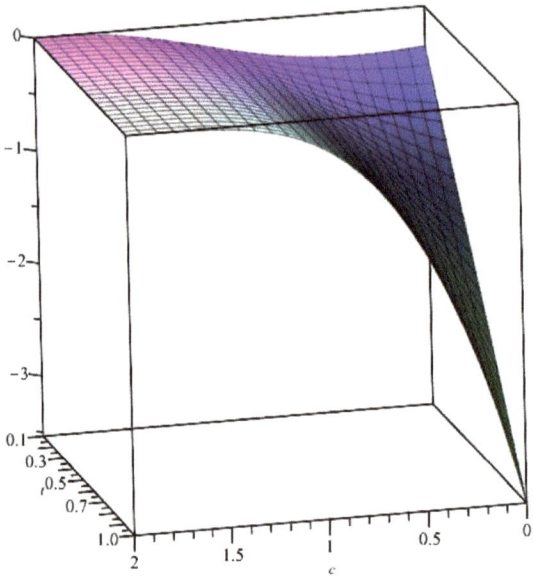

Figure 6. The variation of $V^{\{c\}}$ w.r.t. c and $\theta^2 := t$.

VI—The case of $\hat{g}$. Suppose $\phi(t) := t^c$, with $c \in (0, \frac{3}{2})$ an arbitrary fixed parameter. From Formula (27), we calculate the coefficients

$$\hat{g}_{11} = K_9(c) \cdot (\theta^2)^{c-3} + K_{10}(c) \cdot (\theta^2)^{2c-3},$$

$$\hat{g}_{12} = \hat{g}_{21} = 0,$$

$$\hat{g}_{22} = K_{11}(c) \cdot (\theta^2)^{c-3} + K_{12}(c) \cdot (\theta^2)^{2c-3},$$

where

$$K_9(c) = G'(0) \cdot (\sqrt{2\pi})^{c-1} \cdot (2-c)^{-\frac{3}{2}},$$

$$K_{10}(c) = G''(0) \cdot (\sqrt{2\pi})^{2c-2} \cdot (3-2c)^{-\frac{3}{2}},$$

$$K_{11}(c) = -G'(0) \cdot (\sqrt{2\pi})^{c-1} \cdot (2-c)^{-\frac{5}{2}} \cdot (c^3 - 6c^2 + 10c - 7),$$

$$K_{12}(c) = G''(0) \cdot (\sqrt{2\pi})^{2c-2} \cdot (3-2c)^{-\frac{5}{2}} \cdot (4c^2 - 8c + 6).$$

We suppose that the group logarithm G is chosen such that $\hat{g}$ be non-degenerated. The scalar curvature $\hat{S}^{\{c\}} = \hat{S}^{\{c\}}(\theta)$ of $\hat{g}$ is calculated using MAPLE:

$$\hat{S}^{\{c\}}(\theta) = \frac{1}{4} \cdot (\theta^2)^{-2} \cdot (K_{12}(\theta^2)^c + K_{11})^{-2} (K_{10}(\theta^2)^c + K_9)^{-3} \cdot \Big\{ (\theta^2)^3 \cdot \Big[K_9^3 K_{12} c^2 -$$

$$- K_9^3 K_{12} c - 18 K_9^2 K_{10} K_{11} - 3 K_9^2 K_{10} K_{11} c^2 + 11 K_9 K_{10} K_{11} c - 6 K_9^3 K_{12} \Big] +$$

$$+ (\theta^2)^{3+c} \cdot \Big[-18 K_9^2 K_{10} K_{12} - 18 K_9 K_{10}^2 K_{11} + 2 K_9^2 K_{10} K_{12} c - 5 K_9 K_{10}^2 K_{11} c^2 +$$

$$+ 16 K_9 K_{10}^2 K_{11} c + K_9^2 K_{10} K_{12} c^2 \Big] + (\theta^2)^{3+2c} \cdot \Big[-18 K_9 K_{10}^2 K_{12} - 2 K_{10}^3 K_{11} c^2 +$$

$$+ 7 K_{10}^3 K_{11} c + 7 K_9 K_{10}^2 K_{12} c - 6 K_{10}^3 K_{11} \Big] + (\theta^2)^{3-c} \cdot \Big[2 K_9^3 K_{11} c - 6 K_9^3 K_{11} \Big] +$$

$$+ (\theta^2)^{3+3c} \cdot \Big[4 K_{10}^3 K_{12} c - 6 K_{10}^3 K_{12} \Big] \Big\}.$$

Interestingly, the scalar curvature $\hat{S}^{\{c\}}$ is a rational function of θ^2 and $(\theta^2)^c$.

We particularize now the setting for the BGS group logarithm $G(t) := t$ and replace $G'(0) = 1$ and $G''(0) = 0$ in the previous formulas. Then,

$$\hat{g}_{11} = K_9(c) \cdot (\theta^2)^{c-3}, \quad \hat{g}_{12} = \hat{g}_{21} = 0, \quad \hat{g}_{22} = K_{11}(c) \cdot (\theta^2)^{c-3},$$

where

$$K_9(c) = (\sqrt{2\pi})^{c-1} \cdot (2-c)^{-\frac{3}{2}},$$
$$K_{11}(c) = -(\sqrt{2\pi})^{c-1} \cdot (2-c)^{-\frac{5}{2}} \cdot (c^3 - 6c^2 + 10c - 7).$$

In this particular case, the scalar curvature $\hat{S}^{\{c\}} = \hat{S}^{\{c\}}(\theta)$ of the Riemannian metric $\hat{g}$ has the form:

$$\hat{S}^{\{c\}}(\theta) = \frac{1}{2K_{11}(c)} \cdot (c-3) \cdot (\theta^2)^{1-c}.$$

(The same formula may be recovered, directly, by using Lemma 1.) We mention that $\hat{S}^{\{c\}}$ takes negative values, for every $c \in (0,2)$. In Figure 7, we depicted how this particular $\hat{S}^{\{c\}}$ varies w.r.t. c and θ^2 (denoted t).

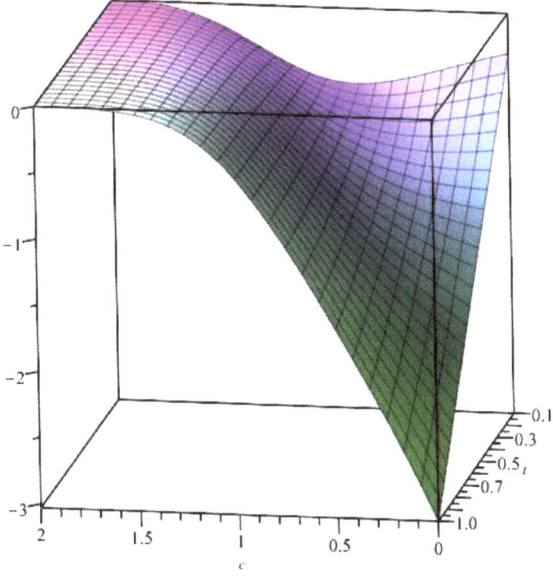

Figure 7. The variation of $\hat{S}^{\{c\}}$ w.r.t. c and $\theta^2 := t$.

VII—The case of $\overline{g}$. From (30), we have the coefficients of $\overline{g}$:

$$\overline{g}_{11} = k_{G,\phi} \cdot (\theta^2)^{-2}, \quad \overline{g}_{12} = \overline{g}_{21} = 0, \quad \overline{g}_{22}^0 = 2k_{G,\phi} \cdot (\theta^2)^{-2},$$

where

$$k_{G,\phi} = G'(0) \cdot \left[\frac{2}{\phi(1)} - \frac{\phi'(1)}{\phi^2(1)}\right] + G''(0) \cdot \frac{1}{\phi^2(1)}.$$

For the moment, we suppose that G and ϕ are suitable chosen, such that $k_{G,\phi} > 0$. It follows that $\overline{g}$ is a Riemannian metric. As the scalar curvature of g^0 is a negative constant $S^0 = -\frac{1}{2}$, we deduce the scalar curvature of $\overline{g}$ is a negative constant $\overline{S} = -\frac{1}{2} \cdot k_{G,\phi}$ w.r.t. θ too. In what follows, we study the variance of $\overline{S}$ in two particular cases.

VII_1. Let $G(t) := t$ be the BGS grup logarithm function and consider $\phi(t) := t^{a^2} + e^{t^{b^3}}$, where the real parameters a and b satisfy $a^2 + eb^3 < 2(1+e)$. Denote the respective metrics by $\overline{g}^{\{a,b\}}$ and their scalar curvatures by $\overline{S}^{\{a,b\}}$. Then,

$$\overline{S}^{\{a,b\}} = -\frac{1}{2} \cdot \left\{ \frac{2}{1+e} - \frac{a^2 + eb^3}{(1+e)^2} \right\}.$$

We mention that $k_{G,\phi} > 0$ (and hence $\overline{S}^{\{a,b\}} < 0$). The dependency of $\overline{S}^{\{a,b\}}$ w.r.t. a and b may be seen in Figure 8.

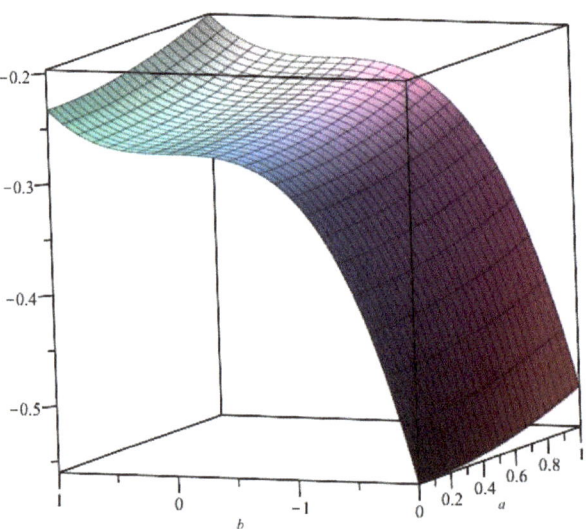

Figure 8. The variation of $\overline{S}^{\{a,b\}}$ w.r.t. a and b.

The family of Fisher-like Riemannian metrics $\overline{g}^{\{a,b\}}$ may be considered as evolving from the classical Fisher metric g^0. Their evolution may be controlled through their scalar curvature.

VII_2. Let $G(t) := \frac{e^{(1-q)t} - 1}{1-q}$ be the Tsallis grup logarithm function, where $q \neq 1$. Let us define $\phi(t) := t^{a^2} + e^{t^{b^3}}$, with real parameters a and b satisfying $a^2 + e \cdot b^3 + q - 1 < 2(1+e)$. We denote the associated metric by $\overline{g}^{\{a,b;q\}}$ and its scalar curvature by $\overline{S}^{\{a,b;q\}}$. Then,

$$\overline{S}^{\{a,b;q\}} = -\frac{1}{2} \cdot \left\{ \frac{2}{1+e} - \frac{a^2 + eb^3 + q - 1}{(1+e)^2} \right\}.$$

We mention that $k_{G,\phi} > 0$ (and hence $\overline{S}^{\{a,b;q\}} < 0$). The dependency of $\overline{S}^{\{a,b;q\}}$ w.r.t. a and b may be seen in Figure 9, for q taking successively the values 1,11,21,31 (from bottom to top). The value $q = 1$ is no longer a forbidden (singular) one!

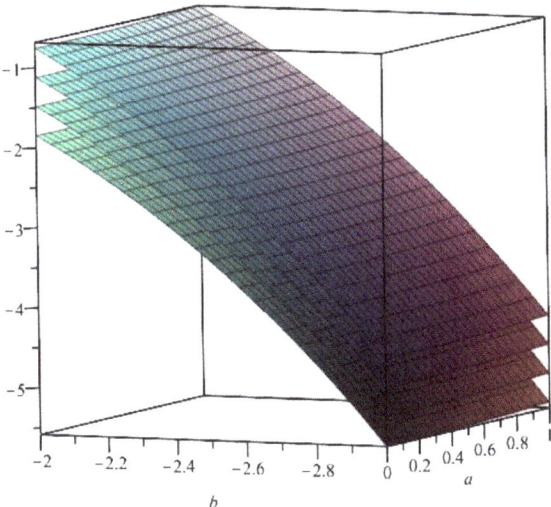

Figure 9. The variation of $\overline{S}^{\{a,b;q\}}$ w.r.t. a and b, when $q \in \{1, 11, 21, 31\}$.

The family of Fisher-like Riemannian metrics $\overline{g}^{\{a,b;q\}}$ may be considered as evolving from the classical Fisher metric g^0, and also as "expanding" from the BGS group logarithm to the q-dependent Tsallis group logarithm. The evolution of these metrics may be controlled through their scalar curvature, which, in addition to the previous case VII_1, "foliates" following the values of q.

Remark 3. *(i) The parameters' domains are subsets of $\mathbb{R} \times (0, \infty)$, which is two-dimensional. Therefore, for all the metrics in this section, the scalar curvature coincides with the Gaussian curvature. The coefficients of the metrics depend on the variable θ^2 only, which has the signification of standard deviation. It follows that the scalar curvature functions are also independent on the mean of the PDF modeled by θ^1. This dependence of the geometric invariants only on the standard deviation suggests applications where a similar property appears: see, for example, [50–54].*

(ii) Using general differential geometric arguments, we knew a priori that the metrics must be (locally) conformal with the Euclidean (or Minkowskian) metric of the plane. However, we obtained more: the conformal factors are explicitly derived, they are global and, as expected, they are also independent of the mean θ^1. Moreover, the metric $\overline{g}$ in example VII is even homothetic with the Euclidean metric.

If we consider a curve in the parameters space, its length (w.r.t any of the respective metrics) depends only on the standard deviation; instead, the angle of two such curves does not depend on either the mean or the standard deviation.

(iii) The statistical significance of the sectional curvature of Fisher-like metrics $g, \tilde{g}, h, \beta, \hat{g}, \overline{g}$ can be obtained by analogy with Ruppeiner's geometric modelization of the Gaussian thermodynamic fluctuations [55]. His "thermodynamic curvature" (R) corresponds to the sectional curvature and measures the inter-particles interaction: when $R = 0$, there is no interaction, and the cases $R > 0$ or $R < 0$ correspond to repulsive or attractive interactions, respectively ([55], apud [48,56]). This approach was developed and generalized by the Geometrothermodynamics theory [57].

Another viewpoint interprets the scalar curvature as a measure of the stability of the statistical model, in a direct proportionality relation ([58], apud [59]).

(iv) It may be worth noting the following special property, apparently collateral to the main path of the discourse. Let us fix a value of the Tsallis parameter q_0 and a value of the scalar curvature $\overline{S}^{\{a,b;q_0\}}$ in example VII_2, denoted by s_0. Then, the solution of the equation

$$s_0 = -\frac{1}{2} \cdot \left\{ \frac{2}{1+e} - \frac{a^2 + eb^3 + q_0 - 1}{(1+e)^2} \right\}$$

is an elliptic curve in the plane of coordinates (a, b), written in Weierstrass form. In Figure 10, we drew these elliptic curves, corresponding to $s_0 = -1$ and to $q_0 \in \{1, -51, -101, -1001\}$ (from left to right).

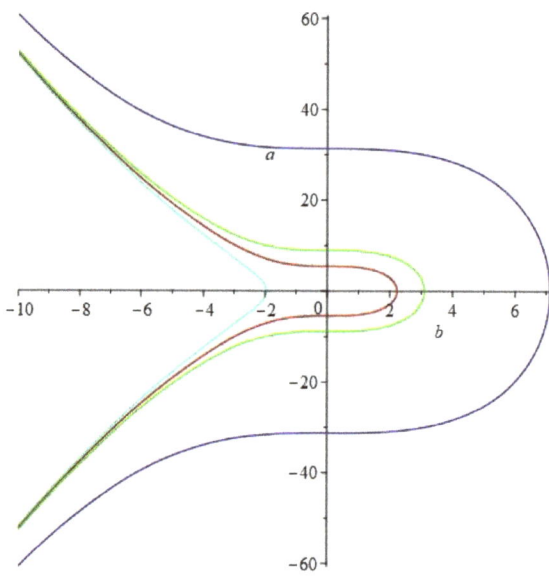

Figure 10. The elliptic curves associated with $s_0 = -1$ and $q_0 \in \{1, -51, -101, -1001\}$.

6. The MaxEnt Problem for the ϕ-Deformed (Naudts) Entropy

Let $V = V(x)$ be a fixed potential energy function, ϕ be a fixed positive strictly-increasing function and $U_0 > 0$ be a fixed real number. Consider $\rho = \rho(x)$ a univariate PDF, satisfying

$$\int_{\mathbb{R}} V(x)\rho(x)dx = U_0$$

and let $H^N_\phi[\rho]$ be its associated ϕ-deformed (Naudts) entropy, based on (5).

Theorem 1. *The optimization problem*

$$\max H^N_\phi[\rho]$$

has the solution

$$\rho^{ME}_\phi(x) = \exp^N_{\{\phi\}}\left[\gamma + \beta V(x)\right], \tag{33}$$

where $\exp^N_{\{\phi\}}$ is the inverse function of $\log^N_{\{\phi\}}$; β and γ are the Lagrange multipliers determined by the constraints, and satisfy the inequality $\gamma + \beta V(x) > 0$.

Proof. The proof is a standard one; see, for example, [60], §12.1. □

Remark 4. Under the previous hypothesis, we denote: the (maximal) ϕ-deformed (Naudts) entropy $H := H^N_\phi[\rho^{ME}_\phi]$; the mean force with respect to ρ^{ME}_ϕ

$$U := \int_{\mathbb{R}} V(x) \cdot \rho^{ME}_\phi(x) dx;$$

the ϕ-deformed generalized free energy

$$F := -\frac{\gamma}{\beta}.$$

We obtain ϕ-deformed generalizations of the thermodynamic relations:

$$F = U + \frac{1}{\beta} H \quad , \quad \frac{d}{d\beta}(\beta F) = U.$$

In the previous relations, all the notions depend on ϕ; we skipped it, in order to keep the formalism simpler. For some physical interpretations, we recommend [29,61,62]. In the particular cases when the ϕ-deformed (Naudts) entropy is of Tsallis or of Kaniadakis type, we recover the formulas from [38,39].

7. Conclusions

(i) In this paper, we refined the search of relevant semi-Riemannian metrics associated in a canonical manner to manifolds of parameterized PDfs, via remarkable entropies and divergences. We stress the main general ideas:

- We made the distinction between quotient divergence and difference divergence, leading to different metrics g and $\tilde{g}$ (see Example 2 (i), (ii) and Formulas (14) and (15));
- We defined the (0,2)-type tensor fields α and β, as possible candidates for Fisher-like metrics (see (17) and (18));
- We gave an interpretation of the GFM1, whose coefficients may be derived from a variation of a generalized (difference) divergence (Remark 1 (i)).

(ii) In particular, based on the ϕ-deformed (Naudts) entropy, we focused on the following topics:

- We calculated the coefficients of the metrics $g, \tilde{g}, h, \alpha, \beta, \hat{g}, \overline{g}$ in terms of $\log^N$ and of the PDF ρ (Propositions 1–3);
- When the PDFs are normal, univariate and depending on two parameters, we provided seven families of examples of the previous metrics; we determined formulas for their scalar curvature and we discussed its variation w.r.t. parameters;
- We proved a MaxEnt result (Theorem 1) for univariate PDFs and some extensions of the thermodynamic relations (Remark 4).

(iii) Future work will be directed toward:

- The search of the statistical relevance of α and β and a statistical interpretation for quotient divergences, similar to that for difference divergences (in the Remark 1 (i));
- The characterization of the case when the quotient divergence coincides with the difference divergence; this kind of result might bring into light unexpected—and eventually important—families of entropies;
- Refining the known families of deformation functions ϕ and finding new ones, relevant for applications. The interplay between the choice of ϕ and of the group logarithm G offers many modeling opportunities.

(iv) There exist two different but connected approaches to entropy: in Thermodynamics and in Statistical mechanics. Its geometrization by means of Fisher metrics follows two apparently different paths. The procedures to construct Fisher-like metrics from entropy are analogous, as they originate from the same general differential geometric methods. Instead, the basic manifold these metrics act upon (i.e., the space of the parameters) is essentially different. Moreover, entropy in Thermodynamics is "more deterministic" and one does not use a log-likelihood function which "produces" it.

The first formalism is dominated by the ideas of Weinhold, Ruppeiner and Quevedo [55,57,63], and is extensively used in models for the entropy of black holes (see [64] and references therein).

Our paper engaged in the second path and is dependent of log-likelihood functions, especially of the ϕ-deformed (Naudts) one. However, we are aware that more connections between the two theories are needed, with refined comparisons of the Riemannian models they both rely on.

Author Contributions: Conceptualization, C.-L.P., I.-E.H., G.-T.P. and V.P. ; validation, C.-L.P., I.-E.H., G.-T.P. and V.P.; writing, C.-L.P., I.-E.H., G.-T.P. and V.P.; visualization, G.-T.P.; supervision, C.-L.P., I.-E.H., G.-T.P. and V.P. All authors have read and agreed to the published version of the manuscript.

Funding: This research received no external funding.

Institutional Review Board Statement: Not applicable.

Informed Consent Statement: Not applicable.

Data Availability Statement: Not applicable.

Acknowledgments: We are grateful to the reviewers for their valuable enlightening remarks.

Conflicts of Interest: The authors declare no conflict of interest.

References

1. Brechtl, J.; Liaw, P.K. *High-Entropy Materials: Theory, Experiments, and Applications*; Springer: Cham, Switzerland, 2021.
2. Calin, O.; Udriste, C. *Geometric Modeling in Probability and Statistics*; Springer: New York, NY, USA, 2014.
3. Di Crescenzo, A.; Longobardi, M. On cumulative entropies and lifetime estimation. In *Methods and Models in Artificial and Natural Computation*; Mira, J.M., Ferrández, J.M., Alvarez-Sachez, J.-P., Paz, F., Toledo, J., Eds.; IWINAC Part I, LNCS 5601; Springer: Berlin, Germany, 2009; pp. 132–141.
4. Furuichi, S. On the maximum entropy principle and the minimization of the Fisher information in Tsallis statistics. *J. Math. Phys.* **2009**, *50*, 013303. [CrossRef]
5. Gell-Mann, M.; Tsallis, C. *Non-Extensive Entropy- Interdisciplinary Applications*; Oxford University Press: Oxford, UK, 2004.
6. Gray, R.M. *Entropy and Information Theory*; Springer: New York, NY, USA, 2011.
7. Guiasu, S. *Information Theory with Applications*; McGraw-Hill: New York, NY, USA, 1977.
8. Kelbert, M.; Stuhlb, I.; Suhov, Y. Weighted entropy: Basic inequalities. *Mod. Stochastics Theory Appl.* **2017**, *4*, 233–252. [CrossRef]
9. Klein, I.; Mangold, B.; Doll, M. Cumulative Paired ϕ-Entropy. *Entropy* **2016**, *18*, 248. [CrossRef]
10. Klein, I.; Doll, M. (Generalized) Maximum Cumulative Direct, Residual, and Paired ϕ Entropy Approach. *Entropy* **2020**, *22*, 91. [CrossRef] [PubMed]
11. Martin, N.F.G.; England, J.W.; Brooks, J.K. *Mathematical Theory of Entropy*; Addison-Wesley: Reading, PA, USA, 1981.
12. Nielsen, F. An Elementary Introduction to Information Geometry. *Entropy* **2020**, *22*, 1100. [CrossRef] [PubMed]
13. Papadimitriou, F. *Spatial Entropy and Landscape Analysis*; Springer: Wiesbaden, Germany, 2022.
14. Sagawa, T. *Entropy, Divergence, and Majorization in Classical and Quantum Thermodynamics*; Springer Nature: Singapore, 2022.
15. Sfetcu, R.-C.; Sfetcu, S.-C.; Preda, V. Ordering Awad–Varma Entropy and Applications to Some Stochastic Models. *Mathematics* **2021**, *9*, 280. [CrossRef]
16. Sherman, T.F. *Energy, Entropy, and the Flow of Nature*; Oxford University Press: Oxford, UK, 2018.
17. Tame, J.R.H. *Approaches to Entropy*; Springer: Singapore, 2019.
18. Popkov, Y.S.; Popkov, A.Y.; Dubnov, Y.A. *Entropy Randomization in Machine Learning*; CRC Press: Boca Raton, FL, USA, 2023.
19. Wei, I.; Ting, K.; Tebourbi, I.; Lu, W.-M.; Kweh, Q.L. The effects of managerial ability on firm performance and the mediating role of capital structure: Evidence from Taiwan. *Financ. Innov.* **2021**, *7*, 89.
20. Gomez, I.; Portesi, M.; Borges, E.P. Universality classes for the Fisher metric derived from relative group entropy. *Phys. A Stat. Mech. Its Appl.* **2020**, *547*, 123827. [CrossRef]
21. Tempesta, P. Multivariate group entropies, super-exponentially growing complex systems and functional equations. *Chaos* **2020**, *30*, 123119. [CrossRef]
22. Amari, S. *Information Geometry and Its Applications*; Springer: Tokyo, Japan, 2016.
23. Ay, N.; Jost, J.; Lê, H.V.; Schwachhöfer, L. *Information Geometry*; Springer: Cham, Switzerland, 2017.
24. Udriste, C.; Tevy, I. Information Geometry in Roegenian Economics. *Entropy* **2022**, *24*, 932. [CrossRef]
25. Eguchi, S.; Komori, O. *Minimum Divergence Methods in Statistical Machine Learning from an Information Geometric Viewpoint*; Springer: Tokyo, Japan, 2022.

26. Sason, I. Divergence Measures: Mathematical Foundations and Applications in Information-Theoretic and Statistical Problems. *Entropy* **2022**, *24*, 712. [CrossRef] [PubMed]
27. Naudts, J. Deformed exponentials and logarithms in generalized thermostatistics. *Phys. A* **2002**, *316*, 323–334. [CrossRef]
28. Naudts, J. Continuity of a class of entropies and relative entropies. *Rev. Math. Phys.* **2004**, *16*, 809–822. [CrossRef]
29. Naudts, J. *Generalized Thermostatistics*; Springer: London, UK, 2011.
30. Korbel, J.; Hanel, R.; Thurner, S. Information Geometric Duality of ϕ-Deformed Exponential Families. *Entropy* **2019**, *21*, 112. [CrossRef]
31. Naudts, J. Update of Prior Probabilities by Minimal Divergence. *Entropy* **2021**, *23*, 1668. [CrossRef]
32. Trivellato, B. Deformed Exponentials and Applications to Finance. *Entropy* **2013**, *15*, 3471–3489. [CrossRef]
33. Matsuzoe, H.; Scarfone, A.M.; Wada, T. A sequential structure of statistical manifolds on deformed exponential family. In *Geometric Science of Information*; GSI 2017, Lecture Notes in Computer Science; Nielsen, F., Barbaresco, F., Eds.; Springer: Berlin, Germany, 2017; Volume 10589, pp. 223–230.
34. Hirica, I.E.; Pripoae, C.-L.; Pripoae, G.-T.; Preda, V. Weighted Relative Group Entropies and Associated Fisher Metrics. *Entropy* **2022**, *24*, 120. [CrossRef]
35. Preda, V.; Balcau, C. Convex quadratic programming with weighted entropic perturbation. *Bull. Math. Soc. Sci. Math. Roum.* **2009**, *52*, 57–64.
36. Preda, V.; Balcau, C. *Entropy Optimization with Applications*; Academiei Romane: Bucharest, Romania, 2010.
37. Sfetcu, R.C.; Sfetcu, S.C.; Preda, V. On Tsallis and Kaniadakis Divergences. *Math. Phys. Anal. Geom.* **2022**, *25*, 7. [CrossRef]
38. Hirica, I.E.; Pripoae, C.-L.; Pripoae, G.-T.; Preda, V. Lie Symmetries of the Nonlinear Fokker–Planck Equation Based on Weighted Kaniadakis Entropy. *Mathematics* **2022**, *10*, 2776. [CrossRef]
39. Pripoae, C.-L.; Hirica, I.E.; Pripoae, G.-T.; Preda, V. Lie symmetries of the nonlinear Fokker–Planck equation based on weighted Tsallis entropy. *Carpathian J. Math.* **2022**, *38*, 597–617. [CrossRef]
40. Scarfone, A.M.; Wada, T. Lie symmetries and related group-invariant solutions of a nonlinear Fokker–Planck equation based on the Sharma–Taneja–Mittal entropy. *Braz. J. Phys.* **2009**, *39*, 475–482. [CrossRef]
41. Tempesta, P. Group entropies, correlation laws, and zeta functions. *Phys. Rev. E* **2011**, *84*, 021121. [CrossRef] [PubMed]
42. Csiszar, I. Why least squares and maximum entropy? An axiomatic approach to inference for linear inverse problems. *Ann. Stat.* **1991**, *19*, 2032–2066. [CrossRef]
43. Sason, I. On f-Divergences: Integral Representations, Local Behavior, and Inequalities. *Entropy* **2018**, *20*, 383. [CrossRef]
44. Birrell, J.; Dupuis, P.; Katsoulakis, M.A.; Pantazis, Y.; Rey-Bellet, L. (f; Γ)-Divergences: Interpolating between f-Divergences and Integral Probability Metrics. *J. Mach. Learn. Res.* **2022**, *23*, 1–70.
45. Suter, F.; Cernat, I.; Dragan, M. Some Information Measures Properties of the GOS-Concomitants from the FGM Family. *Entropy* **2022**, *24*, 1361. [CrossRef]
46. Futami, F.; Iwata, T.; Ueda, N.; Sato, I. Accelerated Diffusion- Based Sampling by the Non-Reversible Dynamics with Skew-Symmetric Matrices. *Entropy* **2021**, *23*, 993. [CrossRef]
47. Udriste, C.; Tevy, I. *Variational Calculus with Engineering Applications*; John Wiley & Sons: Hoboken, NJ, USA, 2023.
48. Dimov, H.; Mladenov, S.; Rashkov, R.C.; Vetsov, T. Entanglement entropy and Fisher information metric for closed bosonic strings in homogeneous plane wave background. *Phys. Rev. D* **2017**, *96*, 126004. [CrossRef]
49. Bauer, M.; Bruveris, M.; Michor, P.W. Uniqueness of the Fisher-Rao metric on the space of smooth densities. *Bull. Lond. Math. Soc.* **2016**, *48*, 499–506. [CrossRef]
50. Javaudin, B.; Gilblas, R.; Sentenac,T.; Le Maoult, Y. Experimental validation of the diffusion function model for accuracy-enhanced thermoreflectometry. *Quant. InfraRed Thermogr. J.* **2021**, *18*, 18–33. [CrossRef]
51. Lederer, A.; Zhang, M.; Tesfazgi, S.; Hirche, S. Networked Online Learning for Control of Safety-Critical Resource-Constrained Systems based on Gaussian Processes. *arXiv* **2022**, arXiv:2202.11491v1.
52. Rajaram, S.; Heinrich, L.E.; Gordan, J.D.; Avva, J.; Bonness, K.M.; Witkiewicz, A.K.; Malter, J.S.; Atreya, C.E.; Warren, R.S.; Wu, L.F.; et al. Sampling to capture single-cell heterogeneity. *Nat. Methods* **2017**, *14*, 967–970. [CrossRef]
53. Sharp, J.A.; Browning, A.P.; Burrage, K.; Simpson, M.J. Parameter estimation and uncertainty quantification using information geometry. *J. R. Soc. Interface* **2022**, *19*, 20210940. [CrossRef]
54. Zhao, T.; Pan, B.; Song, X.; Sui, D.; Xiao, H.; Zhou, J. Heuristic Approaches Based on Modified Three-Parameter Model for Inverse Acoustic Characterisation of Sintered Metal Fibre Materials. *Mathematics* **2022**, *10*, 3264. [CrossRef]
55. Ruppeiner, G. Riemannian geometry in thermodynamic fluctuation theory. *Rev. Mod. Phys.* **1995**, *67*, 605–659. [CrossRef]
56. Dehyadegari, A.; Sheykhi, A.; Wei, S.W. Microstructure of charged AdS black hole via $P-V$ criticality. *Phys. Rev. D* **2020**, *102*, 104013. [CrossRef]
57. Quevedo, H. Geometrothermodynamics. *J. Math. Phys.* **2007**, *48*, 013506. [CrossRef]
58. Janyszek, H.; Mrugala, R. Riemannian geometry and the thermodynamics of model magnetic systems. *Phys. Rev. A* **1989**, *39*, 6515. [CrossRef]
59. Felice, D.; Cafaro, C.; Mancini, S. Information geometric methods for complexity. *Chaos* **2018**, *28*, 032101. [CrossRef]
60. Cover, T.M.; Thomas J.A. *Elements of Information Theory*, 2nd ed.; Wiley-Interscience: Hoboken, NJ, USA, 2006.
61. Wada, T.; Scarfone, A.M. On the nonlinear Fokker–Planck equation associated with k-entropy. *AIP Conf. Proc.* **2007**, *965*, 177–180.

62. Wada, T.; Scarfone, A.M. Asymptotic solutions of a nonlinear diffusive equation in the framework of a k-generalized statistical mechanics. *Eur. Phys. J. B* **2009**, *70*, 65–71. [CrossRef]
63. Brody, D.; Rivier, N. Geometrical aspects of statistical mechanics. *Phys. Rev. E* **1995**, *51*, 1006–1011. [CrossRef] [PubMed]
64. Dimov, H.; Iliev, I.N.; Radomirov, M.; Rashkov, R.C.; Vetsov, T. Holographic Fisher information metric in Schrödinger spacetime. *Eur. Phys. J. Plus* **2021**, *136*, 1128. [CrossRef]

Article

Decomposition of Finitely Additive Markov Chains in Discrete Space

Alexander Zhdanok [1,*] **and Anna Khuruma** [2]

[1] Institute for Information Transmission Problems of the Russian Academy of Sciences, 19, build.1, Bolshoy Karetny Per., 127051 Moscow, Russia
[2] Department of Physics and Mathematics, Tuvan State University, 36 Lenina Street, 667000 Kyzyl, Russia; huruma@list.ru
* Correspondence: zhdanok@iitp.ru

Abstract: In this study, we consider general Markov chains (MC) defined by a transition probability (kernel) that is finitely additive. These Markov chains were constructed by S. Ramakrishnan within the concepts and symbolism of game theory. Here, we study these MCs by using the operator approach. In our work, the state space (phase space) of the MC has any cardinality and the sigma-algebra is discrete. The construction of a phase space allows us to decompose the Markov kernel (and the Markov operators that it generates) into the sum of two components: countably additive and purely finitely additive kernels. We show that the countably additive kernel is atomic. Some properties of Markov operators with a purely finitely additive kernel and their invariant measures are also studied. A class of combined finitely additive MC and two of its subclasses are introduced, and the properties of their invariant measures are proven. Some asymptotic regularities of such MCs were revealed.

Keywords: Markov chains; Markov operators; finitely additive Markov chains; finitely additive measures; invariant measures; decompositions of Markov chains

MSC: 60J05; 60J10; 28A33; 46E27

1. Introduction

In this study, classical Markov chains (MC) are interpreted as random Markov processes with discrete time (in the usual sense) in the phase space (X, Σ), where X is some set (space) and Σ is some sigma-algebra of subsets in X. We also consider time-homogeneous MCs. If X is an arbitrary infinite set that does not highlight any structure other than sigma-algebra Σ, then these MCs are called general.

In 1937, Kryloff and Bogoliouboff [1,2] proposed an operator-theoretical treatment of the general MC study that was then explicitly developed then by Yosida and Kakutani [3]. The essence of the treatment is that the MC is given by a transition function (probability) $P(x, E), x \in X, E \in \Sigma$, which as a kernel defines two dual integral Markov operators T and A in spaces of measurable functions and in spaces of measures, respectively.

A Markov chain is identified with an iterative sequence of probability measures $\{\mu^n\}$. Such sequence is generated by the second Markov operator $\mu^n = A\mu^{n-1} = A^n\mu^1$ with an arbitrary initial probability measure μ^1. We use this treatment in this work.

In the classical theory of MC, the transition function (probability) $P(x, \cdot)$ is assumed by the second argument to be a countably additive measure. At the same time, in economic game theory, developed in the 1960s by Dubbins and Savage [4], and their numerous students and followers, to also involve finitely additive probability measures in the construction of specific random processes became necessary. In particular, in [5], some constructions and investigations of finitely additive measures similar to Markov chains were presented.

Based on the work of [5], in 1981, Ramakrishnan [6] developed a new object construction in the language of strategies, thus named finitely additive Markov chains. These chains are generated by a transition function (strategy) that is finitely additive by the second argument. The phase space (X, Σ) in [6] is a discrete set with the sigma-algebra of all its subsets. In the framework of this construction, the study in [6] contains proof of a number of non-trivial theorems, including ergodic ones, based on these specific chains properties within game theory terms. Some additional questions on this topic were also discussed in further publications by Ramakrishnan (see, e.g., [7]).

Other authors also continued to study some problems of the finitely additive Markov chains theory based on Ramakrishnan findings (see, e.g., [8]). The authors of such works actively used the special apparatus of random variables defined by finitely additive probabilities.

Zhdanok also used finitely additive measures in the study of general classical Markov chains in the works [9,10].

In this paper, we study general Markov chains generated by a transition function that is finitely additive by its second argument, as mentioned above. We consider Markov chains defined on a discrete space. However, it does not use any specific features of game theory, and a different range of problems is solved. We also do not use the apparatus of random variables.

In Section 2, we provide an operator approach for studying general Markov chains with a countably additive transition function on an arbitrary measurable space. We use and develop this construction for finitely additive transition functions.

In Section 3, a discrete topology and a discrete sigma-algebra containing all subsets of the set X are introduced into the phase space (of any cardinality) of finitely additive MCs. We study the properties of countably additive and purely finitely additive transition functions and the Markov operators generated by them in such spaces. We then prove that countably additive transition functions are atomic measures with a finitely or countable support and prove that the Markov operators of MCs with a purely finitely additive transition functions transform all finitely additive measures (including countably additive ones) into purely finitely additive measures.

The transition function of an arbitrary finitely additive MC and the Markov operators generated by it are decomposed into a countably additive component and a purely finitely additive component. Their general properties are studied.

In Section 4, we prove that, for any purely finitely additive MC, all its invariant finitely additive measures are purely finitely additive. The class of combined finitely additive MCs is also introduced here. We then prove that such MCs do not have invariant countably additive measures.

In Section 5, we consider the decomposition of a Markov sequence of measures of combined MCs into a countably additive component and a purely finitely additive component. Combined MCs have two subclasses. The first subclass is when the countably additive component of the Markov operator transforms all purely finitely additive measures into countably additive ones (condition (H_1)). The second subclass is when the same component transforms all purely finitely additive measures into the same ones (condition (H_2)). Under condition (H_1), the norms of countably additive and purely finitely additive components of a Markov sequence of measures were proven to be time-stationary. Additionally, under condition (H_2), the norms of countably additive components of a Markov sequence of measures were proven to converge exponentially to zero. The simple conditions (G_1) and (G_2) on the transition function of the MC are given, under which the "qualitative" conditions (H_1) and (H_2) are also satisfied. The corresponding theorems are then proven.

Examples of finitely additive MCs on a segment are considered in detail in Sections 4 and 5 and their phase portraits are shown.

2. Definitions, Notation and Some Information

Let X be an arbitrary infinite set and Σ be a sigma-algebra of its subsets containing all one-point subsets from X. Let $B(X, \Sigma)$ denote the Banach space of bounded Σ-measurable functions $f : X \to R$ with sup-norm.

We also consider Banach spaces of bounded measures $\mu : \Sigma \to R$, with the norm equal to the total variation of the measure μ (but one can also use the topologically equivalent sup-norm):

$ba(X, \Sigma)$ is the space of finitely additive measures, and
$ca(X, \Sigma)$ is the space of countably additive measures.
If $\mu \geq 0$, then norm $||\mu|| = \mu(X)$.

Definition 1 ([11]). *A finitely additive measure μ, $\mu \geq 0$, is called purely finitely additive (pure charge, pure mean) if any countably additive measure λ satisfying the condition $0 \leq \lambda \leq \mu$ is identically zero. An alternating measure μ is called purely finitely additive if both components of its Jordan decomposition $\mu = \mu^+ - \mu^-$ are purely finitely additive.*

Lemma 1. *If the measure μ is purely finitely additive, then it is equal to zero on every one-point set: $\mu(\{x\}) = 0, \forall x \in X$.*

Proof of Lemma 1. Take a purely finitely additive measure $\mu \geq 0$. Suppose that there is a point $x_0 \in X$ such that $\mu(\{x_0\}) = \alpha > 0$. We take the Dirac measure δ_{x_0} at the point x_0. Then, $\delta_{x_0}(X \setminus x_0) = 0$ and $\alpha \cdot \delta_{x_0}(E) \leq \mu(E)$ for all $E \in \Sigma$, i.e., $\alpha \cdot \delta_{x_0} \leq \mu$. All Dirac measures are countably additive, and this measure $\alpha \cdot \delta_{x_0}$ is also countably additive. Therefore, the statement in Lemma 1 is true for $\mu \geq 0$. This statement is also true for any sign-alternating purely finitely additive measure. $\square$

Obviously, a purely finitely additive measure is equal to zero on any finite set as well. The converse, generally speaking, is not true, for example, for the Lebesgue measure on the segment $[0, 1]$.

Remark 1. *If the measure μ is identically zero, then it can formally be considered both countably additive and purely finitely additive.*

Theorem 1 (Yosida-Hewitt decomposition, see [11]). *Any finitely additive measure μ can be uniquely decomposed into the sum $\mu = \mu_{ca} + \mu_{pfa}$, where μ_{ca} is countably additive and μ_{pfa} is a purely finitely additive measure.*

Bounded purely finitely additive measures also form a Banach space $pfa(X, \Sigma)$ with the same norm and $ba(X, \Sigma) = ca(X, \Sigma) \oplus pfa(X, \Sigma)$.

We denote the sets of non-negative measures:

$V_{ba} = \{\mu \in ba(X, \Sigma) : \mu(X) \leq 1\}$,
$V_{ca} = \{\mu \in ca(X, \Sigma) : \mu(X) \leq 1\}$,
$V_{pfa} = \{\mu \in pfa(X, \Sigma) : \mu(X) \leq 1\}$.

Measures from these sets are called probabilistic if $\mu(X) = 1$.

We also denote by S_{ba}, S_{ca}, and S_{pfa} the sets of all probability measures in V_{ba}, V_{ca}, and V_{pfa}, respectively.

Definition 2. *The classical Markov chains (MCs) on a measurable space (X, Σ) are given by their transition function (probability kernel) $P(x, E), x \in X, E \in \Sigma$, under the usual conditions:*

1. $0 \leq P(x, E) \leq 1, \forall x \in X, \forall E \in \Sigma$;
2. $P(\cdot, E) \in B(X, \Sigma), \forall E \in \Sigma$;
3. $P(x, \cdot) \in ca(X, \Sigma), \forall x \in X$;
4. $P(x, X) = 1, \forall x \in X$.

The numerical value of the function $P(x, E)$ is the probability that the system moves from the point $x \in X$ to the set $E \in \Sigma$ in one step (per unit of time).

We emphasize that the transition function of the classical Markov chain is a countably additive measure in the second argument.

We also call such transition functions countably additive kernels.

The transition function generates two Markov linear bounded positive integral operators:

$$T: B(X, \Sigma) \to B(X, \Sigma), (Tf)(x) = Tf(x) = \int_X f(y) P(x, dy),$$

$\forall f \in B(X, \Sigma), \forall x \in X;$

$$A: ca(X, \Sigma) \to ca(X, \Sigma), (A\mu)(E) = A\mu(E) = \int_X P(x, E) \mu(dx),$$

$\forall \mu \in ca(X, \Sigma), \forall E \in \Sigma.$

The operator A is isometric in the cone of non-negative measures, in particular, $AS_{ca} \subset S_{ca}$.

Let the initial measure be $\mu^1 \in S_{ca}$. Then, the iterative sequence of countably additive probability measures $\mu^{n+1} = A\mu^n \in S_{ca}, n \in N$ is usually identified with the Markov chain. We call $\{\mu^n\}$ a Markov sequence of measures.

Topologically conjugated to the space $B(X, \Sigma)$ is (isomorphically) the space of finitely additive measures: $B^*(X, \Sigma) = ba(X, \Sigma)$ (see, for example, [12]). In this case, the operator $T^*: ba(X, \Sigma) \to ba(X, \Sigma)$ serves as a topological conjugate to the operator T, which is uniquely determined by the well-known rule of integral "scalar products":

$$\langle T^*\mu, f \rangle = \langle \mu, Tf \rangle, \forall f \in B(X, \Sigma), \forall \mu \in ba(X, \Sigma).$$

The operator T^* is the only bounded continuation of the operator A to the space $ba(X, \Sigma)$, preserving its analytic form

$$T^*\mu(E) = \int_X P(x, E) \mu(dx), \forall \mu \in ba(X, \Sigma), \forall E \in \Sigma.$$

The operator T^* has its own invariant subspace $ca(X, \Sigma)$, i.e., $T^*[ca(X, \Sigma)] \subset ca(X, \Sigma)$, on which it coincides with the original operator A. The operator T^* is also isometric, and $T^* S_{ba} \subset S_{ba}$. The construction of the Markov operators T and T^* is now functionally closed. We continue to denote the operator T^* as A.

In such a setting, considering the Markov sequences of probabilistic finitely additive measures

$$\mu^1 \in S_{ba}, \mu^{n+1} = A\mu^n \in S_{ba}, n \in N,$$

and retaining the countable additivity of the transition function $P(x, \cdot)$ by the second argument are natural.

Despite this circumstance, image $A\mu$ of a purely finitely additive measure μ can remain purely finitely additive, i.e., generally speaking,

$$A[ba(X, \Sigma)] \not\subset ca(X, \Sigma).$$

The integral over a finitely additive measure, usually called the Radon integral, is constructed according to the same scheme as the Lebesgue integral over the Lebesgue measure. Its construction was developed in [12] and, in a more modern form, in [13]. Note that, if the original space X is countable and the measure μ is not countably additive, then the integral on X cannot be replaced by a sum (series). Such integrals have other features as well.

Definition 3. *If $A\mu = \mu$ holds for some positive finitely additive measure μ, then we call such a measure invariant for the operator A (and for the Markov chain).*

An invariant probability countably additive measure is often called the stationary distribution of a Markov chain.

The question of the existence of invariant measures and their properties is one of the main questions in the theory of Markov chains.

We denote the sets of all non-zero invariant measures for the operator A as follows:

$$\Delta_{ba} = \{\mu \in V_{ba} : \mu = A\mu\},$$

$$\Delta_{ca} = \{\mu \in V_{ca} : \mu = A\mu\},$$

and

$$\Delta_{pfa} = \{\mu \in V_{pfa} : \mu = A\mu\}.$$

The classical Markov chain with a countably additive transition probability may or may not have invariant countably additive probability measures, i.e., possibly $\Delta_{ca} = \emptyset$ (for example, for a symmetric walk on $\mathbb{Z}$).

In ([14], Theorem 2.2), Šidak proved that any countably additive MC on an arbitrary measurable space (X, Σ) with an operator extended to the space of finitely additive measures has at least one invariant finitely additive measure, i.e., always $\Delta_{ba} \neq \emptyset$.

In ([14], Theorem 2.5), for such MC (in the general case), Šidak established that, if a finitely additive measure μ is invariant, $A\mu = \mu$, and $\mu = \mu_{ca} + \mu_{pfa}$ is its decomposition into countably additive and purely finitely additive components, then each of them is also invariant: $A\mu_{ca} = \mu_{ca}$ and $A\mu_{pfa} = \mu_{pfa}$.

We now give our key definition of finitely additive MCs.

Definition 4. *A transition function of a finitely additive MC on an arbitrary (phase) measurable space (X, Σ) is a function $P(x, E), x \in X, E \in \Sigma$, for which the conditions (1), (2), and (4) from Definition 2 and, instead of condition (3), condition (3') are satisfied: $P(x, \cdot) \in ba(X, \Sigma), \forall x \in X$. We will also call such transition functions finitely additive.*

We consider specific finitely additive MCs that are not countably additive in Examples 2–5 below.

The finitely additive transition function $P(x, E)$ also generates two integral operators: $T : B(X, \Sigma) \to B(X, \Sigma)$ and $A : ba(X, \Sigma) \to ba(X, \Sigma)$ in the same analytical form, with $T^* = A$.

The Markov operators T and $T^* = A$ are linear, bounded, and positive. In addition, the operator A is isometric in the cone of non-negative finitely additive measures, and $AS_{ba} \subset S_{ba}$. However, in this case, generally speaking, the operator A does not transform countably additive measures into the same ones, that is, $Aca(X, \Sigma) \not\subset ca(X, \Sigma)$. Finitely additive MCs are also associated with their Markov sequences of finitely additive measures $\{\mu^n\}$.

Remark 2. *As already noted in the Introduction, in [6], Ramakrishnan introduced the concept of finitely additive Markov chains. This definition uses a number of concepts and constructions used only in game theory. The transition function of such MCs (in our terms) in [6] was interpreted as some conditional strategy, which, as a function of sets, is finitely additive. In Definition 4 and in the following comments about Markov operators, the usual language of functional analysis (measure theory and linear operator theory) is used. Strictly comparing these completely different approaches to constructing the theory of finitely additive Markov chains is very difficult (most likely impossible). However, some analogies for individual results are easy to see.*

It is natural to consider the decomposition of such transition functions (kernels) into two components: countably additive and purely finitely additive.

To define such kernels, we take as a basis Definition 2 and some information from Revuse's book ([15], Chapter 1, §1) and transfer them to the finitely additive case.

Definition 5. *A numerical function $P(x, E)$ of two variables $x \in X$ and $E \in \Sigma$ is called a sub-Markov countably additive kernel if conditions (1), (2), and (3) from Definition 2 are satisfied.*

Similarly, we introduce the terms sub-Markov and Markov kernels for the cases when the kernel $P(x, \cdot)$ is finitely additive or purely finitely additive in the second argument for each $x \in X$.

We can say that, in this case, we replace condition (3) in Definitions 2 and 4 with the following conditions:

(3′) $P(x, \cdot) \in ba(X, \Sigma), \forall x \in X$, and
(3″) $P(x, \cdot) \in pfa(X, \Sigma), \forall x \in X$, respectively.

The integral operators T and A in spaces of functions and measures generated by a sub-Markov (Markov) kernel are also called sub-Markov (Markov).

The already cited Yosida–Hewitt Theorem 1 [11] on the decomposition of a finitely additive measure implies the following statement.

Proposition 1. *Let X be an infinite set and an arbitrary sigma-algebra of its subsets Σ contains all one-point sets. Any Markov finitely additive kernel $P(x, E)$ on (X, Σ) is uniquely presented as the sum of its countably additive and purely finitely additive components: $P(x, E) = P_{ca}(x, E) + P_{pfa}(x, E)$, where $P_{ca}(x, \cdot) \in ca(X, \Sigma), P_{pfa}(x, \cdot) \in pfa(X, \Sigma)$, for all $x \in X, E \in \Sigma$.*

Proof of Proposition 1. The transition function of a finitely additive MC is a probability finitely additive measure $P(x, \cdot)$ on the second argument $P(x, E), E \in \Sigma$ for each fixed $x \in X$, i.e., $P(x, \cdot) \in ba(X, \Sigma)$, by Definition 1. Therefore, for each $x \in X$, the transition function $P(x, \cdot)$ has a unique decomposition $P(x, \cdot) = P_{ca}(x, \cdot) + P_{pfa}(x, \cdot)$ into its countably additive and finitely additive, according to Theorem 1. □

We cannot yet call the components $P_{ca}(x, \cdot)$ and $P_{pfa}(x, \cdot)$ sub-Markov kernels, because the Σ-measurability of the functions $P_{ca}(\cdot, E)$ and $P_{pfa}(\cdot, E)$ for different $E \in \Sigma$ and for an arbitrary sigma-algebra Σ is not guaranteed. Moreover, the original Markov kernel $P(\cdot, E)$ is Σ-measurable for any $E \in \Sigma$ by definition.

If the components $P_{ca}(\cdot, E)$ or $P_{pfa}(\cdot, E)$ are immeasurable, then no sub-Markov operators T and A are integrally expressed in terms of them.

The question of measurability with respect to the first argument of two components in the decompositions of the Markov kernel in Proposition 1 was pointed out by one of the authors of this article in their paper [9]. It was hypothesized that immeasurable decompositions exist. This problem was solved by Gutman and Sotnikov in their work [16].

They proved a number of theorems on the singularities of the decompositions of transition functions (kernels) into the sum of their countably additive and purely finitely additive components in different cases and proved that non-measurable decompositions exist, in particular, on the segment $[0, 1]$ with Lebesgue sigma-algebra.

Later, Sotnikov [17] constructed a class of strongly additive transition functions in which both of their decomposition components are measurable.

In this paper, we use another possibility of ensuring the measurability of the components in the decompositions of the finitely additive Markov kernel, which serves as an introduction to the next subsection in which discrete topologies in an arbitrary MC phase space are discussed.

3. Finitely Additive Markov Kernels in Discrete Space

In the theory of Markov chains, the term "discrete" is used in different senses, and is applied to both the time parameter and the state space of the MC. We use the classical definition from functional analysis (see, for example, [18]), which is also used in some papers on the theory of MCs.

Definition 6. *A topological space (X, τ) is called discrete if all its subsets are simultaneously open and closed (clopen), that is, the topology $\tau = 2^X$ is the set of all subsets of the set X.*

Such a topology in X is generated by the discrete metric $d(x,y)$ equal to 1 for $x \neq y$ and equal to 0 for $x = y$. In discrete space, all points are metrically isolated. Discrete metric (and topology) can be introduced in any set X. In particular, the discrete topology can be introduced in all "principal" number sets: $N, Z, Q, [0,1]$, and $R = R^1$, as well as in R^m ($m \in N$), transforming them into discrete spaces.

If a topological space is discrete, then, obviously, its Borel sigma-algebra $\mathfrak{B} = \tau = 2^X$. This sigma-algebra contains all subsets of the set X. Such a sigma-algebra in X is also called discrete. We will denote it by Σ_d.

Ramakrishnan [6] uses a similar definition of the discrete phase space of an MC.

If the space X is discrete, then, obviously, any bounded numerical function $f : X \to R$ is measurable with respect to the discrete sigma-algebra Σ_d, that is, $f \in B(X, \Sigma_d)$. In particular, Σ_d is measurable in the first argument and the components $P_{ca}(\cdot, E)$ and $P_{pfa}(\cdot, E)$ of the CM transition function in Proposition 1 for all $E \in \Sigma$.

Note that all numeric functions $f : X \to R$ on any discrete space (X, Σ_d) are continuous in the discrete topology $\tau = 2^X$.

Let us introduce the concept of a measure atom, known in different versions (we just need to use a simplified version of its definition).

Definition 7. *Let (X, Σ) be an arbitrary measurable space and $\mu : \Sigma \to R$ be some countably additive measure. An element $x \in X$ is called an atom of the measure μ if $\mu(\{x\}) \neq 0$. If a bounded measure $\mu, \mu \geq 0$, has a support (set of full measure) $D \in \Sigma$, consisting of a finite or countable family of its atoms, then such a measure is called atomic (discrete). Moreover, $D = \{x_1, x_2, \ldots\}$ and $\mu(D) = \sum_n \mu(\{x_n\}) = \mu(X)$.*

The atomic measure $\mu \geq 0$ can be represented as follows

$$\mu(E) = \sum_n \alpha_n \delta_{x_n}(E),$$

where $E \in \Sigma$, δ_{x_n} are Dirac measures concentrated at the points x_n, and $\sum_n \alpha_n = \mu(D) = \mu(X)$.

Note that a countably additive measure on a nondiscrete measurable space (X, Σ) may not have atoms, for example, the Lebesgue measure on $([0,1], \mathfrak{B})$. Additionally, from Definition 7 and Lemma 1, any purely finitely additive measure on any measurable space has no atoms.

If the set X is countable and $\Sigma = \Sigma_d$, then, obviously, any bounded countably additive measure μ on (X, Σ_d) is atomic.

Now, we want to find out how countably additive measures are arranged on an arbitrary discrete space (X, Σ_d). In a wider formulation, this question is considered, for example, in Bourbaki ([19], Chapter III, paragraphs 1 and 2). A locally compact topological space is taken as the initial space X. Countably additive measures are defined as linear continuous functionals on the space of continuous functions. Definitions of a discrete space, a discrete (atomic) measure, and its support are given, which differ from those given above. After proving a number of propositions (theorems), in ([19], Chapter III, paragraph 2, item 5), the following statement is formulated: "on a discrete space, any measure is discrete" (here, countably additive measures).

To apply this statement in this work, we need to give precise definitions of the above and other concepts and translate them into our language. Therefore, in Theorem 2 below, we give our proof of the above statement from [19] in our definitions and refine it.

However, for this, we need one well-known and nontrivial theorem of Ulam, stated, for example, in ([20], Chapter 5, Theorems 5.6 and 5.7) and, in more detail, in ([21], Volume 1, Theorem 1.12.40, and Corollary 1.12.41). We present this theorem under the condition that the continuum hypothesis is accepted, i.e., we assume that $\aleph_1 = c$ (continuum).

Theorem 2. *A finite countably additive measure μ defined on all subsets of the set X of cardinality $\aleph_1$ (c, continuum) is identically zero if it is zero for each one-point subset.*

Obviously, Ulam's theorem holds trivially for sets X with countable cardinality $\aleph_0$. We continue to assume that the continuum hypothesis is true.

Remark 3. *In the books [20,21], the (extended) Ulam Theorem 2 is noted to be true and, for higher, so-called "immeasurable" cardinalities of the set X are found. Immeasurable cardinality includes all cardinalities from an ordered cardinality scale: $\aleph_0$, $\aleph_1 = c$, $\aleph_2$, etc. There is still no example of a set with "measurable" power.*

Definition 8. *A measurable space (X, Σ_d) is called an arbitrary discrete space if $\Sigma_d = 2^X$, and the set X has an arbitrary immeasurable cardinality (including from the ordered cardinality scale). In other words, we consider only discrete spaces for which the (extended) Ulam theorem is valid.*

Now, let us prove the following promised theorem.

Theorem 3. *Any non-zero non-negative bounded countably additive measure $\mu : \Sigma_d \to R$, on an arbitrary discrete space (X, Σ_d) is atomic (discrete) and has a finite or countable support $D = \{x_1, x_2, \ldots\} \subset X$, for which $\mu(\{x_n\}) = \alpha_n > 0, n \in N$, $\sum_n \alpha_n = \mu(D) = \mu(X)$, $\mu(X \setminus D) = 0$.*

Proof. For a countable set X, the assertions of the theorem are trivially fulfilled.

Now, let the set X have uncountable cardinality. Consider an arbitrary bounded non-negative countably additive measure $\mu : \Sigma_d \to R$ for which $0 < \mu(X) = \gamma < \infty$. Because the measure μ is not identically zero, then by Theorem 2, the measure μ has at least one one-point atom $x_0 \in X$ such that $\mu(\{x_0\}) = \alpha_0 > 0$. We denote by D the set of all atoms of measure μ. As we have shown above, $x_0 \in D$ and $D \neq \emptyset$. Let us prove that the set D is finite or countable.

We split the interval $(0, \gamma]$ of possible non-zero values of the measure μ into a countable family of disjoint intervals

$$(0, \gamma] = \cup_{n=1}^{\infty} (\frac{\gamma}{n+1}, \frac{\gamma}{n}].$$

We denote the inverse images of these intervals as

$$D_n = \{x \in X : \mu(\{x\}) \in (\frac{\gamma}{n+1}, \frac{\gamma}{n}]\}, D_n \in \Sigma_d, n = 1, 2, \ldots.$$

Then, the sets D_n are also pairwise disjoint and $D = \cup_{n=1}^{\infty} D_n$. Therefore, since the measure μ is countably additive, then $\mu(D) = \sum_{n=1}^{\infty} \mu(D_n)$.

By construction, for any point $x \in D_n$ performed, $\frac{\gamma}{n+1} < \mu(\{x\}) \leq \frac{\gamma}{n}$, $n = 1, 2, \ldots$. In addition, $\mu(D_n) \leq \gamma < \infty$ for all $n = 1, 2, \ldots$.

If any of the sets D_n was infinite, then by virtue of the inequalities for $\mu(\{x\})$ for $x \in D_n$, it would be $\mu(D_n) = \infty$. This contradiction implies that each set D_n is finite or empty.

Therefore, the set D, as a union of a countable (or finite) family of finite sets, is countable (or finite).

By construction, $D \subset X$ and $\mu(D) \leq \mu(X)$. Let us prove that $\mu(D) = \mu(X)$. Because X has uncountable cardinality and the set D is finite or countable, the set $X \setminus D \neq \emptyset$ and is also uncountable.

Suppose that $\mu(D) < \mu(X)$, i.e., $\mu(X \setminus D) > 0$. By the hypothesis of the theorem, the set X is discrete. Consequently, the set $X \setminus D$ is also discrete.

The restriction μ_D of the measure μ from the set X to the set $X \setminus D$ also satisfies all of the requirements for the measure μ under the conditions of the theorem. Because $\mu(X \setminus D) > 0$, then, again applying Ulam's Theorem 2, we obtain that a point $y_0 \in X \setminus D$ exists such that $\mu_D(\{y_0\}) > 0$. However, then, $\mu(\{y_0\}) > 0$. Therefore, $y_0 \in D$ and $y_0 \neq x$ for any $x \in D$. However, the set D was defined as the set of all points $x \in X$ for which $\mu(\{x\}) > 0$ is satisfied. Thus, we obtain a contradiction. Therefore, $\mu(D) = \mu(X)$ and $\mu(X \setminus D) = 0$.

Because D is finite or countable, we re-number all its points and obtain the last statement of the theorem. □

Surprisingly, all countably additive measures on the discrete segment $[0,1]$ are only atomic. Additionally, the Lebesgue measure does not exist on the discrete segment $[0,1]$. In 1923, Stefan Banach proved that the Lebesgue measure defined on the Borel (generated by the Euclidean topology) sigma-algebra of the segment $[0,1]$ cannot be countably additively extended to the sigma-algebra of all subsets of the segment $[0,1]$. However, it can be extended to a finitely additive measure on a discrete sigma-algebra, and infinitely many such extensions exist. This issue is discussed in many sources; see, for example, ([21], Volume 1, items 1.12.29 and 2.12.91).

Theorem 4. *A finitely additive nonnegative measure μ defined on an arbitrary discrete space (X, Σ_d) is purely finitely additive if and only if the condition $\mu(\{x\}) = 0$ for all $x \in X$ is fulfilled.*

Proof. The necessity of the condition is obvious. Let us show its sufficiency. Let the condition be satisfied but the measure μ be not purely finitely additive. Then, in its decomposition $\mu = \mu_{ca} + \mu_{pfa}$ the countably additive component $\mu_{ca} \neq 0$. In this case, by Theorem 3, a point $x_1 \in X$ exists such that $\mu_{ca}(\{x_1\}) > 0$. From this contradiction, we can see that μ is purely finitely additive. □

Let us now return to Markov chains. Theorem 3 automatically implies the following statement.

Theorem 5. *Let a countably additive sub-Markov kernel $P(x, E)$ be given on an arbitrary discrete space (X, Σ_d), and $P(x, X) > 0$ for all $x \in X$. Then, for any $x \in X$, the measure $P(x, \cdot)$ is atomic and has a finite or countable support $D(x) = \{x_1(x), x_2(x), \ldots\}$, for which*

$$P(x, \{x_n(x)\}) = \alpha_n(x) > 0, n \in \mathbb{N},$$
and $\sum_n \alpha_n(x) = P(x, D(x)) = P(x, X), P(x, X \setminus D(x)) = 0.$

Corollary 1. *(From Theorem 4). Let a finitely additive sub-Markov kernel $P(x, E)$ be given on an arbitrary discrete space (X, Σ_d). For any fixed $x_0 \in X$ the measure $P(x_0, \cdot)$ is purely finitely additive if and only if $P(x_0, \{y\}) = 0$ for all $y \in X$ (including the case $y = x_0$).*

Example 1. *Let $X = [0,1]$ with Euclidean topology, $\Sigma = \mathfrak{B}$, be the Borel sigma-algebra and a countably additive MC given by the kernel $P(x, E) = \lambda(E)$ for all $x \in X$ and $E \in \mathfrak{B}$, where λ is the Lebesgue measure. Such a MC corresponds to a sequence of independent uniformly distributed random variables on the segment $[0,1]$. Obviously, $P(x, \{y\}) = 0$ holds for all $x, y \in X$. However, the phase space $X = [0,1], \Sigma = \mathfrak{B}$ is not discrete, and Theorem 4 is not applicable.*

Example 2. *Let us now take the same $X = [0,1]$ with the discrete sigma-algebra Σ_d. Consider a finitely additive MC defined by the kernel $P(x, E) = \eta(E)$ for all $x \in X$ and $E \in \Sigma_d$, where η is some purely finitely additive measure satisfying the following conditions: $\eta \geq 0, \eta(X) = 1$ and $\eta((0, \varepsilon)) = 1$ for all $\varepsilon > 0$. Then, obviously, the condition $P(x, \{y\}) = 0$ is also satisfied for all $x, y \in X$, and Theorem 4 is applicable.*

The measure η in this example can be informally characterized as follows. It specifies a certain "random variable" that takes a value with probability 1 as close to point 0 as desired but not at point 0.

We then denote by $P^n(x, E)$ the integral convolution of the kernel $P^1(x, E) = P(x, E)$, $n = 1, 2, 3, \ldots$.

The following statement is easily proven by induction.

Corollary 2. *Let a sub-Markov purely finitely additive kernel $P(x,E)$ be given on an arbitrary discrete space (X, Σ_d). Then, for all $x, y \in X$ and $n = 1, 2, 3, \ldots$, $P^n(x, \{y\}) = 0$ (including the case $x = y$).*

In general, the converse is not true. Here is a counter-example.

Example 3. *Let some purely finitely additive probability measure η be given on the discrete space (X, Σ_d), where $X = [0, 1]$. Consider on $([0, 1], \Sigma_d)$ a finitely additive MC with the following rules for passing in one step: $P(0, \{1\}) = 1$, $P(x, E) = \eta(E)$ for all $x \in (0, 1]$ and $E \in \Sigma_d$. In particular, $P(x, \{y\}) = \eta(\{y\}) = 0$ for all $x \in (0, 1]$ and $y \in [0, 1]$.*
Performing the integral convolution of two kernels $P(x, E)$, we obtain that $P^2(x, \{y\}) = 0$ for all $x \in [0, 1]$ and $y \in [0, 1]$. Moreover, $P(0, \{1\}) = 1 > 0$.

As noted above in Section 2, the operator A generated by the countably additive sub-Markov kernel transforms countably additive measures into the same ones, that is, $A[ca(X, \Sigma)] \subset ca(X, \Sigma)$. This property is preserved for the particular discrete case $\Sigma = 2^X$. However, if the measure $\mu \in V_{pfa}$ is purely finitely additive, then both cases are possible: $A\mu \in V_{ca}$ and $A\mu \in V_{pfa}$. However, the situation is different with a purely finitely additive kernel.

Theorem 6. *Let a purely finitely additive sub-Markov kernel $P(x, E)$ be given on an arbitrary discrete space (X, Σ_d). Then, the sub-Markov operator A generated by this kernel transforms all finitely additive measures into purely finitely additive measures, that is, $A[ba(X, \Sigma_d)] \subset pfa(X, \Sigma_d)$, in particular, $A[ca(X, \Sigma_d)] \subset pfa(X, \Sigma_d)$ and $A[pfa(X, \Sigma_d)] \subset pfa(X, \Sigma_d)$.*

Proof. Let the finitely additive measure $\mu \in V_{ba}$ and $\mu(X) > 0$. We denote the measure by $\eta = A\mu$. Clearly, that the measure η is also finitely additive.
If $\eta(X) = 0$, that is, $\eta \equiv 0$ (which is possible), then it can be considered purely finitely additive (see Remark 1) and the theorem is true.
Let $\eta(X) > 0$. Take its decomposition $\eta = \eta_{ca} + \eta_{pfa}$ into a countably additive component η_{ca} and a purely finitely additive component η_{pfa}.
If $\eta_{ca}(X) = 0$, then the measure is $\eta = \eta_{pfa} \in V_{pfa}$ and the theorem is proved.
Suppose that the countably additive measure $\eta_{ca}(X) > 0$. Then, by Theorem 3, the measure η_{ca} has at least one atom $a \in X$, $\eta_{ca}(\{a\}) = \gamma > 0$. Because the measure η_{pfa} is purely finitely additive, then $\eta_{pfa}(\{a\}) = 0$.
By the hypothesis of the theorem, all kernels $P(x, \cdot)$ are purely finitely additive for all $x \in X$. Such measures vanish on any one-point set. Therefore, $P(x, \{a\}) = 0$ for all $x \in X$. Hence,

$$\gamma = \eta_{ca}(\{a\}) = \eta_{ca}(\{a\}) + 0 = \eta_{ca}(\{a\}) + \eta_{pfa}(\{a\}) = \eta(\{a\}) = A\mu(\{a\})$$

$$= \int_X P(x, \{a\}) \mu(dx) = \int_X 0 \cdot \mu(dx) = 0.$$

Thus, we obtain a contradiction. Therefore, $\eta_{ca}(X) = 0$, and the measure $\eta = \eta_{pfa} = A\mu$ is purely finitely additive. □

Now, by using the discrete topology in X, we can complete Proposition 1.

Proposition 2. *Let an arbitrary discrete space (X, Σ_d) be given. Any Markov finitely additive kernel $P(x, E)$ on (X, Σ_d) is uniquely presented as the sum of a sub-Markov countably additive kernel $P_{ca}(x, E)$ and a sub-Markov purely finitely additive kernel $P_{pfa}(x, E)$:*

$$P(x, E) = P_{ca}(x, E) + P_{pfa}(x, E),$$

where $P_{ca}(x, \cdot) \in ca(X, \Sigma_d)$, $P_{pfa}(x, \cdot) \in pfa(X, \Sigma_d)$, and $P_{ca}(\cdot, E) \in B(X, \Sigma_d)$, $P_{pfa}(\cdot, E) \in B(X, \Sigma_d)$ for all $x \in X$ and $E \in \Sigma_d$.

The last inclusions, $P_{ca}(\cdot, E) \in B(X, \Sigma_d)$ and $P_{pfa}(\cdot, E) \in B(X, \Sigma_d)$, mean that the kernels $P_{ca}(\cdot, E)$ and $P_{pfa}(\cdot, E)$ are Σ_d-measurable in the first argument for all $E \in \Sigma_d$.

Proposition 2 makes it possible to introduce integral sub-Markov operators A_{ca} and A_{pfa} generated by the corresponding measurable subkernels. These operators act in the space of measures A_{ca} and $A_{pfa} : ba(X, \Sigma_d) \to ba(X, \Sigma_d)$. They have the same analytical form as the operator A. For any $\mu \in ba(X, \Sigma_d)$ and $E \in \Sigma$,

$$A_{ca}\mu(E) = \int_X P_{ca}(x, E)\mu(dx)$$

and

$$A_{pfa}\mu(E) = \int_X P_{pfa}(x, E)\mu(dx).$$

In this case, $A = A_{ca} + A_{pfa}$.

Because integral kernels of operators are non-negative, the operators A_{ca} and A_{pfa} transform non-negative measures into the same ones, i.e., operators A_{ca} and A_{pfa} are positive. Because $0 \leq P_{ca}(x, E) \leq P(x, E)$ and $0 \leq P_{pfa}(x, E) \leq P(x, E)$ for all $x \in X$ and $E \in \Sigma$, the norms $\|A_{ca}\| \leq \|A\| = 1$ and $\|A_{pfa}\| \leq \|A\| = 1$, i.e., operators are bounded. Thus, both sub-Markov operators A_{ca} and A_{pfa} are linear, bounded (continuous), and positive, and $\|A_{ca}\| \leq 1$ and $\|A_{pfa}\| \leq 1$.

As we have already found out,

$$A_{ca}[ca(X, \Sigma_d)] \subset ca(X, \Sigma_d), A_{pfa}[ba(X, \Sigma_d)] \subset pfa(X, \Sigma_d).$$

Corollary 3. *The following inclusions are true for superpositions of operators A_{ca} and A_{pfa}:*

1. $A_{ca} \cdot A_{ca}[ca(X, \Sigma_d)] \subset ca(X, \Sigma_d)$;
2. $A_{pfa} \cdot A_{pfa}[ba(X, \Sigma_d)] \subset pfa(X, \Sigma_d)$;
3. $A_{pfa} \cdot A_{ca}[ba(X, \Sigma_d)] \subset pfa(X, \Sigma_d)$.

Remark 4. *The operators A_{ca} and A_{pfa}, generally speaking, are non-commutative, i.e., $A_{ca} \cdot A_{pfa} \neq A_{pfa} \cdot A_{ca}$.*

4. Invariant Measures of Markov Operators

In the paper by Zhdanok ([9], Chapter I, §5, Theorem 5.3), the following statement was proven.

Theorem 7. *For any Markov chain with a Markov finitely additive kernel $P(x, E)$ on an arbitrary measurable space (X, Σ), an invariant probability finitely additive measure $\mu = A\mu \in S_{ba}$ exists, that is, $\Delta_{ba} \neq \varnothing$.*

Earlier, a similar theorem (in the language of strategies) was proven by Ramakrishnan ([6], p. 8, Theorem 2) but in the special case of a discrete phase space. In our Theorem 7 given above, no restrictions on the phase space are assumed.

Now let on an arbitrary discrete space (X, Σ_d), $\Sigma_d = 2^X$, a Markov chain with a Markov finitely additive kernel $P(x, E)$ be given. We previously identified two special "extreme" cases. The first is when the kernel $P(x, \cdot)$ is a countably additive measure for every $x \in X$. The second is when the kernel $P(x, \cdot)$ is a purely finitely additive measure for all $x \in X$.

The first case has already been considered in the previous paragraphs of this article and studied in a number of studies by various authors.

Consider now the second special case.

Theorem 8. *Let a Markov chain with a purely finitely additive kernel $P(x, E)$ be given on an arbitrary discrete space (X, Σ_d). Then, for the Markov operator A generated by it, an invariant probabilistic finitely additive measure $\mu = A\mu \in V_{ba}$ exists and all its invariant measures are purely finitely additive, that is, $\Delta_{ba} = \Delta_{pfa} \neq \varnothing$ and $\Delta_{ca} = \varnothing$.*

Proof. Theorem 7 is proven for any sigma-algebra Σ subsets of X and for any Markov finitely additive kernel. Hence, it is also true for the discrete sigma-algebra $\Sigma_d = 2^X$ and for a purely finitely additive kernel.

Therefore, under the conditions of the present theorem, for the operator A, an invariant probabilistic finitely additive measure $\mu = A\mu$ exists, defined on the discrete space (X, Σ_d).

From Theorem 6, the measure μ and all other invariant measures of the operator A are purely finitely additive. $\square$

Definition 9. *We call a finitely additive MC on an arbitrary discrete space (X, Σ_d) combined if its transition function in the decomposition*

$$P(x, E) = P_{ca}(x, E) + P_{pfa}(x, E),$$

satisfies the conditions:

$$P_{ca}(x, X) = q_1, P_{pfa}(x, X) = q_2 \text{ for all } x \in X,$$

where $0 \leq q_1, q_2 \leq 1$, $q_1 + q_2 = 1$.

Let the finitely additive MC be combined. Then, as shown in the comments to Proposition 2, its Markov operator A can also be represented as the sum $A = A_{ca} + A_{pfa}$ of its two components generated by the sub-Markov kernels $P_{ca}(x, E)$ and $P_{pfa}(x, E)$, wherein $\|A_{ca}\| = q_1$, $\|A_{pfa}\| = q_2$.

Definition 10. *A combined MC is called non-degenerate if its decomposition from Definition 9 holds for $0 < q_1, q_2 < 1$ and degenerate if $q_1 = 0$ or $q_2 = 0$.*

Above, in Section 2 and in Theorem 8, we describe the existence of invariant measures and their types for countably additive and purely finitely additive MCs. By Definition 10, they are degenerate cases of combined MCs.

Let the MC be non-degenerate. Let us take functions

$$\tilde{P}_{ca}(x, E) = \frac{1}{q_1} P_{ca}(x, E), \tilde{P}_{pfa}(x, E) = \frac{1}{q_2} P_{pfa}(x, E).$$

Then, the functions $\tilde{P}_{ca}(x, E)$ and $\tilde{P}_{pfa}(x, E)$ satisfy Definition 1 and are transition functions (Markov kernels) of the corresponding Markov operators

$$\tilde{A}_{ca} = \frac{1}{q_1} A_{ca}, \tilde{A}_{pfa} = \frac{1}{q_2} A_{pfa}.$$

Therefore, the Markov operator A of the combined MC is a linear combination

$$A = q_1 \tilde{A}_{ca} + q_2 \tilde{A}_{pfa}$$

for two Markov operators $\tilde{A}_{ca}$ and $\tilde{A}_{pfa}$ (hence, the name of such MCs and operators in Definition 9 is taken).

Recall that, by Theorem 7, any, including combined, finitely additive MC has an invariant finitely additive measure.

Theorem 9. *The combined non-degenerate finitely additive MC on an arbitrary discrete space (X, Σ_d) has no non-zero invariant countably additive measures, that is, $\Delta_{ca} = \emptyset$.*

Proof. We carry out the proof by contradiction. Suppose that $\mu = A\mu \in S_{ca}$, i.e., the invariant measure μ is countably additive. Then,

$$\mu = A\mu = (A_{ca} + A_{pfa})\mu = A_{ca}\mu + A_{pfa}\mu,$$

where A_{ca} is countably additive, and A_{pfa} are purely finitely additive components of the operator A. Then, $A_{ca}\mu$ is also a countably additive measure, and $A_{ca}\mu(X) = q_1 > 0$, that is, the measure $A_{ca}\mu$ is non-zero. By Theorem 6, the measure $A_{pfa}\mu$ is purely finitely additive and non-zero: $A_{pfa}\mu(X) = q_2 > 0$.

Consequently, the measure μ has a non-zero purely finitely additive component $A_{pfa}\mu$ and is not countably additive. The resulting contradiction proves the theorem. □

From Theorem 9, we obtain the following assertion.

Theorem 10. *Let a combined non-degenerate finitely additive MC with invariant probability finitely additive measure $\mu = A\mu \in S_{ba}$ on an arbitrary discrete space (X, Σ_d) be given. Let $\mu = \mu_{ca} + \mu_{pfa}$ be its decomposition into countably additive μ_{ca} and purely finitely additive μ_{pfa} components, $\mu_{ca} \neq 0$, and $\mu_{pfa} \neq 0$.*

Then, the measures μ_{ca} and μ_{pfa} are not invariant for the operator A, that is, $\mu_{ca} \neq A\mu_{ca}$ and $\mu_{pfa} \neq A\mu_{pfa}$.

Recall that by Šidak ([14], Theorem 2.5), for a MC with a countably additive kernel in a similar decomposition of the invariant measure $\mu = \mu_{ca} + \mu_{pfa}$, $\mu_{ca} = A\mu_{ca}$ and $\mu_{pfa} = A\mu_{pfa}$. The difference between such MCs and combined ones turned out to be very significant.

Let us give an example to illustrate the last two theorems.

Example 4. *Consider on the segment $X = [0,1]$ with discrete sigma-algebra Σ_d a combined finitely additive MC with kernel*
$$P(x,E) = P_{ca}(x,E) + P_{pfa}(x,E).$$

These components are set according to the following rules:

$P_{ca}(x,E) = \frac{1}{2}\delta_0(E)$ for all $x \in X$ and $E \subset X$, where δ_0 is the Dirac at point 0;

$P_{pfa}(x,E) = \frac{1}{2}\eta(E)$ for all $x \in X$ and $E \subset X$, where η is some fixed purely finitely additive measure from S_{pfa}. For clarity, we take the measure η from the family of purely finitely additive measures satisfying the condition $\eta((0,\varepsilon)) = 1$ for any $\varepsilon > 0$.

Moreover, $P_{ca}(x,X) = \frac{1}{2} = q_1$ and $P_{pfa}(x,X) = \frac{1}{2} = q_2$ for all $x \in X$.

Essentially, all this means that a Markov chain in one step can move from any point $x \in X$ to point 0 with probability $\frac{1}{2}$ and to any set $E \subset X \setminus \{0\}$ with probability $\frac{1}{2}\eta(E)$. In particular, from any point $x \in X$, the system can move with probability $\frac{1}{2}$ to the open interval $(0,\varepsilon)$ for every $\varepsilon \in (0,1)$. The phase portrait of such a MC with an arbitrary $\varepsilon \in (0,1)$ is shown in the Figure 1.

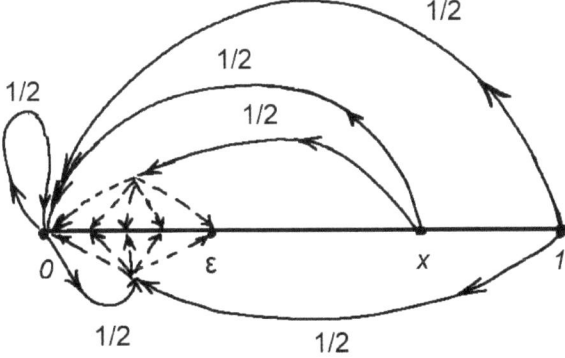

Figure 1. Phase portrait of the MC from Example 4.

Take an arbitrary (initial) finitely additive probability measure $\mu \in S_{ba}$. Then, for any $E \subset X$, the following holds:

$$A\mu(E) = \int_X P(x,E)d\mu(x) = \int_X P_{ca}(x,E)d\mu(x) + \int_X P_{pfa}(x,E)d\mu(x)$$

$$= \frac{1}{2}\int_X \delta_0(E)d\mu(x) + \frac{1}{2}\int_X \eta(E)d\mu(x)$$

$$= \frac{1}{2}\delta_0(E) \cdot \mu(X) + \frac{1}{2}\eta(E) \cdot \mu(X) = \frac{1}{2}\delta_0(E) + \frac{1}{2}\eta(E).$$

Hence, $A\mu = \frac{1}{2}\delta_0 + \frac{1}{2}\eta$ for any initial measure μ.

If $\mu = \frac{1}{2}\delta_0 + \frac{1}{2}\eta$, then $A\mu = \mu$.

Obviously, this is the only invariant probabilistic finitely additive measure for a given MC.

The measures $\mu_{ca} = \frac{1}{2}\delta_0$ and $\mu_{pfa} = \frac{1}{2}\eta$ are non-zero components of the measure μ, countably additive and purely finitely additive, respectively, and $\mu = \mu_{ca} + \mu_{pfa}$. Thus, Theorem 9 is confirmed. Then, also obvious is that $A\mu_{ca} = \mu \neq \mu_{ca}$ and $A\mu_{pfa} = \mu \neq \mu_{pfa}$. Therefore, this example also confirms Theorem 10.

In the combined non-degenerate decomposition $A = A_{ca} + A_{pfa}$ of the finitely additive operator A, its countably additive component A_{ca} and the purely finitely additive component A_{pfa} are equal. One might suppose that Theorem 9 would also be valid for a purely finitely additive invariant measure. However, it is not. Let us give a corresponding counterexample.

Example 5. *We consider a finitely additive combined MC on a discrete segment $X = [0,1]$ under the same conditions as in Example 4, but with a different countably additive component of its kernel: $P_{ca}(x,E) = \frac{1}{2}\delta_x(E)$ for all $x \in X$ and $E \subset X$, where δ_0 is the Dirac measure at point x.*

Meaningfully, this means that, in one step, the Markov system can go from any $x \in X$ to the point x, i.e., go into itself with probability $\frac{1}{2}$ and into any set $E \subset X \setminus \{x\}$ with probability $\frac{1}{2}\eta(E)$. In particular, the probability $P_{pfa}(x,(0,\varepsilon)) = \frac{1}{2}$ for any $\varepsilon \in (0,1)$. The phase portrait of such a MC with an arbitrary $\varepsilon \in (0,1)$ is shown in Figure 2.

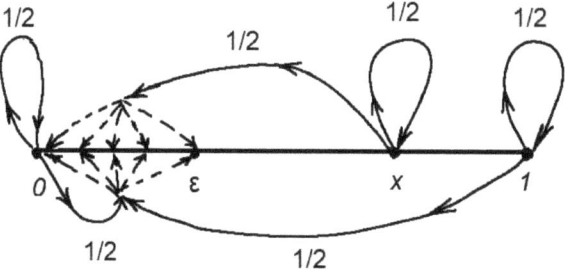

Figure 2. Phase portrait of the MC from Example 5.

Obviously, this MC is a combined non-degenerate chain.

Let us perform integral transformations for an arbitrary initial probability measure $\mu \in S_{ba}$, similar to the transformations in Example 4. As a result (omitting the calculations), we have $A\mu = \frac{1}{2}\mu + \frac{1}{2}\eta$. Then, we solve the equation $\mu = A\mu$. From the last two equalities, we obtain the only solution $\mu = \eta$.

We have shown that this combined non-degenerate MC has a unique invariant finitely additive measure η, which is purely finitely additive, i.e., has no non-zero countably additive component.

5. Norms of Components in the Decomposition of a Markov Sequence of Measures and Their Asymptotic Behavior

Consider a combined non-degenerate finitely additive MC on an arbitrary discrete space (X, Σ_d).

Let an arbitrary initial probability measure $\mu^1 \in S_{ba}$, $\mu^1 = \mu^1_{ca} + \mu^1_{pfa}$, be given, and $\mu^{n+1} = A\mu^n$, $n \in N$ is the Markov sequence of measures generated by this initial measure. Its decomposition is

$$\mu^{n+1} = \mu^{n+1}_{ca} + \mu^{n+1}_{pfa}.$$

Remark 5. *The notation μ^{n+1}_{ca} can be interpreted in two ways: it can be a countably additive component of the measure μ^{n+1}, i.e., $(\mu^{n+1})_{ca}$, or it can be $(n+1)$-th iteration of measure (μ^1_{ca}), i.e., $(\mu^1_{ca})^{(n+1)}$. Generally speaking, these two interpretations do not coincide. Hereafter, we mean that $\mu^{n+1}_{ca} = (\mu^{n+1})_{ca}$ and $\mu^{n+1}_{pfa} = (\mu^{n+1})_{pfa}$, for any $n \in N$.*

Because the operator A is isometric in the cone of positive measures, the norms of $\|\mu^{n+1}\| = \mu^{n+1}(X) = \|\mu^1(X)\| = \mu^1(X) = 1$ for each $n \in N$.

In this section, we consider the norms of the components $\|\mu^{n+1}_{ca}\|$ and $\|\mu^{n+1}_{pfa}\|$ for $n \to \infty$.

Take the second iteration in the Markov sequence of measures $\mu^2 = A\mu^1$. Let us make the appropriate transformations:

$$\mu^2 = \mu^2_{ca} + \mu^2_{pfa} = A\mu^1 = (A_{ca} + A_{pfa})\,(\mu^1_{ca} + \mu^1_{pfa}) \\ = A_{ca}\mu^1_{ca} + A_{ca}\mu^1_{pfa} + A_{pfa}\mu^1_{ca} + A_{pfa}\mu^1_{pfa}. \tag{1}$$

In the last four terms of the decomposition (1), the first is a countably additive measure and the third and fourth are purely finitely additive measures (see Theorem 6).

The second term $A_{ca}\mu^1_{pfa}$ can be a measure of any type. Consider two corresponding main cases: disjoint conditions (H_1) and (H_2).

$$(H_1) \qquad A_{ca}(V_{pfa}) \subset V_{ca},$$

that is, the operator A_{ca} transforms all purely finitely additive measures from V_{pfa} into countably additive measures. Markov chains satisfying this condition (H_1) exist. Let us show that the Markov chain in Example 4 has this property. In Example 4, the Markov chain kernel has a countably additive component $P_{ca} = \frac{1}{2}\delta_0$.

Let μ be an arbitrary purely finitely additive measure: $\mu \in V_{pfa}$. Then, for any $E \subset X$, the following holds:

$$A_{ca}\mu(E) = \int_X P_{ca}(x, E)\mu(dx) = \frac{1}{2}\int_X \delta_0(E)\mu(dx) = \frac{1}{2}\delta_0(E)\mu(X),$$

i.e., $A_{ca}\mu = \frac{1}{2}\delta_0 \cdot \mu(X)$, where the Dirac measure δ_0 is countably additive. Therefore, condition (H_1) is satisfied in Example 4.

Theorem 11. *Let condition (H_1) be satisfied for a combined non-degenerate finitely additive Markov chain on an arbitrary discrete space (X, Σ_d). Then, for any initial measure $\mu^1 \in S_{ba}$ and for any $n \in N$,*

$$\|\mu^{n+1}_{ca}\| = \mu^{n+1}_{ca}(X) = q_1$$

and

$$\|\mu^{n+1}_{pfa}\| = \mu^{n+1}_{pfa}(X) = q_2.$$

Proof. Here, we carry out the proof by induction. Let $n = 1$. Then, by condition (H_1), the second term $A_{ca}\mu^1_{pfa}$ in decomposition (1) is a countably additive measure. Therefore, due to the uniqueness of the decomposition of the Yosida–Hewitt measures, we have

$$\mu^2_{ca} = A_{ca}\mu^1_{ca} + A_{ca}\mu^1_{pfa} = A_{ca}(\mu^1_{ca} + \mu^1_{pfa}) = A_{ca}\mu^1.$$

From here,

$$\|\mu^2_{ca}\| = \mu^2_{ca}(X) = A_{ca}\mu^1(X) = q_1 \cdot \mu^1(X) = q_1.$$

Because

$$1 = \|\mu^2\| = \mu^2_{ca}(X) + \mu^2_{pfa}(X) = \|\mu^2_{ca}\| + \|\mu^2_{pfa}\|,$$

then

$$\|\mu^2_{pfa}\| = 1 - \|\mu^2_{ca}\| = 1 - q_1 = q_2.$$

Thus, the statement of the theorem for $n = 1$ is proven.

Suppose that the statement of the theorem is also true for some $n \in N$.

Let us make the decomposition similar to the decomposition (1) for μ^{n+1} and obtain the following equalities:

$$\mu^{n+1} = \mu^{n+1}_{ca} + A\mu^{n+1}_{pfa} = A\mu^n = (A_{ca} + A_{pfa})(\mu^n_{ca} + \mu^n_{pfa}) \\ = A_{ca}\mu^n_{ca} + A_{ca}\mu^n_{pfa} + A_{pfa}\mu^n_{ca} + A_{pfa}\mu^n_{pfa}. \quad (2)$$

As in the decomposition (1), here, the first term is a countably additive measure, and the third and fourth terms are purely finitely additive measures.

By condition (H_1) the second term $A_{ca}\mu^n_{pfa}$ in (2) is a countably additive measure. Therefore, just as for the measure μ^2_{ca}, we obtain that $\mu^{n+1}_{ca} = A_{ca}\mu^n$. In the same way, we have that

$$\|\mu^{n+1}_{ca}\| = \mu^{n+1}_{ca}(X) = A_{ca}\mu^n(X) = q_1 \cdot \mu^n(X) = q_1$$

and

$$\|\mu^{n+1}_{pfa}\| = \mu^{n+1}_{pfa}(X) = A_{pfa}\mu^n(X) = q_2 \cdot \mu^n(X) = q_2.$$

Therefore, the statement of the theorem is true for any $n \in N$. □

Remark 6. *Norms $\|\mu^{n+1}_{ca}\|$ and $\|\mu^{n+1}_{pfa}\|$ in Theorem 11 are independent of the norms of the components of the initial measure $\|\mu^1_{ca}\|$ and $\|\mu^1_{pfa}\|$. Additionally, this is a very interesting fact.*

Corollary 4. *Let the conditions of Theorem 11 be satisfied. Then, for such a Markov chain there exist invariant finitely additive measures $\mu^* = A\mu^*$, $\mu^* = \mu^*_{ca} + \mu^*_{pfa}$, and for all such measures for their components, the equalities are true:*

$$\|\mu^*_{ca}\| = \mu^*_{ca}(X) = q_1, \|\mu^*_{pfa}\| = \mu^*_{pfa}(X) = q_2.$$

Because Markov chains satisfying the condition (H_1) are not degenerate, that is, $0 < q_1, q_2 < 1$, they do not have invariant countably additive and invariant purely finite additive measures.

Corollary 4 clarifies our Theorem 9 under the additional condition (H_1).

Remark 7. *Obviously, in Example 4, which satisfies condition (H_1), the assertion of Theorem 11 is satisfied. Added to this fact is that, for any initial measure $\mu^1 \in S_{ba}$ the following Markov measure $\mu^2 = A\mu^1$ coincides with the unique invariant measure $\mu^2 = \mu^* = \frac{1}{2}\delta_0 + \frac{1}{2}\eta$ for the given MC. It is not strictly possible to say that the MC from Example 4 "strongly converges" uniformly in the initial measures μ^1 to the only invariant measure μ^*, i.e., this MC has the best ergodic properties.*

We now give the second condition (H_2) related to the decomposition in (1).

$$(H_2) \qquad A_{ca}(V_{pfa}) \subset V_{pfa},$$

that is, the operator A_{ca} transforms all purely finitely additive measures from V_{pfa} into purely finitely additive measures. Such Markov chains exist. Let us show that the Markov chain in Example 5 has this property.

In Example 5, $P_{ca}(x, E) = \frac{1}{2}\delta_x(E)$ for all $x \in X$ and $E \subset X$. We take an arbitrary measure $\mu \in V_{pfa}$. Then, for all $E \subset X$, the following holds:

$$A_{ca}\mu(E) = \int_X P_{ca}(x, E)\mu(dx) = \frac{1}{2}\int_X \delta_x(E)\mu(dx) = \frac{1}{2}\mu(E).$$

Thus, $A_{ca}\mu = \frac{1}{2} \cdot \mu$, where μ is a purely finitely additive measure. Thus, condition (H_2) is satisfied.

Theorem 12. *Let condition (H_2) be satisfied for a combined non-degenerate finitely additive Markov chain on an arbitrary discrete space (X, Σ_d). Then, for any initial finitely additive measure $\mu^1 \in S_{ba}$, for any $n \in N$*

$$\|\mu_{ca}^{n+1}\| = \mu_{ca}^{n+1}(X) = q_1^n \cdot \mu_{ca}^1(X) = q_1^n \cdot \|\mu_{ca}^1\|$$

and

$$\|\mu_{pfa}^{n+1}\| = \mu_{pfa}^{n+1}(X) = 1 - q_1^n \cdot \|\mu_{ca}^1\|.$$

Proof. Let us return to the decomposition (1). From condition (H_2), the second term $A_{ca}\mu_{pfa}^1$ in expansion (1) is a purely finitely additive measure. Therefore, due to the uniqueness of the Yosida–Hewitt decomposition,

$$\mu_{ca}^2 = A_{ca}\mu_{ca}^1,$$
$$\mu_{pfa}^2 = A_{ca}\mu_{pfa}^1 + A_{pfa}\mu_{ca}^1 + A_{pfa}\mu_{pfa}^1 = A_{ca}\mu_{pfa}^1 + A_{pfa}\mu^1. \tag{3}$$

Find the norm of the measure μ_{ca}^2 in equalities (3)

$$\|\mu_{ca}^2\| = \mu_{ca}^2(X) = A_{ca}\mu_{ca}^1(X) = \int_X P_{ca}(x, X)\mu_{ca}^1(dx) = q_1 \cdot \mu_{ca}^1(X) = q_1 \cdot \|\mu_{ca}^1\|.$$

Because $1 = \|\mu^2\| = \|\mu_{ca}^2\| + \|\mu_{pfa}^2\|$, then $\|\mu_{pfa}^2\| = 1 - q_1 \cdot \|\mu_{ca}^1\|$.

From the equalities obtained for $n = 1$ $(n + 1 = 2)$, making an assumption about the general form of the norms of the components of Markov measures is still difficult. Therefore, we now consider another case $n = 2$ $(n + 1 = 3)$.

Let us make transformations for the measure μ^3, similar to transformations (1) for the measure μ^2, relying on the condition (H_2). As a result, we obtain equality for the measure

$$\mu_{ca}^3 = A_{ca}\mu_{ca}^2$$

and the equality for the norm of this measure

$$\|\mu_{ca}^3\| = q_1 \cdot \mu_{ca}^2(X) = q_1^2 \cdot \mu_{ca}^1(X) = q_1^2 \cdot \|\mu_{ca}^1\|.$$

From here,

$$\|\mu_{pfa}^3\| = 1 - q_1^2 \cdot \|\mu_{ca}^1\|.$$

Suppose now that, for arbitrary $n \in N, n \geq 2$ holds for measures $\mu_{ca}^n = A_{ca}\mu_{ca}^{n-1}$, and for the norms of these measures, we have $\|\mu_{ca}^n\| = q_1^{n-1} \cdot \|\mu_{ca}^1\|$.

Then, (omitting transformations) we have

$$\mu_{ca}^{n+1} = A_{ca}\mu_{ca}^n,$$

$$\|\mu_{ca}^{n+1}\| = q_1^n \cdot \|\mu_{ca}^1\|,$$

$$\|\mu_{pfa}^{n+1}\| = 1 - q_1^n \cdot \|\mu_{ca}^1\|.$$

□

Remark 8. *Unlike Theorem 11, in Theorem 12, the norms of the components $\|\mu_{ca}^{n+1}\|$ and $\|\mu_{pfa}^{n+1}\|$ of the measure μ^{n+1} depend (linearly) on the norms of the components of the initial measure μ^1.*

Corollary 5. *Let the conditions of Theorem 12 be satisfied. Then for any finitely additive initial measure $\mu^1 \in S_{ba}$ for the components of the Markov sequence of measures generated by it $\mu^{n+1} = A\mu^n$ as $n \to \infty$,*

$$\|\mu_{ca}^n\| \to 0 \text{ and } \|\mu_{pfa}^n\| \to 1.$$

Moreover, the convergence is uniform with respect to the initial measures $\mu^1 \in S_{ba}$ and exponentially fast.

Corollary 6. *Let the conditions of Theorem 12 be satisfied. Then, for such a Markov chain, all of its invariant finitely additive measures (and such ones always exist, see Theorem 7) are purely finitely additive, i.e., $\Delta_{ba} = \Delta_{pfa} \neq \emptyset, \Delta_{ca} = \emptyset$.*

This statement follows from Theorem 12 or from its Corollary 5, if we take as the initial measure μ^1 its invariant measure $\mu^* = A\mu^*$.

Remark 9. *Let us return to the MC from Example 5. The following assertions are obtained from the properties of the MC obtained above.*

Then, verifying by induction that, for any initial measure $\mu^1 \in S_{ba}$ and for all $E \subset X, n \in N$,

$$|\mu^{n+1}(E) - \eta(E)| = \frac{1}{2^n}|\mu^1(E) - \eta(E)|$$

is easy. Therefore, for each $E \subset X, n \in N$, for the norm of a measure equal to the total variation of the measure, the following estimate is true:

$$\|\mu^{n+1} - \eta\| = \frac{1}{2^n}\|\mu^1 - \eta\| \leq \frac{2}{2^n} = \frac{1}{2^{n-1}}.$$

This implies that the Markov sequence of measures $\{\mu^{n+1}\}$ of a given MC converges strongly (in the metric topology) to a unique invariant purely finitely additive measure η. This convergence is uniform in all initial finitely additive (including countably additive) measures $\mu^1 \in S_{ba}$. In this case, the convergence is exponentially quickly. Thus, the MC in Example 5 is ergodic.

Remark 10. *In the previous Remark 9, we talked about the limiting behavior of Markov sequences of measures, not their Cesaro means. Such an increase in the type of convergence of measures is due to the fact that the MC from Example 5 does not have cycles of measures.*

The article by Zhdanok [22] was devoted to cycles of finitely additive measures. MCs with countably additive transition probability were considered with the Markov operator A extended to the space of finitely additive measures.

The conditions (H_1) and (H_2) are of an understandable qualitative character, but they are difficult to verify for specific MCs. Thus, finding simple analogues of these conditions in terms of the properties of the transition functions considered by the MC is desirable. We offer two such conditions. Here, we present the first of them: the (G_1) condition.

$$(G_1) \begin{cases} \text{There is a finite set } D \subset X \text{ such that for all } x \in X: \\ P_{ca}(x,D) = P_{ca}(x,X) = q_1, \text{ which is equivalent to } P_{ca}(x, X \setminus D) = 0. \end{cases}$$

We still consider an arbitrary discrete phase space and finitely additive combined non-degenerate MCs defined on it.

Theorem 13. *Let condition (G_1) be satisfied for some MC. Then,*
1. *the condition (H_1) is satisfied, and*
2. *the assertion of Theorem 11 is true.*

Proof. Let $\mu \in V_{pfa}, \mu \neq 0$, i.e., the measure μ be purely finitely additive, and the measure $\eta = A_{ca}\mu$. Let condition (G_1) be satisfied. Then,

$$\eta(D) = A_{ca}\mu(D) = \int_X P_{ca}(x,D)\mu(dx) = \int_X q_1 \mu(dx) = q_1 \mu(X) > 0.$$

Similarly, we obtain $\eta(X \setminus D) = 0$ and $\eta(X) = \eta(D)$.

The finitely additive measure $\eta = A_{ca}\mu$ is concentrated on a finite set D. Therefore, it is formally countably additive on D and on the whole space X. This means that $\eta = A_{ca}\mu \in V_{ca}$. Condition (H_1) is satisfied, i.e., $(G_1) \Rightarrow (H_1)$, and the assertion of Theorem 11 is true. □

Consider one more condition (G_2) on the transition function of the MC. For an arbitrary $y \in X$, we denote the set $Q_y = \{x \in X : P(x,\{y\}) > 0\}$.

(G_2) For any $y \in X$ the set Q_y is empty or finite.

Theorem 14. *Let condition (G_2) be satisfied for some MC. Then,*
1. *the condition (H_2) is satisfied, and*
2. *the assertion of Theorem 12 is true.*

Proof. Let $\mu \in V_p fa, \mu \neq 0$, i.e., the measure μ be purely finitely additive, and $\eta = A_{ca}\mu$. Then, for any $y \in X$, the following holds

$$\eta(\{y\}) = A_{ca}\mu(\{y\}) = \int_X P_{ca}(x,\{y\})\,\mu(dx) = \int_{Q_y} P_{ca}(x,\{y\})\mu(dx) + \int_{X \setminus Q_y} P_{ca}(x,\{y\})\mu(dx).$$

Because a purely finitely additive measure is equal to zero on any finite set, then $\mu(Q_y) = 0$, and the first integral in the expansion above is equal to zero.

By condition (G_2) the function $P_{ca}(x,\{y\})$ is equal to zero for all $x \in X \setminus Q_y$. Consequently, the second integral in this expansion is equal to zero. This implies that $\eta(\{y\}) = 0$. Then, the measure η is purely finitely additive by our Theorem 4, Condition (H_2) is satisfied, and the assertion of Theorem 12 is true. □

Remark 11. *Let us show that the MC in Example 4 satisfies the condition (G_1). Recall that the countably additive component $P_{ca}(x,E)$ of the MC transition function in Example 4 has the following form:*

$P_{ca}(x,E) = \frac{1}{2}\delta_0(E)$ for all $x \in X$ and $E \subset X$, where δ_0 is the Dirac measure at point 0. Take a finite set $D = \{0\}$. Then,

$$P_{ca}(x,D) = \frac{1}{2}\delta_0(D) = \frac{1}{2} = q_1, P_{ca}(x, X \setminus D) = 0 \text{ for all } x \in X.$$

Thus, condition (G_1) is fulfilled.
We showed above that the MC in Example 4 also satisfies condition (H_1).

Let us now return to Example 5, in which the countably additive component of the transition function is given by the following rule: $P_{ca}(x,E) = \frac{1}{2}\delta_x(E)$ for all $x \in X$ and $E \subset X$, where δ_0 is the Dirac measure at point x.

Obviously, any point $y \in X = [0,1]$ can be reached in one step only from itself with probability $\frac{1}{2}$. Hence, $Q_y = \{x \in X : P(x,\{y\}) > 0\} = \{y\}$. This set is finite for any $y \in X$. Thus, condition (G_2) is satisfied.

Above, we directly showed (without using Theorem 14) that, in Example 5, condition (H_2) also holds.

6. Conclusions

Work on the theory of finitely additive Markov chains quite naturally appeared in the general theory of random processes and in the economic game theory. Ramakrishnan's pioneering work laid the foundations for such a theory. The main condition in this work is that the transition probability of Markov chains can only be finitely additive. However, the structures he created or used (strategies) are quite complex. They require readers to have a broad outlook in several areas of mathematics.

The authors of this article have been working on problems with using finitely additive measures to study the properties of general Markov chains for a long time. However, attention was primarily paid to classical Markov chains with countably additive transition probability. In this case, finitely additive measures appeared as a result of the extension of Markov operators from the space of countably additive measures to the space of finitely additive measures. All of these studies were carried out within the framework of the operator treatment.

We have seen that combining the problems of the theory of finitely additive Markov chains and the methods we are developing for studying general Markov chains is possible. The result is the present work. Its feature is the absence of concepts and methods of game theory and the apparatus of random variables generated by finitely additive measures. We used the language and methods of classical functional analyses available to a wider readership, and some of our results have a simple proof. However, they provide a basic platform for possible future research conducted by other authors in this direction. In particular, the ergodic properties of finitely additive Markov chains can be considered.

Author Contributions: Conceptualization, A.Z.; methodology, A.Z. and A.K.; writing—original draft preparation, writing—review and editing, A.Z. and A.K.; visualization, A.K.; project administration, A.Z.; funding acquisition, A.Z. and A.K. All authors have read and agreed to the published version of the manuscript.

Funding: This research was funded by the Russian Foundation of Basic Research, RFBR project number 20-01-00575-a.

Institutional Review Board Statement: Not applicable.

Informed Consent Statement: Not applicable.

Data Availability Statement: Not applicable.

Conflicts of Interest: The authors declare no conflict of interest.

References

1. Kryloff, N.; Bogoliouboff, N. Sur les probabilités en chaine. *C. R. Acad. Sci. Paris* **1937**, *204*, 1386–1388.
2. Kryloff, N.; Bogoliouboff, N. Les propriétés ergodiques des suites de probabilités en chaine. *C. R. Acad. Sci. Paris* **1937**, *204*, 1454–1456.
3. Yosida, K.; Kakutani, S. Operator-theoretical treatment of Markoff's processes and mean ergodic theorem. *Ann. Math. Second Ser.* **1941**, *42*, 188–228. [CrossRef]
4. Dubins, L.E.; Savage, L.J. *How to Gamble if You Must: Inequalities for Stochastic Processes*; McGraw-Hill Book Company: New York, NY, USA, 1965.
5. Purves, R.A.; Sudderth, W.D. Some finitely additive probability. *Ann. Probab.* **1976**, *4*, 259–276. [CrossRef]
6. Ramakrishnan, S. Finitely Additive Markov Chains. *Trans. Am. Math. Soc.* **1981**, *265*, 247–272. [CrossRef]

7. Ramakrishnan, S. The tail σ-field of a finitely additive Markov chain starting from a recurrent state. *Proc. Am. Math. Soc.* **1983**, *89*, 493–497. [CrossRef]
8. Gangopadhyay, S.; Rao, B. Some Finitely Additive Probability: Random Walks. *J. Theor. Probab.* **1997**, *7*, 643–657. [CrossRef]
9. Zhdanok, A.I. Finitely additive measures in the ergodic theory of Markov chains I. *Sib. Adv. Math.* **2003**, *13*, 87–125. [CrossRef]
10. Zhdanok, A.I. Finitely additive measures in the ergodic theory of Markov chains II. *Sib. Adv. Math.* **2003**, *13*, 108–125.
11. Yosida, K.; Hewitt, E. Finitely Additive Measures. *Trans. Am. Math. Soc.* **1952**, *72*, 46–66.
12. Dunford, N.; Schwartz, J.T. *Linear Operatiors, Part I: General Theory*; Interscience Publishers, Inc.: New York, NY, USA; London, UK, 1958. [CrossRef]
13. Rao K.P.S.B.; Rao M.B. *Theory of Charges: A Study of Finitely Additive Measures*; Academic Press: London, UK, 1983.
14. Šidak, Z. Integral representations for transition probabilities of Markov chains with a general state space. *Czechoslovak Math. J.* **1962**, *12*, 492–522.
15. Revuz, D. *Markov Chains*, 2nd ed.; North-Holland Mathematical Library: Amsterdam, The Netherlands, 1984. [CrossRef]
16. Gutman, A.E.; Sotnikov, A.I. Order properties of the space of finitely additive transition functions. *Sib. Math. J.* **2004**, *45*, 69–85.
17. Sotnikov, A.I. Order properties of the space of strongly additive transition functions. *Sib. Math. J.* **2005**, *46*, 166–171. [CrossRef]
18. Kolmogorov, A.N.; Fomin, S.V. *Elements of Function Theory and Functional Analysis*; Fizmatlit: Moscow, Russia, 2009. [CrossRef]
19. Bourbaki, N. *Integration: Chapter III-IX*; Nauka: Moscow, Russia, 1977.
20. Oxtoby, J.C. *Measure and Category*; Springer: Berlin, Germany, 1971.
21. Bogachev, V.I. *Measure Theory I*; Springer: Berlin, Germany, 2007.
22. Zhdanok, A.I. Cycles in Spaces of Finitely Additive Measures of General Markov Chains. In *Recent Developments in Stochastic Methods and Applications, Springer Proceedings in Mathematics Statistics*; Shiryaev, A.N., Samouylov, K.E., Kozyrev, D.V., Eds.; Springer: New York, NY, USA, 2021; pp. 131–143.

Article

Fourth Cumulant Bound of Multivariate Normal Approximation on General Functionals of Gaussian Fields

Yoon-Tae Kim and Hyun-Suk Park *

Division of Data Science and Data Science Convergence Research Center, College of Information Science, Hallym University, Chuncheon 200-702, Korea; ytkim@hallym.ac.kr
* Correspondence: hspark@hallym.ac.kr; Tel.: +82-33-248-2036

Abstract: We develop a technique for obtaining the fourth moment bound on the normal approximation of F, where F is an $\mathbb{R}^d$-valued random vector whose components are functionals of Gaussian fields. This study transcends the case of vectors of multiple stochastic integrals, which has been the subject of research so far. We perform this task by investigating the relationship between the expectations of two operators Γ and Γ^*. Here, the operator Γ was introduced in Noreddine and Nourdin (2011) [*On the Gaussian approximation of vector-valued multiple integrals.* J. Multi. Anal.], and Γ^* is a muilti-dimensional version of the operator used in Kim and Park (2018) [*An Edgeworth expansion for functionals of Gaussian fields and its applications*, stoch. proc. their Appl.]. In the specific case where F is a random variable belonging to the vector-valued multiple integrals, the conditions in the general case of F for the fourth moment bound are naturally satisfied and our method yields a better estimate than that obtained by the previous methods. In the case of $d = 1$, the method developed here shows that, even in the case of general functionals of Gaussian fields, the *fourth moment theorem* holds without conditions for the multi-dimensional case.

Keywords: Malliavin calculus; fourth moment theorem; multiple stochastic integrals; multivariate normal approximation; Gaussian fields

MSC: 60H07; 60F25

1. Introduction

For a given real separable Hilbert space $\mathfrak{H}$, we write $X = \{X(h), h \in \mathfrak{H}\}$ to indicate an isonormal Gaussian process defined on a probability space $(\Omega, \mathfrak{F}, \mathbb{P})$. Let $\{F_n, n \geq 1\}$ be a sequence of random variables of functionals of Gaussian fields associated with X. The authors in [1] discovered a central limit theorem (CLT), known as the *fourth moment theorem*, for a sequence of random variables belonging to a fixed Wiener chaos.

Theorem 1. [Fourth moment theorem] *Let $\{F_n, n \geq 1\}$ be a sequence of random variables belonging to the $q(\geq 2)$th Wiener chaos with $\mathbb{E}[F_n^2] = 1$ for all $n \geq 1$. Then, $F_n \xrightarrow{\mathcal{L}} Z$ if and only if $\mathbb{E}[F_n^4] \to 3$, where Z is a standard normal random variable and the notation $\xrightarrow{\mathcal{L}}$ means a convergence in distribution.*

Such a result provides a remarkable simplification of the method of moments or cumulants. In [2], the *fourth moment theorem* is expressed in terms of the Malliavin derivative. However, the results given in [1,2] do not provide any estimates, whereas the authors in [3] find an upper bound for various distances by combining Malliavin calculus (see, e.g., [4–6]) and Stein's method for normal approximation (see, e.g., [7–9]). Moreover, the authors in [10,11] obtain optimal Berry–Esseen bounds as a further refinement of the main results proven in [3] (see, e.g., [12] for a short survey).

For the *fourth moment theorem*, the key step for the proof of this theorem is to show the following inequality:

$$\mathbb{V}ar(\langle DF, -DL^{-1}F\rangle_{\mathfrak{H}}) \leq c(\mathbb{E}[F^4] - 3(\mathbb{E}[F^2])^2), \qquad (1)$$

where DF is the Malliavin derivative of F and L^{-1} is the *pseudo-inverse of the Ornstein–Uhlenbeck generator* (see Section 2). In the particular case where $F = I_q(f), f \in \mathfrak{H}^{\otimes q}$, with $\mathbb{E}[F^2] = 1$, the bound in (1) is given by

$$d_{Kol}(F, Z) \leq \mathbb{V}ar(\langle DF, -DL^{-1}F\rangle_{\mathfrak{H}}) \leq \sqrt{\frac{q-1}{3q}}\sqrt{\mathbb{E}[F^4] - 3}. \qquad (2)$$

where d_{Kol} stands for the *Kolmogorov distance*.

Another research of this line can be found: [13] for multiple Winger integrals in a fixed order of free Winger chaos, and [14–16] for multi-dimensional vectors of multiple stochastic integrals, such that each integral belongs to a fixed order of Wiener chaos. In particular, the new techniques for the proof of the *fourth moment theorem* are also found in [17–19]. In [19], the authors prove this theorem by using the asymptotic independence between blocks of multiple stochastic integrals. At this point, it is important to mention that all of these approaches deal with only the random variables in a fixed chaos, and thus do not cover the cases that are not part of some chaoses. For this reason, we are interested in the conditions that the property of (2) holds for the generalized random variables that are not in a fixed Wiener chaos.

In this paper, we will develop a method for finding a bound on the multivariate normal approximation of a random vector F for which the *fourth moment theorem* holds even when F is a d-dimensional random vector whose components are general functionals of Gaussian fields. By applying this method to a random vector whose components belong to some Wiener chaos, we derive the *fourth moment theorem* with an upper bound more sharply than the previous one given in Theorem 4.3 of [19].

Differently from the *fourth moment theorem* for functionals of Gaussian fields studied so far, the findings of our research represent a further extension and refinement of the *fourth moment theorem*, in the sense that (i) they do not require the involved random vector whose components belong to some Wiener chaos, and (ii) the constant part except for the fourth cumulant may be significantly improved. The main aim in this paper is to discover under what conditions the fourth moment bound holds for vector-valued general functionals of Gaussian fields, where each of which needs not to belong to some Wiener chaos. In the case of vector-valued multiple integrals, the conditions on the *fourth moment theorem* are quite naturally satisfied.

On the other hand, in the case of $d = 1$, the application of the method developed here shows that, even in case of general functionals of Gaussian fields, the *fourth moment theorem* holds without any conditions needed for the case of $d \geq 2$. The only necessary condition is that the fourth cumulant is non-zero. The result in the one-dimensional case is different from the result obtained by substituting $d = 1$ into the multi-dimensional case. For these reasons, we will see how the random vector case can be reformulated in the one-dimensional case.

Our paper is organized in the following way. Section 2 contains some basic notion on Malliavin calculus. Section 3 is devoted to developing a method for obtaining the fourth moment bound for a $\mathbb{R}^d$-valued random vector whose components are functionals of Gaussian fields. In Section 4, we will show the *fourth moment theorem* by applying the new method developed in Section 3 to vector-valued multiple stochastic integrals. In Section 5, we will describe how the random vector case can be reconstructed in the one-dimensional case.

2. Preliminaries

In this section, we describe some basic facts on Malliavin calculus for Gaussian processes. For a more detailed explanation on this subject, see [4,5]. Fix a real separable Hilbert space $\mathfrak{H}$ with an inner product denoted by $\langle \cdot, \cdot \rangle_{\mathfrak{H}}$. Let $B = \{B(h), h \in \mathfrak{H}\}$ be an isonormal Gaussian process that is a centered Gaussian family of random variables, such that $\mathbb{E}[B(h)B(g)] = \langle h, g \rangle_{\mathfrak{H}}$. If H_q is the qth Hermite polynomial, then the closed linear subspace, denoted by $\mathbb{H}_q$ of $L^2(\Omega)$ generated by $\{H_q(B(h)) : h \in \mathfrak{H}, \|h\|_{\mathfrak{H}} = 1\}$ is called the qth *Wiener chaos* of B.

We define a linear isometric mapping $I_q : \mathfrak{H}^{\odot q} \to \mathbb{H}_q$ by $I_q(h^{\otimes n}) = q! H_q(B(h))$, where $\mathfrak{H}^{\odot q}$ is the symmetric qth tensor product. It is well known that any square integrable random variable $F \in L^2(\Omega, \mathcal{G}, \mathbb{P})$, where $\mathcal{G}$ denotes the σ-field generated by B, admits a series expansion of multiple stochastic integrals:

$$F = \sum_{q=0}^{\infty} I_q(f_q),$$

where the series converges in $L^2(\Omega)$ and the functions $f_q \in \mathfrak{H}^{\odot q}$ and $q \geq 0$ are uniquely determined with $f_0 = \mathbb{E}[F]$.

Let $\{e_i, i = 1, 2, \ldots\}$ be a complete orthonormal system of the Hilbert space $\mathfrak{H}$. For $f \in \mathfrak{H}^{\odot p}$ and $g \in \mathfrak{H}^{\odot q}$, the *contraction* $f \otimes_r g$ of f and g, $r \in \{0, 1, \ldots, p \wedge q\}$, is the element of $\mathfrak{H}^{\otimes(p+q-2r)}$ defined by

$$f \otimes_r g = \sum_{i_1, \cdots, i_r = 1}^{\infty} \langle f, e_{i_1} \otimes \cdots \otimes e_{i_r} \rangle_{\mathfrak{H}^{\otimes r}} \otimes \langle g, e_{i_1} \otimes \cdots \otimes e_{i_r} \rangle_{\mathfrak{H}^{\otimes r}}. \quad (3)$$

The product formula for the multiple stochastic integrals is given below.

Proposition 1. *If $f \in \mathfrak{H}^{\odot p}$ and $g \in \mathfrak{H}^{\odot q}$, then*

$$I_p(f) I_q(g) = \sum_{r=0}^{p \wedge q} r! \binom{p}{r} \binom{q}{r} I_{p+q-2r}(f \otimes_r g). \quad (4)$$

We denoted by $\mathcal{S}$ the class of smooth and cylindrical random variables F of the form

$$F = f(B(\varphi_1), \cdots, B(\varphi_n)), \quad n \geq 1, \quad (5)$$

where $f \in \mathcal{C}_b^{\infty}(\mathbb{R}^n)$ and $\varphi_i \in \mathfrak{H}$, $i = 1, \cdots, n$. For these random variables, the *Malliavin derivative* of F with respect to B is the element of $L^2(\Omega, \mathfrak{H})$ defined as

$$DF = \sum_{i=1}^{n} \frac{\partial f}{\partial x_i}(B(\varphi_1), \cdots, B(\varphi_n)) \varphi_i. \quad (6)$$

Let $\mathbb{D}^{q,p}$ be the closure of its associated smooth random variable class with respect to the norm

$$\|F\|_{q,p}^p = \mathbb{E}[|F|^p] + \sum_{k=1}^{q} \mathbb{E}[\|D^k F\|_{\mathfrak{H}^{\otimes k}}^p].$$

Let δ be the adjoint of the Malliavin derivative D. The domain of δ, denoted by $\mathrm{Dom}(\delta)$, is composed of those elements $u \in L^2(\Omega; \mathfrak{H})$ such that there exists a constant C satisfying

$$|\mathbb{E}[\langle D^k F, u \rangle_{\mathfrak{H}^{\otimes l}}]| \leq C (\mathbb{E}[|F|^2])^{1/2} \text{ for all } F \in \mathbb{D}^{k,2}.$$

If $u \in \mathrm{Dom}(\delta)$, then $\delta(u)$ is an element of $L^2(\Omega)$ defined as the following duality formula, called an integration by parts,

$$\mathbb{E}[F \delta(u)] = \mathbb{E}[\langle DF, u \rangle_{\mathfrak{H}}] \text{ for all } F \in \mathbb{D}^{1,2}.$$

Recall that any square integrable random variable F can be expanded as $F = \mathbb{E}[F] + \sum_{q=1}^{\infty} J_q(F)$, where J_q, $q = 0, 1, 2 \ldots$, is the projection of F onto $\mathbb{H}_q$. We say that this random variable belongs to $Dom(L)$ if $\sum_{q=1}^{\infty} q^2 \mathbb{E}[J_q(F)^2] < \infty$. For such a random variable F, we define an operator $L = \sum_{q=0}^{\infty} -qJ_q$, which coincides with the *infinitesimal generator* of the Ornstein–Uhlhenbeck semigroup. Then, $F \in Dom(L)$ if and only if $F \in \mathbb{D}^{1,2}$ and $DF \in Dom(\delta)$, and, in this case, $\delta DF = -LF$. We also define the operator L^{-1}, called the *pseudo-inverse* of L, as $L^{-1}F = \sum_{q=1}^{\infty} \frac{1}{q} J_q(F)$. Then, L^{-1} is an operator with values in $\mathbb{D}^{2,2}$, and $LL^{-1}F = F - \mathbb{E}[F]$ for all $F \in \mathbb{L}^2(\Omega)$.

3. Main Results

In this section, we will find a sufficient condition on the fourth moment bound for a vector-valued random variable whose components are functionals of Gaussian fields. It is important to note that these functionals of Gaussian fields do not necessarily belong to some Wiener chaos. The next lemma will play a fundamental role in this paper.

Lemma 1. *Suppse that $F \in \mathbb{D}^{1,2}$ and $G \in \mathbb{L}^2(\Omega)$. Then, we have that $L^{-1}G \in \mathbb{D}^{2,2}$ and*

$$\mathbb{E}[FG] = \mathbb{E}[F]\mathbb{E}[G] + \mathbb{E}[\langle -DL^{-1}G, DF \rangle_{\mathfrak{H}}].$$

A multi-index is a vector of a non-negative integer of the form $\alpha = (\alpha_1, \ldots, \alpha_d)$. Then, we write

$$|\alpha| = \sum_{j=1}^{d} \alpha_j, \quad \partial_j = \frac{\partial}{\partial x_j}, \quad \partial^\alpha = \partial_1^{\alpha_1} \ldots \partial_d^{\alpha_d}, \quad x^\alpha = \prod_{i=1}^{d} x_i^{\alpha_i},$$

where $x = (x_1, \ldots, x_d)$. By convention, we set $0^0 = 1$.

For the rest of this section, we fix a random vector $F = (F_1, \ldots, F_d)$, $d \geq 2$.

Definition 1. *Assume that $\mathbb{E}[|F|^\alpha] < \infty$ for some $\alpha \in \mathbb{N}^d \setminus \{0\}$. The joint cumulant of order $|\alpha|$ of F is defined by*

$$\kappa_\alpha(F) = (-i)^{|\alpha|} \partial^\alpha \bigg|_{t=0} \log \phi_F(t) \text{ for } t \in \mathbb{R}^d,$$

where $\phi_F(t) = \mathbb{E}\left[e^{i\langle t, F \rangle_{\mathbb{R}^d}}\right]$ is the characteristic function of F.

Suppose that $F_i \in \mathbb{D}^{1,2}$ for each $i = 1, \ldots, d$. Let $l_1, l_2, \ldots$ be a sequence taking values in $\{e_1, \ldots, e_d\}$, where e_i is the multi-index of length d given by

$$e_i = (0, \ldots, 0, 1, 0, \ldots, 0).$$

If $l_1 = e_i$, then $\Gamma_{l_1}^*(F) = F_i$. Suppose that $\Gamma_{l_1,\ldots,l_k}^*(F)$ is a well-defined random variable of $\mathbb{L}^2(\Omega)$. We define

$$\Gamma_{l_1,\ldots,l_{k+1}}^*(F) = \langle -DL^{-1}F^{l_{k+1}}, D\Gamma_{l_1,\ldots,l_k}^*(F) \rangle_{\mathfrak{H}}.$$

For the multivariate Gamma operator $\Gamma_{l_1,\ldots,l_k}^*(F)$, see Definition 4.2 in [14]. For simplicity, we will frequently write $\Gamma_{i_1,\ldots,i_k}^*(F)$ and $\Gamma_{i_1,\ldots,i_k}(F)$ instead of $\Gamma_{e_{i_1},\ldots,e_{i_k}}^*(F)$ and $\Gamma_{e_{i_1},\ldots,e_{i_k}}(F)$, respectively.

Using the Gamma operators $\Gamma_{l_1,\ldots,l_k}$ of F, we can state a formula for the cumulants of any random vector F (see, e.g., [14,20]).

Lemma 2 (Noreddine and Nourdin). *Let $\alpha = (\alpha_1, \ldots, \alpha_d) \in \mathbb{N}^d \setminus \{0\}$ be a d-dimensional multi-index with the unique decomposition $\{l_1, \ldots, l_{|\alpha|}\}$. If $F_i \in \mathbb{D}^{|\alpha|,2^{|\alpha|}}$ for $1 \leq i \leq d$, then*

$$\kappa_\alpha(F) = \sum_\sigma \mathbb{E}\left[\Gamma_{l_1,l_{\sigma(2)},\ldots,l_{\sigma(|\alpha|)}}(F)\right], \tag{7}$$

where the sum $\sum_\sigma$ is taken over all permutations σ of the set $\{2, 3, \ldots, |\alpha|\}$.

Remark 1. *Obviously, the above lemma can be expressed in the one-dimensional case as follows: Let $m \geq 1$ be an integer, and suppose that $F \in \mathbb{D}^{m,2^m}$. Then*

$$\kappa_{m+1}(F) = m! \mathbb{E}[\Gamma_m(F)]. \tag{8}$$

Remark 2. *Successive applications of Lemma 1 yield that*

$$\begin{aligned}
\mathbb{E}[\Gamma_{i,i,j,j}(F)] &= \frac{1}{2}\mathbb{E}[\langle DF_j^2, -DL^{-1}\Gamma_{i,i}(F)\rangle_{\mathfrak{H}}] \\
&= \frac{1}{2}\left\{\mathbb{E}[F_j^2 \Gamma_{i,i}(F)] - \mathbb{E}[F_j^2]\mathbb{E}[\Gamma_{i,i}(F)]\right\} \\
&= \frac{1}{2}\left\{\mathbb{E}[F_i^2 F_j^2] - 2\mathbb{E}[F_i F_j \Gamma_{i,j}(F)] - \mathbb{E}[F_i^2]\mathbb{E}[F_j^2]\right\} \\
&= \frac{1}{2}\left\{\mathbb{E}[F_i^2 F_j^2] - 2(\mathbb{E}[F_i F_j])^2 - \mathbb{E}[F_i^2]\mathbb{E}[F_j^2]\right\} \\
&\quad - \left(\mathbb{E}[\Gamma_{i,j,i,j}(F)] + \mathbb{E}[\Gamma_{i,j,j,i}(F)]\right).
\end{aligned} \tag{9}$$

Equation (9) gives that

$$\begin{aligned}
&\mathbb{E}[\Gamma_{i,i,j,j}(F)] + \mathbb{E}[\Gamma_{i,j,i,j}(F)] + \mathbb{E}[\Gamma_{i,j,j,i}(F)] \\
&= \frac{1}{2}\left\{\mathbb{E}[F_i^2 F_j^2] - 2(\mathbb{E}[F_i F_j])^2 - \mathbb{E}[F_i^2]\mathbb{E}[F_j^2]\right\}.
\end{aligned} \tag{10}$$

For the forthcoming theorem, first we define a set:

$$\mathfrak{E}_{(d)}(F) = \Bigg\{ \mathfrak{e} \in \mathbb{R} : \sum_{i,j=1}^{d} \sum_{l_1+l_2+l_3 = e_i + 2e_j} \mathbb{E}[\Gamma^*_{i,l_1,l_2,l_3}(F)] \\
\geq \mathfrak{e} \sum_{i,j=1}^{d} \sum_{l_1+l_2+l_3 = e_i + 2e_j} \mathbb{E}[\Gamma_{i,l_1,l_2,l_3}(F)] \Bigg\}.$$

Theorem 2. *Let $F = (F_1, \ldots, F_d)$, $d \geq 2$, with $F_i \in \mathbb{D}^{3,2^3}$ and $\mathbb{E}[F_i] = 0$ for $i = 1, \ldots, d$, and Z be a centered normal random vector with the covariance $\Sigma = (\sigma_{ij})_{1 \leq i,j \leq d}$, where $\sigma_{ij} = \mathbb{E}[F_i F_j]$. Suppose that, for $1 \leq i,j \leq d$,*

$$(\alpha) \qquad \mathbb{E}[\Gamma^*_{i,i}(F)\Gamma^*_{j,j}(F)] \geq \mathbb{E}[\Gamma^*_{i,i}(F)]\mathbb{E}[\Gamma^*_{j,j}(F)],$$

$$(\beta) \qquad \mathbb{E}[\Gamma^*_{i,j}(F)\Gamma^*_{j,i}(F)] \geq (\mathbb{E}[\Gamma^*_{i,j}(F)])^2,$$

$$(\gamma) \qquad \mathfrak{e} \in \mathfrak{E}_{(d)}(F).$$

Assume that Σ is invertible. We have that, for any Lipschitz function $h : \mathbb{R}^d \to \mathbb{R}$,

$$\begin{aligned}
&|\mathbb{E}[h(F)] - \mathbb{E}[h(Z)]| \\
&\leq \sqrt{d} \|\Sigma\|_{op}^{1/2} \|\Sigma^{-1}\|_{op} \|h\|_{Lip} \sqrt{\left(\frac{2-\mathfrak{e}}{2}\right) \sum_{i,j=1}^{d} \kappa_{e_i,e_j,e_i,e_j}(F)},
\end{aligned} \tag{11}$$

or, as another expression,

$$\begin{aligned}
&|\mathbb{E}[h(F)] - \mathbb{E}[h(Z)]| \\
&\leq \sqrt{d} \|\Sigma\|_{op}^{1/2} \|\Sigma^{-1}\|_{op} \|h\|_{Lip} \sqrt{\left(\frac{2-\mathfrak{e}}{2}\right) (\mathbb{E}[\|F\|_{\mathbb{R}^d}^4] - \mathbb{E}[\|Z\|_{\mathbb{R}^d}^4])}.
\end{aligned} \tag{12}$$

where $\|\cdot\|_{op}$ and $\|\cdot\|_{\mathbb{R}^d}$ denote the operator norm of a matrix and the euclidean norm in $\mathbb{R}^d$, respectively, and
$$\|h\|_{Lip} = \sup_{x,y \in \mathbb{R}^d} \frac{|h(x) - h(y)|}{\|x-y\|_{\mathbb{R}^d}}.$$

Proof. Recall that, for a Lipschitz function $h : \mathbb{R}^d \to \mathbb{R}$, Theorem 6.1.1 in [4] shows that

$$|\mathbb{E}[h(F)] - \mathbb{E}[h(N)]|$$
$$\leq \sqrt{d} \|\Sigma\|_{op}^{1/2} \|\Sigma^{-1}\|_{op} \|h\|_{Lip} \sqrt{\sum_{i,j=1}^d \mathbb{E}\left[(\sigma_{ij} - \Gamma_{i,j}(F))^2\right]}. \qquad (13)$$

Since $\Gamma_{i,j}^* = \Gamma_{j,i}$ for $1 \leq i,j \leq d$, the right-hand side of (13) can be expressed as

$$|\mathbb{E}[h(F)] - \mathbb{E}[h(N)]|$$
$$\leq \sqrt{d} \|\Sigma\|_{op}^{1/2} \|\Sigma^{-1}\|_{op} \|h\|_{Lip} \sqrt{\sum_{i,j=1}^d \mathbb{E}\left[(\sigma_{ij} - \Gamma_{i,j}^*(F))^2\right]}.$$

By the definition of the operator Γ^*, we have that, for $1 \leq i,j \leq d$,

$$\begin{aligned}
\mathbb{E}[\Gamma_{i,j}^*(F)^2] &= \mathbb{E}[\Gamma_{i,j}^*(F)\langle -DL^{-1}F_j, DF_i\rangle_{\mathfrak{H}}]\\
&= \mathbb{E}[\langle -DL^{-1}F_j, D(F_i\Gamma_{i,j}^*(F))\rangle_{\mathfrak{H}}]\\
&\quad -\mathbb{E}[F_i\langle -DL^{-1}F_j, D\Gamma_{i,j}^*(F)\rangle_{\mathfrak{H}}]\\
&= \mathbb{E}[F_iF_j\Gamma_{i,j}^*(F)] - \mathbb{E}[\Gamma_{i,j,j,i}^*(F)].
\end{aligned} \qquad (14)$$

For $a + b + c = 1$, we write, using Lemma 1 and the definition of Γ^*, the first term in (14) as follows:

$$\begin{aligned}
\mathbb{E}[F_iF_j\Gamma_{i,j}^*(F)] &= a\mathbb{E}[F_iF_j\langle -DL^{-1}F_j, DF_i\rangle_{\mathfrak{H}}]\\
&\quad +b\mathbb{E}[\langle -DL^{-1}F_i, D(F_j\Gamma_{i,j}^*(F))\rangle_{\mathfrak{H}}]\\
&\quad +c\mathbb{E}[\langle -DL^{-1}F_j, D(F_i\Gamma_{i,j}^*(F))\rangle_{\mathfrak{H}}]\\
&:= A_1 + A_2 + A_3.
\end{aligned}$$

It is obvious that

$$\begin{aligned}
A_1 &= a\mathbb{E}[\langle -DL^{-1}F_j, D(F_iF_j \times F_i)\rangle_{\mathfrak{H}}]\\
&\quad -a\mathbb{E}[F_i\langle -DL^{-1}F_j, D(F_iF_j)\rangle_{\mathfrak{H}}]\\
&= a\mathbb{E}[F_i^2F_j^2] - a\mathbb{E}[F_i^2\Gamma_{j,j}^*(F)] - a\mathbb{E}[F_iF_j\Gamma_{i,j}^*(F)]\\
&= a\mathbb{E}[F_i^2F_j^2] - a\mathbb{E}[\Gamma_{i,i}^*(F)\Gamma_{j,j}^*(F)] - a\mathbb{E}[\Gamma_{j,j,i,i}^*(F)]\\
&\quad -A_1.
\end{aligned} \qquad (15)$$

The above Equation (15) gives

$$A_1 = \frac{a}{2}\left\{\mathbb{E}[F_i^2F_j^2] - \mathbb{E}[\Gamma_{i,i}^*(F)\Gamma_{j,j}^*(F)] - \mathbb{E}[\Gamma_{j,j,i,i}^*(F)]\right\}. \qquad (16)$$

Also using Lemma 1 and the definition of Γ^*, the terms A_2 and A_3 can be expressed as

$$A_2 = b\mathbb{E}[\Gamma_{i,j,i,j}^*(F)] + b\mathbb{E}[\Gamma_{i,j}^*(F)\Gamma_{j,i}^*(F)], \qquad (17)$$

$$A_3 = c\mathbb{E}[\Gamma_{i,j,j,i}^*(F)] + c\mathbb{E}[\Gamma_{i,j}^*(F)^2]. \qquad (18)$$

Combining (16)–(18), we obtain, together with (14), that

$$
\begin{aligned}
\mathbb{E}[\Gamma_{i,j}^*(F)^2] &= \frac{a}{2(1-c)}\left\{\mathbb{E}[F_i^2 F_j^2] - \mathbb{E}[\Gamma_{i,i}^*(F)\Gamma_{j,j}^*(F)] - \mathbb{E}[\Gamma_{j,j,i,i}^*(F)]\right\} \\
&\quad + \frac{b}{1-c}\left\{\mathbb{E}[\Gamma_{i,j,i,j}^*(F)] + \mathbb{E}[\Gamma_{i,j}^*(F)\Gamma_{j,i}^*(F)]\right\} \\
&\quad + \frac{c-1}{1-c}\mathbb{E}[\Gamma_{i,j,j,i}^*(F)].
\end{aligned}
\quad (19)
$$

Now, we choose a, b, and c such that $a+b+c=1$ and

$$
-\frac{a}{2(1-c)} = \frac{b}{1-c} = \frac{c-1}{1-c}.
$$

Obviously, we may take $a=1$, $b=-1/2$, and $c=1/2$. The assumptions (α) and (β) yield that the left-hand side of (19) can be bounded by

$$
\begin{aligned}
\mathbb{E}[\Gamma_{i,j}^*(F)^2] &\leq \mathbb{E}[F_i^2 F_j^2] - \mathbb{E}[\Gamma_{j,j,i,i}^*(F)] \\
&\quad - \mathbb{E}[\Gamma_{i,j,i,j}^*(F)] - \mathbb{E}[\Gamma_{i,j,j,i}^*(F)] \\
&\quad - \mathbb{E}[\Gamma_{i,i}^*(F)]\mathbb{E}[\Gamma_{j,j}^*(F)] - (\mathbb{E}[\Gamma_{i,j}^*(F)])^2.
\end{aligned}
\quad (20)
$$

Therefore the Inequality (20) and the assumption (γ) prove that, if $\mathfrak{e} \in \mathfrak{E}_{(d)}(F)$,

$$
\begin{aligned}
\sum_{i,j=1}^d & \mathbb{E}[(\sigma_{ij} - \Gamma_{i,j}^*(F))^2] \\
&\leq \sum_{i,j=1}^d \left\{\mathbb{E}[F_i^2 F_j^2] - \sum_{l_1+l_2+l_3=e_i+2e_j}\mathbb{E}[\Gamma_{i,l_1,l_2,l_3}^*(F)]\right. \\
&\qquad\qquad \left. - 2(\mathbb{E}[F_i F_j])^2 - \mathbb{E}[F_i^2]\mathbb{E}[F_j^2]\right\} \\
&\leq \sum_{i,j=1}^d \left\{\mathbb{E}[F_i^2 F_j^2] - \mathfrak{e}\sum_{l_1+l_2+l_3=e_i+2e_j}\mathbb{E}[\Gamma_{i,l_1,l_2,l_3}(F)]\right. \\
&\qquad\qquad \left. - 2(\mathbb{E}[F_i F_j])^2 - \mathbb{E}[F_i^2]\mathbb{E}[F_j^2]\right\}.
\end{aligned}
\quad (21)
$$

Applying (10) in Remark 2 (or Lemma 2) to the right-hand side of (21), we have, together with the assumptions (α) and (β), that

$$
\begin{aligned}
\sum_{i,j=1}^d & \mathbb{E}[(\sigma_{ij} - \Gamma_{i,j}^*(F))^2] \\
&\leq \sum_{i,j=1}^d \left\{\mathbb{E}[F_i^2 F_j^2] - \frac{\mathfrak{e}}{2}\mathbb{E}[F_i^2 F_j^2] + (\mathfrak{e}-2)(\mathbb{E}[F_i F_j])^2\right. \\
&\qquad\qquad \left. + \frac{\mathfrak{e}-2}{2}\mathbb{E}[F_i^2]\mathbb{E}[F_j^2]\right\} \\
&= \left(\frac{2-\mathfrak{e}}{2}\right)\sum_{i,j=1}^d (\mathbb{E}[F_i^2 F_j^2] - 2(\mathbb{E}[F_i F_j])^2 - \mathbb{E}[F_i^2]\mathbb{E}[F_j^2]) \\
&= \left(\frac{2-\mathfrak{e}}{2}\right)\sum_{i,j=1}^d \kappa_{e_i,e_j,e_i,e_j}(F).
\end{aligned}
\quad (22)
$$

The Inequality (22) proves the desired conclusion (11). Since $\mathbb{E}[Z_i^2 Z_j^2] = 2(\mathbb{E}[Z_i Z_j])^2 + \mathbb{E}[Z_i^2]\mathbb{E}[Z_j^2]$, the identity $\mathbb{E}[\|Z\|_{\mathbb{R}^d}^4] = \sum_{i,j=1}^{d}(2\sigma_{ij}^2 + \sigma_{ii}\sigma_{jj})$ holds, which gives another expression (12). Hence, the proof of this theorem is completed. □

Remark 3. *Our techniques do not require the components of a random vector $F = (F_1, \ldots, F_d)$ to belong to a fixed Wiener chaos. Since the assumptions (α), (β), and (γ) are satisfied in the case of a random vector whose entries are element of some Wiener chaos, our result is an extension of Theorem 4.3 in [19]. This fact makes it possible to estimate how restrictive the assumptions given in Theorem 2 are in practice. In addition, for this random vector, the constant of the estimate in Theorem 4.3 in [19] corresponds to $\mathfrak{e} = 0$ in (12).*

4. Vector-Valued Multiple Stochastic Integrals

In this section, we consider a special case of the previous result such that F is a vector-valued multiple stochastic integral. First, for an explicit expression of Γ^*, we introduce the combinatorial constants

$$\beta^*_{q_{i_1},\ldots,q_{i_a}}(r_1,\ldots,r_a)$$

recursively defined by the relation

$$\beta^*_{q_{i_1},q_{i_2}}(r_2) = q_{i_2}(r_2-1)!\binom{q_{i_1}-1}{r_2-1}\binom{q_{i_2}-1}{r_2-1},$$

and for any $a \geq 3$,

$$\begin{aligned}
&\beta^*_{q_{i_1},\ldots,q_{i_a}}(r_2,\ldots,r_a) \\
&= \beta^*_{q_{i_1},\ldots,q_{i_{a-1}}}(r_2,\ldots,r_{a-1})(q_{i_1}+\cdots+q_{i_{a-1}}-2r_2-\cdots-2r_{a-1})(r_a-1)! \\
&\quad \times \binom{q_{i_1}+\cdots+q_{i_{a-1}}-2r_2-\cdots-2r_{a-1}-1}{r_a-1}\binom{q_{i_a}-1}{r_a-1}.
\end{aligned}$$

For an explicit expression of Γ, we use the notations

$$\beta_{q_{i_1},q_{i_2}}(r_2) = q_{i_2}(r_2-1)!\binom{q_{i_1}-1}{r_2-1}\binom{q_{i_2}-1}{r_2-1},$$

and

$$\begin{aligned}
&\beta_{q_{i_1},\ldots,q_{i_a}}(r_2,\ldots,r_a) \\
&= \beta_{q_{i_1},\ldots,q_{i_{a-1}}}(r_2,\ldots,r_{a-1})q_{i_a}(r_a-1)! \\
&\quad \times \binom{q_{i_1}+\cdots+q_{i_{a-1}}-2r_2-\cdots-2r_{a-1}-1}{r_a-1}\binom{q_{i_a}-1}{r_a-1} \text{ for } a \geq 3.
\end{aligned}$$

Theorem 3. *Fix $d \geq 2$. Let $q_i \geq 2$, $i = 1, \ldots, d$, be positive integers, and let F be a random vector*

$$F = (F_1, \ldots, F_d) = (I_{q_1}(f_{q_1}), \ldots, I_{q_d}(f_{q_d})),$$

where $f_{q_i} \in \mathfrak{H}^{\odot q_i}$ for $i = 1, \ldots, d$. Let Z be a centered multivariate normal random variable with the covariance $\Sigma = (\sigma_{ij})_{1 \leq i,j \leq d}$, where $\sigma_{ij} = \mathbb{E}[F_i F_j]$. For any Lipschitz function $h: \mathbb{R}^d \to \mathbb{R}$, it holds that

$$\begin{aligned}
&|\mathbb{E}[h(F)] - \mathbb{E}[h(Z)]| \\
&\leq \sqrt{\frac{2-\mathfrak{e}}{2}}\sqrt{d}\|\Sigma\|_{op}^{1/2}\|\Sigma^{-1}\|_{op}\|h\|_{Lip}\sqrt{\sum_{i,j=1}^{d}\kappa_{e_i,e_j,e_i,e_j}(F)}, \quad (23)
\end{aligned}$$

or

$$|\mathbb{E}[h(F)] - \mathbb{E}[h(Z)]| \leq \sqrt{\frac{2-\mathfrak{e}}{2}} \sqrt{d} \|\Sigma\|_{op}^{1/2} \|\Sigma^{-1}\|_{op} \|h\|_{Lip} \sqrt{\mathbb{E}[\|F\|_{\mathbb{R}^d}^4] - \mathbb{E}[\|Z\|_{\mathbb{R}^d}^4]}, \quad (24)$$

where a constant $\mathfrak{e}$ is given by

$$\mathfrak{e} = \frac{1}{\max_{1 \leq i \leq d} q_i}.$$

Moreover, if $q_1 = \cdots = q_d = q$, then $\mathfrak{e}$ is given by

$$\mathfrak{e} = \frac{2}{q}. \quad (25)$$

Proof. It is sufficient to prove that F satisfies the assumptions (α), (β), and (γ) in Theorem 2. For the condition (α): By the definition of Γ^*, we have that

$$\Gamma_{ii}^*(F)\Gamma_{jj}^*(F)$$
$$= q_i q_j \sum_{r_1=1}^{q_i} \sum_{r_2=1}^{q_j} (r_1-1)!(r_2-1)!\binom{q_i-1}{r_1-1}^2 \binom{q_j-1}{r_2-1}^2$$
$$\times I_{2q_i-2r_1}(f_{q_i} \tilde{\otimes}_{r_1} f_{q_i}) I_{2q_j-2r_2}(f_{q_j} \tilde{\otimes}_{r_2} f_{q_j}),$$

which yields

$$\mathbb{E}[\Gamma_{ii}^*(F)\Gamma_{jj}^*(F)]$$
$$= q_i q_j \sum_{r=1}^{q_i} (r_1-1)!(q_j-q_i+r-1)!\binom{q_i-1}{r-1}^2 \binom{q_j-1}{q_j-q_i+r-1}^2$$
$$\times (2q_i-2r)! \langle f_{q_i} \tilde{\otimes}_r f_{q_i}, f_{q_j} \tilde{\otimes}_{q_j-q_i+r} f_{q_j} \rangle_{\mathfrak{H}^{\otimes(2q_i-2r)}}$$
$$= q_i! q_j! (f_{q_i} \tilde{\otimes}_{q_i} f_{q_i})(f_{q_j} \tilde{\otimes}_{q_j} f_{q_j})$$
$$+ q_i q_j \sum_{r=1}^{q_i-1} (r-1)!(q_j-q_i+r-1)!\binom{q_i-1}{r-1}^2 \binom{q_j-1}{q_j-q_i+r-1}^2$$
$$\times (2q_i-2r)! \langle f_{q_i} \tilde{\otimes}_r f_{q_i}, f_{q_j} \tilde{\otimes}_{q_j-q_i+r} f_{q_j} \rangle_{\mathfrak{H}^{\otimes(2q_i-2r)}}. \quad (26)$$

On the other hand,

$$\mathbb{E}[\Gamma_{ii}^*(F)]\mathbb{E}[\Gamma_{jj}^*(F)] = q_i!(f_{q_i} \tilde{\otimes}_{q_i} f_{q_i}) \times q_j!(f_{q_j} \tilde{\otimes}_{q_j} f_{q_j}). \quad (27)$$

Denote by $\ell(\mathbf{a})$ the length of a vector $\mathbf{a}$. To prove (α), we need to show that, for every $1 \leq i, j \leq d$, the inner products in (26)

$$\langle f_{q_i} \tilde{\otimes}_r f_{q_i}, f_{q_j} \tilde{\otimes}_{q_j-q_i+r} f_{q_j} \rangle_{\mathfrak{H}^{\otimes(2q_i-2r)}} \geq 0.$$

For this, it is sufficient, from the symmetry of f_{q_i}, $i = 1, \ldots, d$, and symmetrization of contractions, to show that, for every $1 \leq i, j \leq d$,

$$\int_{\mathcal{Z}^{2(q_i+q_j)}} f_{q_i}(\mathbf{u}_1, \mathbf{w}) f_{q_i}(\mathbf{u}_2, \mathbf{w}) f_{q_j}(\mathbf{u}_1, \mathbf{v})$$
$$\times f_{q_j}(\mathbf{u}_2, \mathbf{v}) \mu^{\otimes 2(q_i+q_j)}(d\mathbf{u}_1, d\mathbf{u}_2, d\mathbf{v}, d\mathbf{w}) \geq 0, \quad (28)$$

where $\ell(\mathbf{w}) = r$ and $\ell(\mathbf{u}_1) + \ell(\mathbf{u}_2) = 2q_i - 2r$. Since $\ell(\mathbf{u}_1) = \ell(\mathbf{u}_2) = q_i - r$, the integral in (28) can be expressed as

$$\int_{\mathcal{Z}^{q_j-q_i+2r}} (f_{q_i} \otimes_{\ell(\mathbf{u}_1)} f_{q_j})(\mathbf{w},\mathbf{v})(f_{q_i} \otimes_{\ell(\mathbf{u}_2)} f_{q_j})(\mathbf{w},\mathbf{v}) \mu^{\otimes q_j+r_1+r_2}(d\mathbf{w},d\mathbf{v})$$

$$= \int_{\mathcal{Z}^{q_j-q_i+2r}} (f_{q_i} \otimes_{\ell(\mathbf{u}_1)} f_{q_j})^2(\mathbf{w},\mathbf{v}) \mu^{\otimes q_j+r_1+r_2}(d\mathbf{w},d\mathbf{v}) \geq 0. \qquad (29)$$

Using (26) and (27) together with (29) yields that, for $1 \leq i, j \leq d$,

$$\mathbb{E}[\Gamma_{ii}^*(F)\Gamma_{jj}^*(F)] \geq \mathbb{E}[\Gamma_{ii}^*(F)]\mathbb{E}[\Gamma_{jj}^*(F)].$$

For the condition (β): Obviously,

$$\Gamma_{ij}^*(F)\Gamma_{ji}^*(F) \qquad (30)$$

$$= q_i q_j \sum_{r_1=1}^{q_i \wedge q_j} \sum_{r_2=1}^{q_i \wedge q_j} (r_1-1)!(r_2-1)! \binom{q_i-1}{r_1-1}^2 \binom{q_j-1}{r_2-1}^2$$

$$\times I_{q_i+q_j-2r_1}(f_{q_i} \widetilde{\otimes}_{r_1} f_{q_j}) I_{q_i+q_j-2r_2}(f_{q_i} \widetilde{\otimes}_{r_2} f_{q_j}).$$

The expectation of (30) gives

$$\mathbb{E}[\Gamma_{ij}^*(F)\Gamma_{ji}^*(F)] \qquad (31)$$

$$= q_i q_j \sum_{r=1}^{q_i \wedge q_j} [(r-1)!]^2 \binom{q_i-1}{r-1}^2 \binom{q_j-1}{r-1}^2$$

$$\times (q_i+q_j-2r)! \|f_{q_i} \widetilde{\otimes}_r f_{q_j}\|_{\mathfrak{H}^{\otimes(q_i+q_j-2r)}}^2.$$

For $q_i < q_j$, the expectation (31) can be written as

$$\mathbb{E}[\Gamma_{ij}^*(F)\Gamma_{ji}^*(F)] = q_i q_j [(q_i-1)!]^2 \|f_{q_i} \widetilde{\otimes}_{q_i} f_{q_j}\|_{\mathfrak{H}^{\otimes(q_i+q_j-2r)}}^2$$

$$+ \sum_{r=1}^{q_i-1} [(r-1)!]^2 \binom{q_i-1}{r-1}^2 \binom{q_j-1}{r-1}^2$$

$$\times (q_i+q_j-2r)! \|f_{q_i} \widetilde{\otimes}_r f_{q_j}\|_{\mathfrak{H}^{\otimes(q_i+q_j-2r)}}^2. \qquad (32)$$

Since $\mathbb{E}[\Gamma_{ij}^*(F)] = 0$ for $q_i < q_j$, we deduce, from (32), that

$$\mathbb{E}[\Gamma_{ij}^*(F)\Gamma_{ji}^*(F)] \geq (\mathbb{E}[\Gamma_{ij}^*(F)])^2 \text{ for } q_i < q_j.$$

On the other hand, if $q_i = q_j$, then

$$\mathbb{E}[\Gamma_{ij}^*(F)\Gamma_{ji}^*(F)] = (q_i!)^2 \|f_{q_i}\|_{\mathfrak{H}^{\otimes q_i}}^4 \qquad (33)$$

$$+ \sum_{r=1}^{q_i-1} [(r-1)!]^2 \binom{q_i-1}{r-1}^2 \binom{q_j-1}{r-1}^2$$

$$\times (2q_i-2r)! \|f_{q_i} \widetilde{\otimes}_r f_{q_i}\|_{\mathfrak{H}^{\otimes(2q_i-2r)}}^2$$

$$\geq (\mathbb{E}[\Gamma_{ij}^*(F)])^2.$$

For the condition (γ): First, write

$$\sum_{l_1+l_2+l_3 = e_i + 2e_j} \mathbb{E}[\Gamma_{i,l_1,l_2,l_3}^*(F)]$$

$$= \mathbb{E}[\Gamma_{i,i,j,j}^*(F)] + \mathbb{E}[\Gamma_{i,j,i,j}^*(F)] + \mathbb{E}[\Gamma_{i,j,j,i}^*(F)]. \qquad (34)$$

Next, we compute the three expectations in (34). By the definition of the operator Γ^*, we obtain

$$\Gamma^*_{i_1,i_2,i_3,i_4}(F) \tag{35}$$

$$= \sum_{r_2=1}^{q_{i_1} \wedge q_{i_2}} \sum_{r_3=1}^{(q_{i_1}+q_{i_2}-2r_1)\wedge q_{i_3}} \sum_{r_4=1}^{(q_{i_1}+q_{i_2}+q_{i_3}-2r_1-2r_2)\wedge q_{i_4}}$$

$$\times \beta^*_{q_{i_1},\ldots,q_{i_4}}(r_2,r_3,r_4)\mathbf{1}_{\{2r_2<q_{i_1}+q_{i_2}\}}\mathbf{1}_{\{2r_2+2r_3<q_{i_1}+q_{i_2}+q_{i_3}\}}$$

$$\times I_{q_{i_1}+\cdots+q_{i_4}-2r_2-2r_3-2r_4}(((f_{q_{i_1}}\tilde{\otimes}_{r_2}f_{q_{i_2}})\tilde{\otimes}_{r_3}f_{q_{i_3}})\tilde{\otimes}_{r_4}f_{q_{i_4}}),$$

and

$$\Gamma_{i_1,i_2,i_3,i_4}(F) \tag{36}$$

$$= \sum_{r_2=1}^{q_{i_1} \wedge q_{i_2}} \sum_{r_3=1}^{(q_{i_1}+q_{i_2}-2r_1)\wedge q_{i_3}} \sum_{r_4=1}^{(q_{i_1}+q_{i_2}+q_{i_3}-2r_1-2r_2)\wedge q_{i_4}}$$

$$\times \beta_{q_{i_1},\ldots,q_{i_4}}(r_2,r_3,r_4)\mathbf{1}_{\{2r_2<q_{i_1}+q_{i_2}\}}\mathbf{1}_{\{2r_2+2r_3<q_{i_1}+q_{i_2}+q_{i_3}\}}$$

$$\times I_{q_{i_1}+\cdots+q_{i_4}-2r_2-2r_3-2r_4}(((f_{q_{i_1}}\tilde{\otimes}_{r_2}f_{q_{i_2}})\tilde{\otimes}_{r_3}f_{q_{i_3}})\tilde{\otimes}_{r_4}f_{q_{i_4}}).$$

When $q_{i_1}+\cdots+q_{i_4} = 2r_2+2r_3+2r_4$ and $r_3 \leq q_{i_1}+q_{i_2}+q_{i_3}-2r_2-2r_3$, we have that $q_{i_4} \geq r_4$. Hence, $r_4 = q_{i_4}$. Taking an expectation on (35) and (36) yields that

$$\mathbb{E}[\Gamma^*_{i_1,i_2,i_3,i_4}(F)] = \sum_{r_2=1}^{q_{i_1}\wedge q_{i_2}} \sum_{r_3=1}^{(q_{i_1}+q_{i_2}-2r_2)\wedge q_{i_3}} \beta^*_{q_{i_1},\ldots,q_{i_4}}(r_2,r_3,q_{i_4}) \tag{37}$$

$$\times J_1(i_1,\ldots,i_4;r_2,r_3)\mathbf{1}_{\{2r_2<q_{i_1}+q_{i_2}\}}$$

$$\times \mathbf{1}_{\{2r_2+2r_3=q_{i_1}+q_{i_2}+q_{i_3}-q_{i_4}\}},$$

and

$$\mathbb{E}[\Gamma_{i_1,i_2,i_3,i_4}(F)] = \sum_{r_2=1}^{q_{i_1}\wedge q_{i_2}} \sum_{r_3=1}^{(q_{i_1}+q_{i_2}-2r_2)\wedge q_{i_3}} \beta_{q_{i_1},\ldots,q_{i_4}}(r_2,r_3,q_{i_4}) \tag{38}$$

$$\times J_1(i_1,\ldots,i_4;r_2,r_3)\mathbf{1}_{\{2r_2<q_{i_1}+q_{i_2}\}}$$

$$\times \mathbf{1}_{\{2r_2+2r_3=q_{i_1}+q_{i_2}+q_{i_3}-q_{i_4}\}},$$

where

$$J_1(i_1,\ldots,i_4;r_2,r_3) = \langle (f_{q_{i_1}}\tilde{\otimes}_{r_2}f_{q_{i_2}})\tilde{\otimes}_{r_3}f_{q_{i_3}}, f_{q_{i_4}}\rangle_{\mathfrak{H}^{\otimes q_{i_4}}}.$$

Using the definition of coefficients β^* and β, we compute

$$\beta^*_{q_{i_1},\ldots,q_{i_4}}(r_2,r_3,q_{i_4}) - \epsilon\beta_{q_{i_1},\ldots,q_{i_4}}(r_2,r_3,q_{i_4}) \tag{39}$$

$$= (q_{i_4})!\left\{\beta^*_{q_{i_1},q_{i_2},q_{i_3}}(r_2,r_3) - \epsilon\beta_{q_{i_1},q_{i_2},q_{i_3}}(r_2,r_3)\right\}$$

$$= (q_{i_1}+q_{i_2}-2r_2-\epsilon q_{i_3})J_2(i_1,\ldots,i_4;r_2,r_3),$$

where

$$J_2(i_1,\ldots,i_4;r_2,r_3) = (q_{i_4})!\beta_{q_{i_1},q_{i_2}}(r_2)(r_3-1)!$$

$$\times \binom{q_{i_1}+q_{i_2}-2r_2-1}{r_3-1}\binom{q_{i_3}-1}{r_3-1}.$$

If $(i_1,\ldots,i_4) = (i,i,j,j), (i,j,i,j)$ or (i,j,j,i), then we have, from a similar estimate as for (29), that, for $1 \leq r_2 \leq q_{i_1} \wedge q_{i_2}$ and $1 \leq r_3 \leq (q_{i_1} + q_{i_2} - 2r_2) \wedge q_{i_3}$,

$$J_1(i_1,\ldots,i_4;r_2,r_3) \geq 0.$$

Indeed, for $(i_1,\ldots,i_4) = (i,i,j,j)$, it is sufficient to show that

$$\int_{\mathcal{Z}^{2(q_i+q_j)}} f_{q_i}(\mathbf{u}_1,\mathbf{v}_1,\mathbf{w}) f_{q_i}(\mathbf{u}_2,\mathbf{v}_2,\mathbf{w}) f_{q_j}(\mathbf{u}_1,\mathbf{u}_2,\mathbf{v}_3)$$
$$\times f_{q_j}(\mathbf{v}_1,\mathbf{v}_2,\mathbf{v}_3) \mu^{\otimes 2(q_i+q_j)}(d\mathbf{u}_1,d\mathbf{u}_2,\mathbf{w},d\mathbf{v}_1,d\mathbf{v}_2,d\mathbf{v}_3)$$
$$= \int_{\mathcal{Z}^{2(q_i+q_j)}} (f_{q_i} \otimes_{\ell(\mathbf{u}_1)} f_{q_j})(\mathbf{v}_1,\mathbf{u}_2,\mathbf{w},\mathbf{v}_3)$$
$$\times (f_{q_i} \otimes_{\ell(\mathbf{v}_2)} f_{q_j})(\mathbf{v}_1,\mathbf{u}_2,\mathbf{w},\mathbf{v}_3)(d\mathbf{v}_1,d\mathbf{u}_2,\mathbf{w},d\mathbf{v}_3) \geq 0, \quad (40)$$

where $\ell(\mathbf{u}_1) = \ell(\mathbf{v}_2)$. Similarly, we can show that, for $(i_1,\ldots,i_4) = (i,j,i,j)$ or (i,j,j,i),

$$J_1(i_1,\ldots,i_4;r_2,r_3) \geq 0.$$

These facts lead us to $\mathbb{E}[\Gamma_{i_1,i_2,i_3,i_4}(F)] \geq 0$ and $\mathbb{E}[\Gamma^*_{i_1,i_2,i_3,i_4}(F)] \geq 0$ for $(i_1,\ldots,i_4) = (i,i,j,j)$, (i,j,i,j) or (i,j,j,i), which implies that $\mathfrak{E}_{(d)}(F) \neq \emptyset$. Now, we find a constant $\mathfrak{e} > 0$ such that $\mathfrak{e} \in \mathfrak{E}_{(d)}(F)$. Let us set $J(\cdots) = J_1(\cdots) \times J_2(\cdots)$. From (37) and (38), we have, together with (39), that

$$\sum_{i,j=1}^{d} \left\{ \sum_{l_1+l_2+l_3=e_i+2e_j} \left(\mathbb{E}[\Gamma^*_{i,l_1,l_2,l_3}(F)] - \mathfrak{e}\mathbb{E}[\Gamma_{i,l_1,l_2,l_3}(F)] \right) \right\}$$
$$= \sum_{i,j=1}^{d} \left\{ \mathbb{E}[\Gamma^*_{i,i,j,j}(F)] - \mathfrak{e}\mathbb{E}[\Gamma_{i,i,j,j}(F)] + \mathbb{E}[\Gamma^*_{i,j,i,j}(F)] \right.$$
$$\left. - \mathfrak{e}\mathbb{E}[\Gamma_{i,j,i,j}(F)] + \mathbb{E}[\Gamma^*_{i,j,j,i}(F)] - \mathfrak{e}\mathbb{E}[\Gamma_{i,j,j,i}(F)] \right\}$$
$$= V_{1,d} + V_{2,d} + V_{3,d}, \quad (41)$$

where

$$V_{1,d} = \sum_{i,j=1}^{d} \sum_{r_2=1}^{q_i} (2q_i - 2r_2 - \mathfrak{e}q_j) J(i,i,j,j;r_2,r_3)$$
$$\times \mathbf{1}_{\{r_2<q_i\}} \mathbf{1}_{\{r_2+r_3=q_i\}},$$

$$V_{2,d} = \sum_{i,j=1}^{d} \sum_{r_2=1}^{q_i \wedge q_j} (q_i + q_j - 2r_2 - \mathfrak{e}q_j) J(i,j,i,j;r_2,r_3)$$
$$\times \mathbf{1}_{\{2r_2<q_i+q_j\}} \mathbf{1}_{\{r_2+r_3=q_i\}},$$

and

$$V_{3,d} = \sum_{i,j=1}^{d} \sum_{r_2=1}^{q_i \wedge q_j} (q_i + q_j - 2r_2 - \mathfrak{e}q_j) J(i,j,j,i;r_2,r_3)$$
$$\times \mathbf{1}_{\{2r_2<q_i+q_j\}} \mathbf{1}_{\{r_2+r_3=q_j\}}.$$

For every $i,j \in \{1,\ldots,d\}$ and $r_2 \in \{1,\ldots,q_i-1\}$, we have

$$(2q_i - 2r_2 - \mathfrak{e}q_j) \geq (2 - \mathfrak{e} \max_{1 \leq i \leq d} q_i).$$

This leads us to
$$V_{1,d} \geq (2 - \varepsilon \max_{1\leq i \leq d} q_i)\tilde{V}_{1,d}, \qquad (42)$$
where
$$\tilde{V}_{1,d} = \sum_{i,j=1}^{d} \sum_{r_2=1}^{q_i} J(i,i,j,j;r_2,r_3)\mathbf{1}_{\{r_2<q_i\}}\mathbf{1}_{\{r_2+r_3=q_i\}}.$$

For the second sum $V_{2,d}$ in (41), we change the range of r_2 from the inequality $2r_2 < q_i + q_j$ to
$$r_2 \leq \frac{q_i + q_j}{2} - \alpha_{i,j} \text{ for } \alpha_{i,j} \in (0,1],$$
where $[(q_i + q_j)/2] - \alpha_{i,j}$ is a positive integer. For fixed $i,j \in \{1,\ldots,d\}$,
$$(q_i + q_j - 2r_2 - \varepsilon q_j) \geq \left(q_i + q_j - 2\left[\left(\frac{q_i+q_j}{2} - \alpha_{i,j}\right) \wedge q_i\right] - \varepsilon q_j\right). \qquad (43)$$

If $q_i = q_j$ for $1 \leq i,j \leq d$, then, from (43), we have
$$\begin{aligned}(q_i + q_j - 2r_2 - \varepsilon q_j) &\geq (2q_i - 2(q_i - 1) - \varepsilon q_i) \\ &\geq (2 - \varepsilon \max_{1\leq i \leq d} q_i)\end{aligned} \qquad (44)$$

for every $i,j \in \{1,\ldots,d\}$ and $r_2 \in \{1,\ldots,q_i - 1\}$. For $q_j - q_i \geq 2$, we deduce, from (43), for fixed $i,j \in \{1,\ldots,d\}$, that
$$\begin{aligned}(q_i + q_j - 2r_2 - \varepsilon q_j) &\geq (q_i + q_j - 2q_i - \varepsilon q_j) \\ &\geq (2 - \varepsilon \max_{1\leq i \leq d} q_i).\end{aligned} \qquad (45)$$

For $q_j = q_i + 1$ and $0 < \alpha_{i,j} \leq 0.5$, the Inequality (43) yields
$$\begin{aligned}(q_i + q_j - 2r_2 - \varepsilon q_j) &\geq (2q_i + 1 - 2q_i - \varepsilon q_j) \\ &\geq (1 - \varepsilon \max_{1\leq i \leq d} q_i).\end{aligned} \qquad (46)$$

On the other hand, if $q_j = q_i + 1$ and $0.5 < \alpha_{i,j} \leq 1$, then we obtain, from (43), that
$$\begin{aligned}(q_i + q_j - 2r_2 - \varepsilon q_j) &\geq \left[2q_i + 1 - 2\left(q_i + \frac{1}{2} - \alpha_{i,j}\right) - \varepsilon q_j\right] \\ &\geq (2\alpha_{i,j} - \varepsilon q_j) \\ &\geq (1 - \varepsilon \max_{1\leq i \leq d} q_i).\end{aligned} \qquad (47)$$

Combining the above results (44)–(47), we obtain
$$V_{2,d} \geq (1 - \varepsilon \max_{1\leq i \leq d} q_i)\tilde{V}_{2,d}, \qquad (48)$$
where
$$\tilde{V}_{2,d} = \sum_{i,j=1}^{d} \sum_{r_2=1}^{q_i \wedge q_j} J(i,j,i,j;r_2,r_3)\mathbf{1}_{\{2r_2<q_i+q_j\}}\mathbf{1}_{\{r_2+r_3=q_i\}}.$$

Similarly,
$$V_{3,d} \geq (1 - \varepsilon \max_{1\leq i \leq d} q_i)\tilde{V}_{3,d}, \qquad (49)$$

where
$$\tilde{V}_{3,d} = \sum_{i,j=1}^{d} \sum_{r_2=1}^{q_i \wedge q_j} J(i,j,j,i;r_2,r_3)\mathbf{1}_{\{2r_2 < q_i+q_j\}}\mathbf{1}_{\{r_2+r_3=q_j\}}.$$

The Inequalities (42), (48), and (49) yield

$$\sum_{i,j=1}^{d} \left\{ \sum_{l_1+l_2+l_3=e_i+2e_j} \left(\mathbb{E}[\Gamma^*_{i,l_1,l_2,l_3}(F)] - \mathfrak{e}\mathbb{E}[\Gamma_{i,l_1,l_2,l_3}(F)] \right) \right\}$$
$$\geq (1 - \mathfrak{e} \max_{1 \leq i \leq d} q_i)(\tilde{V}_{1,d} + \tilde{V}_{2,d} + \tilde{V}_{3,d})$$
$$\geq 0 \text{ for } \mathfrak{e} \in \left[0, \frac{1}{\max_{1 \leq i \leq d} q_i}\right],$$

so that the condition (γ) is satisfied. Hence, applying Theorem 2 gives the desired conclusion. If $q_1 = \cdots = q_d = q$, the estimate in (42) yields a constant $\mathfrak{e}$ given in (25). □

Remark 4. 1. Theorem 3 proves that the three assumptions in Theorem 2 are satisfied under the same conditions as in Theorem 4.3 of [19]. To achieve this, we just need to explicitly compute the expected values of Gamma operators and compare them.
2. The estimate in Theorem 4.3 of [19] corresponds to the estimate (24) with $\mathfrak{e} = 0$. Hence, our approach improves the rate of constants appearing in the previous estimate given in [19]. If $q_1 = \cdots = q_d = 1$, then $\mathfrak{e} = 2$, which implies that F has the same distribution with Z.

5. Results in Dimension One ($d = 1$)

In this section, we specialize the results given in the previous Sections 3 and 4 to the one-dimensional case. We begin with a one-dimensional version of Gamma operators Γ and Γ^* (for these operators, see [21,22]). We set $\Gamma_1(F) = F$ and $\Gamma_1^*(F) = F$. If F is a well-defined element in $\mathbb{L}^2(\Omega)$, we set $\Gamma_{k+1}(F) = \langle DF, -DL^{-1}\Gamma_k(F)\rangle_{\mathfrak{H}}$ and $\Gamma_{k+1}^*(F) = \langle -DL^{-1}F, D\Gamma_k^*(F)\rangle_{\mathfrak{H}}$ for $k = 1, 2, \ldots$.

Theorem 4. If $d = 1$, the conditions (α), (β), and (γ) are satisfied under the assumption $\mathbb{E}[\Gamma_4(F)] \neq 0$.

Proof. The assumptions (α) and (β) obviously hold. Indeed, the Cauchy–Schwartz inequality proves that
$$\mathbb{E}[\Gamma_2^*(F)^2] \geq (\mathbb{E}[\Gamma_2^*(F)])^2,$$
where $\Gamma_2^*(F) = \Gamma_2(F) = \langle -DL^{-1}F, DF\rangle_{\mathfrak{H}}$. A repeated application of Lemma 1 proves that
$$\mathbb{E}[\Gamma_2(F)^2] = \mathbb{E}[F^2\Gamma_2(F)] - \mathbb{E}[\Gamma_4^*(F)]$$
$$= 2\mathbb{E}[\Gamma_4(F)] + (\mathbb{E}[F^2])^2 - \mathbb{E}[\Gamma_4^*(F)].$$

This shows that $\mathbb{V}ar(\Gamma_2(F)) = 2\mathbb{E}[\Gamma_4(F)] - \mathbb{E}[\Gamma_4^*(F)]$. Let $\phi(x) = \mathbb{E}[\Gamma_4(F)]x - \mathbb{E}[\Gamma_4^*(F)]$. Then, $\phi(2) \geq 0$. Since $\mathbb{E}[\Gamma_4(F)] \neq 0$, there exists a constant $\mathfrak{e} \in \mathbb{R}$ such that $\phi(\mathfrak{e}) \leq 0$. This implies that the condition (γ) is satisfied. □

Remark 5. If $\mathbb{E}[F] = 0$, it follows from (8) that
$$\mathbb{E}[\Gamma_4(F)] = \frac{1}{6}\left(\mathbb{E}[F^4] - 3(\mathbb{E}[F^2])^2\right). \tag{50}$$

Studies so far have shown that Inequality (1) holds true only when F belongs to a fixed Wiener chaos. However, the technique developed here can be applied to prove that the fourth moment theorem (1) holds even if F is not an element of a fixed Wiener chaos. The proof in Theorem 4 yields, together with (50), that

$$\operatorname{Var}(\Gamma_2(F)) \leq \frac{2-\mathfrak{e}}{6}\left(\mathbb{E}[F^4] - 3(\mathbb{E}[F^2])^2\right), \tag{51}$$

where a constant $\mathfrak{e}$ satisfies $\phi(\mathfrak{e}) \leq 0$. Note that the constant given in (12) is three times that in (51).

Proposition 2. *Let ϕ be a linear function in the proof of Theorem 4. Let $F = I_q(f)$ with $f \in \mathfrak{H}^{\odot q}$ ($q \geq 2$). Then, there exists a constant $\mathfrak{e} \in [2/q, 2)$ such that $\phi(\mathfrak{e}) \leq 0$, and $(-\infty, 2/q] \subseteq \mathfrak{E}_{(1)}(F)$.*

Proof. A direct computation yields that

$$\begin{aligned}
\mathbb{E}[\Gamma_4^*(F)] &= q! \sum_{r=1}^{q-1} \beta_{q,q}^*(r)(2q-2r)(q-r-1)! \binom{2q-2r-1}{q-r-1} \\
&\quad \times \binom{q-1}{q-r-1} \|f \tilde{\otimes}_r f\|_{\mathfrak{H}^{\odot(2q-2r)}}^2 > 0.
\end{aligned} \tag{52}$$

On the other hand, Theorem 5.1 in [22] shows that

$$\begin{aligned}
\mathbb{E}[\Gamma_4(F)] &= q! \sum_{r=1}^{q-1} \beta_{q,q}(r) q (q-r-1)! \binom{2q-2r-1}{q-r-1} \\
&\quad \times \binom{q-1}{q-r-1} \|f \tilde{\otimes}_r f\|_{\mathfrak{H}^{\odot(2q-2r)}}^2 > 0.
\end{aligned} \tag{53}$$

Combining (52) and (53) (or $V_{1,d}$ for $d = 1$ in (41) in the proof of Theorem 3) together with $\beta_{q,q}^* = \beta_{q,q}$, we obtain that

$$\begin{aligned}
-\phi(\mathfrak{e}) &= \mathbb{E}[\Gamma_4^*(F)] - \mathfrak{e}\mathbb{E}[\Gamma_4(F)] \\
&= q! \sum_{r=1}^{q-1} \beta_{q,q}(r)(2q - 2r - \mathfrak{e}q)(q-r-1)! \binom{2q-2r-1}{q-r-1} \\
&\quad \times \binom{q-1}{q-r-1} \|f \tilde{\otimes}_r f\|_{\mathfrak{H}^{\odot(2q-2r)}}^2 \\
&\geq (2 - \mathfrak{e}q) q! \sum_{r=1}^{q-1} \beta_{q,q}(r)(q-r-1)! \binom{2q-2r-1}{q-r-1} \\
&\quad \times \binom{q-1}{q-r-1} \|f \tilde{\otimes}_r f\|_{\mathfrak{H}^{\odot(2q-2r)}}^2.
\end{aligned} \tag{54}$$

This Inequality (54) shows that $\phi(2/q) \leq 0$. Since $\mathbb{E}[\Gamma_4^*(F)] > 0$ and $\mathbb{E}[\Gamma_4(F)] > 0$, it may be possible for $\mathfrak{e}$ to belong to $[2/q, 2)$. □

Remark 6. *Substituting $2/q$ for $\mathfrak{e}$ in (51), we can derive the* fourth moment theorem *in (2). By using the new method developed in this paper, we show that the constant term given in (51) is less than or equal to the one in (2). This means that*

$$\frac{2 - \mathfrak{e}}{6} \leq \frac{q-1}{3}. \tag{55}$$

Let's take an example that satisfies (55).

Example 1. *We consider the case of $q = 3$. Let $F = I_3(h^{\otimes 3})$ with $h \in \mathfrak{H}$. A similar computation as for (54) proves that*

$$\begin{aligned}
&\mathbb{E}[\Gamma_4^*(F)] - \mathfrak{e}\mathbb{E}[\Gamma_4(F)] \\
&= 3! \times 3 \sum_{r=1}^{2}(r-1)!\binom{2}{r-1}^2 (6 - 2r - \mathfrak{e}q)(3-r-1)! \\
&\quad \times \binom{6-2r-1}{3-r-1}\binom{2}{3-r-1}\|h^{\otimes 3}\tilde{\otimes}_r h^{\otimes 3}\|_{\mathfrak{H}^{\otimes(6-2r)}}^2 \\
&= (3! \times 18)(4 - 3\mathfrak{e})\|h^{\otimes 3}\tilde{\otimes}_1 h^{\otimes 3}\|_{\mathfrak{H}^{\otimes 4}}^2 \\
&\quad + (3! \times 12)(2 - 3\mathfrak{e})\|h^{\otimes 3}\tilde{\otimes}_2 h^{\otimes 3}\|_{\mathfrak{H}^{\otimes 2}}^2 \\
&= 72\left(8 - \frac{15}{2}\mathfrak{e}\right)\|h\|_{\mathfrak{H}}^6.
\end{aligned} \quad (56)$$

From (56), it follows that $(-\infty, 16/15] = \mathfrak{C}_{(1)}(F)$ and

$$\mathfrak{e} = \frac{\mathbb{E}[\Gamma_4^*(F)]}{\mathbb{E}[\Gamma_4(F)]} = 16/15.$$

As a consequence of (51), the upper bound is given by

$$\mathbb{V}ar(\Gamma_2(F)) \leq \sqrt{\frac{7}{45}}\sqrt{\mathbb{E}[F^4] - 3(\mathbb{E}[F^2])^2}. \quad (57)$$

On the other hand, the estimate (2) ($q = 3$) gives

$$\mathbb{V}ar(\Gamma_2(F)) \leq \sqrt{\frac{30}{45}}\sqrt{\mathbb{E}[F^4] - 3(\mathbb{E}[F^2])^2}. \quad (58)$$

Compare the constant in (57) with that in (58).

6. Conclusions and Future Works

This paper finds a method to obtain the fourth moment bound on the normal approximation of F, where F is a d-dimensional random vector whose components are general functionals of Gaussian fields. In order to prove the *fourth moment theorem*, all we need to do is to show that the conditions (α), (β), and (γ) in Theorem 2 are satisfied. The significant feature of our works is that these conditions are naturally satisfied in the specific case where F is a random variable belonging to the vector-valued multiple integrals. In addition, our technique yields a much better estimate than the conventional method. Comparing with the studies in literatures [3,14–16,19,20], our study is not only an extension of these studies, but it is also possible to naturally derive the results of existing studies.

As future research directions, we will apply our approach for the *fourth moment theorem*, developed here, to more general processes, including Markov diffusion processes and Poisson processes. Our developed approach is expected to integrate the *fourth moment theorem* for many processes.

Author Contributions: Conceptualization, Y.-T.K. and H.-S.P.; methodology, Y.-T.K.; writing and original draft preparation, Y.-T.K. and H.-S.P.; co-review and validation, H.-S.P.; writing—editing and funding acquisition. All authors have read and agreed to the published version of the manuscript.

Funding: This research was supported by Hallym University Research Fund 2021 (HRF-202112-005).

Institutional Review Board Statement: Not applicable.

Informed Consent Statement: Not applicable.

Data Availability Statement: Not applicable.

Acknowledgments: We are very grateful to the anonymous Referees for their suggestions and valuable advice.

Conflicts of Interest: The authors declare no conflict of interest.

References

1. Nualart, D.; Peccati, G. Central limit theorems for sequences of multiple stochastic integrals. *Ann. Probab.* **2005**, *33*, 177–193. [CrossRef]
2. Nualart, D.; Ortiz-Latorre, S. Central limit theorems for multiple stochastic integrals and Malliavin calculus. *Ann. Probab.* **2008**, *33*, 177–193. [CrossRef]
3. Nourdin, I.; Peccati, G. Stein's method on Wiener chaos. *Probab. Theory Related Fields* **2009**, *145*, 75–118. [CrossRef]
4. Nourdin, I.; Peccati, G. *Normal Approximations with Malliavin Calculus: From Stein's Method to Universality*; Cambridge Tracts in Mathematica; Cambridge University Press: Cambridge, MA, USA, 2012; Volume 192.
5. Nualart, D. *Malliavin Calculus and Related Topics*, 2nd ed.; Probability and Its Applications; Springer: Berlin, Germany, 2006.
6. Nualart, D. *Malliavin Calculus and Its Applications*; Regional Conference Series in Mathematics Number 110; American Mathematical Society: Providence, RI, USA, 2008.
7. Stein, C. A bound for the error in the normal approximation to the distribution of a sum of dependent random variables. In *Proceedings of the Sixth Berkeley Symposium on Mathematical Statistics and Probabiltiy*; University of California Press: Berkeley, CA, USA, 1972; Voume II, pp. 583–602.
8. Stein, C. *Approximate Computation of Expectations*; IMS: Hayward, CA, USA, 1986.
9. Chen, L.H.Y.; Goldstein, L.; Shao, Q.-M. *Normal Approximation by Stein's Method*; Springer: Heidelberg/Berin, Germany, 2011.
10. Nourdin, I.; Peccati, G. Stein's method and exact Berry-Esseen asymptotics for functionals of Gaussian fields. *Ann. Probab.* **2009**, *37*, 2231–2261. [CrossRef]
11. Nourdin, I.; Peccati, G. The optimal fourth moment theorem. *Proc. Am. Math. Soc.* **2015**, *143*, 3123–3133. [CrossRef]
12. Nourdin, I.; Peccati, G. Stein's method meets Malliavin calculus: A short survey with new estimates. In *Recent Development in Stochastic Dynamics and Stochasdtic Analysis*; World Sci. Publ.: Hackensack, NJ, USA, 2010; Volume 8, pp. 207–236
13. Kemp, T.; Nourdin, I.; Peccati, G.; Speicher, R. Winger chaos and the fourth moment. *Ann. Probab.* **2012**, *40*, 1577–1635. [CrossRef]
14. Noreddine, S.; Nourdin, I. On the Gaussian approximation of vector-valued multiple integrals. *J. Multi. Anal.* **2011**, *102*, 1008–1017. [CrossRef]
15. Nourdin, I.; Peccati, G.; Réveillac, A. Multivariate normal approximation using Stein's method and Malliavin calcululus. *Ann. L'Institut Henri-PoincarÉ-Probab. Atstistiques* **2010**, *46*, 45–58.
16. Peccati, G.; Tudor, C. Gaussian limits for vector-valued multiple stochastic integrals. In *Séminaire de Probabilités XXXVIII*; Springer: Berlin, Germany, 2005; Volume 1857, pp. 247–262.
17. Azmoodeh, E.; Campese, S.; Poly, G. Fourth moment theorems for Markov diffusion generators. *J. Funct. Anal.* **2014**, *9*, 473–500. [CrossRef]
18. Ledoux, M. Chaos of a Markov operator and the fourth moment theorem. *Ann. Probab.* **2012**, *40*, 2439–2459. [CrossRef]
19. Nourdin, I.; Rosinski, J. Asymptotic independence of multiple Wiener-Itô integrals and the resulting limit laws. *Ann. Probab.* **2014**, *42*, 497–526. [CrossRef]
20. Campese, S. Optimal convergence rates and one-term Edgeworth expansions for multidimensional functionals of Gaussian fields. *ALeA Lat. Am. J. Probab. Math. Stat.* **2013**, *10*, 881–919.
21. Kim, Y.T.; Park, H.S. An Edeworth expansion for functionals of Gaussian fields and its applications. *Stoch. Proc. Their Appl.* **2018**, *44*, 312–320.
22. Nourdin, I.; Peccati, G. Cumulants on the Wiener space. *J. Funct. Anal.* **2010**, *258*, 3775–3791. [CrossRef]

Article

Testing for the Rayleigh Distribution: A New Test with Comparisons to Tests for Exponentiality Based on Transformed Data

Gerrit Lodewicus Grobler, Elzanie Bothma * and James Samuel Allison

School of Mathematical and Statistical Sciences, Faculty of Natural and Agricultural Sciences, North-West University, Potchefstroom 2531, South Africa; gerrit.grobler@nwu.ac.za (G.L.G.); james.allison@nwu.ac.za (J.S.A.)
* Correspondence: elzanie.bothma@nwu.ac.za

Abstract: We propose a new goodness-of-fit test for the Rayleigh distribution which is based on a distributional fixed-point property of the Stein characterization. The limiting null distribution of the test is derived and the consistency against fixed alternatives is also shown. The results of a finite-sample comparison is presented, where we compare the power performance of the new test to a variety of other tests. In addition to existing tests for the Rayleigh distribution we also exploit the link between the exponential and Rayleigh distributions. This allows us to include some powerful tests developed specifically for the exponential distribution in the comparison. It is found that the new test outperforms competing tests for many of the alternative distributions. Interestingly, the highest estimated power, against all alternative distributions considered, is obtained by one of the tests specifically developed for the Rayleigh distribution and not by any of the exponentiality tests based on the transformed data. The use of the new test is illustrated on a real-world COVID-19 data set.

Keywords: asymptotics; goodness-of-fit; Monte Carlo simulation; Rayleigh distribution; Stein characterization

MSC: 62F03; 62F05

1. Introduction

In 1880 an acoustics problem gave rise to a distribution that nowadays plays a prominent role in research fields such as reliability theory, life testing and survival analysis (see, e.g., [1]). The Rayleigh distribution was introduced by [2], while undertaking a study regarding the resultant of a great number of sound waves with differing phases. Refs. [3,4] demonstrated the importance of the Rayleigh distribution in communication engineering and electro-vacuum devices, respectively. Ref. [5] found that the Rayleigh distribution has clinical applications, specifically estimating the noise variance of Magnetic Resonance Images (MRI). Ref. [6] discusses this phenomenon and proposed that this estimation can be done by fitting the density function of the Rayleigh distribution to the partial histogram of the MRI. Ref. [7] improved this estimation with the use of background segmentation, by fitting the density function of the Rayleigh distribution to the histogram of the segmented background in order to estimate the noise variance. The estimation of the noise forms a crucial part in efficiently denoising the MRI as well as in the quality assessment of these images. The Rayleigh distribution has also become a popular model in survival analysis and reliability theory, see, e.g., [8,9].

For any of the above-mentioned applications to be relevant, it is crucial to test the hypothesis that the observed data are indeed realisations from a Rayleigh distribution. Since the square of a Rayleigh distributed variable is exponentially distributed, goodness-of-fit tests designed for the exponential distribution can be used to test for the Rayleigh

distribution—a fact that we investigate further in Section 4. However, even though the applications of the Rayleigh distribution increased significantly over the past few decades, literature on tests specifically developed for the Rayleigh distribution is relatively scarce. Some of these include a test proposed by [10] based on the empirical Laplace transform, a test based on entropy suggested by [11] as well as [12] and an empirical likelihood based test by [13]. It has become a common approach to use distributional characterizations to propose goodness-of-fit testing procedures, see, e.g., Ref. [14] and the references therein. In this paper, we propose a new test for the Rayleigh distribution based on a modification of Stein's characterization discussed by [15].

The standard Stein characterization (see [16]) of the normal distribution states that Z is standard normal if, and only if,

$$\mathbb{E}[g'(Z) - Zg(Z)] = 0 \tag{1}$$

is true for all absolute continuous functions g for which the expectation exists. Some applications, such as goodness-of-fit tests based on (1), are rather complicated, since the results depend on the choice of g. Instead of using this relationship, Ref. [17] characterised the standard normal distribution based on the zero bias distribution. A real valued random variable X^* is said to have a X zero-bias distribution if

$$\mathbb{E}[g'(X^*)] = \mathbb{E}[Xg(X)]$$

holds for all absolutely continuous functions g for which the expectation exists. If $\mathbb{E}X = 0$ and $\mathrm{Var}(X) = 1$, the X zero-bias distribution exists, is unique and has distribution function

$$F(t) = \mathbb{E}[X(X-t)\mathbb{1}\{X \leq t\}], t \in \mathbb{R}.$$

Using this distribution function, ref. [17] showed that Z is standard normal if, and only if, the distribution function of Z is given by $F(t)$. Ref. [15] generalised this method to a wide range of continuous distributions by generalising Stein's characterization. They showed that if X has support $[0, \infty)$, then it has distribution F if, and only if, the distribution function of X is given by

$$F(t) = \mathbb{E}\left[-\frac{f'(X)}{f(X)} \min\{X, t\}\right], t \in (0, \infty), \tag{2}$$

where f is the density of X. The result in (2) is true under some regularity conditions on f, which will be discussed in Section 2. The characterization in (2) will be used to develop a new goodness-of-fit test specifically for the Rayleigh distribution.

Before proceeding some notation is introduced. Let $X_1, \ldots, X_n$ be independent and identically distributed (i.i.d.) continuous realisations of a positive random variable X with unknown distribution function F and density f. If X follows a Rayleigh distribution with density function

$$f(x) = \frac{x}{\theta^2} e^{-\frac{x^2}{2\theta^2}}, x \geq 0, \theta > 0,$$

it will be denoted by $X \sim Ral(\theta)$. The composite goodness-of-fit hypothesis to be tested is

$$H_0: \text{the distribution of } X \text{ is } Ral(\theta), \tag{3}$$

for some $\theta > 0$, against general alternatives.

The remainder of the article is organised as follows: In Section 2, the new test statistic is introduced. Section 3 contains the basic theoretical results pertaining to the asymptotic behaviour of the test. The results of a Monte Carlo study, where the power performance of the newly proposed test is compared to some existing tests, is given in Section 4. The competing tests also include five powerful tests for exponentiality based on transformed data.

The paper concludes in Section 5 with an application of the test to a real-world COVID-19 data set and some concluding remarks.

2. Test Statistic

For the characterization in (2) to be true the following regularity conditions, see [15], should hold:

(I) f is continuously differentiable on $[0, \infty)$;
(II) $f(x) > 0$ for every $x \in [0, \infty)$;
(III) for $\kappa_f(x) = \left| \frac{f'(x) \min\{F(x), 1-F(x)\}}{f^2(x)} \right|$ we have $\sup_{x \in [0, \infty]} \kappa_f(x) < \infty$;
(IV) $\int_0^\infty (1 + |x|) |f'(x)| dx < \infty$;
(V) $\lim_{x \to 0} \frac{F(x)}{f(x)} = 0$;
(VI) $\lim_{x \to \infty} \frac{1-F(x)}{f(x)} = 0$.

It can easily be seen that conditions (I), (II), (V) and (VI) hold for the Rayleigh distribution. For $X \sim Ral(\theta)$, κ_f in condition (III) becomes

$$\kappa_f(x) = \frac{\theta^2 e^{x^2/2\theta^2}}{x^2} \min\{F(x), 1 - F(x)\} \left| 1 - \frac{x^2}{\theta^2} \right|$$

and for $x^2 > \theta^2$; $\left| 1 - \frac{x^2}{\theta^2} \right| = \frac{x^2}{\theta^2} - 1$. For x large enough we have that $1 - F(x) < F(x)$; thus,

$$\lim_{x \to \infty} \kappa_f(x) = \theta^2 \lim_{x \to \infty} \left(\frac{\exp(x^2/2\theta^2)}{x^2} \right) (1 - F(x)) \left(\frac{x^2}{\theta^2} - 1 \right) = 1$$

Because x is sufficiently small, we have that $F(x) < 1 - F(x)$; thus, we have

$$\lim_{x \to 0} \kappa_f(x) = \theta^2 \lim_{x \to 0} \exp(-x^2/2\theta^2) \left(1 - \frac{x^2}{\theta^2} \right) \frac{\left(1 - e^{x^2/2\theta^2}\right)}{x^2} = \frac{1}{2\theta^2} \theta^2 = \frac{1}{2}.$$

Since $\kappa_f(x)$ is continuous with limits 1 and $\frac{1}{2}$ as x tends to infinity and zero, respectively, it implies that $\sup_{x \in [0, \infty)} \kappa_f(x) < \infty$.

The integral in condition (IV) can be written as follows in terms of expectations:

$$\int_0^\infty (1 + |x|) \left(1 - \frac{x^2}{\theta^2} \right) \left(\frac{1}{\theta^2} \right) e^{-x^2/2\theta^2} dx = \mathbb{E}\left(\{1 + X\} \left\{ 1 - \frac{X^2}{\theta^2} \right\} \right),$$

where X is Rayleigh distributed. The finite moments of the Rayleigh distribution exist, i.e., $\mathbb{E}(X^k) < \infty$, $k \in \mathbb{N}$. Therefore,

$$\int_0^\infty (1 + |x|) |f'(x)| dx < \infty.$$

In Proposition 1 below, the characterization in (2) is re-stated specifically for the Rayleigh distribution.

Proposition 1. *Let $X : \Omega \to (0, \infty)$ be a random variable with distribution function F and density function f that satisfies conditions (I)–(VI) and $\mathbb{E}[X] < \infty$. Then $X \sim Ral(\theta)$ if, and only if,*

$$\mathbb{E}\left[\left(\frac{X}{\theta^2} - \frac{1}{X} \right) \min\{X, t\} \right] - F(t) = 0, t > 0.$$

Note that $X \sim Ral(\theta)$ if, and only if, $Y = \frac{X}{\theta} \sim Ral(1)$. This follows from the invariance property of the Rayleigh distribution with respect to scale transformations. This implies that $Y \sim Ral(1)$ if, and only if, for all $t > 0$

$$\psi(t) = T^Y(t) - F^Y(t) = 0, \tag{4}$$

where $T^Y(t) = \mathbb{E}[(Y - 1/Y) \min(Y, t)]$ and F^Y is the distribution function of Y. Our newly proposed test is motivated by (4). Since $\psi(t)$ will be unknown, we estimate it by its empirical counterpart,

$$\hat{\psi}_n(t) = T_n^Y(t) - F_n^Y(t),$$

where $T_n^Y(t) = \frac{1}{n} \sum_{j=1}^n (Y_j - 1/Y_j) \min(Y_j, t)$, $F_n^Y(t) = \frac{1}{n} \sum_{j=1}^n I(Y_j \leq t)$ and $Y_j = X_j/\hat{\theta}_n$, with $\hat{\theta}_n = \sqrt{(2n)^{-1} \sum_{j=1}^n X_j^2}$ the maximum likelihood estimator for θ.

We propose the following weighted L^2–distance between $\hat{\psi}(t)$ and 0 to test the hypothesis in (3):

$$R_{n,a} = n \int_0^\infty \hat{\psi}_n^2(t) w_a(t) dt, \tag{5}$$

where $w_a(t)$ is a positive, continuous weight function depending on a positive tuning parameter a. The test rejects for large values of $R_{n,a}$. Throughout the paper we use $w_a(t) = e^{-at}$ as the weight function, which results in the following easily calculable form of the test statistic:

$$R_{n,a} = \frac{1}{n} \sum_{j=1}^n \left(-\frac{1}{a} e^{-aY_{(j)}} \left[\left\{ Y_{(j)} - \frac{1}{Y_{(j)}} \right\}^2 \left\{ \frac{2}{a} Y_{(j)} + \frac{2}{a^2} \right\} + 2Y_{(j)}^2 - 3 \right] + \frac{2}{a^3} \left[Y_{(j)}^2 - 2 + \frac{1}{Y_{(j)}^2} \right] \right)$$

$$+ \frac{2}{n} \sum_{1 \leq j < k \leq n} \left(\left\{ Y_{(j)} - \frac{1}{Y_{(j)}} \right\} \left\{ Y_{(k)} - \frac{1}{Y_{(k)}} \right\} \left(-\frac{1}{a} e^{-aY_{(j)}} \left\{ \frac{1}{a} Y_{(j)} + \frac{2}{a^2} \right\} + \frac{2}{a^3} - \frac{Y_{(j)}}{a^2} e^{-aY_{(k)}} \right) \right.$$

$$+ \left\{ Y_{(j)} - \frac{1}{Y_{(j)}} \right\} \left\{ -\frac{Y_{(j)}}{a} e^{-aY_{(k)}} \right\}$$

$$\left. + \left\{ Y_{(k)} - \frac{1}{Y_{(k)}} \right\} \left\{ \frac{1}{a^2} e^{-aY_{(k)}} - \frac{1}{a} e^{-aY_{(j)}} \left(Y_{(j)} + \frac{1}{a} \right) \right\} + \frac{1}{a} e^{-aY_{(k)}} \right),$$

where $Y_{(1)} < Y_{(2)} < \cdots < Y_{(n)}$ denotes the order statistics of $Y_1, \ldots, Y_n$.

Remark 1. *The most commonly used choices for the weight function $w_a(\cdot)$ are $w_a(t) = e^{-a|t|}$ and $w_a(t) = e^{-at^2}$ (see, e.g., [18,19]). Due to the positive support of the Rayleigh distribution, we use $w_a(t) = e^{-a|t|} = e^{-at}$, $t \geq 0$. This choice does not only provide a close form expression for the test statistic, but also competitive powers which are reported in the Monte Carlo simulation study (see Section 4).*

3. Asymptotics

In this section, we will first show that, under the null hypothesis, $R_{n,a}$ converges in distribution to a norm of a Gaussian element of the Hilbert space $\mathcal{H} = L^2((0, \infty), \mathcal{B})$ of measurable, square integrable functions. The norm $\|\cdot\|_\mathcal{H}$ that will be used is defined in terms of a random element G_n of $\mathcal{H}$, $n \in \mathbb{N}$, by

$$\|G_n\|_\mathcal{H} = \left(\int_0^\infty \{G_n(t)\}^2 e^{-at} dt \right)^{\frac{1}{2}}.$$

We will also show that the newly proposed test is consistent.

First note that by substituting t with $\frac{s}{\hat{\theta}_n}$ and Y_j with $\frac{X_j}{\hat{\theta}_n}$ in (5) the test statistic $R_{n,a}$ can be rewritten as

$$R_{n,a} = \frac{1}{\hat{\theta}_n} \int_0^\infty \left(\sqrt{n} \left\{ \hat{T}_n^X(s) - F_n^X(s) \right\} \right)^2 e^{-as/\hat{\theta}_n} ds, \qquad (6)$$

where

$$\hat{T}_n^X(s) = \frac{1}{n\hat{\theta}_n^2} \sum_{j=1}^n \left(X_j - \frac{\hat{\theta}_n^2}{X_j} \right) \min\{X_j, s\} \qquad (7)$$

is a continuous function.

To obtain our two main results, we use the following Lemma, in which the notation $G_n \approx H_n$ is used when $||G_n - H_n||_{\mathcal{H}}^2 = o_{\mathbb{P}}(1)$, where $o_{\mathbb{P}}(1)$ denotes a sequence of random variables that converge to zero in probability. We also assume, w.l.o.g., that $\theta = 1$.

Lemma 1. *Suppose $X, X_1, X_2, \ldots$ are i.i.d. random variables with distribution function F^X and $\mathbb{E}[X^4] < \infty$. Let $\hat{T}_n^X(s)$ be defined as in (7), then*

$$\hat{T}_n^X(s) = \frac{1}{\hat{\theta}_n^2} \left\{ T_n^X(s) + \left(1 - \hat{\theta}_n^2\right) r_n^X(s) \right\},$$

where

$$r_n^X(s) = \frac{1}{n} \sum_{j=1}^n \frac{1}{X_j} \min\{X_j, s\},$$

and

$$T_n^X(s) = \frac{1}{n} \sum_{j=1}^n \left(X_j - \frac{1}{X_j} \right) \min(X_j, s).$$

We also have that

$$\sqrt{n} \hat{T}_n^X(s) \approx \frac{\sqrt{n}}{\hat{\theta}_n^2} \left\{ T_n^X(s) + \left(1 - \hat{\theta}_n^2\right) r^X(s) \right\},$$

where

$$r^X(s) = \mathbb{E}\left[\frac{1}{X} \min\{X, s\}\right].$$

Proof. The first result follows immediately by rewriting $\hat{T}_n^X(s)$ in (7) as

$$\hat{T}_n^X(s) = \frac{1}{n\hat{\theta}_n^2} \sum_{j=1}^n \left[\left(X_j - \frac{1}{X_j} \right) \min\{X_j, s\} + \left(\frac{1}{X_j} - \frac{\hat{\theta}_n^2}{X_j} \right) \min\{X_j, s\} \right].$$

To show the second result we notice that

$$\sqrt{n} \left\{ \hat{T}_n^X(s) - \frac{1}{\hat{\theta}_n^2} \left[T_n^X(s) + \left(1 - \hat{\theta}_n^2\right) r^X(s) \right] \right\} = \frac{\sqrt{n}(1 - \hat{\theta}_n^2)}{\hat{\theta}_n^2} \left\{ r_n^X(s) - r^X(s) \right\}.$$

Applying a weak form of the law of large numbers in separable Hilbert spaces, we have that $r_n^X(s) = r^X(s) + o_{\mathbb{P}}(1)$ and by the continuous mapping theorem $||r^X - r_n^X||_{\mathcal{H}}^2 = o_{\mathbb{P}}(1)$. Since $\hat{\theta}_n^2$ is the maximum likelihood estimator of θ^2, we have that $\sqrt{n}(1 - \hat{\theta}_n^2) = \mathcal{O}_{\mathbb{P}}(1)$, where $\mathcal{O}_{\mathbb{P}}(1)$ denotes a sequence of random variables that is bounded in probability. The result then follows from Slutsky's theorem. □

Theorem 1. *Let $X, X_1, X_2, \ldots$ be i.i.d. standard Rayleigh random variables. There exists a centred Gaussian element $\mathcal{W}$ of $\mathcal{H}$ such that $R_{n,a} \xrightarrow{\mathcal{D}} ||\mathcal{W}||_{\mathcal{H}}^2$, where the covariance kernel of $\mathcal{W}$ is given by*

$$K(s,t) = \text{Cov}[W_j(s), W_j(t)]$$
$$= F^X(s \wedge t) + (s \wedge t)[I_3(s \wedge t, s \vee t) - 2I_1(s \wedge t, s \vee t) + I_{-1}(s \wedge t, s \vee t)]$$
$$+ st\left[2F^X(s \vee t) - 2 + I_2(s \vee t, \infty) + I_{-2}(s \vee t, \infty)\right] + I_4(0, s \wedge t) - 2I_2(0, s \wedge t)$$
$$+ r^X(s)r^X(t) + 2F^X(s)F^X(t)$$
$$+ \left\{-\frac{1}{2}I_4(0,s) + \frac{3}{2}I_2(0,s) + s\left[-\frac{1}{2}I_3(s,\infty) + \frac{3}{2}I_1(s,\infty) + I_{-1}(s,\infty)\right]\right\}r^X(t)$$
$$+ \left\{-\frac{1}{2}I_4(0,t) + \frac{3}{2}I_2(0,t) + t\left[-\frac{1}{2}I_3(t,\infty) + \frac{3}{2}I_1(t,\infty) + I_{-1}(t,\infty)\right]\right\}r^X(s)$$
$$- \frac{1}{2}\{I_4(0,s) - I_2(0,s) + s[I_3(s,\infty) + I_1(s,\infty)]\}F_X(t)$$
$$- \frac{1}{2}\{I_4(0,t) - I_2(0,t) + t[I_3(t,\infty) + I_1(t,\infty)]\}F_X(s),$$

where
$$I_k(a,b) = \mathbb{E}\left[X_j^k \mathbb{1}(a \leq X_j \leq b)\right]$$

and
$$I_k(a,\infty) = \lim_{b \to \infty} I_k(a,b).$$

Proof. First note that
$$\sqrt{n}\{\hat{T}_n^X(s) - F_n^X(s)\} \approx \frac{\sqrt{n}}{\hat{\theta}_n^2}\left\{T_n^X(s) + \left(1 - \hat{\theta}_n^2\right)r^X(s) - \hat{\theta}_n^2 F^X(s)\right\},$$

since $||F^X - F_n^X||_{\mathcal{H}}^2 = o_\mathbb{P}(1)$. We can therefore write
$$\sqrt{n}\{\hat{T}_n^X(s) - F_n^X(s)\} \approx \frac{1}{\sqrt{n}\hat{\theta}_n^2}\sum_{j=1}^n W_j(s),$$

where
$$W_j(s) = \left(X_j - \frac{1}{X_j}\right)\min\{X_j, s\} + \left(1 - \frac{1}{2}X_j^2\right)r^X(s) - \frac{1}{2}X_j^2 F^X(s).$$

We note that $W_1, \ldots, W_n$ are i.i.d. random variables with $E(W_1) = 0$ and $E||W_1||_{\mathcal{H}}^2 < \infty$. Therefore, by the central limit theorem for separable Hilbert spaces (see [20]) there exists a centred Gaussian element $\mathcal{W} \in \mathcal{H}$ with
$$\frac{1}{\sqrt{n}}\sum_{j=1}^n W_j(\cdot) \xrightarrow{\mathcal{D}} \mathcal{W}(\cdot).$$

From this we have that $\sqrt{n}\{\hat{T}_n^X(s) - F_n^X(s)\} = \mathcal{O}_\mathbb{P}(1)$. Therefore, since $\hat{\theta}_n = 1 + o_\mathbb{P}(1)$ and by Holder's inequality we have that
$$\left|\int_0^\infty \left(\sqrt{n}\{\hat{T}_n^X(s) - F_n^X(s)\}\right)^2 e^{-as/\hat{\theta}_n}ds - \int_0^\infty \left(\sqrt{n}\{\hat{T}_n^X(s) - F_n^X(s)\}\right)^2 e^{-as}ds\right|$$
$$\leq \sup_{s>0}\left|e^{-as\left(\frac{1}{\hat{\theta}_n} - 1\right)} - 1\right|\left|\left|\sqrt{n}\{\hat{T}_n^X - F_n^X\}\right|\right|_{\mathcal{H}}^2 = o_\mathbb{P}(1).$$

Therefore,
$$R_{n,a} = ||\sqrt{n}\{\hat{T}_n^X - F_n^X\}||_{\mathcal{H}}^2 + o_\mathbb{P}(1). \tag{8}$$

The final result then follows from Slutsky's theorem. □

Remark 2. *A closed form expression for the covariance kernel for the limiting centred Gaussian distribution does not exist. However, for non-negative even numbers of k closed form formulas for functions $I_k(a,b)$ exist by using the following recursive formulas*

$$I_0(a,b) = F^X(b) - F^X(a)$$

$$I_k(a,b) = a^k e^{-1/2a^2} - b^k e^{-1/2b^2} + k I_{k-2}(a,b).$$

Now that we have shown that, under the null hypothesis, $R_{n,a}$ converges in distribution to a norm of a Gaussian element of the Hilbert space $\mathcal{H}$, we can continue to show that the newly proposed test is consistent. Therefore, we will show that $\frac{R_{n,a}}{n} = \Delta + o_{\mathbb{P}}(1)$, where $\Delta = ||T^X - F^X||_{\mathcal{H}}^2$ with the properties that $\Delta = 0$ under the null hypothesis and $\Delta > 0$ under fixed alternatives. This is as a result of the characterization of the Rayleigh distribution in Proposition 1.

Theorem 2. *Suppose $X, X_1, X_2, \ldots$ are i.i.d. random variables with distribution function F^X and $\mathbb{E}[X^2] < \infty$. As $n \to \infty$, we have*

$$\frac{R_{n,a}}{n} = ||T^X - F^X||_{\mathcal{H}}^2 + o_{\mathbb{P}}(1).$$

Proof. From (8) we have that

$$\frac{R_{n,a}}{n} = ||\hat{T}_n^X - F_n^X||_{\mathcal{H}}^2 + o_{\mathbb{P}}(1).$$

To prove the theorem we need to show that

$$||\hat{T}_n^X - F_n^X||_{\mathcal{H}}^2 = ||T^X - F^X||_{\mathcal{H}}^2 + o_{\mathbb{P}}(1).$$

By a weak form of the law of large numbers for separable Hilbert spaces we have that $T_n^X(s) = T^X(s) + o_{\mathbb{P}}(1)$ and $F_n^X(s) = F^X(s) + o_{\mathbb{P}}(1)$. Moreover, from Lemma 1 we have that $\hat{T}_n^X(s) = T_n^X(s) + o_{\mathbb{P}}(1)$ and hence $\hat{T}_n^X(s) = T^X(s) + o_{\mathbb{P}}(1)$. We also have that

$$\hat{T}_n^X(s) - F_n^X(s) = \left(\hat{T}_n^X(s) - T^X(s)\right) + \left(T^X(s) - F^X(s)\right) + \left(F^X(s) - F_n^X(s)\right),$$

and by the continuous mapping theorem the result follows. □

4. Simulation Study

In this section, Monte Carlo simulations are used to compare the finite sample performance of the newly proposed test to the following existing goodness-of-fit tests for the Rayleigh distribution:

- The traditional Kolmogorov–Smirnov (KS_n), Cramér-von Mises (CM_n) and Anderson–Darling (AD_n) tests;
- A test based on the empirical Laplace transform proposed by [10], $EL_{n,a}$;
- A test based on the cumulative residual entropy proposed by [11], CR_n, and
- A test based on an estimator of the Kullback–Leibler divergence proposed by [12], $KL_{n,a}$.

The estimated powers of $R_{n,a}$, $EL_{n,a}$ and $KL_{n,a}$ are functions of a tuning parameter, a. For $R_{n,a}$ we report the results for $a = 1$ and $a = 5$, for $EL_{n,a}$ a is 1 and 5 and for $KL_{n,a}$ results are reported for $a = 3$ and $a = 4$. The motivation for these choices of a will be discussed in Section 4.2.

In addition to the existing tests, we also compare the performance of the new test to the following five powerful tests for exponentiality (see, e.g., the overview papers by [21] as well as [22] for a discussion on a variety of tests for exponentiality);

- The modified Kolmogorov–Smirnov ($\widetilde{KS}_n$) and Cramér-von Mises ($\widetilde{CM}_n$) tests based on the mean residual life proposed by [23];
- Two tests based on the empirical Laplace transform; one proposed by [24], $BH_{n,a}$, and the other one by [25], $HM_{n,a}$, and
- A test based on the empirical characteristic function proposed by [26], EP_n.

Here, we test for the Rayleigh distribution by testing for exponentiality of the transformed data (using the well known property that the square of a Rayleigh distributed random variable follows an exponential distribution). The estimated powers of $BH_{n,a}$ and $HM_{n,a}$ are functions of a tuning parameter, a. For both $BH_{n,a}$ and $HM_{n,a}$ we report the results for $a = 0.75, 1$ and 1.25.

4.1. Simulation Setting

A significance level of 5% is used throughout. Critical values of all the tests are obtained using 50,000 independent Monte Carlo replications drawn from a standard Rayleigh distribution (all the test statistics are invariant with respect to scale transformations). Power estimates are calculated and reported for sample sizes $n = 20$ and $n = 30$ using 10,000 independent Monte Carlo replications obtained from various alternative distributions. These include some 'local' alternatives as well as those given in Table 1. These alternative distributions were chosen since they are frequently used alternatives for the Rayleigh distribution, which has an increasing hazard rate. The hazard rates of the considered alternative distributions include constant hazard rates (CHR), increasing hazard rates (IHR), decreasing hazard rates (DHR) and non-monotone hazard rates (NMHR). These alternatives all have support in $\mathbb{R}^+$ and are used in many other empirical studies for goodness-of-fit tests of lifetime distributions (see, e.g., [10,21,27]). In Table 1, all scale parameters are set to one due to the scale transformation $Y_j = X_j/\hat{\theta}_n, j = 1, \ldots, n$. All simulations and calculations are done in Ref. [28]. The tables are produced using the *Stargazer* package, see [29].

Table 1. Probability density functions of the alternative distributions considered in the Monte Carlo study.

Alternative	f(x)	Notation
Gamma	$\frac{1}{\Gamma(\theta)} x^{\theta-1} \exp(-x)$	$\Gamma(\theta)$
Weibull	$\theta x^{\theta-1} \exp(-x^\theta)$	$W(\theta)$
Power	$\frac{1}{\theta} x^{(1-\theta)/\theta}, 0 < x < 1$	$PW(\theta)$
Linear Failure Rate	$(1 + \theta x) \exp\left(-x - \frac{\theta x^2}{2}\right)$	$LFR(\theta)$
Lognormal	$\exp\left\{-\frac{1}{2}\left(\frac{\log(x)}{\theta}\right)^2\right\} \{\theta x \sqrt{2\pi}\}^{-1}$	$LN(\theta)$
Inverse Gaussian	$\left(\frac{\theta}{2\pi x^3}\right)^{1/2} \exp\left\{\frac{-\theta(x-1)^2}{2x}\right\}$	$IG(\theta)$
Gompertz	$\exp(-\theta x) \exp\left\{-\left(\frac{1}{\theta}\right)(\exp(\theta x) - 1)\right\}$	$GO(\theta)$
Exponential	$\theta \exp(-\theta x)$	$Exp(\theta)$
Extreme value	$\frac{1}{\theta} \exp\left(x + \frac{1-\exp(x)}{\theta}\right)$	$EV(\theta)$
Exponential geometric	$(1-\theta) \exp(-x)(1 - \theta \exp(-x))^{-2}$	$EG(\theta)$

We first consider some local power estimates. Here, we consider a mixture distribution, which is obtained by sampling with probability p from a standard exponential distribution ($Exp(1)$) and with probability $(1-p)$ from a $Ral(1)$ distribution. The value $p = 0$ corresponds to the standard Rayleigh distribution, whereas increasing values of p implies a larger deviation from the null distribution. These estimated powers are given in Table 2 and the estimated powers for the exponentiality tests based on the transformed data are given in Table 3. The estimated powers for sample sizes 20 and 30 against every alternative distribution in Table 1 are given in Tables 4 and 5, respectively. The estimated powers, obtained using the tests for exponentiality based on the transformed data, for sample sizes 20 and 30 are given in Tables 6 and 7, respectively. The entries in these tables are the percentages of 10,000 independent Monte Carlo samples that resulted in the rejection of the null hypothesis (rounded to the nearest integer). For the reader's convenience, the highest estimated power for each alternative distribution among the existing tests, as well as the tests for exponentiality based on the square of the data, are displayed separately in bold in each of their respective tables. The last column of Tables 2, 4 and 5 contain the highest estimated powers from the corresponding exponentiality tests based on the transformed data (i.e., the highest powers obtained from Tables 3, 6 and 7 are also reported in the last column of Tables 2, 4 and 5); this will make comparison easier.

Table 2. Estimated local powers for the mixture of the Rayleigh and exponential distributions for various choices of the mixture parameter, p.

p	n	KS_n	CM_n	AD_n	$EL_{n,1}$	$EL_{n,5}$	CR_n	$KL_{n,3}$	$KL_{n,4}$	$R_{n,1}$	$R_{n,5}$	Exp
0	20	5	5	5	5	5	5	5	5	5	5	5
	30	5	4	5	4	5	4	5	5	6	5	5
0.05	20	6	6	7	8	7	7	6	5	7	9	7
	30	6	7	8	9	8	9	6	6	8	9	8
0.1	20	8	8	12	**15**	10	10	6	6	10	13	10
	30	8	9	14	**16**	13	13	8	7	13	**16**	12
0.15	20	9	11	17	**20**	15	14	8	8	14	**20**	14
	30	12	14	21	**25**	19	16	12	11	18	23	17
0.2	20	12	14	22	**27**	19	17	11	11	19	**27**	18
	30	15	17	27	**34**	25	21	14	15	25	**34**	23
0.25	20	15	18	29	**34**	25	21	14	14	24	**34**	25
	30	21	24	36	**44**	34	27	19	20	32	**44**	18
0.3	20	19	22	35	**42**	30	24	16	15	30	**42**	30
	30	26	30	44	**54**	41	32	25	27	41	53	42
0.35	20	22	27	42	**50**	37	30	21	22	37	**50**	36
	30	32	37	54	**62**	49	38	31	32	50	61	49
0.4	20	28	32	48	**56**	43	35	26	27	42	**56**	43
	30	41	45	62	**70**	58	44	39	38	57	**70**	57
0.45	20	34	39	56	**64**	52	41	32	32	49	62	51
	30	46	51	69	**77**	65	52	46	46	64	76	66
0.5	20	39	43	61	**69**	57	45	36	36	55	**69**	57
	30	51	59	76	82	72	57	52	53	71	**83**	72

Table 3. Estimated local powers for the mixture of the Rayleigh and exponential distributions, using transformed data, for various choices of the mixture parameter, p.

p	n	$\widetilde{KS}_n$	$\widetilde{CV}_n$	EP_n	$BH_{n,0.75}$	$BH_{n,1}$	$BH_{n,1.25}$	$HM_{n,0.75}$	$HM_{n,1}$	$HM_{n,1.25}$
0	20	5	5	5	5	5	5	5	5	5
	30	5	5	5	5	5	5	5	5	5
0.05	20	6	6	7	7	7	7	7	6	7
	30	6	7	7	8	7	8	7	7	7
0.1	20	7	9	10	10	10	10	10	9	9
	30	8	10	11	11	12	10	12	12	11
0.15	20	8	12	12	14	13	13	14	13	13
	30	10	15	15	17	16	17	17	16	16
0.2	20	10	15	16	18	17	17	18	18	17
	30	14	19	20	23	22	22	23	22	22

Table 3. Cont.

p	n	$\widetilde{KS}_n$	$\widetilde{CV}_n$	EP_n	$BH_{n,0.75}$	$BH_{n,1}$	$BH_{n,1.25}$	$HM_{n,0.75}$	$HM_{n,1}$	$HM_{n,1.25}$
0.25	20	14	18	20	23	22	22	**25**	23	22
	30	18	25	27	31	30	29	**34**	31	31
0.3	20	15	23	24	28	28	26	**30**	28	27
	30	23	31	34	40	37	36	**42**	39	38
0.35	20	19	29	30	35	33	33	**36**	34	34
	30	27	38	40	46	44	44	**49**	46	45
0.4	20	23	35	36	41	39	38	**43**	41	40
	30	36	46	49	55	54	52	**57**	55	55
0.45	20	29	41	43	49	46	46	**51**	48	48
	30	42	53	55	63	61	59	**66**	63	62
0.5	20	32	46	47	53	52	51	**57**	54	53
	30	47	60	62	70	67	67	**72**	70	69

Table 4. Estimated powers for general alternatives for the Rayleigh distribution for sample size $n = 20$.

F	KS_n	CM_n	AD_n	$EL_{n,1}$	$EL_{n,5}$	CR_n	$KL_{n,3}$	$KL_{n,4}$	$R_{n,1}$	$R_{n,5}$	Exp
CHR											
$Exp(1)$	86	90	96	**97**	94	89	84	85	94	**97**	95
IHR											
$\Gamma(1.5)$	57	63	73	75	73	64	44	44	72	**77**	72
$\Gamma(2)$	32	38	44	43	**46**	41	19	18	44	44	44
$W(1.2)$	64	69	80	84	79	68	54	55	79	**85**	79
$W(1.4)$	37	42	53	58	53	43	26	25	52	**60**	52
$PW(1)$	16	20	40	42	13	21	45	**46**	18	41	21
$LFR(2)$	38	45	63	**70**	56	42	36	36	56	69	59
$LFR(4)$	26	29	47	**56**	41	29	25	25	40	55	42
$EV(0.5)$	56	61	79	**84**	74	58	54	55	73	**84**	76
$EV(1.5)$	22	24	46	**56**	33	20	26	28	35	**56**	38
$GO(0.5)$	56	62	79	**84**	74	57	54	54	75	**84**	76
$GO(1.5)$	22	25	44	54	33	20	27	29	33	**55**	38
DHR											
$\Gamma(0.4)$	100	100	100	100	100	100	100	100	100	100	100
$\Gamma(0.7)$	97	98	**100**	**100**	99	97	98	98	99	**100**	99
$W(0.8)$	97	98	**100**	**100**	**100**	98	98	98	**100**	**100**	**100**
$EG(0.2)$	94	96	99	**100**	99	95	95	95	98	96	98
$EG(0.5)$	97	98	99	88	**100**	97	98	98	92	71	99
$EG(0.8)$	86	90	95	55	**100**	99	**100**	99	75	60	94
NMHR											
$PW(2)$	87	89	98	**99**	93	83	96	96	95	**99**	95
$PW(3)$	99	99	**100**	**100**	**100**	99	**100**	**100**	99	**100**	**100**
$LN(0.8)$	67	71	72	66	**75**	74	51	50	**75**	68	**75**
$LN(1)$	90	92	94	93	**95**	92	82	82	94	94	94
$LN(1.5)$	**100**	**100**	**100**	**100**	**100**	**100**	99	99	**100**	**100**	**100**
$IG(0.5)$	97	98	98	98	98	97	94	93	**99**	98	98
$IG(1.5)$	56	61	60	48	62	**64**	42	42	**64**	52	63

Table 5. Estimated powers for general alternatives for the Rayleigh distribution for sample size $n = 30$.

F	KS_n	CM_n	AD_n	$EL_{n,1}$	$EL_{n,5}$	CR_n	$KL_{n,3}$	$KL_{n,4}$	$R_{n,1}$	$R_{n,5}$	Exp
					CHR						
$Exp(1)$	96	98	99	**100**	99	97	96	96	99	**100**	99
					IHR						
$\Gamma(1.5)$	76	81	87	89	88	79	63	65	88	**90**	87
$\Gamma(2)$	47	53	57	56	59	54	28	28	**60**	57	59
$W(1.2)$	81	86	92	94	92	83	74	76	91	**95**	92
$W(1.4)$	53	58	69	72	69	56	37	39	68	**74**	68
$PW(1)$	22	28	55	51	14	37	66	**68**	24	50	27
$LFR(2)$	53	59	76	83	71	53	51	53	72	**84**	74
$LFR(4)$	36	43	61	**69**	55	37	37	37	54	68	56
$EV(0.5)$	74	80	90	**94**	88	72	71	73	88	**94**	89
$EV(1.5)$	32	35	58	68	42	23	39	41	46	**69**	51
$GO(0.5)$	74	78	91	**94**	88	72	73	74	88	**94**	89
$GO(1.5)$	33	37	58	**68**	44	25	41	42	47	**68**	51
					DHR						
$\Gamma(0.4)$	100	100	100	100	100	100	100	100	100	100	100
$\Gamma(0.7)$	100	100	100	100	100	100	100	100	100	100	100
$W(0.8)$	100	100	100	100	100	100	100	100	100	100	100
$EG(0.2)$	99	99	100	100	100	99	100	99	99	96	100
$EG(0.5)$	100	100	100	87	100	100	100	100	93	68	100
$EG(0.8)$	96	98	99	52	**100**	**100**	99	99	75	59	99
					NMHR						
$PW(2)$	97	98	**100**	**100**	98	94	**100**	**100**	99	**100**	99
$PW(3)$	100	100	100	100	100	100	100	99	100	100	100
$LN(0.8)$	83	86	87	81	88	87	70	71	**89**	82	88
$LN(1)$	97	98	**99**	**99**	**99**	98	94	95	**99**	**99**	99
$LN(1.5)$	100	100	100	100	100	100	100	100	100	100	100
$IG(0.5)$	100	100	100	100	100	100	99	99	100	100	100
$IG(1.5)$	73	77	77	62	78	79	62	62	**80**	67	80

Table 6. Estimated powers for general alternatives for the exponential distribution for sample size $n = 20$.

F	$\widetilde{KS}_n$	$\widetilde{CV}_n$	EP_n	$BH_{n,0.75}$	$BH_{n,1}$	$BH_{n,1.25}$	$HM_{n,0.75}$	$HM_{n,1}$	$HM_{n,1.25}$
					CHR				
$Exp(1)$	82	90	90	94	93	93	**95**	94	93
					IHR				
$\Gamma(1.5)$	52	66	68	**72**	71	70	**72**	71	71
$\Gamma(2)$	29	40	43	43	43	43	43	43	**44**
$W(1.2)$	57	70	72	77	77	76	**79**	78	76
$W(1.4)$	31	44	46	**52**	50	50	**52**	**52**	51
$PW(1)$	12	11	7	17	14	11	**21**	17	14
$LFR(2)$	30	43	46	55	53	52	**59**	57	54
$LFR(4)$	20	30	31	40	36	36	**42**	39	39
$EV(0.5)$	48	61	62	72	71	68	**76**	72	71
$EV(1.5)$	15	21	22	34	30	27	**38**	35	33
$GO(0.5)$	47	62	63	72	71	68	**76**	72	71
$GO(1.5)$	14	22	23	33	29	28	**38**	34	31

Table 6. *Cont.*

F	$\widetilde{KS}_n$	$\widetilde{CV}_n$	EP_n	$BH_{n,0.75}$	$BH_{n,1}$	$BH_{n,1.25}$	$HM_{n,0.75}$	$HM_{n,1}$	$HM_{n,1.25}$
				DHR					
$\Gamma(0.4)$	100	100	100	100	100	100	100	100	100
$\Gamma(0.7)$	95	98	98	99	99	99	99	99	99
$W(0.8)$	96	98	98	99	99	99	100	100	99
$EG(0.2)$	91	95	95	98	98	97	98	98	98
$EG(0.5)$	95	98	98	99	99	99	99	99	99
$EG(0.8)$	82	90	90	93	93	93	94	94	93
				NMHR					
$PW(2)$	75	84	79	93	91	89	95	93	92
$PW(3)$	97	99	98	100	100	99	100	100	100
$LN(0.8)$	64	73	74	74	75	75	72	73	73
$LN(1)$	88	93	93	94	94	94	94	94	94
$LN(1.5)$	99	100	100	100	100	100	100	100	100
$IG(0.5)$	96	98	98	98	98	98	98	98	98
$IG(1.5)$	53	64	64	62	63	63	58	59	61

Table 7. Estimated powers for general alternatives for the exponential distribution for sample size $n = 30$.

F	$\widetilde{KS}_n$	$\widetilde{CV}_n$	EP_n	$BH_{n,0.75}$	$BH_{n,1}$	$BH_{n,1.25}$	$HM_{n,0.75}$	$HM_{n,1}$	$HM_{n,1.25}$
				CHR					
$Exp(1)$	95	98	98	99	99	99	99	99	99
				IHR					
$\Gamma(1.5)$	73	82	84	87	86	85	87	86	87
$\Gamma(2)$	43	57	58	57	59	59	58	57	58
$W(1.2)$	78	87	87	91	90	90	92	91	91
$W(1.4)$	47	60	62	67	66	65	68	68	66
$PW(1)$	17	15	6	21	18	14	27	22	18
$LFR(2)$	44	58	60	68	67	66	74	70	68
$LFR(4)$	31	43	44	53	51	48	56	54	51
$EV(0.5)$	67	79	80	87	86	84	89	87	87
$EV(1.5)$	22	30	29	45	41	37	51	46	42
$GO(0.5)$	67	78	79	87	85	84	89	88	86
$GO(1.5)$	22	31	29	46	42	39	51	47	44
				DHR					
$\Gamma(0.4)$	100	100	100	100	100	100	100	100	100
$\Gamma(0.7)$	100	100	100	100	100	100	100	100	100
$W(0.8)$	100	100	100	100	100	100	100	100	100
$EG(0.2)$	99	99	99	100	100	100	100	100	100
$EG(0.5)$	100	100	100	100	100	100	100	100	100
$EG(0.8)$	95	98	98	99	99	99	99	99	99
				NMHR					
$PW(2)$	93	96	91	99	98	97	99	99	98
$PW(3)$	100	100	100	100	100	100	100	100	100
$LN(0.8)$	82	88	89	88	88	88	86	87	88
$LN(1)$	97	98	99	99	99	99	99	99	99
$LN(1.5)$	100	100	100	100	100	100	100	100	100
$IG(0.5)$	99	100	100	100	100	100	100	100	100
$IG(1.5)$	72	80	80	78	78	80	73	75	76

4.2. Simulation Results

We will now present some general conclusions regarding the tabulated estimated powers of the different tests considered. Since the performance of the tests are affected by the type of hazard rate of the alternative distribution, we will discuss the overall performance as well as the performance when the results are grouped according to the type of hazard rate.

First, we will consider the estimated local powers, presented in Tables 2 and 3. We find that KS_n and CM_n exhibit poor power performance, displaying the lowest powers among the tests for the majority of the choices of the mixture probability, p. We note that $EL_{n,1}$ and $R_{n,5}$ are tied for the best test for the majority of mixture proportions. Figure 1 displays the local powers of AD, $EL_{n,1}$, CR and $R_{n,5}$ over the complete range of mixture probabilities. The superior performance of $EL_{n,1}$ and $R_{n,5}$, for this mixture distribution, is clear from this figure.

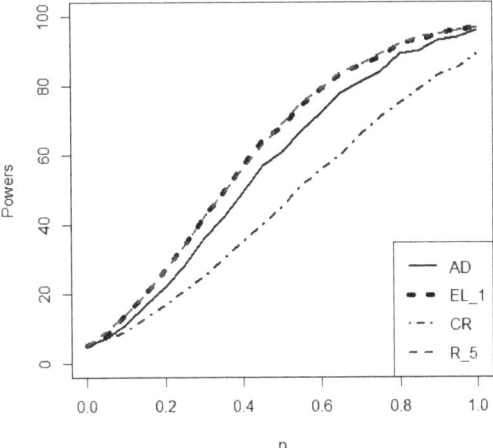

Figure 1. Local powers for some of the tests over the entire range of mixture probabilities of the Rayleigh exponential mixture distribution for $n = 20$.

For the transformed data, $\widetilde{KS}_n$ exhibits the lowest powers overall and $HM_{n,0.75}$ has the highest overall powers for the majority of the alternatives considered.

We will now consider the performance of the tests, developed specifically for the Rayleigh distribution, in general against all of the general alternative distributions listed in Table 1. From both Tables 4 and 5 we see that, in general, the powers of KS_n and CR_n are lower for the majority of the alternatives considered and perform unfavourably in comparison to the other tests, for both sample sizes. On the other hand, $EL_{n,1}$ and $R_{n,5}$ perform quite well as we find that they outperform the other tests, having the highest estimated power for the majority of the alternatives considered. All tests considered perform quite well against the standard exponential distribution (which has a constant hazard rate) for both sample sizes.

Shifting our attention now to results associated with alternatives with increasing hazard rates, one finds, once again, that KS_n and CR_n have lower powers for both sample sizes considered. For most of the alternatives in this category $EL_{n,1}$ and $R_{n,5}$ have the highest power, only being outperformed, or equaled, for a handful of these alternatives by other tests.

Moving our attention to alternatives with a decreasing hazard, we see that all the tests considered perform very well and, since there are such minor differences in the power performance between all the tests, it is difficult to identify a single 'best' test for this set of alternatives. However, for the smaller sample size, KS_n still attains powers that are slightly lower than the rest of the tests.

We now observe the results associated with alternatives with non-monotone hazard rates. The tests that generally perform well are AD_n, $EL_{n,1}$ and $R_{n,1}$. However, the test that exhibits the highest power for the majority of the alternatives, for both sample sizes, is $R_{n,5}$.

Finally, we consider the performance of the tests for exponentiality based on the transformed data. The tests with the lowest powers are $\widetilde{KS}_n$ and $\widetilde{CM}_n$. $BH_{n,1}$ and $HM_{n,1.25}$ perform very well, exhibiting high powers for most of the alternatives considered, especially for alternatives with decreasing or non-monotone hazard rates. $HM_{n,0.75}$ displays the highest overall powers for the majority of the alternatives considered. However, the highest estimated power, against all alternative distributions considered, is obtained by one of the tests specifically developed for the Rayleigh distribution and not by any of the exponentiality tests based on the transformed data. Therefore, we recommend that the tests proposed specifically for the Rayleigh distribution is used when goodness-of-fit testing is performed for the Rayleigh distribution.

To conclude, we provide a brief demonstration of how the choice of the tuning parameter, a, influences the powers of the newly proposed test. In order to visualise the behaviour of the powers for different values of a, Figure 2 present the powers for $R_{n,a}$ over a grid of a values and six different alternative distributions. This figure is also used to motivate the choice of a values included in the study.

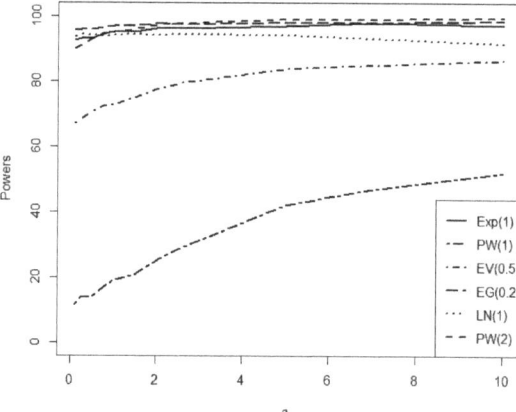

Figure 2. Estimated powers for $R_{100,a}$ for some alternatives appearing in Table 1.

The choice of $a = 1$ was made since it is the point where the powers for most of the alternative distributions start to stabilize and reach a plateau. The choice for $a = 5$ is due to the fact that it is the point where the powers for most of the alternative distributions reach their maximum value.

5. Practical Application

As noted in Section 1, the Rayleigh distribution found various applications in the fields of survival analysis and reliability theory. In this section we demonstrate the use of the tests specifically developed for the Rayleigh distribution by applying them to a real-world survival data set: the COVID-19 data set of Italy given in Table 8—for a discussion on the data set, see [30]. The data set displays the COVID-19 mortality rates recorded for 59 days in Italy from 27 February 2020 to 27 April 2020. Ref. [30] discussed and analysed the use of an extended three parameter Rayleigh distribution to model the data. They concluded that the newly extended Rayleigh distribution is a good fit to the data. We, however, will investigate the goodness-of-fit of the traditional one parameter Rayleigh distribution as well as that of the exponential distribution. Figure 3 represents the probability plots of both the Rayleigh (grey dots) and exponential (black dots) distribution fitted to the data, where $\hat{\theta} = 6.583$ and $\hat{\lambda} = 0.123$ in the case of the exponential distribution.

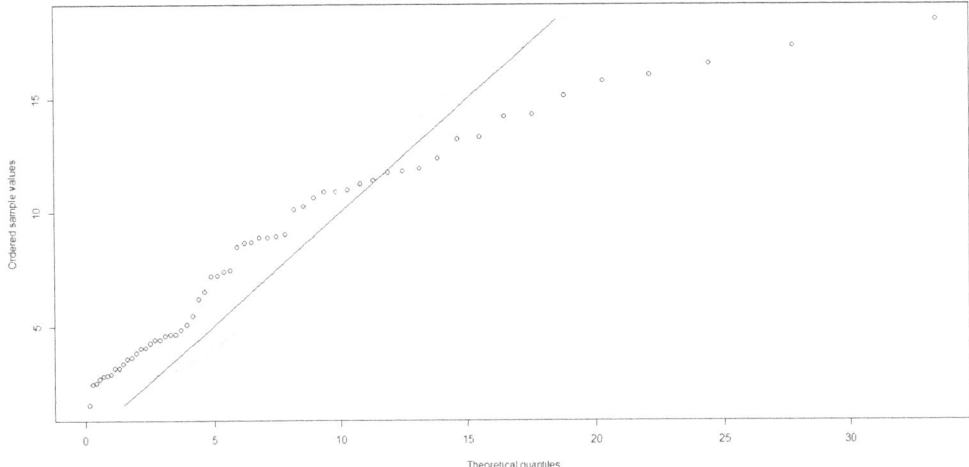

Figure 3. Probability plot of a fitted Rayleigh (grey dots) and exponential (black dots) distribution.

The probability plot suggests that the underlying distribution of the data might be the Rayleigh distribution instead of the exponential distribution.

Table 8. COVID-19 data set of Italy.

1.518	2.450	2.508	2.686	2.780	2.814	2.881	3.134	3.148	3.341
3.564	3.606	3.827	4.011	4.040	4.253	4.408	4.416	4.571	4.639
4.640	4.859	5.073	5.452	6.194	6.503	7.201	7.214	7.407	7.445
8.479	8.646	8.697	8.905	8.906	8.961	9.037	10.138	10.282	10.644
10.908	10.919	11.010	11.273	11.410	11.775	11.822	11.950	12.396	13.226
13.333	14.242	14.330	15.137	15.787	16.046	16.561	17.337	18.474	

Table 9 contains the estimated p-value (calculated based on 50,000 samples of size 59 simulated from the standard Rayleigh distribution) of each test for testing formally whether the data originated from a Rayleigh distribution.

Table 9. p-values for the COVID-19 data of Italy.

TestStatistic	KS_n	CM_n	AD_n	$EL_{n,1}$	$EL_{n,5}$	CR_n	$KL_{n,3}$	$KL_{n,4}$	$R_{n,1}$	$R_{n,5}$
p-value	0.05974	0.12038	0.12906	0.62786	0.5679	0.4104	0.09604	0.07	0.8903	0.91866

From these p-values it is clear that all the tests do not reject the null hypothesis in (3) at a 5% significance level and we can therefore conclude that the Rayleigh distribution is also a feasible option to model the data.

Having found that the Rayleigh distribution is a good fit to the observed data, one can now go about calculating quantiles, moments and other useful distributional properties by using the theoretical Rayleigh distribution with estimated parameter $\hat{\theta} = 6.583$. For example, by fitting this Rayleigh distribution we find that the mean mortality rate over the 59 days is 8.2506.

6. Conclusions and Future Research

In this article, a new goodness-of-fit test statistic specifically designed for the Rayleigh distribution was considered. The finite-sample performance of this newly suggested test was studied via the use of a Monte Carlo simulation. From the results, it is clear that this new test is not only feasible when testing goodness-of-fit for the Rayleigh distribution, it also outperforms or equals competitor tests for the majority of the alternative distributions considered. For practical implementation we suggest using the choice $a = 5$ for $R_{n,a}$. Alternatively, one can use a data-dependent choice of this tuning parameter suggested, e.g., in [31].

In analysing mortality or survival data (like the COVID-19 data set) one will, more often than not, deal with observations that are censored. For our newly proposed test to be applicable in these kinds of situations, it needs to be modified to accommodate censoring. Naturally, this modification will complicate some of the asymptotic derivations and might be an avenue for future research. Some work in this regard has been started by [32] as well as [33].

Author Contributions: The authors (G.L.G., E.B., J.S.A.) contributed equally. All authors have read and agreed to the published version of the manuscript

Funding: This research received no external funding.

Institutional Review Board Statement: Not applicable.

Informed Consent Statement: Not applicable.

Data Availability Statement: Not applicable.

Acknowledgments: The work of E. Bothma and J.S. Allison are based on research supported by the National Research Foundation (NRF). Any opinion, finding and conclusion or recommendation expressed in this material is that of the authors and the NRF does not accept any liability in this regard.

Conflicts of Interest: The authors declare no conflict of interest.

References

1. Johnson, N.L.; Kotz, S.; Balakrishnan, N. *Continuous Univariate Distributions*, 2nd ed.; Wiley: New York, NY, USA, 1994.
2. Rayleigh, F.R.S. Xii. On the resultant of a large number of vibrations of the same pitch and of arbitrary phase. *Lond. Edinb. Dublin Philisophical Mag. J. Sci.* **1880**, *10*, 73–78. [CrossRef]
3. Dyer, D.; Whisenand, C. Best linear unbiased estimator of the parameter of the Rayleigh distribution. *IEEE Trans. Reliab.* **1973**, *22*, 229–231. [CrossRef]
4. Polovko, A. *Fundamentals of Reliability Theory*; Academic Press: Cambridge, MA, USA, 1968.
5. Brummer, M.; Mersereau, R.; Eisner, R.; Lewine, R. Automatic detection of brain contours in MRI data sets. *IEEE Trans. Med. Imaging* **1993**, *12*, 153–166. [CrossRef] [PubMed]
6. Sijbers, J.; Poot, D.; den Dekker, A.; Pintjens, W. Automatic estimation of the noise variance from the histogram of a magnetic resonance image. *Phys. Med. Biol.* **2007**, *52*, 1335–1348. [CrossRef]
7. Rajan, J.; Poot, D.; Juntu, J.; Sijbers, J. *Segmentation Based Noise Variance Estimation from Background MRI Data*; ICIAR 2010 Part I LNCS; Springer: Berlin/Heidelberg, Germany, 2010; Volume 6111, pp. 62–70.
8. Guemana, M.; Hafaifa, A.; Mohamed, B.R. Reliability modeling using Rayleigh distribution: Industrial pump application. In Proceedings of the 19th European Conference on Mathematics for Industry ECMI2016, Santiago de Compostela, Spain, 13–17 June 2016.
9. Elviana, E.; Purwadi, J. *Parameters Estimation of Rayleigh Distribution in Survival Analysis on Type II Censored Data Using the Bayesian Method*; Journal of Physics: Conference Series; IOP Publishing: Bristol, UK, 2020; Volume 1503, p. 012004.
10. Meintanis, S.G.; Iliopoulos, G. Tests of fit for the Rayleigh distribution based on the empirical Laplace transform. *Ann. Inst. Stat. Math.* **2003**, *55*, 137–151. [CrossRef]
11. Baratpour, B.S.; Khodadadi, F. A cumulative residual entropy characterization of the Rayleigh distribution and related goodness-of-fit test. *J. Stat. Res. Iran* **2012**, *9*, 115–1294. [CrossRef]
12. Alizadeh Noughabi, R.; Alizadeh Noughabi, H.; Ebrahimi Moghaddam Behabadi, A. An entropy test for the Rayleigh distribution and power comparison. *J. Stat. Comput. Simul.* **2014**, *84*, 151–158. [CrossRef]
13. Safavinejad, M.; Jomhoori, S.; Alizadeh Noughabi, H. A density-based empirical likelihood ratio goodness-of-fit test for the Rayleigh distribution and power comparison. *J. Stat. Comput. Simul.* **2015**, *85*, 3322–3334. [CrossRef]
14. Nikitin, Y.Y. Tests based on characterizations, and their efficiencies: A survey. *arXiv* **2017**, arXiv:1707.01522.

15. Betsch, S.; Ebner, B. Characterizations of continuous univariate probability distributions with applications to goodness-of-fit testing. *arXiv* **2018**, arXiv:1810.06226.
16. Stein, C. A bound for the error in the normal approximation to the distribution of a sum of dependent random variables. In Proceedings of the Sixth Berkeley Symposium on Mathematical Statistics and Probability, Berkeley, CA, USA, 9–22 July 1971; Volume 2: Probability Theory; University of California Press: Berkeley, CA, USA, 1972; Volume 6, pp. 583–603.
17. Betsch, S.; Ebner, B. Testing normality via a distributional fixed point property in the Stein characterization. *TEST* **2018**, *29*, 105–138. [CrossRef]
18. Henze, N.; Meintanis, S.G.; Ebner, B. Goodness-of-fit tests for the gamma distribution based on the empirical Laplace transform. *Commun. -Stat.-Theory Methods* **2012**, *41*, 1543–1556. [CrossRef]
19. Allison, J.S.; Pretorius, C. A Monte Carlo evaluation of the performance of two new tests for symmetry. *Comput. Stat.* **2017**, *32*, 1323–1338. [CrossRef]
20. Ledoux, M.; Talagrand, M. *Probability in Banach Spaces: Isoperimetry and Processes*; Springer Science & Business Media: Berlin/Heidelberg, Germany, 2013.
21. Allison, J.S.; Santana, L.; Smit, N.; Visagie, I.J.H. An "apples-to-apples" comparison of various tests for exponentiality. *Comput. Stat.* **2017**, *32*, 1241–1283. [CrossRef]
22. Henze, N.; Meintanis, S.G. Recent and classical tests for exponentiality: A partial review with comparisons. *Metrika* **2005**, *61*, 29–45. [CrossRef]
23. Baringhaus, L.; Henze, N. Tests of fit for exponentiality based on a characterization via the mean residual life function. *Stat. Pap.* **2000**, *41*, 225–236. [CrossRef]
24. Baringhaus, L.; Henze, N. A class of consistent tests for exponentiality based on the empirical Laplace transform. *Ann. Inst. Stat. Math.* **1991**, *43*, 551–564. [CrossRef]
25. Henze, N.; Meintanis, S.G. Tests of fit for exponentiality based on the empirical Laplace transform. *Statistics* **2002**, *36*, 147–161. [CrossRef]
26. Epps, T.; Pulley, L. A test of exponentiality vs. monotone-hazard alternatives derived from the empirical characteristic function. *J. R. Stat. Soc. Ser. (Methodol.)* **1986**, *48*, 206–213. [CrossRef]
27. Allison, J.; Milošević, B.; Obradović, M.; Smuts, M. Distribution-free goodness-of-fit tests for the pareto distribution based on a characterization. *Comput. Stat.* **2022**, *37*, 403–418. [CrossRef]
28. R Core Team. *R: A Language and Environment for Statistical Computing*; R Foundation for Statistical Computing: Vienna, Austria, 2019.
29. Hlavac, M. Stargazer: Well-formatted regression and summary statistics tables. *R Package Version* **2018**, *5*, 2.
30. Almongy, H.M.; Almetwally, E.M.; Aljohani, H.M.; Alghamdi, A.S.; Hafez, E. A new extended rayleigh distribution with applications of COVID-19 data. *Results Phys.* **2021**, *23*, 104012. [CrossRef]
31. Allison, J.; Santana, L. On a data-dependent choice of the tuning parameter appearing in certain goodness-of-fit tests. *J. Stat. Comput. Simul.* **2015**, *85*, 3276–3288. [CrossRef]
32. Bothma, E.; Allison, J.S.; Cockeran, M.; Visagie, I.J.H. Characteristic function and Laplace transform-based tests for exponentiality in the presence of random right censoring. *Stat* **2021**, *10*, e394. [CrossRef]
33. Cuparić, M.; Milošević, B. New characterization based exponentiality tests for randomly censored data. *arXiv* **2020**, arXiv:2011.07998.

Article

Optimal Test Plan of Step Stress Partially Accelerated Life Testing for Alpha Power Inverse Weibull Distribution under Adaptive Progressive Hybrid Censored Data and Different Loss Functions

Refah Alotaibi [1], Ehab M. Almetwally [2,3], Qiuchen Hai [4] and Hoda Rezk [5,*]

1. Department of Mathematical Sciences, College of Science, Princess Nourah bint Abdulrahman University, P.O. Box 84428, Riyadh 11671, Saudi Arabia
2. Department of Mathematical Statistical, Faculty of Graduate Studies for Statistical Research, Cairo University, Cairo 12613, Egypt
3. Department of Statistical, Faculty of Business Administration, Delta University for Science and Technology, Talkha 7730103, Egypt
4. Department of Mathematical, Physical, and Engineering Sciences, Texas A&M University-San Antonio, San Antonio, TX 78224, USA
5. Department of Statistics, Al-Azhar University, Cairo 4434003, Egypt
* Correspondence: hodaragab2009@yahoo.com

Abstract: Accelerated life tests are used to explore the lifetime of extremely reliable items by subjecting them to elevated stress levels from stressors to cause early failures, such as temperature, voltage, pressure, and so on. The alpha power inverse Weibull (APIW) distribution is of great significance and practical applications due to its appealing characteristics, such as its flexibilities in the probability density function and the hazard rate function. We analyze the step stress partially accelerated life testing model with samples from the APIW distribution under adaptive type II progressively hybrid censoring. We first obtain the maximum likelihood estimates and two types of approximate confidence intervals of the distributional parameters and then derive Bayes estimates of the unknown parameters under different loss functions. Furthermore, we analyze three probable optimum test techniques for identifying the best censoring under different optimality criteria methods. We conduct simulation studies to assess the finite sample performance of the proposed methodology. Finally, we provide a real data example to further demonstrate the proposed technique.

Keywords: the alpha power inverse Weibull distribution; step stress partially accelerated life testing; adaptive progressive hybrid censored data; loss functions

MSC: 65C20; 60E05; 62P30; 62L15

1. Introduction

The reliability of products has recently grown greatly in the present era of technical achievements due to an ongoing effort for improving manufacturing processes in various companies. Under the presence of high competition to launch their products within a short time period, direct use of traditional life testing methodologies will be an expensive and time-consuming operation for evaluating the lifetime of a product to predict product failures. As a result, accelerated life tests (ALTs) are usually employed to explore the lifetime of extremely reliable products, as they can be used with elevated stress levels of stressors to trigger early failures, such as temperature, voltage (electric field), pressure, and so on. Thereafter, the constant-stress and step-stress models in the ALTs have been studied in life testing and reliability analyses; see, for example, [1–4].

It is known that each product sample in the ALTs is typically analyzed under a constant-stress scenario, subjected to some continuous amounts of constant stress until all units fail or the test is cancelled for any reason, such as censoring plan. However, the test conditions associated with step-stress models do not remain constant throughout the tests, since the stress on a sample of test units could increase step by step at a prescribed period or concurrently when a fixed number of failures occurs. In addition, the ALTs often use a suitable physical model to extrapolate the collected breakdown information under accelerated settings, whereas it is difficult to select a proper physical model to describe the life stress relationships in practical situations [5]. To overcome these drawbacks of ALTs, researchers may employ partially accelerated life testing (PALT), which is classified into two types: constant-stress loading and step-stress loading. In the constant-stress PALT (CSPALT), each sample of tested items is subjected to normal and accelerated levels of constant stress until all units fail or the test is terminated; see, for example, [6,7]. In the step-stress PALT (SSPALT), certain objects or materials are initially tested under normal or usage settings for a predetermined amount of time before being subjected to accelerated test conditions until the termination time; see, for example, [8–10].

In life-testing and reliability trials, data are commonly censored due to time and cost constraints. The hybrid censoring scheme [11], which includes Type-I and Type-II censorings as special cases, is commonly utilized in reliability analysis. We, here, refer the interested reader to [12] for a nice overview of the hybrid censoring. However, the hybrid censoring scheme lacks an option to delete units during the testing period due to time and cost constraints. To address this issue, a progressive censoring scheme was developed by allowing for the deletion of experimental units at various periods of time throughout the test; see, for example, [13,14] in detail. It is worth pointing out that in the progressively Type-II hybrid censoring, the number of required failures and the number of items that must be deleted are determined in advance, whereas there is no time constraint on the experiment, leading to a very long period.

To address this issue, [15] proposed the Type-I Progressive Hybrid Censoring Scheme (TIPHCS), with an additional time and failure constraint that the experiment will run until a predetermined time point or a predetermined number of failures, whichever comes first. However, since the sample size in TIPHCS is random, only a few or even no failure would occur before a pre-specified time limit, resulting in poor efficiency of the parameter estimation. The authors of [16] proposed an adaptive type-II PHCS (AT-II PHCS), in which n units are placed on a life test with a predetermined number of failures m and a pre-fixed progressive censoring scheme $\varepsilon_1, \varepsilon_2, \ldots, \varepsilon_m$, but the experimenter is allowed to change some of the ε_{iw}s during the experiment depending on situations. At the initial failure time, $z_{1:m:n}$, ε_1 units are randomly selected from the remaining $n-1$ alive items and are then removed from the experiment. At the second failure time, $z_{2:m:n}$, ε_2 units of the remaining $n - 1 - \varepsilon_1$ units are eliminated at random, and so on. If the m-th failure time $z_{m:m:n}$, occurs before the predetermined time δ, all the remaining $\varepsilon_m = n - m - \sum_{i=1}^{m} \varepsilon_i$ units are removed and the experiment terminates at time $z_{m:m:n}$. The AT-II PHCS allows the experiment to run over the test termination time restriction. As a result, if $z_{m:m:n} > \delta$, the experiment will soon be stopped by setting $\varepsilon_{c+1}, \varepsilon_{c+2}, \ldots, \varepsilon_{m-1} = 0$. This means that if $z_{c:m:n} < \delta < z_{c+1:m::n}$, with $c+1 < m$ and $y_{c:m:n}$ is the $c-th$ failure time that occurred before δ, no surviving item will be removed from the experiment until the effective sample of m failures is attained, resulting in the remaining units $\varepsilon_m = n - c - \sum_{i=1}^{c} \varepsilon_i$.

Due to the importance of the AT-II PHCS, numerous authors have investigated the problem of parameter estimation in different statistical models based on this censoring scheme; see, for example, Refs. [17–19] for the Weibull distribution, Ref. [20] for the log-normal distribution, Ref. [21] for the exponentiated Weibull distribution, Refs. [22,23] for the extended Weibull distribution, Ref. [24] for the Burr Type-XII distribution, Ref. [25] for the exponentiated Pareto distribution, Ref. [26] for the inverted NH distribution, Ref. [27] for the Weibull generalized exponential distribution, Ref. [28] for the exponentiated exponential distribution, Ref. [29] for the exponentiated power Lindley distribution, and references cited therein. To the best of our knowledge, little research attention has been devoted to the alpha power inverse Weibull (APIW) distribution [30]. This observation motivates us to investigate statistical inference of the APIW distribution under AT-II PHCS.

Due to flexibilities in its probability density function (PDF) and hazard rate function (HRF), the APIW distribution has become a useful model in the study of life testing and reliability analyses. The cumulative distribution function (CDF), PDF, survival function (SF), and HRF for an APIW random variable T are given by

$$F(t;\alpha,\beta,\theta) = \frac{\alpha^{e^{-\beta t^{-\theta}}} - 1}{\alpha - 1}, \ \alpha,\beta,\theta,t > 0, \tag{1}$$

$$f(t;\alpha,\beta,\theta) = \frac{\log(\alpha)\,\theta\beta e^{-\beta t^{-\theta}} t^{-\theta-1} \alpha^{e^{-\beta t^{-\theta}}}}{\alpha - 1}, \ \alpha,\beta,\theta,t > 0, \tag{2}$$

$$S(t;\alpha,\beta,\theta) = \frac{\alpha}{\alpha - 1}\left(1 - \alpha^{e^{-\beta t^{-\theta}} - 1}\right), \ \alpha,\beta,\theta,t > 0, \tag{3}$$

and

$$h(t;\alpha,\beta,\theta) = \frac{\log(\alpha)\,\theta\beta e^{-\beta t^{-\theta}} t^{-\theta-1} \alpha^{e^{-\beta t^{-\theta}} - 1}}{\left(1 - \alpha^{e^{-\beta t^{-\theta}} - 1}\right)}, \ \alpha,\beta,\theta,t > 0, \tag{4}$$

respectively, where $\alpha > 0$ and $\theta > 0$ are the shape parameters and $\beta > 0$ is a scale parameter. This distribution includes many well-known distributions as special cases, such as the alpha power Fréchet, alpha power inverse Rayleigh, alpha power inverse exponential, inverse Weibull, Fréchet, inverse Rayleigh, and the inverse exponential distributions. In addition, it has closed-form expressions of the SF and HRF, which make the distribution a good alternative to commonly used distributions in life-testing analysis.

In this paper, we analyze the step stress partially accelerated life testing model with samples from the APIW distribution under the AT-II PHCS. We first consider the MLEs and derive asymptotic confidence interval and bootstrap confidence intervals of the model parameters. We then propose Bayes estimates of the unknown parameters with non-informative and informative priors under the symmetric and asymmetric loss functions. In addition, we identify the best progressive censoring scheme to the most information about the unknown parameters among all conceivable progressive censoring schemes. Numerical results from simulation studies and a real-data application show that the performance of the proposed technique is quite satisfactory for analyzing censored data under different sampling schemes.

The rest of this paper is organized as follows. Section 2 describes the lifetime model and the test assumptions. Section 3 derives the MLEs of the APIW parameters under the AT-II PHCS. Section 4 constructs the confidence intervals of the unknown parameters. Bayesian analysis of the unknown parameters is provided in Section 5. We carry out simulations in Section 6 to investigate the finite sample performance of the proposed model. In Section 7, a real-data example is provided for illustrative purposes. Finally, concluding remarks are provided in Section 8 with Fisher information of the model deferred to the Appendix A.

2. Assumptions and Procedure for Testing

Suppose that in a simple SSPALT, the test employs only two stress levels, S_u (normal operating circumstances) and S_a (accelerated condition), such that $S_u < S_a$, where S_u and S_a are twins. Under each stress level, at least one failure should occur. We assume that at both stress levels, the failures of the test items follow the APIW distribution in (2). Then, the lifetime Z of a test item follows a TRV model given by

$$Z = \begin{cases} T, & if\ T < \tau \\ \tau + \frac{T-\tau}{\lambda}, & T > \tau \end{cases}$$

where T indicates the lifetime of an item under the stress ST and represents the time point at which stress ST is switched from u to a, and $\lambda > 1$ is an accelerated factor (AF). Then, under the TRV model, we obtain the PDF, CDF, and SF of Z given by

$$f_u(z; \alpha, \beta, \theta) = \frac{\log(\alpha)\, \theta \beta e^{-\beta z^{-\theta}} z^{-\theta-1} \alpha^{e^{-\beta z^{-\theta}}}}{\alpha - 1}, \qquad (5)$$

$$F_u(z; \alpha, \beta, \theta) = \frac{\alpha^{e^{-\beta z^{-\theta}}} - 1}{\alpha - 1}, \qquad (6)$$

$$S_u(z; \alpha, \beta, \theta) = \frac{\alpha}{\alpha - 1}\left(1 - \alpha^{e^{-\alpha z^{-\theta}} - 1}\right) \qquad (7)$$

Now, at stress ST $= a$, the PDF, CDF, and SF of Z are produced as follows:

$$f_a(z; \alpha, \beta, \theta, \lambda) = \frac{\log(\alpha)\, \theta \beta e^{-\beta[\tau+\lambda(z-\tau)]^{-\theta}} [\tau + \lambda(z-\tau)]^{-\theta-1} \alpha^{e^{-\beta[\tau+\lambda(z-\tau)]^{-\theta}}}}{\alpha - 1}, \qquad (8)$$

$$F_a(z; \alpha, \beta, \theta, \lambda) = \frac{\alpha^{e^{-\beta[\tau+\lambda(z-\tau)]^{-\theta}}} - 1}{\alpha - 1}, \quad \alpha, \beta, \theta, z > 0, \lambda > 1, \qquad (9)$$

$$S_a(z; \alpha, \beta, \theta, \lambda) = \frac{\alpha}{\alpha - 1}\left(1 - \alpha^{e^{-\alpha[\tau+\lambda(z-\tau)]^{-\theta}} - 1}\right), \qquad (10)$$

where $\alpha, \beta, \theta, z > 0, \lambda > 1$. We assume that a sample of n items is assigned to the stress level S_u to test according to the SSPALT and a known progressive censoring scheme $\varepsilon_1, \varepsilon_2, \ldots, \varepsilon_m$. The test will proceed and the items from n that do not fail up to time S_u are placed through S_a to test, and the test will continue until the censorship time is reached. If the $m-th$ failure does not occur within the censoring point δ, no item will be removed from the test. The testing will continue until the $m-th$ failure is registered, at which point it will be terminated when all remaining items are eliminated. As a result, the implemented scheme is $\varepsilon_1, \varepsilon_2, \ldots, \varepsilon_c, 0, 0, \ldots, 0, \varepsilon_m$. Thus, we obtain the observed samples given by

$z_{1:m:n} < z_{2:m:n} < \ldots < z_{m_u:m:n} < \tau < z_{m_u+1:m:n} < \ldots < z_{c:m:n} < \delta < z_{c+1:m:n} < \ldots < z_{m:m:n}$,

illustrated in Figure 1.

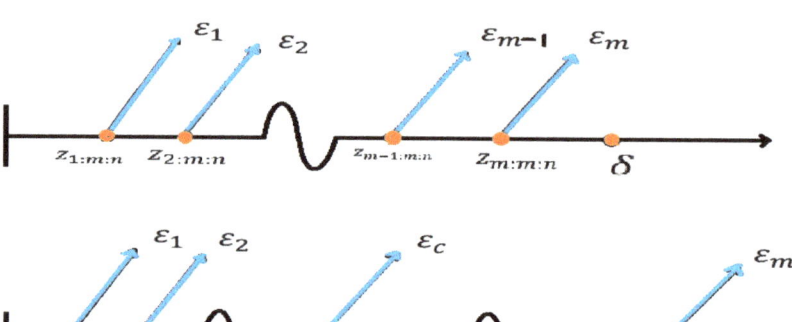

Figure 1. Illustration of the AT-II PHCS scheme.

We observe from this figure that the AT-II PHCS is a special instance of the AT-II PHCS as $\delta \to 0$ and that the AT-II PHCS reduces to the classical Type-II PHCS as $\delta \to \infty$.

3. The Parameter Estimation

The resulting likelihood function of the data under the AT-II PHCS is given by

$$L(z;\alpha,\beta,\theta,\lambda) \propto \prod_{i=1}^{m_u}\{f_u(z_i)[R_u(z_i)]^{\varepsilon_i}\} \prod_{i=m_u+1}^{m}\{f_a(z_i)[R_a(z_i)]^{\varepsilon_i}[R_a(z_m)]^{\varepsilon_m}\}, \quad (11)$$

where $z_i = z_{i:m:n}$, $\varepsilon_m = n - m - \sum_{i=1}^{c}\varepsilon_i$. Then it follows

$$L(z;\alpha,\beta,\theta,\lambda) \propto \prod_{i=1}^{m_u}\left\{\frac{\log(\alpha)\,\theta\beta e^{-\beta z_i^{-\theta}} z_i^{-\theta-1}\alpha^{e^{-\beta z_i^{-\theta}}}}{\alpha - 1}\left[\frac{\alpha}{\alpha-1}\left(1 - \alpha^{e^{-\beta z_i^{-\theta}}-1}\right)\right]^{\varepsilon_i}\right\}$$

$$\times \prod_{i=m_u+1}^{m}\left\{\frac{\log(\alpha)\,\theta\beta e^{-\beta[\tau+\lambda(z_i-\tau)]^{-\theta}}[\tau+\lambda(z_i-\tau)]^{-\theta-1}\alpha^{e^{-\beta[\tau+\lambda(z_i-\tau)]^{-\theta}}}}{\alpha-1}\left[\frac{\alpha}{\alpha-1}\left(1 - \alpha^{e^{-\beta[\tau+\lambda(z_i-\tau)]^{-\theta}}-1}\right)\right]^{\varepsilon_i}\left[\frac{\alpha}{\alpha-1}\left(1 - \alpha^{e^{-\beta[\tau+\lambda(z_m-\tau)]^{-\theta}}-1}\right)\right]^{\varepsilon_m}\right\} \quad (12)$$

The MLE is commonly used to estimate the unknown parameters, as it effectively and efficiently yields estimates with good statistical properties. By taking the natural logarithm on both sides of Equation (12), we obtain the log-likelihood equation $L(z;\alpha,\beta,\theta,\lambda) = \ell$ as follows

$$\ell = m_u\log(\log(\alpha)) - m_u\log(\alpha-1) + m_u\log(\theta) + m_u\log(\beta) - \beta\sum_{i=1}^{m_u}z_i^{-\theta} - (\theta+1)\sum_{i=1}^{m_u}\log(z_i)$$

$$+\log(\alpha)\sum_{i=1}^{m_u}e^{-\beta z_i^{-\theta}} + \sum_{i=1}^{m_u}\varepsilon_i\log(\alpha) - \sum_{i=1}^{m_u}\varepsilon_i\log(\alpha-1) + \sum_{i=1}^{m_u}\varepsilon_i\log\left(1 - \alpha^{e^{-\beta z_i^{-\theta}}-1}\right)$$

$$+m\log(\log(\alpha)) - m\log(\alpha-1) + m\log(\theta) + m\log(\beta) - \beta\sum_{i=m_u+1}^{m}[\tau+\lambda(z_i-\tau)]^{-\theta}$$

$$-(\theta+1)\sum_{i=m_u+1}^{m}\log[\tau+\lambda(z_i-\tau)] + \log(\alpha)\sum_{i=m_u+1}^{m}e^{-\beta[\tau+\lambda(z_i-\tau)]^{-\theta}} + \sum_{i=m_u+1}^{m}(\varepsilon_i)\log(\alpha)$$

$$-\sum_{i=m_u+1}^{m}(\varepsilon_i)\log(\alpha-1) + \sum_{i=m_u+1}^{m}\varepsilon_i\log\left(1 - \alpha^{e^{-\beta[\tau+\lambda(z_i-\tau)]^{-\theta}}-1}\right) + \varepsilon_m\log(\alpha) - \varepsilon_m\log(\alpha-1)$$

$$+\varepsilon_m\log\left(1 - \alpha^{e^{-\beta[\tau+\lambda(z_m-\tau)]^{-\theta}}-1}\right) \quad (13)$$

The MLEs of the parameters α, β, θ and λ can be obtained by solving the following nonlinear system equations

$$\frac{\partial\ell}{\partial\alpha} = \frac{m_u+m}{\alpha\log\alpha} - \frac{(m_u+m)}{(\alpha-1)} + \frac{1}{\alpha}\sum_{i=1}^{m_u}e^{-\beta z_i^{-\theta}} - \frac{1}{\alpha}\sum_{i=1}^{m_u}\varepsilon_i - \frac{1}{\alpha-1}\sum_{i=1}^{m_u}\varepsilon_i - \log(\alpha)\sum_{i=1}^{m_u}\varepsilon_i\alpha^{e^{-\beta z_i^{-\theta}}-1}$$

$$+\frac{1}{\alpha}\sum_{i=m_u+1}^{m}\varepsilon_i e^{-\beta[\tau+\lambda(z_i-\tau)]^{-\theta}} + \frac{1}{\alpha}\sum_{i=m_u+1}^{m}(\varepsilon_i) + \frac{1}{(\alpha-1)}\sum_{i=m_u+1}^{m}(\varepsilon_i) \quad (14)$$

$$+\log(\alpha)\sum_{i=m_u+1}^{m}\varepsilon_i\frac{\alpha^{e^{-\beta[\tau+\lambda(z_i-\tau)]^{-\theta}}-1}}{\left(1-\alpha^{e^{-\beta[\tau+\lambda(z_i-\tau)]^{-\theta}}-1}\right)} + \frac{\varepsilon_m}{\alpha} - \frac{\varepsilon_m}{(\alpha-1)} + \frac{\varepsilon_m\log(\alpha)\alpha^{e^{-\beta[\tau+\lambda(z_m-\tau)]^{-\theta}}-1}}{1-\alpha^{e^{-\beta[\tau+\lambda(z_m-\tau)]^{-\theta}}-1}},$$

$$\begin{aligned}
\frac{\partial \ell}{\partial \theta} &= \frac{m_u+m}{\theta} + \beta \sum_{i=1}^{m_u} z_i^{-\theta} \log(z_i) - \sum_{i=1}^{m_u} \log(z_i) \\
&+ \log(\alpha) \sum_{i=1}^{m_u} \beta z_i^{-\theta} \log(z_i) e^{-\beta z_i^{-\theta}} + \sum_{i=1}^{m_u} e^{-\beta z_i^{-\theta}} \beta z_i^{-\theta} \log(z_i) \left(e^{-\beta z_i^{-\theta}} - 1 \right) \varepsilon_i \alpha e^{-\beta z_i^{-\theta}} - 2 \\
&+ \beta \sum_{i=m_u+1}^{m} [\tau + \lambda(z_i - \tau)]^{-\theta} \log[\tau + \lambda(z_i - \tau)] \\
&- \sum_{i=m_u+1}^{m} \log[\tau + \lambda(z_i - \tau)] + \log(\alpha) \sum_{i=m_u+1}^{m} e^{-\beta[\tau+\lambda(z_i-\tau)]^{-\theta}} \beta[\tau + \lambda(z_i - \tau)]^{-\theta} \log[\tau + \lambda(z_i - \tau)] \\
&+ \sum_{i=m_u+1}^{m} \frac{\varepsilon_i e^{-\beta[\tau+\lambda(z_i-\tau)]^{-\theta}} \beta[\tau+\lambda(z_i-\tau)]^{-\theta} \log[\tau+\lambda(z_i-\tau)] \left(e^{-\beta[\tau+\lambda(z_i-\tau)]^{-\theta}} - 1 \right) \left(\alpha e^{-\beta[\tau+\lambda(z_i-\tau)]^{-\theta}} - 2 \right)}{\left(1 - \alpha e^{-\beta[\tau+\lambda(z_i-\tau)]^{-\theta}} - 1 \right)} \\
&+ \frac{\varepsilon_m e^{-\beta[\tau+\lambda(z_m-\tau)]^{-\theta}} \beta[\tau+\lambda(z_m-\tau)]^{-\theta} \log[\tau+\lambda(z_m-\tau)] \left(e^{-\beta[\tau+\lambda(z_m-\tau)]^{-\theta}} - 1 \right) \left(\alpha e^{-\beta[\tau+\lambda(z_m-\tau)]^{-\theta}} - 2 \right)}{\alpha e^{-\beta[\tau+\lambda(z_m-\tau)]^{-\theta}} - 1},
\end{aligned}$$ (15)

$$\begin{aligned}
\frac{\partial \ell}{\partial \beta} &= \frac{m_u}{\beta} - \sum_{i=1}^{m_u} z_i^{-\theta} - \log(\alpha) \sum_{i=1}^{m_u} z_i^{-\theta} e^{-\beta z_i^{-\theta}} - \sum_{i=1}^{m_u} \varepsilon_i z_i^{-\theta} e^{-\beta z_i^{-\theta}} \left(\alpha e^{-\beta z_i^{-\theta}} - 1 \right) + \frac{m}{\beta} + \sum_{i=m_u+1}^{m} [\tau + \lambda(z_i - \tau)]^{-\theta} \\
&+ \log(\alpha) \sum_{i=m_u+1}^{m} [\tau + \lambda(z_i - \tau)]^{-\theta} e^{-\beta[\tau+\lambda(z_i-\tau)]^{-\theta}} \\
&+ \sum_{i=m_u+1}^{m} \varepsilon_i \frac{\alpha e^{-\beta[\tau+\lambda(z_i-\tau)]^{-\theta}} - 1 \left(e^{-\beta[\tau+\lambda(z_i-\tau)]^{-\theta}} - 1 \right)}{1 - \alpha e^{-\beta[\tau+\lambda(z_i-\tau)]^{-\theta}} - 1} \\
&+ \frac{\varepsilon_m \left(e^{-\beta[\tau+\lambda(z_m-\tau)]^{-\theta}} - 1 \right) [\tau+\lambda(z_m-\tau)]^{-\theta} \left(\alpha e^{-\beta[\tau+\lambda(z_m-\tau)]^{-\theta}} - 1 \right)}{1 - \alpha e^{-\beta[\tau+\lambda(z_m-\tau)]^{-\theta}} - 1},
\end{aligned}$$ (16)

$$\begin{aligned}
\frac{\partial \ell}{\partial \lambda} &= -\beta \sum_{i=m_u+1}^{m} (z_i - \tau)[\tau + \lambda(z_i - \tau)]^{-\theta-1} - \sum_{i=m_u+1}^{m} \frac{(\theta+1)(z_i-\tau)}{[\tau+\lambda(z_i-\tau)]} \\
&+ \beta \log(\alpha) \sum_{i=m_u+1}^{m} e^{-\beta[\tau+\lambda(z_i-\tau)]^{-\theta}} (z_i - \tau)[\tau + \lambda(z_i - \tau)]^{-\theta-1} \\
&+ \frac{\sum_{i=m_u+1}^{m} \varepsilon_i e^{-\beta[\tau+\lambda(z_i-\tau)]^{-\theta}} \beta(z_i-\tau)[\tau+\lambda(z_i-\tau)]^{-\theta-1} \left(e^{-\beta[\tau+\lambda(z_i-\tau)]^{-\theta}} - 1 \right) \alpha e^{-\beta[\tau+\lambda(z_i-\tau)]^{-\theta}} - 2}{\left(1 - \alpha e^{-\beta[\tau+\lambda(z_i-\tau)]^{-\theta}} - 1 \right)} \\
&+ \frac{\varepsilon_m e^{-\beta[\tau+\lambda(z_m-\tau)]^{-\theta}} \beta(z_m-\tau)[\tau+\lambda(z_m-\tau)]^{-\theta-1} \left(e^{-\beta[\tau+\lambda(z_m-\tau)]^{-\theta}} - 1 \right) \alpha e^{-\beta[\tau+\lambda(z_m-\tau)]^{-\theta}} - 2}{1 - \alpha e^{-\beta[\tau+\lambda(z_m-\tau)]^{-\theta}} - 1}.
\end{aligned}$$ (17)

We observe that it is difficult to get closed-form solutions of the parameters from the above nonlinear equations. As a result, we employ an iterative approach, such as Newton–Raphson, to find numerical solutions to the nonlinear systems.

4. Confidence Intervals

A confidence interval (CI) is a collection of numbers that serves as reasonable approximations to an unknown population characteristic (e.g., [31]). We consider two types of CIs for the unknown parameters as follows.

4.1. Approximate Confidence Intervals

According to large sample theory, the MLEs are consistent and regularly distributed under certain regularity conditions. To be more specific, $[(\hat{\alpha} - \alpha), (\hat{\theta} - \theta), (\hat{\beta} - \beta), (\hat{\lambda} - \lambda)] \sim N(0, \sigma)$ is known to yield the asymptotic distribution of MLEs of α, θ, β and λ, where $\sigma = \sigma_{ij}, i, j = 1, 2, 3, 4$ is the unknown parameters' in the variance–covariance matrix. The inverse of the Fisher information matrix is an estimate of the variance–covariance matrix. The estimated $100(1-\pi)\%$ two-sided CIs for the unknown parameter are provided by

$$(\hat{\pi}_{iL}, \hat{\pi}_{iU}): \hat{\pi}_i \mp z_{1-\frac{\pi}{2}} \sqrt{\hat{\sigma}_{ij}}, i = 1, 2, 3, 4,$$

where $z_{1-\pi/2}$ is the π-th percentile of the standard normal distribution. However, the above asymptotic CIs may not perform well due to an asymmetric property of the APIW distribution. To deal with this issue, we consider the parametric bootstrap percentile intervals as an alternative [32].

4.2. Bootstrap Confidence Intervals

We consider the parametric bootstrap sampling with percentile intervals, which can be implemented using Algorithm 1.

Algorithm 1. Bootstrap
---
1. Step 0, basic setup:
2. Set b = 1
3. Determine the MLE values of $\omega = (\alpha, \theta, \beta, \lambda)$, as showing by $\hat{\omega} = (\hat{\alpha}, \hat{\theta}, \hat{\beta}, \hat{\lambda})$.
4. Step 1: Sample
5. Get the *bth* bootstrap resample t_p^* from $F(.|\hat{\omega})$, where is the MLE from Step 0.
6. Step 2: Estimates from the bootstrap:
7. Calculate the *bth* bootstrap estimations.
8. $\hat{\omega}^{*b} = \left(\hat{\alpha}^{*b}, \hat{\theta}^{*b}, \hat{\beta}^{*b}, \hat{\lambda}^{*b}\right)$,
9. Utilize the t_p^* resample obtained in Step 1.
10. Step three, repeat:
11. Set b←b+1,
12. Steps 1–3 are then repeated until b = G.
13. Step 4: In ascending sequence, begin:
14. Sort the estimates in increasing order so that
15. $\left\{\hat{\alpha}^{*[1]}, \hat{\alpha}^{*[2]}, \ldots, \hat{\alpha}^{*[G]}\right\}, \left\{\hat{\theta}^{*[1]}, \hat{\theta}^{*[2]}, \ldots, \hat{\theta}^{*[G]}\right\}, \left\{\hat{\beta}^{*[1]}, \hat{\beta}^{*[2]}, \ldots, \hat{\beta}^{*[G]}\right\}, \left\{\hat{\lambda}^{*[1]}, \hat{\lambda}^{*[2]}, \ldots, \hat{\lambda}^{*[G]}\right\}$

The $100(1-\omega)\%$ percentile bootstrap CIs for the unknown parameter are computed as follows

$$(\hat{\omega}_{iL}, \hat{\omega}_{iU}) = \left(\hat{\omega}_i^{*[\frac{\pi}{2}]G}, \hat{\omega}_i^{*[(1-\frac{\pi}{2})G]}\right), i = 1, 2, 3, 4,$$

where $\hat{\omega}_1^* = \alpha^*, \hat{\omega}_2^* = \theta^*, \hat{\omega}_3^* = \beta^*$, and $\hat{\omega}_4^* = \lambda^*$.

5. Bayesian Estimation

In this section, we focus on Bayes estimation for the unknown parameters. Bayesian analysis begins with prior specifications for the unknown parameters. In this paper, we assume that the parameters α, θ, β, and λ are statistically independent and follow independent gamma distributions, denoted by $gamma(a_j, b_j); j = 1, \ldots, 4$, respectively. The joint priors for the APIW parameters can be written as

$$\varphi(\alpha, \theta, \beta, \lambda) \propto \alpha^{a_1-1} e^{-b_1 \alpha} \theta^{a_2-1} e^{-b_2 \theta} \beta^{a_3-1} e^{-b_3 \beta} \lambda^{a_4-1} e^{-b_4 \lambda}, \tag{18}$$

where $a_j \geq 0$ and $b_j \geq 0; j = 1, \ldots, 4$ are pre-determined hyperparameters that reflect prior knowledge of the unknown parameters. The resulting joint posterior distribution of the unknown parameters is given by

$$L(\alpha, \theta, \beta, \lambda | \underline{t}) \propto \varphi(\alpha, \theta, \beta, \lambda) \prod_{i=1}^{4} \prod_{j=1}^{n_i} f(t_{ij})(1 - F(t_{ij}))^{d_i}, \tag{19}$$

which is usually unidentifiable. Thus, we employ Markov chain Monte Carlo (MCMC) methods to generate posterior samples of the unknown parameters for making posterior inference. In particular, the acquired samples will also be used to approximate Bayes estimates and obtain the corresponding highest posterior density (HPD) credible ranges for the unknown parameters [33]. In this paper, we obtain the Bayes estimates of the unknown parameters under the symmetric (SLF) and asymmetric (ELF) loss functions, which are denoted as

$$\ell(\alpha,\tilde{\alpha}) = (\tilde{\alpha}-\alpha)^2, \ell(\theta,\tilde{\theta}) = (\tilde{\theta}-\theta)^2, \ell(\beta,\tilde{\beta}) = (\tilde{\beta}-\beta)^2, \ell(\lambda,\tilde{\lambda}) = (\tilde{\lambda}-\lambda)^2, \quad (20)$$

where $\tilde{\alpha}, \tilde{\theta}, \tilde{\beta}$ and $\tilde{\lambda}$ denote the estimated posterior means of α, θ, β and λ, respectively.

The generalized entropy (GE), an asymmetric loss function, is a simple generalization of the entropy loss with the shape parameter q being 1 and is given by

$$\ell(\omega,\tilde{\omega}) \propto \left(\frac{\tilde{\omega}}{\omega}\right)^q - q\ln\left(\frac{\tilde{\omega}}{\omega}\right) - 1, \, q \neq 1, \quad (21)$$

where $\tilde{\omega}$ is an approximated estimation of ω given by

$$\tilde{\omega}_{GE} = [E_\omega(\omega^{-q})]^{\frac{-1}{q}}, \quad (22)$$

assuming that ω^{-q} exists and is finite and E_ω represents the anticipated value [34]. It should be emphasized that other loss functions may easily be substituted in the same way.

6. Optimization Criterion

There has been a lot of interest in identifying the best censoring scheme in recent years; see [35–39]. For values of n and m determined by the samples under a test, possible censoring schemes are all combinations of $R_1, \ldots, R_m$. We are interested in selecting the best sample technique, as it entails identifying the progressive censoring scheme that provides the most information about the unknown parameters among all conceivable progressive censoring schemes. The first challenge is to determine a way to generate the unknown parameter information based on specific progressive censoring data, and the second is to compare two distinct information measures based on two different progressive censoring techniques. We, here, provide some of the optimality criteria as follows. We choose the censoring method that provides the most information about the unknown parameters. Table 1 provides a variety of commonly used measures in selecting the proper progressive censoring strategy, C_i.

Table 1. Some practical censoring plan optimum criteria.

Criterion	Method
C_1	Maximize trace $[I_{4\times 4}(.)]$
C_2	Minimize trace $[I_{4\times 4}(.)]^{-1}$
C_3	Minimize det $[I_{4\times 4}(.)]^{-1}$

We are interested in maximizing the observed Fisher information $I_{4\times 4}(.)$ for C_1. Furthermore, for criteria C_2 and C_3, we reduce the determinant and trace of $[I_{4\times 4}(.)]^{-1}$. Comparing multiple criteria is simple when dealing with a distribution with a single parameter; however, comparing the two Fisher information matrices becomes difficult for multiparameter distributions, because C_2 and C_3 are not scale invariant. As a result, the logarithm of the APIW distribution for $\hat{t}_p$ is provided by

$$\log(\hat{t}_p) = \log\left\{\frac{-1}{\beta}\log\left[1 - \frac{\log(1+p(\alpha-1))}{\log\alpha}\right]\right\}^{\frac{1}{\theta}}, \, 0 < p < 1, \quad (23)$$

We apply the delta approach to (23) to obtain the approximated variance for $\log(\hat{t}_p)$ of the APIW distribution as

$$Var(\log(\hat{t}_p)) = [\nabla \log(\hat{t}_p)]^T I_{4\times 4}^{-1}(\hat{\alpha}, \hat{\theta}, \hat{\beta}, \hat{\lambda})[\nabla \log(\hat{t}_p)],$$

where

$$[\nabla \log(\hat{t}_p)]^T = \left[\frac{\partial}{\partial \alpha}\log(\hat{t}_p), \frac{\partial}{\partial \theta}\log(\hat{t}_p), \frac{\partial}{\partial \beta}\log(\hat{t}_p), \frac{\partial}{\partial \lambda}\log(\hat{t}_p)\right]_{(\alpha=\hat{\alpha},\theta=\hat{\theta},\beta=\hat{\beta},\lambda=\hat{\lambda})}$$

The optimal progressive censoring corresponds to a maximum value of C_1 and a minimum value of C_i, $i = 1, 2, 3$.

7. Simulation

In this section, simulation experiments are carried out to evaluate the MLEs and Bayesian estimators' performances under the SLF and ELF in terms of their bias, mean square error (MSE), length of asymptotic CIs (LACI), and length of credible CIs (LCCI). The 95% CIs are generated using the asymptotic distribution of the MLEs. Two MLE bootstrap confidence intervals are additionally attained. The HPD is used to calculate the 95% credible intervals. Two schemes of progressive censoring are taken into consideration:

Scheme I: $R_1 = \ldots = R_{m-1} = 0$, and $R_m = n - m$.
Scheme II: $R_2 = \ldots = R_m = 0$ and $R_1 = n - m$.

For more information, see [40]. To choose the best strategy for the determinant and trace of the variance–covariance matrices, maximization of the principal diagonal elements of the Fisher information matrices, minimization of the determinant and trace of the variance–covariance matrix, and minimization of the variance in the logarithmic MLE of the p-th quantile, we used various optimization criteria. The following algorithm is used to carry out the estimation procedure:

1. Give the numbers n, m, and τ. The total sample size in complete case is $n = 100$ and 200; the censored sample size is $m = 75$ and 90 m when $n = 100$ and $m = 150$ and 185 when $n = 200$.
2. Give the parameters, $\alpha = 2$, $\beta = 2$, $\lambda = 1.6$, $\theta = 0.7$, and $\alpha = 0.6$, $\beta = 0.7$, $\lambda = 0.8$, $\theta = 1.4$.
3. Make a sample of size n of the randomness from the random variable t in Equation (1), then sort it. It is easy to create a random variable with the APIW distribution. If the uniform random variable U is drawn from the interval $[0, 1]$, then

$$z = \begin{cases} \left\{\frac{-1}{\beta}\ln\left[\frac{\ln(1+(\alpha-1)U)}{\ln(\alpha)}\right]\right\}^{\frac{-1}{\theta}} & t < \tau \\ \tau - \tau^* + \left\{\frac{-1}{\lambda}\ln\left[\frac{\ln(1+(\alpha-1)u)}{\ln(\alpha)}\right]\right\}^{\frac{-1}{\theta}} & t > \tau \end{cases}.$$

4. To generate the adaptive progressive hybrid censored data for given n, m, and δ, we use the model in (7). The data can be thought of as:

$$z_{1:m:n} < z_{2:m:n} < \ldots < z_{u:m:n} < \tau < z_{u+1:m:n} < \ldots z_{c:m:n} < \delta < z_{c+1:m:n} < z_{m:m:n}$$

5. To obtain the MLEs of the parameters, the nonlinear system is solved by using the Newton–Raphson method.
6. To obtain the Bayes estimation of the parameters, we obtain posterior samples from the MCMC algorithm.
7. Repeat Steps 3 through 6 for 1000 iterations.
8. Calculate the MLEs and Bayes parameter-related average values of bias, MSE, and LCI.
9. Calculate various parameter estimations and their confidence intervals.
10. Calculate the various optimization criteria.

Numerical simulation studies are provided in Tables 2–7 and Figures 2 and 3. Several conclusions can be drawn as follows.

- By increasing the censored sample sizes m, the bias, MSE, and LCI of the estimates for the two alternative censored methods decrease for fixed values of n and δ.

- By increasing the censored sample sizes δ, the bias, MSE, and LCI of the estimates for the two alternative censored methods decrease for fixed values of n and m.
- By increasing the censored sample sizes n, the bias, MSE, and LCI of the estimates for the two alternative censored methods decrease for fixed values of the sample sizes δ and m.
- Bayes estimations of the parameters under the two loss functions outperform the MLE in terms of bias and MSE for the scenarios under consideration.
- The bias and MSE of Bayes estimations of the parameters increase under the considered scenarios when we used negative weight for ELF.
- The HPDs of the unknown parameters outperform the CIs based on the MLEs with respect to ACIs and LCIs. In addition, we observe that the lengths of the bootstrap CIs are the shortest.

Table 2. Bias, MSE, LACI, LBCI, and LCCI with scheme 1 in case 1.

$\alpha=2, \beta=2, \lambda=1.6, \theta=0.7$				MLE				SELF			ELF c = −1.25			ELF c = 1.25		
n	τ, δ	m		Bias	MSE	LACI	LBPCI	LBTCI	Bias	MSE	LCCI	Bias	MSE	LCCI	Bias	MSE	LCCI
100	2, 10	75	α	0.3263	0.3997	2.1248	0.0965	0.0947	−0.2602	0.3062	1.8368	−0.2458	0.2894	1.7968	−0.4100	0.5367	2.2491
			β	−1.3825	1.9408	0.6726	0.0302	0.0301	−0.5628	0.3439	0.6222	−0.5578	0.3379	0.6157	−0.6050	0.3980	0.6726
			λ	−0.3294	0.1665	0.9447	0.0406	0.0406	0.2863	0.1435	0.7539	0.6361	0.4416	0.7597	0.5878	0.3778	0.6959
			θ	0.8792	0.8010	0.6577	0.0301	0.0300	0.0546	0.0395	0.3513	0.0563	0.0097	0.3143	0.0389	0.0079	0.3100
		90	α	0.1289	0.3267	2.1851	0.1033	0.1031	−0.0321	0.0331	0.7063	−0.0309	0.0329	0.7056	−0.0423	0.0351	0.7149
			β	−1.3616	1.8885	0.7287	0.0325	0.0327	−0.2817	0.1017	0.5869	−0.2789	0.0997	0.5807	−0.3071	0.1212	0.6382
			λ	−0.2883	0.1568	1.0653	0.0484	0.0484	0.1990	0.0575	0.5284	0.2005	0.0583	0.5303	0.1850	0.0506	0.4982
			θ	0.8403	0.7273	0.5710	0.0257	0.0253	0.0464	0.0241	0.3401	0.1281	0.0246	0.3411	0.1123	0.0198	0.3214
	3.5, 18	75	α	1.2072	2.6719	4.3243	0.1911	0.1921	−0.1065	0.2610	1.8586	−0.0961	0.2537	1.8425	−0.2112	0.3636	2.1097
			β	−1.1084	1.2923	0.9910	0.0427	0.0432	−0.6102	0.4100	0.7449	−0.6050	0.4028	0.7387	−0.6526	0.4709	0.7836
			λ	0.4902	0.4963	1.9853	0.0901	0.0900	0.2893	0.2940	0.6019	0.9399	0.9551	1.0307	0.8542	0.7929	0.9038
			θ	0.6934	0.5379	0.9372	0.0414	0.0410	0.1369	0.0546	0.4633	0.1387	0.0550	0.4645	0.1201	0.0390	0.4486
		90	α	1.3165	2.5775	3.6059	0.1659	0.1640	−0.0176	0.0289	0.6324	−0.0166	0.0288	0.6321	−0.0262	0.0298	0.6365
			β	−0.7230	0.9408	0.6724	0.0317	0.0317	−0.2981	0.1098	0.5521	−0.2953	0.1077	0.5458	−0.3236	0.1297	0.6095
			λ	0.3408	0.2248	1.2936	0.0615	0.0615	0.2828	0.0994	0.5239	0.2850	0.1009	0.5256	0.2630	0.0863	0.4918
			θ	0.5154	0.5080	0.4873	0.0216	0.0217	0.1171	0.0185	0.2572	0.1185	0.0188	0.2583	0.1050	0.0154	0.2438
200	2, 10	150	α	0.4348	0.3536	1.5917	0.0687	0.0686	−0.3758	0.3113	1.5792	−0.3615	0.2930	1.5336	−0.5182	0.5351	1.9342
			β	−1.4213	2.0289	0.3648	0.0164	0.0164	−0.5234	0.2866	0.4452	−0.5207	0.2836	0.4421	−0.5462	0.3127	0.4733
			λ	−0.3996	0.1784	0.5367	0.0252	0.0251	0.3067	0.1470	0.4559	0.6752	0.4750	0.5652	0.6380	0.4234	0.5026
			θ	0.8859	0.7991	0.4679	0.0216	0.0216	0.1493	0.0536	0.2133	0.0502	0.0055	0.2140	0.0411	0.0046	0.2089
		185	α	0.3155	0.2366	1.4526	0.0660	0.0657	−0.0758	0.0305	0.6101	−0.0749	0.0303	0.6091	−0.0847	0.0331	0.6135
			β	−1.4129	2.0049	0.3619	0.0153	0.0150	−0.3626	0.1448	0.4347	−0.3595	0.1423	0.4300	−0.3899	0.1677	0.4811
			λ	−0.3822	0.1643	0.5300	0.0236	0.0241	0.2720	0.0855	0.4317	0.2737	0.0866	0.4337	0.2565	0.0760	0.4061
			θ	0.8609	0.7536	0.4379	0.0193	0.0194	0.1081	0.0367	0.2046	0.1822	0.0372	0.2442	0.1678	0.0318	0.2363
	3.5, 18	150	α	0.4026	0.2824	1.4873	0.0552	0.0567	−0.1721	0.2094	1.5946	−0.1630	0.2006	1.5636	−0.2593	0.3096	1.8659
			β	−0.9198	1.4616	0.3652	0.0129	0.0128	−0.5550	0.3255	0.5263	−0.5521	0.3219	0.5242	−0.5792	0.3553	0.5561
			λ	0.2994	0.1698	0.5294	0.0258	0.0255	0.1025	0.1085	0.4657	1.0326	1.1012	0.6591	0.9497	0.9289	0.5761
			θ	0.7250	0.5558	0.6811	0.0314	0.0309	0.1129	0.0419	0.2710	0.1138	0.0197	0.2710	0.1047	0.0168	0.2699
		185	α	0.4004	0.2704	1.0908	0.0425	0.0416	−0.0208	0.0234	0.5713	−0.0200	0.0233	0.5702	−0.0283	0.0244	0.5746
			β	−0.2134	0.8482	0.3493	0.0109	0.0119	−0.3858	0.1599	0.3899	−0.3823	0.1570	0.3850	−0.4166	0.1867	0.4370
			λ	0.2444	0.0915	0.5070	0.0219	0.0214	0.2369	0.0877	0.4251	0.3718	0.1509	0.4277	0.3447	0.1295	0.3881
			θ	0.6121	0.4589	0.3919	0.0174	0.0174	0.1670	0.0305	0.1924	0.1681	0.0309	0.1941	0.1565	0.0268	0.1823

Table 3. Bias, MSE, LACI, LBCI, and LCCI with scheme 2 in case 1.

$\alpha=2, \beta=2, \lambda=1.6, \theta=0.7$			MLE					SELF			ELF c = −1.25			ELF c = 1.25		
n	τ, δ	m	Bias	MSE	LACI	LBPCI	LBTCI	Bias	MSE	LCCI	Bias	MSE	LCCI	Bias	MSE	LCCI
100	2, 10	75	α	0.4624	0.5714	2.3474	0.1201	0.1205	−0.2218	0.2633	1.8289	−0.2105	0.2495	1.7748	−0.3394	0.4512	2.2924
			β	−1.3916	1.9624	0.6328	0.0319	0.0321	−0.5221	0.2971	0.6066	−0.5175	0.2918	0.5994	−0.5610	0.3430	0.6561
			λ	−0.3496	0.1814	0.9551	0.0496	0.0499	0.3042	0.1802	0.7407	0.4214	0.2150	0.7430	0.3813	0.1781	0.7106
			θ	1.0136	1.0650	0.7624	0.0425	0.0421	0.5739	0.3628	0.7099	0.5790	0.3695	0.7194	0.5214	0.2973	0.6187
		90	α	0.5295	0.5660	2.4170	0.0765	0.0770	−0.2670	0.2579	1.7531	−0.2544	0.2632	1.6937	−0.4003	0.5122	2.3486
			β	−1.4030	1.9596	0.6540	0.0210	0.0206	−0.5261	0.2965	0.5475	−0.5217	0.2915	0.5396	−0.5636	0.3405	0.5825
			λ	−0.3740	0.1798	1.3282	0.0431	0.0425	0.4374	0.1800	0.7370	0.4412	0.2313	0.7418	0.4023	0.1940	0.6995
			θ	0.9861	1.0122	0.7831	0.0251	0.0249	0.5751	0.3640	0.6653	0.5798	0.3701	0.6715	0.5259	0.3017	0.6024
	3.5, 18	75	α	0.4601	0.5524	2.2904	0.1124	0.1125	−0.1171	0.2100	1.6852	−0.1090	0.2033	1.6784	−0.1962	0.2943	1.8787
			β	−1.1979	1.4732	0.7660	0.0243	0.0246	−0.5480	0.2832	0.5410	−0.5432	0.3140	0.5365	−0.5884	0.3679	0.5782
			λ	0.2992	0.1722	0.9408	0.0444	0.0438	0.6883	0.1526	0.9032	0.6950	0.5369	0.9078	0.6229	0.4307	0.8363
			θ	0.8304	0.7148	0.6230	0.0188	0.0188	0.4609	0.2310	0.5173	0.4644	0.2346	0.5208	0.4256	0.1959	0.4685
		90	α	0.5074	0.5339	2.2637	0.0712	0.0716	−0.0227	0.0252	0.5770	−0.0219	0.0251	0.5750	−0.0300	0.0263	0.5855
			β	−1.1968	1.4705	0.7666	0.0240	0.0241	−0.2323	0.0708	0.5093	−0.2303	0.0697	0.5044	−0.2500	0.0822	0.5517
			λ	0.2893	0.1719	0.9128	0.0292	0.0298	0.2058	0.0585	0.4962	0.2073	0.0593	0.4986	0.1917	0.0513	0.4786
			θ	0.8319	0.7175	0.6251	0.0204	0.0205	0.2410	0.0649	0.3098	0.2432	0.0661	0.3141	0.2204	0.0542	0.2832
200	2, 10	150	α	0.4968	0.4611	1.8157	0.0594	0.0594	−0.4156	0.3868	1.7927	−0.3966	0.3570	1.7173	−0.6259	0.8221	2.3011
			β	−1.4238	2.0385	0.4153	0.0131	0.0131	−0.5478	0.3116	0.4096	−0.5445	0.3078	0.4078	−0.5748	0.3434	0.4355
			λ	−0.4137	0.1950	0.6052	0.0186	0.0184	0.4819	0.1826	0.5607	0.4852	0.2608	0.6138	0.4507	0.2244	0.5572
			θ	0.9426	0.9101	0.5755	0.0177	0.0173	0.5626	0.3389	0.5679	0.5658	0.3428	0.5713	0.5291	0.2985	0.5178
		185	α	0.5008	0.4615	1.8002	0.0559	0.0563	−0.0585	0.0268	0.5996	−0.0576	0.0265	0.5964	−0.0668	0.0293	0.6242
			β	−1.4305	2.0554	0.3718	0.0120	0.0118	−0.3356	0.1240	0.4175	−0.3328	0.1220	0.4126	−0.3604	0.1433	0.4485
			λ	−0.4246	0.1920	0.5577	0.0183	0.0180	0.2406	0.0689	0.4180	0.2421	0.0698	0.4216	0.2260	0.0609	0.3888
			θ	0.9422	0.9061	0.5310	0.0167	0.0167	0.3808	0.1519	0.3178	0.3844	0.1548	0.3210	0.3454	0.1245	0.2811
	3.5, 18	150	α	0.4717	0.3649	1.7284	0.0574	0.0570	−0.2171	0.2180	1.5888	−0.2071	0.2071	1.5436	−0.3190	0.3637	2.0831
			β	−1.2425	1.5586	0.4772	0.0152	0.0148	−0.5556	0.3018	0.3705	−0.5524	0.3143	0.3680	−0.5818	0.3487	0.3847
			λ	0.1907	0.0833	0.8496	0.0252	0.0254	0.8361	0.0733	0.7085	0.8428	0.7451	0.7166	0.7687	0.6179	0.6418
			θ	0.7916	0.6403	0.4600	0.0147	0.0148	0.4665	0.2287	0.4089	0.4688	0.2310	0.4112	0.4432	0.2060	0.3780
		185	α	1.5699	0.3267	3.5125	0.1158	0.1166	−0.0406	0.0260	0.6052	−0.0398	0.0259	0.6024	−0.0483	0.0275	0.6174
			β	−1.2296	1.5242	0.4327	0.0146	0.0144	−0.3682	0.1148	0.4297	−0.3648	0.1450	0.4256	−0.3978	0.1727	0.4703
			λ	0.2119	0.0832	0.7672	0.0246	0.0253	0.3420	0.0513	0.4309	0.3447	0.1319	0.4339	0.3172	0.1117	0.4069
			θ	0.7923	0.6399	0.4322	0.0138	0.0138	0.3183	0.1058	0.2583	0.3207	0.1074	0.2611	0.2952	0.0908	0.2329

Table 4. Bias, MSE, LACI, LBCI, and LCCI with scheme 1 in case 2.

$\alpha=0.6, \beta=0.7, \lambda=0.8, \theta=1.4$			MLE					SELF			ELF c = −1.25			ELF c = 1.25		
n	τ, δ	m		Bias	MSE	LACI	LBPCI	LBTCI	Bias	MSE	LCCI	Bias	MSE	LCCI	Bias	MSE	LCCI
100	0.6, 1.3	75	α	−0.5240	0.2747	0.1405	0.0022	0.0022	−0.1110	0.0206	0.3572	−0.1057	0.0196	0.3578	−0.1615	0.0343	0.3626
			β	−0.2999	0.0922	0.2150	0.0086	0.0083	−0.2663	0.0740	0.2063	−0.2641	0.0728	0.2066	−0.2856	0.0848	0.2194
			λ	0.0052	0.0093	0.4453	0.0177	0.0177	0.0200	0.0083	0.3513	0.0222	0.0084	0.3514	0.0008	0.0081	0.3521
			θ	0.2704	0.0885	0.4687	0.0205	0.0209	0.0732	0.0181	0.4339	0.0750	0.0184	0.4339	0.0574	0.0156	0.4351
		90	α	−0.4477	0.2017	0.0482	0.0061	0.0061	−0.0486	0.0051	0.2093	−0.0475	0.0050	0.2086	−0.0591	0.0064	0.2144
			β	−0.2570	0.0691	0.1885	0.0098	0.0100	−0.2212	0.0516	0.2015	−0.2192	0.0507	0.1992	−0.2383	0.0599	0.2146
			λ	0.0945	0.0082	0.3785	0.0203	0.0203	0.0211	0.0056	0.2751	0.0220	0.0056	0.2750	0.0129	0.0055	0.2783
			θ	0.1132	0.0271	0.4865	0.0212	0.0202	0.0282	0.0104	0.3800	0.0289	0.0105	0.3799	0.0218	0.0099	0.3766

Table 4. Cont.

$\alpha=0.6, \beta=0.7, \lambda=0.8, \theta=1.4$				MLE				SELF			ELF c = −1.25			ELF c = 1.25		
n	τ, δ	m		Bias	MSE	LACI	LBPCI	LBTCI	Bias	MSE	LCCI	Bias	MSE	LCCI	Bias	MSE	LCCI
200	0.8, 1.5	75	α	−0.5342	0.2856	0.1804	0.0019	0.0019	−0.0505	0.0780	0.5301	−0.0449	0.0815	0.5360	−0.0990	0.0461	0.5708
			β	−0.1805	0.0375	0.3960	0.0082	0.0082	−0.2799	0.0528	0.2684	−0.2775	0.0820	0.2668	−0.3001	0.0953	0.2745
			λ	0.3202	0.1212	0.8482	0.0163	0.0161	0.1205	0.0312	0.4830	0.1232	0.0318	0.4820	0.0957	0.0263	0.4838
			θ	0.2652	0.0891	0.5336	0.0169	0.0173	0.2184	0.0708	0.5753	0.2206	0.0720	0.5783	0.1984	0.0606	0.5573
		90	α	−0.5122	0.2644	0.0611	0.0056	0.0057	−0.0334	0.0081	0.2086	−0.0323	0.0037	0.2086	−0.0431	0.0047	0.2083
			β	−0.0762	0.0160	0.2736	0.0124	0.0127	−0.2306	0.0506	0.1998	−0.2285	0.0548	0.1982	−0.2477	0.0644	0.2139
			λ	0.2548	0.1135	0.5362	0.0258	0.0258	0.1086	0.0193	0.3247	0.1096	0.0195	0.3253	0.0994	0.0171	0.3165
			θ	0.0780	0.0246	0.5238	0.0167	0.0165	0.0940	0.0189	0.3921	0.0949	0.0191	0.3931	0.0858	0.0169	0.3768
	0.6, 1.3	150	α	−0.5503	0.3029	0.1706	0.0008	0.0008	−0.1207	0.0200	0.2611	−0.1166	0.0189	0.2599	−0.1571	0.0303	0.2621
			β	−0.2948	0.0882	0.1971	0.0044	0.0044	−0.2850	0.0833	0.1726	−0.2835	0.0824	0.1715	−0.2982	0.0911	0.1726
			λ	0.0074	0.0524	0.4162	0.0089	0.0090	0.0116	0.0057	0.2784	0.0131	0.0057	0.2773	−0.0023	0.0057	0.2796
			θ	0.3037	0.1005	0.3554	0.0109	0.0109	0.0952	0.0189	0.3662	0.0964	0.0192	0.3668	0.0848	0.0166	0.3599
		185	α	−0.4551	0.2090	0.0259	0.0055	0.0055	−0.0324	0.0051	0.0733	−0.0320	0.0014	0.0732	−0.0362	0.0017	0.0757
			β	−0.1976	0.0416	0.1409	0.0063	0.0062	−0.2553	0.0663	0.1278	−0.2536	0.0654	0.1269	−0.2687	0.0734	0.1345
			λ	0.2050	0.0053	0.2817	0.0136	0.0137	−0.0202	0.0031	0.1965	−0.0193	0.0031	0.1962	−0.0277	0.0036	0.2046
			θ	0.0212	0.0074	0.3277	0.0110	0.0110	0.0694	0.0068	0.2919	0.0701	0.0108	0.2922	0.0638	0.0097	0.2890
	0.8, 1.5	150	α	−0.5588	0.3131	0.1154	0.0054	0.0054	−0.0395	0.2423	0.8773	−0.0266	0.4469	0.8702	−0.1289	0.1863	0.8322
			β	0.0655	0.0179	0.4586	0.0212	0.0213	−0.0833	0.0109	0.3543	−0.2813	0.0898	0.4482	−0.3004	0.1008	0.4510
			λ	0.8364	0.7483	0.8673	0.0399	0.0395	0.1402	0.0585	0.8695	0.1427	0.0593	0.8679	0.1171	0.0513	0.8502
			θ	−0.0539	0.0232	0.5586	0.0267	0.0267	0.2571	0.0194	0.5065	0.2587	0.0953	0.6570	0.2422	0.0843	0.6294
		185	α	−0.5559	0.3091	0.0279	0.0010	0.0010	−0.0218	0.0594	0.0401	−0.0214	0.0006	0.0400	−0.0256	0.0008	0.0424
			β	−0.0517	0.0133	0.1916	0.0058	0.0059	−0.3182	0.0102	0.1041	−0.3169	0.1011	0.1039	−0.3293	0.1092	0.1060
			λ	0.3258	0.1151	0.3711	0.0120	0.0120	0.0068	0.0027	0.1917	0.0082	0.0027	0.1917	−0.0056	0.0027	0.1963
			θ	0.0429	0.0193	0.3909	0.0122	0.0122	0.0290	0.0190	0.3326	0.2915	0.0924	0.3330	0.2772	0.0838	0.3223

Table 5. Bias, MSE, LACI, LBCI, and LCCI with scheme 2 in case 2.

$\alpha=0.6, \beta=0.7, \lambda=0.8, \theta=1.4$				MLE				SELF			ELF c = −1.25			ELF c = 1.25		
n	τ, δ	m		Bias	MSE	LACI	LBPCI	LBTCI	Bias	MSE	LCCI	Bias	MSE	LCCI	Bias	MSE	LCCI
100	0.6, 1.3	75	α	−0.6947	0.4827	0.6661	0.0015	0.0015	−0.0664	0.0453	0.6946	−0.0642	0.0425	0.6770	−0.0647	0.0439	0.6710
			β	−0.2988	0.0909	0.1620	0.0357	0.0364	−0.3179	0.0906	0.3675	−0.3146	0.0902	0.3623	−0.2934	0.0901	0.3400
			λ	−0.0135	0.0093	0.3837	0.0865	0.0825	−0.1626	0.0090	0.4409	−0.1595	0.0383	0.4353	−0.1589	0.0085	0.4282
			θ	0.6069	0.3911	0.6072	0.1366	0.1323	0.3054	0.1329	0.8110	0.3081	0.1351	0.8130	0.2801	0.1132	0.7882
		90	α	−0.6950	0.4830	0.6182	0.0030	0.0026	−0.0019	0.0411	0.0079	−0.0018	0.0009	0.0073	−0.0013	0.0250	0.0013
			β	−0.2316	0.0718	0.1572	0.0346	0.0345	−0.2133	0.0712	0.2092	−0.2033	0.0691	0.2085	−0.2104	0.0714	0.2008
			λ	−0.0455	0.0074	0.3045	0.1013	0.1010	−0.1628	0.0068	0.2907	−0.1591	0.0063	0.2908	−0.1595	0.0062	0.2801
			θ	0.5775	0.3441	0.4313	0.1406	0.1400	0.2543	0.1010	0.6715	0.2581	0.1036	0.6755	0.2197	0.0787	0.6262
	0.8, 1.5	75	α	−0.5943	0.3532	0.4910	0.0016	0.0016	0.0584	0.0421	0.5866	0.0626	0.2306	0.5715	0.0198	0.0370	0.5360
			β	−0.1657	0.0340	0.3209	0.0554	0.0552	−0.3376	0.0291	0.3288	−0.3337	0.1182	0.3236	−0.3267	0.0214	0.3036
			λ	0.3389	0.0090	0.6334	0.1018	0.1016	−0.0575	0.0079	0.6268	−0.0537	0.0270	0.6184	−0.0491	0.0063	0.6080
			θ	0.4365	0.2228	0.7154	0.1166	0.1156	0.3705	0.1272	0.6530	0.3735	0.1275	0.6568	0.3411	0.1146	0.6132
		90	α	−0.5941	0.3529	0.4108	0.0021	0.0020	0.0677	0.0412	0.4675	0.2800	1.1994	3.1964	0.0612	0.0326	0.4268
			β	−0.1699	0.0315	0.3000	0.0550	0.0556	−0.3659	0.0139	0.2499	−0.3616	0.1357	0.2466	−0.3399	0.0167	0.2317
			λ	0.3172	0.0012	0.5363	0.1035	0.1007	−0.1149	0.0012	0.4647	−0.1103	0.0273	0.4588	−0.1056	0.0015	0.4510
			θ	0.4460	0.2231	0.6214	0.1171	0.1176	0.4044	0.1010	0.6072	0.4082	0.2037	0.4728	0.3688	0.0917	0.5640

Table 5. Cont.

				MLE				SELF		ELF c = −1.25			ELF c = 1.25		
	α = 0.6, β = 0.7, λ = 0.8, θ = 1.4														
n	τ, δ	m		Bias	MSE	LACI	LBPCI	LBTCI	Bias	MSE	LCCI	Bias	MSE	LCCI	Bias	MSE	LCCI
200	0.6, 1.3	150	α	−0.5964	0.3557	0.0039	0.0007	0.0006	−0.0005	0.0011	0.0031	−0.0005	0.0001	0.0031	−0.0006	0.0001	0.0031
			β	−0.2865	0.0831	0.1284	0.0229	0.0226	−0.2953	0.0793	0.1128	−0.2927	0.0914	0.2801	−0.2315	0.0658	0.1030
			λ	0.0095	0.0029	0.2102	0.0385	0.0364	−0.0012	0.0023	0.2034	−0.1163	0.0221	0.3416	−0.0014	0.0229	0.2036
			θ	0.5218	0.2802	0.3539	0.0606	0.0602	0.2415	0.0756	0.3044	0.2434	0.0767	0.4460	0.2244	0.0656	0.3042
		185	α	−0.4695	0.3248	0.0037	0.0006	0.0005	−0.0043	0.0005	0.0025	−0.0034	0.0001	0.0242	−0.0041	0.0001	0.0025
			β	−0.2321	0.0810	0.1210	0.0242	0.0237	−0.2402	0.0692	0.1028	−0.2840	0.0817	0.2766	−0.2143	0.0519	0.1030
			λ	−0.0157	0.0027	0.2039	0.0426	0.0427	−0.2624	0.0022	0.1931	−0.2583	0.0804	0.4188	−0.2594	0.0022	0.1845
			θ	0.4604	0.2372	0.3384	0.0614	0.0612	0.4370	0.0622	0.2613	0.4406	0.2277	0.6197	0.4028	0.0619	0.2546
	0.8, 1.5	150	α	−0.4693	0.3248	0.0038	0.0015	0.0015	0.1955	0.0013	0.0025	0.2065	1.2956	0.6617	0.0749	0.0123	0.0022
			β	−0.1932	0.0418	0.2645	0.0396	0.0393	−0.3756	0.0415	0.2195	−0.3719	0.1504	0.2897	−0.3403	0.0402	0.2132
			λ	0.0029	0.0020	0.2051	0.0806	0.0806	−0.1400	0.0020	0.1499	−0.1361	0.0399	0.4920	−0.1373	0.0016	0.1542
			θ	0.4195	0.2318	0.2620	0.0925	0.0930	0.5393	0.0720	0.2279	0.5434	0.3563	0.7944	0.4997	0.0630	0.2175
		185	α	−0.3692	0.3048	0.0010	0.0011	0.0011	−0.0521	0.0004	0.0023	−0.0475	0.0905	0.6529	−0.0471	0.0047	0.1700
			β	−0.1882	0.0415	0.2329	0.0269	0.0268	−0.3041	0.0315	0.1925	−0.2409	0.1746	0.2626	−0.2944	0.0302	0.1832
			λ	0.0025	0.0018	0.1943	0.0503	0.0487	−0.1873	0.0014	0.1476	−0.1829	0.0494	0.4703	−0.1822	0.0014	0.1490
			θ	0.3560	0.2033	0.2150	0.0605	0.0613	0.4586	0.0519	0.1597	0.5908	0.4063	0.9854	0.4154	0.0434	0.1486

Table 6. Optimization criterion with different schemes and cases.

		Scheme		1			2		
Case	n	τ, δ	m	C1	C2	C3	C1	C2	C3
1	100	2, 10	75	8.9523	3.860×10⁻⁵	758.8371	7.9682	4.248×10⁻⁵	679.5787
			90	7.1809	6.359×10⁻⁶	766.3755	7.4242	3.969×10⁻⁵	769.7234
		3.5, 18	75	4.7788	3.619×10⁻⁵	765.5838	7.6918	1.605×10⁻⁵	690.4161
			90	3.4849	3.370×10⁻⁶	778.3303	7.4603	1.503×10⁻⁵	777.0073
	200	2, 10	150	3.4486	7.767×10⁻⁷	1616.8601	4.0384	1.900×10⁻⁶	1306.3727
			185	3.1947	5.709×10⁻⁷	1645.6376	3.3101	8.940×10⁻⁷	1619.5660
		3.5, 18	150	3.1965	6.971×10⁻⁷	1731.1179	4.0136	1.163×10⁻⁶	1561.8482
			185	2.9820	2.556×10⁻⁷	1735.4056	3.0424	2.965×10⁻⁷	1607.0823
2	100	2, 10	75	7.9682	4.248×10⁻⁴	679.5787	0.3979	3.289×10⁻¹⁰	6985.3086
			90	7.4242	6.873×10⁻⁴	769.7234	0.3933	2.030×10⁻¹⁰	72883.3960
		3.5, 18	75	6.9178	1.605×10⁻⁴	690.4161	0.3869	9.505×10⁻¹⁰	104,014.7057
			90	6.6033	1.503×10⁻⁴	779.0073	0.3773	1.246×10⁻¹⁰	117,561.7575
	200	2, 10	150	4.0384	1.900×10⁻⁶	1306.3727	0.3284	3.465×10⁻¹¹	410,484.9941
			185	3.3101	8.940×10⁻⁶	1619.5660	0.3244	1.216×10⁻¹²	214,081.1995
		3.5, 18	150	3.3625	1.163×10⁻⁶	1761.8482	0.2731	1.068×10⁻¹¹	140,775.1960
			185	3.0424	2.965×10⁻⁶	1807.0823	0.2412	1.554×10⁻¹²	178,754.3036

Table 7. MLE, SE, and different measures of goodness of fit.

	Estimates	SE	AIC	CAIC	BIC	HQIC	CVM	AD	KS	PVKS
α	26.9222	74.2080	121.2031	121.6099	127.6326	123.7319	0.0997	0.5233	0.0976	0.5859
β	235.4901	222.2091								
λ	6.4564	0.6125								

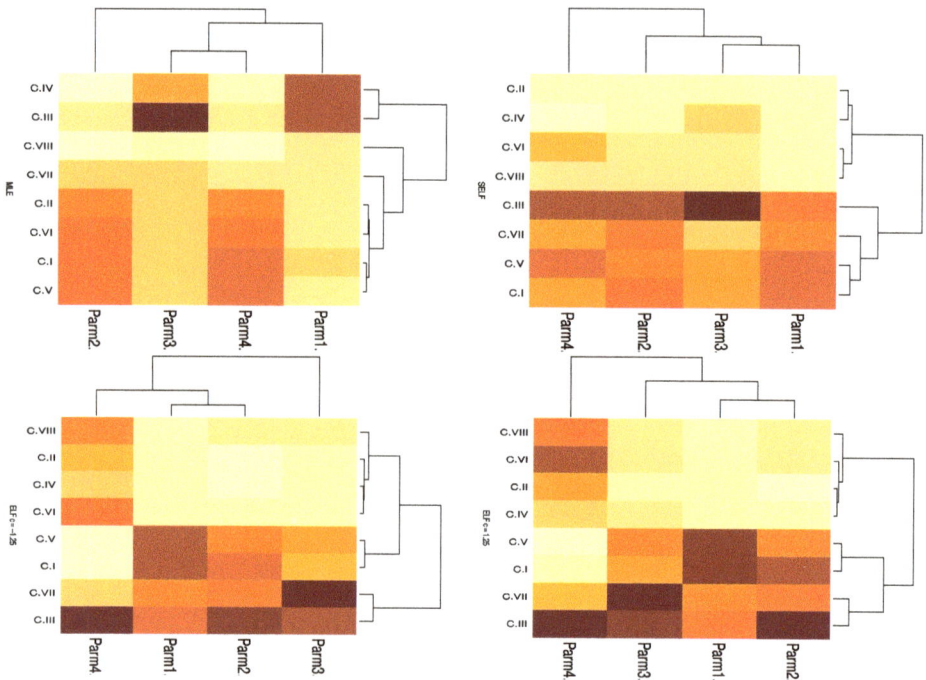

Figure 2. Heatmap for MSE with scheme 1 in case 1.

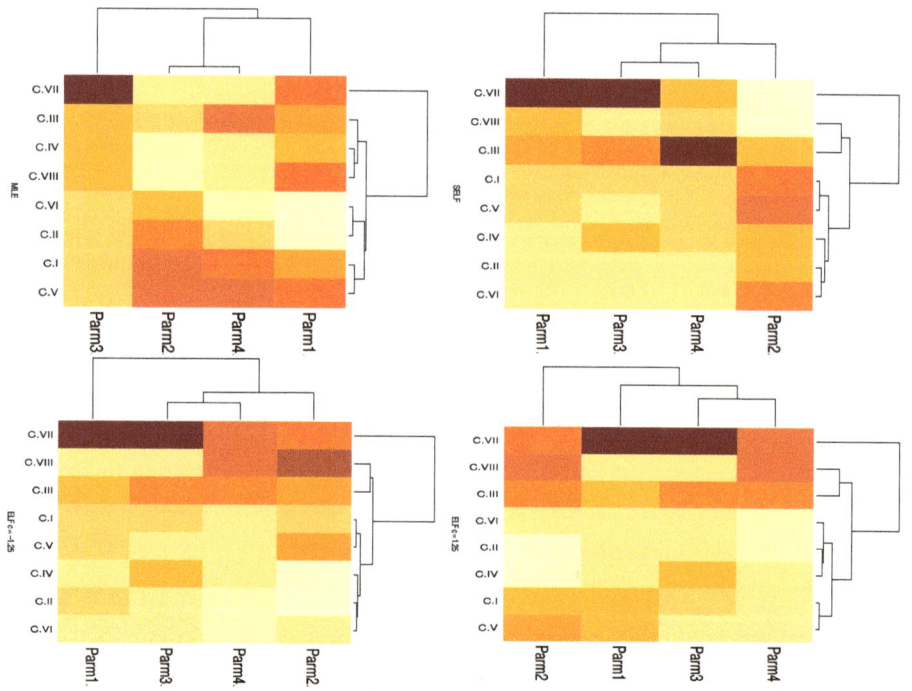

Figure 3. Heatmap for MSE with scheme 1 in case 2.

8. A Real-Data Application

We use examination data from [41] to illustrate the practical application of the proposed model. The following information represents the strength measured in GPA for single carbon fibers with gauge lengths of 10 mm and sample size of 63: 1.901, 2.132, 2.203, 2.228, 2.257, 2.350, 2.361, 2.396, 2.397, 2.445, 2.454, 2.474, 2.518, 2.522, 2.525, 2.532, 2.575, 2.614, 2.616, 2.618, 2.624, 2.659, 2.675, 2.738, 2.740, 2.856, 2.917, 2.928, 2.937, 2.937, 2.977, 2.996, 3.030, 3.125, 3.139, 3.145, 3.220, 3.223, 3.235, 3.243, 3.264, 3.272, 3.294, 3.332, 3.346, 3.377, 3.408, 3.435, 3.493, 3.501, 3.537, 3.554, 3.562, 3.628, 3.852, 3.871, 3.886, 3.971, 4.024, 4.027, 4.225, 4.395, and 5.020. Here, we use the modified Kolmogorov–Smirnov as a method for the goodness-of-fit test as follows:

The computational formula for the modified Kolmogorov–Smirnov statistic is then given by

$$D_{m:n} = \max(D^+_{m:n}, D^-_{m:n}),$$

where

$$D^+_{m:n} = \max_i \left(\omega_{i:m:n} - F(z_{i:m:n}; \hat{\alpha}, \hat{\beta}, \hat{\theta}, \hat{\lambda}) \right)$$

$$D^-_{m:n} = \max_i \left(F(z_{i:m:n}; \hat{\alpha}, \hat{\beta}, \hat{\theta}, \hat{\lambda}) - \omega_{i-1:m:n} \right),$$

$$\omega_{i:m:n} = 1 - \prod_{j=m-i+1}^{m} \frac{j + R_{m-j+1} + \ldots + R_m}{j + 1 + R_{m-j+1} + \ldots + R_m}.$$

Ref. [42] proposed a general-purpose goodness-of-fit test by first estimating the unknown parameters of the hypothesized distribution, then transforming the data to normality, and then testing the goodness of fit of the transformed data to normality. Then, along the lines of [42], the proposed test procedure is as follows:

1. Find the maximum likelihood estimate of the unknown parameter $\alpha, \beta, \theta, \lambda$, denoted by $\hat{\alpha}, \hat{\beta}, \hat{\theta}, \hat{\lambda}$, under the hypothesized model and calculate $v_{i:m:n} = F(z_{i:m:n}; \hat{\alpha}, \hat{\beta}, \hat{\theta}, \hat{\lambda})$ for $i = 1, \ldots, m$.
2. Generate $y_{i:m:n}$ as $F^{-1}(v_{i:m:n})$ for $i = 1, \ldots, m$.
3. Considering $y_{1:m:n}, \ldots, y_{m:m:n}$ as a progressively Type-II censored data from an APIW distribution with $\alpha, \beta, \theta, \lambda$ and calculate the maximum likelihood estimates $\hat{\alpha}, \hat{\beta}, \hat{\theta}, \hat{\lambda}$.
4. Calculate $u_{i:m:n} = \Phi(y_{i:m:n})$ for $i = 1, \ldots, m$.
5. Calculate $D_{m:n}$
6. Reject the null hypothesis at significance level δ if the test statistic exceeds the upper tail significance points.

For more information about the p-value for KS test for SSPALT samples, see [42–46].

In Table 7, we provide the MLEs with their standard errors (SEs) for the APIW parameters and different measures of goodness of fit as Akaike information criterion (AIC), Bayesian information criterion (BIC), corrected Akaike information criterion (CAIC), Hannan–Quinn information criterion (HQIC), Kolmogorov–Smirnov (KS) test and its p-value (PVKS), Anderson–Darling (AD), and Cramèr–von Mises (CVM).

The empirical CDF and its CDF fitted (left panel), and the histogram of the data and its fitted density function to the single carbon fiber data (right panel) are displayed in the top of Figure 4. Further, a graph of the PP plot (left panel) and QQ plot (right panel) of the APIW distribution is shown in bottom Figure 4.

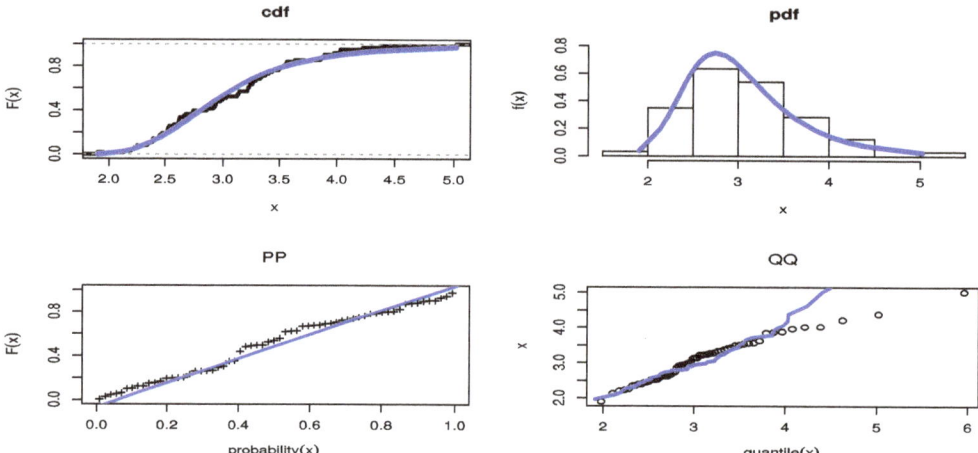

Figure 4. Fitting plot of APIW distribution of single carbon fibers.

Figure 5 shows the profile log-likelihood function plots for the parameters of the APIW distribution. Figure 6 displays contour plots of the log-likelihood function for the APIW parameters, indicating that the MLEs can be uniquely estimated.

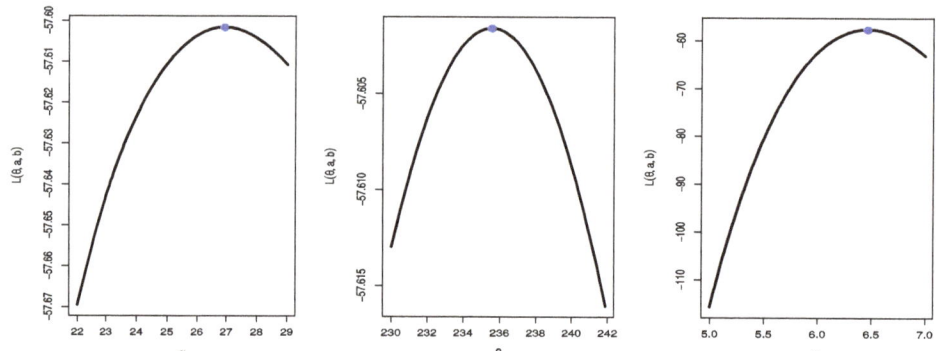

Figure 5. Graphs of profile log-likelihood function for the parameters for the APIW model.

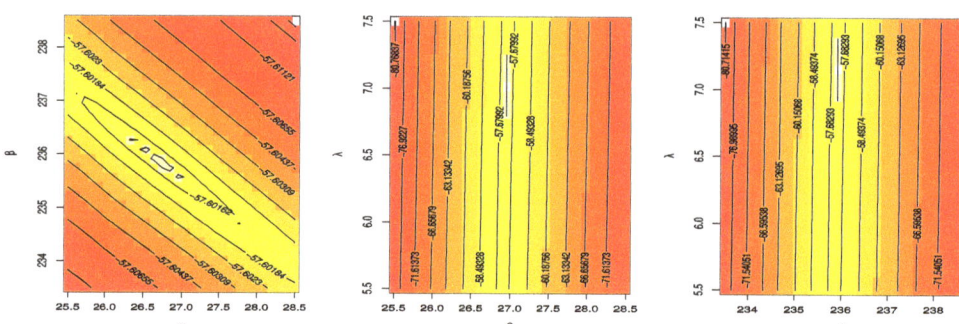

Figure 6. Contour plots of the log-likelihood function for the parameters for the APIW model.

Numerical results for the single carbon fiber study are provided in Table 8. Table 9 contains the estimations based on the censored data. For a given fixed scheme, we observe that Bayes estimates of the unknown parameters are close to the MLEs. Table 10 discusses the estimation of τ, which is given by equating $F_1(\tau) = F_2(\tau^*)$. Table 11 discusses different optimality measures for the MLE based on different schemes, illustrating that the proposed technique is quite satisfactory.

Table 8. The single carbon fiber study data based on SSPALT when $\tau = 3$ and $\delta = 3.8$.

Scheme	Before τ	After τ
I	1.901 2.132 2.203 2.228 2.257 2.350 2.361 2.396 2.397 2.445 2.454 2.474 2.518 2.522 2.525 2.532 2.575 2.614 2.616 2.618 2.624 2.659 2.675 2.738 2.740 2.856 2.917 2.928 2.937 2.937 2.977 2.996	3.030 3.125 3.139 3.145 3.220 3.223 3.235 3.243 3.264 3.272 3.294 3.332 3.346 3.377 3.408 3.435 3.493 3.501
II	1.901 2.132 2.203 2.257 2.350 2.361 2.396 2.397 2.445 2.454 2.474 2.518 2.522 2.575 2.614 2.616 2.618 2.624 2.659 2.675 2.738 2.740 2.917 2.928 2.937 2.937 2.977	3.030 3.125 3.139 3.145 3.220 3.235 3.243 3.264 3.272 3.346 3.377 3.408 3.435 3.493 3.501 3.628 3.871 3.886 3.971 4.024 4.225 4.395 5.020

Table 9. The MLE and its SE and Bayesian and its SD with confidence intervals.

			MLE				Bayesian			
	m		Estimates	SE	Lower	Upper	Estimates	SD	Lower	Upper
Complete	63	α	71.8806	22.7927	27.2070	116.5542	75.6191	18.5540	38.7075	111.2613
		β	162.0261	66.5356	31.6163	292.4359	190.3651	30.1964	135.8759	251.3891
		λ	229.3353	91.8064	49.3948	409.2759	269.1464	40.5281	189.3768	340.9331
		θ	7.4069	0.4585	6.5082	8.3056	7.5259	0.2519	7.0329	7.9940
I	50	α	156.2681	73.6006	12.0110	300.5253	167.0087	52.8410	71.6085	266.4320
		β	200.3566	99.6606	5.0219	395.6913	214.5642	42.8232	134.4151	288.3952
		λ	287.9273	113.3318	65.7969	510.0577	302.9877	57.5639	207.9282	407.4394
		θ	7.8263	0.6827	6.4882	9.1643	7.8582	0.3078	7.2443	8.4240
II	50	α	218.2157	108.2157	6.1130	430.3184	226.5631	77.5768	95.4818	369.4948
		β	270.8559	93.4996	87.5967	454.1151	279.5810	48.5672	176.8138	367.8409
		λ	377.6384	117.2506	147.8272	607.4497	389.1168	65.6272	248.3191	499.9688
		θ	8.1569	0.6178	6.9461	9.3678	8.1828	0.3113	7.6173	8.8183

Table 10. Estimated τ.

Scheme	MLE	Bayes
complete	3.14407	3.14130
I	3.14227	3.13465
II	3.12476	3.12368

Table 11. Optimality measures.

	Complete	I	II
C1	15,642.68	74,500.21	124,729.4
C2	26,415,630	1.24×10^9	9.09×10^9
C3	36.46753	35.4808	29.99117

9. Conclusions

It is known that in life-testing and reliability trials, many data may exhibit different shapes and are censored due to time and cost constraints. Thus, accelerated life tests are commonly used to explore the lifetime of reliable items by subjecting them to elevated stress levels of stressors that could cause early failures. This observation motivated us to investigate the step stress partially accelerated life testing model with samples from the APIW distribution under the adaptive type II progressively hybrid censoring. We considered statistical inferences of the unknown model parameters of the APIW distribution from both likelihood and Bayesian perspectives. We first considered the maximum likelihood estimates for the unknown model parameters and used these estimates to construct two types of approximate confidence intervals of the distributional parameters. We then conducted Bayesian inference for the unknown parameters with non-informative and informative priors under the symmetric and asymmetric loss functions. Moreover, we analyzed three different probable optimum test techniques for the proposed model under different optimal criteria. Numerical results from both simulations and a real-data application illustrated that the performance of the proposed method is quite satisfactory for estimating the APIW parameters under different sampling schemes. We may, thus, conclude that the proposed model has great potential for analyzing censored data under the AT-II PHCS in the study of life testing and reliability analyses.

Author Contributions: R.A., E.M.A., Q.H., and H.R. have contributed equally. All authors have read and agreed to the published version of the manuscript.

Funding: This research was funded by Princess Nourah bint Abdulrahman University Researchers Supporting Project number (PNURSP2022R50), Princess Nourah bint Abdulrahman University, Riyadh, Saudi Arabia.

Institutional Review Board Statement: Not applicable.

Informed Consent Statement: Not applicable.

Data Availability Statement: The data used to support the findings of this study are included within the article.

Acknowledgments: Princess Nourah bint Abdulrahman University Researchers Supporting Project number (PNURSP2022R50), Princess Nourah bint Abdulrahman University, Riyadh, Saudi Arabia.

Conflicts of Interest: The authors declare no conflict of interest.

Appendix A. Fisher Information Matrix

The Fisher information matrix is a fundamental statistical construct that describes how much information data offer on a variable that is unknown. It can be used to calculate the variance in an estimator as well as the asymptotic behavior of maximum-likelihood estimations. The inverse of the Fisher information matrix is an estimator of the asymptotic covariance matrix. The Fisher information matrix is computed by taking the expected values of the negative second-partial and mixed-partial derivatives of the log-likelihood function with respect to α, θ, β and λ. It is further explained below.

$$I_{4\times 4} = -E \begin{bmatrix} a_{11} & a_{12} & a_{13} & a_{14} \\ a_{21} & a_{22} & a_{23} & a_{24} \\ a_{31} & a_{32} & a_{33} & a_{34} \\ a_{41} & a_{42} & a_{43} & a_{44} \end{bmatrix}, \quad (A1)$$

where $a_{11} = E\left(\frac{\partial^2 \ell}{\partial \alpha^2}\right)$, $a_{12} = a_{21} = E\left(\frac{\partial^2 \ell}{\partial \alpha \partial \theta}\right)$, $a_{13} = a_{31} = E\left(\frac{\partial^2 \ell}{\partial \alpha \partial \beta}\right)$, $a_{14} = a_{41} = E\left(\frac{\partial^2 \ell}{\partial \alpha \partial \lambda}\right)$, $a_{22} = E\left(\frac{\partial^2 \ell}{\partial \theta^2}\right)$, $a_{33} = E\left(\frac{\partial^2 \ell}{\partial \beta^2}\right)$, $a_{32} = a_{23} = E\left(\frac{\partial^2 \ell}{\partial \theta \partial \beta}\right)$, $a_{44} = E\left(\frac{\partial^2 \ell}{\partial \lambda^2}\right)$, $a_{42} = a_{24} = E\left(\frac{\partial^2 \ell}{\partial \theta \partial \lambda}\right)$, and $a_{34} = a_{34} = E\left(\frac{\partial^2 \ell}{\partial \beta \partial \lambda}\right)$.

The relevant matrices' elements are computed. As a result, the variance–covariance matrix for MLEs can be constructed as follows:

$$\begin{aligned}
\frac{\partial^2 \ell}{\partial \alpha^2} =\; & -\frac{(m_u+m)}{(\alpha \log \alpha)^2} + \frac{(m_u+m+\varepsilon_m)}{(\alpha-1)^2} - \frac{1}{\alpha^2}\sum_{i=1}^{m_u} e^{-\beta z_i^{-\theta}} + \frac{1}{\alpha^2}\sum_{i=1}^{m_u}\varepsilon_i + \frac{1}{(\alpha-1)^2}\sum_{i=1}^{m_u}\varepsilon_i \\
& - \left[\frac{1}{\alpha}\sum_{i=1}^{m_u}\varepsilon_i \alpha^{e^{-\beta z_i^{-\theta}}-1} + (\log(\alpha))^2 \sum_{i=1}^{m_u}\varepsilon_i \alpha^{e^{-\beta z_i^{-\theta}}-1}\right] - \frac{1}{\alpha^2}\sum_{i=m_u+1}^{m}\varepsilon_i e^{-\beta[\tau+\lambda(z_i-\tau)]^{-\theta}} \\
& - \frac{1}{\alpha^2}\sum_{i=m_u+1}^{m}(\varepsilon_i) + \frac{1}{(\alpha-1)^2}\sum_{i=m_u+1}^{m}(\varepsilon_i) \\
& + \left[\frac{1}{\alpha}\sum_{i=m_u+1}^{m}\varepsilon_i \frac{\alpha^{e^{-\beta[\tau+\lambda(z_i-\tau)]^{-\theta}}-1}}{\left(1-\alpha^{e^{-\beta[\tau+\lambda(z_i-\tau)]^{-\theta}}-1}\right)} \right. \\
& + \log(\alpha)\sum_{i=m_u+1}^{m}\varepsilon_i \left(e^{-\beta[\tau+\lambda(z_i-\tau)]^{-\theta}}\right. \\
& \left. -1\right)\left(\alpha^{e^{-\beta[\tau+\lambda(z_i-\tau)]^{-\theta}}-2}\right)\left(\frac{\left(1-\alpha^{e^{-\beta[\tau+\lambda(z_i-\tau)]^{-\theta}}-1}\right)+1}{\left(1-\alpha^{e^{-\beta[\tau+\lambda(z_i-\tau)]^{-\theta}}-1}\right)^2}\right)\right] - \frac{\varepsilon_m}{\alpha^2} \\
& + \left[\frac{1}{\alpha}\sum_{i=m_u+1}^{m}\varepsilon_i \frac{\alpha^{e^{-\beta[\tau+\lambda(z_m-\tau)]^{-\theta}}-1}}{\left(1-\alpha^{e^{-\beta[\tau+\lambda(z_m-\tau)]^{-\theta}}-1}\right)}\right. \\
& + \log(\alpha)\sum_{i=m_u+1}^{m}\varepsilon_i \left(e^{-\beta[\tau+\lambda(z_m-\tau)]^{-\theta}}\right. \\
& \left.\left. -1\right)\left(\alpha^{e^{-\beta[\tau+\lambda(z_m-\tau)]^{-\theta}}-2}\right)\left(\frac{\left(1-\alpha^{e^{-\beta[\tau+\lambda(z_m-\tau)]^{-\theta}}-1}\right)+1}{\left(1-\alpha^{e^{-\beta[\tau+\lambda(z_m-\tau)]^{-\theta}}-1}\right)^2}\right)\right],
\end{aligned} \qquad (A2)$$

$$\begin{aligned}
\frac{\partial^2 \ell}{\partial \alpha \partial \theta} =\; & \frac{1}{\alpha}\sum_{i=1}^{m_u} e^{-\beta z_i^{-\theta}}\log(\beta z_i) - \log(\alpha)\sum_{i=1}^{m_u}\varepsilon_i e^{-\beta z_i^{-\theta}}\log(\beta z_i)\alpha^{e^{-\beta z_i^{-\theta}}-1} + \frac{1}{\alpha}\sum_{i=m_u+1}^{m}\varepsilon_i \log(\beta[\tau+\\
& \lambda(z_i-\tau)])e^{-\beta[\tau+\lambda(z_i-\tau)]^{-\theta}} + \log(\alpha)\sum_{i=m_u+1}^{m}\varepsilon_i\left(\alpha^{e^{-\beta[\tau+\lambda(z_i-\tau)]^{-\theta}}-1}\right)e^{-\beta[\tau+\lambda(z_i-\tau)]^{-\theta}}\log(\beta[\tau+\\
& \lambda(z_i-\tau)]\left(\frac{\left(1-\alpha^{e^{-\beta[\tau+\lambda(z_i-\tau)]^{-\theta}}-1}\right)+\left(\alpha^{e^{-\beta[\tau+\lambda(z_i-\tau)]^{-\theta}}-1}\right)}{\left(1-\alpha^{e^{-\beta[\tau+\lambda(z_i-\tau)]^{-\theta}}-1}\right)^2}\right) + \\
& \varepsilon_m \log(\alpha)\left(\alpha^{e^{-\beta[\tau+\lambda(z_m-\tau)]^{-\theta}}-1}\right)e^{-\beta[\tau+\lambda(z_m-\tau)]^{-\theta}}\log(\beta[\tau+\lambda(z_m-\\
& \tau)])\left[\frac{\left(1-\alpha^{e^{-\beta[\tau+\lambda(z_m-\tau)]^{-\theta}}-1}\right)+\left(\alpha^{e^{-\beta[\tau+\lambda(z_m-\tau)]^{-\theta}}-1}\right)}{\left(1-\alpha^{e^{-\beta[\tau+\lambda(z_m-\tau)]^{-\theta}}-1}\right)^2}\right],
\end{aligned} \qquad (A3)$$

$$\begin{aligned}
\frac{\partial^2 \ell}{\partial \alpha \partial \beta} =\; & -\frac{1}{\alpha}\sum_{i=1}^{m_u} e^{-\beta z_i^{-\theta}} z_i^{-\theta} - \log(\alpha)\sum_{i=1}^{m_u}\varepsilon_i \alpha^{e^{-\beta z_i^{-\theta}}-1}e^{-\beta z_i^{-\theta}} z_i^{-\theta} - \frac{1}{\alpha}\sum_{i=m_u+1}^{m}\varepsilon_i [\tau+\lambda(z_i-\tau)]^{-\theta}e^{-\beta[\tau+\lambda(z_i-\tau)]^{-\theta}}\\
& + \log(\alpha)\sum_{i=m_u+1}^{m}\varepsilon_i \left(\alpha^{e^{-\beta[\tau+\lambda(z_i-\tau)]^{-\theta}}-1}\right)[\tau\\
& + \lambda(z_i-\tau)]^{-\theta}e^{-\beta[\tau+\lambda(z_i-\tau)]^{-\theta}}\left[\frac{\left(\alpha^{e^{-\beta[\tau+\lambda(z_i-\tau)]^{-\theta}}-1}\right)+1}{\left(1-\alpha^{e^{-\beta[\tau+\lambda(z_i-\tau)]^{-\theta}}-1}\right)^2}\right]\\
& + \varepsilon_m \log(\alpha)\left(\alpha^{e^{-\beta[\tau+\lambda(z_m-\tau),]^{-\theta}}-1}\right)[\tau+\lambda(z_m-\tau)]^{-\theta}e^{-\beta[\tau+\lambda(z_m-\tau)]^{-\theta}},
\end{aligned} \qquad (A4)$$

$$\frac{\partial^2 \ell}{\partial \alpha \partial \lambda} = +\frac{1}{\alpha} \sum_{i=m_u+1}^{m} \varepsilon_i(z_i - \tau) e^{-\beta[\tau+\lambda(z_i-\tau)]^{-\theta}}$$
$$+ \log(\alpha) \sum_{i=m_u+1}^{m} \varepsilon_i e^{-\beta[\tau+\lambda(z_i-\tau)]^{-\theta}} \beta(z_i - \tau)[\tau$$
$$+ \lambda(z_i - \tau)]^{-\theta-1} \alpha^{e^{-\beta[\tau+\lambda(z_i-\tau)]^{-\theta}}-1} \left(\frac{\left(1-\alpha^{e^{-\beta[\tau+\lambda(z_i-\tau)]^{-\theta}}-1}\right)+1}{\left(1-\alpha^{e^{-\beta[\tau+\lambda(z_i-\tau)]^{-\theta}}-1}\right)^2} \right) \quad \text{(A5)}$$
$$+ \varepsilon_m \log(\alpha) e^{-\beta[\tau+\lambda(z_m-\tau)]^{-\theta}} \beta(z_m - \tau)[\tau$$
$$+ \lambda(z_m - \tau)]^{-\theta-1} \alpha^{e^{-\beta[\tau+\lambda(z_m-\tau)]^{-\theta}}-1} \left(\frac{\alpha^{e^{-\beta[\tau+\lambda(z_m-\tau)]^{-\theta}}-1}+1}{\left(1-\alpha^{e^{-\beta[\tau+\lambda(z_m-\tau)]^{-\theta}}-1}\right)^2} \right),$$

$$\frac{\partial^2 \ell}{\partial \theta^2}$$
$$= \beta \sum_{i=1}^{m_u} z_i^{-\theta} (\log(z_i))^2$$
$$+ \log(\alpha) \beta \sum_{i=1}^{m_u} \left(z_i^{-\theta} (\log(z_i))^2 e^{-\beta z_i^{-\theta}} - z_i^{-2\theta} \log(z_i) e^{-\beta z_i^{-\theta}} \right)$$
$$+ \beta \sum_{i=1}^{m_u} \varepsilon_i e^{-\beta z_i^{-\theta}} z_i^{-\theta} \log(z_i) \left(e^{-\beta z_i^{-\theta}} - 1 \right) \alpha^{e^{-\beta z_i^{-\theta}}-2} + \beta \sum_{i=m_u+1}^{m} [\tau + \lambda(z_i - \tau)]^{-\theta} \log[\tau + \lambda(z_i - \tau)]$$
$$- \sum_{i=m_u+1}^{m} \log[\tau + \lambda(z_i - \tau)] + \log(\alpha) \sum_{i=m_u+1}^{m} e^{-\beta[\tau+\lambda(z_i-\tau)]^{-\theta}} \beta[\tau + \lambda(z_i - \tau)]^{-\theta} \log[\tau + \lambda(z_i - \tau)]$$
$$+ \sum_{i=m_u+1}^{m} \beta \varepsilon_i [\log[\tau + \lambda(z_i - \tau)]]^2 [\tau + \lambda(z_i - \tau)]^{-\theta} \left(e^{-\beta[\tau+\lambda(z_i-\tau)]^{-\theta}} \right) \left(\alpha^{e^{-\beta[\tau+\lambda(z_i-\tau)]^{-\theta}}-2} \right) \quad \text{(A6)}$$
$$+ \left\{ \frac{\left[\left(e^{-\beta[\tau+\lambda(z_i-\tau)]^{-\theta}} - 1 \right) \left[1 + \left(\alpha^{e^{-\beta[\tau+\lambda(z_i-\tau)]^{-\theta}}-1} \right) - [\tau+\lambda(z_i-\tau)]^{-\theta} + (\alpha e)^{-1} + \alpha^{e^{-\beta[\tau+\lambda(z_i-\tau)]^{-\theta}}-1} \right] \right]}{1 - \alpha^{-\beta[\tau+\lambda(z_i-\tau)]^{-\theta}-1}} \right\}$$
$$+ \beta \varepsilon_m (\log[\tau + \lambda(z_m - \tau)])^2 [\tau + \lambda(z_m - \tau)]^{-\theta} e^{-\beta[\tau+\lambda(z_m-\tau)]^{-\theta}} \left(\alpha^{e^{-\beta[\tau+\lambda(z_m-\tau)]^{-\theta}}-2} \right)$$
$$+ \left\{ \frac{\left(e^{-\beta[\tau+\lambda(z_m-\tau)]^{-\theta}} - 1 \right) \left[1 + \left(\alpha^{e^{-\beta[\tau+\lambda(z_m-\tau)]^{-\theta}}-1} \right) - [\tau+\lambda(z_m-\tau)]^{-\theta} + (\alpha e)^{-1} + \alpha^{e^{-\beta[\tau+\lambda(z_m-\tau)]^{-\theta}}-1} \right]}{\left(1 - \alpha^{e^{-\beta[\tau+\lambda(z_m-\tau)]^{-\theta}}-1} \right)} \right\},$$

$$\frac{\partial^2 \ell}{\partial \theta \partial \beta} = \sum_{i=1}^{m_u} z_i^{-\theta} \log(z_i) + \log(\alpha) \sum_{i=1}^{m_u} z_i^{-\theta} \log(z_i) e^{-\beta z_i^{-\theta}} \left(1 - \beta z_i^{-\theta} \right) + \sum_{i=1}^{m_u} \varepsilon_i \left(e^{-\beta z_i^{-\theta}} - 1 \right) z_i^{-\theta} \log(z_i) e^{-\beta z_i^{-\theta}} \left(\alpha^{e^{-\beta[\tau+\lambda(z_m-\tau)]^{-\theta}}-2} \right) \left[1 - \beta z_i^{-\theta} \left(1 + \frac{1}{\alpha} e^{-\beta z_i^{-\theta}} z_i^{-\theta} \left(e^{-\beta z_i^{-\theta}} - 2 \right) \right) \right] + \sum_{i=m_u+1}^{m} [\tau + \lambda(z_i - \tau)]^{-\theta} \log[\tau + \lambda(z_i - \tau)] + \log(\alpha) \sum_{i=m_u+1}^{m} e^{-\beta[\tau+\lambda(z_i-\tau)]^{-\theta}} [\tau + \lambda(z_i - \tau)]^{-\theta} \log[\tau + \lambda(z_i - \tau)] (1 - \beta[\tau + \lambda(z_i - \tau)]^{-\theta}) + \sum_{i=m_u+1}^{m} \varepsilon_i [\tau + \lambda(z_i - \tau)]^{-\theta} \log[\tau + \lambda(z_i - \tau)] e^{-\beta[\tau+\lambda(z_i-\tau)]^{-\theta}} \times$$
$$\left[\frac{\left(e^{-\beta[\tau+\lambda(z_i-\tau)]^{-\theta}} - 1 \right) \left(\alpha^{e^{-\beta[\tau+\lambda(z_i-\tau)]^{-\theta}}-2} \right) \left(1 - \frac{\beta}{e\alpha}[\tau+\lambda(z_i-\tau)]^{-\theta} \right) - \beta[\tau+\lambda(z_i-\tau)]^{-\theta} \left(1 - \alpha^{e^{-\beta[\tau+\lambda(z_i-\tau)]^{-\theta}}-1} \right)}{\left(1 - \alpha^{e^{-\beta[\tau+\lambda(z_i-\tau)]^{-\theta}}-1} \right)^2} \right] + \quad \text{(A7)}$$
$$\varepsilon_m [\tau + \lambda(z_m - \tau)]^{-\theta} \log[\tau + \lambda(z_m - \tau)] e^{-\beta[\tau+\lambda(z_m-\tau)]^{-\theta}} \times$$
$$\left[\frac{\left(e^{-\beta[\tau+\lambda(z_m-\tau)]^{-\theta}} - 1 \right) \left(\alpha^{e^{-\beta[\tau+\lambda(z_m-\tau)]^{-\theta}}-2} \right) \left(1 - \frac{\beta}{e\alpha}[\tau+\lambda(z_m-\tau)]^{-\theta} \right) - \beta[\tau+\lambda(z_m-\tau)]^{-\theta} \left(1 - \alpha^{e^{-\beta[\tau+\lambda(z_m-\tau)]^{-\theta}}-1} \right)}{\left(1 - \alpha^{e^{-\beta[\tau+\lambda(z_m-\tau)]^{-\theta}}-1} \right)^2} \right],$$

$$
\begin{aligned}
\frac{\partial^2 \ell}{\partial \lambda \partial \theta} =\ & \beta \sum_{i=m_u+1}^{m} (z_i - \tau)[\tau + \lambda(z_i - \tau)]^{-\theta-1}(1 - \theta \log[\tau + \lambda(z_i - \tau)]) \\
& - \sum_{i=m_u+1}^{m} \frac{(z_i - \tau)}{[\tau + \lambda(z_i - \tau)]} \\
& + \log(\alpha) \sum_{i=m_u+1}^{m} \left\{ \left(-\beta^2 e^{-\beta[\tau + \lambda(z_i - \tau)]^{-\theta}} (z_i - \tau)[\tau + \lambda(z_i - \tau)]^{-2\theta-1} \log[\tau + \lambda(z_i - \tau)] \right) \right. \\
& + (z_i - \tau)[\tau + \lambda(z_i - \tau)]^{-\theta} e^{-\beta[\tau + \lambda(z_i - \tau)]^{-\theta}} \log[\tau + \lambda(z_i - \tau)] \\
& \left. + (z_i - \tau)[\tau + \lambda(z_i - \tau)]^{-\theta-1} e^{-\beta[\tau + \lambda(z_i - \tau)]^{-\theta}} \right\} \\
& + \sum_{i=m_u+1}^{m} \frac{\beta \varepsilon_i}{\left(1 - \alpha^{e^{-\beta[\tau + \lambda(z_i - \tau)]^{-\theta}} - 1}\right)^2} \\
& \times \left(\theta \beta(z_i - \tau) e^{-\beta[\tau + \lambda(z_i - \tau)]^{-\theta}} [\tau + \lambda(z_i - \tau)]^{-\theta-1} \log[\tau + \lambda(z_i - \tau)] \left(e^{-\beta[\tau + \lambda(z_i - \tau)]^{-\theta}} - 1 \right) \left(\alpha^{e^{-\beta[\tau + \lambda(z_i - \tau)]^{-\theta}} - 2} \right) \right. \\
& - \theta[\tau + \lambda(z_i - \tau)]^{-\theta-1}(z_i - \tau) e^{-\beta[\tau + \lambda(z_i - \tau)]^{-\theta}} \left(e^{-\beta[\tau + \lambda(z_i - \tau)]^{-\theta}} - 1 \right) \left(\alpha^{e^{-\beta[\tau + \lambda(z_i - \tau)]^{-\theta}} - 2} \right) \\
& + \frac{(z_i - \tau) e^{-\beta[\tau + \lambda(z_i - \tau)]^{-\theta}} \left(e^{-\beta[\tau + \lambda(z_i - \tau)]^{-\theta}} - 1 \right) \left(\alpha^{e^{-\beta[\tau + \lambda(z_i - \tau)]^{-\theta}} - 2} \right)}{[\tau + \lambda(z_i - \tau)]} \\
& + e^{-\beta[\tau + \lambda(z_i - \tau)]^{-\theta}} [\tau + \lambda(z_i - \tau)]^{-\theta-1} \log[\tau + \lambda(z_i - \tau)] \left(e^{-\beta[\tau + \lambda(z_i - \tau)]^{-\theta}} - 1 \right) \left(e^{-\beta[\tau + \lambda(z_i - \tau)]^{-\theta}} - 2 \right) \left(\alpha^{e^{-\beta[\tau + \lambda(z_i - \tau)]^{-\theta}} - 3} \right) \\
& \left. e^{-\beta[\tau + \lambda(z_i - \tau)]^{-\theta}} \beta [\tau + \lambda(z_i - \tau)]^{-\theta-1} \right) \\
& + \frac{\beta \varepsilon_m}{\left(1 - \alpha^{e^{-\beta[\tau + \lambda(z_m - \tau)]^{-\theta}} - 1}\right)^2} \\
& \times \left(\theta \beta(z_m - \tau) e^{-\beta[\tau + \lambda(z_m - \tau)]^{-\theta}} [\tau + \lambda(z_m - \tau)]^{-\theta-1} \log[\tau + \lambda(z_m - \tau)] \left(e^{-\beta[\tau + \lambda(z_m - \tau)]^{-\theta}} - 1 \right) \left(\alpha^{e^{-\beta[\tau + \lambda(z_m - \tau)]^{-\theta}} - 2} \right) \right. \\
& - \theta[\tau + \lambda(z_m - \tau)]^{-\theta-1}(z_m - \tau) e^{-\beta[\tau + \lambda(z_m - \tau)]^{-\theta}} \left(e^{-\beta[\tau + \lambda(z_m - \tau)]^{-\theta}} - 1 \right) \left(\alpha^{e^{-\beta[\tau + \lambda(z_m - \tau)]^{-\theta}} - 2} \right) \\
& + \frac{(z_m - \tau) e^{-\beta[\tau + \lambda(z_m - \tau)]^{-\theta}} \left(e^{-\beta[\tau + \lambda(z_m - \tau)]^{-\theta}} - 1 \right) \left(\alpha^{e^{-\beta[\tau + \lambda(z_m - \tau)]^{-\theta}} - 2} \right)}{[\tau + \lambda(z_m - \tau)]} \\
& + e^{-\beta[\tau + \lambda(z_m - \tau)]^{-\theta}} [\tau + \lambda(z_m - \tau)]^{-\theta-1} \log[\tau + \lambda(z_m - \tau)] \left(e^{-\beta[\tau + \lambda(z_m - \tau)]^{-\theta}} - 1 \right) \\
& \left. \left(e^{-\beta[\tau + \lambda(z_m - \tau)]^{-\theta}} - 2 \right) \left(\alpha^{e^{-\beta[\tau + \lambda(z_m - \tau)]^{-\theta}} - 3} \right) e^{-\beta[\tau + \lambda(z_m - \tau)]^{-\theta}} \beta [\tau + \lambda(z_m - \tau)]^{-\theta-1} \right),
\end{aligned}
\tag{A8}
$$

$$
\begin{aligned}
\frac{\partial^2 \ell}{\partial \beta^2} =\ & -\frac{(m_u + m)}{\beta^2} - \log(\alpha) \sum_{i=1}^{m_u} z_i^{-2\theta} e^{-\beta z_i^{-\theta}} - \sum_{i=1}^{m_u} \varepsilon_i z_i^{-2\theta} e^{-\beta z_i^{-\theta}} \left(\alpha^{e^{-\beta z_i^{-\theta}}} - 1 \right) \\
& + \log(\alpha) \sum_{i=m_u+1}^{m} [\tau + \lambda(z_i - \tau)]^{-2\theta} e^{-\beta[\tau + \lambda(z_i - \tau)]^{-\theta}} \\
& + \sum_{i=m_u+1}^{m} \varepsilon_i \alpha^{e^{-\beta[\tau + \lambda(z_i - \tau)]^{-\theta}} - 1} [\tau + \lambda(z_i - \tau)]^{-\theta} \frac{\left(\left(e^{-\beta[\tau + \lambda(z_i - \tau)]^{-\theta}} - 1 \right)^2 + e^{-\beta[\tau + \lambda(z_i - \tau)]^{-\theta}} \right)}{\left(1 - \alpha^{e^{-\beta[\tau + \lambda(z_i - \tau)]^{-\theta}} - 1} \right)^2} \\
& + \frac{\varepsilon_m \left(e^{-\beta[\tau + \lambda(z_m - \tau)]^{-\theta}} - 1 \right) [\tau + \lambda(z_m - \tau)]^{-\theta} \left(\left(\alpha^{-\beta[\tau + \lambda(z_m - \tau)]^{-\theta}} - 1 \right)^2 + e^{-\beta[\tau + \lambda(z_m - \tau)]^{-\theta}} \right)}{\left(1 - \alpha^{e^{-\beta[\tau + \lambda(z_m - \tau)]^{-\theta}} - 1} \right)^2},
\end{aligned}
\tag{A9}
$$

$$
\begin{aligned}
\frac{\partial^2 \ell}{\partial \beta \partial \lambda} = &-\theta \sum_{i=m_u+1}^{m} (z_i - \tau)[\tau + \lambda(z_i - \tau)]^{-\theta-1} \\
&-\theta \log(\alpha) \sum_{i=m_u+1}^{m} \left((z_i - \tau)[\tau + \lambda(z_i - \tau)]^{-\theta-1} e^{-\beta[\tau+\lambda(z_i-\tau)]^{-\theta}} \right. \\
&\left. + \beta[\tau + \lambda(z_i - \tau)]^{-2\theta-1}(z_i - \tau)e^{-\beta[\tau+\lambda(z_i-\tau)]^{-\theta}} \right) \\
&+ \sum_{i=m_u+1}^{m} \frac{\beta \varepsilon_i}{\alpha}(z_i - \tau)[\tau + \lambda(z_i - \tau)]^{-\theta-1}\left(e^{-\beta[\tau+\lambda(z_i-\tau)]^{-\theta}} - 1 \right)^2 \frac{\left(\alpha e^{-\beta[\tau+\lambda(z_i-\tau)]^{-\theta}} - 2 + 1 \right)}{\left(1 - \alpha^{e^{-\beta[\tau+\lambda(z_i-\tau)]^{-\theta}} - 1} \right)^2} \\
&+ \frac{\varepsilon_m \beta}{\alpha}(z_m - \tau)\left(e^{-\beta[\tau+\lambda(z_m-\tau)]^{-\theta}} - 1 \right)^2 [\tau + \lambda(z_m - \tau)]^{-\theta-1} \frac{\left(\alpha e^{-\beta[\tau+\lambda(z_m-\tau)]^{-\theta}} - 2 + 1 \right)}{\left(1 - \alpha^{e^{-\beta[\tau+\lambda(z_m-\tau)]^{-\theta}} - 1} \right)^2},
\end{aligned} \quad (A10)
$$

$$
\begin{aligned}
\frac{\partial^2 \ell}{\partial \lambda^2} = &\beta(\theta - 1)\sum_{i=m_u+1}^{m}(z_i - \tau)^2[\tau + \lambda(z_i - \tau)]^{-\theta-2} - (\theta + 1)\sum_{i=m_u+1}^{m}\frac{(z_i-\tau)^2}{[\tau+\lambda(z_i-\tau)]^2} + \beta\theta\log(\alpha)\sum_{i=m_u+1}^{m}(z_i- \\
&\tau)e^{-\beta[\tau+\lambda(z_i-\tau)]^{-\theta}}[\tau+\lambda(z_i-\tau)]^{-2(\theta-1)}\left([\tau+\lambda(z_i-\tau)]^{-(\theta-1)} + 1\right) + \sum_{i=m_u+1}^{m}\theta\varepsilon_i\beta^2(z_i- \\
&\tau)^2 e^{-\beta[\tau+\lambda(z_i-\tau)]^{-\theta}}[\tau+\lambda(z_i-\tau)]^{-\theta-1}\left(e^{-\beta[\tau+\lambda(z_i-\tau)]^{-\theta}} - \right. \\
&\left. 1\right)\alpha e^{-\beta[\tau+\lambda(z_i-\tau)]^{-\theta}} - 2\left(\frac{1+[\tau+\lambda(z_i-\tau)]^{-(\theta+1)}+e^{-\beta[\tau+\lambda(z_i-\tau)]^{-\theta}}+[\tau+\lambda(z_i-\tau)]^{-1}}{\left(1-\alpha^{e^{-\beta[\tau+\lambda(z_i-\tau)]^{-\theta}}-1}\right)^2}\right) + \varepsilon_m\beta^2(z_m-\tau)^2[\tau+ \\
&\lambda(z_m-\tau)]^{-\theta-1}\left(e^{-\beta[\tau+\lambda(z_m-\tau)]^{-\theta}} - 1\right)\alpha e^{-\beta[\tau+\lambda(z_m-\tau)]^{-\theta}} - 2\left(\frac{1+[\tau+\lambda(z_m-\tau)]^{-(\theta+1)}+e^{-\beta[\tau+\lambda(z_m-\tau)]^{-\theta}}+[\tau+\lambda(z_m-\tau)]^{-1}}{\left(1-\alpha^{e^{-\beta[\tau+\lambda(z_m-\tau)]^{-\theta}}-1}\right)^2}\right).
\end{aligned} \quad (A11)
$$

References

1. Rahman, A.; Sindhu, T.N.; Lone, S.A.; Kamal, M. Statistical inference for Burr Type X distribution using geometric process in accelerated life testing design for time censored data. *Pak. J. Stat. Oper. Res.* **2020**, *16*, 577–586. [CrossRef]
2. Zhang, X.; Yang, J.; Kong, X. Planning constant-stress accelerated life tests with multiple stresses based on D-optimal design. *Qual. Reliab. Eng. Int.* **2021**, *37*, 60–77. [CrossRef]
3. Dusmez, S.; Akin, B. Remaining useful lifetime estimation for degraded power MOSFETs under cyclic thermal stress. In Proceedings of the 2015 IEEE Energy Conversion Congress and Exposition (ECCE), Montreal, QC, Canada, 20–24 September 2015; pp. 3846–3851. [CrossRef]
4. Stojadinovic, N.; Dankovic, D.; Manic, I.; Davidovic, V.; Djoric-Veljkovic, S.; Golubovic, S. Impact of Negative Bias Temperature Instabilities on Lifetime in p-channel Power VDMOSFETs. In Proceedings of the 2007 8th International Conference on Telecommunications in Modern Satellite, Cable and Broadcasting Services, Nis, Serbia and Montenegro, 26–28 September 2007; pp. 275–282. [CrossRef]
5. Alotaibi, R.; Mutairi, A.; Almetwally, E.M.; Park, C.; Rezk, H. Optimal Design for a Bivariate Step-Stress Accelerated Life Test with Alpha Power Exponential Distribution Based on Type-I Progressive Censored Samples. *Symmetry* **2022**, *14*, 830. [CrossRef]
6. Hassan, A.S.; Nassr, S.G.; Pramanik, S.; Maiti, S.S. Estimation in constant stress partially accelerated life tests for Weibull distribution based on censored competing risks data. *Ann. Data Sci.* **2020**, *7*, 45–62. [CrossRef]
7. Rabie, A. E-Bayesian estimation for a constant-stress partially accelerated life test based on Burr-X Type-I hybrid censored data. *J. Stat. Manag. Syst.* **2021**, *24*, 1649–1667. [CrossRef]
8. Goel, P.K. Some Estimation Problems in the Study of Tampered Random Variables. Ph.D. Thesis, Department of Statistics, Carnegie Mellon University, Pittsburgh, Pennsylvania, 1971.
9. DeGroot, M.H.; Goel, P.K. Bayesian estimation and optimal designs in partially accelerated life testing. *Nav. Res. Logist.* **1979**, *26*, 223–235. [CrossRef]
10. Rahman, A.; Lone, S.A.; Islam, A. Analysis of exponentiated exponential model under step stress partially accelerated life testing plan using progressive type-II censored data. *Investig. Oper.* **2019**, *39*, 551–559.
11. Epstein, B. Truncated life tests in the exponential case. *Ann. Math. Stat.* **1954**, *25*, 555–564. [CrossRef]

12. Balakrishnan, N.; Kundu, D. Hybrid censoring: Models, inferential results and applications. *Comput. Stat. Data Anal.* **2013**, *57*, 166–209. [CrossRef]
13. Balakrishnan, N. Progressive censoring methodology: An appraisal. *Test* **2007**, *16*, 211–296. [CrossRef]
14. Balakrishnan, N.; Cramer, E. *The Art of Progressive Censoring: Applications to Reliability and Quality, Statistics for Industry and Technology*; Springer: New York, NY, USA, 2014.
15. Kundu, D.; Joarder, A. Analysis of Type-II progressively hybrid censored data. *Comput. Stat. Data Anal.* **2006**, *50*, 2509–2528. [CrossRef]
16. Ng, H.K.T.; Kundu, D.; Chan, P.S. Statistical analysis of exponential lifetimes under an adaptive Type-II progressive censoring scheme. *Nav. Res. Logist. (NRL)* **2009**, *56*, 687–698. [CrossRef]
17. Lin, C.T.; Ng, H.K.T.; Chan, P.S. Statistical inference of Type-II progressively hybrid censored data with Weibull lifetimes. *Commun. Stat. Meth.* **2009**, *38*, 1710–1729. [CrossRef]
18. Ismail, A.A. Inference for a step-stress partially accelerated life test model with an adaptive Type-II progressively hybrid censored data from Weibull distribution. *J. Comput. Appl. Math.* **2014**, *260*, 533–542. [CrossRef]
19. Almetwally, E.M.; Almongy, H.M.; Rastogi, M.K.; Ibrahim, M. Maximum product spacing estimation of Weibull distribution under adaptive type-II progressive censoring schemes. *Ann. Data Sci.* **2020**, *7*, 257–279. [CrossRef]
20. Hemmati, F.; Khorram, E. Statistical analysis of the lognormal distribution under type-II progressive hybrid censoring schemes. *Commun. Stat. Simulat. Comput.* **2013**, *42*, 52–75. [CrossRef]
21. Sobhi, M.M.A.; Soliman, A.A. Estimation for the exponentiated Weibull model with adaptive Type-II progressive censored schemes. *Appl. Math. Model.* **2016**, *40*, 1180–1192. [CrossRef]
22. Zhang, C.; Shi, Y. Estimation of the extended Weibull parameters and acceleration factors in the step-stress accelerated life tests under an adaptive progressively hybrid censoring data. *J. Stat. Comput. Simulat.* **2016**, *86*, 3303–3314. [CrossRef]
23. Nassr, S.G.; Almetwally, E.M.; El Azm, W.S.A. Statistical inference for the extended Weibull distribution based on adaptive type-II progressive hybrid censored competing risks data. *Thail. Stat.* **2021**, *19*, 547–564.
24. Nassar, M.; Nassr, S.G.; Dey, S. Analysis of burr Type-XII distribution under step stress partially accelerated life tests with Type-I and adaptive Type-II progressively hybrid censoring schemes. *Ann. Data Sci.* **2017**, *4*, 227–248. [CrossRef]
25. Abo-Kasem, O.E.; Almetwally, E.M.; Abu El Azm, W.S. Inferential Survival Analysis for Inverted NH Distribution Under Adaptive Progressive Hybrid Censoring with Application of Transformer Insulation. *Ann. Data Sci.* **2022**, 1–48. [CrossRef]
26. Alam, I.; Ahmed, A. Parametric and Interval Estimation Under Step-Stress Partially Accelerated Life Tests Using Adaptive Type-II Progressive Hybrid Censoring. *Ann. Data Sci.* **2020**, 1–13. [CrossRef]
27. Almongy, H.M.; Almetwally, E.M.; Alharbi, R.; Alnagar, D.; Hafez, E.H.; Mohie El-Din, M.M. The Weibull generalized exponential distribution with censored sample: Estimation and application on real data. *Complexity* **2021**, *2021*, 6653534. [CrossRef]
28. Selim, M.A. Estimation and prediction for Nadarajah-Haghighi distribution based on record values. *Pak. J. Stat.* **2018**, *34*, 77–90. [CrossRef]
29. Haj Ahmad, H.; Salah, M.M.; Eliwa, M.S.; Ali Alhussain, Z.; Almetwally, E.M.; Ahmed, E.A. Bayesian and non-Bayesian inference under adaptive type-II progressive censored sample with exponentiated power Lindley distribution. *J. Appl. Stat.* **2022**, *49*, 2981–3001. [CrossRef] [PubMed]
30. Basheer, A.M. Marshall-Olkin alpha power inverse exponential distribution: Properties and applications. *Ann. Data Sci.* **2019**, *9*, 301–313. [CrossRef]
31. Neyman, J. Outline of a theory of statistical estimation based on the classical theory of probability. *Philos. Trans. R. Soc. Lond.-Ser. A Math. Phys. Sci.* **1937**, *236*, 333–380.
32. Efron, B. Bootstrap Methods: Another Look at the Jackknife. *Ann. Stat.* **1979**, *7*, 1–26. [CrossRef]
33. Gelman, A.; Carlin, J.B.; Stern, H.S.; Rubin, D.B. *Bayesian Data Analysis*, 2nd ed.; Chapman and Hall/CRC: Boca Raton, FL, USA, 2004. [CrossRef]
34. Dey, S. Bayesian estimation of the shape parameter of the generalized exponential distribution under different loss functions. *Pak. J. Stat. Oper. Res.* **2010**, *6*, 163–174. [CrossRef]
35. Burkschat, M.; Cramer, E.; Kamps, U. On optimal schemes in progressive censoring. *Stat. Probab. Lett.* **2006**, *76*, 1032–1036. [CrossRef]
36. Burkschat, M.; Cramer, E.; Kamps, U. Optimality criteria and optimal schemes in progressive censoring. *Commun. Stat.—Theory Methods* **2007**, *36*, 1419–1431. [CrossRef]
37. Burkschat, M. On optimality of extremal schemes in progressive type II censoring. *J. Stat. Plan. Inference* **2008**, *138*, 1647–1659. [CrossRef]
38. Pradhan, B.; Kundu, D. On progressively censored generalized exponential distribution. *TEST* **2009**, *18*, 497–515. [CrossRef]
39. Elshahhat, A.; Rastogi, M.K. Estimation of parameters of life for an inverted Nadarajah–Haghighi distribution from type-II progressively censored samples. *J. Indian Soc. Probab. Stat.* **2021**, *22*, 113–154. [CrossRef]
40. Long, C.; Chen, W.; Yang, R. Ratio estimation of the population mean using auxiliary information under the optimal sampling design. *Probab. Eng. Inf. Sci.* **2022**, *36*, 449–460. [CrossRef]
41. Badar, M.G.; Priest, A.M. Statistical aspects of fibre and bundle strength in hybrid composites. In *Progress in Science and Engineering Composites*; Hayashi, T., Kawata, K., Umekawa, S., Eds.; ICCM-IV: Tokyo, Japan, 1982; pp. 1129–1136.
42. Chen, G.; Balakrishnan, N. A general-purpose approximate goodness-of-fit test. *J. Qual. Technol.* **1995**, *27*, 154–161. [CrossRef]

43. Pakyari, R.; Balakrishnan, N. A general-purpose approximate goodness-of-fit test for progressively type-II censored data. *IEEE Trans. Reliab.* **2012**, *61*, 238–244. [CrossRef]
44. El-Din, M.M.; Abu-Youssef, S.E.; Ali, N.S.; Abd El-Raheem, A.M. Estimation in constant-stress accelerated life tests for extension of the exponential distribution under progressive censoring. *Metron* **2016**, *74*, 253–273. [CrossRef]
45. Abd El-Raheem, A.M.; Almetwally, E.M.; Mohamed, M.S.; Hafez, E.H. Accelerated life tests for modified Kies exponential lifetime distribution: Binomial removal, transformers turn insulation application and numerical results. *AIMS Math.* **2021**, *6*, 5222–5255. [CrossRef]
46. Dimitrova, D.S.; Kaishev, V.K.; Tan, S. Computing the Kolmogorov-Smirnov Distribution When the Underlying CDF is Purely Discrete, Mixed, or Continuous. *J. Sta. Softw.* **2020**, *95*, 1–42. [CrossRef]

Article

Stabilization of Stochastic Dynamical Systems of a Random Structure with Markov Switches and Poisson Perturbations

Taras Lukashiv [1,2,3,*,†], Yuliia Litvinchuk [3,†], Igor V. Malyk [3,†], Anna Golebiewska [2] and Petr V. Nazarov [1,*]

1. Multiomics Data Science Research Group, Department of Cancer Research, Luxembourg Institute of Health, L-1445 Strassen, Luxembourg
2. NORLUX Neuro-Oncology Laboratory, Department of Cancer Research, Luxembourg Institute of Health, L-1210 Luxembourg, Luxembourg
3. Department of Mathematical Problems of Control and Cybernetics, Yuriy Fedkovych Chernivtsi National University, 58000 Chernivtsi, Ukraine
* Correspondence: t.lukashiv@gmail.com (T.L.); petr.nazarov@lih.lu (P.V.N.)
† These authors contributed equally to this work.

Abstract: An optimal control for a dynamical system optimizes a certain objective function. Here, we consider the construction of an optimal control for a stochastic dynamical system with a random structure, Poisson perturbations and random jumps, which makes the system stable in probability. Sufficient conditions of the stability in probability are obtained, using the second Lyapunov method, in which the construction of the corresponding functions plays an important role. Here, we provide a solution to the problem of optimal stabilization in a general case. For a linear system with a quadratic quality function, we give a method of synthesis of optimal control based on the solution of Riccati equations. Finally, in an autonomous case, a system of differential equations was constructed to obtain unknown matrices that are used for the construction of an optimal control. The method using a small parameter is justified for the algorithmic search of an optimal control. This approach brings a novel solution to the problem of optimal stabilization for a stochastic dynamical system with a random structure, Markov switches and Poisson perturbations.

Keywords: optimal control; Lyapunov function; system of stochastic differential equations; Markov switches; Poisson perturbations

MSC: 60J25; 93C73; 93E03; 93E15

1. Introduction

The main problem considered in this paper is the synthesis of an optimal control for a controlled dynamical system, described by a stochastic differential equation (SDE) with Poisson perturbations and external random jumps [1,2]. The importance of this problem is linked to the fact that the dynamics of many real processes cannot be described by continuous models such as ordinary differential equations or Ito's stochastic differential equations [3]. More complex systems include the presence of jumps, and these jumps can occur at random $\tau_k, k \geq 1$, or deterministic time moments, $t_m, m \geq 1$. In the first case, the jump-like change can be described by point processes [4,5], or in a more specific case by generalized Poisson processes, the dynamics of which are characterized only by the intensity of the jumps. The jumps of the system at deterministic moments of time, t_m, can be described by the relation:

$$\Delta x(t_m) = x(t_m) - x(t_m-) = g(\ldots), \qquad (1)$$

where $x(t), t \geq 0$, is a random process describing the dynamics of the system, the function g is a finite-valued function that reflects the magnitude of a jump which depends on time t and process x in the time t_m-. According to the works of Katz I. Ya. [1], Yasinsky

V.K., Yurchenko I.V. and Lukashiv T.O. [6], the description of jumps at deterministic time moments, t_m, are quite accurately described using the Equation (1). It allows a relatively simple transfer of the basic properties of stochastic systems of differential equations without jumps ($g \equiv 0$) to systems with jumps. Such properties, as will be noted below, include the Markovian property, $x(t), t \geq 0$, concerning natural filtering, and the martingale properties, $\|x(t)\|^2, t \geq 0$ [7,8]. It should be noted that the description of real dynamical systems is not limited to the Wiener process and point processes (Poisson process). A more general approach is based on the use of semimartingales [9]. The disadvantage of this approach is that it is impossible to link it with the methods used for systems described by ordinary differential equations or stochastic Ito's differential equations. The second approach to describe jump processes, $x(t)$, is based on the use of semi-Markov processes, considered in the works of Korolyuk V.S. [10] and Malyk I.V. [2,11]. In particular, the works of Malyk I.V. are devoted to the convergence of semi-Markov evolutions in the averaging scheme and diffusion approximation. The results derived in these works together with the results of the works on large deviations (e.g., [12]) can also be used to investigate the considered problems.

Since we consider generalized classical differential equations, the approaches used will also be classical. The basic research method is based on the Lyapunov methods described in the papers by Katz I. Ya. [1] and Lukashiv T.O. and Malyk I.V. [13]. It should be noted that the application of this method makes it possible to find the optimal control for linear systems with a quadratic quality functional, which also corresponds to classical dynamical systems [14].

It should be noted that a large number of works are devoted to the issues of stability of systems with jumping Markov processes. For example, the works [15,16] consider sufficient conditions for the stability of Ito stochastic differential equations with Markov switching and the presence of variable delay. In the work [15], this theory has gained logical use for modeling neural networks with a decentralized event-triggered mechanism and finding sufficient conditions for stabilizing the process that describe dynamic of the neural network. Note that the authors of this work also considered systems of stochastic differential equations in which the deterministic term near dt is quasi-linear; that is, the linear component plays the main role in this research. This assumption of quasi-linearity allows, with additional conditions on the value of the nonlinear part, the discovery of sufficient stability conditions of the $x(t), t \geq 0$, by constructing suboptimal control $u(t), t \geq 0$. Similar results were obtained also in the work [16], where authors described an algorithm of stabilization by construction of the non-fragile event-triggered controller for Ito stochastic differential equations with varying delay. The authors chose a specific class of admissible controls, which makes it possible to solve the optimization problem for finding a suboptimal control.

The structure of the paper is as follows. In Section 2, we consider the mathematical model of a dynamical system with jumps. It is described by a system of stochastic differential equations with Poisson's integral and external jumps. Sufficient conditions for the existence and uniqueness of the solution of this system are given there. In Section 3, we investigate the stability in probability of the solution $x(t), t \geq 0$. In this section, we consider the notion of the Lyapunov function and prove the sufficient conditions for stability in probability (Theorem 1). The algorithm for computing the quality functional, $J_u(y, h, x_0)$, from the known control, $u(t)$, is given in Section 4. Moreover, we further present sufficient conditions for the existence of an optimal control (Theorem 2), which are based on the existence of a Lyapunov function for the given system. Section 5 considers constructing an optimal control for linear non-autonomous systems via the coefficients of the system. The optimal control is found by solving auxiliary Ricatti equations (Theorem 3). For the analysis of linear autonomous systems, we consider the construction of a quadratic functional. Finally, we formulate sufficient conditions of existence of an optimal control (Theorem 4), and present the explicit form of such a control in the case of a quadratic quality functional.

2. Task Definition

On the probability basis $(\Omega, \mathfrak{F}, F, \mathbf{P})$ [7], consider a stochastic dynamical system of a random structure given by Ito's stochastic differential Equation (SDE) with Poisson perturbations:

$$dx(t) = a(t-, \xi(t-), x(t-), u(t-))dt +$$
$$+ b(t-, \xi(t-), x(t-), u(t-))dw(t) +$$
$$+ \int_{\mathbb{R}^m} (c(t-, \xi(t-), x(t-), u(t-), z))\tilde{\nu}(dz, dt), \ t \in \mathbb{R}_+ \setminus K, \quad (2)$$

with Markov switches

$$\Delta x(t)\big|_{t=t_k} = g(t_k-, \xi(t_k-), \eta_k, x(t_k-)), \quad t_k \in K = \{t_n \uparrow\} \quad (3)$$

for $\lim_{n \to +\infty} t_n = +\infty$ and initial conditions

$$x(0) = x_0 \in \mathbb{R}^m, \ \xi(0) = y \in \mathbf{Y}, \eta_0 = h \in \mathbf{H}. \quad (4)$$

Here, $\xi(t), t \geq 0$, is a homogeneous continuous Markov process with a finite number of states $\mathbf{Y} := \{y_1, \ldots, y_N\}$ and a generator Q; $\{\eta_k, k \geq 0\}$ is a Markov chain with values in the space $\mathbf{H}$ and the transition probability matrix $\mathbb{P}_H$; $x : [0, +\infty) \times \Omega \to \mathbb{R}^m$; $w(t)$ is an m-dimensional standard Wiener process; $\tilde{\nu}(dz, dt) = \nu(dz, dt) - \mathbb{E}\nu(dz, dt)$ is a centered Poisson measure; and the processes w, ν, ξ and η are independent [3,7]. We denote by

$$\mathfrak{F}_{t_k} = \sigma(\xi(s), w(s), \nu(s, *), \eta_e, s \leq t_k, t_e \leq t_k)$$

a minimal σ-algebra, with respect to which $\xi(t)$ is measurable for all $t \in [0, t_k]$ and η_n for $n \leq k$.

The process $x(t), t \geq 0$ is càdlàg and the control $u(t) := u(t, x(t)) : [0, T] \times \mathbb{R}^m \to \mathbb{R}^m$ is an m-measure function from the class of admissible controls U [14].

The following mappings are measurable by a set of variables $a : \mathbb{R}_+ \times \mathbf{Y} \times \mathbb{R}^m \times \mathbb{R}^m \to \mathbb{R}^m$, $b : \mathbb{R}_+ \times \mathbf{Y} \times \mathbb{R}^m \times \mathbb{R}^m \to \mathbb{R}^m \times \mathbb{R}^m$, $c : \mathbb{R}_+ \times \mathbf{Y} \times \mathbb{R}^m \times \mathbb{R}^m \times \mathbb{R}^m \to \mathbb{R}^m$ and function $g : \mathbb{R}_+ \times \mathbf{Y} \times \mathbf{H} \times \mathbb{R}^m \to \mathbb{R}^m$ satisfies the Lipschitz condition

$$|a(t, y, x_1, u) - a(t, y, x_2, u)| + |b(t, y, x_1, u) - b(t, y, x_2, u)| +$$
$$+ \int_{\mathbb{R}^m} |c(t, y, x_1, u, z) - c(t, y, x_2, u, z)|\Pi(dz) +$$
$$+ |g(t, y, h, x_1) - g(t, y, h, x_2)| \leq L|x_1 - x_2|, \quad (5)$$

where $\Pi(dz)$ is defined by $\mathbb{E}\nu(dz, dt) = \Pi(dz)dt$, $L > 0$, $x_1, x_2 \in \mathbb{R}^m$ for $\forall t \geq 0, y \in \mathbf{Y}$, $h \in \mathbf{H}$, and the condition

$$|a(t, y, 0, u)| + |b(t, y, 0, u)| + \int_{\mathbb{R}^m} |c(t, y, 0, u, z)|\Pi(dz) +$$
$$+ |g(t, y, h, 0)| \leq C < \infty, \quad (6)$$

The conditions defined above, with respect to the mappings a, b, c and g, guarantee the existence of a strong solution to Equations (2)–(4) with the exact stochastic equivalence [13].

Let us denote

$$\mathbf{P}_k((y, h, x), \Gamma \times G \times \mathbf{C}) :=$$
$$:= P(\xi(t_{k+1}), \eta_{k+1}, x(t_{k+1}) \in \Gamma \times G \times \mathbf{C} | (\xi(t_k), \eta_k, x(t_k)) = (y, h, x))$$

the transition probability of a Markov chain $(\xi(t_k), \eta_k, x(t_k))$, determining the solution to the Equations (2)–(4) $x(t)$, at the k-th step.

3. Stability in Probability

Here we used the definitions from classical works in this area [14,17].

Definition 1. *The discrete Lyapunov operator $(lv_k)(y, h, x)$ on a sequence of measurable scalar functions $v_k(y, h, x)$: $\mathbf{Y} \times \mathbf{H} \times \mathbb{R}^m \to \mathbb{R}^1, k \in \mathbb{N} \cup \{0\}$ for SDE (2) with Markov switches (3) is defined by the equation:*

$$(lv_k)(y, h, x) := \int_{\mathbf{Y} \times \mathbf{H} \times \mathbb{R}^m} \mathbf{P}_k((y, h, x), du \times dz \times dl) v_{k+1}(u, z, l) - v_k(y, h, x), k \geq 0. \quad (7)$$

When applying the second Lyapunov method to the SDE (2) with Markov switches (3), special sequences of the above mentioned functions $v_k(y, h, x), k \in \mathbb{N}$ are required.

Definition 2. *The Lyapunov function for the system of the random structure (2)–(4) is a sequence of non-negative functions $\{v_k(y, h, x), k \geq 0\}$, for which*

1. *for all $k \geq 0, y \in \mathbf{Y}, h \in \mathbf{H}, x \in \mathbb{R}^m$ the discrete Lyapunov operator is defined $(lv_k)(y, h, x)$ (7),*
2. *for $r \to \infty$*

$$\bar{v}(r) \equiv \inf_{\substack{k \in \mathbb{N}, y \in \mathbf{Y}, \\ h \in \mathbf{H}, |x| \geq r}} v_k(y, h, x) \to +\infty$$

3. *for $r \to 0$*

$$\underline{v}(r) \equiv \sup_{\substack{k \in \mathbb{N}, y \in \mathbf{Y}, \\ h \in \mathbf{H}, |x| \leq r}} v_k(y, h, x) \to 0,$$

Moreover, $\bar{v}(r)$ and $\underline{v}(r)$ are continuous and strictly monotonous.

Definition 3. *Let us call a system of random structure (2)–(4) stable in probability on the whole, and if for $\forall \varepsilon_1 > 0, \varepsilon_2 > 0$ one can specify, as $\delta > 0$, that from the inequality $|x| < \delta$ follows the inequality*

$$\mathbf{P}\left\{\sup_{t \geq 0} |x(t)| > \varepsilon_1\right\} < \varepsilon_2 \quad (8)$$

for all $x_0 \in \mathbb{R}^m, y \in \mathbf{Y}, h \in \mathbf{H}$.

To solve the Equations (2)–(4) in the intervals $[t_k, t_{k+1})$, the following estimate takes place

Lemma 1. *Let the coefficients of Equation (2), a, b, c and function g, satisfy the Lipschitz condition (5) and the uniform boundedness condition (6).*
Then, for all $k \geq 0$, the inequality for the strong solution of the Cauchy problem (2)–(4) holds

$$\mathbf{E}\left\{\sup_{t_k \leq t < t_{k+1}} |x(t)|^2\right\} \leq 7\left[\mathbb{E}|x(t_k)|^2 + 3C^2(t_{k+1} - t_k)\right] \times$$

$$\times \exp\left\{7L^2((t_{k+1} - t_k) + 8)\right\}, t \in (t_k, t_{k+1}). \quad (9)$$

Proof of Lemma 1. Using the integral form of the strong solution of Equation (2) [8], for all $t \in [t_k, t_{k+1}), t_k \geq 0$, the following inequality is true:

$$|x(t)| \leq |x(t_k)| + \int_{t_k}^{t} |a(\tau, \xi(\tau), x(\tau), u(\tau)) - a(\tau, \xi(\tau), 0, u(\tau))| d\tau +$$

$$+ \int_{t_k}^{t} |a(\tau, \xi(\tau), 0, u(\tau))| d\tau +$$

$$+ \int_{t_k}^{t} |b(\tau, \xi(\tau), x(\tau), u(\tau)) - b(\tau, \xi(\tau), 0, u(\tau))| dw(\tau) +$$

$$+ \int_{t_k}^{t} |b(\tau, \xi(\tau), 0, u(\tau))| dw(\tau) +$$

$$+ \int_{t_k}^{t} \int_{\mathbb{R}^m} |c(\tau, \xi(\tau), x(\tau), u(\tau), z) - c(\tau, \xi(\tau), 0, u(\tau), z)| \tilde{\nu}(dz, d\tau) +$$

$$+ \int_{t_k}^{t} \int_{\mathbb{R}^m} |c(\tau, \xi(\tau), 0, u(\tau), z)| \tilde{\nu}(dz, d\tau)$$

Given (5) and (6) and the inequality $(\sum_{i=1}^{n} x_i)^2 \leq n \sum_{i=1}^{n} x_i^2$ we get:

$$\sup_{t_k \leq t < t_{k+1}} |x(t)|^2 \leq 7 \sup_{t_k \leq t < t_{k+1}} \Big[|x(t_k)|^2 +$$

$$+ \left| \int_{t_k}^{t} |a(\tau, \xi(\tau), x(\tau), u(\tau)) - a(\tau, \xi(\tau), 0, u(\tau))| d\tau \right|^2 +$$

$$+ \left| \int_{t_k}^{t} |a(\tau, \xi(\tau), 0, u(\tau))| d\tau \right|^2 +$$

$$+ \left| \int_{t_k}^{t} |b(\tau, \xi(\tau), x(\tau), u(\tau)) - b(\tau, \xi(\tau), 0, u(\tau))| dw(\tau) \right|^2 +$$

$$+ \left| \int_{t_k}^{t} |b(\tau, \xi(\tau), 0, u(\tau))| dw(\tau) \right|^2 +$$

$$+ \left| \int_{t_k}^{t} \int_{\mathbb{R}^m} |c(\tau, \xi(\tau), x(\tau), u(\tau), z) - c(\tau, \xi(\tau), 0, u(\tau), z)| \tilde{\nu}(dz, d\tau) \right|^2 +$$

$$+ \left| \int_{t_k}^{t} \int_{\mathbb{R}^m} |c(\tau, \xi(\tau), 0, u(\tau), z)| \tilde{\nu}(dz, d\tau) \right|^2 \Big] \leq$$

$$\leq 7 \Big[\sup_{t_k \leq t < t_{k+1}} |x(t)|^2 + \sup_{t_k \leq t < t_{k+1}} L^2 \left| \int_{t_k}^{t} |x(\tau)| d\tau \right|^2 +$$

$$+ C^2(t_{k+1} - t_k) + \sup_{t_k \leq t < t_{k+1}} L^2 \left| \int_{t_k}^{t} |x(\tau)| dw(\tau) \right|^2 + C^2(t_{k+1} - t_k) +$$

$$+ \sup_{t_k \leq t < t_{k+1}} \left| \int_{t_k}^{t} \int_{\mathbb{R}^m} |c(\tau, \xi(\tau), x(\tau), u(\tau), z) - c(\tau, \xi(\tau), 0, u(\tau), z)| \tilde{\nu}(dz, d\tau) \right|^2 +$$

$$+ \sup_{t_k \leq t < t_{k+1}} \left| \int_{t_k}^{t} \int_{\mathbb{R}^m} |c(\tau, \xi(\tau), 0, u(\tau), z)| \tilde{\nu}(dz, d\tau) \right|^2 \Big].$$

Consider the designation:

$$y(t) = \mathbb{E}\left\{ \sup_{t_k \leq s < t} |x(s)|^2 / \mathfrak{F}_{t_k} \right\}.$$

Then, according to the last inequality, $y(t)$ satisfies the ratio:

$$y(t) \leq 7\left[\mathbb{E}\left\{|x(t)|^2/\mathfrak{F}_{t_k}\right\} + 3C^2(t_{k+1} - t_k) + L^2((t_{k+1} - t_k) + 8) \cdot \int_{t_k}^{t} y(\tau)d\tau\right].$$

Using the Gronwall inequality, we obtain an estimate of:

$$\mathbb{E}\left\{\sup_{t_k \leq t < t_{k+1}} |x(t)|^2/\mathfrak{F}_{t_k}\right\} \leq$$

$$\leq 7\left[\mathbb{E}|x(t_k)|^2 + 3C^2(t_{k+1} - t_k)\right]e^{7L^2((t_{k+1}-t_k)+8)},$$

as required as proof. □

Remark 1. *We will consider the stability of the trivial solution $x \equiv 0$ of the system (2)–(4); that is, the fulfillment of (6) when $C = 0$ [17–19].*

Theorem 1. *Let:*
(1) Interval lengths $[t_k, t_{k+1})$ do not exceed $\Delta > 0$, i.e., $|t_{k+1} - t_k| \leq \Delta, k \geq 0$;
(2) The Lipschitz condition is satisfied (5);
(3) There exists Lyapunov functions $v_k(y, h, x), k \geq 0$ such that the following inequality holds true

$$(lv_k)(y, h, x) \leq 0, k \geq 0. \tag{10}$$

Then, the system of random structure (2)–(4) is stable in probability on the whole.

Remark 2. *It should be noted that if condition 1 is not satisfied, the number of jumps (3) is finite and the system (2)–(4) turns into a system without jumps after $\max t_k$. In this case, we can use the results presented in [1].*

Proof of Theorem 1. The conditional expectation of the Lyapunov function is:

$$\mathbb{E}\{v_{k+1}(\xi(t_{k+1}), \eta_{k+1}, x(t_{k+1}))/\mathfrak{F}_{t_k}\} = \int_{Y \times H \times \mathbb{R}^m} \mathbf{P}_k((\xi(t_k), \eta_k, x(t_k))(du \times dz \times dl)v_{k+1}(u, z, l)). \tag{11}$$

Then, by the definition of the discrete Lyapunov operator $(lv_k)(y, h, x)$ (see (7)) and from Equation (11), taking into account (10), we obtain the following inequality:

$$\mathbb{E}\{v_{k+1}(\xi(t_{k+1}), \eta_{k+1}, x(t_{k+1}))/\mathfrak{F}_{t_k}\} = v_k(\xi(t_k), \eta_k, x(t_k)) + (lv_k)(\xi(t_k), \eta_k, x(t_k)) \leq \bar{v}(|x(t_k)|). \tag{12}$$

From Lemma 1 and the properties of the function $\bar{v}$, it follows that the conditional expectation of the left part of inequality (12) exists.

Using (11) and (12), let us write the discrete Lyapunov operator $(lv_k)(y, h, x)$, defined by the solutions of (2)–(4):

$$(lv_k)(\xi(t_k), \eta_k, x(t_k)) = \mathbb{E}\{v_{k+1}(\xi(t_{k+1}), \eta_{k+1}, x(t_{k+1}))/\mathfrak{F}_{t_k}\} - v_k(\xi(t_k), \eta_k, x(t_k)) \leq 0. \tag{13}$$

Then, when $k \geq 0$, the following inequality is satisfied:

$$\mathbb{E}\{v_{k+1}(\xi(t_{k+1}), \eta_{k+1}, x(t_{k+1}))/\mathfrak{F}_{t_k}\} \leq v_k(\xi(t_k), \eta_k, x(t_k)).$$

This means that the sequence of random variables $v_k(\xi(t_k), \eta_k, x(t_k))$ is a supermartingale with respect to $\mathfrak{F}_{t_k}$ [5].

Thus, the following inequality holds:

$$\mathbb{E}\{v_{N+1}(\xi(t_{N+1}), \eta_{N+1}, x(t_{N+1}))\} - \mathbb{E}\{v_n(\xi(t_n), \eta_n, x(t_n))\} =$$

$$= \sum_{k=n}^{N} \mathbf{E}\{(lv_k)(\xi(t_k), \eta_k, x(t_k))\} \leq 0.$$

Since the random variable $\sup_{t_k \leq t < t_{k+1}} |x(t)|^2$ is independent of events of σ-algebra $\mathfrak{F}_{t_k}$ [4], then

$$\mathbf{E}\left\{\sup_{t_k \leq t < t_{k+1}} |x(t)|^2 \bigg/ \mathfrak{F}_{t_k}\right\} = \mathbf{E}\left\{\sup_{t_k \leq t < t_{k+1}} |x(t)|^2\right\},$$

i.e., the inequality (9) also holds for the usual expectation

$$\mathbf{E}\left\{\sup_{t_k \leq t < t_{k+1}} |x(t)|^2\right\} \leq 7\left[\mathbb{E}|x|^2\right] e^{7L^2(\Delta+8)}$$

at $C = 0$, assuming that the stability of the trivial solution is investigated.

Then,

$$\mathbf{P}\left\{\sup_{t \geq 0} |x(t)| > \varepsilon_1\right\} =$$

$$= \mathbf{P}\left\{\sup_{n \in \mathbb{N}} \sup_{t_{n-1} \leq t < t_n} |x(t)| > \varepsilon_1\right\} \leq$$

$$\leq \mathbf{P}\left\{\sup_{n \in \mathbb{N}} 7 e^{7L^2(\Delta+8)} |x(t_{n-1})| > \varepsilon_1\right\} \leq$$

$$\leq \mathbf{P}\left\{\sup_{n \in \mathbb{N}} |x(t_{n-1})| > \frac{\varepsilon_1}{7} e^{-7L^2(\Delta+8)}\right\} \leq$$

$$\leq \mathbf{P}\left\{\sup_{n \in \mathbb{N}} v_{n-1}(\xi(t_{n-1}), \eta_{n-1}, x(t_{n-1})) \geq \bar{v}(\frac{\varepsilon_1}{7} e^{-7L^2(\Delta+8)})\right\} \quad (14)$$

If $\sup|x(t_k)| \geq r$, then based on the definition of the Lyapunov function, the inequality is fulfilled

$$\sup_{k \geq 0} v_k(\xi(t_k), \eta_k, x(t_k)) \geq \inf_{k \geq 0, y \in \mathbf{Y}, h \in \mathbf{H}, |x| \geq r} v_k(y, h, x) = \bar{v}(r). \quad (15)$$

Using the inequality for non-negative supermartingales [5,7], we obtain an estimate of the right-hand side of (14):

$$\mathbf{P}\left\{\sup_{n \in \mathbb{N}} v_{n-1}(\xi(t_{n-1}), \eta_{n-1}, x(t_{n-1})) \geq \bar{v}(\frac{\varepsilon_1}{7} e^{-7L^2(\Delta+8)})\right\} \leq$$

$$\leq \frac{1}{\bar{v}(\frac{\varepsilon_1}{7} e^{-7L^2(\Delta+8)})} v_0(y, h, x) \leq \frac{\bar{v}(|x|)}{\bar{v}(\frac{\varepsilon_1}{7} e^{-7L^2(\Delta+8)})}. \quad (16)$$

Given the inequality (14), the inequality (16) guarantees that the inequality (8) of stability in probability holds for the whole system (2)–(4). □

4. Stabilization

The optimal stabilization problem is such that for an SDE (2) with switches (3), one should construct a control $u(t, x(t))$ such that the unperturbed motion $x(t) \equiv 0$ of the system (2)–(4) is stable in probability on the whole.

It is assumed that the control, u, will be determined by the full feedback principle. In addition, the condition of continuity of $u(t)$ on t is in the range

$$t \geq 0, \, x \in \mathbb{R}^m, \, y \in \mathbf{Y}, \, h \in \mathbf{H}. \quad (17)$$

for every fixed $\zeta(t) = y \in \mathbf{Y}$ and $\eta_k = h \in \mathbf{H}$.

It is also assumed that the structure of the system at time $t \geq 0$, which is independent of the Markov chain η_k ($k \geq 0$ corresponds to time $t_k \in K$), is known.

Obviously, there is an infinite set of controls. The only control should be chosen from the requirement of the best quality of the process, which is expressed in the form of the minimization condition of the functional:

$$I_u(y, h, x_0) := \sum_{k=0}^{\infty} \int_{t_k}^{\infty} E\{W(t, x(t), u(t))/\zeta(0) = y, \eta_0 = h, x(0) = x_0\} dt, \quad (18)$$

where $W(t, x, u) \geq 0$ is a non-negative function defined in the region $t \geq 0, x \in \mathbb{R}^m, u \in \mathbb{R}^r$.

The algorithm for calculating the functional (18) for a given control, $u(t, x)$, is as follows:
(A) Find the trajectory $x(t)$ with an SDE (2) at $u \equiv u(t, y, h, x)$, for example, by the Euler–Maruyama method [20];
(B) Substitute $x(t), \zeta(t)$ and $u(t) = u(t, x(t))$ into the functional (18);
(C) Calculate the value of the function (18) by statistical modeling (Monte Carlo);
(D) The problem of choosing the functional $W(t, x, u)$, which determines the estimate I_u and the quality of the process $x(t)$ as a strong solution of the SDE (2), is related to the specific features of the problem and the following three conditions can be identified:

1. The minimization conditions of the functional (18) must ensure that the strong solution, $x(t)$, of the SDE (2) fades fast enough on average with high probability;
2. The value of the integral should satisfactorily estimate the computation time spent on generating the control, $u(t)$;
3. The value of the quality functional should satisfactorily estimate the computation time spent on forming the control, $u(t)$;
4. The functional $W(t, x, u)$ must be such that the solution of the stabilization problem can be constructed.

Remark 3. *For a linear SDE (2), in many cases the quadratic form with respect to the variables x and u is satisfactory*

$$W(t, x, u) = x^T M(t) x + u^T D(t) u, \quad (19)$$

where $M(t)$ is a symmetric non-negative matrix of size $m \times m$ and $D(t)$ is a positively determined matrix of the size $r \times r$ for all $t \geq 0$.

Remark 4. *Note that according to the feedback principle, $M(t)$ and $D(t)$ depend indirectly on the values of $\zeta(t)$ and η_k. Therefore, in the examples below, we will calculate the values of $M(t)$ and $D(t)$ for fixed $\zeta(t)$ and η_k.*

The value I_u in the case of the quadratic form of the variables x and u evaluates the quality of the transition process quite well on average. The presence of the term $u^T D u$ and the minimum condition simultaneously limit the amount of the control action $u \in \mathbb{R}^r$.

Remark 5. *If the jump condition of the phase trajectory is linear, then the solution of the stabilization problem belongs to the class of linear on the phase vector $x \in \mathbb{R}^m$ controls $u(t, x)$. Such problems are called linear-quadratic stabilization problems.*

Definition 4. *The control $u^0(t)$, which satisfies the condition:*

$$I_{u^0}(y, h, x_0) = \min I_u(y, h, x_0),$$

where the minimum should be searched for all controls continuous variables t and x at each $\zeta(0) = y \in \mathbf{Y}$ and $\eta_0 = h \in \mathbf{H}$, let us call it optimal in the sense of optimal stabilization of the strong solution $x \in \mathbb{R}^m$ of the system (2)–(4).

Theorem 2. Let the system (2)–(4) have a scalar function $v^0(t_k, y, h, x)$ and an r-vector function $u^0(t, y, h, x) \in \mathbb{R}^r$ in the region (17) and fulfill the conditions:

1. The sequence of the functions $v_k^0(y, h, x) \equiv v^0(t_k, y, h, x)$ is the Lyapunov functional;
2. The sequence of r-measured functions-control

$$u_k^0(y, h, x) \equiv u^0(t_k, y, h, x) \in \mathbb{R}^r; \qquad (20)$$

   is measurable in all arguments where $0 \leq t_k < t_{k+1}, k \geq 0$;
3. The sequence of functions from the criterion (18) by $x \in \mathbb{R}^m$ is positive definite, i.e., for $\forall t \in [t_k, t_{k+1}), k \geq 0$,

$$W(t, x, u_k^0(y, h, x)) > 0; \qquad (21)$$

4. The sequence of infinitesimal operators $(lv_k^0)|_{u_k^0}$, calculated for $u_k^0 \equiv u^0(y, h, x)$, satisfies the condition for $\forall t \in [t_k, t_{k+1})$

$$(lv_k^0)|_{u_k^0} = -W(t, x, u_k^0); \qquad (22)$$

5. The value of $(lv_k^0) + W(t, x, u)$ reaches a minimum at $u = u^0, k \geq 0$, i.e.,

$$(lv_k^0)|_{u_k^0} + W(t, x, u_k^0) = \min_{u \in \mathbb{R}^r}\{(lv_k^0)|_u + W(t, x, u)\} = 0; \qquad (23)$$

6. The series

$$\sum_{k=0}^{\infty} \int_{t_k}^{\infty} \mathbf{E}\{W(t, x(t), u(t))/x(t_{k-1})\}dt < \infty \qquad (24)$$

converges.

Then, the control $u_k^0 \equiv u^0(t_k, y, h, x), k \geq 0$ stabilizes the solution of Equations (2)–/(4). In this case, the equality

$$v^0(y, h, x_0) \equiv$$

$$\equiv \sum_{k=0}^{\infty} \int_{t_k}^{\infty} \mathbf{E}\{W(t, x(t), u(t))/x(t_{k-1})\}dt =$$

$$= \min_{u \in \mathbb{R}^r} \sum_{k=0}^{\infty} \int_{t_k}^{\infty} \mathbf{E}\{W(t, x(t), u(t))/x_{(}t_k)\}dt \equiv I_{u^0}(y, h, x_0) \qquad (25)$$

is held.

Proof of Theorem 2. I. Stability in probability in the whole of a dynamical system of a random structure (2)–(4) for $u \equiv u^0(t_k, x), k \geq 0$ immediately follows from Theorem 1, since the functionals $v^0(y, h, x)$ for any $t \in [t_k, t_{k+1}), k \geq 0$ satisfy the conditions of this theorem.

II. The equality (25) is obviously also a consequence of Theorem 1.

III. Proof by contradiction that the stabilization of a strong solution of a dynamical system of random structure (2)–(4) is controlled by $u^0(t_k, x), t_k \leq t < t_{k+1}, k \geq 0$.

Let the control $u^*(t_k, x) \neq u^0(t_k, x)$ exist, which, when substituted into the SDE (2), realizes a solution $x^*(t)$ with initial conditions (3) and (4), such that the equality

$$I_{u^*}(y, h, x_0) \leq I_{u^0}(y, h, x_0). \qquad (26)$$

is held.

The fulfilment of conditions (1)–(6) of Theorem 2 will lead to an inequality (see (27)) in contrast to (26).

From the condition (5) (see (23)) follows the inequality:

$$(lv_k^0)|_{u^*} \geq -W(t, x, u^*(t, y, h, x)). \qquad (27)$$

Averaging (27) over random variables $\{x^*(t), \xi(t), \eta_k\}$ over intervals $[t_k, t_{k+1}), k \geq 0$ and integrating over t from 0 to T, we obtain n inequalities:

$$\mathbf{E}\{v^0(t_1, \xi(t_1), \eta_{k_1}, x^*(t_1))/y_1, \eta_{k_1}, x^*(t_1)\} - v^0(y, h, x_0) \geq$$

$$\geq -\int_0^{t_1} \mathbf{E}\{W(t, x^*(t), u^*(t))/x_0\}dt, \qquad (28)$$

$$\mathbf{E}\{v^0(t_2, \xi(t_2), \eta_{k_2}, x^*(t_2))/y_1, \eta_{k_1}, x^*(t_1)\} - $$
$$- \{v^0(t_1, \xi(t_1), \eta_{k_1}, x^*(t_1))/y, h, x_0\} \geq$$

$$\geq -\int_{t_1}^{t_2} \mathbf{E}\{W(t, x^*(t), u^*(t))/x^*(t_1)\}dt, \qquad (29)$$

$$\cdots$$

$$\mathbf{E}\{v^0(t_n, \xi(t_n), \eta_{k_n}, x^*(t_n))\big/y_{n-1}, \eta_{k_{n-1}}, x^*(t_{n-1})\} -$$
$$- \{v^0(t_{n-1}, \xi(t_{n-1}), \eta_{k_{n-1}}, x^*(t_{n-1}))\big/y_{n-2}, \eta_{k_{n-2}}, x^*(t_{n-2})\} \geq$$

$$\geq -\int_{t_{n-1}}^{t_n} \mathbf{E}\{W(t, x^*(t), u^*(t))/x^*(t_{n-1})\} \qquad (30)$$

Taking into account the martingale property of the Lyapunov functions $v^0(t, \xi(t), h, x^*(t)$ (see condition (1) of the theorem) due to the system (2)–(4), i.e., by the definition of a martingale, we have n equalities with the probability of one being:

$$\mathbf{E}\{v^0(t_k, \xi(t_k), \eta_k, x^*(t_k))/y_{k-1}, \eta_{k-1}, x^*(t_{k-1})\} =$$

$$= v^0(t_{k-1}, \xi(t_{k-1}), \eta_{k-1}, x^*(t_{k-1})), k = \overline{1, n}. \qquad (31)$$

Substituting (31) into the inequalities (28)–(30), we obtain the inequality:

$$\mathbf{E}\{v^0(t_n, \xi(t_n), \eta_{k_n}, x^*(t_n))/t_{n-1}, \xi(t_{n-1}), \eta_{k_{n-1}}, x^*(t_{n-1})\} - v^0(y, h, x_0) \geq$$

$$\geq -\sum_{k=0}^{n} \int_{t_k}^{t_{k+1}} \mathbf{E}\{W(t, x^*(t), u^*(t))/x^*(t_{k-1})\}dt \geq$$

$$\geq -\sum_{k=0}^{\infty} \int_{t_k}^{\infty} \mathbf{E}\{W(t, x^*(t), u^*(t))/x^*(t_{k-1})\}dt. \qquad (32)$$

According to the assumption (26), it follows that for $t_n \to \infty$, the integrals on the right-hand side of (32) converge and, taking into account the convergence of the series (24) (condition (6)), we obtain the inequality:

$$v^0(y, h, x_0) = I_{u^0}(y, h, x_0) \leq$$

$$\leq \sum_{k=0}^{\infty} \int_{t_k}^{\infty} \mathbf{E}\{W(t, x^*(t), u^*(t))/x^*(t_{k-1})\}dt =$$

$$= I_{u^*}(y, h, x_0). \qquad (33)$$

Indeed, from the convergence of the series (32) (under condition (6)), it follows that the integrands in (33) tend to zero as $t \to \infty$. In this way, $\lim_{n \to \infty} \mathbf{E}\{v^0(t_n, y_n, \eta_{k_n}, x^*(t_n))\} = 0$.

Note that it makes sense to consider natural cases when from the condition

$$E\{W\} \underset{t \to \infty}{\to} 0$$

it follows that $E\{v^0\} \underset{t \to \infty}{\to} 0$.

Thus, the inequality (33) contradicts the inequality (26). This contradiction proves the statement regarding the optimality of the control $u^0(t_k, x), k \geq 0$.

□

In cases when the Markov process with a finite number of states $\xi(t_k)$ admits a conditional expansion of the conditional transition probability

$$P\{\omega : \xi(t + \Delta t) = y_j / \xi(t) = y_i, y_i \neq y_j\} =$$

$$= q_{ij}(t)\Delta t + o(\Delta t), i, j = \overline{1, N}, \tag{34}$$

we obtain an equation that must be satisfied by the optimal Lyapunov functions, $v_k^0(y, h, x)$, and the optimal control, $u_k^0(t, x), \forall t \in [t_k, t_{k+1})$.

Note that according to [6,21], the weak infinitesimal operator (7) has the form:

$$(lv_k)(y, h, x) = \frac{\partial v_k(y, h, x)}{\partial t} + (\nabla v_k(y, h, x), a(t, y, x, u)) +$$

$$+ \frac{1}{2} Sp(b^T(t, y, x, u) \cdot \nabla^2 v_k(y, h, x) \cdot b(t, y, x, u)) +$$

$$+ \int_{\mathbb{R}^m} [v_k(y, h, x + c(t, y, x, u, z)) - v_k(y, h, x) - (\nabla v_k(y, h, x))^T \cdot c(t, y, x, u, z)] \Pi(dz) +$$

$$+ \sum_{j \neq i}^{N} [\int_{\mathbb{R}^m} v_j(t, x) p_{ij}(t, z/x) dz - v_i(t, x)] q_{ij}, \tag{35}$$

where $(\cdot, \cdot)$ is a scalar product, $\nabla v_k = \left(\frac{\partial v_k}{\partial x_1}, \ldots, \frac{\partial v_k}{\partial x_m}\right)^T$, $\nabla^2 v_k = \left[\frac{\partial^2 v_k}{\partial x_i \partial x_j}\right]_{i,j=1}^m$, $k \geq 0$, "T" stands for a transposition, Sp is a trace of matrix and $p_{ij}(t, z/x)$ is a conditional probability density:

$$Px(\tau) \in [z, z + dz]/x(\tau - 0) = x = p_{ij}(\tau, z/x)dz + o(dz)$$

assuming that $\xi(\tau - 0) = y_i$, $\xi(\tau) = y_j$.

Taking into account Formula (35), the first equation for v^0 can be obtained by replacing the left side of (23) with the expression for the averaged infinitesimal operator, $(lv_k^0)|_{u^*}$ [1]. Then, the desired equation at the points (t_k, y_j, η_k, x) has the form:

$$\frac{\partial v_k^0}{\partial t} + \left(\left(\frac{\partial v_k^0}{\partial x}\right)^T \cdot a(t, y, x, u)\right) + \frac{1}{2} Sp\left(\left(b^T(t, y_i, x) \cdot \frac{\partial^2 v_k^0}{\partial x^2} \cdot b(t, y_i, x)\right)\right) +$$

$$+ \int_{\mathbb{R}^m} [v_k^0(\cdot, \cdot, x + c(t, y, x, u, z)) - v_k^0 - (\frac{\partial v_k^0}{\partial x})^T \cdot c(t, y, x, u, z)] \Pi(dz) +$$

$$+ \sum_{j \neq i}^{l} \left[\int_{-\infty}^{+\infty} v_j^0(y_j, h, x_j) p_{ij}(t, z/x) dz - v_i^0(y_i, h, x)\right] q_{ij}(t) dt +$$

$$+ W(t, x, u) = 0. \tag{36}$$

The second equation for optimal control, $u_k^0(t, y, h, x)$, can be obtained from (36) by differentiation with respect to the variable u, since $u = u^0$ delivers the minimum of the left side of (36):

$$\left[\left(\frac{\partial v^0}{\partial x}\right)^T \cdot \left(\frac{\partial a}{\partial u}\right) + \left(\frac{\partial W}{\partial u}\right)^T\right]\bigg|_{u=u_k^0} = 0, \quad (37)$$

where $\frac{\partial a}{\partial u}$ – $m \times r$-matrix of Jacobi, stacked with elements $\left\{\frac{\partial a_n}{\partial u_s}, n = \overline{1, m}, s = \overline{1, r}\right\}$; $\left(\frac{\partial W}{\partial u}\right) \equiv \left(\frac{\partial W}{\partial u_1}, \ldots, \frac{\partial W}{\partial u_r}\right), k \geq 0$.

Thus, the problem of optimal stabilization, according to the Theorem 2, consists of solving the complex nonlinear system of Equation (23) with partial derivatives to, determine the unknown Lyapunov functions, $v_{ik}^0 \equiv v_k^0(y, h, x), i = \overline{1, l}, k \geq 0$.

Note that this system is obtained by eliminating the control $u_k^0 = u^0(t, y, h, x)$ from Equations (36) and (37).

It is quite difficult to solve such a system; therefore, we will further consider linear stochastic systems for which convenient solution schemes can be constructed.

5. Stabilization of Linear Systems

Consider a controlled stochastic system defined by a linear Ito's SDE with Markov parameters and Poisson perturbations:

$$dx(t) = [A(t-,\xi(t-))x(t-) + B(t-,\xi(t-))u(t-)]dt + \sigma(t-,\xi(t-))x(t-)dw(t)+$$

$$+ \int_{\mathbb{R}^m} c(t-,\xi(t-),u(t-),z)x(t-)\widetilde{\nu}(dz,dt), \ t \in \mathbb{R}_+ \setminus K, \quad (38)$$

with Markov switching

$$\Delta x(t)\big|_{t=t_k} = g(t_k-,\xi(t_k-),\eta_k,x(t_k-)), \quad t_k \in K = \{t_n \Uparrow\} \quad (39)$$

for $\lim_{n \to +\infty} t_n = +\infty$ and initial conditions

$$x(0) = x_0 \in \mathbb{R}^m, \ \xi(0) = y \in \mathbf{Y}, \eta_0 = h \in \mathbf{H}. \quad (40)$$

Here, A, B, σ and C are piecewise continuous integrable matrix functions of appropriate dimensions.

Let us assume that the conditions for the jump of the phase vector $x \in \mathbb{R}^m$ at the moment when $t = t^*$ of the change in the structure of the system due to the transition $\xi(t^*-) = y_i$ in $\xi(t^*) = y_j \neq y_i$ are linear and given in the form:

$$x(t^*) = K_{ij}x(t^*-) + \sum_{s=1}^{N} \zeta_s Q_s x(t^*-), \quad (41)$$

where $\zeta_s := \zeta_s(\omega)$ are independent random variables for which $\mathbf{E}\zeta_s = 0, \mathbf{E}\zeta_s^2 = 1$ and K_{ij} and Q_s are given as $(m \times m)$-matrices.

Note that the equality (41) can replace the general jump conditions [6]:
- The case of non-random jumps will be at $Q_s = 0$, i.e.,

$$x(t^*) = K_{ij}x(t^*-);$$

- The continuous change in the phase vector means that $Q_s = 0$ and $K_{ij} = A_{ij} = I$ (identity $(m \times m)$-matrix).

The quality of the transition process will be estimated by the quadratic functional

$$I_u(y, h, x_0) := \sum_{k=0}^{\infty} \int_{t_k}^{\infty} \mathbf{E}\{x^T(t)M(t)x(t) + u^T(t)D(t)u(t) / y, h, x_0\} dt, \qquad (42)$$

where $M(t) \geq 0, D(t) > 0$ are symmetric matrices of dimensions $(m \times m)$ and $(r \times r)$, respectively.

According to the Theorem 2, we need to find optimal Lyapunov functions, $v_k^0(y, h, x)$, and a control, $u_k^0(t, x)$, for $\forall t \in [t_k, t_{k+1}), t_k \in K, k = 0, 1, 2, \ldots$

The optimal Lyapunov functions are sought in the form:

$$v_k^0(y, h, x) = x^T G(t, y, h) x, \qquad (43)$$

where $G(t, y, h)$ is a positive-definite symmetric matrix of the size $(m \times m)$.

Hereafter, when $\xi(t)$ describes a Markov chain with a finite number of states $\mathbf{Y} = \{y_1, y_2, \ldots, y_l\}$, and $\eta_k, k \geq 0$ describes a Markov chain with values h_k in metric space $\mathbf{H}$ and with transition probability at the k-th step $\mathbf{P}_k(h, G)$, we introduce the following notation:

$$A_i(t) := A(t, y_i), \quad B_i(t) := B(t, y_i), \quad \sigma_i(t) := \sigma(t, y_i), \quad C_i(t, z) := C(t, y_i, z),$$

$$G_{ik}(t) := G(t, y_i, h_k), \quad v_{ik} := v(y_i, h_k, x).$$

Let us substitute the functional (43) into Equations (36) and (38) to find an optimal Lyapunov function, $v_k^0(y, h, x)$, and an optimal control, $u_k^0(t, x)$, for $\forall t \in [t_k, t_{k+1})$. Given the form of a weak infinitesimal operator (35), we obtain:

$$x^T(t) \frac{dG_{ik}(t)}{dt} x(t) + 2[A_i(t)x(t) + B_i(t)u(t)] G_{ik}(t) x(t) +$$

$$+ Sp(x^T(t)\sigma_i^T(t)G_{ik}(t)\sigma_i(t)x(t)) + \int_{\mathbb{R}^m} x^T(t) C_i^T(t,z) G_{ik}(t) C_i(t,z) x(t) \Pi(dz) +$$

$$+ x^T(t) \sum_{j \neq i}^{N} \left[K_{ij}^T G_{ik}(t) K_{ij} + \sum_{s=0}^{l} Q_s^T G_{ik}(t) Q_s - G_{ik}(t) \right] q_{ij} x(t) +$$

$$+ x^T(t) M_{ik}(t) x(t) + u^T(t) D_{ik}(t) u(t) = 0, \qquad (44)$$

$$2x^T(t) G_{ik}(t) B_i(t) + 2u^T(t) D_{ik}(t) = 0. \qquad (45)$$

Note that the partial derivative with respect to u of the operator (lv) is equal to zero, which confirms the conjecture about constructing an optimal control that does not depend on switching (39) for the system (40).

From (45), we find an optimal control for $\xi(t) = y_i$, when switching (39) $\eta_k = h_k, k \geq 0$,

$$u_{ik}^0(t, x) = -D_{ik}^{-1}(t) B_i^T(t) G_{ik}(t) x(t). \qquad (46)$$

Given the matrix equality

$$2x^T(t) G_{ik}(t) A_i(t) x = x^T(t) (G_{ik}(t) A_i(t) + A_i^T(t) G_{ik}(t)) x(t)$$

and excluding u_{ik}^0 from (44) and equating the resulting matrix with a quadratic form to zero, we can obtain a system of matrix differential equations of Riccati type for finding the matrices $G_{ik}(t)$, where $i = 1, 2, \ldots, l, k \geq 0$, corresponding to the interval $[t_k, t_{k+1})$:

$$\frac{dG_{ik}(t)}{dt} + G_{ik}(t) A_i(t) - B_i(t) D_{ik}^{-1}(t) B_i^T(t) G_{ik}(t) +$$

$$+Sp(\sigma_i^T(t)G_{ik}(t)\sigma_i(t))+\int_{\mathbb{R}^m}C_i^T(t,z)G_{ik}(t)C_i(t,z)\Pi(dz)+$$

$$+\sum_{j\neq i}^{N}\left[K_{ij}^TG_{ik}(t)K_{ij}+\sum_{s=0}^{l}Q_s^TG_{ik}(t)Q_s-G_{ik}(t)\right]q_{ij}+M_{ik}(t)=0, \qquad (47)$$

$$\lim_{t\to\infty}G_{ik}(t)=0, i=\overline{1,N}, k\geq 0. \qquad (48)$$

Thus, we obtain the following statement, which is actually a corollary to Theorem 2.

Theorem 3. *Let the system of matrix Equations (47) and (48) have positive-definite solutions of the order $(m\times m)$*

$$G_{1k}(t)>0, G_{2k}(t)>0,\ldots, G_{lk}(t)>0.$$

Then, the control (46) gives a solution to the problem of optimal stabilization of the system (38)–(40) with jump condition (41) and the criterion of optimality (42).

6. Stabilization of Autonomous Systems

Consider the case of an autonomous system that is given by the SDE

$$dx=[A(\zeta(t))x+B(\zeta(t))u]dt+\sigma(\zeta(t))xdw(t)+C(\zeta(t))xdN(t),\ t\in\mathbb{R}_+\setminus K, \qquad (49)$$

with Markov switching (39) and initial conditions (40). Here, $x\in\mathbb{R}^m$, $u\in\mathbb{R}^r$, $A(y)$, $B(y)$, $\sigma(y)$ and $C(y)$ are known matrix functions defined in the set $\mathbf{Y}=\{y_1,y_2,\ldots,y_k\}$ of possible values of the Markov chain ζ. $N(t), t\geq 0$ is a Poisson process with intensity λ [4].

In the case of phase vector jumps (41) and the quadratic quality functional (42), the systems (47) and (48) for finding unknown matrices $G_{ik}, i=\overline{1,N}, k\geq 0$, will take the form:

$$G_{ik}A_i+A_i^TG_{ik}-B_iD_{ik}^{-1}B_i^TG_{ik}+\sigma_i^TG_{ik}\sigma_i+$$

$$+\lambda C_i^TG_{ik}C_i+$$

$$+\sum_{j\neq i}^{N}\left[K_{ij}^TG_{ik}K_{ij}+\sum_{s=0}^{l}Q_s^TG_{ik}Q_s-G_{ik}\right]q_{ij}+M_{ik}=0, i=\overline{1,N}, k\geq 0. \qquad (50)$$

Remark 6. *Note that any differential system written in the normal form (such as the system (38), where the dependence of x on t is explicitly indicated) can be reduced to an autonomous system by increasing the number of unknown functions (coordinates) by one.*

Small Parameter Method for Solving the Problem of the Optimal Stabilization

The algorithmic solution to the problem of optimal stabilization of a linear autonomous system of random structure ((43), (39) and (40)) is achieved by introducing a small parameter [1]. There are two ways to introduce the small parameter:

Case I. Transition probabilities $y_i\to y_j$ of Markov chains ζ are small, i.e., the transition intensities, q_{ij}, due to the small parameter ($\varepsilon>0$) can be represented as:

$$q_{ij}=\varepsilon r_{ij}. \qquad (51)$$

Case II. Small jumps of the phase vector $x(t)\in R^m$, i.e., matrices K_{ij} and Q_s from (41), should be presented in the form:

$$K_{ij}=I+\varepsilon K_{ij};\ Q_s=\varepsilon Q_s. \qquad (52)$$

In these cases, we will search for the optimal Lyapunov function $v_k^0(y, x, h), k \geq 0$, in the form of a convergent power series with a base $\varepsilon > 0$

$$v_k^0(y, h, x) = x^T \sum_{r=0}^{\infty} \varepsilon^r G^{(r)}(y, h) x. \tag{53}$$

According to (46), the optimal control, u^0, should be sought in the form of a convergent series:

$$u_k^0(y, h, x) = -[D^{-1}(y) B^T(y) \sum_{r=0}^{\infty} \varepsilon^r G^{(r)}(y, h)] x. \tag{54}$$

Case I. Let us substitute the series (53) and (54), taking into account (51), into (44):

$$G_{ik} A_i + (A_i)^T G_{ik} - B_i D_{ik}^{-1} B_i^T G_{ik} + \sigma_i^T G_{ik} \sigma_i +$$

$$+ \lambda C_i^T G_{ik} C_i +$$

$$+ \sum_{\substack{j=1 \\ j \neq i}}^{l} K_{ij}^T G_{ik} K_{ij} + \sum_{s=1}^{N} Q_s^T (G_{ik} Q_s - G_{ik}) \varepsilon r_{ij} + C_{ik} = 0; i = \overline{1,l}, k \geq 0.$$

Equating the coefficients at the same powers of $\varepsilon > 0$, we get:

$$A_i^T G_i^{(0)} + G_{ik}^{(0)} A_i - B_i D_{ik}^{-1} B_{ik}^T G_{ik}^{(0)} +$$

$$+ \sigma_{ik}^T G_{ik}^{(0)} \sigma_{ik} + \lambda C_i^T G_{ik}^{(0)} C_i + M_{ik} = 0, i = \overline{1,l}, k \geq 0, \tag{55}$$

$$\tilde{A}_{ik}^T G_{ik}^{(r)} + G_{ik}^{(r)} \tilde{A}_{ik} + \sigma_i^T G_{ik}^{(r)} \sigma_i + \lambda C_i^T G_{ik}^{(0)} C_i =$$
$$= -\sum_{j \neq i}^{l} (K_{ik}^T G_{ik}^{(r-1)} K_{ij} + \sum_{s=1}^{N} Q_s^T G_{ik}^{(r-1)} Q_s - G_{ik}^{(r-1)}) r_{ij} +$$

$$+ \sum_{q=1}^{r-1} B_i D_{ik}^{-1} B_i^T G_{ik}^{(r-q)}, \tag{56}$$

$$r > 1; \tilde{A}_{ik} \equiv A_i - B_i D_{ik}^{-1} B_i^T G_{ik}^{(0)}, i = \overline{1,l}, k \geq 0.$$

Note that the system (55) consists of independent matrix equations which, for a fixed $i = 1, 2, \ldots, l$, gives a solution to the problem of optimal stabilization of the system

$$dx(t) = (A_i x(t) + B_i u(t)) dt + \sigma_i x(t) dw(t) + C_i x(t) dN(t), \tag{57}$$

with the quality criterion

$$I_u(y, h, x_0) = \sum_{k=0}^{\infty} \int_{t_k}^{\infty} E\{x^T(t) M_{ik} x(t) + u^T(t) D_{ik} u(t) / x_0\} dt,$$

$$i = \overline{1,l}, k \geq 0, M_{ik} > 0, D_{ik} > 0. \tag{58}$$

A necessary and sufficient condition for the solvability of the system (55) is the existence of linear admissible control in the system (57), which provides exponential stability in the mean square of the unperturbed motion of this system [17].

Let us assume that the system of matrix quadratic Equation (55) has a unique positive definite solution, $G_{ik}^{(0)} > 0, i = \overline{1,l}, k \geq 0$.

Equation (56) to find $G_{ik}^{(r)} > 0, r \geq 1, k \geq 0$ is linear, so it has a unique solution for a fixed $i = \overline{1,l}, k \geq 0, r \geq 1$ and any matrices that are on the right side of (56).

Indeed, the system

$$dx(t) = \tilde{A}_{ik}x(t)dt + \sigma_i x(t)dw(t) + C_i x(t)dN(t) \tag{59}$$

is obtained by closing the system (57) with the optimal control

$$u_k^0 = -D_{ik}^{-1}B_{ik}^T G_{ik}^{(0)}x(t),$$

which provides exponential stability in the mean square. Then, there is a unique solution to the system (56). Note that in the linear case for autonomous systems, the asymptotic stability is equivalent to the exponential stability [2]. Consider a theorem which originates from the results of this work.

Theorem 4. *If a strong solution, $x(t)$, of the system (57) is exponentially stable in the mean square, then there exists Lyapunov functions $v_k(y, h, x), k \geq 0$, which satisfy the conditions:*

$$c_1\|x\|^2 \leq v_k(y, h, x) \leq c_1\|x\|;$$

$$\frac{dE[v_k]}{dt} \leq -c_3\|x\|^2.$$

Thus, the system of matrix Equations (55) and (56) allows us to consistently find the coefficients $G_{ik}^{(r)} > 0$ of the corresponding series (53) and (54), starting with a positive solution $G_{ik}^{(0)} > 0, i = \overline{1, l}, k \geq 0$ of the system (55).

The next step is to prove the convergence of the series (53) and (54). Without the loss of generality, we simplify notations by fixing $k \geq 0$. Let $L_r := \max_{\substack{i=\overline{1,l},\\ k \geq 0}} \left\|G_i^{(r)}\right\|$. Then, from (56), it follows that there is a constant $c > 0$, such that for any $r > 0$ the following estimate is correct:

$$L_r \leq c\left[\sum_{q=1}^{r-1} L_q L_{r-q} + L_{r-1}\right]. \tag{60}$$

Next, we use the method of majorant series.
Consider the quadratic equation

$$\rho^2 + (a + \varepsilon)\rho + b = 0, \tag{61}$$

where the coefficients a and b are chosen such that the power series expansion of one of the roots of this equation is a majorant series for (53).

We obtain

$$\rho_{1,2} = -\frac{a+\varepsilon}{2} \pm \sqrt{\frac{(a+\varepsilon)^2}{4} - b} = \sum_{r=0}^{\infty} \varepsilon^r \rho_r. \tag{62}$$

Let us substitute (62) into (61), and equate coefficients at equal powers of ε. Then, we get an expression for ρ_r through $\rho_0, \ldots, \rho_{r-1}$:

$$\rho_r = -\frac{1}{2\rho_0 + a}\left[\sum_{q=1}^{r-1}\rho_q \rho_{r-q} + \rho_{r-1}\right], \tag{63}$$

where ρ_0 should be found from the Equation

$$\rho_0^2 + a\rho_0 + b = 0. \tag{64}$$

Comparing (60) and (63), we find that the series (62) will be major for (53), if we consider

$$c = -\frac{1}{2\rho_0 + a} > 0; \rho_0 = L_0 > 0.$$

Thus, the values of the coefficients a and b in Equation (61) are

$$a = -\left[\frac{1}{c} + 2L_0\right] < 0;$$
$$b = \frac{L_0}{c} + L_0^2 > 0.$$

Using the known a and b from (61), we find that the majorant series for (53) will be the expansion one of the roots of (61). This root is such that its values are determined by

$$\rho_0 = L_0 = -\frac{a}{2} - \sqrt{\frac{a^2}{4} - b}.$$

Convergence of the series (53) for $v_k^0(y, h, x)$ follows from the obvious inequality

$$\left\|\sum_{r=0}^{\infty} \varepsilon^r G^{(r)}(y, h)\right\| \leq \sum_{r=0}^{\infty} L_r \varepsilon^r.$$

Thus, we have proved the assertion which is formalized below as Theorem 5:

Theorem 5. 1. For $\forall i = \overline{1, l}, k \geq 0$, the system (57) has a linear admissible control;
2. Transition intensities, q_{ij}, of a homogeneous Markov chain ξ satisfy the condition (51).
Then,

1. There is a unique solution to the problem of optimal stabilization of the system (43), (39) and (40) with the jump condition (41) of the phase vector $x \in R^m$;
2. The optimal Lyapunov function $v_k^0(y, h, x)$ and optimal control $u_k^0(y, h, x)$ are determined by the convergent series (53) and (54), whose coefficients are found from the corresponding systems (55) and (56).

Case II. Let us substitute the series $G_{ik} = \sum_{r=0}^{\infty} \varepsilon^r G_{ik}^{(r)}$ into (44) and equate the coefficients at the same powers ε. Then, taking into account (52), we obtain the following equations:

$$G_{ik}^{(0)} A_i + A_i^T G_{ik}^{(0)} + \sigma_i^T G_{ik}^{(0)} \sigma_i - B_i D_{ik}^{-1} B_i^T G_{ik}^{(0)} +$$

$$+ \lambda C_i^T G_{ik} C_i + \sum_{j \neq i}^{l} (G_{jk}^{(0)} - G_{ik}^{(0)}) q_{ij} + M_{ik} = 0, k \geq 0, \tag{65}$$

$$G_{ik}^{(r)} \tilde{A}_{ik} + \tilde{A}_{ik}^T G_{ik}^{(r)} + \sigma_i^T G_{ik}^{(r)} \sigma_i + \lambda C_i^T G_{ik} C_i + \sum_{j \neq i}^{l} (G_{jk}^{(r)} - G_{ik}^{(r)}) q_{ij} = \Phi_{ik}^{(r)}, \tag{66}$$

where $i = \overline{1, l} k \geq 0$, $\tilde{A}_{ik} = A_i - B_i D_{ik}^{-1} B_i^T G_{ik}^{(0)}$,

$$\Phi_{ik}^{(r)} = \sum_{q=1}^{r-1} B_i D_{ik}^{-1} B_i^T G_{ik}^{(r-q)} -$$

$$-\sum_{j \neq i}^{l} (K_{ij}^T G_{jk}^{(r-1)} + G_{jk}^{(r-1)} K_{ij} + K_{ij}^T G_{jk}^{(r-2)} K_{ij} + \sum_{s=1}^{N} Q_s^T G_{jk}^{(r-2)} Q_s) q_{ij}.$$

Based on the equations above, the following theorem is correct:

Theorem 6. 1. *The system of matrix Equation (65) has a unique positive definite solution* $G_{ik}^{(0)} > 0, i = \overline{1,l}; k \geq 0;$
2. *Jumps of the phase vector $x \in R^m$ satisfy the condition (52).*
Then, the linear-quadratic optimal stabilization problem (43), (39) and (40) of minimizing the functional (42) has a unique solution, which is given in the form of convergent series (53) and (54), and the matrices $G_{ik}^{(r)}, i = \overline{1,l}; r \geq 1, k \geq 0$ is the only solution to the linear matrix Equation (66).

7. Model Example

To illustrate the above theoretical results, consider an example with the following parameters:

- The continuous Markov chain $\zeta(t), t \geq 0$ is defined by generator

$$Q = \begin{pmatrix} -7 & 7 \\ 3 & -3 \end{pmatrix};$$

- $t_k = k, k \geq 1;$
- The values of the function g in the times t_k depend only on the value of x:

$$g(t, \zeta, \eta, x) = K_{ij}x = \alpha x, Q_s = 0;$$

where $\alpha \in [-1, 1]$. For example, below we use $\alpha = 0.2$;
- The intensity of the Poisson process is $\lambda = 0.2$;
- The values of the matrices $A(\zeta)$ for $\zeta(t) \in \{1, 2\}$ are

$$A_1 = \begin{pmatrix} -2 & 1 & 1 \\ 3 & -3 & 0 \\ 0 & 6 & -2 \end{pmatrix}, A_2 = \begin{pmatrix} -4 & 8 & 0 \\ 0 & 1 & 2 \\ 3 & -2 & -1 \end{pmatrix};$$

- The values of the matrices $B(\zeta)$ for $\zeta(t) \in \{1, 2\}$ are

$$B_1 = \begin{pmatrix} 4 & 2 \\ 0 & -2 \\ 1 & 1 \end{pmatrix}, B_2 = \begin{pmatrix} 0 & 1 \\ 4 & -3 \\ -1 & 1 \end{pmatrix};$$

- The values of the matrices $\sigma(\zeta)$ for $\zeta(t) \in \{1, 2\}$ are

$$\sigma_1 = \begin{pmatrix} 1 & 0 & 0 \\ -1 & 1 & 1 \\ -1 & -1 & 1 \end{pmatrix}, \sigma_2 = \begin{pmatrix} 1 & -1 & -1 \\ 0 & 1 & -1 \\ 0 & 0 & 1 \end{pmatrix}.$$

- The values of the matrices $C(\zeta)$ for $\zeta(t) \in \{1, 2\}$ are

$$C_1 = \begin{pmatrix} 0.3 & 0.2 & 0.1 \\ -0.2 & 0.4 & 0.8 \\ 0.1 & 0.1 & 0.2 \end{pmatrix}, C_2 = \begin{pmatrix} -0.5 & 0.1 & -0.2 \\ 0.4 & 0.5 & -1.1 \\ -0.7 & -0.6 & 0.3 \end{pmatrix};$$

- The control parameters are

$$M_{ik} = \begin{pmatrix} 1 & 0 & 0 \\ 0 & 2 & 0 \\ 0 & 0 & 3 \end{pmatrix}, D_{ik} = \begin{pmatrix} 10 & 0 \\ 0 & 40 \end{pmatrix}.$$

For simplicity, we will assume that the random variables η_k are constants and the solution, $x(t)$, and optimal control, $u(t)$, depend only on the random process, $\zeta(t)$.

The main problem of optimal control is the solution of the Riccati Equation (50). There are several basic approaches to finding an approximate solution to this equation. However, in our example, we used the particle swarm optimization method, which allows us to relatively quickly find the solution to Equation (50). The results of finding this equation will be the matrices

$$G_1 = \begin{pmatrix} 0.2044 & 0.0943 & 0.0043 \\ 0.1258 & 0.3605 & 0.165 \\ 0.0139 & 0.1575 & 0.3146 \end{pmatrix}, G_2 = \begin{pmatrix} 0.1268 & 0.5538 & -0.0962 \\ 0.2533 & 2.8729 & 0.2214 \\ 0.1096 & 0.2075 & 2.0079 \end{pmatrix}.$$

Both solutions are positively defined, so by Theorem 3 there exists an optimal control, which stabilizes system (57) and is defined by

$$u(t)_{\xi(t)=i} = -D^{-1}B^T G_i x(t)$$

for $i \in \{1, 2\}$. Two realization of the solution, $x(t)$, and corresponding control, $u(t)$, are shown in Figures 1 and 2.

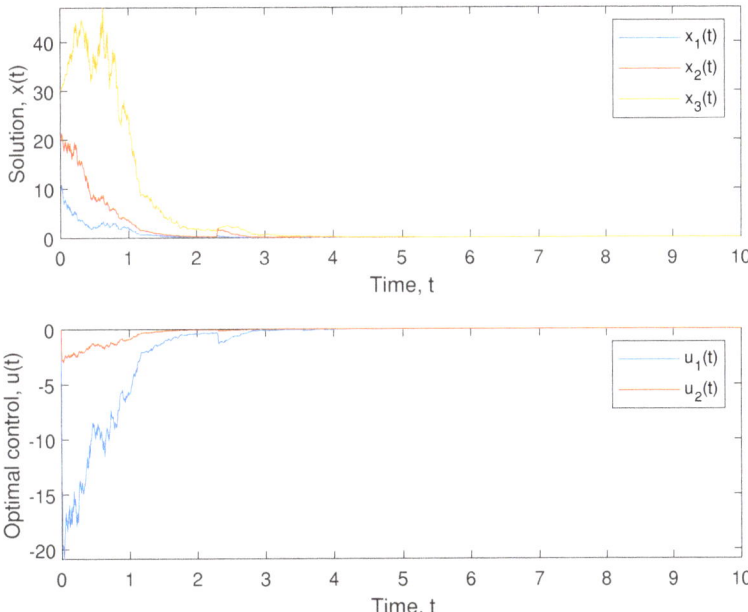

Figure 1. Realizations of the solution and optimal control with initial conditions $(10, 20, 30)$.

As we can see from the above examples, the resulting optimal control, $u(t)$, stabilizes the system, and therefore minimizes the functional $I_u(y, h, x_0)$. In addition, considering the form of the matrix D from (42), we can see that $u_2(t)$ is close to 0, because

$$u^T(t)Du(t) = 100u_1^2(t) + 1600u_2^2(t).$$

In this way, the optimal control found will agree with the given quality functional $I_u(y, h, x_0)$.

An analysis of the solution showed that there is an optimal control for an arbitrary $\alpha \in [-1, 1]$. The $|\alpha| < 1$ case corresponds to the compressive case, since in this case the solution is compressed by the α coefficient at each step in the point, t_k. The $|\alpha| = 1$ case is not compressible, but the existence of an optimal control can be found based on Theorem 3. The case of $|\alpha| > 1$ is not included in the theory of this work, since in this case, the solution of Equation (50) either does not exist or is not positively defined. This case needs further investigation.

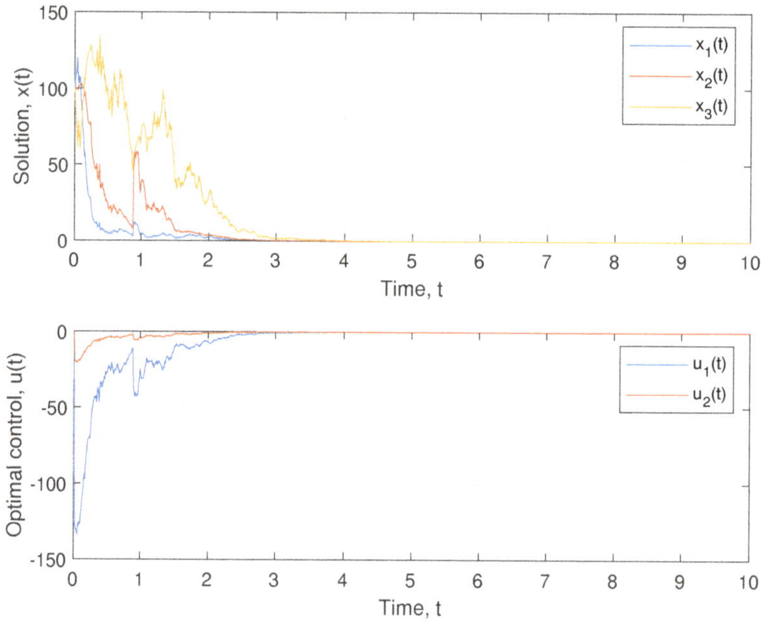

Figure 2. Realizations of solution and optimal control with initial conditions $(100, 100, 100)$.

8. Discussion

In this work, we have obtained sufficient conditions for the existence of an optimal solution for a stochastic dynamical system with jumps, which transform the system to a stable one in probability. The second Lyapunov method was used to investigate the existence of an optimal solution. This method is efficient both for ordinary differential equations (ODE) and for stochastic differential equations (SDE). As it can be seen from the proof of the Theorem 2, the existence of finite bounds for jumps at non-random time moments, t_m ($\lim_{m \to \infty} t_m = T^* < \infty$), does not impact the stability of the solution. On the other hand, $|t_{m+} - t_m| > \delta, m \geq 1$ was used for proving the existence of the optimal control (Theorem 3). This restriction is also present in the works of other authors. Thus, a goal of future work could be to construct an optimal control without the assumption $|t_{m+} - t_m| > \delta, m \geq 1$, which will considerably expand the scope of the second Lyapunov method.

The limitation of the proposed method is linked to the need for a solution to Riccati's equations that can be computationally heavy. For small dimensions of m, Riccati's equations can be solved either by iteration or by genetic algorithms, but for large dimensions of m, only genetic algorithms work.

9. Conclusions

In this work, we obtained sufficient conditions for the existence of a solution to an optimal stabilization problem for dynamical systems with jumps. We considered the case of a linear system with a quadratic quality functional. We showed that by designing an optimal control that stabilizes the system to a stable one in probability reduces the problem of solving the Riccati equations. Additionally, for a linear autonomous system, the method using a small parameter is substantiated for solving the problem of optimal stabilization. The obtained solutions can be used to describe a stock market in economics, biological systems, including models of response to treatment of cancer, and other complex dynamical systems.

In addition, this work serves as a basis for the study of systems of type (3)–(4) under the conditions of the presence of condensation point, i.e.,

$$\lim_{k \to \infty} t_k = t^* < \infty.$$

Systems with this condition are a mathematical model of real phenomena, in which exceptional events accumulate very quickly over a finite period of time, which can lead to a collapse of the system. For example, paper [22] examines the mathematical model of the collapse of the bridge in Tacoma. At the same time, the authors of this work took into account only deterministic influences, and did not include random events affecting the dynamics of the bridge. Considering both deterministic and random influences can provide a more precise picture for the understanding of such dramatic effects.

Author Contributions: Conceptualization, T.L. and I.V.M.; methodology, T.L. and I.V.M.; validation, T.L., Y.L., I.V.M. and P.V.N.; formal analysis, T.L., Y.L., I.V.M. and P.V.N.; writing—original draft preparation, T.L., Y.L. and I.V.M.; writing—review and editing, T.L., P.V.N. and A.G.; supervision, I.V.M. and P.V.N.; project administration, P.V.N. and A.G.; funding acquisition, A.G. and P.V.N. All authors have read and agreed to the published version of the manuscript.

Funding: This work was supported by the Luxembourg National Research Fund C21/BM/15739125/DIOMEDES to T.L., P.V.N. and A.G.

Institutional Review Board Statement: Not applicable.

Informed Consent Statement: Not applicable.

Data Availability Statement: Not applicable.

Acknowledgments: We would like to acknowledge the administrations of the Luxembourg Institute of Health (LIH) and the Luxembourg National Research Fund (FNR) for their support in organizing scientific contacts between research groups in Luxembourg and Ukraine.

Conflicts of Interest: The authors declare no conflicts of interest.

Abbreviations

The following abbreviations are used in this manuscript:

ODE   ordinary differential equation
SDE   stochastic differential equation

References

1. Kats, I.Ya. *Lyapunov Function Method in Problems of Stability and Stabilization of Random-Structure Systems*; Izd. Uralsk. Gosakademii Putei Soobshcheniya: Yekaterinburg, Russia, 1998. (In Russian)
2. Tsarkov, Y.F.; Yasinsky, V.K.; Malyk, I.V. Stability in impulsive systems with Markov perturbations in averaging scheme. 2. Averaging principle for impulsive Markov systems and stability analysis based on averaged equations. *Cybern. Syst. Anal.* **2011**, *47*, 44–54. [CrossRef]
3. Oksendal, B. *Stochastic Differential Equations*; Springer: New York, NY, USA, 2013.
4. Doob, J.L. *Stochastic Processes*; Wiley: New York, NY, USA, 1953.
5. Jacod, J.; Shiryaev, A.N. *Limit Theorems for Stochastic Processes. Vols. 1 and 2*; Fizmatlit: Moscow, Russia, 1994. (In Russian)
6. Lukashiv, T.O.; Yurchenko, I.V.; Yasinskii, V.K. Lyapunov function method for investigation of stability of stochastic Ito random-structure systems with impulse Markov switchings. I. General theorems on the stability of stochastic impulse systems. *Cybern. Syst. Anal.* **2009**, *45*, 281–290.
7. Dynkin, E.B. *Markov Processes*; Academic Press: New York, NY, USA, 1965.
8. Korolyuk, V.S.; Tsarkov, E.F.; Yasinskii, V.K. *Probability, Statistics, and Random Processes. Theory and Computer Practice, Vol. 3, Random Processes. Theory and Computer Practice*; Zoloti Lytavry: Chernivtsi, Ukraine, 2009. (In Ukrainian)
9. Protter, P.E. *Stochastic Integration and Differential Equations*, 2nd ed.; Springer: New York, NY, USA, 2004.
10. Koroliouk, V.S.; Samoilenko, I.V. Asymptotic expansion of a functional constructed from a semi-Markov random evolution in the scheme of diffusion approximation. *Theory Probab. Math. Stat.* **2018**, *96*, 83–100. [CrossRef]
11. Tsarkov, Y.F.; Yasinsky, V.K.; Malyk, I.V. Stability in impulsive systems with Markov perturbations in averaging scheme. I. Averaging principle for impulsive Markov systems. *Cybern. Syst. Anal.* **2010**, *46*, 975–985. [CrossRef]

12. Koroliuk, V.S.; Limnios, N. *Stochastic Systems in Merging Phase Space*; World Scientific Publishing Company: Singapore, 2005.
13. Lukashiv, T.O.; Malyk, I.V. Stability of controlled stochastic dynamic systems of random structure with Markov switches and Poisson perturbations. *Bukovinian Math. J.* **2022**, *10*, 85–99. [CrossRef]
14. Andreeva, E.A.; Kolmanovskii V.B.; Shaikhet L.E. *Control of Hereditary Systems*; Nauka: Moskow, Russia, 1992. (In Russian)
15. Vadivel, R.; Ali, M. S.; Alzahranib, F. Robust H_∞ synchronization of Markov jump stochastic uncertain neural networks with decentralized event-triggered mechanism. *Chin. J. Phys.* **2019**, *60*, 68–87. [CrossRef]
16. Vadivel, R.; Hammachukiattikul, P.; Zhu, Q.; Gunasekaran, N. Event-triggered synchronization for stochastic delayed neural networks: Passivity and passification case . *Asian J. Control.* **2022**. [CrossRef]
17. Hasminsky, R.Z. *Stability of Systems of Differential Equations under Random Parameter Perturbations*; Nauka: Moscow, Russia, 1969. (In Russian)
18. Skorokhod, A.V. *Asymptotic Methods in the Theory of Stochastic Differential Equations*; Naukova Dumka: Kyiv, Ukraine, 1987. (In Russian).
19. Sverdan, M.L.; Tsar'kov, E.F. *Stability of Stochastic Impulse Systems*; RTU: Riga, Latvia, 1994. (In Russian)
20. Kloeden, P.E.; Platen, E. *Numerical Solution of Stochastic Differential Equations*; Springer: Berlin, Germany, 1992.
21. Lukashiv, T. One Form of Lyapunov Operator for Stochastic Dynamic System with Markov Parameters. *J. Math.* **2016**, *2016*, 1694935. [CrossRef]
22. Arioli, G.; Gazzola, F. A new mathematical explanation of what triggered the catastrophic torsional mode of the Tacoma Narrows Bridge. *Appl. Math. Model.* **2015**, *39*, 901–912. [CrossRef]

Disclaimer/Publisher's Note: The statements, opinions and data contained in all publications are solely those of the individual author(s) and contributor(s) and not of MDPI and/or the editor(s). MDPI and/or the editor(s) disclaim responsibility for any injury to people or property resulting from any ideas, methods, instructions or products referred to in the content.

Article

Approximation of the Statistical Characteristics of Piecewise Linear Systems with Asymmetric Damping and Stiffness under Stationary Random Excitation

Tudor Sireteanu [1], Ana-Maria Mitu [1,*], Ovidiu Solomon [1,2] and Marius Giuclea [1,2]

1 Institute of Solid Mechanics, Romanian Academy, 15 Constantin Mille, RO-010141 Bucharest, Romania
2 Department of Applied Mathematics, Bucharest University of Economic Studies, 6 Romana Square, RO-010374 Bucharest, Romania
* Correspondence: anamaria.mitu@imsar.ro

Abstract: In this paper, the dynamic response of piecewise linear systems with asymmetric damping and stiffness for random excitation is studied. In order to approximate the statistical characteristics for each significant output of piecewise linear system, a method based on transmissibility factors is applied. A stochastic linear system with the same transmissibility factor is attached, and the statistical parameters of the studied output corresponding to random excitation having rational spectral densities are determined by solving the associated Lyapunov equation. Using the attached linear systems for root mean square and for standard deviation of displacement, the shift of the sprung mass average position in a dynamic regime, due to damping or stiffness asymmetry, can be predicted with a good accuracy for stationary random input. The obtained results are compared with those determined by the Gaussian equivalent linearization method and by the numerical integration of asymmetric piecewise linear system equations. It is shown that the piecewise linear systems with asymmetrical damping and stiffness characteristics can provide a better vibration isolation (lower force transmissibility) than the linear system.

Keywords: asymmetric piecewise linear systems; transmissibility factors; Lyapunov equation

MSC: 60H35

1. Introduction

The limitations of vibration isolation systems with linear passive damping and stiffness characteristics are well known. A high damping ratio is effective in the resonance frequency range but increases the dynamic response of isolation system for higher frequencies. On the other hand, lower damping ratios could be effective above the resonance range with the cost of an unacceptable increase in the dynamic response within the resonance range. Piecewise linear (PWL) systems with asymmetric damping and stiffness characteristics can provide a lower transmissibility factor over the entire frequency range than linear systems.

Many approximate methods have been proposed for studying the vibration of systems with PWL stiffness and damping characteristics [1–6]. The dynamic behavior of PWL systems was studied in [7–9]. A piecewise linear aeroelastic system with and without a tuned vibration absorber was investigated [10]. The experimental results show that the introduction of the piecewise linear stiffness and damping significantly decreases the response amplitude at the primary resonance [11]. The beneficial effect for ride comfort of road vehicles, mainly due to the suspension damping asymmetry, which introduces a downward shift in the mean position of the sprung mass in addition to the vibratory response, has been studied [12–18]. The classical dynamics of the systems with both the statistically uncertain piecewise constant drift and diffusion were extended in [19]. Asymmetric damping forces induce the equilibrium position of the isolated body to shift downward [20]. A nonlinear interval optimization of asymmetric damper parameters for a racing car is proposed to improve road holding [21].

Various linearization methods have been developed for the analysis of nonlinear systems [22–24]. A very useful property of piecewise linear systems is the independence of their transmissibility factors with respect to the excitation amplitude [25,26]. These factors could be defined as the ratios of root mean square (rms) or standard deviation (std) of output for the same parameters of the harmonic input within the frequency range of practical interest. Therefore, a first order linear differential system can be attached to the considered piecewise linear system so that the first vector component of the attached system has the same transmissibility factor as the chosen output of the nonlinear system. This approach was employed to obtain approximate solutions of PWL systems with piecewise-linear damping with variable friction for application to semi-active control of vibration [23] and for the comparison of the on–off control strategies of vehicle suspensions [24].

In the present work, the Lyapunov equation for attached linear systems is used to approximate the first and second order statistical moments of any significant output of PWL systems with passive asymmetric damping and stiffness. In classical linearization methods, the nonlinear system is replaced by a single equivalent linear system. In the framework of the method used in the present paper, a set of attached linear systems is employed to approximate the statistical characteristics of the PWL system output. Using the attached linear systems for rms and std displacement, the shift of sprung mass average position in dynamic regime, due to damping or stiffness asymmetry, can be predicted with a good accuracy for stationary random input, as confirmed by the numerical results.

In Section 2, the asymmetrical piecewise characteristics are described. In Section 3, the mathematical model of single degree of freedom (SDOF) vibration isolation system with PWL characteristics is presented. In Section 4, the effect of asymmetry of damping and restoring characteristics on the dynamic behavior of piecewise linear systems under stationary random excitation is illustrated. In Section 5, the Gaussian equivalent linearization method for PWL systems is applied. In Section 6, the results obtained by the proposed approach are compared with those given by the Gaussian equivalent linearization method. In order to estimate the statistical characteristics for the output of asymmetric PWL systems, the corresponding attached linear systems are determined in Section 7. In the last section, the statistical characteristics of the simulated output with those calculated by solving Lyapunov equation for corresponding attached linear system are compared. The relative errors show the efficiency and applicability of this method for PWL systems.

2. Modeling the Asymmetrical Piecewise Characteristics

Figure 1 shows the plots of asymmetrical PWL stiffness in Figure 1a and damping characteristics in Figure 1b, given by

$$F_s(x) = \begin{cases} k_1 x, & x \leq 0 \\ k_2 x, & x > 0 \end{cases}, \quad F_d(\dot{x}) = \begin{cases} c_1 \dot{x}, & \dot{x} \leq 0 \\ c_2 \dot{x}, & \dot{x} > 0 \end{cases} \tag{1}$$

where $k_1, k_2 \geq 0$ are the stiffness coefficients and $c_1, c_2 \geq 0$ are the damping coefficients and x is the travel of vibration isolation system.

Total hysteretic force developed by vibration isolation system for imposed harmonic motion $x(t) = X \sin \omega t$, where $\omega = 2\pi f$, f is the frequency and X is the amplitude, is $F_h(x, \dot{x}) = F_s(x) + F_d(\dot{x})$. The time histories of hysteretic force $F_h(x, \dot{x})$, stiffness force $F_s(x)$ and damping force $F_d(\dot{x})$ are illustrated in Figure 2, for parameters values shown in Table 1.

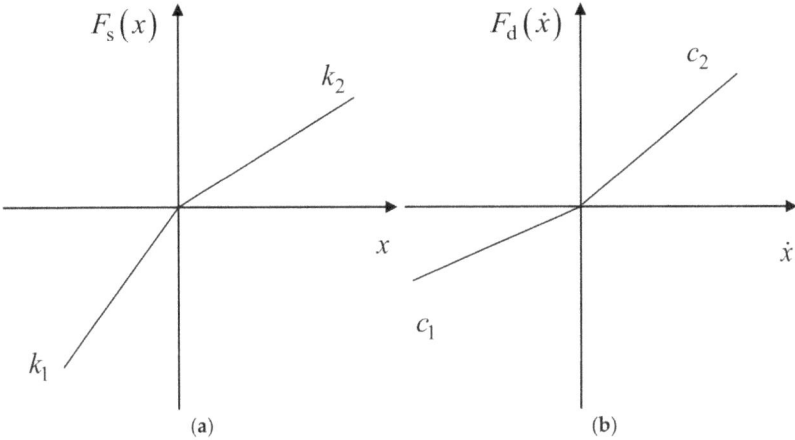

Figure 1. Asymmetrical PWL: (**a**) stiffness characteristics; (**b**) damping characteristics.

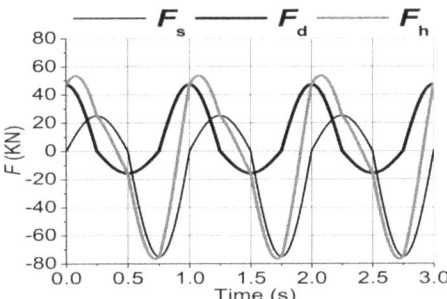

Figure 2. Time histories of forces developed by a vibration isolation system with asymmetric PWL.

Table 1. Values of parameters for hysteretic force.

k_1 [KN/m]	k_2 [KN/m]	c_1 [KNs/m]	c_2 [KNs/m]	X [m]	f [Hz]
1500	500	50	150	0.05	1

The loops portraying the variation of damping force F_d and total hysteretic force F_h versus the imposed displacement x are shown in Figure 3.

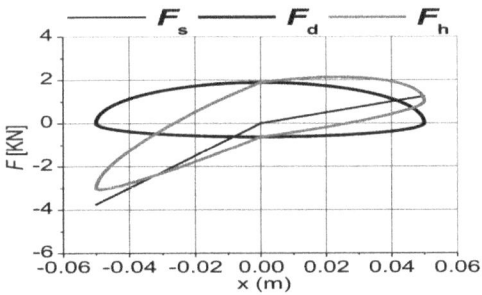

Figure 3. The stiffness characteristic and hysteresis loops portraying the variation of damping force.

The enclosed area by these loops represents E_d, the energy dissipated per cycle:

$$E_d = \int_0^{\frac{2\pi}{\omega}} F_d(\dot{x})\dot{x}dt = 0.5\pi\omega X^2(c_1+c_2) \qquad (2)$$

Figure 4 depicts the schematic model of a device with asymmetrical damping and stiffness characteristics.

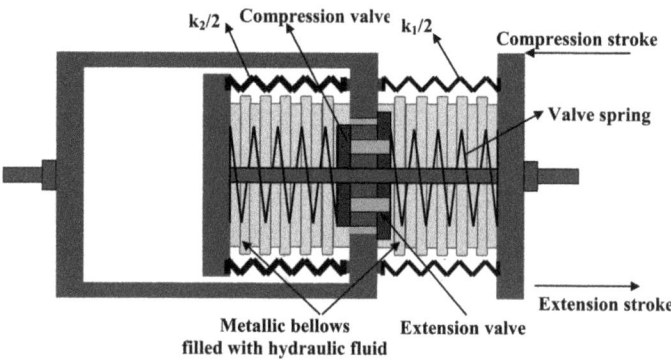

Figure 4. Design principle of a device with PWL asymmetric damping and stiffness characteristics.

The metallic bellows, filled with hydraulic fluid, are welded at both ends, and, therefore, the fluid damper is leak proof. The asymmetry of damping force is controlled by the openings of extension and compression valves. The dimensions of valve openings and fluid viscosity must be assessed such that to have laminar flow within the range of damper operating conditions. Since the bellows geometry is identical, there is no need for any volume compensation system. The suspension springs with different stiffness are in the unloaded condition (free length) when the isolation system is in the equilibrium position. Each of them has only one end fixed on the device structure. Therefore, they work only as compression springs for both extension and compression strokes. The bellows longitudinal stiffness, being much smaller than the stiffness of springs, is neglected.

3. Mathematical Model of SDOF Vibration Isolation System with PWL Characteristics

Vibration isolation systems are widely used to reduce the dynamic forces transmitted from the base input to sprung mass (Figure 5) or from the sprung mass to the system base (Figure 6).

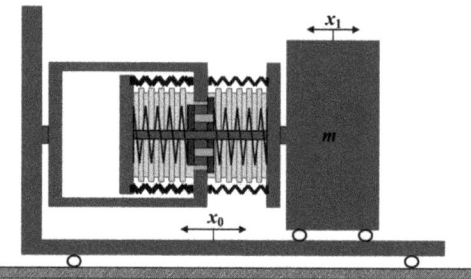

Figure 5. PWL system for mitigation the dynamic forces transmitted from the base input to the sprung mass.

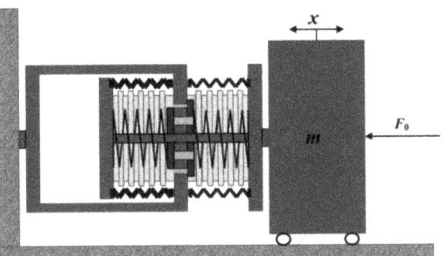

Figure 6. PWL system for mitigation the dynamic forces transmitted from the sprung mass to the system base.

The equation of motion for both vibration isolation systems, shown in Figures 5 and 6, can be written as:

$$m\ddot{x} + F_d(\dot{x}) + F_s(x) = P_0(t) \qquad (3)$$

where $x = x_1 - x_0$ is the relative displacement of sprung mass, $P_0(t) = -m\ddot{x}_0$ is the input of system shown in Figure 5, x_1 is the absolute displacement and x_0 is the base displacement. For the system depicted in Figure 6, x is the absolute displacement of sprung mass, relative to its static equilibrium position, and $P_0(t) = F_0(t)$ is the force applied to the sprung mass. In both cases, x is the stroke (travel) of sprung mass suspension and will be called displacement (disp). The main output of interest for vibration isolation systems are the absolute accelerations of sprung mass $\ddot{x}_1$, for system shown in Figure 5, and $\ddot{x}$, for system shown in Figure 6. The absolute acceleration is a measure for mitigation of dynamic forces transmitted through the sprung mass suspension. In the rest of the paper it will be called acceleration and abbreviated as acc. The analytic expressions of asymmetric damping and elastic characteristics $F_d(\dot{x})$ and $F_s(x)$ can be written as

$$\begin{aligned} F_d(\dot{x}) &= 0.5\left[c_1(1-\operatorname{sgn}\dot{x}) + c_2(1+\operatorname{sgn}\dot{x})\right]\dot{x}, \\ F_s(x) &= 0.5\left[k_1(1-\operatorname{sgn}x) + k_2(1+\operatorname{sgn}x)\right]x. \end{aligned} \qquad (4)$$

Introducing the notations

$$\begin{aligned} &\omega_1 = 2\pi f_1 = \sqrt{\tfrac{k_1}{m}},\; \omega_2 = 2\pi f_2 = \sqrt{\tfrac{k_2}{m}},\; \zeta_1 = \tfrac{c_1}{2\omega_1 m},\; \zeta_2 = \tfrac{c_2}{2\omega_2 m} \\ &\beta = \tfrac{c_2}{c_1} = \tfrac{\zeta_2 f_2}{\zeta_1 f_1},\; \gamma = \sqrt{\tfrac{k_2}{k_1}} = \tfrac{f_2}{f_1} \\ &f_d(\dot{x}) = \tfrac{F_d(\dot{x})}{m},\; f_s(x) = \tfrac{F_s(x)}{m} \text{ and } p_0(t) = \tfrac{P_0(t)}{m}, \end{aligned} \qquad (5)$$

the equation of motion (3) becomes

$$\ddot{x} + f_d(\dot{x}) + f_s(x) = p_0(t) \qquad (6)$$

where

$$\begin{aligned} f_d(\dot{x}) &= \zeta_1\omega_1\left[(\beta+1)\dot{x} + (\beta-1)|\dot{x}|\right], \\ f_s(x) &= 0.5\omega_1^2\left[(\gamma^2+1)x + (\gamma^2-1)|x|\right]. \end{aligned} \qquad (7)$$

From (2) and (5), one can see that asymmetry parameter β is the ratio of dissipated energy per rebound $(E_{d2} = 0.5\pi\omega X^2 c_2)$ and bound $(E_{d1} = 0.5\pi\omega X^2 c_1)$ strokes for an imposed harmonic motion.

4. The Effect of Asymmetry of Damping and Restoring Characteristics on the Dynamic Behavior of Piecewise Linear Systems under Stationary Random Excitation

In general, the asymmetry of damping or stiffness characteristics leads to a drift of sprung mass average position in dynamic regime, different from its static equilibrium position. Nevertheless, by a suitable combination of the asymmetry parameters β and γ, one can obtain outputs of PWL systems with almost no drift.

Suppose that $p_0(t)$ is a stationary Gaussian random process with zero mean and standard deviation σ_0. If $x(t)$ is the steady state stationary solution of Equation (6), with constant mean value $m_x = E[x]$ then $E[\ddot{x}] = E[\dot{x}] = 0$. Therefore, by applying the average operator corresponding to joint distribution of the output of Equation (6), m_x is obtained as follows:

$$m_x = -\frac{m_{|x|}}{\gamma^2 + 1}\left[\left(\gamma^2 - 1\right) + 2(\beta - 1)\zeta_1 \frac{m_{|\dot{x}|}}{\omega_1 m_{|x|}}\right] \tag{8}$$

where

$$m_{|x|} = E[|x|] \text{ and } m_{|\dot{x}|} = E[|\dot{x}|] \tag{9}$$

The relation (8) shows that $m_x = 0$ if $\gamma = 1$, $\beta = 1$; $m_x < 0$ if $\gamma > 1$, $\beta > 1$ and $m_x > 0$ if $\gamma < 1$, $\beta < 1$. It is worth noting that by assuming $m_{|\dot{x}|}/\omega_1 m_{|x|} \approx 1$, for all case studies considered in this work (including $\gamma > 1$, $\beta < 1$ or $\gamma < 1$, $\beta > 1$), the sign of m_x could be predicted by determining the sign of expression $S(\gamma, \beta, \zeta_1) = -[(\gamma^2 - 1) + 2(\beta - 1)\zeta_1]$, without being necessary the numerical simulation values from (9).

5. Gaussian Equivalent Linearization Method of PWL Systems

The Gaussian equivalent linear system (LinEq) of system (6), where $p_0(t)$ is a stationary Gaussian process, $E[p_0(t)] = 0$ and $E[p_0^2(t)] = \sigma_0^2$ is written as

$$\ddot{x} + 2\zeta_e \omega_e \dot{x} + \omega_e^2 x = p_0(t) \tag{10}$$

The joint probability density function of the Gaussian stationary solution of equivalent linear system is

$$g(x, \dot{x}) = g_1(x)g_2(\dot{x})$$
$$g_1(x) = \frac{1}{\sqrt{2\pi}\sigma_x}\exp\left[-\frac{x^2}{2\sigma_x^2}\right], g_2(\dot{x}) = \frac{1}{\sqrt{2\pi}\sigma_{\dot{x}}}\exp\left[-\frac{\dot{x}^2}{2\sigma_{\dot{x}}^2}\right], \tag{11}$$

where $\sigma_x = \sigma_x(\omega_e, \zeta_e)$ and $\sigma_{\dot{x}} = \sigma_{\dot{x}}(\omega_e, \zeta_e)$ are the standard deviations for the solution of Equation (10).

The variance of the acceleration $\ddot{x}_1 = 2\zeta_e \omega_e \dot{x} + \omega_e^2 x$ of the equivalent linear system is

$$\sigma_{\ddot{x}_1}^2 = E[\ddot{x}_1^2] = 4\zeta_e^2 \omega_e^2 E[\dot{x}^2] + \omega_e^4 E[x^2] = \omega_e^2\left[4\zeta_e^2 \sigma_{\dot{x}}^2 + \omega_e^2 \sigma_x^2\right] \tag{12}$$

Applying the linearization criteria,

$$\varepsilon_e(\omega_e) = E\left[(f_s(x) - \omega_e^2 x)^2\right] = \min, \quad \frac{\partial \varepsilon_e(\omega_e)}{\partial \omega_e} = 0$$
$$\varepsilon_d(\zeta_e, \omega_e) = E\left[(f_d(\dot{x}) - 2\zeta_e \omega_e \dot{x})^2\right] = \min, \quad \frac{\partial \varepsilon_d(\zeta_e, \omega_e)}{\partial \zeta_e} = 0 \tag{13}$$

the linear equivalent stiffness and damping coefficients are obtained using (6), (11) and (13):

$$\omega_e^2 = \frac{E[x f_s(x)]}{E[x^2]} = \frac{\omega_1^2 + \omega_2^2}{2} = \frac{\omega_1^2(1 + \gamma^2)}{2},$$
$$\zeta_e = \frac{E[\dot{x} f_d(\dot{x})]}{2\omega_e E[\dot{x}^2]} = \frac{\zeta_1 \omega_1 + \zeta_2 \omega_2}{2\omega_e} = \frac{\zeta_1 \omega_1 (1 + \beta)}{2\omega_e}. \tag{14}$$

Using (14) one can write

$$f_e = f_1 \sqrt{\frac{1 + \gamma^2}{2}}, \quad \zeta_e = \frac{\zeta_1(1 + \beta)}{\sqrt{2(1 + \gamma^2)}}, \quad f_e = \omega_e/2\pi, \quad f_1 = \omega_1/2\pi \tag{15}$$

In order to highlight the advantage of using the vibration isolation systems with asymmetric PWL characteristics, the obtained results are compared with those of optimal linear equivalent system.

For given values of linear equivalent system ζ_e, f_e and chosen values of asymmetry parameters γ, β, relations (15) yield:

$$f_1 = f_e\sqrt{\frac{2}{1+\gamma^2}},\ f_2 = \gamma f_1,\ \zeta_1 = \frac{\zeta_e\sqrt{2(1+\gamma^2)}}{1+\beta}\ \text{and}\ \zeta_2 = \frac{\beta}{\gamma}\zeta_1 \quad (16)$$

From (16) one can obtain the balance equation between the energy dissipated by PWL asymmetric system and its linear equivalent system per cycle for same imposed harmonic motion:

$$\zeta_1 f_1 + \zeta_2 f_2 = 2 f_e \zeta_e \quad (17)$$

As one can see from previous relations, there are an infinite number of PWL asymmetric systems having same linear equivalent system.

Following [27], the standard deviation of the stationary steady state acceleration of sprung mass for stochastic linear system (10) with Gaussian white noise excitation $p_0(t)$ and constant spectral density S_0 is

$$\sigma_{\ddot{x}_1 e} = \sqrt{2S_0 \int_0^\infty A^2_{\ddot{x}_1 e}(\omega)\, d\omega} = \sqrt{\frac{\pi \omega_e S_0(1 + 4\zeta_e^2)}{2\zeta_e}}, \quad (18)$$

where $A_{\ddot{x}_1 e}(\omega)$ is the acceleration transmissibility factor of linear equivalent system:

$$A_{\ddot{x}_1 e}(\omega) = \sqrt{\frac{4\zeta_e^2 \omega_e^2 \omega^2 + \omega_e^4}{\omega^4 + 2(2\zeta_e^2 - 1)\omega_e^2 \omega^2 + \omega_e^4}} \quad (19)$$

The optimum value of damping ratio ζ_e, which minimizes the std value of sprung mass acceleration is $\zeta_e = 0.5$, and its minimum value is $\sigma_{\ddot{x}_1 \min} = \sqrt{2\pi\omega_e S_0}$. Taking $S_0 = 1\ \text{m}^2\text{s}^{-3}$ and $\omega_e = 2\pi\ \text{rad/s}$, the optimum std value of acceleration is $\sigma_{\ddot{x}_1 \min} \cong 6.28\ \text{ms}^{-2}$. For numerical integration, the input is a limited bandwidth white noise, and std value of acceleration is calculated as

$$\sigma_{\ddot{x}_1 e} \cong \sqrt{2\int_{\omega_{\min}}^{\omega_{\max}} A^2_{\ddot{x}_1 e}(\omega;\zeta_e,\omega_e)\, d\omega} \cong 6.21\ \text{ms}^{-2}, \quad (20)$$

where $0.2 \le \omega \le 128$ and ω is measured in rad/s, which is a good approximation of optimum value $\sigma_{\ddot{x}_1 \min}$, calculated over the whole range of angular frequency $[0, \infty)$. The results obtained by the proposed approach will be compared with those obtained by the Gaussian equivalent linearization method.

6. The Response of PWL Systems to Stationary Gaussian Random Input with Rational Spectral Density (Shape Filtered White Noise)

According to [28], the covariance function and spectral density of stationary Gaussian random input $p_0(t)$ are

$$\begin{aligned}C_0(\tau) &= \sigma_0^2 e^{-a|\tau|}\cos b\tau,\ a > 0,\ b \ge 0,\\ S_0(\omega) &= \frac{\sigma_0^2}{\pi}\frac{a(\omega^2+a^2+b^2)}{\omega^4+2(a^2-b^2)\omega^2+(a^2+b^2)^2},\end{aligned} \quad (21)$$

where $\sigma_0^2 = \int_{-\infty}^{\infty} S_0(\omega)d\omega = 2\int_0^{\infty} S_0(\omega)d\omega$. The above expression of $S_0(\omega)$ can be viewed as the spectral density of the Gaussian stationary random process $p_0(t)$, obtained as the output of a second order shape filter to a stationary Gaussian white noise process $z(t)$ with $E[z(t)] = 0$, $E[z(t)z(t+\tau)] = 2\pi S_0 \delta(\tau)$, where $\delta(\tau)$ is the Dirac delta function. In order to determine the equations of the second order shape filter, the spectral density (21) is written under the form

$$S_0(\omega) = \frac{|P(i\omega)|^2}{|Q(i\omega)|^2} = \frac{|b_0(i\omega) + b_1|^2}{\left|a_0(i\omega)^2 + a_1(i\omega) + a_2\right|^2}, \quad (22)$$

where $b_0 = \sigma_0\sqrt{\frac{a}{\pi}}$, $b_1 = \sigma_0\sqrt{\frac{a(a^2+b^2)}{\pi}}$, $a_0 = 1$, $a_1 = 2a$, $a_2 = a^2 + b^2$.

The output $u_1(t)$ of the following first order differential system with the white noise excitation $z(t)$ is a Gaussian stationary random process with spectral density $S_0(\omega)$:

$$\dot{\mathbf{u}} = \mathbf{A}\mathbf{u} + \mathbf{g}z, \quad (23)$$

where

$$\mathbf{A} = \begin{bmatrix} 0 & 1 \\ -a_2 & -a_1 \end{bmatrix}, \quad \mathbf{u} = \begin{bmatrix} u_1 \\ u_2 \end{bmatrix}, \quad \mathbf{g} = \begin{bmatrix} g_1 \\ g_2 \end{bmatrix} \quad (24)$$

$g_1 = \sigma_0\sqrt{\frac{a}{\pi}}$, $g_2 = \sigma_0\sqrt{\frac{a}{\pi}}\left(\sqrt{a^2+b^2} - 2a\right)$ and $p_0(t) = u_1(t)$.

In order to study the behavior of asymmetric PWL systems excited by stationary random input with rational spectral density, a linear system of first order stochastic equations is assessed such as the first component of its solution vector has the same transmissibility factor as the chosen output of the considered piecewise linear system [23]. The statistical parameters of obtained stochastic differential equations are determined by solving the associated Lyapunov equation.

Since the mean value of PWL acceleration response system has zero mean, the transmissibility factors corresponding to standard deviation and root mean square values are identical.

The discrete values of transmissibility factor corresponding to standard deviation of acceleration $\ddot{x}_1(t)$ is defined as:

$$\tilde{A}_{\ddot{x}_1}(\omega_i) = \frac{\sigma_{\ddot{x}_1}(\omega_i)}{\sigma_{p_{0i}}} = \frac{\sqrt{2}\,\sigma_{\ddot{x}_1}(\omega_i)}{P_0}, \quad i = \overline{1,N} \quad (25)$$

These values are obtained by numerical integration of Equation (6), using Matlab Simulink, for harmonic inputs with constant amplitude and different frequencies in the twelfth octave band:

$$p_{0i}(t) = P_0 \sin \omega_i t, \quad \omega_i = 2\pi f_i, \quad f_1 = 0.3\,\text{Hz}, f_N = 20.05\,\text{Hz}, \quad f_i = 2^{\frac{i-1}{12}} f_1, \quad i = \overline{1,N} \quad (26)$$

where $P_0 = 1\,\text{m/s}^2$, $N = \left[\frac{\log(f_N/f_1)}{\log(f_2/f_1)}\right] + 2 = 114$.

It should be mentioned that the transmissibility factors of PWL systems, with asymmetry type (affine) [29], considered in this paper, do not depend on the amplitude P_0 of the applied harmonic input with variable frequency, as long as they are computed for the stationary regime. The numerical values $\tilde{A}_{\ddot{x}_1}(\omega_i)$, $i = \overline{1,N}$, can be fitted using the Least Squares Method, by analytical expressions having the form

$$A_{\ddot{x}_1}(\omega) = \sqrt{\frac{P_1\omega^2 + P_2}{\omega^4 + Q_1\omega^2 + Q_2}}. \quad (27)$$

The transmissibility factor $A_{\ddot{x}_1}(\omega)$ is written as:

$$A_{\ddot{x}_1}(\omega) = \left|\frac{b_0(i\omega) + b_1}{(i\omega)^2 + a_1(i\omega) + a_2}\right| = \sqrt{\frac{b_0^2\omega^2 + b_1^2}{\omega^4 + (a_1^2 - 2a_2)\omega^2 + a_2^2}} \quad (28)$$

From relations (27) and (28), the following nonlinear algebraic systems of equations for unknown coefficients b_0, b_1, a_1, a_2, are obtained

$$\begin{cases} b_0^2 = P_1 \\ b_1^2 = P_2 \end{cases}, \quad \begin{cases} a_1^2 - 2a_2 = Q_1 \\ a_2^2 = Q_2 \end{cases} \tag{29}$$

The attached linear system corresponding to transmissibility factor (28) can be written as

$$\dot{\mathbf{u}} = \mathbf{A}\mathbf{u} + \mathbf{c}p_0, \tag{30}$$

where

$$\mathbf{A} = \begin{bmatrix} 0 & 1 \\ -a_2 & -a_1 \end{bmatrix}, \quad \mathbf{u} = \begin{bmatrix} u_1 \\ u_2 \end{bmatrix}, \quad \mathbf{c} = \begin{bmatrix} c_1 \\ c_2 \end{bmatrix}, \quad \begin{cases} c_1 = b_0 \\ c_2 = b_1 - a_1 c_1 \end{cases} \tag{31}$$

The transmissibility factor $A_{\ddot{x}_1}(\omega) \cong A_{\sigma_{u_1}}(\omega) = \sqrt{2}\sigma_{u_1}/P_0$, where u_1 is the first component of the solution vector $\mathbf{u}$. The system (30) is asymptotically stable if $a_1, a_2 > 0$. Therefore, from the sets of real solutions of (29), one must select only the solutions that fulfill these conditions.

In what follows, the study is carried out for several asymmetric PWL systems for which the stochastic equivalent linear system is the optimal one. The parameters of PWL systems, given in Table 2, were obtained by using relations (16).

Table 2. The parameters of PWL systems.

Case	ζ_1	f_1 [Hz]	γ	β	ζ_2	f_2 [Hz]
1	0.05	0.25	5.57	79	0.71	1.39
2	0.1	0.5	2.65	19	0.72	1.33
3	0.1	0.7	1.76	13.31	0.76	1.23
4	0.2	0.4	3.39	11.5	0.68	1.36
5	0.3	0.6	2.13	4.55	0.64	1.28
6	0.7	1.1	0.81	0.3	0.26	0.89

In Figure 7, the transmissibility factor $\tilde{A}_{\ddot{x}_1}(\omega_i)$ obtained by numerical integration for the asymmetric PWL systems from Table 2 is compared with transmissibility factor of their stochastic equivalent linear system ($\zeta_1 = \zeta_2 = 0.5$, $\gamma = \beta = 1$, $f_1 = f_2 = 1$ Hz).

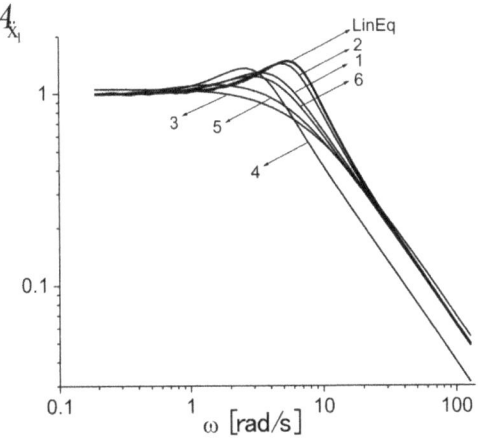

Figure 7. The transmissibility factors for linear and asymmetric PWL systems.

Table 3 presents the standard deviation values of the acceleration obtained by using a similar relation to (20), for the transmissibility factors of asymmetric PWL systems shown in Figure 7.

Table 3. The transmissibility factors of asymmetric PWL systems.

Case	ζ_1	f_1 [Hz]	ζ_2	f_2 [Hz]	$\sigma_{\ddot{x}_1}$ [m/s^2]
1	0.05	0.25	0.71	1.39	4.52
2	0.1	0.5	0.72	1.33	4.98
3	0.1	0.7	0.76	1.23	5.35
4	0.2	0.4	0.68	1.36	4.71
5	0.3	0.6	0.64	1.28	5.12
6	0.7	1.1	0.26	0.89	5.97

The above results show that the piecewise linear systems with asymmetrical damping and stiffness characteristics can provide a better vibration isolation (lower force transmissibility) than the optimum equivalent linear system ($\sigma_{\ddot{x}_1} = 6.21$ [m/s^2]).

7. Attached Linear System for Different Outputs of PWL Systems Excited by a Second Order Shape Filtered White Noise

In order to estimate the statistical characteristics for the output of asymmetric PWL systems, the corresponding attached linear systems will be determined in the next sections. The stochastic equations of attached linear system for the piecewise linear system (6), with shape filtered white noise excitation, is obtained by combining Equations (23) and (30):

$$\dot{\mathbf{u}} = \mathbf{A}\mathbf{u} + \mathbf{g}z, \tag{32}$$

where

$$\mathbf{A} = \begin{bmatrix} 0 & 1 & c_1 & 0 \\ -a_2 & -a_1 & c_2 & 0 \\ 0 & 0 & 0 & 1 \\ 0 & 0 & -a_4 & -a_3 \end{bmatrix}, \quad \mathbf{u} = \begin{bmatrix} u_1 \\ u_2 \\ u_3 \\ u_4 \end{bmatrix}, \quad \mathbf{g} = \begin{bmatrix} 0 \\ 0 \\ g_1 \\ g_2 \end{bmatrix} \tag{33}$$

$$u_1(t) = \ddot{x}_1(t), \ u_3(t) = p_0(t)$$
$$a_3 = 2a, \ a_4 = a^2 + b^2, g_1 = \sigma_0\sqrt{\tfrac{a}{\pi}}, \ g_2 = \sigma_0\sqrt{\tfrac{a}{\pi}}\left(\sqrt{a^2+b^2} - 2a\right)$$

The covariance matrix $\mathbf{C} = (c_{ij})$, $c_{ij} = c_{ji} = \lim_{t\to\infty} E[u_i(t)u_j(t)]$, $i,j = \overline{1,4}$ of the steady state stationary solution of stochastic linear system (32) satisfies [30] the Lyapunov Equation:

$$\mathbf{AC} + \mathbf{CA}^T + 2\pi S_0 \mathbf{g}\mathbf{g}^T = 0 \tag{34}$$

The standard deviation of the acceleration is estimated by $\sigma_{\ddot{x}_1} \cong \sigma_{u_1}$ where $\sigma_{u_1} = \sqrt{c_{11}}$. The values of $\sigma_{\ddot{x}_1}$ obtained by using Lyapunov equation will be compared with those determined for linear equivalent system (10) where $\zeta_e = 0.5$ and $\omega_e = 2\pi$ rad/s.

The values of transmissibility factors $\tilde{A}_{\text{xrms}}(\omega_i) = \frac{\Psi_x(\omega_i)}{\sigma_{P_{0i}}} = \frac{\sqrt{2}\Psi_x(\omega_i)}{P_0}$, $i = \overline{1,N}$, and $\tilde{A}_{\text{xstd}}(\omega_i) = \frac{\sigma_x(\omega_i)}{\sigma_{P_{0i}}} = \frac{\sqrt{2}\sigma_x(\omega_i)}{P_0}$, $i = \overline{1,N}$ corresponding to rms Ψ_x and std σ_x of relative displacement $x(t)$ are obtained by numerical integrations. These values can be approximated by rational expressions having the form

$$A_x(\omega) = \sqrt{\frac{P_1\omega^4 + P_2\omega^2 + P_3}{\omega^6 + Q_1\omega^4 + Q_2\omega^2 + Q_3}} \tag{35}$$

The transmissibility factor is written as

$$A_x(\omega) = \left| \frac{b_0(i\omega)^2 + b_1(i\omega) + b_2}{(i\omega)^3 + a_1(i\omega)^2 + a_2(i\omega) + a_3} \right| = \sqrt{\frac{b_0^2 \omega^4 + (b_1^2 - 2b_0 b_2)\omega^2 + b_2^2}{\omega^6 + (a_1^2 - 2a_2)\omega^4 + (a_2^2 - 2a_1 a_3)\omega^2 + a_3^2}} \tag{36}$$

From relations (35) and (36) one can obtain the following algebraic systems of equations for unknown coefficients $b_0, b_1, b_2, a_1, a_2, a_3$:

$$\begin{cases} b_0^2 = P_1 \\ b_1^2 - 2b_0 b_2 = P_2 \\ b_2^2 = P_3 \end{cases}, \quad \begin{cases} a_1^2 - 2a_2 = Q_1 \\ a_2^2 - 2a_1 a_3 = Q_2 \\ a_3^2 = Q_3 \end{cases} \tag{37}$$

The equations of the attached linear system having the same transmissibility factor (35) can be written as

$$\dot{\mathbf{u}} = \mathbf{A}\mathbf{u} + \mathbf{c} p_0 \tag{38}$$

where

$$\mathbf{A} = \begin{bmatrix} 0 & 1 & 0 \\ 0 & 0 & 1 \\ -a_3 & -a_2 & -a_1 \end{bmatrix}, \quad \mathbf{u} = \begin{bmatrix} u_1 \\ u_2 \\ u_3 \end{bmatrix}, \quad \mathbf{c} = \begin{bmatrix} c_1 \\ c_2 \\ c_3 \end{bmatrix}, \quad \begin{cases} c_1 = b_0 \\ c_2 = b_1 - a_1 c_1 \\ c_3 = b_2 - a_2 c_1 - a_1 c_2 \end{cases} \quad u_1(t) = x(t), \tag{39}$$

The system (38) is asymptotically stable if $a_i > 0$, for $i = 1, 2, 3$. The covariance function and spectral density of system input $p_0(t)$ are given by (21). The attached system of stochastic differential equations with white noise excitation is given by

$$\dot{\mathbf{u}} = \mathbf{A}\mathbf{u} + \mathbf{g} z \tag{40}$$

where

$$u_1(t) = x, \ u_2(t) = \dot{x}(t), \ u_4 = p_0(t), \ \mathbf{A} = \begin{bmatrix} 0 & 1 & 0 & c_1 & 0 \\ 0 & 0 & 1 & c_2 & 0 \\ -a_3 & -a_2 & -a_1 & c_3 & 0 \\ 0 & 0 & 0 & 0 & 1 \\ 0 & 0 & 0 & -a_5 & -a_4 \end{bmatrix}, \quad \mathbf{u} = \begin{bmatrix} u_1 \\ u_2 \\ u_3 \\ u_4 \\ u_5 \end{bmatrix}, \quad \mathbf{g} = \begin{bmatrix} 0 \\ 0 \\ 0 \\ g_1 \\ g_2 \end{bmatrix} \tag{41}$$

$a_4 = 2a$, $a_5 = a^2 + b^2$, $g_1 = \sigma_0 \sqrt{\frac{a}{\pi}}$, $g_2 = \sigma_0 \sqrt{\frac{a}{\pi}} \left(\sqrt{a^2 + b^2} - 2a \right)$

The rms and std values of relative displacements of PWL system, Ψ_x and σ_x, can be approximated as $\Psi_x \cong \sqrt{c_{11\,\text{rms}}}$ and $\sigma_x \cong \sqrt{c_{11\,\text{std}}}$. The values of $c_{11\,\text{rms}}$ and $c_{11\,\text{std}}$ are the first elements of covariance matrices $\mathbf{C}_{\text{rms}}(c_{ij\text{rms}})$, $\mathbf{C}_{\text{std}}(c_{ij\text{std}})$, $i, j = \overline{1, 4}$, obtained by solving the Lyapunov Equation (34), corresponding to attached linear systems for the transmissibility factors $A_{x\text{rms}}(\omega)$ and $A_{x\text{std}}(\omega)$, respectively. The mean displacement of asymmetric PWL system is approximated by

$$m_{x\text{Lyap}} \cong \sqrt{c_{11\,\text{rms}} - c_{11\,\text{std}}} \,\text{sgn}(S(\gamma, \beta, \zeta_1)) \tag{42}$$

8. Numerical Results

In this section, the statistical characteristics of simulated output are compared with those calculated by solving the Lyapunov Equation (34) for corresponding attached linear systems. The length and sampling interval of simulated filtered white noise input $p_0(t)$ were $T = 100\,\text{s}$ and $\Delta t = 0.001\,\text{s}$. The results obtained for the study cases, given in Table 2 for PWL asymmetric systems and for their linear equivalent system ($\zeta_e = 0.5$, $\omega_e = 2\pi\,\text{rad/s}$), are presented in Tables 4–6.

Table 4. The std values and relative errors for absolute accelerations.

Case	$\sigma_{\ddot{x}_1 sim}$ [m/s^2]	$\sigma_{\ddot{x}_1 Lyap}$ [m/s^2]	Relative Error (%)	$\sigma_{\ddot{x}_1 LinEq}$ [m/s^2]	Relative Error (%)
1	0.537	0.516	3.9	0.742	38
2	0.597	0.559	6.4	0.742	24
3	0.665	0.618	7.1	0.742	11
4	0.564	0.536	5	0.742	31
5	0.634	0.587	7.4	0.742	17
6	0.720	0.709	1.5	0.742	3

Table 5. The rms values and relative errors for relative displacements.

Case	rms$_{xsim}$ [m]	rms$_{xLyap}$ [m]	Relative Error (%)	rms$_{LinEq}$ [m]	Relative Error (%)
1	0.181	0.185	0.022	0.013	0.928
2	0.0488	0.048	0.016	0.013	0.737
3	0.0277	0.026	0.061	0.013	0.535
4	0.0658	0.067	0.018	0.013	0.804
5	0.0285	0.028	0.018	0.013	0.546
6	0.0174	0.017	0.023	0.013	0.257

Table 6. The mean values and relative errors for relative displacements.

Case	m_{xsim} [m]	c_{11rms} [m^2]	c_{11std} [m^2]	m_{xLyap} [m]	Relative Error (%)	m_x [m]
1	−0.167	0.0343	0.0019	−0.18	7.8	−0.168
2	−0.039	0.0023	0.0005	−0.042	7.7	−0.04
3	−0.02	0.0007	0.0002	−0.022	10	−0.02
4	−0.055	0.0045	0.0007	−0.062	12.7	−0.056
5	−0.02	0.0008	0.0003	−0.022	10	−0.021
6	0.009	0.0003	0.0002	0.01	11.1	0.009

The last column of Table 6 shows the mean values of displacement, evaluated by using in (8) the values $m_{|x|}, m_{|\dot{x}|}$ obtained by numerical integration of PWL equation of motion (6). It worth noting that the optimum value of damping ratio for a linear system with undamped eigenfrequency $\omega_1 = 2\pi$ rad/s and considered random input $p_0(t)$, is $\zeta_{opt} = 0.55$. The value of standard deviation of simulated acceleration output obtained in this case is $\sigma_{\ddot{x}_1 opt} = 0.741$ m/s^2.

Table 4 shows that the simulated values $\sigma_{\ddot{x}_1 sim}$ are better approximated by using the proposed method than the Gaussian equivalent linearization method. Therefore, in all case studies the asymmetric PWL systems provide better vibration isolation than the optimum linear system, for both considered random inputs (band limited and shape filtered white noise).

The results presented in Tables 4 and 6 show that the relative errors of approximation between the results obtained by numerical integration of asymmetric PWL systems and those calculated by using the Lyapunov equation for linear attached systems are less than 7.5% for standard deviation of acceleration and less than 13% for mean value of displacement. As one can see, from Tables 2 and 6, as nonlinearity increases, the mean value displacement is better approximated. It should be mentioned that the Gaussian equivalent linearization method cannot provide any information about the drift of sprung mass average position in dynamic regime, as it is shown in Table 5.

In order to illustrate the application of presented method, the case 1 from Table 2, which display the strongest nonlinearity, has been chosen. In Figures 8 and 9 are plotted the transmissibility factors, simulated and fitted for this case, as well as the values of parameters from fitting the curves given by the expressions (27) and (35).

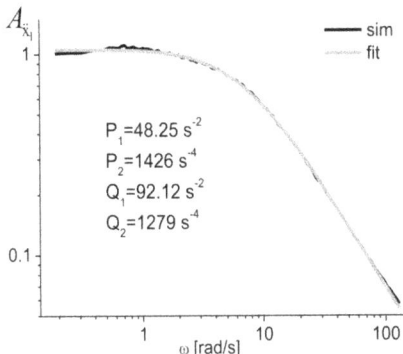

Figure 8. Simulated and fitted transmissibility factors for acceleration.

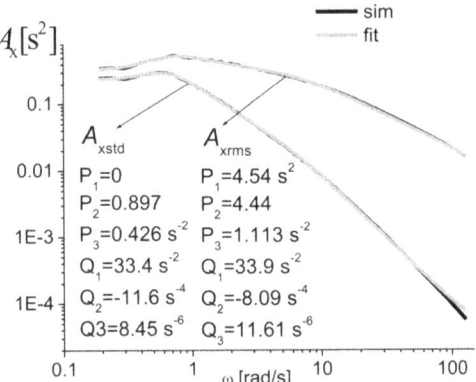

Figure 9. Simulated and fitted transmissibility factors for std and rms displacement.

In Tables 7 and 8 are given the coefficients of attached linear systems corresponding to acceleration and displacement, obtained by solving the algebraic Equations (29), (31), (37) and (39) for parameters shown in Figures 8 and 9.

Table 7. Coefficients of attached linear system for std acceleration.

a_1 [s^{-1}]	a_2 [s^{-2}]	c_1	c_2 [s^{-1}]	c_{11} [$m^2 s^{-4}$]
13.07	37.35	6.96	−130.4	0.265

Table 8. Coefficients of attached linear system for std and rms displacement.

	a_1 [s^{-1}]	a_2 [s^{-2}]	a_3 [s^{-3}]	c_1	c_2 [s^{-1}]	c_2 [s^{-2}]	c_{11} [m^2]	$|m_x|_{Lyap}$ [m]
Coefficients for std disp	6.45	5.05	2.82	0.0158	−1.036	7.236	0.0019	0.18
Coefficients for rms disp	6.8	6.19	3.41	2.13	−17.5	106.8	0.0343	

In the last column of these tables are given the values of elements c_{11} from covariance matrices obtained by solving the Lyapunov Equation (34), for the corresponding attached linear systems. Using these coefficients, are obtained the values of std acceleration $\sigma_{\ddot{x}_1 \text{Lyap}} = \sqrt{c_{11}} = 0.515$ ms^{-2} and the mean value of displacement $m_{x\text{Lyap}} \cong -\sqrt{c_{11\,\text{rms}} - c_{11\,\text{std}}} = -0.18$ m, according to (8). Figure 10 shows the first 30 s from the simulated time histories of input, acceleration and displacements outputs for PWL, attached linear (rms for displacement) and linear equivalent systems, obtained for case study 1.

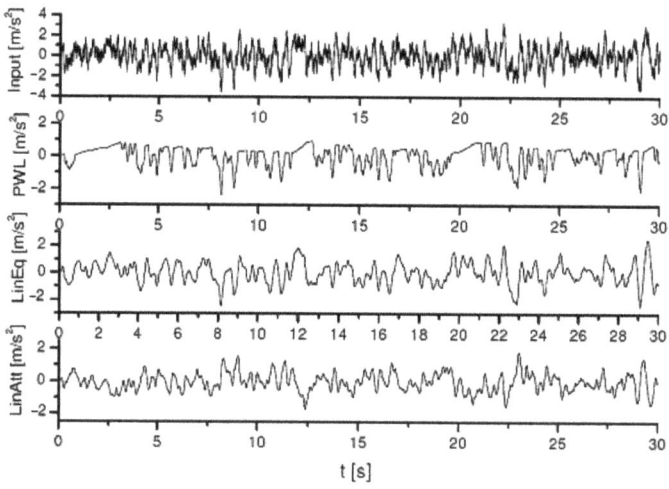

Figure 10. Acceleration output of PWL, equivalent linear and attached linear systems for case 1.

In Figure 11 are plotted the spectral densities of acceleration output, determined by 1/3 octave band-pass filtering for PWL, linear equivalent and the attached linear systems.

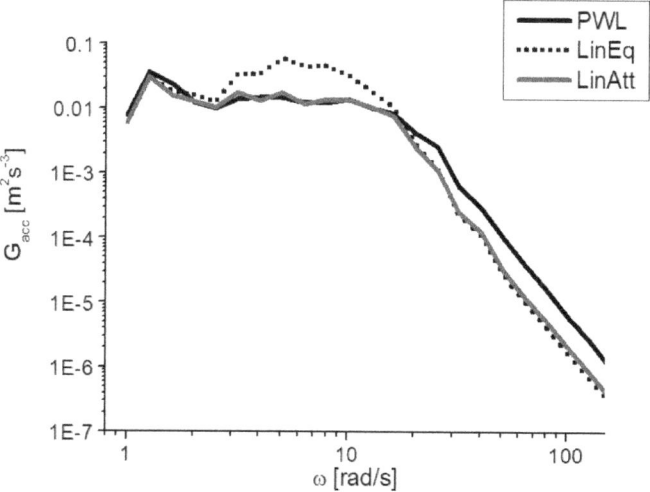

Figure 11. Spectral densities of acceleration for PWL, linear equivalent and attached linear systems.

The relative errors between the areas under spectral densities that represent the variances of acceleration, given in Table 9, advocate the efficiency of the proposed method.

Table 9. Variances of acceleration for PWL, LinEq and LinAtt systems.

System	Area G_{acc} [m^2/s^4]	Relative Error %
PWL	0.254	-
LinEq	0.503	98
LinAtt	0.23	9.4

9. Conclusions

The dynamic response of piecewise linear systems with asymmetric damping and stiffness for random inputs is approximated by a method based on transmissibility factors. The application of this method does not require the numerical simulation of input and output time histories, except for obtaining the transmissibility factors by using harmonic inputs. Using these frequency characteristics, a stochastic linear system is attached for each variable of interest. The statistical parameters of the studied output corresponding to random excitations having rational spectral densities are determined by solving the associated Lyapunov equation.

The obtained results are compared with those determined by the numerical integration of asymmetric PWL response. The relative errors show the efficiency and applicability of this method for PWL systems. In addition, this approach allows the realization of vibration isolation systems with better performance than those with linear characteristics. Using the attached linear systems for rms and std displacement, the shift of sprung mass average position in dynamic regime, due to damping or stiffness asymmetry, can be predicted with a good accuracy for stationary random input.

Author Contributions: Conceptualization, T.S., A.-M.M., O.S. and M.G.; methodology, T.S., A.-M.M., O.S. and M.G.; writing—original draft preparation, T.S., A.-M.M., O.S. and M.G.; writing—review and editing, T.S., A.-M.M., O.S. and M.G. All authors have read and agreed to the published version of the manuscript.

Funding: This research received no external funding.

Institutional Review Board Statement: Not applicable.

Informed Consent Statement: Not applicable.

Data Availability Statement: Not applicable.

Conflicts of Interest: The authors declare no conflict of interest.

Abbreviations

The following abbreviations are used in this manuscript:

acc	acceleration
disp	displacement
LinAtt	Linear attached
LinEq	Linear equivalent
Lyap	Lyapunov
PWL	piecewise linear
rms	root mean square
SDOF	single degree of freedom
sim	simulated
std	standard deviation

References

1. Xu, L.; Lu, M.W.; Cao, Q. Bifurcation and chaos of a harmonically excited oscillator with both stiffness and viscous damping piecewise nonlinearity by incremental harmonic balance method. *J. Sound Vib.* **2003**, *264*, 873–882. [CrossRef]
2. Narimani, A.; Golnaraghi, M.F.; Nakhaie, J.G. Frequency response of a piecewise linear vibration isolator. *J. Vib. Control* **2004**, *10*, 1775–1894. [CrossRef]

3. Ji, J.C.; Hansen, C.H. On the approximate solution of a piecewise nonlinear oscillator under super-harmonic resonance. *J. Sound Vib.* **2005**, *283*, 467–474. [CrossRef]
4. Yu, S.D. An efficient computational method for vibration analysis of unsymmetric piecewise-linear dynamical systems with multiple degrees of freedom. *Nonlinear Dyn.* **2013**, *71*, 493–504. [CrossRef]
5. Silveira, M.; Wahi, P.; Fernandes, J.C.M. Exact and approximate analytical solutions of oscillator with piecewise linear asymmetrical damping. *Int. J. Non-Linear Mech.* **2019**, *110*, 115–122. [CrossRef]
6. Ranjbarzadeh, H.H.; Kakavand, F. Determination of nonlinear vibration of 2DOF system with an asymmetric piecewise-linear compression spring using incremental harmonic balance method. *Eur. J. Mech. A/Solids* **2019**, *73*, 161–168. [CrossRef]
7. Natsiavas, S. Dynamics of Piecewise Linear Oscillators. *World Sci. Ser. Nonlinear Sci.* **2000**, *28*, 127–153. [CrossRef]
8. Qigang, L.; Luyu, L. Dynamic Performance of Time-Domain Piecewise Linear Stiffness System. *J. Eng. Mech.* **2021**, *147*, 04021037. [CrossRef]
9. Yurchenko, D.; Iwankiewicz, R.; Alevras, P. Control and dynamics of a SDOF system with piecewise linear stiffness and combined external excitations. *Probabil. Eng. Mech.* **2014**, *35*, 118–124. [CrossRef]
10. Lelkes, J.; Kalmár-Nagy, T. Analysis of a piecewise linear aeroelastic system with and without tuned vibration absorber. *Nonlinear Dyn.* **2021**, *103*, 2997–3018. [CrossRef]
11. Sun, Y. Experimental Modelling and Amplitude-Frequency Response Analysis of a Piecewise Linear Vibration System. *IEEE* **2020**, *9*, 4279–4290. [CrossRef]
12. Rajalingham, C.; Rakheja, S. Influence of Suspension Damper Asymmetry on Vehicle Vibration Response to Ground Excitation. *J. Sound Vib.* **2003**, *266*, 1117–1129. [CrossRef]
13. Silveira, M.; Pontes, B.R., Jr.; Balthazar, J.M. Use of nonlinear asymmetrical shock absorber to improve comfort on passenger vehicles. *J. Sound Vib.* **2014**, *333*, 2114–2129. [CrossRef]
14. Seifi, A.; Hassannejad, R.; Hamed, M. Use of nonlinear asymmetrical shock absorbers in multi-objective optimization of the suspension system in a variety of road excitations. *Proc. Inst. Mech. Eng. Part K J. Multi-Body Dyn.* **2016**, *231*, 372–387. [CrossRef]
15. Doiphode, S.; Chaudhari, S.; Shendge, P.D.; Phadke, S.B. Analysis of asymmetrical damper for improving ride comfort of passenger cars. In Proceedings of the 3rd IEEE International Conference on Recent Trends in Electronics, Information & Communication Technology (RTEICT), Bangalore, India, 18–19 May 2018. [CrossRef]
16. Fernandes, J.C.M.; Goncalves, P.J.P.; Silveira, M. Interaction between asymmetrical damping and geometrical nonlinearity in vehicle suspension systems improves comfort. *Nonlinear Dyn.* **2020**, *99*, 1561–1576. [CrossRef]
17. Guntur, H.L.; Setiawan, L.F. The influence of asymmetry ratio and average of the damping force on the performance and ride comfort of a vehicle. *Int. J. Veh. Syst. Model. Tes* **2016**, *11*, 97–115. [CrossRef]
18. Pazooki, A.; Goodarzi, A.; Khajepour, A.; Soltani, A.; Porlier, C. A novel approach for the design and analysis of nonlinear dampers for automotive suspensions. *J. Vib. Control* **2018**, *24*, 3132–3147. [CrossRef]
19. Borisov, A.; Bosov, A.; Miller, G. Optimal Stabilization of Linear Stochastic System with Statistically Uncertain Piecewise Constant Drift. *Mathematics* **2022**, *10*, 184. [CrossRef]
20. Li, Z.; Yao, J.; Xu, Y. Controlling the vertical shift of an isolated body based on the vibration of nonlinear systems with asymmetric damping forces. *Meccanica* **2022**, *57*, 1173–1191. [CrossRef]
21. Tian, C.; Han, X.; Liu, J.; Zhou, B.; Lei, F.; Li, F. Nonlinear Interval Optimization of Asymmetric Damper Parameters for a Racing Car. *Int. J. Comput. Methods* **2021**, *18*, 2150013. [CrossRef]
22. Bozhko, A.E.; Shteinvol'f, A.L. A statistical linearization method of piecewise-linear characteristics of mechanical systems with asymmetric distribution laws of the vibrations. *Int. Appl. Mech.* **1985**, *21*, 1106–1111. [CrossRef]
23. Sireteanu, T.; Solomon, O.; Mitu, A.M.; Giuclea, M. A linearization method of piecewise linear systems based on frequency domain characteristics with application to semi-active control of vibration. *J. Vib. Acoust.* **2018**, *140*, 061006. [CrossRef]
24. Sireteanu, T.; Solomon, O.; Mitu, A.M.; Giuclea, M. Application of a novel linearization method to compare the on–off control strategies modeled by piecewise linear systems. *J. Vib. Control* **2020**, *26*, 23–24. [CrossRef]
25. Hac, A. Optimal linear preview control of active vehicle suspension. *Veh. Syst. Dyn.* **1992**, *21*, 167–195. [CrossRef]
26. Stammers, C.W.; Sireteanu, T. Vibration control of machines by use of semi-active dry friction. *J. Sound Vib.* **1998**, *209*, 671–684. [CrossRef]
27. Dinca, F.; Teodosiu, C. *Nonlinear and Random Vibrations*; Academic Press Inc.: New York, NY, USA; London, UK, 1973; ISBN 0122167503.
28. Mitu, A.M.; Sireteanu, T.; Giuclea, M.; Solomon, O. Simulation of wide-sense stationary random time-series with specified spectral densities. *J. Vib. Acoust.* **2016**, *138*, 031011. [CrossRef]
29. Johansson, M. Piecewise Linear Control Systems. Ph.D. Thesis, Lunds Tekniska Högskola Kansliet, Lund, Sweden, 1999.
30. Särkkä, S.; Solin, A. *Applied Stochastic Differential Equations*; Cambridge University Press: Cambridge, UK, 2019; Volume 10.

Article

Estimating the Coefficients of a System of Ordinary Differential Equations Based on Inaccurate Observations

Gurami Tsitsiashvili [1,*,†], Marina Osipova [1,2] and Yury Kharchenko [1]

[1] Institute for Applied Mathematics, Far Eastern Branch of Russian Academy of Sciences, 690041 Vladivostok, Russia; mao1975@list.ru (M.O.); har@iam.dvo.ru (Y.K.)
[2] Institute for Applied Mathematics, Far Eastern Federal University, 690922 Vladivostok, Russia
* Correspondence: guram@iam.dvo.ru; Tel.: +7-914-693-2749
† Current address: IAM FEB RAS, Radio Str. 7, 690041 Vladivostok, Russia.

Abstract: In this paper, we solve the problem of estimating the parameters of a system of ordinary differential equations from observations on a short interval of argument values. By analogy with linear regression analysis, a sufficiently large number of observations are selected on this segment and the values of the functions on the right side of the system and the values of the derivatives are estimated. According to the obtained estimates, unknown parameters are determined, using the differential equations system. The consistency of the estimates obtained in this way is proved with an increase in the number of observations over a short period of argument values. Here, an algorithm for estimating parameters acts as a system. The error of the obtained estimate is an indicator of its quality. A sequence of inaccurate measurements is a random process. The method of linear regression analysis applied to an almost linear regression function is used as an optimization procedure.

Keywords: system of ordinary differential equations; linear regression analysis; theorem of existence and uniqueness; implicit function theorem; method of moments

MSC: 60J28

1. Introduction

The problem of estimating the parameters of a system of nonlinear ordinary differential equations, based on inaccurate deterministic observations, using known optimization algorithms, is solved in the papers [1–3]. An alternative approach for estimating the parameters of a deterministic recurrent sequence, observed with random additive and multiplicative errors, based on the relationships between the trajectory averages and their approximation from inaccurate observations, is proposed in [4,5].

The advantage of the first approach is the possibility of using known optimization algorithms, and the disadvantage of it is the lack of analytical estimates of the convergence rate to the estimated parameters. The advantage of the second approach is the availability of theoretical estimates of the convergence rate to the estimated parameters, and the disadvantage of it is the need to establish limit cycles or limit distributions for recurrent sequences.

Despite all the differences in these approaches, the common fact is that by increasing in the length of the observation segment, the accuracy of estimates increases and, under certain conditions, may tend to zero. At the same time, the problem of estimating parameters over a small observation interval is interesting, which is closely related to discrete optimization methods of experiment planning (see, for example, [6,7]).

In this paper, this problem is solved for a system of non-linear ordinary differential equations. At the same time, the estimation of the parameters of this system, based on inaccurate observations, is solved under the assumption that a large number of observations may be carried out over a relatively short segment. To estimate the parameters, the method of linear regression analysis is used in relation to a regression function that slightly deviates from the original function in a small neighbourhood of some time moment [8–13].

This method is based on minimizing the standard deviation of a sequence of observations from a linear regression function. In this case, such a relationship is selected between the number of observations and the interval between neighbouring observations so that the resulting error in determining the parameters tends to zero when the number of observations tends to infinity.

The final stage of the parameter estimation algorithm is the substitution of estimates of the values of functions and the values of their derivatives into the original system of equations at the selected point. Further, by analogy with the method of moments, unknown parameters of the system of equations are estimated and the consistency of the estimates obtained is proved. This paper also uses the implicit function theorem, which allows us to establish that the obtained parameter estimates are consistent depending on the number of observations. Based on the results obtained, computational experiments were carried out.

Thus, elements of system analysis have been introduced into the solution of the task. Here, an algorithm for estimating parameters acts as a system. The error of the obtained estimate is an indicator of its quality. A sequence of inaccurate measurements is a random process. Furthermore, the process and the method of linear regression analysis applied to an almost linear regression function is used as an optimization procedure. It is evaluated using the theorem on the existence and uniqueness of the solution of a system of ordinary differential equations and with the help of the implicit function theorem. Additionally, known error estimates in the linear regression analysis method are used.

2. Estimating the Coefficients of a System of Ordinary Differential Equations by Inaccurate Observations

2.1. Preliminaries

Consider a system of ordinary differential equations with fixed values of parameters $\beta_i = \beta_i^0$, $i = 1, \ldots, m$,

$$\frac{dx_i}{dt} = F_i(x_1, \ldots, x_m, \beta_1^0, \ldots, \beta_m^0), \quad i = 1, \ldots, m, \qquad (1)$$

where $x_1 = x_1(t), \ldots, x_m = x_m(t)$ are unknown functions. In well-known monographs on the theory of ordinary differential equations (see, for example, [14,15]), the theorem of the existence and uniqueness of the solution of this system in a small neighbourhood of a certain point is formulated and proved in Theorem 1.

Theorem 1. *Assume that functions $F_i = F_i(x_1, \ldots, x_m, \beta_1^0, \ldots, \beta_m^0)$ are continuous in a rectangular parallelepiped $Q = \{(x_1, \ldots, x_m) \in R^m : x_i^0 - a_i \leq x_i \leq x_i^0 + a_i, i = 1, \ldots, m\}$ together with their partial derivatives $\dfrac{\partial F_i}{\partial x_i}$, $i = 1, \ldots, m$. Then there is a segment $t_0 - r \leq t \leq t_0 + r$, on which the system of Equation (1) has a unique solution satisfying the initial conditions $x_i(t_0) = x_i^0$, $i = 1, \ldots, m$.*

Remark 1. *From the Weierstrass theorem for continuous functions on a compact, it follows that the functions $x_i(t)$, $i = 1, \ldots, m$, on the segment $[t_0 - r, t_0 + r]$ (continuity follows from differentiability) and function $\left|F_i \cdot \dfrac{\partial F_i}{\partial x_i}\right|$, $i = 1, \ldots, m$, on a set Q (due to the continuity of the multipliers) reach their highest final values C_i.*

Denote

$$M_0 = (x_1^0, \ldots, x_m^0, \beta_1^0, \ldots, \beta_m^0), \quad F_i(M_0) = F_i^0, \quad i = 1, \ldots, m,$$

$$M_0' = (x_1^0, \ldots, x_m^0, F_1^0, \ldots, F_m^0, \beta_1^0, \ldots, \beta_m^0),$$

$$G_i(x_1,\ldots,x_m,f_1,\ldots,f_m,\beta_1,\ldots,\beta_m) = F_i(x_1,\ldots,x_m,\beta_1,\ldots,\beta_m) - f_i,$$

where F_i are described in Theorem 1, and consider the system of equations

$$G_i(x_1,\ldots,x_m,f_1,\ldots,f_m,\beta_1,\ldots,\beta_m) = 0, \; i=1,\ldots,m. \quad (2)$$

In monographs on mathematical analysis (see, for example, [16,17]), conditions are formulated, under which the system (2) may be resolved with respect to variables $\beta_1,\ldots,\beta_m$ (see for example Theorem 2).

Theorem 2. *If the functions G_i, $i=1,\ldots,m$ are continuously differentiable in the neighbourhood of the point M'_0 and the Jacobian*

$$\left.\frac{\partial(G_1,\ldots,G_m)}{\partial(\beta_1,\ldots,\beta_m)}\right|_{M'_0} \neq 0, \quad (3)$$

then there are neighbourhoods U, V, W of points $(x_1^0,\ldots,x_m^0)$, $(F_1^0,\ldots,F_m^0)$, $(\beta_1^0,\ldots,\beta_m^0)$, respectively, such that the system of Equation (2) is uniquely solvable in the neighbourhood of $U \times V \times W$ of the point M'_0 relative to the variables $\beta_1,\ldots,\beta_m$. Moreover, if $\beta_i = g_i(x_1,\ldots,x_m,f_1,\ldots,f_m)$, $i=1,\ldots,m$, is the specified solution, then all functions g_i are continuously differentiable in the neighbourhood $U \times V$ and $\beta_i^0 = g_i(x_1^0,\ldots,x_m^0,F_1^0,\ldots,F_m^0)$.

Remark 2. *When the conditions of Theorem 2 are met, the functions g_i, $i=1,\ldots,m$, are continuous at the point $(x_1^0,\ldots,x_m^0,F_1^0,\ldots,F_m^0)$.*

2.2. Ordinary Differential Equation

Consider the differential equation for a fixed value of the parameter $\beta = \beta_0$

$$\frac{dx}{dt} = F(x,\beta_0) \quad (4)$$

with the initial condition $x(0) = x_0$, assuming that the function $F(x,\beta)$ is continuously differentiable in the neighbourhood of a point $M_0 = (x_0,\beta_0)$ and $\left.\frac{\partial F}{\partial \beta}\right|_{M_0} \neq 0$. Let the inaccurate observations $y(t) = x(t) + \varepsilon(t)$ are known for the state of $x(t)$ at the moments $t = kh$, $k = 0,\pm 1,\ldots,\pm n$, $hn \leq r$. Denote

$$\varepsilon_k = \varepsilon(kh), \; x_k = x(kh), \; y_k = y(kh) = x_k + \varepsilon_k, \; F_0 = F(x_0,\beta_0)$$

and suppose that ε_k, $k=0,\pm 1,\ldots,\pm n$, is a set of independent and identically distributed random variables with zero mean and variance σ^2. The problem of estimating the parameter β_0 of the differential Equation (4) from these observations is posed.

The solution of this problem is carried out in two stages. First, they are constructed using a modification of the least squares estimation method $\hat{x}_0$, $\hat{F}_0$ and their convergence to the estimated parameters x_0, F_0 is investigated. Then, by analogy with the method of moments, an estimate of $\hat{\beta}_0$ is constructed and its convergence to the estimated parameter β_0 is investigated.

Evaluation of values x_0, F_0. Let us introduce the notations, outlining the method for defining $\hat{x}_0$, $\hat{F}_0$

$$\hat{x}_0 = \frac{\sum_{k=-n}^{n} y_k}{2n+1}, \; \hat{F}_0 = \frac{\sum_{k=-n}^{n} y_k kh}{\sum_{k=-n}^{n}(kh)^2}. \quad (5)$$

Theorem 3. *If $\sigma^2 < \infty$ and $h = n^{-\alpha}$, then, for $\alpha > 1$, the estimate of $\hat{x}_0$ is an asymptotically unbiased and consistent estimate of the parameter x_0. The estimate $\hat{F}_0$ is an asymptotically unbiased estimate of the parameter F_0. At $1 < \alpha < 3/2$; the estimate $\hat{F}_0$ is a consistent estimate of F_0.*

Proof of Theorem 3. Denote $\tilde{y}_k = x_0 + F_0 kh + \varepsilon_k$ and put

$$\tilde{x}_0 = \frac{\sum_{k=-n}^{n} \tilde{y}_k}{2n+1}, \quad \tilde{F}_0 = \frac{\sum_{k=-n}^{n} \tilde{y}_k kh}{\sum_{k=-n}^{n} (kh)^2}.$$

Estimates of $\tilde{x}_0$, $\tilde{F}_0$ are obtained by the least squares method for coefficients x_0, F_0 of linear regression [9] and satisfy the following relations

$$E\tilde{x}_0 = x_0, \quad E\tilde{F}_0 = F_0, \quad Var\tilde{x}_0 = \frac{\sigma^2}{2n+1}, \quad Var\tilde{F}_0 = \frac{\sigma^2}{\sum_{k=-n}^{n}(kh)^2}. \tag{6}$$

Here, Ex is mathematical expectation of arbitrary random variable x and $Varx = E(x - Ex)^2$ is its variance. In turn, the following equalities are almost certainly fulfilled

$$\widehat{x}_0 - \tilde{x}_0 = \frac{\sum_{k=-n}^{n}(\widehat{y}_k - \tilde{y}_k)}{2n+1}, \quad \widehat{F}_0 - \tilde{F}_0 = \frac{\sum_{k=-n}^{n}(\widehat{y}_k - \tilde{y}_k)kh}{\sum_{k=-n}^{n}(kh)^2}. \tag{7}$$

Moreover, the differences $\widehat{y}_k - \tilde{y}_k = x_k - x_0 - F_0 kh$, $k = 0, \pm 1, \ldots, \pm n$ are deterministic quantities.

The Remark 1 implies the existence of a number C satisfying the inequality

$$\sup_{|t| \leq nh} |x''(t)| = \sup_{|t| \leq nh} \left| \frac{\partial F(x(t), \beta_0)}{\partial x} F(x(t), \beta_0) \right| = 2C < \infty.$$

Then, from the Taylor formula with a residual term in the Lagrange form,

$$x(kh) = x(0) + F_0 kh + \frac{(kh)^2}{2} x''(kh\tau_k), \quad |\tau_k| \leq 1, \; k = 0, \pm 1, \ldots, \pm n,$$

inequalities follow

$$|x_k - x_0 - F_0 kh| \leq C(kh)^2, \; k = 0, \pm 1, \ldots, \pm n. \tag{8}$$

From the Formulas (7) and (8) for $n \to \infty$, the relations follow

$$|\widehat{x}_0 - \tilde{x}_0| \leq \frac{\sum_{k=-n}^{n}|x_k - x_0 - F_0 kh|}{2n+1} \leq \frac{2Ch^2 \sum_{k=1}^{n} k^2}{2n+1} \sim \frac{Ch^2 n^2}{3}, \tag{9}$$

$$|\widehat{F}_0 - \tilde{F}_0| \leq \frac{\sum_{k=-n}^{n}|(x_k - x_0 - F_0 kh)kh|}{\sum_{k=-n}^{n}(kh)^2} \leq \frac{Ch^3 \sum_{k=1}^{n} k^3}{\sum_{k=1}^{n} h^2 k^2} \sim \frac{Chn}{4}. \tag{10}$$

The Formulas (6), (9) and (10) lead to the relations

$$|E\widehat{x}_0 - x_0| = |E\widehat{x}_0 - E\tilde{x}_0| \preceq \frac{Ch^2 n^2}{2}, \quad Var\widehat{x}_0 = Var\tilde{x}_0, \tag{11}$$

$$|E\widehat{F}_0 - F_0| = |E\widehat{F}_0 - E\tilde{F}_0| \preceq \frac{3Chn}{4}, \quad Var\widehat{F}_0 = Var\tilde{F}_0. \tag{12}$$

Here $a_n \preceq b_n$ means that $\limsup_{n \to \infty} a_n/b_n \leq 1$. Then from the condition $h = n^{-\alpha}$, $\alpha > 1$, and the Relations (11) and (12) we have

$$|E\widehat{x}_0 - x_0| \to 0, \; |E\widehat{F}_0 - F_0| \to 0, \; n \to \infty, \tag{13}$$

that $\widehat{x}_0$, $\widehat{F}_0$ are asymptotic unbiased estimates of x_0, F_0.

From the Bieneme–Chebyshev inequality, the Relations (9) and (11) and the conditions $h = n^{-\alpha}$, $\alpha > 1$, we get for any $\delta > 0$

$$P(|\hat{x}_0 - x_0| > \delta) \leq P(|\hat{x}_0 - \tilde{x}_0| + |\tilde{x}_0 - x_0|) > \delta) = P(|\tilde{x}_0 - x_0| \geq \delta - |\hat{x}_0 - \tilde{x}_0|) \leq$$

$$\leq \frac{\sigma^2}{(2n+1)(\delta - |\hat{x}_0 - \tilde{x}_0|)^2} \to 0, \; n \to \infty. \tag{14}$$

Thus, for $h = n^{-\alpha}$, $\alpha > 1$, estimate $\hat{x}_0$ is a consistent estimate of x_0.
At the same time, from the Relations (10), (12) and (13) for $h = n^{-\alpha}$, $1 < \alpha < 3/2$, we get for any $\delta > 0$

$$P(|\hat{F}_0 - F_0| > \delta) \leq P(|\hat{F}_0 - \tilde{F}_0| + |\tilde{F}_0 - F_0|) > \delta)) =$$

$$P(|\tilde{F}_0 - F_0| > \delta - |\hat{F}_0 - \tilde{F}_0|) \leq \frac{3\sigma^2}{h^2 n^3(\delta - |\hat{F}_0 - \tilde{F}_0|)^2} \to 0, \; n \to \infty. \tag{15}$$

Therefore, if the condition $h = n^{-\alpha}$, $1 < \alpha < 3/2$, is true, the estimate $\hat{F}_0$ is a consistent estimate of F_0. □

Remark 3. *It is worth noting that Theorem 3 is true for any distribution of random variables ε_k with finite variance σ^2. Indeed it is necessary to prove limit relation $H_n = \frac{\sum_{k=-n}^{n} \varepsilon_k k}{h \sum_{k=-n}^{n} k^2} \to 0, \; n \to \infty$. However, the most reasonable way to solve this question is to consider such distributions of random variables ε_k as normal for $\sigma^2 < \infty$ / or stable for $\sigma^2 = \infty$, because H_n has normal/stable distribution also.*

Evaluation of parameter β_0. Consider the equation

$$F(\hat{x}_0, \beta) = \hat{F}_0. \tag{16}$$

Theorem 4. *In conditions of Theorem 3, Equation (16) has a unique solution $\hat{\beta}_0$, which is a consistent estimate of the parameter β_0.*

Proof of Theorem 4. Since the function $F(x, \beta)$ is continuously differentiable in the neighbourhood of the point $M_0 = (x_0, \beta_0)$ and $\frac{\partial F}{\partial \beta}\big|_{M_0} \neq 0$,, then the conditions of the theorem for the function $G(x, f, \beta) = F(x, \beta) - f$ are fulfilled. So, in some neighbourhood of the point $M'_0 = (x_0, F_0, \beta_0)$, the equation is solvable with respect to $\beta = g(x, f)$, while $\beta_0 = g(x_0, F_0)$. Then, from the Remark 2, we get that for any $\varepsilon > 0$ there exists $\delta(\varepsilon) > 0$ such that in the neighbourhood $\{(x, f) : |x - x_0| \leq \delta(\varepsilon), |f - F_0| \leq \delta(\varepsilon)\}$ of the point (x_0, F_0) the inequality $|\beta - \beta_0| \leq \varepsilon$ is executed.
It follows that with the specified choice of $\delta(\varepsilon)$, the relation is fulfilled

$$|\hat{x}_0 - x_0| \leq \delta(\varepsilon), \; |\hat{F}_0 - F_0| \leq \delta(\varepsilon) \Rightarrow |\hat{\beta}_0 - \beta_0| \leq \varepsilon. \tag{17}$$

In turn, from the Relations (14) and (15) it follows that for any ε and $\delta(\varepsilon)$ there is such a $n_0(\varepsilon, \delta(\varepsilon))$, that for any $n > n_0(\varepsilon, \delta(\varepsilon))$ inequalities are fair

$$P(|\hat{x}_0 - x_0| \leq \delta(\varepsilon)) \geq 1 - \frac{\varepsilon}{2}, \; P(|\hat{F}_0 - F_0| \leq \delta(\varepsilon)) \geq 1 - \frac{\varepsilon}{2}. \tag{18}$$

Therefore, from the Relations (17) and (18) we have $P(|\hat{\beta}_0 - \beta_0| \leq \varepsilon) \geq 1 - \varepsilon$. Thus, for any $\varepsilon > 0$, there exists $n_0(\varepsilon)$ such that for $n > n_0(\varepsilon)$, the inequality holds $P(|\hat{\beta}_0 - \beta_0| > \varepsilon) < \varepsilon$, which means consistency (convergence in probability at $n \to \infty$) of the constructed estimate. □

2.3. System of Differential Equations

Consider a system (1) with initial conditions $x_i(0) = x_i^0$, $i = 1, \ldots, m$. We assume that the functions $F_i(x_1, \ldots, x_m, \beta_1, \ldots, \beta_m)$, $i = 1, \ldots, m$, are continuously differentiable in the neighbourhood of the point M_0 and the Jacobian $\left.\frac{\partial(F_1, \ldots, F_m)}{\partial(\beta_1, \ldots, \beta_m)}\right|_{M_0} \neq 0$. Inaccurate observations are known $y_i(t) = x_i(t) + \varepsilon_i(t)$ for the state $x_i(t)$, $i = 1, \ldots, m$, at moments $t = kh$, $k = 0, \pm 1, \ldots, \pm n$, $hn \leq r$. Let $\varepsilon_i(kh)$, $k = 0, \pm 1, \ldots, \pm nh$, $i = 1, \ldots, m$, is a set of independent and identically distributed random variables with zero mean and variance σ^2. The task is to estimate the vector of parameters $(\beta_1^0, \ldots, \beta_m^0)$ of a system of differential Equation (1) based on these observations.

Denote

$$\widehat{x}_i^0 = \frac{\sum_{k=-n}^{n} y_i(kh)}{2n+1}, \quad \widehat{F}_i^0 = \frac{\sum_{k=-n}^{n} y_i(kh)}{\sum_{k=-n}^{n} (kh)^2}, \quad i = 1, \ldots, m. \tag{19}$$

Theorem 5. *If $\sigma^2 < \infty$ and $h = n^{-\alpha}$, then, for $\alpha > 1$, the estimate $\widehat{x}_i^0$ is an asymptotically unbiased and consistent estimate of the parameter x_i^0. The estimate $\widehat{F}_i^0$ is an asymptotically unbiased estimate of the parameter F_i^0. For $1 < \alpha < 3/2$, the estimate $\widehat{F}_i^0$ is a consistent estimate of the value F_i^0, $i = 1, \ldots, m$.*

Consider a system of equations

$$F_i(\widehat{x}_1, \ldots, \widehat{x}_m, \beta_1, \ldots, \beta_m) = F_i^0, \quad i = 1, \ldots, m. \tag{20}$$

Theorem 6. *In conditions of Theorem 5 the system of Equation (20) has a unique solution $(\widehat{\beta}_1^0, \ldots \widehat{\beta}_m^0)$, which is a consistent estimate of the vector of parameters $(\beta_1^0, \ldots, \beta_m^0)$.*

The proofs of the Theorems 5 and 6 almost verbatim repeat the proofs of the Theorems 3 and 4.

Remark 4. *Theorems 3–6 are devoted to ordinary differential equations of the first order and their systems. However, it is possible to spread them to ordinary differential equations and their systems of arbitrary order. For this purpose it is possible to use for examples results of [12,13].*

2.4. Computational Experiment

Example 1. *The computational experiment was conducted first for the Cauchy problem*

$$\frac{dx}{dt} = F(x, \beta_0) = \beta_0 x, \quad x(0) = 1, \quad \beta_0 = 0.5.$$

The solution of this equation has the form $x = e^{b_0 t}$. We assumed that by observing the process described by this equation, $\pm kh$, $k = 0, 1, \ldots, n$, $h = n^{-5/4}$, $n = 10{,}000$, inaccurate observations were obtained at time points $y_{\pm k} = e^{\pm b_0 hk} + \varepsilon_{\pm k}$, $k = 0, 1, \ldots, n$.

Here, independent random variables $\varepsilon_{\pm k}$, $k = 0, 1, \ldots, n$, are distributed uniformly on the segment $[-1/2, 1/2]$ left and on the segment $[-1/4, 1/4]$ right. According to the Formula (5), the parameters x_0, $F_0 = F(x_0, \beta_0)$ in our notation $\widehat{x}_0$, $\widehat{F}_0$, were evaluated first, then the formula for evaluating the parameter β_0 was found from the equation $\widehat{F}_0 = \widehat{x}_0 \widehat{\beta}_0$. Table 1 shows the results of a computational experiment conducted 1000 times, namely, the interval distribution (5 intervals) of relative frequencies $\widehat{\beta}_0$.

Table 1. Interval distribution of estimate $\hat{\beta}_0$ when $\varepsilon_{\pm k}$ has variance $\sigma^2 = 1/12$ left and variance $\sigma^2 = 1/48$ right.

Distribution Intervals	Relative Frequencies	Distribution Intervals	Relative Frequencies
0.387413–0.432612	0.027	0.437796–0.460889	0.011
0.432612–0.477811	0.238	0.460889–0.483983	0.171
0.477811–0.52301	0.477	0.483983–0.507076	0.494
0.52301–0.568209	0.229	0.507076–0.53017	0.29
0.568209–0.613408	0.029	0.53017–0.553263	0.034

Consequently, a decrease in variance σ^2 improves the quality of the obtained estimates sufficiently clearly.

Now, consider the case in which independent random variables $\varepsilon_{\pm k}$, $k = 0, 1, ..., n$, are distributed normally with mean 0 and variance σ^2. Table 2 shows the results of a computational experiment conducted 1000 times, namely, the interval distribution (five intervals) of relative frequencies $\hat{\beta}_0$.

Table 2. Interval distribution of estimate $\hat{\beta}_0$ when $\varepsilon_{\pm k}$ has variance $\sigma^2 = 1/12$ left and variance $\sigma^2 = 1/48$ right.

Distribution Intervals	Relative Frequencies	Distribution Intervals	Relative Frequencies
0.393462–0.442011	0.062	0.435015–0.458419	0.014
0.442011–0.49056	0.328	0.458419–0.481824	0.144
0.49056–0.53911	0.458	0.481824–0.505228	0.47
0.53911–0.587659	0.143	0.505228–0.528632	0.322
0.587659–0.636208	0.009	0.528632–0.552036	0.05

Consequently, the quality of obtained results for disturbances distributed normally behaves like in a case of uniform distribution.

Example 2. A computational experiment was also carried out for the system of Lorentz equations

$$\begin{cases} \dfrac{dx}{dt} = F_1(x, y, z, \sigma_0, r_0, b_0) = \sigma_0(y - x), \\ \dfrac{dy}{dt} = F_2(x, y, z, \sigma_0, r_0, b_0) = x(r_0 - z) - y, \\ \dfrac{dz}{dt} = F_3(x, y, z, \sigma_0, r_0, b_0) = xy - b_0 z, \end{cases} \quad (21)$$

with the given initial conditions $x(0) = 1$, $y(0) = 2$, $z(0) = 1$, in the case of $\sigma_0 = 1$, $r_0 = 2$, $b_0 = 3$. The solution of this system is not written out explicitly, but it is solved by the finite difference method. We write out the corresponding equations for the grid $\{\pm kh, k = 0, 1, ..., n\}$ in increments of $h = n^{-5/4}$, $n = 10{,}000$:

$$\begin{cases} x_{\pm(k+1)} = x_{\pm k} \pm \sigma_0 h(y_{\pm k} - x_{\pm k}), \\ y_{\pm(k+1)} = y_{\pm k} \pm h(x_{\pm k}(r_0 - z_{\pm k}) - y_{\pm k}), \\ z_{\pm(k+1)} = z_{\pm k} \pm h(x_{\pm k} y_{\pm k} - b_0 z_{\pm k}), \end{cases} \quad (22)$$

$x_0 = 1$, $y_0 = 2$, $z_0 = 1$. We assumed that by observing the process described by these equations, inaccurate observations were obtained

$$X_{\pm k} = x_{\pm k} + \varepsilon_1(\pm hk), \quad Y_{\pm k} = y_{\pm k} + \varepsilon_2(\pm hk), \quad Z_{\pm k} = z_{\pm k} + \varepsilon_3(\pm hk), \quad k = 0, 1, ..., n,$$

where $\varepsilon_i(\pm hk)$, $i = 1, 2, 3$, $k = 0, 1, \ldots, n$, are independent random variables, distributed uniformly over a segment $[-1/2, 1/2]$. According to the Formula (19), the parameters were evaluated first x_0, y_0, z_0, $F_i^0 = F_i(x_0, y_0, z_0, \sigma_0, r_0, b_0)$, $i = 1, 2, 3$, in our notation

$\widehat{x}_0, \widehat{y}_0, \widehat{z}_0, \widehat{F}_i^0, i = 1, 2, 3$. Further, the estimates of the parameters σ_0, r_0, b_0 were found from the relations

$$\begin{cases} \widehat{F}_1^0 = \sigma(\widehat{y}_0 - \widehat{x}_0), \\ \widehat{F}_2^0 = \widehat{x}_0(r - \widehat{z}_0) - \widehat{y}_0, \\ \widehat{F}_3^0 = \widehat{x}_0\widehat{y}_0 - b\widehat{z}_0. \end{cases} \quad (23)$$

Table 3 shows the results of a computational experiment conducted 1000 times, namely, the interval distribution of relative frequencies $\widehat{\sigma}_0, \widehat{r}_0, \widehat{\beta}_0$.

Table 3. Interval distribution of estimates $\widehat{\sigma}_0, \widehat{r}_0, \widehat{b}_0$.

distribution intervals $\widehat{\sigma}_0$	relative frequencies $\widehat{\sigma}_0$
0.883607–0.931473	0.035
0.931473–0.979339	0.275
0.979339–1.0272	0.486
1.0272–1.07507	0.192
1.07507–1.12294	0.015
distribution intervals $\widehat{r}_0$	relative frequencies $\widehat{r}_0$
1.89817–1.94253	0.038
1.94253–1.98689	0.242
1.98689–2.031262	0.471
2.03126–2.07562	0.224
2.07562–2.11998	0.025
distribution intervals $\widehat{b}_0$	relative frequencies $\widehat{b}_0$
2.87579–2.92301	0.021
2.92301–2.97022	0.267
2.97022–3.01744	0.457
3.01744–3.06466	0.231
3.06466–3.11188	0.024

3. Conclusions

Remarks 3 and 4 indicate the following possible generalizations of the results obtained in Theorems 3–6. First, we should consider the case when the variance of random perturbations σ^2 decreases and so quality of obtained estimates improves. However, if the variance $\sigma^2 = \infty$ like in a case of heavy tails of disturbances distributions, then it is necessary to consider stable distribution of random variables ε_k. Secondly, we should consider the case of ordinary differential Equations (and systems) of higher than the unit order.

Furthermore, at last, along with systems of ordinary differential equations, the proposed method for estimating parameters may be applied to equations or systems of partial differential equations. As a basis for the development of this method of parameter estimation, the theorem of the existence of a solution of partial differential equations system in the vicinity of a certain point may be taken (see, for example, [18]).

4. Discussion

The solution of the considered problem involves the choice of an experimental plan, the use of the theorem of existence and uniqueness for a system of ordinary differential equations, the implicit function theorem and the method of linear regression analysis. Linear regression analysis is based on minimizing of the root-mean-square deviation of the sequence of observations from the linear regression function.

Practically, all the considered generalizations of the results obtained in the paper arise at the junction of several scientific directions. These include probability theory and mathematical statistics, ordinary differential and partial differential equations and their systems, and mathematical analysis. Such tasks arising at the junction of several research directions are usually considered in the system analysis, management and information processing. This circumstance determines the choice of this research topic and the ways to solve the task and an application of optimization procedures.

Author Contributions: Conceptualization, G.T. and Y.K.; methodology and formal analysis, G.T.; analysis of instrument capabilities in parameter estimation, Y.K.; checking the received formulas and numerical experiments, M.O. All authors have read and agreed to the published version of the manuscript.

Funding: This research received no external funding.

Institutional Review Board Statement: Not applicable.

Informed Consent Statement: Not applicable.

Data Availability Statement: Data supporting reported results were obtained by Yu. Kharchenko and M. Osipova.

Conflicts of Interest: The authors declare no conflict of interest.

References

1. Penenko, A.V. Consistent numerical schemes for solving nonlinear inverse source problems with the gradient-type algorithms and the Newton–Kantorovich methods. *Num. Anal. Appl.* **2018** *11*, 73–88. [CrossRef]
2. Penenko, A.V. The Newton–Kantorovich method in inverse source problems for production-destruction models with time series-type measurement data. *Num. Anal. Appl.* **2019** *12*, 51–69. [CrossRef]
3. Penenko, A.V.; Khassenova, Z.T.; Penenko, V.V.; Pyanova, E.A. Numerical study of a direct variational data assimilation algorithm in Almaty city conditions. *Eurasian J. Math. Comput. Appl.* **2019** *7*, 53–64.
4. Tsitsiashvili, G.S. Study of Synergistic Effects in Complex Stochastic Systems. *Mathematics* **2021** *9*, 1396. [CrossRef]
5. Tsitsiashvili, G.S.; Osipova, M.A. Estimation of parameters of nonlinear recurrent relations. *Bull. Voronezh State Univ. Ser. Syst. Anal. Inf. Technol.* **2021** *3*, 27–37. (In Russian)
6. Cox, D.R.; Reid, N. *The Theory of the Design of Experiments*; Chapman and Hall/CRC: Boca Raton, FL, USA; London, UK; New York, NY, USA; Washington, DC, USA, 2000.
7. Shih-Kung, L. *Planning Behaviour. Theories and Experiments*; Cambridge Scholars Publishing: Cambridge, UK, 2019.
8. Krugman, P.R.; Obstfeld, M.; Melitz, M.J. *International Economics: Theory and Policy*, 9th Global ed.; Pearson: Harlow, UK, 2012.
9. Freedman, D.A. *Statistical Models: Theory and Practice*; Cambridge University Press: Cambridge, UK, 2009.
10. Husin, S.F.; Mamat, M.; Ibrahim, M.A.H.; Rivaie, M. An Efficient Three-Term Iterative Method for Estimating Linear Approximation Models in Regression Analysis. *Mathematics* **2020**, *8*, 977. [CrossRef]
11. Hu, Y.; Wu, S.; Feng, S.; Jin, J. Estimation in Partial Functional Linear Spatial Autoregressive Model. *Mathematics* **2020**, *8*, 1680. [CrossRef]
12. Shokri, A.; Tahmourasi, M. A new two-step Obrechkoff method with vanished phase-lag and some of its derivatives for the numerical solution of radial Schrodinger equation and related IVPs with oscillating solutions. *Iran. J. Math. Chem.* **2017**, *8*, 137–159.
13. Mehdizadeh Khalsaraei, M.; Shokri, A. A new explicit singularly P-stable four-step method for the numerical solution of second order IVPs. *Iran. J. Math. Chem.* **2020**, *11*, 17–31.
14. Teschl, G. *Ordinary Differential Equations and Dynamical Systems*; American Mathematical Society: Providence, RI, USA, 2012.
15. Hartman, P. *Ordinary Differential Equations, Classics in Applied Mathematics*; Society for Industrial and Applied Mathematics: Philadelphia, PA, USA, 2002; p. 38.
16. Garling, D.J.H. *A Course in Mathematical Analysis*; Cambridge University Press: Cambridge, UK, 2013; Volume 1.
17. Zorich, V.A. *Mathematical Analysis I*; Springer: Berlin/Heidelberg, Germany, 2016.
18. Folland, G.B. *Introduction to Partial Differential Equations*, 2nd ed.; Princeton University Press: Princeton, RI, USA, 1995.

Article

Exploring the Predictors of Co-Nationals' Preference over Immigrants in Accessing Jobs—Evidence from World Values Survey

Daniel Homocianu

Department of Accounting, Business Information Systems, and Statistics, Faculty of Economics and Business Administration, Alexandru Ioan Cuza University, 700505 Jassy, Romania; daniel.homocianu@uaic.ro

Abstract: This paper presents the results of an exploration of the most resilient influences determining the attitude regarding prioritizing co-nationals over immigrants for access to employment. The source data were from the World Values Survey. After many selection and testing steps, a set of the seven most significant determinants was produced (a fair-to-good model as prediction accuracy). These seven determinants (a hepta-core model) correspond to some features, beliefs, and attitudes regarding emancipative values, gender discrimination, immigrant policy, trust in people of another nationality, inverse devoutness or making parents proud as a life goal, attitude towards work, the post-materialist index, and job preferences as more inclined towards self rather than community benefits. Additional controls revealed the significant influence of some socio-demographic variables. They correspond to gender, the number of children, the highest education level attained, employment status, income scale positioning, settlement size, and the interview year. All selection and testing steps considered many principles, methods, and techniques (e.g., triangulation via adaptive boosting (in the Rattle library of R), and pairwise correlation-based data mining—PCDM, LASSO, OLS, binary and ordered logistic regressions (LOGIT, OLOGIT), prediction nomograms, together with tools for reporting default and custom model evaluation metrics, such as ESTOUT and MEM in Stata). Cross-validations relied on random subsamples (CVLASSO) and well-established ones (mixed-effects). In addition, overfitting removal (RLASSO), reverse causality, and collinearity checks succeeded under full conditions for replicating the results. The prediction nomogram corresponding to the most resistant predictors identified in this paper is also a powerful tool for identifying risks. Therefore, it can provide strong support for decision makers in matters related to immigration and access to employment. The paper's novelty also results from the many robust supporting techniques that allow randomly, and non-randomly cross-validated and fully reproducible results based on a large amount and variety of source data. The findings also represent a step forward in migration and access-to-job research.

Keywords: immigration; access to employment; regression and classification models; collinearity and reverse causality checks; performance comparisons and reporting; triangulation; cross-validations; full support for replication of results

MSC: 60-02

1. Introduction

A well-known saying by Andrew Smith states: "People fear what they don't understand and hate what they can't conquer". Migration is a generalized phenomenon as old as humanity [1]. Moreover, it seems to belong to all historical periods and all continents. Consequently, it became an issue of growing public concern [2]. In today's highly globalized and knowledge-based economies [3], migration is responsible for affecting individuals and societies multi-dimensionally [4]. According to Kanbur and Rapoport (2005) [5], its effects apply to both countries of origin and destination, and some of them relate to brain drain and widening income gaps [6].

In terms of migration motivations, the search for jobs [7,8] is one of them and the basis for the hope of a stable [9], if not better, life [10]. The latter seems natural to human beings [11]. Sensitivity to immigration, a process that affects both the immigrants and the native population [12], depends significantly on the country under consideration [13]. A well-known example of negative public perception is related to the concern that immigrants take the jobs of native-born workers [14–16]. Additionally, this will be translated into negative feelings of native residents towards immigrants and even less supportive attitudes towards pro-immigration policies [17], more as an expression of fear. These labor-market-related concerns [18] considered together with some other economic worries, such as the competition for economic and political power, social status, and the concern for crimes affecting individual security and material welfare form a large category known as realistic threats [19], the latter perhaps is even an expression of hatred.

In the same category of realistic threats (many of macroeconomic nature), we can find another explanation for negative perceptions of immigrants. This explanation seems to be related to the competition for limited resources [20–22] as a primary source of the conflict of interests between groups [23], mainly focused on cost–benefit reasons coupled with some other considerations such as geographical disproportions [24].

Other studies are more focused on socio-demographic and individual features. They show that women and those with higher education and income were more positive toward immigration, whereas older people and people with more seniority at work were considerably more negative [25]. The latter is confirmed in studies focused on comparing young people with adults in such specific terms [26]. Still, recent studies indicate that younger generations may, in fact, harbor more negative attitudes towards immigrants [27]. In addition, people who subscribe to conservative political ideologies are more likely to show negative attitudes toward immigrants [28]. Moreover, some personality traits, such as social domination orientation and right-wing authoritarianism, which reflect attitudes toward social hierarchy, equality, respect for authority, and traditional values, can condition individual perceptions of immigrants as inferior or even a threat [29,30].

Regarding another category of threats, namely the symbolic ones, Mangum and Block (2018) [31] consider that social identity affects public opinion on immigration and immigrants. In these terms, cultural differences coupled with the size of the minority group can act as threats to the values and identity of the majority [32]. Closely related to individual traits, other scholars [33] have shown that more educated people place a much higher value on the cultural diversity of society, believing that immigration generates benefits for society. The latter suggests that education is a transformative force capable of changing individual and collective values, and also encouraging people to be more confident, tolerant, and open [34].

Therefore, in addition to apparent reasons such as fear or hatred, attitudes towards immigrants and their access to jobs depend to a large extent on a whole range of more complex reasons related to individual and group characteristics, including personality traits, age, level of education, values and attitudes transmitted and developed, cultural diversity, and policies related to these phenomena. And this, of course, without claiming that this list is exhaustive.

The article further reviews the literature on the perceptions related to both migration and migrants as potential occupants of jobs. Then, it describes the data and methodology used, before presenting and discussing the main findings in a dedicated section. The latter captures the focus of the current study, namely the discovery of the determinants of the public perception's preference for citizens over immigrants regarding access to jobs. Additionally, this is achieved by insisting on emphasizing causal relations and eliminating redundancies after performing many robustness checks in advance.

2. Related Work

According to Ambrosini (2013) [35], at a certain point, many local governments developed a policy of excluding immigrants, motivated by reasons of security, the priority of national citizens' access to various social benefits, and the defense of the cultural identity of the territory. Additionally, the opposite could work here, which means that such policies inevitably generate some perceptions [36] and indirectly change the public perception of immigrants. In some cases, they can destabilize the moral panics nurtured by it [37]. However, the relationship between the two exists and was a source of some debates and discussions in the literature [2,38,39]. Ivarsflaten (2005) [40] even compared the impact that some elites exert, which has the potential to impact change in the public perception that diversity poses a threat. This author concluded that the former would undoubtedly be less significant.

Regarding the Big Five personality traits and their potential impact on immigration acceptance, Rueda (2018) [41] stated that altruism is an important omitted variable in many political economy studies, which focuses on self-interest rather than on aversion to inequality. Stafford (2020) [42] examined the relationship between attitudes towards immigration and the Big Five personality traits. She found that personality traits, especially those related to altruism, are not just simple influences but essential determinants of attitudes toward immigrants, even with controls for political predispositions and socio-demographic characteristics.

Kunst et al. (2015) [43] discuss the common identity notion, which seems to be crucial for securing the altruistic efforts of the majority to integrate immigrants and, thus, for achieving functional multiculturalism. Still, some research on multicultural beliefs [44] has shown that multiculturalism can cause negative reactions against immigrants and minority groups. This is because the members of the majority sometimes perceive it as threatening their position and identity [45]. Moreover, other studies [46,47] suggest a strong relation between immigration acceptance and emancipative and democratic values. The latter is not necessarily incompatible with the idea of multiculturalism [48]. On the other hand, the perceived high discrimination and lack of acceptance hinder the positive impact of any integration guidelines [49].

In terms of interpersonal trust, according to Pellegrini et al. (2021) [50], this is a mediator between the experienced social exclusion and anti-immigrant attitudes. The experience of being socially excluded reduces feelings of generalized interpersonal trust that, in turn, promote hostile attitudes towards immigrants. Rustenbach (2010) [51] found this type of trust to be a strong predictor of anti-immigrant attitudes.

According to Ensign and Robinson (2011) [52], conventional thinking suggests that immigrants have no choice but to work as entrepreneurs or be self-employed, which is somehow to the detriment of the idea that entrepreneurial attitudes make them migrate. Moreover, it is worth mentioning that employers assign particular meanings to the migrant identity [53], which allows them to enjoy the benefits of cheap, exploitable, and hard-working employees. In some cases, migrants use this identity to obtain jobs, enduring exploitation, including the peculiar form of working below their skill level. Still, accepting hard work at lower wages [54] is explained by the dreams of future self-employment of the immigrant workers.

Therefore, considering the arguments presented here and in the Introduction section, the main hypotheses of this paper are:

H1. *The opinion on immigration policy is closely related to or even a determinant of the level of public acceptance of immigrants as potential job occupants [35,55].*

H2. *Those who subscribe to altruism [56], including working in the benefit of large communities, emancipative values [57], and against any discrimination no matter the type [58], ideologies including multiculturalism [59], and trust in people no matter their origins, are more inclined to accept immigrants when it comes to access to jobs.*

H3. *The ones being more attached to their cultural values and traditions [60] as part of their national identity [61–63] are more likely to be against immigrants as potential job occupants.*

H4. *The attitude towards work and entrepreneurship (as an expression of independence) could be a determinant for this specific type of immigrant acceptance [64–66].*

H5. *The respondent's socio-demographic features are also significant predictors for this kind of acceptance [67,68].*

3. Materials and Methods

This article started from one of the most comprehensive datasets of the World Values Survey (WVS). The latter (version 1.6, WVS_TimeSeries_stata_v1_6.dta) includes 1045 variables and 426,452 observations. Its .csv export followed the simple binary derivation (C002bin) of the original variable to analyze (C002, Jobs scarce: Employers should prioritize nation people than immigrants). Additionally, this was achieved by considering the two extremes of its original three-point scale (Agree, Disagree, Neither—Tables A1 and A2, Appendix A). The option to generate numerical values for labeled variables was enabled when exporting.

The next step was to load this .csv export into the Rattle data mining interface (version 5.4.0) of R, then set C002bin as the target, ignore its source (C002) from the list of inputs and apply the adaptive boosting technique for the decision tree classifiers [69]. This step was performed [70,71] using default settings (Figure 1) to discover the most important related variables. The latter was the 1st data mining and selection round.

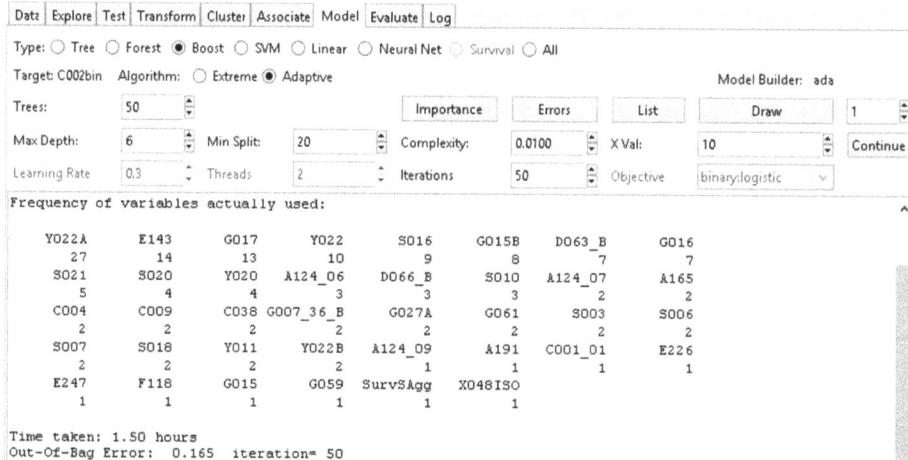

Figure 1. The results of the first selection round using adaptive (Ada) boosting in Rattle.

A consolidation of the set of variables used followed. It involved the ones remaining after the previous step. In some cases, such as with aggregate indexes, it included their sources.

The 2nd selection round stood on a set of filters applied. First, they met a minimum threshold of 0.1 [72] for the absolute values of pairwise correlation coefficients [73] between each recoded variable from the previous step and the one that was to be analyzed. In addition, there was a minimum value of the corresponding significance (min $p = 0.001$) and a minimum support afferent to a minimum number of valid observations (at least a third of the total number) for each pair.

A processing/recoding phase followed. It involved all remaining variables (after the 2nd selection phase). Additionally, some socio-demographic ones for control and cross-validations purposes benefited this treatment. It mostly meant removing the missing and DK/NA (do not know/no answer) values [74] and reversing the scales in the case of larger values which do not reflect higher intensities, but vice versa.

Next, the 3rd selection phase occurred using mixed-effects modeling [75–77] in Stata 17 MP (64-bit version). The latter included both fixed-effects (the remaining variables after the 2nd selection phase and recoded at the previous step—top of Table A1, Appendix A) and random effects (clusters on gender, age, marital status, number of children, education level, income level, professional situation, region, settlement size, and survey year—bottom of Tables A1 and A2, Appendix A). Only those variables not losing significance no matter the clustering criteria and the mixed-effects regression type (both the melogit for the binary form of the response variable and the meologit for the one having values on a scale) resulted in this selection point.

Next, the 4th selection round took place also in Stata. It consisted of successive invocations (stages) of two powerful commands in the LASSO [78] package (CVLASSO to perform random cross-validations and RLASSO for controlling overfitting) until there was no loss in selections.

At the next step (5th round), reverse causality checks served the selection. The latter meant using pairs of individual models built by taking only each of the remaining influences and the variable to analyze (wished roles) and by reversing their roles (the response becomes an input and vice versa or reversed roles). Only some resulted after using ordered logit regressions. It is about the ones generating more explanatory power [79]/larger R-squared (or pseudo R-squared in the form of McFadden's R-squared as reported by Stata for non-OLS regressions such as logit, ologit, meologit, etc.—explanations by Professor Richard Williams of the University of Notre Dame, https://www3.nd.edu/~rwilliam/stats3/L05.pdf (accessed on 25 January 2023) and more information gain/smaller values for both AIC and BIC [80] for the wished roles vs. the reversed ones. They acted as determinants (predictors).

The 6th selection phase focused on testing the existing collinearity between the remaining influences (those emerging after the 3rd phase) and the selected predictors (those resulting after the 4th). Ordinary least squares (OLS) regressions served, and the computed VIF (variance inflation factor) stood against (Equation (1)) the maximum accepted VIF threshold of the model [81,82]. In addition, the maximum absolute values from the matrices with correlation coefficients (maxAbsVPMCC) [83] corresponding to both influences and predictors were objects of evaluation [72,84].

$$\text{Model's maximum accepted VIF} = 1/(1 - \text{model's R-squared}) \tag{1}$$

Additionally, a prediction nomogram [85] resulted when using the *nomolog* command (after its previous installation using the following command: *net install st0391_1, replace from (http://www.stata-journal.com/software/sj15-3)*, and considering the most stalwart remaining predictors).

Finally, each socio-demographic variable previously used for cross-validations served controlling purposes (new models). The latter meant adding them one by one on top of the existing most robust model. They included the most resilient predictors emerging after the previous selection round.

All data processing and tests took place on a Windows Server Datacenter virtual machine (Intel Xeon Gold 6240 CascadeLake CPU and ~32 Gigabytes of memory) in a private cloud. The reporting of the results mainly benefited from the *estout* prerequisite package (*ssc install estout, replace*) with support for both the *eststo* and *esttab* commands [86,87], allowing the direct generation of tables (in the console and as external files, respectively) with default performance metrics, as well as some additional ones [83] of well-known statistical models.

As the reviewers of this manuscript have suggested (and I thank them very much for this observation), there are significant differences between data mining and statistics. Among others, they concern the approaches and techniques used, the propositions and hypothesis statement (loosely vs. well-defined), and the considered type and volume of data (all available vs. sample; several million to a few billion data points vs. hundreds to thousands). In addition, there are also consistent differences between exploratory approaches and those specific to empirical science. This paper benefits from the advantages of all these categories. The letter is coupled with those emerging when comparing the results obtained this way with the ones from the existing scientific theory.

4. Results

After performing the first selection step using adaptive boosting (in the Rattle library —https://rattle.togaware.com of R, accessed on 22 October 2022), a set of 38 variables resulted (Figure 1).

As seen in Figure 1, one way to look at the importance of the resulting variables is by considering their corresponding frequencies of use in the tree construction.

The next concern before going to the second selection step, dedicated to filters on absolute values of pairwise correlation coefficients, was to find and keep (consolidation) only the sources of the following variables:

(a) Y011 as DEFIANCE—Welzel defiance sub-index with three components (AUTHORITY or inverse respect for it, NATIONALISM or inverse national pride, and DEVOUT or Inverse Devoutness) derived from E018 (Future changes: Greater respect for the authority), G006 (How proud of nationality), and D054 (One of the main goals in life has been to make my parents proud);

(b) Y020 as RESEMAVAL—Welzel emancipative values index (https://www.worldvaluessurvey.org/WVSContents.jsp?CMSID=welzelidx&CMSID=welzelidx, accessed on 22 October 2022) with four classes of components dedicated to AUTONOMY (A029 as Important child qualities: independence, A034 as Important child qualities: imagination, and A042 as Important child qualities: obedience), EQUALITY (C001_01 as Jobs scarce: Men should have more right to a job than women, D059 as Men make better political leaders than women do, and D060 as University is more important for a boy than for a girl), CHOICE (F118 as Justifiable: Homosexuality, F120 as Justifiable: Abortion, and F121 as Justifiable: Divorce), and VOICE (E001 as Aims of the country: first choice, E002 as Aims of the country: second choice, E003 as Aims of respondent: first choice, and E004 as Aims of respondent: second choice);

(c) Y022 as EQUALITY—Welzel equality sub-index as C001, D059, and D060;

(d) SurvSAgg that served to build the cultural map (https://www.worldvaluessurvey.org/WVSContents.jsp?CMSID=tradrat&CMSID=tradrat, accessed on 22 October 2022) starting from a set of source variables:

- A008 (Feeling of happiness).
- A165 (Can most people be trusted?).
- E018 (Future changes such as greater respect for authority).
- E025 (Political action such as signing a petition).
- F063 (How important is God in your life?).
- F118 (Is homosexuality justifiable?).
- F120 (Is abortion justifiable?).
- G006 (How proud of nationality?).
- Y002 (Post-materialist index 4-item).
- Y003 (Autonomy index).

After this consolidation point, 51 unique variables resulted: A008 (Section 4 (d) above), A029, A034, and A042 (Section 4 (b) above), A124_06 (Neighbors: Immigrants/foreign workers), A124_07 (Neighbors: People who have AIDS), A124_09 (Neighbors: Homosexuals), A165 (Section 4 (d) above), A191 (It is important to this person living in secure surroundings), C001_01 (Section 4 (b) above), C004 (Jobs scarce: older people should be forced to retire) C009 (First choice, if looking for a job), C038 (People who don't work turn lazy), D054 (Section 4 (a) above), D059, and D060 (Section 4 (b) above), D063_B (Job best way for women to be independent), D066_B (Problem if women have more income than husband), E001, E002, E003, and E004 (Section 4 (b) above), E018 (Section 4 (a) and above), E025 (Section 4 (d) above), E143 (Immigrant policy), E226 (Democracy: People choose their leaders in free elections), E247 (Priority: Global poverty versus National problems), F063, F118, and F120 (Section 4 (d) above), F121 (Section 4 (b) above), G006 (Section 4 (d) above), G007_36_B (Trust: People of another nationality), G015 and G015B (citizenship), G016

(Language at home), G017 (birth country), G027A (Respondent immigrant), G059 (Effects of immigrants on the development of own country), G061 (Measures taken by the government when people from other countries are coming here to work), S003 (ISO 3166-1 numeric country code), S006 (Original respondent number), S007 (Unified respondent number), S010 (Total length of interview), S016 (Language in which interview was conducted), S018 (weight), S020 (Year of survey), S021 (Country-wave-study-set-year), X048ISO (Counties and Country Macroregions ISO 3166-2), Y002, and Y003 (Section 4 (d) above).

After performing the second phase meant for filters starting from pairwise correlation coefficients as absolute values (≥ 0.1), together with their significance ($p < 0.001$) and support (at least a third of the data or N > 142,150), 19 variables resulted as indicated in Table 1. The same results were more easily achieved using the PCDM command (Stata script at https://tinyurl.com/25pd6mx6, accessed on 30 January 2023) in Stata [73] and three parameters (minacc (0.1) minn (142,150) maxp (0.001)) corresponding to those three filters above.

Table 1. Tabular view of the results of the second selection round based on magnitude of correlation coefficients, support, and significance.

Outcome(y)	Input(x)	Correl.Coef.(CC)	Abs.Val.CC(ACC)	No.Obs.(Nobs)	Signif.(p)
C002bin	A124_06	0.107909689	0.107909689	319909	0
C002bin	A124_07	0.142095439	0.142095439	317298	0
C002bin	A124_09	0.149715072	0.149715072	311613	0
C002bin	A165	0.100856547	0.100856547	318679	0
C002bin	C001_01	−0.127478411	0.127478411	327400	0
C002bin	C009	−0.134529402	0.134529402	154481	0
C002bin	C038	−0.160784424	0.160784424	150894	0
C002bin	D054	−0.138970602	0.138970602	297639	0
C002bin	D059	−0.207249289	0.207249289	292549	0
C002bin	D060	−0.136010212	0.136010212	298000	0
C002bin	E025	0.142892051	0.142892051	298829	0
C002bin	E143	0.162277299	0.162277299	162113	0
C002bin	F063	0.138614001	0.138614001	314495	0
C002bin	F118	−0.215562546	0.215562546	298557	0
C002bin	F120	−0.158791514	0.158791514	309204	0
C002bin	F121	−0.132066862	0.132066862	316046	0
C002bin	G007_36_B	0.15077934	0.15077934	181140	0
C002bin	Y002	−0.133265316	0.133265316	316151	0
C002bin	Y003	−0.104665323	0.104665323	326701	0

The next concern before going to the third selection step (dedicated to cross-validations on specified criteria) was to recode ("nt" call sign meaning null treatment) the remaining variables (all 19 in Table 1). In addition to these, the ones to be used as clustering criteria in cross-validations or for further controls were recorded as well. The main concern here was to remove missing and DK/NA answers and adapt the scales to the original meaning of the source questions (Listing A1 and Tables A1 and A2, Appendix A).

The results after the third selection phase relied on mixed-effects modeling. They consisted of discovering and emphasizing the resisting influences (ten from 19, Table A3) no matter the chosen clustering criteria from the set of socio-demographic variables (bottom of Listing A1, lines 49–70, Appendix A section), including the year of the survey (S020, which did not require processing). Just ten influences from the previous list of 19 proved to be robust in this third selection round (Table A3), namely: A124_06nt, C001_01nt, C009nt, C038nt, D054nt, D059nt, E143nt, F118nt, G007_36_Bnt, and Y002nt. The remaining eight influences failed at least in one scenario (A124_07nt-models 6, 9, 11–22; A124_09nt-models 6, 7, 10, 11, and 22; A165nt-model 11; D060nt-models 2–11, 21, and 22; E025nt-models 1–8, 10–19, 21, and 22; F063nt-models 9, and 20; F120nt-models 9, 20, and 22; F121nt–models 9, 11, 20, and 22; Y003nt-models 1–11, 12–15, and 17–22).

The fourth selection round (Stata script at https://tinyurl.com/4x3ez5y9, accessed on 30 January 2023) used CVLASSO and RLASSO and the remaining ten variables. It encountered no loss in selection.

The fifth selection round dedicated itself to reversing causality checks. In addition, it removed one influence from the remaining ten (ordered logit—Table A4) when focusing on the predictors/determinants (the sense of the influences was counted). It gave up A124_06Cnt (Neighbors: Immigrants/foreign workers).

The sixth selection round, responsible for discovering evidence of collinearity (OLS max.Comput.VIF overpassing OLS max.Accept.VIF), further eliminated two variables (D059nt and F118nt—Table A5). Consequently, four matrices with correlation coefficients (only for the predictors in Models 1 and 2, 5 and 6, 9 and 10, and 15—Figure 2) additionally resulted. D054nt was temporarily removed (Models 9 and 10) because of being collinear with F118nt. The latter brought a higher accuracy and an R-squared value (Model 7 vs. Model 8 in Table A5). However, later, after removing F118nt (collinear with C001_01nt, Models 11 and 12), D054nt was added back (Logit Model 15 had the highest accuracy—AUCROC = 0.7852) and generated no collinearity (Table A5—Model 16).

Figure 2. Assessing collinearity using consecutive matrices with correlation coefficients only for predictors (Stata script at https://tinyurl.com/ueefxfmd, accessed on 30 January 2023).

When cross-validating again (second stage: Stata script at https://tinyurl.com/mwb6nher, accessed on 30 January 2023) starting from these seven remaining determinants and the same clustering criteria for cross-validations (including counties and country macroregions—X048WVSnt), no loss in selection occurred.

In terms of support (Stata script at https://tinyurl.com/f868yab4, accessed on 30 January 2023), more than 45,000 observations corresponding to a single wave served in most cases. Additionally, this is because all seven predictors and the response variable were considered simultaneously only in Wave 5 (2005–2009).

A prediction nomogram (Figure 3, *nomolog* command in Stata) starting from binary logistic regressions (Table A5—Model 15) served visual interpretations for all seven remaining determinants. This model, which has seven predictors, generated an R^2 of 0.1799 and a fair-to-good accuracy (AUCROC of 0.7852). The maximum theoretical probability for the most advantageous combination of variable values (Figure 3) is more than 0.99. The latter corresponds to a total score of 39.55 (second X-axis—bottom of Figure 3) as the top-down sum of 3.5, 6.75, 7.6, 4.6, 4.4, 2.7, and 10, values determined relatively easily after drawing perpendiculars to the first X-axis (Score). For other combinations of values (e.g., right edge of Figure 3), these seven predictors were identified as the most important ones; lower total scores emerged (e.g., 21.95). They indicated less critical cases and a lower corresponding probability (e.g., >0.8) of prioritizing the nation's people to the detriment of immigrants regarding access to jobs. This nomogram also suggests the magnitude of the marginal effects (visually as segments corresponding to the unit difference on any scale—Figure 3 and Model 1, Table A7, Appendix A) for those seven robust determinants. In addition, it serves to understand the cumulated effect size by considering the amplitude of any scale visible in this representation.

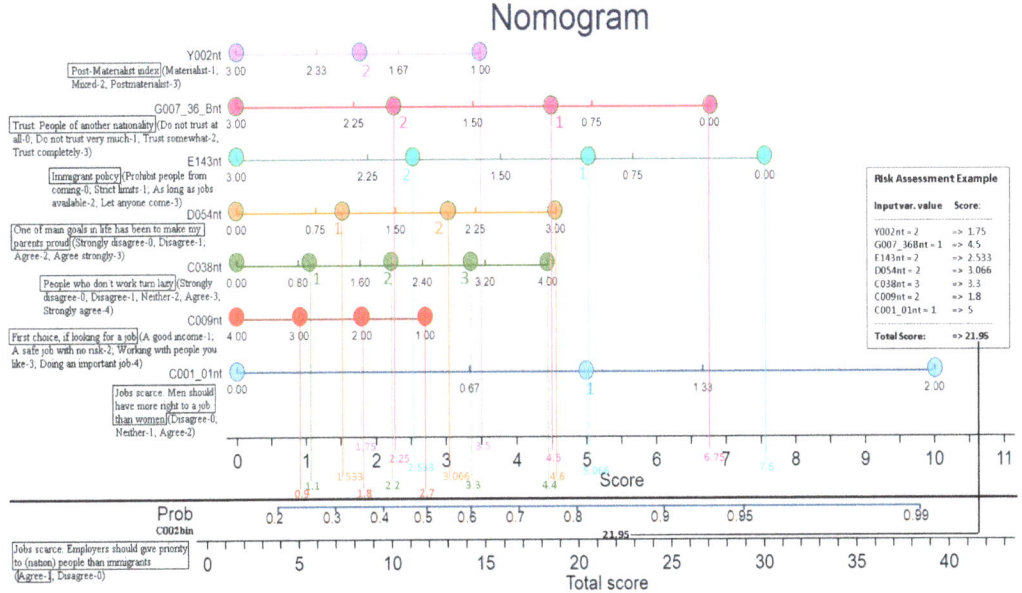

Figure 3. Risk prediction nomogram corresponding to the most resilient predictors (generated using the *nomolog* command in Stata).

Further controls (Table A6, Appendix A) are based on all seven most resilient predictors (Figure 3) and each of those eleven socio-demographic variables already used in cross-validations. All confirmed the robustness of the already identified hepta-core base model (Figure 3 and Models 1 and 13, Table A6, Appendix A), but only seven of them (Models 2, 6–9, 11, 12, 14, 18–21, 23, and 24, Table A6, Appendix A) proved to be significant. The best models here are those additionally emphasizing the role of the settlement size (X049nt, Model 11, based on a logit regression, and Model 23, based on an ologit one, Table A6, Appendix A). They have the highest McFadden's pseudo R-squared (0.1937 for logit and 0.1108 for ologit), AUC-ROC (0.7946), and the lowest AIC (29162.5254 and 58024.8556) and BIC (29238.7119 and 58110.7761) if compared to the base ones (containing only those seven predictors—Models 1 and 13, Table A6, Appendix A).

Moreover, only for these seven additional confirmed influences were the corresponding models also reported using coefficients computed as average marginal effects (Table A7,

Appendix A) and containing direct references to the hypothesis codes. The performance metrics (e.g., pseudo R-squared, AUC-ROC, AIC, and BIC) are the same as in the case of Models 1, 2, 6–9, 11, and 12, Table A6, Appendix A). The interpretation of the coefficients in Table A7 (Appendix A, immediately above the errors reported between round parentheses) follows a simple rule. Each such value indicates the effect of an increase (for positive coefficients)/decrease (for negative ones) by one unit in the value of the corresponding variable (for a given model) on the target variable. This effect translates into the probability of finding it acceptable for employers to prioritize their employees over immigrants increasing by the same value (as the one of the coefficient) but in percentage points.

5. Discussion

The most important of these seven predictors is magnitude (the descending order of scale amplitudes as a visual representation can be found in Figure 3), which corresponds to the attitude towards gender inequality in terms of jobs. It indicates that people agreeing that men should have more rights to a job than women. It is a fact that they are also more likely to accept the idea that employers should prioritize co-nationals than immigrants in case of job scarcity (positive influence or the maximum value of 2 on the right—Figure 3). The latter means that the attitude to the first type of inequality regarding access to jobs (the gender-related one) is the best predictor of the one towards the second type (the immigration-related one). This finding is in line with the already documented relations between gender and migration when it comes to various kinds of discrimination, as mentioned in the scientific literature [88–90].

The second most important determinant when considering the same magnitude criterion seems to correspond to the permissiveness level of the immigration policy. As expected, the latter shows that the ones manifesting a lower level of this type of permissiveness are also more likely (negative influence or the minimum value of 0 on the right—Figure 3) to accept the idea of prioritizing citizens over immigrants in the event of job shortages (validation of H1). Although this finding seems almost obvious, the relationship between migration policy and job discrimination is a complex and well-studied one [91–93].

The third most potent predictor found (Figure 3 and Model 15 in Table A5) is related to the level of trust in people of another nationality. It means that the people with a lower level for this type of trust are also more likely (negative influence or the minimum value of 0 on the right—Figure 3) to accept that employers should prioritize citizens over immigrants in case of lack of jobs. The latter is in line with the findings of other scholars [94–96] and contributes to the validation of H2.

The fourth mightiest determinant corresponds to extrinsic motivations (one of the principal life goals of the respondents is to make their parents proud, also known as devoutness and partially related with traditions due to the interpretation of familism as one of their foundations [97]). That has a positive influence on the response variable. Its maximum value of 3 on the right is observable in Figure 3. It means that people more motivated this way (or devoted to parents in these terms) are also more likely to prioritize their co-nationals in case of job shortages. This finding also stands when considering the existing scientific literature [98,99]. Additionally, it applies if starting from the connection of both items with the notion of power distance. More specifically, the question specifying whether agreeing with making one's own parents proud is assumed to extend to the family. Moreover, it captures the obedience and hierarchy in the family concepts. The one as to whether nationals are privileged over immigrants when jobs are scarce is directly related to the definition of power distance. The particular way the devoutness works contributes to validating H3.

The next most important predictor (fifth) relates to the acceptance level regarding the idea that people who do not work turn lazy (also with a positive influence—the maximum value of 4 on the right, as seen in Figure 3). The latter shows that people more inclined to accept this attitude towards work are also more protective of the nation's people's access to jobs. This finding complements other findings in the scientific literature, revealing the limitations of migrant working identity [53,100].

The sixth most potent determinant concerns the post-materialist index (the version with four items), which has a negative influence (the minimum of 1 on the right—Figure 3). The latter refers to people with a lower appetite for postmaterialist values or less need for independence and fulfillment of personal objectives in life [101]. They are also more likely to prioritize their co-nationals at the expense of immigrants as access to employment. This finding is in line with the ones of [102], through the concept of subjective well-being associated with endorsement of democracy, greater emphasis on postmaterialist values, and less intolerance (more tolerance) of immigrants and members of different racial and ethnic groups.

The specific way these two predictors function means a complete validation of H4.

The last most important predictor in terms of magnitude corresponds to the variable measuring the preference regarding a job with benefits for the community rather than individual ones (negative influence—the minimum value of 1 on the right—Figure 3). It indicates that people are less likely to prefer community-oriented jobs; on the contrary, they are more oriented towards individual benefits when it comes to a job or are simply more selfish [103]. They are more inclined to protect the nation's people in case of job shortages. The latter contributes to the full validation of H2.

Next, all seven resilient predictors previously found (Figure 3) stood as a strong base for further controls (Table A6, Appendix A). Those used all socio-demographic criteria involved in cross-validations. Only seven of those criteria indicated significance.

First, the gender influence (Models 2 and 14, Table A6, Appendix A) indicates that female respondents are more protective of citizens than immigrants regarding access to jobs. It means that women are more likely to consider it more justifiable for employers to prioritize the people of their nation than men. The latter is in line with some findings in the literature [104,105] and contradicts others [106].

An additional socio-demographic variable was found significant (income scale, Models 9 and 21, Table A6, Appendix A). By its sign (negative), the latter indicates that those who earn more are less inclined to consider it justifiable for employers to prioritize nationals than immigrants. This idea stands in the light of the findings of Chandler and Tsai (2001) [107], Tucci (2005) [108], Tavakoli and Chatterjee (2021) [109], and Ruhs (2018) [110]. For the last author, this is especially true for high-skilled migrants. The same applies to those with a higher education level (Models 7 and 19, Table A6, Appendix A). Additionally, this is also in line with the findings of Tavakoli and Chatterjee (2021) [109]. They concluded that an additional level of education on the earnings of an individual and his family income will bring better financial welfare and security. In turn, the latter will reduce the perception of the economic threat of immigrants. The same is true for those with an employment status more near a full-time job (Models 8 and 20, Table A6, Appendix A) and the opposite (positive coefficient sign) for the ones having more children (Models 6 and 18, Table A6, Appendix A). These last two findings are consistent with those on the income dependence of the response variable. The latter state that people in higher-income groups are more tolerant towards immigrants [111], more positive in their attitudes to them [112], and show significantly lower levels of welfare chauvinism [113].

Another significant control variable corresponds to the settlement size (Models 11 and 23, Table A6, Appendix A). The latter contributes to the best models (largest McFadden pseudo R-squared, AUC-ROC, and lowest AIC and BIC) with eight predictors (hepta-core plus each additional control), as already emphasized at the end of the Results section above. Due to its sign (negative), it shows that people from larger communities (bigger cities) are also less inclined to consider it acceptable for employers to prioritize nationals to the detriment of immigrants. In the case of Europe, this finding stands, and such respondents are more likely to have more tolerant attitudes towards immigrants [111]. Similarly, with direct reference to the case of Canada, other scholars [114] highlighted a particularity of large urban areas when compared with the small ones, namely, the existence of immigrant service providers and language-training venues. By contrast, in Russia, for example, people living in the countryside are the least xenophobic, while the population of big cities is the most xenophobic [115]. All these mean the partial validation of H5, when considering that some socio-demographic variables were not found to be significant (e.g., age, marital status).

Due to its positive coefficient sign, the last significant control variable (the survey year, Models 12 and 24, Table A6, Appendix A) indicates a relevant finding. Despite the undeniable globalization and the rise of multiculturalism, over time, people have increasingly come to believe that it is more acceptable for employers to prioritize citizens over immigrants. The latter contradicts studies focused on general attitudes towards immigration [116] or integration of immigrants [117] based on considering specific regions and expanding for a shorter time.

As expected, due to its nature (nominal numerical codes originally unrelated to a specific intensity scale), the variable corresponding to the counties and country macroregions (X048WVS—in the given form) in which the interview took place did not prove to be statistically significant as a control variable. Still, it has proven to be extremely important [118,119] for cross-validations. The same argument (numerical codes originally unrelated to an intensity scale but useful for cross-validation) applies to the values of the variable corresponding to the country code (S003—ISO 3166-1 numeric country code). Still, the latter was identified in the first selection round (adaptive boosting—right side of Figure 1). Therefore, differences among countries are expected beyond these seven common predictors, referred to as a hepta-core model. However, the specific features of countries and particular regions (e.g., a dummy variable referring to whether a country is ex-communist or not [120], some country-dependent measures of economic activity such as GDP or the ratio between stock market capitalization and GDP defined in The World Bank Data Catalog or even the Worldwide Governance Indicators defined by Kaufmann et al. in 2010 [121] and used in many other studies, including recent ones [122,123]) will be the object of future research on the same topic but with more focus on certain local peculiarities.

6. Conclusions

An accurate model with seven strong influences emerged in this paper. These act more as determinants because of passing reverse causality checks. They indicate a specific type of world values survey respondents. It is about the ones less likely to consider it acceptable for employers to prioritize their people over immigrants. These are as follows: those who believe in emancipative values, namely, the ones of gender equality for jobs, those choosing a profession more relevant for the community than for themselves, those disagreeing that people who do not work will turn lazy, the ones with higher values if inverse devoutness (less inclined to make their own parents proud), the ones agreeing with a less prohibitive immigrant policy, those who trust more in people of another nationality, and the ones with a profile corresponding to a higher value for the post-materialist index. In addition, some controls generally emphasized the positive roles of three socio-demographic variables. There are the female gender, the number of children, and the survey year. It is also worth mentioning the negative ones, which are education level, employment status in terms of involvement in a full-time job, income scale, and settlement size (the most important control variable in terms of performance added to the basic hepta-core model), when considering whether it is justifiable for employers to prioritize the people of their nation rather than immigrants. By allowing visual interpretations corresponding to the seven most resilient determinants, the prediction nomogram presented in this paper serves both as a powerful probability identification instrument and as a decision support tool that serves management systems under conditions of uncertainty and risk. All conclusions related to the identified determinants stand on models with fair-to-good classification accuracy. They resulted after performing many selection rounds and robustness checks.

Funding: This research received no external funding.

Institutional Review Board Statement: The data used in this study belongs to the World Values Survey, which conducted surveys following the Declaration of Helsinki.

Informed Consent Statement: The World Values Survey obtained informed consent from all subjects involved in the study.

Data Availability Statement: The dataset used in this study belongs to the World Values Survey is the .dta file inside the "WVS TimeSeries 1981 2020 Stata v1 6.zip" archive (https://www.worldvaluessurvey.org/WVSDocumentationWVL.jsp, accessed on 22 October 2022, the "Data and Documentation" menu, the "Data Download" option, the "Timeseries (1981–2022)" entry).

Acknowledgments: For allowing the exploration of the dataset and the agreement to publish the research results, the author would like to thank the World Values Survey and supporting projects. In terms of technical assistance (https://cloud.raas.uaic.ro, (accessed on 22 October 2022), as a private cloud of the Alexandru Ioan Cuza University of Iași, Romania), this paper benefited from the support of the Competitiveness Operational Programme Romania. More precisely, project number SMIS 124759—RaaS-IS (Research as a Service Iasi) id POC/398/1/124759.

Conflicts of Interest: The author declares no conflict of interest.

Appendix A

Listing A1. Recoding the remaining variables using a Stata script with numbered lines—numbers displayed separately, as when opened with the Stata editor (Stata script at: https://tinyurl.com/5n6bdfss, accessed on 30 January 2023).

```
1. use ''F:\ WVS_TimeSeries_stata_v1_6.dta'' //19x: A124_06
   A124_07 A124_09 A165 C001_01 C009 C038 D054 D059 D060 E025
   E143 F063 F118 F120 F121 G007_36_B Y002 Y003
2. generate C002nt=.
3. replace C002nt=2 if C002==1
4. replace C002nt=0 if C002==2
5. replace C002nt=1 if C002==3 // or Jobs scarce: Employers
   should give priority to (nation) people than immigrants
6. gen C002bin=.
7. replace C002bin=1 if C002==1
8. replace C002bin=0 if C002==2 // or Jobs scarce: Employers
   should give priority to (nation) people than immigrants
9. gen A124_06nt =.
10. replace A124_06nt=A124_06 if A124_06!=. & A124_06>=0 //or
    Neighbors: Immigrants/foreign workers
11. gen A124_07nt =.
12. replace A124_07nt=A124_07 if A124_07!=. & A124_07>=0 //or
    Neighbors: People who have AIDS
13. gen A124_09nt =.
14. replace A124_09nt=A124_09 if A124_09!=. & A124_09>=0 //or
    Neighbors: Homosexuals
15. generate A165nt=.
16. replace A165nt=2-A165 if A165!=. & A165>0 //or Most people
    can be trusted
17. generate C001_01nt=.
18. replace C001_01nt=2 if C001_01==1
19. replace C001_01nt=0 if C001_01==2
20. replace C001_01nt=1 if C001_01==3 //or Jobs scarce: Men
    should have more right to a job than women (source for
    Y022A=WOMJOB- Welzel equality -1: Gender equality: job)
```

```
21. generate C009nt=.
22. replace C009nt=C009 if C009!=. & C009>0  //or First choice,
    if looking for a job:1.good income,2.safe job,3.wrk &people
    u like ,4.Do an import.job,5.Do someth.for community
23. generate C038nt = .
24. replace C038nt=5-C038 if C038!=. & C038>0  //or People who
    don't work turn lazy
25. generate D054nt = .
26. replace D054nt=4-D054 if D054!=. & D054>0  //or One of main
    goals in life has been to make my parents proud (source for
    Y011C=DEVOUT- Welzel defiance -3: Inverse devoutness)
27. generate D059nt=.
28. replace D059nt=4-D059 if D059!=. & D059>0  //or Men make
    better political leaders than women do (source for Y022B=
    WOMPOL- Welzel equality -2: Gender equality: politics)
29. generate D060nt=.
30. replace D060nt=4-D060 if D060!=. & D060>0  //or University is
    more important for a boy than for a girl (source for Y022C=
    WOMEDU- Welzel equality -3: Gender equality: education)
31. generate E025nt=.
32. replace E025nt=3-E025 if E025!=. & E025>0  //or Political
    action: Signing a petition
33. generate E143nt = .
34. replace E143nt=4-E143 if E143!=. & E143>0  //or Immigrant
    policy: 1 Let anyone come . 4 Prohibit people from coming
35. generate F063nt=.
36. replace F063nt=F063 if F063!=. & F063>0  //or How important is
    God in your life
37. generate F118nt=.
38. replace F118nt=F118 if F118!=. & F118>0  //or Justifiable:
    Homosexuality
39. generate F120nt=.
40. replace F120nt=F120 if F120!=. & F120>0  //or Justifiable:
    Abortion
41. generate F121nt=.
42. replace F121nt=F121 if F121!=. & F121>0  //or Justifiable:
    Divorce
43. generate G007_36_Bnt=.
44. replace G007_36_Bnt=4-G007_36_B if G007_36_B!=. & G007_36_B>0
    //Trust: People of another nationality (B)
45. generate Y002nt=.
46. replace Y002nt=Y002 if Y002!=. & Y002>0  //or Post-Materialist
    index 4-item: 1 Materialist, 2 Mixed, 3 Postmaterialist
47. generate Y003nt=.
48. replace Y003nt=2+Y003 if Y003!=. & Y003>-5  //or Autonomy
    Index: -2 Obedience/Religious Faith .. 2 Determination,
    perseverance/Independence
49. *FOR BUILDING CLUSTERS WHEN PERFORMING CROSS-VALIDATIONS:
50. generate X001nt = .
51. replace X001nt=X001 if X001!=. & X001>0  //Gender
52. generate X003nt = .
53. replace X003nt=X003 if X003!=. & X003>0  //Age
54. generate X007nt = .
```

```
55. replace X007nt=8-X007 if X007!=. & X007>0 //Marital status
56. generate X007bin=.
57. replace X007bin=1 if X007==1 | X007==2
58. replace X007bin=0 if X007!=. & X007>2 //Marital status as
    with someone or not
59. generate X011nt=.
60. replace X011nt=X011 if X011!=. & X011>=0 //How many children
    do you have
61. generate X025nt=.
62. replace X025nt=X025 if X025!=. & X025>0 //Highest educational
    level attained
63. generate X028nt=.
64. replace X028nt=8-X028 if X028!=. & X028>0 & X028<9 //
    Employment status
65. generate X047nt=.
66. replace X047nt=X047 if X047!=. & X047>0 //Scale of incomes
67. generate X048WVSnt=.
68. replace X048WVSnt=X048WVS if X048WVS!=. & X048WVS>0 //Regions
69. generate X049nt=.
70. replace X049nt=X049 if X049!=. & X049>0 //Settlement size
```

Table A1. The most relevant items of this study.

Variable	Short Description	Coding Details
C002	Jobs scarce: Employers should give priority to (nation) people than immigrants (original format)	<0 for Do not know/No Answer/Not applicable/Not Asked/Missing (DK/NA/M); 1-Agree; 2-Disagree; 3-Neither
C002nt	The same as above but with a reversed scale and with null and DK/NA/M treatment	Null (.)-DK/NA/M; 2-Agree; 1-Neither; 0-Disagree
C002bin	The same as above in its binary form and with null and DK/NA/M treatment	Null (.)-DK/NA/M or Neither; 1-Agree; 0-Disagree
A124_06	Neighbors: Immigrants/foreign workers (original format)	<0 for DK/NA/M; 1-Mentioned; 0-Not mentioned
A124_06nt	The same as above with null and DK/NA/M treatment	Null (.)-DK/NA/M; 1-Mentioned; 0-Not mentioned
A124_07	Neighbors: People who have AIDS (original format)	<0 for DK/NA/M; 1-Mentioned; 0-Not mentioned
A124_07nt	The same as above with null and DK/NA/M treatment	Null (.)-DK/NA/M; 1-Mentioned; 0-Not mentioned
A124_09	Neighbors: Homosexuals (original format)	<0 for DK/NA/M; 1-Mentioned; 0-Not mentioned
A124_09nt	The same as above with null and DK/NA/M treatment	Null (.)-DK/NA/M; 1-Mentioned; 0-Not mentioned
A165	Most people can be trusted (original format)	<0 for DK/NA/M; 1-You can trust most people; 2-Need to be very careful
A165nt	The same as above but with a reversed scale and with null and DK/NA/M treatment	Null (.)-DK/NA/M; 1-You can trust most people; 0-Need to be very careful
C001_01	Jobs scarce: Men should have more rights to a job than women (original format)	<0 for DK/NA/M; 1-Agree; 2-Disagree; 3-Neither
C001_01nt	The same as above but with a reversed scale and with null and DK/NA/M treatment	Null (.)-DK/NA/M; 2-Agree; 1-Neither; 0-Disagree

Table A1. Cont.

Variable	Short Description	Coding Details
C009	The first choice, if looking for a job (original format)	<0 for DK/NA/M; 1-A good income; 2-A safe job with no risk; 3-Working with people you like; 4-Doing important work; 5-Do something for the community
C009nt	The same as above with null and DK/NA/M treatment	Null (.)-DK/NA/M; 1-A good income ... 5-Do something for the community
C038	People who do not work turn lazy (original format)	<0 for DK/NA/M; 1-Strongly agree; 2- Agree; 3-Neither agree nor disagree; 4-Disagree; 5-Strongly disagree
C038nt	The same as above but with a reversed scale and with null and DK/NA/M treatment	Null (.)-DK/NA/M; 0-Strongly disagree ... 4-Strongly agree
D054	One of my main goals in life has been to make my parents proud (original format)	<0 for DK/NA/M; 1-Strongly agree; 2- Agree; 3-Disagree; 4-Strongly disagree
D054nt	The same as above but with a reversed scale and with null and DK/NA/M treatment	Null (.)-DK/NA/M; 0-Strongly disagree ... 3-Strongly agree
D059	Men make better political leaders than women do (original format)	<0 for DK/NA/M; 1-Strongly agree; 2- Agree; 3-Disagree; 4-Strongly disagree
D059nt	The same as above but with a reversed scale and with null and DK/NA/M treatment	Null (.)-DK/NA/M; 0-Strongly disagree .. 3-Strongly agree
D060	University is more important for a boy than for a girl (original format)	<0 for DK/NA/M; 1-Strongly agree; 2- Agree; 3-Disagree; 4-Strongly disagree
D060nt	The same as above but with a reversed scale and with null and DK/NA/M treatment	Null (.)-DK/NA/M; 0-Strongly disagree ... 3-Strongly agree
E025	Political action: Signing a petition (original format)	<0 for DK/NA/M; 1-Have done; 2- Might do; 3-Would never do
E025nt	The same as above but with a reversed scale and with null and DK/NA/M treatment	Null (.)-DK/NA/M; 0-Would never do; 1- Might do; 2-Have done
E143	Immigrant policy (original format)	<0 for DK/NA/M; 1-Let anyone come; 2- As long as jobs available; 3-Strict limits; 4-Prohibit people from coming
E143nt	The same as above but with a reversed scale and with null and DK/NA/M treatment	Null (.)-DK/NA/M; 0-Prohibit people from coming ... 3-Let anyone come
F063	How important is God in your life (original format)	<0 for DK/NA/M; 1-Not at all important ... 10-Very important
F063nt	The same as above with null and DK/NA/M treatment	Null (.)-DK/NA/M; 1-Not at all important ... 10-Very important
F118	Justifiable: Homosexuality (original format)	<0 for DK/NA/M; 1-Never justifiable ... 10-Always justifiable
F118nt	The same as above with null and DK/NA/M treatment	Null (.)-DK/NA/M; 1-Never justifiable ... 10-Always justifiable
F120	Justifiable: Abortion (original format)	<0 for DK/NA/M; 1-Never justifiable ... 10-Always justifiable
F120nt	The same as above with null and DK/NA/M treatment	Null (.)-DK/NA/M; 1-Never justifiable ... 10-Always justifiable
F121	Justifiable: Divorce (original format)	<0 for DK/NA/M; 1-Never justifiable ... 10-Always justifiable
F121nt	The same as above with null and DK/NA/M treatment	Null (.)-DK/NA/M; 1-Never justifiable ... 10-Always justifiable

Table A1. *Cont.*

Variable	Short Description	Coding Details
G007_36_B	Trust: People of another nationality (original format)	<0 for DK/NA/M; 1-Trust completely; 2- Trust somewhat; 3-Not very much; 4-Not at all
G007_36_Bnt	The same as above but with a reversed scale and with null and DK/NA/M treatment	Null (.)-DK/NA/M; 0-Not at all .. 3-Trust completely
Y002	Post-Materialist index 4-item (original format)	<0 for DK/NA/M; 1-Materialist; 2- Mixed; 3-Postmaterialist
Y002nt	The same as above with null and DK/NA/M treatment	Null (.)-DK/NA/M; 1-Materialist; 2- Mixed; 3-Postmaterialist
Y003	Autonomy index (original format)	<0 for DK/NA/M; -2-Obedience/Religious Faith ... 2-Determination, perseverance/Independence
Y003nt	The same as above but with a positive (raised) scale and with null and DK/NA/M treatment	Null (.)-DK/NA/M; 0-Obedience/Religious Faith ... 4-Determination, perseverance/Independence
X001	Gender (original format)	<0 for DK/NA/M; 1-Male; 2-Female
X001nt	The same as above with null and DK/NA/M treatment	Null (.)-DK/NA/M; 1-Male; 2-Female
X003	Age (original format)	<0-DK/NA/M
X003nt	The same as above with null and DK/NA/M treatment	Null (.)-DK/NA/M
X007	Marital status (original format)	<0-DK/NA/M; 1-Married; 2-Living together as married; 3-Divorced; 4-Separated; 5-Widowed; 6-Single/Never married; 7 and 8-other values considered the most distant from the status of a married person
X007nt	The same as above but with a reversed scale and with null and DK/NA/M treatment	Null (.)-DK/NA/M; 0 and 1-other values considered the most distant from the status of a married person; 2-Single/Never married .. 7-Married
X007bin	The same as above in its binary form and with null and DK/NA/M treatment	Null (.)-DK/NA/M; 1-Married/ Living together as married; 0-Otherwise
X011	How many children do you have (original format)	<0-DK/NA/M; 0-No child; 1-1 child; 2-2 children .. 5-5 children or more
X011nt	The same as above with null and DK/NA/M treatment	Null (.)-DK/NA/M; 0-No child .. 5-5 children or more
X025	The highest educational level attained (original format)	<0-DK/NA/M; 1-Inadequately completed elementary education; 2-Completed (compulsory) elementary education; 3-Incomplete secondary school: technical/vocational type; 4-Complete secondary school: technical/vocational type; 5-Incomplete secondary: university-preparatory type; 6-Complete secondary: university-preparatory type; 7-Some university without degree/Higher education-lower-level; 8-University with degree/Higher education-upper-level tertiary
X025nt	The same as above with null and DK/NA/M treatment	Null (.)-DK/NA/M; 1-Inadequately completed elementary education .. 8-University with degree/Higher education-upper-level tertiary
X028	Employment status (original format)	<0-DK/NA/M; 1-Full time; 2-Part time; 3-Self employed; 4-Retired; 5-Housewife; 6-Students; 7-Unemployed; 8-Other

Table A1. Cont.

Variable	Short Description	Coding Details
X028nt	The same as above but with a reversed scale and with null and DK/NA/M treatment	Null (.)-DK/NA/M; 0-Other .. 7-Full time
X047	The scale of incomes (original format)	<0-DK/NA/M; 1-Lowest step; 2-Second step .. 10-Tenth step; 11-Highest step
X047nt	The same as above with null and DK/NA/M treatment	Null (.)-DK/NA/M; 1-Lowest step .. 11-Highest step
X048WVS	Counties and Country Macroregions (numeric code) where the interview was conducted (original format)	<0-DK/NA/M; 8001 Albania: Tirana .. 7360013 SD: River Nile
X048WVSnt	The same as above with null and DK/NA/M treatment	Null (.)-DK/NA/M; 8001 Albania: Tirana .. 7360013 SD: River Nile
X049	Settlement size (original format)	<0-DK/NA/M; 1—Under 2000; 2—2000—5000; 3—5000—10,000; 4—10,000—20,000; 5—20,000—50,000; 6—50,000—100,000; 7—100,000—500,000; 8—500,000 and more
X049nt	The same as above with null and DK/NA/M treatment	Null (.)-DK/NA/M; 1-Under 2000 .. 8-500,000 and more
S020	Year of survey (original format)	Years between 1981 and 2020 (limited to 2017-2020-non-NULL observations for the response variable)

Source: WVS data.

Table A2. Descriptive statistics for the most relevant WVS items used in this study.

Variable	n	Mean	Std.Dev.	Min	0.25	Median	0.75	Max
C002nt	377,345	1.55	0.75	0	1	2	2	2
C002bin	330,509	0.82	0.39	0	1	1	1	1
A124_06nt	396,205	0.21	0.41	0	0	0	0	1
A124_07nt	384,956	0.44	0.5	0	0	0	1	1
A124_09nt	376,865	0.5	0.5	0	0	1	1	1
A165nt	409,115	0.26	0.44	0	0	0	1	1
C001_01nt	395,652	0.97	0.91	0	0	1	2	2
C009nt	183,875	2.15	1.12	1	1	2	3	5
C038nt	175,111	2.86	1.09	0	2	3	4	4
D054nt	360,660	2.27	0.78	0	2	2	3	3
D059nt	357,860	1.53	0.98	0	1	1	2	3
D060nt	364,765	1.04	0.92	0	0	1	1	3
E025nt	379,840	0.83	0.81	0	0	1	2	2
E143nt	186,246	1.54	0.84	0	1	2	2	3
F063nt	402,066	7.7	3.02	1	6	10	10	10
F118nt	380,939	3.21	3.04	1	1	1	5	10
F120nt	398,878	3.37	2.85	1	1	2	5	10
F121nt	403,700	4.65	3.1	1	1	5	7	10
G007_36_Bnt	220,047	1.19	0.86	0	1	1	2	3
Y002nt	396,977	1.77	0.62	1	1	2	2	3
Y003nt	414,123	2.05	1.16	0	1	2	3	4
X001nt	421,634	1.52	0.5	1	1	2	2	2
X003nt	421,892	41.14	16.23	13	28	39	53	103
X007nt	421,264	5.34	2.18	0	3	7	7	7
X007bin	421,264	0.64	0.48	0	0	1	1	1
X011nt	410,849	1.89	1.81	0	0	2	3	24
X025nt	300,306	4.71	2.23	1	3	5	6	8
X028nt	413,665	4.69	2.16	0	3	5	7	7
X047nt	389,150	4.65	2.3	1	3	5	6	10
X048WVSnt	380,027	450,000	260,000	8,001	230,000	420,000	700,000	890,000
X049nt	303,252	4.95	2.51	1	3	5	7	8
S020	426,452	2005.05	9.57	1981	1998	2006	2012	2020

Source: own calculation in Stata (Stata script at https://tinyurl.com/yt872hcs, accessed on 31 January 2023).

Table A3. The results of cross-validations on some socio-demographic variables using mixed-effects binary (first 11 models) and ordered logit (last 11 ones).

Table A3. Cont.

Model	(1)	(2)	(3)	(4)	(5)	(6)	(7)	(8)	(9)	(10)	(11)	(12)	(13)	(14)	(15)	(16)	(17)	(18)	(19)	(20)	(21)	(22)
Input/Response	C002bin	C002bin	C002bin	C002bin	C002bin	C002bin	C002bin	C002bin	C002bin	C002bin	C002bin	C002nt	C002nt	C002nt	C002nt	C002nt	C002nt	C002nt	C002nt	C002nt	C002nt	C002nt
_cons	1.7591 *** (0.3016)	1.7618 *** (0.1248)	1.7621 *** (0.1023)	1.7606 *** (0.1674)	1.7858 *** (0.0626)	1.8108 *** (0.1440)	1.7951 *** (0.2164)	1.6956 *** (0.2091)	2.1114 *** (0.2154)	1.8087 *** (0.1656)	1.9660 *** (0.5685)											
varf_cons[X001nt]]	0.0068 ** (0.0025)											0.0024 (0.0019)										
varf_cons[X003nt]]		0.0017 (0.0023)											0.0012 (0.0016)									
varf_cons[X007bin]]			0.0003 (0.0010)											0.0004 (0.0005)								
varf_cons[X007bin]]				0.0000 (0.0000)																		
varf_cons[X011nt]]					0.0000 (0.0000)										0.0000 (0.0000)							
varf_cons[X025nt]]						0.0094 *** (0.0026)										0.0000 (0.0000)						
varf_cons[X028nt]]							0.0256 (0.0276)										0.0036 * (0.0022)					
varf_cons[X047nt]]								0.0407 * (0.0182)										0.0155 (0.0147)				
varf_cons[X048WV5nt]]									0.9769 (0.1090)										0.0322 * (0.0134)			
varf_cons[X049nt]]										0.0122 (0.0066)										0.6856 (0.0706)		
varf_cons[S020]]											0.3847 (0.2663)										0.0074 (0.0051)	0.1051 (0.0699)
N	33,646	33,601	33,623	33,623	32,706	32,019	32,205	31,586	33,103	27,549	33,665	38,468	38,412	38,436	38,436	37,260	36,628	36,949	36,108	37,864	31,523	38,489
AIC	28,976.6072	28,980.5107	28,995.2304	28,983.3193	28,173.1051	27,603.3404	28,431.6436	27,065.5576	26,470.2628	23,067.7451	26,724.7783	57,631.2925	57,566.6483	57,593.4617	57,586.0935	55,506.4302	54,929.4457	56,506.1179	53,920.0443	54,208.1111	47,271.6480	57,459.9627
BIC	28,993.4545	29,157.3793	29,045.7682	28,993.7422	28,240.2676	27,661.5400	28,480.3027	27,140.8018	26,946.8178	23,697.3112	26,781.1752	57,648.4076	57,754.8800	57,626.2454	57,594.6933	55,376.6556	54,097.5142	56,563.7790	54,004.9670	54,076.0298	47,338.5158	57,465.6571

Source: own calculation in Stata (Stata script at https://tinyurl.com/susvkppj, accessed on 30 January 2023). Notes: var (_cons []) relates to the cross-validation criterion. Robust standard errors are between round parentheses. The raw coefficients emphasized using *, **, and *** are significant at 5‰, 1‰, and 1%. Red vs. green indicates a loss of significance (not selected variables) vs. the opposite (the selected ones).

Table A4. The results of the first stage of reverse causality checks using ordered logit.

Ologit Model	(1)	(2)	(3)	(4)	(5)	(6)	(7)	(8)	(9)	(10)	(11)	(12)	(13)	(14)	(15)	(16)	(17)	(18)	(19)	(20)
Input/Response	C002nt	A1241_0mt	C002nt	C001_01nt	C002nt	L009nt	C002nt	C019nt	C002nt	D054nt	C002nt	D059nt	C002nt	L143nt	C002nt	L143nt	C002nt	G007_3n_Bnt	C002nt	Y002nt
A1241_0mt	0.6682 *** (0.0095)																			
C001_01nt		0.6370 *** (0.0042)																		
C009nt				−0.2307 *** (0.0048)																
C019nt						0.3211 *** (0.0048)														
D054nt								0.3915 *** (0.0047)												
D059nt										0.4651 *** (0.0042)										
L143nt												0.4734 *** (0.0065)								
T118nt															−0.1426 *** (0.0012)					
G007_3n_Bnt																	−0.3915 *** (0.0058)			
Y002nt																				−0.3374 *** (0.0046)
C002nt		0.3864 *** (0.0061)		0.7017 *** (0.0045)		−0.2817 *** (0.0061)		0.3957 *** (0.0062)		0.3454 *** (0.0045)		0.5046 *** (0.0043)		−0.4273 *** (0.0058)		0.4942 *** (0.0045)		−0.3817 *** (0.0056)	0.4489 *** (0.0060)	
N	364,886	364,886	373,890	373,890	173,676	173,676	171,085	171,085	339,416	339,416	333,481	333,481	181,744	181,744	341,555	341,555	209,101	209,101	359,823	359,823
chi²	4075.6756	4077.5373	22,654.9698	24,630.4358	2334.3676	2124.2002	4434.4490	4132.8212	68079723	5946.5022	12,262.6181	13,692.4046	5317.2469	5372.7167	14,504.4671	12,026.1077	4612.6482	4628.3237	5633.7297	5493.3756
P	0.0000	0.0000	0.0000	0.0000	0.0000	0.0000	0.0000	0.0000	0.0000	0.0000	0.0000	0.0000	0.0000	0.0000	0.0000	0.0000	0.0000	0.0000	0.0000	0.0000
Pseudo R² (McFadden)	0.0074	0.0117	0.0402	0.0343	0.0260	0.0052	0.0169	0.0097	0.0128	0.0086	0.0252	0.0159	0.0199	0.0121	0.0272	0.0119	0.0145	0.0098	0.0103	0.0088
AIC	573,486.7251	380,867.1659	569,329.7561	743,787.6208	346,870.8392	445,301.0113	267,052.432	408,574.0556	528,500.762	732,454.3935	514,743.012	874,678.1394	276,760.648	441,719.4397	512,401.6024	1,114,113.9416	195,803.616	506,403.8567	541,172.692	663,326.2812
BIC	573,521.1451	380,518.7826	569,362.7511	743,820.1159	346,903.3041	445,341.2711	267,084.570	408,624.3052	528,562.633	732,497.5534	514,706.430	874,521.0267	276,728.076	441,759.8811	512,372.662	1,114,221.3543	195,414.103	506,441.8590	541,230.0753	663,386.6613

Source: own calculation in Stata (Stata script at https://tinyurl.com/4a2778m42, accessed on 30 January 2023). Notes: robust standard errors are between round parentheses. The raw coefficients emphasized using *** are significant at 1‰. Colors are applied to emphasize better model scores and selected variables (green) and lower model scores and variables not selected (red).

Table A5. Identified collinearity issues.

Model	(1)	(2)	(3)	(4)	(5)	(6)	(7)	(8)	(9)	(10)	(11)	(12)	(13)	(14)	(15)	(16)	(17)	(18)
Regression Type	Logit	OLS	Logit	Logit	Logit	OLS	Logit	Logit	Logit	OLS	Logit	Logit	Logit	OLS	Logit	OLS	Logit	OLS
Filter condition	N/A	N/A	C001_01nt=	D054nt!=	N/A	N/A	D054nt!=	F118nt!=	N/A	N/A	C001_01nt!=	F118nt!=	N/A	N/A	N/A	N/A	N/A	N/A
C001_01nt	0.7086 *** (0.0211)	0.0808 *** (0.0022)		0.7867 *** (0.0204)	0.7829 *** (0.0201)	0.0908 *** (0.0021)	0.7908 *** (0.0201)	0.8391 *** (0.0199)	0.7941 *** (0.0199)	0.0928 *** (0.0020)		0.8651 *** (0.0196)	0.8861 *** (0.0186)	0.1021 *** (0.0018)	0.8647 *** (0.0189)	0.8967 *** (0.0018)	0.7867 *** (0.0191)	0.7947 *** (0.0019)
C009nt	−0.1240 ***	−0.0229 ***	−0.1489 ***	−0.1320 ***	−0.1334 ***	−0.1243 ***	−0.1396 ***	−0.1619 ***	−0.1375 ***	−0.0248 ***	−0.1797 ***	−0.1735 ***	−0.1690 ***	−0.0291 ***	−0.1558 ***	−0.0275 ***	−0.1427 ***	−0.0270 ***
	(0.0122)	(0.0019)	(0.0120)	(0.0121)	(0.0120)	(0.0019)	(0.0119)	(0.0118)	(0.0119)	(0.0018)	(0.0115)	(0.0117)	(0.0112)	(0.0017)	(0.0114)	(0.0017)	(0.0114)	(0.0018)
C038nt	0.1451 *** (0.0121)	0.0244 *** (0.0019)	0.1493 *** (0.0120)	0.1570 *** (0.0120)	0.1555 *** (0.0119)	0.0257 *** (0.0018)	0.1722 *** (0.0117)	0.1928 *** (0.0116)	0.1714 *** (0.0116)	0.0286 *** (0.0018)	0.1937 *** (0.0112)	0.2235 *** (0.0113)	0.2239 *** (0.0109)	0.0354 *** (0.0017)	0.1922 *** (0.0112)	0.0299 *** (0.0017)	0.1812 *** (0.0113)	0.0303 *** (0.0018)
D054nt	0.1594 *** (0.0174)	0.0276 *** (0.0027)	0.1824 *** (0.0171)	0.1791 *** (0.0172)	0.1771 *** (0.0170)	0.0304 *** (0.0026)									0.2629 *** (0.0160)	0.0429 *** (0.0024)	0.2474 *** (0.0160)	0.0429 *** (0.0025)
D059nt	0.2404 *** (0.0177)	0.0318 *** (0.0023)	0.4303 *** (0.0165)															
E143nt	−0.4715 ***	−0.0626 ***	−0.4764 ***	−0.4673 ***	−0.4607 ***	−0.0617 ***	−0.4593 ***	−0.4663 ***	−0.4604 ***	−0.0618 ***	−0.4631 ***	−0.4668 ***	−0.4381 ***	−0.0543 ***	−0.4358 ***	−0.0535 ***	−0.4099 ***	−0.0547 ***
	(0.0183)	(0.0023)	(0.0178)	(0.0181)	(0.0179)	(0.0023)	(0.0178)	(0.0176)	(0.0177)	(0.0022)	(0.0169)	(0.0173)	(0.0163)	(0.0020)	(0.0167)	(0.0020)	(0.0169)	(0.0021)
F118nt	−0.0724 ***	−0.0148 ***	−0.0912 ***	−0.0825 ***	−0.0831 ***	−0.0162 ***	−0.0927 ***		−0.0928 ***	−0.0178 ***	−0.1280 ***							
	(0.0042)	(0.0007)	(0.0041)	(0.0041)	(0.0041)	(0.0007)	(0.0040)		(0.0040)	(0.0007)	(0.0038)							
G007_36_Bnt	−0.3044 ***	−0.0441 ***	−0.3252 ***	−0.3111 ***	−0.3108 ***	−0.0447 ***	−0.3198 ***	−0.3600 ***	−0.3185 ***	−0.0457 ***	−0.3500 ***	−0.3796 ***	−0.4114 ***	−0.0554 ***	−0.3906 ***	−0.0526 ***	−0.3636 ***	−0.0529 ***
	(0.0178)	(0.0023)	(0.0173)	(0.0177)	(0.0175)	(0.0023)	(0.0175)	(0.0173)	(0.0173)	(0.0023)	(0.0166)	(0.0171)	(0.0162)	(0.0020)	(0.0164)	(0.0020)	(0.0165)	(0.0022)
Y002nt	−0.2362 ***	−0.0394 ***	−0.2819 ***	−0.2543 ***	−0.2590 ***	−0.0419 ***	−0.2648 ***	−0.3170 ***	−0.2639 ***	−0.0423 ***	−0.3362 ***	−0.3348 ***	−0.3201 ***	−0.0494 ***	−0.3025 ***	−0.0473 ***	−0.2909 ***	−0.0479 ***
	(0.0223)	(0.0032)	(0.0219)	(0.0222)	(0.0220)	(0.0031)	(0.0219)	(0.0215)	(0.0217)	(0.0031)	(0.0212)	(0.0213)	(0.0204)	(0.0028)	(0.0207)	(0.0028)	(0.0207)	(0.0030)
A124_0ent																	0.4291 *** (0.0397)	0.0420 *** (0.0039)
_cons	2.0665 *** (0.0832)	0.8702 *** (0.0118)	2.4117 *** (0.0812)	2.3386 *** (0.0805)	2.3603 *** (0.0798)	0.9100 *** (0.0114)	2.7547 *** (0.0718)	1.9727 *** (0.0760)	2.7500 *** (0.0712)	0.9752 *** (0.0099)	3.3529 *** (0.0681)	2.4915 *** (0.0689)	2.5401 *** (0.0662)	0.9129 *** (0.0089)	1.9563 *** (0.0733)	0.8268 *** (0.0100)	1.8357 *** (0.0741)	0.8206 *** (0.0106)
N	39,409	39,409	39,409	39,409	40,337	40,337	40,337	40,337	41,042	41,042	41,042	41,042	47,618	47,618	46,794	46,794	43,679	43,679
chi² / F	5397.0323		4678.7274	5263.4820	5340.8593		5284.0049	4874.1607	5358.1703		4410.4134	4788.2363	5579.7515		5685.7433		4994.4131	
P	0.0000	0.0000	0.0000	0.0000	0.0000	0.0000	0.0000	0.0000	0.0000	0.0000	0.0000	0.0000	0.0000	0.0000	0.0000	0.0000	0.0000	0.0000
R² (OLS) / McFadden's Pseudo R² (logit)	0.1853	0.1816	0.1512	0.1806	0.1793	0.1760	0.1768	0.1701	0.1769	0.1729	0.1284	0.1648	0.1745	0.1574	0.1799	0.1637	0.1645	0.1549
RMSE		0.3759				0.3760				0.3765				0.3672		0.3659		0.3766
AIC	34,006.3629	34,733.5721	35,424.2274	34,190.1829	34,899.1207	35,578.0705	35,801.8603	35,285.0073	35,573.9850	36,293.2589	37,667.6077	36,093.7725	39,348.4448	39,717.3424	38,428.2481	38,705.2740	37,842.0569	38,648.3166
BIC	34,092.1804	34,819.3896	35,501.4632	34,275.4187	34,976.5659	35,655.3157	35,870.2005	35,353.8475	35,642.9638	36,362.2377	37,727.9642	36,154.1289	39,409.8416	39,778.7392	38,498.2762	38,775.3021	37,920.2185	38,726.4782
AUCROC	0.7844		0.7796	0.7808	0.7799		0.7780	0.7799	0.7791		0.7287	0.7776	0.7828		0.7852		0.7724	
chi² GOF	24,317.90		18,676.12	16,884.76	17,091.77	11,106.98	7158.41	11,231.56	6291.07		3573.21	3592.05		7381.92		10,453.02		
p GOF	0.0000		0.0000	0.0000	0.0000		0.0000	0.0000	0.0000		0.0000	0.0000						
Max.Abs.VPMCC	0.4094	0.4094	0.2971	0.2940	0.2932	0.2932	0.2732	0.2091	0.2747	0.2747	0.2378	0.1745	0.1819	0.1819	0.2159	0.2159	0.2022	0.2022
OLSmax.Accept.VIF		1.2219				1.2134				1.2090				1.1868		1.1957		1.1833
OLSmax.Comput.VIF		1.3027				1.2741				1.2181				1.0911		1.1121		1.1012

Source and notes: same as in Table A4 (Stata scripts at https://tinyurl.com/yc26vjzd, accessed on 30 January 2023).

Table A6. Controlling using the most relevant seven remaining predictors (hepta-core) and most of the socio-demographic variables in logit (first 12) and ologit models (last 12).

Model	(1)	(2)	(3)	(4)	(5)	(6)	(7)	(8)	(9)	(10)	(11)	(12)	(13)	(14)	(15)	(16)	(17)	(18)	(19)	(20)	(21)	(22)	(23)	(24)
Input/Response	C002bin	C002bin	C002bin	C002bin	C002bin	C002bin	C002bin	C002bin	C002bin	C002bin	C002bin	C002bin	C002nt	C002nt	C002nt	C002nt	C002nt	C002nt	C002nt	C002nt	C002nt	C002nt	C002nt	C002nt
C001_01nt	0.8647 ***	0.8755 ***	0.8675 ***	0.8670 ***	0.8661 ***	0.8527 ***	0.8396 ***	0.8441 ***	0.8666 ***	0.8660 ***	0.9469 ***	0.8504 ***	0.6261 ***	0.6356 ***	0.6304 ***	0.6305 ***	0.6299 ***	0.6186 ***	0.6024 ***	0.6076 ***	0.6258 ***	0.6308 ***	0.6576 ***	0.6129 ***
	(0.0189)	(0.0192)	(0.0190)	(0.0190)	(0.0190)	(0.0191)	(0.0199)	(0.0192)	(0.0197)	(0.0190)	(0.0232)	(0.0191)	(0.0126)	(0.0128)	(0.0126)	(0.0126)	(0.0126)	(0.0128)	(0.0132)	(0.0128)	(0.0131)	(0.0127)	(0.0146)	(0.0127)
C009nt	−0.1558 ***	−0.1572 ***	−0.1534 ***	−0.1562 ***	−0.1562 ***	−0.1524 ***	−0.1546 ***	−0.1505 ***	−0.1454 ***	−0.1547 ***	−0.1388 ***	−0.1493 ***	−0.1075 ***	−0.1083 ***	−0.1056 ***	−0.1076 ***	−0.1076 ***	−0.1050 ***	−0.1056 ***	−0.1033 ***	−0.0994 ***	−0.1059 ***	−0.0944 ***	−0.1011 ***
	(0.0114)	(0.0114)	(0.0114)	(0.0114)	(0.0114)	(0.0116)	(0.0117)	(0.0115)	(0.0119)	(0.0115)	(0.0130)	(0.0114)	(0.0093)	(0.0093)	(0.0093)	(0.0093)	(0.0093)	(0.0095)	(0.0095)	(0.0093)	(0.0097)	(0.0093)	(0.0106)	(0.0093)
C038nt	0.1922 ***	0.1946 ***	0.1933 ***	0.1922 ***	0.1920 ***	0.1916 ***	0.1972 ***	0.1931 ***	0.1888 ***	0.1936 ***	0.1778 ***	0.1899 ***	0.1749 ***	0.1766 ***	0.1759 ***	0.1751 ***	0.1749 ***	0.1733 ***	0.1782 ***	0.1730 ***	0.1718 ***	0.1754 ***	0.1647 ***	0.1733 ***
	(0.0112)	(0.0112)	(0.0112)	(0.0112)	(0.0112)	(0.0114)	(0.0115)	(0.0113)	(0.0117)	(0.0113)	(0.0129)	(0.0112)	(0.0092)	(0.0092)	(0.0092)	(0.0092)	(0.0092)	(0.0094)	(0.0095)	(0.0093)	(0.0096)	(0.0093)	(0.0105)	(0.0092)
D054nt	0.2629 ***	0.2619 ***	0.2577 ***	0.2618 ***	0.2630 ***	0.2654 ***	0.2607 ***	0.2463 ***	0.2651 ***	0.2669 ***	0.2836 ***	0.2505 ***	0.2702 ***	0.2693 ***	0.2658 ***	0.2686 ***	0.2694 ***	0.2741 ***	0.2655 ***	0.2554 ***	0.2740 ***	0.2686 ***	0.2820 ***	0.2548 ***
	(0.0160)	(0.0160)	(0.0162)	(0.0160)	(0.0160)	(0.0162)	(0.0165)	(0.0161)	(0.0166)	(0.0161)	(0.0183)	(0.0161)	(0.0130)	(0.0131)	(0.0132)	(0.0131)	(0.0131)	(0.0132)	(0.0135)	(0.0132)	(0.0135)	(0.0132)	(0.0150)	(0.0132)
E143nt	−0.4358 ***	−0.4336 ***	−0.4380 ***	−0.4357 ***	−0.4355 ***	−0.4234 ***	−0.4497 ***	−0.4336 ***	−0.4279 ***	−0.4344 ***	−0.4409 ***	−0.4354 ***	−0.3978 ***	−0.3968 ***	−0.3994 ***	−0.3980 ***	−0.3979 ***	−0.3909 ***	−0.4142 ***	−0.3957 ***	−0.3921 ***	−0.3954 ***	−0.3965 ***	−0.3965 ***
	(0.0167)	(0.0167)	(0.0168)	(0.0167)	(0.0167)	(0.0169)	(0.0176)	(0.0169)	(0.0174)	(0.0168)	(0.0191)	(0.0167)	(0.0130)	(0.0130)	(0.0131)	(0.0130)	(0.0130)	(0.0132)	(0.0138)	(0.0132)	(0.0135)	(0.0131)	(0.0149)	(0.0130)
C007_36_Bnt	−0.3906 ***	−0.3884 ***	−0.3885 ***	−0.3900 ***	−0.3903 ***	−0.3943 ***	−0.4015 ***	−0.3891 ***	−0.3839 ***	−0.3916 ***	−0.4267 ***	−0.3948 ***	−0.3549 ***	−0.3535 ***	−0.3533 ***	−0.3545 ***	−0.3548 ***	−0.3562 ***	−0.3618 ***	−0.3546 ***	−0.3452 ***	−0.3561 ***	−0.3865 ***	−0.3574 ***
	(0.0164)	(0.0164)	(0.0163)	(0.0164)	(0.0164)	(0.0166)	(0.0173)	(0.0166)	(0.0172)	(0.0164)	(0.0190)	(0.0165)	(0.0130)	(0.0130)	(0.0131)	(0.0130)	(0.0130)	(0.0132)	(0.0137)	(0.0132)	(0.0135)	(0.0130)	(0.0150)	(0.0130)
Y002nt	−0.3025 ***	−0.2976 ***	−0.3072 ***	−0.3031 ***	−0.3024 ***	−0.3013 ***	−0.2891 ***	−0.3000 ***	−0.2955 ***	−0.3013 ***	−0.2972 ***	−0.2949 ***	−0.2423 ***	−0.2387 ***	−0.2448 ***	−0.2432 ***	−0.2427 ***	−0.2298 ***	−0.2274 ***	−0.2296 ***	−0.2285 ***	−0.2412 ***	−0.2385 ***	−0.2347 ***
	(0.0207)	(0.0208)	(0.0207)	(0.0207)	(0.0207)	(0.0210)	(0.0215)	(0.0209)	(0.0216)	(0.0208)	(0.0239)	(0.0208)	(0.0165)	(0.0165)	(0.0165)	(0.0165)	(0.0165)	(0.0169)	(0.0171)	(0.0167)	(0.0172)	(0.0166)	(0.0189)	(0.0165)
X001nt		0.1338 ***												0.0943 ***										
		(0.0258)												(0.0206)										
X003nt			−0.0016 *												−0.0013 *									
			(0.0008)												(0.0006)									
X007nt				−0.0061												−0.0060								
				(0.0058)												(0.0047)								
X007bin					−0.0086												−0.0160							
					(0.0261)												(0.0210)							
X011nt						0.0374 ***												0.0395 ***						
						(0.0078)												(0.0061)						
X025nt							0.0217 ***												−0.0226 ***					
							(0.0061)												(0.0049)					

Table A6. Cont.

Model	(1)	(2)	(3)	(4)	(5)	(6)	(7)	(8)	(9)	(10)	(11)	(12)	(13)	(14)	(15)	(16)	(17)	(18)	(19)	(20)	(21)	(22)	(23)	(24)
Input/Response	C002bin	C002bin	C002bin	C002bin	C002bin	C002bin	C002bin	C002bin	C002bin	C002bin	C002bin	C002bin	C002nt	C002nt	C002nt	C002nt	C002nt	C002nt	C002nt	C002nt	C002nt	C002nt	C002nt	C002nt
X028nt								−0.0510*** (0.0059)												−0.0421*** (0.0047)				
X047nt									−0.0563*** (0.0060)												−0.0654*** (0.0048)			
X048WV5nt										0.0000 (0.0000)												0.0000 (0.0000)		
X049nt											−0.0399*** (0.0061)												−0.0267*** (0.0048)	
5020												0.1014*** (0.0137) −201.5337 (27.4591)												0.1061*** (0.0110)
_cons	1.9563*** (0.0733)	1.7297*** (0.0854)	2.0320*** (0.0825)	1.9899*** (0.0803)	1.9609*** (0.0753)	1.8580*** (0.0755)	2.0661*** (0.0802)	2.2076*** (0.0798)	2.1746*** (0.0807)	1.9210*** (0.0765)	2.1135*** (0.0891)													
N	46,794	46,765	46,672	46,758	46,758	46,758	42,847	45,155	43,697	46,022	35,072	46,794	52,847	52,816	52,707	52,778	52,778	51,342	48,532	51,109	49,322	51,994	39,817	52,847
chi2	5685.7433	5688.5318	5672.4660	5683.4406	5683.3776	5611.6102	5201.4993	5466.7913	5423.3517	5646.8899	4503.3261	5724.3055	7305.0666	7346.2792	7286.6653	7302.4065	7302.4264	7187.7236	6701.7632	6990.7162	7002.7849	7254.7074	5812.3052	7360.6229
P	0.0000	0.0000	0.0000	0.0000	0.0000	0.0000	0.0000	0.0000	0.0000	0.0000	0.0000	0.0000	0.0000	0.0000	0.0000	0.0000	0.0000	0.0000	0.0000	0.0000	0.0000	0.0000	0.0000	0.0000
Pseudo R² (McFadden)	0.1799	0.1806	0.1803	0.1801	0.1801	0.1806	0.1784	0.1776	0.1849	0.1809	0.1937	0.1810	0.1061	0.1064	0.1064	0.1063	0.1063	0.1069	0.1050	0.1037	0.1102	0.1068	0.1108	0.1072
AIC	38,428.2481	38,374.9837	38,312.8451	38,371.4277	38,372.4109	37,574.4499	36,060.042	37,637.9773	35,541.8175	37,919.9773	29,162.5254	38,382.4131	75,309.910	75,446.2792	75,266.0253	75,381.7813	75,382.8895	72,658.0117	70,647.1644	73,988.3821	69,993.0322	74,871.0248	56,024.8556	75,423.8842
BIC	38,498.2762	38,452.7947	38,391.6032	38,450.1817	38,451.1817	37,658.0187	36,123.9027	37,716.4390	35,619.9828	37,999.6092	29,236.7119	38,461.1847	75,398.8354	75,535.6189	75,376.6104	75,470.3198	75,471.6280	72,945.3644	70,735.0042	74,076.7593	70,086.4934	74,958.6137	58,110.7761	75,512.6558
AUCROC	0.7852	0.7857	0.7855	0.7854	0.7853	0.7856	0.7827	0.7827	0.7880	0.7859	0.7946	0.7858												
chi2 GOF	7381.92	10,953.57	38,671.11	15,346.54	10,824.82	18,332.19	19,780.57	19,606.24	21,480.62	44,368.52	17,832.45	15,449.12												
p GOF	0.0000	0.0000	0.0000	0.0000	0.0000	0.0000	0.0000	0.0000	0.0000	0.0000	0.0000	0.0000												
Max.Abs.VPMCC	0.2159	0.2160	0.2159	0.2157	0.2157	0.2158	0.2120	0.2111	0.2177	0.2164	0.2288	0.2160	0.2159	0.2160	0.2159	0.2157	0.2157	0.2158	0.2120	0.2111	0.2177	0.2164	0.2288	0.2160

Source and notes: same as in Table A3 (Stata scripts at https://tinyurl.com/puw7nd3n, and https://tinyurl.com/wcnwtvra, both accessed on 30 January 2023).

Table A7. The average marginal effects identified after controlling using the most relevant seven predictors (hepta-core) and each of the other seven most significant socio-demographic control variables in logit models.

Model	(1)	(2)	(3)	(4)	(5)	(6)	(7)	(8)
C001_01nt (H2)	0.1132 ***	0.1145 ***	0.1113 ***	0.1131 ***	0.1124 ***	0.1122 ***	0.1264 ***	0.1112 ***
	(0.0024)	(0.0024)	(0.0024)	(0.0026)	(0.0024)	(0.0024)	(0.0029)	(0.0024)
C009nt (H2)	−0.0204 ***	−0.0206 ***	−0.0199 ***	−0.0208 ***	−0.0200 ***	−0.0188 ***	−0.0185 ***	−0.0195 ***
	(0.0015)	(0.0015)	(0.0015)	(0.0016)	(0.0015)	(0.0015)	(0.0017)	(0.0015)
C038nt (H4)	0.0252 ***	0.0254 ***	0.0250 ***	0.0266 ***	0.0257 ***	0.0244 ***	0.0237 ***	0.0248 ***
	(0.0015)	(0.0015)	(0.0015)	(0.0015)	(0.0015)	(0.0015)	(0.0017)	(0.0015)
D054nt (H3)	0.0344 ***	0.0343 ***	0.0347 ***	0.0351 ***	0.0328 ***	0.0343 ***	0.0379 ***	0.0328 ***
	(0.0021)	(0.0021)	(0.0021)	(0.0022)	(0.0021)	(0.0021)	(0.0024)	(0.0021)
E143nt (H1)	−0.0570 ***	−0.0567 ***	−0.0553 ***	−0.0605 ***	−0.0577 ***	−0.0554 ***	−0.0589 ***	−0.0569 ***
	(0.0021)	(0.0021)	(0.0021)	(0.0023)	(0.0022)	(0.0022)	(0.0025)	(0.0021)
G007_36_Bnt (H2)	−0.0511 ***	−0.0508 ***	−0.0515 ***	−0.0541 ***	−0.0518 ***	−0.0497 ***	−0.0569 ***	−0.0516 ***
	(0.0021)	(0.0021)	(0.0021)	(0.0023)	(0.0021)	(0.0022)	(0.0024)	(0.0021)
Y002nt (H2, H4)	−0.0396 ***	−0.0389 ***	−0.0393 ***	−0.0389 ***	−0.0399 ***	−0.0382 ***	−0.0397 ***	−0.0386 ***
	(0.0027)	(0.0027)	(0.0027)	(0.0029)	(0.0028)	(0.0028)	(0.0032)	(0.0027)
X001nt (H5)		0.0175 ***						
		(0.0034)						
X011nt (H5)			0.0049 ***					
			(0.0010)					
X025nt (H5)				−0.0029 ***				
				(0.0008)				
X028nt (H5)					−0.0068 ***			
					(0.0008)			
X047nt (H5)						−0.0073 ***		
						(0.0008)		
X049nt (H5)							−0.0053 ***	
							(0.0008)	
S020 (H5)								0.0133 ***
								(0.0018)
N	46,794	46,765	45,604	42,847	45,155	43,697	35,072	46,794

Source: own calculation in Stata (Stata script at https://tinyurl.com/yvc3py3u, accessed on 30 January 2023)
Notes: robust standard errors are between round parentheses. Coefficients computed as average marginal effects and emphasized using *** are significant at 1‰. The H codes on the left indicate the hypotheses to which the variables next to them belong.

References

1. Pronk, J.P. Migration: The nomand in each of Us. *Popul. Dev. Rev.* **1993**, *19*, 323. [CrossRef]
2. Beutin, R.; Canoy, M.; Horvath, A.; Hubert, A.; Lerais, F.; Sochacki, M. Reassessing the link between public perception and migration policy. *Eur. J. Migr. Law* **2007**, *9*, 389–418. [CrossRef]
3. Širá, E.; Vavrek, R.; Kravčáková Vozárová, I.; Kotulič, R. Knowledge economy indicators and their impact on the sus-tainable competitiveness of the EU countries. *Sustainability* **2020**, *12*, 4172. [CrossRef]
4. Çelik, S. Evaluation of the Migration Phenomenon as an Economics Dimension. In *Social Considera-tions of Migration Movements and Immigration Policies*; Erçetin, Ş., Ed.; IGI Global: Hershey, PA, USA, 2018; pp. 58–65. [CrossRef]
5. Kanbur, R.; Rapoport, H. Migration selectivity and the evolution of spatial inequality. *J. Econ. Geogr.* **2005**, *5*, 43–57. [CrossRef]
6. Miyagiwa, K. Scale economies in education and the brain drain problem. *Int. Econ. Rev.* **1991**, *32*, 743. [CrossRef]
7. Geist, C.; McManus, P.A. Different reasons, different results: Implications of migration by gender and family status. *Demography* **2011**, *49*, 197–217. [CrossRef] [PubMed]
8. Migali, S.; Scipioni, M. A Global Analysis of Intentions to Migrate. European Commission 2018, JRC111207. Available online: https://knowledge4policy.ec.europa.eu/sites/default/files/technical_report_on_gallup_v7_finalpubsy.pdf (accessed on 9 July 2021).
9. White, A. Double return migration: Failed returns to Poland leading to settlement abroad and New Transnational Strategies. *Int. Migr.* **2013**, *52*, 72–84. [CrossRef]
10. Zuberi, D.; Ptashnick, M. In search of a better life: The experiences of working poor immigrants in Vancouver, Canada. *Int. Migr.* **2011**, *50*, e60–e93. [CrossRef]
11. de Haas, H. A theory of migration: The aspirations-capabilities framework. *Comp. Migr. Stud.* **2021**, *9*, 1–35. [CrossRef] [PubMed]
12. Bazán-Monasterio, V.; Gil-Lacruz, A.I.; Gil-Lacruz, M. Life satisfaction in relation to attitudes towards immigrants among Europeans by generational cohorts. *Int. J. Intercult. Relat.* **2021**, *80*, 121–133. [CrossRef]

13. Sarrasin, O.; Green, E.G.; Bolzman, C.; Visintin, E.P.; Politi, E. Competition- and identity-based roots of an-ti-immigration prejudice among individuals with and without an immigrant background. *Int. Rev. Soc. Psychol.* **2018**, *31*, 12. [CrossRef]
14. Mayda, A.M. Who is against immigration? A cross-country investigation of individual attitudes toward immigrants. *Rev. Econ. Stat.* **2006**, *88*, 510–530. [CrossRef]
15. Constant, A. Do migrants take the jobs of Native Workers? *IZA World Labor* **2014**. [CrossRef]
16. Fierro, J.; Parella, S. Social Trust and support for immigrants' social rights in Spain. *J. Ethn. Migr. Stud.* **2021**, 1–17. [CrossRef]
17. Hainmueller, J.; Hopkins, D.J. Public attitudes toward immigration. *Annu. Rev. Political Sci.* **2014**, *17*, 225–249. [CrossRef]
18. Gang, I.N.; Rivera-Batiz, F.; Yun, M.-S. Economic strain, ethnic concentration and attitudes towards foreigners in the European Union. *SSRN Electron. J.* **2002**. [CrossRef]
19. Stephan, W.G.; Ybarra, O.; Bachman, G. Prejudice toward Immigrants1. *J. Appl. Soc. Psychol.* **1999**, *29*, 2221–2237. [CrossRef]
20. Hjerm, M. Anti-immigrant attitudes and cross-municipal variation in the proportion of immigrants. *Acta Sociol.* **2009**, *52*, 47–62. [CrossRef]
21. Parla, A.Y.S.E. Remembering across the border: Postsocialist nostalgia among Turkish immigrants from Bulgaria. *Am. Ethnol.* **2009**, *36*, 750–767. [CrossRef]
22. Liu, H. Beyond co-ethnicity: The politics of differentiating and integrating new immigrants in Singapore. *Ethn. Racial Stud.* **2014**, *37*, 1225–1238. [CrossRef]
23. Pondy, L.R. Organizational conflict: Concepts and Models. *Adm. Sci. Q.* **1967**, *12*, 296. [CrossRef]
24. Freeman, G.P. Comparative analysis of immigration politics. *Am. Behav. Sci.* **2011**, *55*, 1541–1560. [CrossRef]
25. Davidov, E.; Meulemann, B.; Schwartz, S.H.; Schmidt, P. Individual values, cultural embeddedness, and anti-immigration sentiments: Explaining differences in the effect of values on attitudes toward immigration across Europe. *KZfSS Kölner Z. Soziologie Soz.* **2014**, *66*, 263–285. [CrossRef]
26. Debrael, M.; d'Haenens, L.; De Cock, R.; De Coninck, D. Media use, fear of terrorism, and attitudes towards immigrants and refugees: Young people and adults compared. *Int. Commun. Gaz.* **2019**, *83*, 148–168. [CrossRef]
27. McCann, W.S.; Boateng, F.D. An examination of American perceptions of the immigrant-crime relationship. *Am. J. Crim. Justice* **2020**, *45*, 973–1002. [CrossRef]
28. Semyonov, M.; Raijman, R.; Gorodzeisky, A. Foreigners' Impact on European Societies: Public Views and Perceptions in a Cross-National Comparative Perspective. *Int. J. Comp. Sociol.* **2008**, *49*, 5–29. [CrossRef]
29. Markaki, Y.; Longhi, S. What determines attitudes to immigration in European countries? an analysis at the regional level. *Migr. Stud.* **2013**, *1*, 311–337. [CrossRef]
30. Gregurović, M.; Kuti, S.; Župarić-Iljić, D. Attitudes towards immigrant workers and asylum seekers in eastern Croatia: Dimensions, determinants, and differences. *Migr. I Etničke Teme/Migr. Ethn. Themes* **2016**, *32*, 91–122. [CrossRef]
31. Mangum, M.; Block, R. Social Identity Theory and public opinion towards immigration. *Soc. Sci.* **2018**, *7*, 41. [CrossRef]
32. Valentova, M.; Alieva, A. Gender differences in the perception of immigration-related threats. *Int. J. Intercult. Relat.* **2014**, *39*, 175–182. [CrossRef]
33. Hainmueller, J.; Hiscox, M. Educated Preferences: Explaining Attitudes toward Immigration in Europe. *Int. Organ.* **2007**, *61*, 399–442. [CrossRef]
34. Borgonovi, F. The relationship between education and levels of trust and tolerance in europe1. *Br. J. Sociol.* **2012**, *63*, 146–167. [CrossRef] [PubMed]
35. Ambrosini, M. Immigration in Italy: Between economic acceptance and political rejection. *J. Int. Migr. Integr.* **2013**, *14*, 175–194. [CrossRef]
36. Citrin, J.; Green, D.P.; Muste, C.; Wong, C. Public opinion toward immigration reform: The role of economic motivations. *J. Politics* **1997**, *59*, 858–881. [CrossRef]
37. Flynn, D. New Borders, new management: The Dilemmas of Modern Immigration Policies. *Ethn. Racial Stud.* **2005**, *28*, 463–490. [CrossRef]
38. Hood, M.V., III; Morris, I.L. ¿Amigo o enemigo?: Context, attitudes, and Anglo public opinion toward immigration. *Soc. Sci. Q.* **1997**, *78*, 309–323.
39. Ford, R.; Jennings, W.; Somerville, W. Public opinion, responsiveness and constraint: Britain's three immigration policy regimes. *J. Ethn. Migr. Stud.* **2015**, *41*, 1391–1411. [CrossRef]
40. Ivarsflaten, E. Threatened by diversity: Why restrictive asylum and immigration policies appeal to Western Europeans. *J. Elect. Public Opin. Parties* **2005**, *15*, 21–45. [CrossRef]
41. Rueda, D. Food comes First, then morals: Redistribution preferences, parochial altruism, and immigration in Western Europe. *J. Politics* **2018**, *80*, 225–239. [CrossRef]
42. Stafford, K.E. Predicting Positive Attitudes toward Immigrants with Altruism. Master's Thesis, University of Kentucky, Lexington, KY, USA, 2020. [CrossRef]
43. Kunst, J.R.; Thomsen, L.; Sam, D.L.; Berry, J.W. We are in this together. *Personal. Soc. Psychol. Bull.* **2015**, *41*, 1438–1453. [CrossRef]
44. Verkuyten, M.; Martinovic, B.; Smeekes, A. The Multicultural Jigsaw Puzzle. *Personal. Soc. Psychol. Bull.* **2014**, *40*, 1480–1493. [CrossRef]
45. Esses, V.M.; Wagner, U.; Wolf, C.; Preiser, M.; Wilbur, C.J. Perceptions of national identity and attitudes toward im-migrants and immigration in Canada and Germany. *Int. J. Intercult. Relat.* **2006**, *30*, 653–669. [CrossRef]

46. Grigoryev, D.; Batkhina, A.; van de Vijver, F.; Berry, J.W. Towards an integration of models of discrimination of im-migrants: From Ultimate (functional) to proximate (sociofunctional) explanations. *J. Int. Migr. Integr.* **2019**, *21*, 667–691. [CrossRef]
47. Akaliyski, P.; Welzel, C.; Hien, J. A community of shared values? dimensions and dynamics of cultural integration in the European Union. *J. Eur. Integr.* **2022**, *44*, 569–590. [CrossRef]
48. Awad, I. Critical multiculturalism and deliberative democracy. *Javn. Public* **2011**, *18*, 39–54. [CrossRef]
49. Guerra, R.; Rodrigues, R.B.; Aguiar, C.; Carmona, M.; Alexandre, J.; Lopes, R.C. School achievement and well-being of immigrant children: The role of acculturation orientations and perceived discrimination. *J. Sch. Psychol.* **2019**, *75*, 104–118. [CrossRef]
50. Pellegrini, V.; De Cristofaro, V.; Salvati, M.; Giacomantonio, M.; Leone, L. Social Exclusion and anti-immigration attitudes in Europe: The mediating role of Interpersonal Trust. *Soc. Indic. Res.* **2021**, *155*, 697–724. [CrossRef]
51. Rustenbach, E. Sources of negative attitudes toward immigrants in Europe: A multi-level analysis. *Int. Migr. Rev.* **2010**, *44*, 53–77. [CrossRef]
52. Ensign, P.C.; Robinson, N.P. Entrepreneurs because they are immigrants or immigrants because they are entrepreneurs? *J. Entrep.* **2011**, *20*, 33–53. [CrossRef]
53. McAreavey, R. Migrant Identities in a New Immigration Destination: Revealing the Limitations of the 'Hard working' Migrant Identity. *Popul. Space Place* **2017**, *23*, e2044. [CrossRef]
54. Iyer, G.R.; Shapiro, J.M. Ethnic entrepreneurial and marketing systems: Implications for the global economy. *J. Int. Mark.* **1999**, *7*, 83–110. [CrossRef]
55. Karreth, J.; Singh, S.P.; Stojek, S.M. Explaining attitudes toward immigration: The role of Regional Context and individual predispositions. *West Eur. Politics* **2015**, *38*, 1174–1202. [CrossRef]
56. Gu, Y.; Zhang, X.; Lin, Z. Factors affecting attitudes toward migrants: An International Comparative Study. *Chin. Political Sci. Rev.* **2022**, *7*, 234–258. [CrossRef]
57. Kapitány-Fövény, M.; Richman, M.J.; Demetrovics, Z.; Sulyok, M. Do you let me symptomatize? the potential role of cultural values in cross-national variability of mental disorders' prevalence. *Int. J. Soc. Psychiatry* **2018**, *64*, 756–766. [CrossRef]
58. Yang, K.-E.; Ham, S.-H. Truancy as systemic discrimination: Anti-discrimination legislation and its effect on school attendance among immigrant children. *Soc. Sci. J.* **2017**, *54*, 216–226. [CrossRef]
59. Ward, C.; Masgoret, A.-M. Attitudes toward immigrants, immigration, and multiculturalism in New Zealand: A Social Psychological Analysis. *Int. Migr. Rev.* **2008**, *42*, 227–248. [CrossRef]
60. Badea, C.; Bender, M.; Korda, H. Threat to national identity continuity: When affirmation procedures increase the acceptance of Muslim immigrants. *Int. J. Intercult. Relat.* **2020**, *78*, 65–72. [CrossRef]
61. Schnapper, D. The debate on immigration and the crisis of National Identity. *West Eur. Politics* **1994**, *17*, 127–139. [CrossRef]
62. Triandafyllidou, A.; Veikou, M. The hierarchy of greekness. *Ethnicities* **2002**, *2*, 189–208. [CrossRef]
63. Pehrson, S.; Green, E.G. Who we are and who can join us: National identity content and entry criteria for new immigrants. *J. Soc. Issues* **2010**, *66*, 695–716. [CrossRef]
64. Holland, K.M. A history of Chinese immigration in the United States and Canada. *Am. Rev. Can. Stud.* **2007**, *37*, 150–160. [CrossRef]
65. Brzozowski, J. Immigrant Entrepreneurship and economic adaptation: A critical analysis. *Entrep. Bus. Econ. Rev.* **2017**, *5*, 159–176. [CrossRef]
66. Mäkinen, K. Struggles of citizenship and class: Anti-immigration activism in Finland. *Sociol. Rev.* **2017**, *65*, 218–234. [CrossRef]
67. Gorodzeisky, A.; Semyonov, M. Terms of exclusion: Public views towards admission and allocation of rights to immigrants in European countries. *Ethn. Racial Stud.* **2009**, *32*, 401–423. [CrossRef]
68. Nowicka, M.; Krzyżowski, Ł. The social distance of Poles to other minorities: A study of four cities in Germany and Britain. *J. Ethn. Migr. Stud.* **2016**, *43*, 359–378. [CrossRef]
69. Karabulut, E.M.; Ibrikci, T. Analysis of Cardiotocogram Data for Fetal Distress Determination by Decision Tree-Based Adaptive Boosting Approach. *J. Comput. Commun.* **2014**, *2*, 32–37. [CrossRef]
70. Chen, Y.-K.; Li, W.; Tong, X. Parallelization of AdaBoost algorithm on multi-core processors. In Proceedings of the 2008 IEEE Workshop on Signal Processing Systems, Washington, DC, USA, 8–10 October 2008; pp. 275–280. [CrossRef]
71. Williams, G. *Data Mining with Rattle and R: The Art of Excavating Data for Knowledge Discovery*; Springer: Berlin/Heidelberg, Germany, 2011; pp. 269–291.
72. Schober, P.; Boer, C.; Schwarte, L.A. Correlation Coefficients. *Anesth. Analg.* **2018**, *126*, 1763–1768. [CrossRef] [PubMed]
73. Homocianu, D.; Airinei, D. PCDM and PCDM4MP: New Pairwise Correlation-Based Data Mining Tools for Parallel Pro-862 cessing of Large Tabular Datasets. *Mathematics* **2022**, *10*, 2671. [CrossRef]
74. Tsikriktsis, N. A review of techniques for treating missing data in OM survey research. *J. Oper. Manag.* **2005**, *24*, 53–62. [CrossRef]
75. DeBruine, L.M.; Barr, D.J. Understanding Mixed-Effects Models Through Data Simulation. *Adv. Methods Pract. Psychol. Sci.* **2021**, *4*, 1–15. [CrossRef]
76. Roberts, D.R.; Bahn, V.; Ciuti, S.; Boyce, M.S.; Elith, J.; Guillera-Arroita, G.; Hauenstein, S.; Lahoz-Monfort, J.J.; Schrö-der, B.; Thuiller, W.; et al. Cross-validation strategies for data with temporal, spatial, hierarchical, or phylogenetic structure. *Ecography* **2017**, *40*, 913–929. [CrossRef]
77. Picard, R.R.; Cook, R.D. Cross-validation of Regression Models. *J. Am. Stat. Assoc.* **1984**, *79*, 575–583. [CrossRef]

78. Ahrens, A.; Hansen, C.B.; Schaffer, M.E. Lassopack: Model selection and prediction with regularized regression in Stata. *Stata J. Promot. Commun. Stat. Stata* **2020**, *20*, 176–235. [CrossRef]
79. Irandoukht, A. Optimum ridge regression parameter using R-squared of prediction as a criterion for regression analysis. *J. Stat. Theory Appl.* **2021**, *20*, 242. [CrossRef]
80. Lai, K. Using Information Criteria Under Missing Data: Full Information Maximum Likelihood Versus Two-Stage Estimation. *Struct. Equ. Model. A Multidiscip. J.* **2021**, *28*, 278–291. [CrossRef]
81. Vatcheva, K.P.; Lee, M.; McCormick, J.B.; Rahbar, M.H. Multicollinearity in Regression Analyses Conducted in Epi-de-miologic Studies. *Epidemiology* **2016**, *6*, 227. [CrossRef]
82. Mironiuc, I.-C.; Homocianu, D. Incipient tests of exploring the influences on accepting the priority of compatriots vs. immigrants in terms of access to employment, Race. *Ethn. Identity Politics eJournal (SSRN Electron. J.)* **2021**. [CrossRef]
83. Homocianu, D.; Tîrnăucă, C. MEM and MEM4PP: New Tools Supporting the Parallel Generation of Critical Metrics in the Evaluation of Statistical Models. *Axioms* **2022**, *11*, 549. [CrossRef]
84. Mukaka, M.M. Statistics corner: A guide to appropriate use of correlation coefficient in medical research. *Malawi Med. J.* **2012**, *24*, 69–71.
85. Zlotnik, A.; Abraira, V. A general-purpose nomogram generator for predictive logistic regression models. *Stata J. Promot. Commun. Stat. Stata* **2015**, *15*, 537–546. [CrossRef]
86. Jann, B. Making regression tables from stored estimates. *Stata J.* **2005**, *5*, 288–308. [CrossRef]
87. Jann, B. Making regression tables simplified. *Stata J.* **2007**, *7*, 227–244. [CrossRef]
88. Pittaway, E.; Bartolomei, L. Refugees, Race, and Gender: The Multiple Discrimination against Refugee Women. *Refug. Can. J. Refug.* **2001**, *19*, 21–32. [CrossRef]
89. Ferrant, G.; Tuccio, M. *How Do Female Migration and Gender Discrimination in Social Institutions Mutually Influence Each Other?* OECD Development Centre Working Papers, No. 326; OECD Publishing: Paris, France, 2015. [CrossRef]
90. Ruyssen, I.; Salomone, S. Female migration: A way out of discrimination? *J. Dev. Econ.* **2018**, *130*, 224–241. [CrossRef]
91. Berríos-Riquelme, J. Labor market insertion of professional Venezuelan immigrants in northern Chile: Precariousness and discrimination in the light of migration policy. *REMHU Rev. Interdiscip. Mobilidade Hum.* **2021**, *29*, 117–132. [CrossRef]
92. Kuznetsova, I.; Round, J. Postcolonial migrations in Russia: The racism, informality, and discrimination nexus. *Int. J. Sociol. Soc. Policy* **2019**, *39*, 52–67. [CrossRef]
93. Valfort, M. Do anti-discrimination policies work? *IZA World Labor* **2018**, *450*. [CrossRef]
94. Cooray, A.; Marfouk, A.; Nazir, M. Public Opinion and Immigration: Who Favours Employment Discrimination against Immigrants? *Int. Migr.* **2018**, *56*, 5–23. [CrossRef]
95. Evangelist, M. Narrowing Racial Differences in Trust: How Discrimination Shapes Trust in a Racialized Society. *Soc. Probl.* **2021**, *69*, 1109–1136. [CrossRef]
96. Dinesen, P.T. Upbringing, Early Experiences of Discrimination and Social Identity: Explaining Generalised Trust among Immigrants in Denmark. *Scand. Political Stud.* **2010**, *33*, 93–111. [CrossRef]
97. Dalton, R.J.; Ong, N.-N.T. Authority orientations and Democratic attitudes: A test of the 'Asian Values' hypothesis. *Jpn. J. Political Sci.* **2005**, *6*, 211–231. [CrossRef]
98. Hofstede, G. *Culture's Consequences: Comparing Values, Behaviors, Institutions, and Organizations across Nations*; SAGE: Thousand Oaks, CA, USA, 2001.
99. Beugelsdijk, S.; Welzel, C. Dimensions and dynamics of national culture: Synthesizing Hofstede with Inglehart. *J. Cross-Cult. Psychol.* **2018**, *49*, 1469–1505. [CrossRef] [PubMed]
100. Zhou, M.; Yang, A.Y. Divergent experiences, and patterns of integration: Contemporary Chinese immigrants in Metropolitan Los Angeles, USA. *J. Ethn. Migr. Stud.* **2022**, *48*, 913–932. [CrossRef]
101. Scheling, L.; Richter, D. Generation Y: Do millennials need a partner to be happy? *J. Adolesc.* **2021**, *90*, 23–31. [CrossRef]
102. Diener, E.; Tov, W. Subjective well-being and peace. *J. Soc. Issues* **2007**, *63*, 421–440. [CrossRef]
103. Lieber, E.; Nihira, K.; Mink, I.T. Filial piety, modernization, and the challenges of raising children for Chinese immigrants: Quantitative and qualitative evidence. *Ethos* **2004**, *32*, 324–347. [CrossRef]
104. Czymara, C.S.; Schmidt-Catran, A.W. Refugees unwelcome? Changes in the public acceptance of immigrants and refugees in Germany in the course of Europe's 'immigration crisis'. *Eur. Sociol. Rev.* **2017**, *33*, 735–751. [CrossRef]
105. Deole, S.S.; Huang, Y. Suffering and prejudice: Do negative emotions predict immigration concerns? *Immigr. Refug. Citizsh. Law eJournal* **2020**. [CrossRef]
106. Korol, L.; Fietzer, A.W.; Bevelander, P.; Pasichnyk, I. Are immigrants scapegoats? The reciprocal relationships between subjective well-being, political distrust, and anti-immigrant attitudes in young adulthood. *Psychol. Rep.* **2022**, 003329412110659. [CrossRef]
107. Chandler, C.R.; Tsai, Y. Social factors influencing immigration attitudes: An analysis of data from the General Social Survey. *Soc. Sci. J.* **2001**, *38*, 177–188. [CrossRef]
108. Tucci, I. *Explaining Attitudes towards Immigration: New Pieces to the Puzzle*; DIW Discussion Papers; Deutsches Institut für Wirtschaftsforschung (DIW): Berlin, Germany, 2005; p. 484. Available online: http://hdl.handle.net/10419/18335 (accessed on 25 January 2023).
109. Tavakoli, Z.; Chatterjee, S. The Mediating Role of Level of Education and Income on the Relationship between Political Ideology and Attitude towards Immigration. *Int. J. Humanit. Soc. Sci.* **2021**, *15*, 756–759.

10. Ruhs, M. Labor immigration policies in high-income countries: Variations across political regimes and varieties of capitalism. *J. Leg. Stud.* **2018**, *47*, S89–S127. [CrossRef]
11. Paas, T.; Halapuu, V. Attitudes towards immigrants and the integration of ethnically diverse societies. *East. J. Eur. Stud.* **2012**, *3*, 161–176. Available online: http://ejes.uaic.ro/articles/EJES2012_0302_PAA.pdf (accessed on 25 January 2023).
12. Hernes, G.; Knudsen, K. Norwegians' Attitudes Toward New Immigrants. *Acta Sociol.* **1992**, *35*, 123–139. [CrossRef]
13. Crepaz, M.M.L.; Damron, R. Constructing Tolerance: How the Welfare State Shapes Attitudes About Immigrants. *Comp. Political Stud.* **2008**, *42*, 437–463. [CrossRef]
14. Walton-Roberts, M. Research on Immigration and Integration in the Metropolis. In Proceedings of the National Metropolis Conference, Edmonton, AB, Canada, 21–24 March 2004.
15. Bessudnov, A. Ethnic hierarchy and public attitudes towards immigrants in Russia. *Eur. Sociol. Rev.* **2016**, *32*, 567–580. [CrossRef]
16. Wilkes, R.; Corrigall-Brown, C. Explaining time trends in public opinion: Attitudes towards immigration and immigrants. *Int. J. Comp. Sociol.* **2010**, *52*, 79–99. [CrossRef]
17. Callens, M.-S.; Valentová, M.; Meuleman, B. Do attitudes towards the integration of immigrants change over time? A comparative study of Natives, second-generation immigrants and foreign-born residents in Luxembourg. *J. Int. Migr. Integr.* **2013**, *15*, 135–157. [CrossRef]
18. Böckerman, P.; Skedinger, P.; Uusitalo, R. Seniority rules, worker mobility and wages: Evidence from multi-country linked employer-employee data. *Labour Econ.* **2018**, *51*, 48–62. [CrossRef]
19. Zhu, C.; Zhao, Q.; He, J.; Böckerman, P.; Luo, S.; Chen, Q. Genetic basis of STEM Occupational Choice and Regional Economic Performance: A UK Biobank Genome-Wide Association Study. 2022. Available online: https://www.researchsquare.com/article/rs-2040131/v1 (accessed on 25 January 2023). [CrossRef]
20. Homocianu, D.; Dospinescu, O.; Sireteanu, N.A. Exploring the Influences of Job Satisfaction for Europeans Aged 50+ from Ex-communist vs. Non-communist Countries. *Soc. Indic. Res.* **2022**, *159*, 235–279. [CrossRef]
21. Kaufmann, D.; Kraay, A.; Mastruzzi, M. The Worldwide Governance Indicators: Methodology and Analytical Issues. Draft Policy Research Working Paper. Retrieved 22 January 2020. 2010. Available online: http://info.worldbank.org/governance/wgi/pdf/wgi.pdf (accessed on 25 January 2023).
22. Abegaz, M.B.; Debela, K.L.; Hundie, R.M. The effect of governance on entrepreneurship: From all income economies perspective. *J. Innov. Entrep.* **2023**, *12*, 1. [CrossRef]
23. Antón, J.I.; Grande, R.; Muñoz de Bustillo, R.; Pinto, F. Gender Gaps in Working Conditions. *Soc. Indic. Res.* **2023**. [CrossRef]

Disclaimer/Publisher's Note: The statements, opinions and data contained in all publications are solely those of the individual author(s) and contributor(s) and not of MDPI and/or the editor(s). MDPI and/or the editor(s) disclaim responsibility for any injury to people or property resulting from any ideas, methods, instructions or products referred to in the content.

Article

Algorithmic Strategies for Precious Metals Price Forecasting

Gil Cohen

Department of Management, Western Galilee Academic College, P.O. Box 2125, Acre 2412101, Israel; gilc@wgalil.ac.il

Abstract: This research is the first attempt to create machine learning (ML) algorithmic systems that would be able to automatically trade precious metals. The algorithm uses three forecast methodologies: linear regression (LR), Darvas boxes (DB), and Bollinger bands (BB). Our data consists of 20 years of daily price data concerning five precious metals futures: gold, silver, copper, platinum, and palladium. We found that all of the examined precious metals' current daily returns are negatively autocorrelated to their former day's returns and identified lagged interdependencies among the examined metals. Silver futures prices were found to be best forecasted by our systems, and platinum the worst. Moreover, our system better forecasts price-up trends than downtrends for all examined techniques and commodities. Linear regression was found to be the best technique to forecast silver and gold prices trends, while the Bollinger band technique best fits palladium forecasting.

Keywords: precious metals; gold; silver; algorithmic trading; futures

MSC: 37M22

Citation: Cohen, G. Algorithmic Strategies for Precious Metals Price Forecasting. *Mathematics* **2022**, *10*, 1134. https://doi.org/10.3390/math10071134

Academic Editors: Alexandru Agapie, Denis Enachescu, Vlad Stefan Barbu and Bogdan Iftimie

Received: 24 February 2022
Accepted: 30 March 2022
Published: 1 April 2022

Publisher's Note: MDPI stays neutral with regard to jurisdictional claims in published maps and institutional affiliations.

Copyright: © 2022 by the author. Licensee MDPI, Basel, Switzerland. This article is an open access article distributed under the terms and conditions of the Creative Commons Attribution (CC BY) license (https:// creativecommons.org/licenses/by/ 4.0/).

1. Introduction

The use of artificial intelligence (AI) in financial assets price forecasting and trading has become more and more frequent as the amount and speed of the flow of new financial data increased dramatically. Algorithms are used to analyze simultaneous multi-sourced data. Those systems are developed by market experts and are usually applied to stocks and currencies markets. The following research develops and tests such an AI system and applies it to the precious metals' futures market. Precious metals have always been perceived by investors as a hedging tool against inflation (see, for example, [1]) or stock market crashes. In the following research, we designed, optimized, and tested three algorithmic trading systems suitable for precious metal futures trading. Our long period of time data enables us to test the performance of our system over changing economic conditions. The technical analysis approach used here, commonly used by practitioners to trade stocks and foreign exchanges, relies on historical data for the sake of forecasting future prices. We used the particle swarm optimization (PSO) algorithm as our primary optimization tool because of its ability to handle multi-objective optimization simultaneously.

Many researchers have tried to prove the ability of such algorithmic trading systems to achieve abnormal returns for stocks, currencies, and indices. However, many researchers focus on stocks and foreign exchange and partly neglected commodity futures and especially precious metal futures. The following research aims to fill that gap with an insight into three algorithmic trading strategies that were programmed in accordance with the uniqueness of the precious metal financial markets. We use 20 years of daily futures data corresponding to five major precious metals, including gold, silver, copper, platinum, and palladium, to test three algorithmic trading strategies: linear regression (LR), Darvas boxes (DB), and Bollinger bands (BB). We followed [2], that concluded that LR and DB could help traders predict Bitcoin short-term price trends. Our 20 years of data were split into 10 years of training and optimization and 10 years of testing the trading results. We found that it is possible to forecast short-term price trends of precious metals. Silver futures prices were found to be best forecasted by our systems, and platinum was the worst. Our system better forecasts price-up trends than downtrends for all examined techniques and commodities. Linear regression was found to be the best technique to forecast silver and gold prices, while the Bollinger band technique best fits palladium forecasting.

2. Literature Review

Our system is based on pattern recognition which is a developing AI field that helps us to understand different chaotic phenomena. Ref. [3] argued that the applicability of Bayesian methods was greatly enhanced through the development of a range of approximate inference algorithms such as variational Bayes and expectation propagation. An important foundation for learning input–output mapping from a set of examples was presented by [4]. They developed a theoretical framework for the approximation method based on regularization networks that are closely related to pattern recognition. Their methodologies included task-dependent clustering and dimensionality reduction. Other researchers provided an understanding of the mathematical concepts behind forecasting methods that are based on probabilistic derivations. Ref. [5] provided a joint introduction to Gaussian processes (GP) and relevance vector machines (RVM-developed by [6]). They found that RVMs allow the choice of more general basis functions, whereas the behavior of predictive variance is generally counterintuitive. Ref. [7] examined the GP and RVM models and concluded that probabilistic models could produce predictive distributions instead of point predictions.

Most researchers that tried to explain precious metals prices have done so by linking the stock market to the precious metal market. Ref. [8] explained that precious metal futures have higher returns when investor sentiment is pessimistic rather than optimistic. Ref. [9] argued that the price of precious metals and their volatility are driven by shocks originating in the economic uncertainty and risk appetite of investors that prevail in the equity market. Other researchers focused on the interrelations between the prices of the leading precious metals. Ref. [10] showed that precious metals were strongly correlated with each other in the last decade. Ref. [11] documented that weekly changes in traders' positions have a destabilizing impact on subsequent conditional volatility in gold, silver, and palladium futures markets.

Other researchers linked precious metals prices to each other and other commodities. Ref. [12] examined spillover effects among six commodity futures markets and found that both gold and silver are information transmitters to other commodity futures markets. Ref. [13] have examined the impact of oil price changes on precious metals prices. They identified the safe-haven nature of precious metals against an oil price drop.

Past researchers also attempted to construct AI systems to predict precious metals prices. Ref. [14] proposed a model that combines the adaptive neuro-fuzzy inference system and genetic algorithm. Ref. [15] discovered hidden patterns governing systems' evolution. Unlike these attempts to predict precious metals prices, we designed algorithmic trading systems and tested their ability to predict precious metals prices.

3. Data and Methodologies

Our data consists of 20 years of daily data of open–closed, high–low prices of five precious metals futures. We used a lagged multi-dimension stepwise regression model to examine lagged correlations between the daily return of the examined precious metals, including autocorrelations, as described in Equation (1).

$$(G, S, C, P, Pa)_i = \beta_1 G_{i=-1\ldots-3} + \beta_2 S_{i=-1\ldots-3} + \beta_3 C_{i=-1\ldots-3} + \beta_4 P_{i=-1\ldots-3} + \beta_5 Pa_{i=-1\ldots-3} \tag{1}$$

where: $(G, S, C, P, Pa)_i$ = the daily return of gold, silver copper, platinum, and palladium, $(G, S, C, P, Pa)_{i=-1\ldots-3}$ is 1 ... 3 days ago daily returns of gold, silver, copper, platinum, and palladium.

The results of this model enabled us to better understand short term autocorrelations of returns and lagged dependencies between the precious metals price movements and helped us design our trading systems.

3.1. Algorithmic Trading System

We designed our algorithmic trading system to report the actual trading results: net profit (NP), percent of profitable trades of all trades (PP), and the profit factor (PF). NP is the dollar value of the total net profit generated by the trading system, PP is the percentage number of winning trades out of the entire set of trades generated by the system, and PF is defined as gross profits divided by gross losses. We programmed three algorithmic systems based on three sophisticated trading technical tools and altered their configuration until we achieved maximum profitability in terms of NP and PF. The designed systems are based on three methodologies: linear regression, Darvas boxes, and Bollinger bands which are well-known technical formations that are commonly used to analyze investment opportunities for stock and currencies traders. We then optimized NP and PF by altering the setups behind our systems and splitting the system's performance into long and short positions.

The complexity of our systems requires multi-objective optimization formulas. We selected particle swarm optimization (PSO), developed by Kennedy and Eberhart ([16,17]) as our primary optimization method. This methodology enabled us to train the system in the initial period and test it in the latter period. The 20 years of our examined period were split into two separate periods, 10 years of training and optimizing and 10 years of testing and reporting results. We started the process with a random trading setup that included the trading time frames and the various tools ingredients. Next, for each setup, we evaluated the desired fitness of the trading results to our predefined goals: Maximum NP, PF, and PP. We then compared each result to its former maximum and set a new maximum if needed. The process is described in Equation (2).

$$V(1)_{i+1,d} = V_{id} + C_1 Rand \times P_{id} - X_{id} + C_2 R \text{ and } P_{gd} - X_{id} \qquad (2)$$

$$X(2)_{i+1,d} = X_{id} + V_{id} \qquad (3)$$

where V_{id} = the value of each setup, Rand = random number, P_{id} = the setups initial identification, and P_{gd} = the setups' maximum identification.

Last, we looped the process using Equation (3) until the highest multiple objectives were achieved.

3.2. Linear Regression Strategy

Figure 1 demonstrate how we used the linear regressions technique for algorithmic trading platforms.

Figure 1. Linear regression algorithmic trading strategy. Notes: Every candlestick in Figure 1 represent the high/low open/close of the commodity futures' daily prices. The middle line in Figure 1 represent the linear regression line, while the other two lines represent one standard deviation from it.

A linear regression strategy demands the length of time for the line formation and the span from that line that determines the entry and exit from the trading positions. The regression line in Figure 1, for example, is based on 50 trading days when one standard deviation from that line determines the entry and exit points to the trading position. We started our PSO procedure with a random variable for both the daily time length and for the span that determined the actual entry and exits of trades. The system altered those variables in order to maximize our trading targets.

3.3. Darvas Boxes Strategy

Figure 2 show an example of an automated trading platform using Darvas boxes.

Figure 2. Darvas boxes algorithmic trading strategy. Notes: Every candlestick in Figure 2 represent the high/low open/close Bitcoin daily prices. A green daily candle means that the close price is above the opening price and a red candle means that the close price is lower than the opening price. The green and red lines indicate the upper and lower boundaries of Darvas's boxes.

Figure 2 show how Darvas boxes are designed and how they generate a long and short signal. This algorithmic trading system assumes that the trader is always exposed to price shifts between long and short positions. Darvas boxes use the notation that deviation from overtime horizontal support and resistance lines can be used to construct a winning trading strategy. The idea is that the asset's price should move within a specific box formation when no external news is provided and break formation when important news concerning the commodity is introduced to the financial markets. Boxes can be formed using any predetermined time frame according to the financial asset's volatility. A high volatility financial asset demands a shorter time frame for box formation than a low volatility asset. The PSO process starts with a random number of days to construct the boxes and alter them to achieve better trading performances. Once the size and shape of the boxes are formed in the training period, it is used for the tested period for which performances are remeasured.

3.4. Bollinger Bands Strategy

Bollinger bands (BB) (developed by John Bollinger) use two standard deviations away from a simple moving average. The trading strategy demonstrated in Figure 3 uses 14 days for the moving average calculation with the original two standard deviations. When the price of the commodity crosses the lower band, the system opens, a buy long order is placed, and when it crosses the upper band, a sell short order is generated.

Figure 3. Bollinger Bands algorithmic trading strategy. Notes: A green daily candle means that the close price is above the opening price and a red candle means that the close price is lower than the opening price. The middle brown line is a simple moving average and the blue lines are the upper and lower boundaries of the BB.

The PSO procedures start with random setups for both the moving average and the standard deviations and optimize both particles of our trading system.

The three methodologies that were tested in this research are based on the pattern recognition of price movements of the precious metals. The LR tries to adjust a linear model (horizontal or diagonal) to the data and determine price direction through a deviation from that linear formation. The DB methodology works on a shorter-term formation of boxes that represent the horizontal support and resistance lines. A deviation from that formation can be used to identify price trends shifts and support trading decision making. The concept that lies behind the BB structure does not demand the identification of a predetermined formation but rather determines a zone in which the financial assets are expected to move within a specific time frame. A break-out of the price from the expected zone can indicate irregularities of movements and can be used to make profits.

4. Results

We start the results section by presenting 10 years of (until the end of April 2021) monthly and daily correlations matrix between the returns of the examined precious metals.

From Table 1, we learn that all examine precious metal monthly returns are positively correlated. However, on a daily level, the correlations between the precious metals prices do not have the same sign. While gold and silver and copper and silver are negatively correlated, platinum and palladium and silver and platinum are positively correlated. We now apply to the daily data our designated multi-dimension regression model (Equation (1)), and report the results for the standard stepwise regression model is presented in Table 2. This model enables us to better understand the one to three day lag dependencies of each metal to its previous price changes and to the other precious metals.

Table 2 show an interesting phenomenon, all precious metals' current daily returns are negatively autocorrelated to their former days' returns: gold and silver to their former three consecutive days returns, platinum to its two consecutive days returns, and copper and palladium to their single former day returns. In terms of interdependencies, Table 2 exhibit that gold current daily returns are negatively affected by silver's former days' returns. However, silver's current daily returns are positively correlated to gold's returns two and three days ago. Platinum's current daily returns were found to be positively affected by gold, silver, and palladium's past returns. Palladium's current daily return was found to be positively correlated to yesterday's returns of silver and platinum and two days ago of gold's returns. The observations described above about the precious metals' daily autocorrelations helped us better understand the fluency of daily prices to construct our trading strategy. All the designed trading systems are based on daily trading data. However, because of the different nature of these strategies, the number of days used for each of them which is determined solely by the optimization process, is different. For example, the linear regression system needs more days than the other methodologies to construct its formations; therefore, the algorithm needs a higher number of days to analyze the price trends and produce profitable trading signals than the systems that are based on Darvas boxes and Bollinger bands which are more dynamic in nature and demand fewer days to achieve their best performances.

Table 1. Correlations matrix of monthly and daily returns.

	Period	Gold	Silver	Copper	Platinum	Palladium
Gold	M	1	0.75	0.25	0.51	0.28
Silver	M	0.75	1	0.45	0.61	0.44
Copper	M	0.25	0.45	1	0.56	0.51
Platinum	M	0.51	0.61	0.56	1	0.55
Palladium	M	0.28	0.44	0.51	0.55	1
Gold	D	1	−0.032	0.015	−0.015	−0.032
Silver	D	−0.032	1	−0.029	0.017	0.031
Copper	D	0.015	−0.029	1	0.015	−0.029
Platinum	D	−0.015	0.017	0.015	1	0.030
Palladium	D	−0.032	0.031	−0.029	0.030	1

Table 2. Results of the regression model.

Gold

	G_{-1}	G_{-2}	G_{-3}	S_{-2}	S_{-3}	C_{-2}	C_{-3}	P_{-1}	P_{-2}	
Coeff	−0.20 *	−0.17 *	−0.04 *	−0.02 *	−0.02 *	0.02	0.04	0.03	0.04	$R^2 = 0.14$
T stat	−11.00	−9.48	−2.14	−2.82	−2.04	0.97	1.86	1.57	1.73	F = 21.6

Silver

	G_{-1}	G_{-2}	G_{-3}	S_{-1}	S_{-2}	S_{-3}	C_{-1}	C_{-2}	
Coeff	−0.04	0.09 *	0.06 *	−0.48 *	−0.26 *	−0.14 *	0.26 *	0.06	$R^2 = 0.19$
T stat	−1.18	2.44	1.82	−25.3	−12.36	−7.33	5.93	1.62	F = 83.9

Copper

	G_{-1}	G_{-2}	G_{-3}	S_{-1}	S_{-2}	S_{-3}	C_{-1}	P_{-1}	
Coeff	0.01	0.01	−0.01	0.01	0.01	−0.02	−0.05 *	0.02	$R^2 = 0.07$
T stat	0.75	0.72	0.73	1.26	0.15	−1.41	−2.42	1.14	F = 2.7

Platinum

	G_{-1}	S_{-1}	S_{-2}	S_{-3}	C_{-3}	P_{-1}	P_{-2}	Pa_{-1}	Pa_{-2}	
Coeff	0.03 *	0.11 *	0.09 *	0.04 *	−0.02	−0.07 *	−0.03 *	0.09 *	0.08 *	$R^2 = 0.21$
T stat	1.95	14.65	10.65	5.60	1.27	−3.93	−2.05	6.73	5.85	F = 39.4

Palladium

	G_{-2}	G_{-3}	S_{-1}	S_{-2}	S_{-3}	C_{-2}	C_{-3}	P_{-1}	Pa_{-1}	
Coeff	0.04 *	−0.02	0.04 *	0.01	0.02	0.02	−0.05	0.06 *	0.08 *	$R^2 = 0.15$
T stat	2.17	−1.04	3.78	1.39	1.75	0.76	−1.85	2.26	4.33	F = 16.64

Notes: $(G, S, C, P, Pa)_i$ = daily returns of gold, silver, copper, platinum, and palladium, $(G, S, C, P, Pa)_{i=-1...-3}$ is 1 ... 3 days ago daily returns of gold, silver, copper, platinum, and palladium. * = significant at 95% confidence level. R^2 = the proportion of the variation in the dependent variable that is predictable from the independent variable(s). F = Statistic test results that measure the fitness of the model to the data. T stat = the ratio of the departure of the estimated value of a parameter from its hypothesized value to its standard error.

4.1. Linear Regression Trading Strategy

The linear regression strategy requires determining the number of days on which the linear regression line is formed. We start with a random number of days for each metal and optimize the trading results through our PSO system. The best trading results are summarized in Table 3 and Figure 4.

Table 3. Linear regression strategy trading results.

Days		Gold	Silver	Copper	Platinum	Palladium
20	NP	53,390	315,150	72,612	−9705	235,950 **
	PP	45.48%	44.54%	43.88%	42.92%	40.67%
	PF	1.06	1.25	1.14	0.98	1.30
25	NP	90,680	415,175	122,662 **	46,715	174,050
	PP	42.96%	44.18%	44.71%	43.5%	39.14%
	PF	1.13	1.40	1.22	1.10	1.23
30	NP	159,810	600,750	121,450	51,955	−4300
	PP	45.55%	46.26%	43.87%	42.7%	39.7%
	PF	1.26	1.67	1.24	1.13	0.99
35	NP	171,040	589,150	112,862	73,445 **	−133,650
	PP	43.89%	44.4%	44.41%	43.92%	8.8%
	PF	1.31	1.71	1.26	1.18	0.83
36	NP	165,180	558,975	119,837	59,225	−132,400
	PP	42.6%	43.91%	44.48%	43.25%	37.78%
	PF	1.30	1.64	1.28	1.15	0.83
37	NP	172,600	539,700	122,187	59,005	−159,950
	PP	42.63%	45.1%	44.65%	42.53%	37.76%
	PF	1.30	1.65	1.29	1.15	0.80
38	NP	177,190 **	561,425 **	96,737	40,110	−177,300
	PP	42.48%	44.15%	42.46%	41.72%	38.04%
	PF	1.32	1.69	1.22	1.09	0.78
39	NP	174,600	523,050	96,787	22,160	−219,000
	PP	43.78%	43.46%	41.62%	39.93%	37.09%
	PF	1.32	1.63	1.22	1.05	0.73
40	NP	167,460	480,000	79,400	27,700	−224,150
	PP	43%	41.64%	42.5%	40.14%	36.55%
	PF	1.31	1.58	1.18	1.069	0.73

Notes: NP = Net profit, PP = Percent of profitable trades of all trades, PF = Profit factor, Days= The number of days on which the linear regression is constructed. ** = The highest NP.

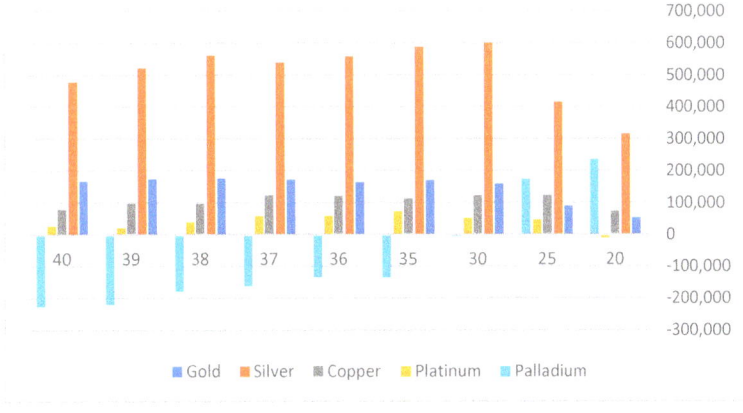

Figure 4. Net profits trading results of linear regression strategy.

Table 3 and Figure 4 demonstrate that the linear regression methodology best fits to the trade of silver, palladium, and gold and fits less to the trade of copper and platinum. The best setup for gold and silver trading systems is 38 days, for which the system generated USD 177,198 and USD 561,425 NP, respectively. For palladium, the best setup is 20 days achieving an NP of USD 235,950 with a PF of 1.30. In Table 4, we split our trades into long and short trades to examine whether a difference in profitability will occur.

Table 4. Linear regression trading results of long/short strategies.

Days		Gold	Silver	Copper	Platinum	Palladium
	NP	163,650	341,900	79,500	54,460	213,600
Long	PP	44.4%	45.6%	49.3%	46.5%	44.3%
	PF	1.6	1.82	1.39	1.3	1.67
	NP	13,540	219,525	42,687	18,985	22,350
Short	PP	41%	42.5%	39.8%	41.3%	37.3%
	PF	1.05	1.55	1.2	1.09	1.05

Notes: NP = Net profit, PP = Percent of profitable trades of all trades, PF = Profit factor. The results for gold and silver are calculated according to their optimum setups of 38 days, copper 37 days, platinum 35 days, and palladium 20 days.

Table 4 indicate that the linear regression technique fits both long and short trades. However, it is a better strategy for long trades than for short trades for all the examined commodities. The difference in long and short trades is significant for all metals in terms of NP and PF. Silver, again, leads the other metals in both long and short trades, resulting in a PF of 1.8 for long trades and 1.55 for short trades.

4.2. Darvas Box Strategy

Darvas box strategy requires determining the number of days on which the system will build the boxes formations and deliver buy or sell signals. Again, we start with a random number of days and let our PSO system optimize our goal functions. The best trading results are summarized in Table 5 and Figure 5.

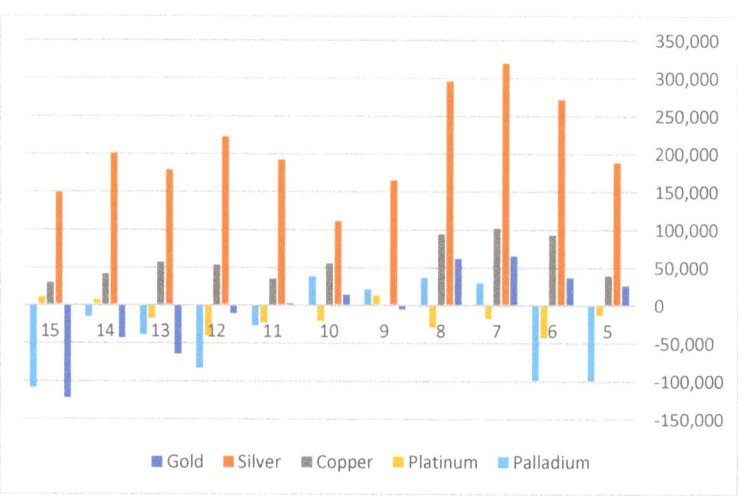

Figure 5. Net profits trading results of Darvas boxes strategy.

The trading results according to the Darvas boxes methodology described in Table 5 and Figure 5 show that this methodology, like the linear regression technique, best forecasts silver price trends than copper and gold, and it is less effective in forecasting future prices of platinum and palladium. Our system generated an NP of USD 319,200 for silver, with a PF of 1.55, using a 7-day setup. This setup was found to be useful also for gold and copper trading. Table 6 divide all the trades into long and short trades using the optimized setups for each metal.

Table 5. Darvas boxes strategy trading results.

Days		Gold	Silver	Copper	Platinum	Palladium
5	NP	26,080	188,475	39,487	−12,725	−98,550
	PP	37.30%	36%	35.45%	37.8%	34.12%
	PF	1.05	1.22	1.09	0.97	0.86
6	NP	36,990	271,625	93,087	−42,775	−97,950
	PP	36.67%	36.24%	36%	37.9%	33%
	PF	1.08	1.36	1.26	0.88	0.85
7	NP	65,290 **	319,200 **	102,175 **	−17,735	29,550
	PP	39.54%	37.75%	35.19%	36.36%	33.06%
	PF	1.17	1.55	1.31	0.95	1.06
8	NP	61,830	295,650	94,425	−29,445	36,750
	PP	38.49%	37.54%	37.81%	37.13%	33.18%
	PF	1.17	1.55	1.31	0.91	1.07
9	NP	−5290	164,800	94,925	13,035 **	21,150
	PP	36.33%	35.07%	40.11%	37%	33.51%
	PF	0.98	1.28	1.35	1.05	1.04
10	NP	13,610	111,125	55,662	−21,020	38,650 **
	PP	33.62%	33.59%	38.79%	32.32%	33.14%
	PF	1.04	1.19	1.20	0.93	1.09
11	NP	2500	191,875	35,412	−22,795	−26,250
	PP	35.61%	34.05%	39.1%	29.94%	32.7%
	PF	1.00	1.38	1.13	0.92	0.94
12	NP	−10,760	222,425	53,537	−40,555	−82,450
	PP	35.68%	36.89%	39.86%	29.7%	31.37%
	PF	0.97	1.52	1.21	0.85	0.83
13	NP	−63,780	178,125	56,737	−17,490	−38,350
	PP	30.415	34 %	39%	30.61%	34%
	PF	0.83	1.39	1.24	0.93	0.91
14	NP	−43,000	200,275	41,762	6990	−14,950
	PP	32.15	35.71%	37.3%	32.33%	36.22%
	PF	0.87	1.47	1.18	1.03	0.96
15	NP	−122,000	148,125	29,212	10,590	−108,550
	PP	34%	32.56%	35.45%	31.93%	33.88%
	PF	0.96	1.32	1.13	1.05	0.75

Notes: NP = Net profit, PP = Percent of profitable trades of all trades, PF = Profit factor, Days = The number of days on which the Darvas box is constructed. ** = The highest NP.

Table 6. Darvas boxes trading results of long/short strategies.

Days		Gold	Silver	Copper	Platinum	Palladium
Long	NP	111,170	222,425	95,863	28,335	152,550
	PP	41.815	39.55%	39.32%	42.155	39.77%
	PF	1.77	1.93	1.79	1.28	2.02
Short	NP	−45,880	96,775	6312	−15,300	−113,900
	PP	37.25%	35.96%	31.03%	31.7%	26.44%
	PF	0.81	1.28	1.03	0.91	0.58

Notes: NP = Net profit, PP = Percent of profitable trades of all trades, PF = Profit factor. The results for gold, silver, and copper are calculated according to their optimum setups of 7 days, platinum 9 days, and palladium 10 days.

The table shows that for all five precious metals, the system again performed better for long trades than for short trades. Moreover, short trades have produced losses for gold, platinum, and palladium. The only precious metals for which the Darvas boxes technique fits both long and short trade are silver and copper. These results indicate that the system based on the Darvas boxes methodology can better predict positive future price trends than negative trends.

4.3. Bollinger Band Strategy

Table 7 summarize the results of the examined metals prices using the Bollinger band (BB) technique. This methodology calculates a moving average of a predetermined number of the trading day and contrasts the upper and lower bands using two standard deviations from that moving average. Using our PSO system, we optimized the trading results for each commodity in terms of NP, PP, and PF. The results are presented in Table 7 and Figure 6.

Table 7. Bollinger bands strategy trading results.

Days		Gold	Silver	Copper	Platinum	Palladium
7	NP	−60	381,325 **	12,462	−8450	279,350
	PP	60.2%	62.5%	64.7%	61.1%	56.1%
	PF	1.0	1.67	1.03	0.97	1.80
8	NP	37,470	248,425	−84,162	−80,850	311,950 **
	PP	59.8%	61%	63.6%	63.3%	61%
	PF	1.08	1.34	0.82	0.77	1.70
9	NP	39,690	203,425	−89,450	−88,335	223,700
	PP	59.2%	63%	62.5%	65%	58.4%
	PF	1.08	1.27	0.81	0.75	1.43
10	NP	8730	179,175	−90,262	−72,165	162,600
	PP	58.2%	65.5%	63.1%	65%	60%
	PF	1.02	1.26	0.80	0.80	1.30
11	NP	56,330	233,175	−64,937	−28,080	−118,800
	PP	60.6%	65.9%	62.4%	65.5%	57.9%
	PF	1.13	1.35	0.85	0.92	0.80
12	NP	69,310	61,925	−84,000	−31,120	−87,400
	PP	63.8%	65.9%	65.1%	66.5%	59.2%
	PF	1.16	1.09	0.81	0.90	0.85
13	NP	103,760 **	7100	−63,812	5690	−116,000
	PP	63.7%	63.5%	65.6%	64.5%	58.7%
	PF	1.25	1.01	0.85	1.02	0.79
14	NP	88,190	−21,100	−68,412	−6050	−22,100
	PP	63.6%	62.8%	64.3%	63.1%	59.6%
	PF	1.22	0.97	0.83	0.98	0.96
15	NP	83,580	14,950	−67,437	4660	114,150
	PP	62.6%	64.3%	64.5%	65.6%	61.3%
	PF	1.21	1.02	0.83	1.02	1.25
16	NP	83,890	700	−4562	6300	104,650
	PP	63%	65.5%	66.7%	66.3%	60.8%
	PF	1.21	1.0	0.98	1.02	1.24
17	NP	77,980	67,225	−46,887	24,120	37,750
	PP	62.5%	66.1%	61.9%	66%	60.3%
	PF	1.2	1.1	0.87	1.09	1.08
18	NP	54,520	187,975	−13,837	28,780	33,950
	PP	62.3%	67.4%	63.8%	67.8%	62.3%
	PF	1.14	1.33	0.96	1.11	1.07
19	NP	48,340	280,495	59,812 **	19,250	50,950
	PP	63.6%	67.5%	65.7%	68.8%	63%
	PF	1.13	1.54	1.18	1.07	1.10
20	NP	33,920	203,975	5262	52,500 **	10,550
	PP	61.2%	66.8%	65.8%	69.8%	62.9%
	PF	1.09	1.41	1.02	1.19	1.02

Notes: NP = Net profit, PP = Percent of profitable trades of all trades, PF = Profit factor, Days = The number of days on which the Bollinger band is constructed. ** = The highest.

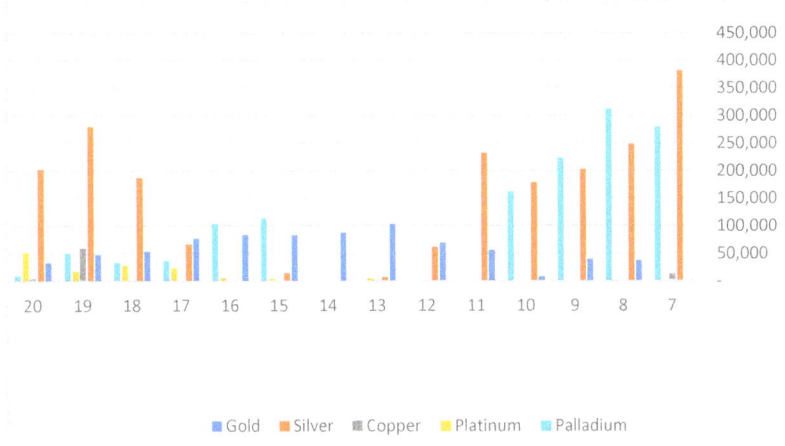

Figure 6. Net profits trading results of Bollinger bands strategy.

Table 7 and Figure 6 indicate that BB best forecasts silver and palladium futures prices, and it is less effective for copper and platinum. Seven days was found to be the best setup for silver and palladium, while 13 days best fit the gold price forecast. It is worth noting that silver and palladium prices are more volatile than the other metals, as was demonstrated in Table 1, resulting in relatively fewer preferred days setups for the BB methodology. The BB technique provided better percent of profitable (PP) results for all metals than the linear regression or the Darvas boxes techniques making it the lowest risk algorithmic trading system. Table 8 split the trades for long and short trades.

Table 8. Bollinger bands trading results of long/short strategies.

Days		Gold	Silver	Copper	Platinum	Palladium
Long	NP	134,490	252,425	57,137	48,370	262,800
	PP	65.7%	63.5%	64.7%	73.2%	64.7%
	PF	1.85	2.12	1.37	1.35	2.65
Short	NP	−30,730	128,900	2675	4130	49,150
	PP	61.7%	61.5%	66.7%	66.4%	57.5%
	PF	0.88	1.37	1.02	1.03	1.17

Notes: NP = Net profit, PP = Percent of profitable trades of all trades, PF = Profit factor. The results for gold, silver, and copper are calculated according to their optimum setups of 7 days, platinum 9 days, and palladium 10 days.

Table 8 indicate that, again, the BB methodology also fits long than short trades better. This technique fails to predict the negative price trends of gold.

5. Summary and Implications

In this research, we examined the short-term behavior of five major precious metals and tried to determine whether prices can be predicted and traded accordingly to algorithmic trading systems. By using a multidimensional regression model, we found that all precious metals' current daily returns are negatively autocorrelated to their former days' returns. Gold and silver are negatively correlated to the former three consecutive days' returns, platinum to two former days returns, and copper and palladium to a single former days' returns. The model also identified lagged interdependencies among the examined metals. These findings helped us to better understand the daily price fluctuation of each metal and to improve the trading systems. The trading systems used three forecasts' methodologies: linear regression (LR), Darvas boxes (DB), and Bollinger bands (BB). Our data consisted of 20 years of daily price data concerning five precious metals futures:

gold, silver, copper, platinum, and palladium. During that long time, the precious metals experienced high and low price volatility under different economic conditions. We used PSO as our primary optimization tool because of the complexity of our target function. For that optimization process, we split our data into two equal time periods, 10 years of training and optimization of our system and 10 years of testing and reporting results.

We found that it is possible to forecast the short-term price trends of all the examined precious metals. Moreover, we documented that our system better forecasts price-up trends than downtrends for all examined techniques and commodities. Our systems best predict silver future prices and forecasts platinum prices the worst. Linear regression was found to be the best forecasting technique for silver and gold price trends, while the Bollinger band technique best fits palladium. This research has proven that precious metals prices can be predicted using an algorithmic trading system and, therefore, can be used by researchers, traders, and hedgers.

Funding: This research was funded by Western Galilee Academic College.

Institutional Review Board Statement: Not applicable.

Informed Consent Statement: Not applicable.

Data Availability Statement: Not applicable.

Conflicts of Interest: The author declares no conflict of interest.

References

1. Chebbi, T. The response of precious metal futures markets to unconventional monetary surprises in the presence of uncertainty. *Int. J. Financ. Econ.* **2020**, *26*, 1897–1916. [CrossRef]
2. Cohen, G. Forecasting Bitcoin Trends Using Algorithmic Learning Systems. *Entropy* **2020**, *22*, 838. [CrossRef] [PubMed]
3. Bishop, C.M. *Pattern Recognition and Machine Learning*; Springer: Cambridge, UK, 2006.
4. Poggio, T.; Girosi, F. Networks for approximation and learning. *Proc. IEEE* **1990**, *78*, 1481–1497. [CrossRef]
5. Martino, L.; Read, J. Joint introduction to Gaussian Processes and Relevance Vector Machines with Connections to Kalman filtering and other Kernel Smoothers. *Inf. Fusion* **2021**, *74*, 17–38. [CrossRef]
6. Tipping, M.E. Sparse Bayesian Learning and the Relevance Vector Machine. *J. Mach. Learn. Res.* **2001**, *1*, 211–244.
7. Candela, J.Q. *Learning with Uncertainty—Gaussian Processes and Relevance Vector Machines*; Technical University of Denmark: Copenhagen, Denmark, 2004; pp. 1–152.
8. Zheng, Y. The linkage between aggregate investor sentiment and metal futures returns: A nonlinear approach. *Q. Rev. Econ. Financ.* **2015**, *58*, 128–142. [CrossRef]
9. Qadan, M. Risk appetite and the prices of precious metals. *Resour. Policy* **2019**, *62*, 138–153. [CrossRef]
10. Sensoy, A. Dynamic relationship between precious metals. *Resour. Policy* **2013**, *38*, 504–511. [CrossRef]
11. Bosch, D.; Pradkhan, E. The impact of speculation on precious metals futures markets. *Resour. Policy* **2015**, *44*, 118–134. [CrossRef]
12. Kang, S.H.; McIver, R.; Yoon, S.M. Dynamic spillover effects among crude oil, precious metal, and agricultural commodity futures markets. *Energy Econ.* **2017**, *62*, 19–32. [CrossRef]
13. Shahzad, J.H.; Rehman, M.U.; Jammazi, R. Spillovers from oil to precious metals: Quantile approaches. *Resour. Policy* **2019**, *61*, 508–521. [CrossRef]
14. Alameer, Z.; Elaziz, M.A.; Ewees, A.A.; Haiwang, Y.; Zhang, J. Forecasting Copper Prices Using Hybrid Adaptive Neuro-Fuzzy Inference System and Genetic Algorithms. *Nat. Resour. Res.* **2019**, *28*, 1385–1401. [CrossRef]
15. Cortez, C.A.T.; Saydam, S.; Coulton, J.; Sammut, C. Alternative techniques for forecasting mineral commodity prices. *Int. J. Min. Sci. Technol.* **2018**, *28*, 309–322. [CrossRef]
16. Kennedy, J.; Eberhart, R.C. Practical Swarm Optimization. In Proceedings of the International Conference on Neural Networks, Perth, Australia, 27 November–1 December 1995; pp. 1942–1948.
17. Eberhart, R.C.; Simpson, P.K.; Dobbins, R.W. *Computational Intelligence PC Tools*; Academic Press Professional: Boston, MA, USA, 1996.

MDPI
St. Alban-Anlage 66
4052 Basel
Switzerland
www.mdpi.com

Mathematics Editorial Office
E-mail: mathematics@mdpi.com
www.mdpi.com/journal/mathematics

Disclaimer/Publisher's Note: The statements, opinions and data contained in all publications are solely those of the individual author(s) and contributor(s) and not of MDPI and/or the editor(s). MDPI and/or the editor(s) disclaim responsibility for any injury to people or property resulting from any ideas, methods, instructions or products referred to in the content.